How Much Have Global Problems Cost the World?

There are often blanket claims that the world is facing more problems than ever but there is a lack of empirical data to show where things have deteriorated or in fact improved. In this book, some of the world's leading economists discuss ten problems that have blighted human development, ranging from malnutrition, education, and climate change, to trade barriers and armed conflicts. Costs of the problems are quantified in percent of GDP, giving readers a unique opportunity to understand the development of each problem over the past century and the likely development into the middle of this century, and to compare the size of the challenges. For example: How bad was air pollution in 1900? How has it deteriorated and what about the future? Did climate change cost more than malnutrition in 2010? This pioneering initiative to provide answers to many of these questions will undoubtedly spark debate amongst a wide readership.

BJØRN LOMBORG is Director of the Copenhagen Consensus Center and Adjunct Professor in the Department of Management, Politics and Philosophy at Copenhagen Business School. He is the author of the controversial bestseller *The Skeptical Environmentalist* (Cambridge University Press, 2001) and was named one of the "Top 100 Global Thinkers" by *Foreign Policy* magazine in 2010, 2011, and 2012, one of the world's "100 Most Influential People" by *Time*, and one of the "50 people who could save the planet" by The *Guardian*.

How Much Have Global Problems Cost the World?

A Scorecard from 1900 to 2050

Edited by
BJØRN LOMBORG

CAMBRIDGE
UNIVERSITY PRESS

University Printing House, Cambridge CB2 8BS, United Kingdom

Published in the United States of America by Cambridge University Press, New York

Cambridge University Press is part of the University of Cambridge.

It furthers the University's mission by disseminating knowledge in the pursuit of education, learning, and research at the highest international levels of excellence.

www.cambridge.org
Information on this title: www.cambridge.org/9781107679337

© Copenhagen Consensus Center 2013

First published 2013

Printing in the United Kingdom by TJ International Ltd. Padstow Cornwall

A catalogue record for this publication is available from the British Library

Library of Congress Cataloging in Publication data
How much have global problems cost the world? : a scorecard from 1900 to 2050 / edited by Bjørn Lomborg.
   pages   cm
Includes index.
ISBN 978-1-107-67933-7
ISBN 978-1-107-02733-6
1. Social problems – Economic aspects – History.   I. Lomborg, Bjørn, 1965–
HN13.H676   2013
303.3′72–dc23

2013000579

ISBN 978-1-107-02733-6 Hardback
ISBN 978-1-107-67933-7 Paperback

Contents

Figures

Tables

Contributors

Editor

Bjørn Lomborg is the Director of the Copenhagen Consensus Center and Adjunct Professor at Copenhagen Business School

Authors

Maura Allaire is a Ph.D. student in the Department of Environmental Sciences and Engineering, University of North Carolina at Chapel Hill, NC

Kym Anderson is the George Gollin Professor of Economics, in the School of Economics, University of Adelaide, Australia and Professor of Economics, Crawford School of Public Policy, Australian National University

S. Brock Blomberg is the Robin and Peter Barker Professor of Economics, at Claremont McKenna College, Clarement, CA

Aline Chiabai is an Associate Researcher at the Basque Centre for Climate Change in the Basque Country, Bilbao, Spain

David Fuente is a Ph.D. student in the Department of City and Regional Planning, University of North Carolina at Chapel Hill, NC

Gregory D. Hess is Vice President for Academic Affairs, Dean of the Faculty, James G. Boswell Professor of Economics and George R. Roberts Fellow at Claremont McKenna College, Claremont, CA

Sue Horton holds the CIGI Chair in Global Health Economics in the Balsillie School of the University of Waterloo, Ontario

Guy Hutton is an international development economist

Joyce P. Jacobsen is the Andrews Professor of Economics at Wesleyan University, Middletown, CT

Dean T. Jamison is Professor of Global Health at the Institute for Health Metrics and Evaluation (IHME) at the University of Washington, Seattle, WA

Marc Jeuland is an Assistant Professor in the Sanford School of Public Policy, Duke University, Durham, NC

Prabhat Jha is Professor of Economics, Canada Research Chair of Health and Development at the University of Toronto, founding Director of the Centre for Global Health Research, St. Michael's Hospital, Associate Professor in the Department of Public Health Sciences, University of Toronto, research scholar at the McLaughlin Centre for Molecular Medicine, University of Toronto, and professeur extraordinaire at the University of Lausanne, Switzerland

Varun Malhotra is a Researcher at the Centre for Global Health Research, St. Michael's Hospital and Dalla Lana School of Public Health, University of Toronto

Anil Markandya is Professor of Economics at the University of Bath, UK and Scientific Director of the Basque Centre for Climate Change in the Basque Country, Bilbao, Spain

Semra Özdemir is a Ph.D. student in the Department of Environmental Sciences and Engineering, University of North Carolina at Chapel Hill, NC

Harry Anthony Patrinos is a Senior Education Economist with the World Bank

George Psacharopoulos is an economist, formerly at the London School of Economics and the World Bank

Richard H. Steckel is SBS Distinguished Professor of Economics, Anthropology and History, Ohio State University, Columbus, OH and Research Associate, National Bureau of Economic Research, Cambrige, MA

Richard S. J. Tol is Professor of Economics at the University of Sussex, Brighton, UK and Professor of the Economics of Climate Change, Institute for Environmental Studies and Department of Spatial Economics, Vrije Universiteit, Amsterdam

Stéphane Verguet is a Researcher at the Institute for Health Metrics and Evaluation, University of Washington, Seattle, WA

Dale Whittington is Professor at the Departments of Environmental Sciences and Engineering and of City and Regional Planning, University of North Carolina at Chapel Hill, NC and at the Manchester Business School, UK

Acknowledgments

This book was made possible because of the efforts of many dedicated people.

I would like to start by thanking our advisory board; Nobel Laureates Finn Kydland, Douglass North, Vernon Smith, and renowned economist Nancy Stokey, for their invaluable advice and assistance.

I am grateful for the commitment of staff members at the Copenhagen Consensus Center: Henrik Meyer, David Young, Ulrik Larsen, Sasha Beckmann, Sibylle Aebi, Sandra Andresen, and Zsuzsa Horvath. I would particularly like to thank the project manager, Kasper Thede Anderskov, for his exceptional dedication and enthusiasm.

And I would like to express my deep and sincere appreciation to each of the authors of the outstanding research in this volume, and to the 28 excellent reviewers connected to this project.

Introduction

BJØRN LOMBORG

The Costs of Human Challenges

The human race has always faced a wide range of challenges and, despite great progress, continues to do so. This book aims to produce a 150-year view of some of humanity's biggest challenges, and to present these in a new and thought-provoking way. The research presented here uses in-depth economic data analysis to establish the cost to humankind caused by its biggest challenges, and how the impact of these challenges evolved over the twentieth century and will continue to change until the middle of this century.

Understanding the change in impact of the different problems across centuries or even just their relative sizes at a particular moment is fraught with difficulty, since our understanding of world problems and progress is to a large extent shaped by vocal interest groups, the length of the media's attention span, and our perceptions – shaped by personal experience – of what matters and what does not.

In the developed world, the challenges that we hear the most about are not necessarily those that cause the biggest problems to humanity. Issues come and go from the front pages of newspapers: an African famine can be news one day, superseded by a terror threat in the developed world the next. Issues like the Y2K bug can create considerable alarm, and then fade away to nothing. Other times, there might be a perception that we have solved an issue – malnutrition, or the HIV epidemic, for example – because we hear a lot less about it than we once did.

What role can economic analysis play in helping us to get a clearer picture? One of my favorite examples comes from the USA in the late 1990s, and it shows how the media's focus can easily cloud our perspective.

In 1997–8, the weather pattern El Niño affected the United States – and it was widely covered on the TV news and in newspapers. The weather pattern was blamed for everything from wrecking tourism, causing more allergies, melting the ski-slopes, creating snow-storms, and even for causing a dip in Disney's share price. Based on the media's reporting, the average reader or viewer was left with the clear impression that El Niño was an overwhelmingly negative phenomenon.

But economic research provides a fuller picture. A peer-reviewed article tallied, in financial terms, all of the problems and all the benefits (which had been seldom reported) from El Niño in the USA.

The weather pattern caused storm damage – but it also raised winter temperatures which reduced the number of people who died from the cold and cut heating bills, reduced spring flood damage, led to transportation savings, and reduced Atlantic hurricanes. The total damages were estimated at $4 billion, whereas the total benefits were estimated at $19 billion. In this case, the economic analysis helps us to gain a better perspective on the true scale and impact of the challenge, in this case in the USA.

Economics can also serve to show us whether or not particular challenges are becoming more or less problematic for humanity over time. That is what this book will attempt to do.

Such an endeavor is important. If we don't focus on the right things, we will not respond adequately to the challenges that matter. If we worry that things are getting worse and spiraling out of control, we are likely to panic and such a state of mind is hardly conducive to making good decisions.

It is entirely possible to gain the impression that the world's challenges are piling up, and that humanity is failing to respond to them. For instance, we often hear doomsday-style rhetoric from campaigners who paint a picture of ever-escalating pollution. It is easy to counter such claims with particular data and facts. You might remember stories of London's smog in the 1940s and 1950s when on bad days you literally could not see 10 feet ahead of you. Data clearly tells us that London air has gotten cleaner since the late nineteenth century, and is likely cleaner now than it has been since 1585.

Yet, it is easy to present data from other places that makes the opposite point: in many places, air pollution has increased (such as in Beijing and many other cities in developing nations). Moreover, if we only talk about outdoor air pollution, we ignore the much larger problem of indoor air pollution which causes perhaps 2 million deaths through people trying to cook or keep warm with dirty fuels.

This is where we need an analysis which takes into account *all* of the data across the world and looks at *both* indoor and outdoor air pollution, showing the individual and impact across the century and the likely development ahead. That is what the chapter on air pollution in this book has done.

Of course, we need to not only look at air pollution, but also at health, war, gender, food, and a host of other issues. Likewise, we need to realize that problems have not been evenly spread, and nor has progress. OECD members – the club of the world's richest countries – have a combined population smaller than China's, while in the rest of the world, nearly a billion people still suffer from chronic malnutrition. Yet, over a period when world population has tripled, the absolute number of malnourished people has remained pretty much the same. There are still far too many people who go to bed hungry, but global farming has managed to produce enough food for an ever-larger proportion of the world's rapidly burgeoning population.

This Book's Contents

In this volume, we include contributions from a range of authors who have been asked to do the seemingly impossible – to quantify the cost to humanity from ten diverse challenges:

- Air pollution
- Conflicts
- Climate change
- Biodiversity
- Education
- Gender inequality
- Health
- Malnutrition
- Trade barriers
- Water and sanitation.

In trying to find a common language, we have asked authors to evaluate the impacts in their area in terms of "percentage of GDP." With such a wide range of topics, this framework enables us to make more sensible comparisons of relative impacts in such diverse areas as biodiversity changes, malnutrition and trade barriers.

There are those who question the use of economics to put a cost on things that they would regard as beyond price: human life or biodiversity, for example. The simple if uncomfortable truth is that we do this all the time. For instance, politicians and bureaucrats regularly decide whether to build an extra roundabout or a safer road, which will save lives but comes at an extra cost. When we decide not to adopt the safest course in order to save money, we implicitly set a value on human lives. Likewise, policies to cut down forests have to weigh the benefits in timber and employment against values like biodiversity.

Rather as Churchill considered democracy to be the worst form of government – with the exception of all the others that have been tried – we could view placing an economic cost perspective on the human condition as the least bad approach to gaining an overview of the problems.

Based on the best available data and case studies, the authors in each case have used statistical modeling tools and descriptive historical economics to portray the trend, state, and outlook for each of the challenges. Their economic analysis provides one of the best possible estimates of the historic, present and future welfare cost from a given challenge.

To overcome data availability constraints and to ensure that credible cost estimates are made for each challenge, especially for the first half of the twentieth century and for less developed countries, many authors provide a sensitivity

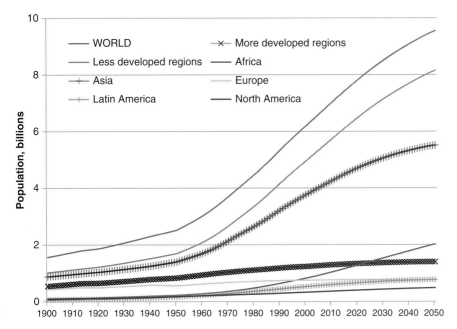

Figure I.1 *Population (billions)*

analysis to establish a better range for measuring uncertainties.

This is an ambitious project, pushing the frontier of economic historic assessments and forecasts, and one that required us to ask authors to broadly use the same assumptions about growth and population levels.

To guarantee a harmonious set of assumptions across the economic assessments, the Copenhagen Consensus – which commissioned the research – created a resource base for the authors including historic and future data for key economic variables – and population growth (see Figures I.1 and I.2). The smoothed data set only draws from credible sources; mainly United Nation Statistics and Historical Statistics of the World Economy by Angus Maddison.[1] Regions and income groups are defined according to the United Nations disaggregation (Table I.1).

While this may seem like a very rough generalization of the world divided in only two income categories or five regions, this has not been the real constraint on the authors when it comes to detail. The real constraint is the lack of the complementary challenge-specific time-series data which has in several cases made the disaggregation proposed by the Copenhagen Consensus Center impossible.

Yet we are proud to learn that this project has forced the authors to think creatively and look in new places for better historical data that can tell the story of our human development, and in some cases this has created new longer time-series data, making the way for better economic statistical analysis. One can only hope that statistical databases continue to grow as that is necessary for good economic assessments help us make better judgments and investments for our common good, based on historic proof.

The high and low regional growth rate estimates are based on literature review of key economic institutions such as United Nations and the World Bank (Table I.2). As it is impossible to create a consensus on future growth rates, the ones used are indeed conservative estimates of a hopefully even brighter future.

Of course this geographical disaggregation covers great variations within regions and even within countries just as overall economic growth may hide the

[1] Maddison, A. (2006): *The World Economy: A Millennial Perspective (vol. 1), Historical Statistics (vol. 2)*. Paris: OECD.

Table I.1 Regions and income groups

- **More developed** regions comprise Europe, Northern America, Australia/New Zealand and Japan
- **Less developed** regions comprise Africa, Asia (excluding Japan/Australia/New Zealand), Latin America and the Caribbean
- **Africa** (includes all regions of Africa)
- **Asia** (includes Oceania)
- **Europe**
- **Latin America** (includes the Caribbean)
- **North America**

Table I.2 The low/high growth prospect is based on the following GDP growth rates

Low growth scenario	High growth scenario
• World: 2.5%	• World: 3.5%
• More developed: 1.5%	• More developed: 2.5%
• Less developed: 3.5%	• Less developed: 4.5%
• Africa: 2.5%	• Africa: 3.5%
• Asia: 3.5%	• Asia: 4.5%
• Europe: 1.5%	• Europe: 2.5%
• Latin America: 2.5%	• Latin America: 3.5%
• North America: 2.0%	• North America: 3.0%

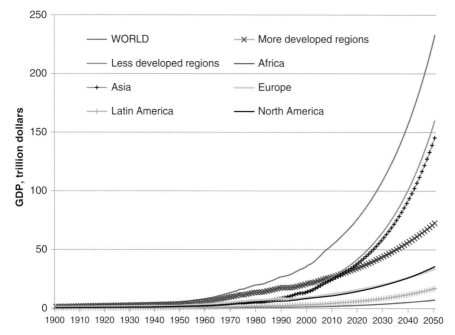

Figure I.2 *GDP 1900–2050; high growth scenario for 2010–2050 (trillion 1990 International Geary–Khamis dollars)*

inequality beneath. However, as this book shows it does achieve the objective of telling a detailed story of development in different tempi across different regions. The full data set is available on the Copenhagen Consensus Center Website.

Methodology and Coverage

It is important to realize that when we ask researchers to look at any area, the problems (or benefits)

from several other areas will also influence their results. So, one cannot just add the GDP costs from the many different areas, because they will partially overlap.

For instance, much of the development in nutrition would not have been possible if it had not been for improved education making progress in food research possible as well as the development of better global infrastructure and distribution networks. Separating the challenges and our achievements into different categories is more a didactic instrument that makes it easier to pinpoint progress or decline.

Moreover, when we look at the entire world across 150 years, it is impossible to include everything. We simply undertook a valiant first attempt to cover the world. Yet, it is perhaps worth briefly touching on the areas that we did not study. Common to them all was that we were not able to get sufficient numbers of researchers to study them in the time-frame available. Below, I've tried to indicate the likely direction of more studies to look at these problems.

Finance

It is clear – the 2008 crisis notwithstanding – that the increased availability of credit and finance has been important for the economic development across the last century and likely to be so for the coming decades. One can point to access to finance for consumers in terms of allowing consumption smoothing; for small businesses as start-up credit; for large businesses as access to bond issues or private equity; interest-rate swaps and exchange-rate insurance; for governments the ability to borrow large amounts, especially during the development phase, and a number of other areas. In total, it is likely that the increased access to financial tools has contributed and will continue to contribute positively to global development.

Demographics and Population

This has for a long time been a major concern, perhaps most poignantly described in *The Population Bomb*.[2] The worry has been that increasing populations could reduce life quality by stretching resources (see below), increasing pollution and diluting growth. In the current set-up of the question that we have asked the authors to address – namely measuring the size of the problems in terms of percentage of GDP at any given time – the issue of demographics is implicitly present in and contributing to all areas, since we are essentially measuring per capita impacts. Thus, if increasing populations have indeed increased pollution, this will show up as an increasing pollution problem in the studies.

However, there are also other impacts that could have been interesting to look at. For instance, one

reaction to population concerns was the one-child policy in China, which has probably caused a severely skewed gender ratio in China today. Moreover, in many industrialized (and increasingly in many developing) countries the worry is about shrinking populations, aging demographic, and increasing welfare costs. Yet, increasing life expectancy is also an uncontroversial good for the individual, and this is measured in the health chapter.

The impact of population is included in the assessments in the individual chapters, and life expectancy in the health chapter, whereas the impact of the other demographic variables is hard to assess up-front.

Resources and Energy

It is clear that much of the development of the twentieth century is due to the abundant availability of energy (especially fossil fuels) and resources (like iron and cement). Concerns about global warming are dealt with in the chapter on global warming.

Many have expressed concerns for the depletion of resources, in the vein of a Club of Rome argument (1972). They have worried that by using so much fossil fuels and other resources we have left the world with fewer and less easily accessible options for the future, which would obviously indicate a negative impact on the development across the century. Against these theoretical worries, the empirical indicators show that we have generally found more new resources (including fossil fuels) than we have used, mostly through technological innovation. Most major resources have longer years-of-consumption, and show increasing availability, and for the past 150 years, the general price trend has been downwards. Thus it seems reasonable to expect that if energy and resources had been included, the increased access to lower-priced available resources has contributed and will continue to contribute positively to global development.

---

[2] Ehrlich, P. (1968) *The Population Bomb*. Cutchogue, NY: Buccaneer Books.

Physical and Communications Infrastructure

It is obvious that many of the developments in modern civilization (and into its future) have come about because information, goods, and services can move ever more easily. This is both because of increased availability of roads, trains, and ships for goods and people, as well as the advent of telegraphs, telephones, faxes, cell phones, and the internet for ideas and communication. Although we were unsuccessful in commissioning sufficiently high-quality papers to bear on these issues, it is clear that increased access to physical and communications infrastructure resources has contributed and will continue to contribute positively to global development.

Civil Rights/Human Rights/Democracy/Racism

While economics and statistics are powerful tools when it comes to measuring the world around us, there are many important issues and challenges that are almost impossible to measure. This does not mean that they are not important. Below you will see that we did manage to estimate a similar topic, namely gender. Overall, it seems difficult to say with great confidence whether civil rights and democracy have contributed and will contribute positively to human development, but it appears harder to claim that their development across the past 110 years has and will impact human development negatively.

Corruption

It is obvious that corruption constitutes a significant cost on human development, estimated today at around 1% of GDP. However, it seems almost impossible to estimate with any degree of precision what its signigicance across the past century has been. Thus, while important, the current project has not found it possible to estimate its change in importance going forward.

Politics

It is clear that politics and the ability to implement social decisions have a large impact on human welfare, and many observers agree that politicians often seem to be doing very badly compared to our loftiest hopes. Again, though, it appears almost impossible at present to show whether politicians and political structures have become less or more capable at advancing human well-being, and as such, the projects have not explored this important measure.

Happiness

Finally, there is the issue of happiness. This is important in two related respects. First, since human happiness arguably is the most fundamental measure of utility, maybe we should have tried to measure it across the past century and estimate it into the future. While an intriguing concept, the problem is that as happiness is almost entirely self-evaluated, it is necessarily relative and hard to compare across cultures and across time. Thus, it has not been included in this evaluation.

Second, many have suggested that happiness is potentially a better measure of human welfare than GDP, and thus questions the basic unit of comparison in this project. The problem is that none of the current attempts to make a 'better' GDP estimate on e.g. happiness have been broadly accepted, nor are the data available in high detail throughout the twentieth century and till 2050. Moreover, while no one would argue that GDP is a perfect measure, it is clear that higher GDP correlates with other attractive outcomes like economic freedom, freedom from corruption, better health and social outcomes, lower poverty, life satisfaction, etc.[3] Thus, for the current project, GDP is a reasonable first proxy for human welfare and happiness.

Development of Human Welfare

After these methodological considerations, it is worth looking at the actual results from the individual papers and then estimating the total costs imposed by some of the major human challenges

---

[3] See   http://filipspagnoli.wordpress.com/stats-on-human-rights/statistics-on-gross-domestic-product-correlations/

over the twentieth century and their likely impact during the first half of the twenty-first.

This is very much a first attempt at an ambitious project, but the overall picture clearly is of major improvements to the lives of most, with many problems remaining and some issues moving in the wrong direction.

Let us look at the individual chapters. In Chapter 1, Guy Hutton examines the problem of air pollution. Today we associate this issue largely with urbanization, in both industrialized and developing countries. The soot from coal fires and industry may no longer be a problem in European cities, but there remains an issue with traffic emissions on busy roads, sometimes compounded by local weather conditions as in the infamous Los Angeles smog. In major cities in rapidly developing countries, domestic stoves and industry are still the main problem, highlighted by the Chinese authorities shutting down many local factories during the Beijing Olympics in 2008.

More overlooked, but in terms of deaths ultimately more important, is indoor air pollution. This is especially a problem in developing countries, where families often rely on dirty and inefficient fuels to cook and keep warm. Since women and children often spend more time indoors, they are especially prone to the consequences of indoor air pollution, from respiratory disease to premature death.

Looking at the first graph measuring deaths per year, the importance of indoor air pollution through the last 110 years is obvious. Hutton estimates that the total annual deaths from indoor air pollution in 1900 were about 2.7 million, with 2.6 million deaths in the developing countries and 100,000 in the developed world. Contrast this to about 177,000 annual deaths from outdoor air pollution, with 160,000 in the developed world. Across the past century, indoor air pollution deaths in the developed world almost disappeared. At the same time, more people, more frequently living in cities, with ever more cars, were a primary cause of increasing deaths in both the developed and the developing world. With environmental legislation and car saturation, deaths started declining in the First World after 1970. In the developing world, with increasing pollution, increasing urbanization and growing populations, deaths will continue to increase towards the mid twenty-first century.

However, the amazing story, which is somewhat hidden in this figure, is that the number of people dying from indoor air pollution in the Third World, although terribly high, has actually declined to about 1.85 millon today and is likely to drop below 1 million by 2050. Why is it amazing, when there are still so many people dying? Because at the same time the number of people in the developing world has increased eightfold, the annual risk of dying per person has dropped from 0.25% to 0.01% – or 25 times.

But clearly outdoor air pollution in the developing world has shot up at the same time. Is this not an indication that things are getting worse? Yes, it is unequivocally bad that the number of people dying is increasing. And even if we measure this in terms of risk per person, it has been increasing. However, even the outdoor air pollution is *only half as bad* for a person in a developing country in 2050 than it was for a developed country citizen in 1970, likely because of cleaner technology. And ultimately, while more people die from outdoor air pollution, many fewer people die from indoor air pollution in the Third World, making the entire number still decline (Figure I.3).

Moreover, death is not the only problem stemming from air pollution. There are also sickness days as well as indirect costs such as damage to buildings and crops, as well as costs of time required to collect firewood. Taking all of those costs into account, Hutton shows that the total cost of air pollution in 1900 ran to $446 billion 1990 dollars (all dollar amounts described here are in Gheary–Khamis 1990 US$) or about 23% of Gross World Product (GWP) in 1900, as is evident in Figure I.3.

Remember, this does *not* mean that the nations of the world in 1900 were suffering a 23% loss of their GDP, or that if there had been no air pollution, GDP would have been 23% higher. Most of the losses were in human lives cut short, which while a definite loss of human welfare would only obliquely show up in GDP (and possibly as a cost of care for older people). Rather the 23% indicates the size of the problem, the size of the loss of human welfare in an easily comparable metric.

From a loss of 23% in 1900, we see a loss of $3 trillion in 2010, or 5.6% of GWP, and a loss of 4% of GWP by 2050 ($7.5 trillion). So, has air pollution become a bigger problem or a smaller one?

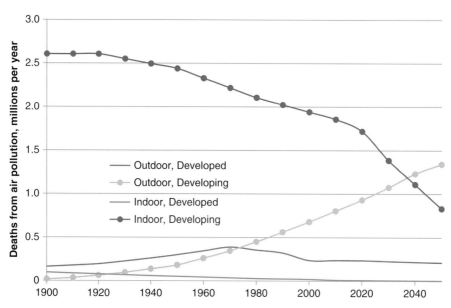

Figure I.3 *Deaths from air pollution*

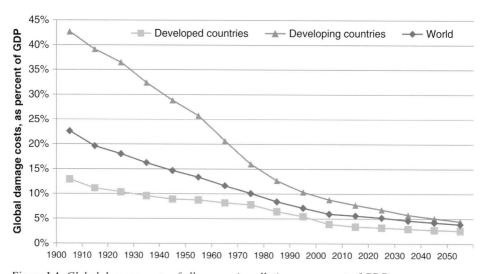

Figure I.4 *Global damage costs of all-cause air pollution, as percent of GDP*

The total cost has certainly gone up, which could indicate that air pollution has gotten worse. But this analysis neglects that at the same time, there are many more people living (which means that any air pollution can kill more people) while each person has gotten much richer (and hence each life is valued much higher). This is why a more accurate way to describe the problem is how big the problem is compared to the total wealth at the current time, as is

evident in Figure I.4. Here, the problem has become less significant for both developed and developing countries, perhaps most dramatically for the developing world, where welfare damages of 43% were occurring around 1900, but have now declined to 8% and likely will end up at 4% by mid-century.

Another way to see why percentage of GDP is a more accurate way to describe whether the problem is growing or declining is to recast it as a risk issue (since deaths are by far the biggest contributor to the damage cost, we can just look at death risks). If we look at the annual risk of dying across the 150-year period in Figure I.5, in 1900 it stood at about 0.18% – or one person in 550 would die each year from air pollution (mostly in the developing world from indoor air pollution). Now, that risk is about 0.04% or 1 in 2,500, and by mid-century it will be almost 0.02% or 1 in 5,000. When we ask if air pollution has gotten better or worse, we could reformulate that as a question behind the Rawlsian veil of ignorance – which time-version of society would you rather be a part of, if risk of death from air pollution was your only consideration? It is clear that this would be the latter part, or the lower part of the risk curve.

Notice that although the absolute number of deaths remains steady or slightly declining across the period, this is not important for the point here. Even if the *absolute* number of deaths had increased, what matters is that the *relative* numbers go down. (If you had to make a choice about which society to be born into, your decision is not influenced by whether there are absolutely more people dying from air pollution, if there are also even more people in total; what matters is your risk of being one of the people who die from air pollution.)

Indoor air pollution has been by far the most important air pollutant through the twentieth century, as is evident in Figure I.6.

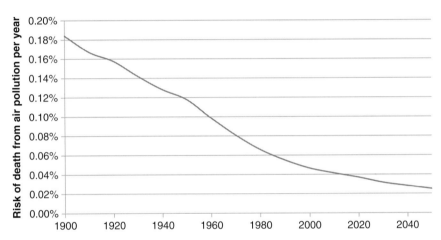

Figure I.5 *Risk of death from air pollution per year*

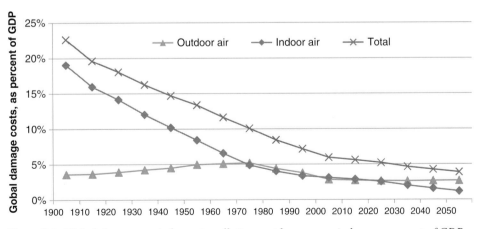

Figure I.6 *Global damage costs from air pollution, outdoor versus indoor, as percent of GDP*

However, Hutton's chapter also signals a change on the horizon: before mid-century, it is reckoned that outdoor pollution will become more important than indoor, as urbanization increases but most people have access to improved cooking stoves. Although absolute numbers affected continue to decline, the economic cost of mortality rises with increasing prosperity.

As Hutton explains, the decreasing trend of air pollution is encouraging. However, he points out that the projected reductions in damage costs beyond 2010 depend on the success of current and future policies to reduce exposure to air pollution in both urban and indoor environments. Maintaining progress requires us to ensure that appropriate policies are implemented, and sustainable economic growth continues.

Pollution is an unwanted side effect of developments which have also provided many benefits for humans: the burning of fossil fuels, and urbanization. However, the most-discussed and major impact of greater use of fossil fuel energy is clearly climate change, and in Chapter 3 Richard Tol addresses its economic costs. In particular, he tries to estimate past costs as a way to improve confidence in projections of future impacts. Generally, attention focuses on the likely negative impact of climate change, but Tol's chapter takes a more nuanced and balanced view. The model he uses includes a range of impacts: agriculture and forestry, sea level rise, various health issues, energy consumption, water resources, ecosystem effects and storms.

In some cases – agriculture in particular – the impact over the twentieth century has been very positive. In others, such as water, the impact has been generally negative, while for health effects the impact has been both negative and positive at different times.

Projecting forward through the twenty-first century, cold-related cardiovascular deaths fall steadily, while those caused by heat rise rapidly. Deaths from respiratory disease also increase, but those due to malaria and diarrhea fall with improving healthcare as a consequence of economic growth.

Overall, the greatest losses towards the end of the twenty-first century come from the energy sector. In the twentieth century most countries gained slightly from the moderate warming, because the higher costs of cooling were somewhat outweighed by

reduced costs of heating. From 2035, however, extra cooling costs will increasingly outweigh the reduced heating costs, leading to a significant net cost of about 2% GDP by the end of the century.

It is important to emphasize that there is a clear divide between the rich, temperate countries which have overall benefitted from warming and poor, tropical countries, for whom the impact has been mostly negative. This trend looks set to become even more marked over the twenty-first century, highlighting the need to pursue an effective response to climate change.

Overall, Tol finds, the pattern of climate change over the twentieth century improved human welfare. In the first part of the twentieth century, climate change caused a welfare increase of 0.5% GDP, edging up to 1.4% by 2000. For the future, he estimates the welfare benefit will reach its maximum at 1.5% by 2025; it will be reduced to about 1.2% by mid-century, before going rapidly negative in the last two decades of the century, ending at −1.2% in 2100 (Figure I.7).

In Chapter 2, S. Brock Blomberg and Gregory Hess look at the cost of conflict. Military expenditures and the cost of human lives make war inherently wasteful but, for a range of reasons, it sadly still persists. Indeed, wars have led to an appalling loss of life during the twentieth century: 140 million or more deaths, with 78–90 million of those resulting from the two world wars.

Blomberg and Hess look at the balance between "Guns" and "Butter" – a convenient shorthand for military and consumption. A simple way to look at the cost of guns is, of course, how this spending cannot be used for consumption spending; that is simply to look at the cost of guns across time as the cost of conflict. However, the chapter also analytically looks at the utility of a decline in military spending, or essentially to estimate the amount which people would be willing to pay to avoid returning to a time of previous conflict and provide point estimates for this.

For the future, the authors look at three potential scenarios:

- High-conflict scenario – conflict and military spending, due to the events following 9/11, continues to grow at the trend rate from 2000 to 2007
- Medium-conflict scenario – conflict and military spending remain steady at the current ratios

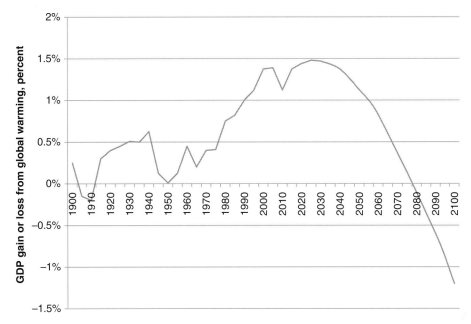

Figure I.7 *The global average economic impact of climate change in the twentieth and twenty-first centuries*

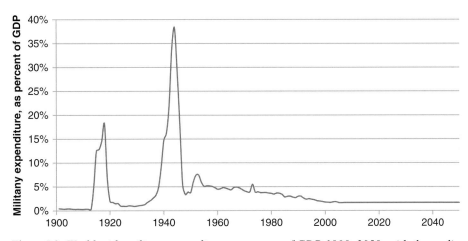

Figure I.8 *World-wide military expenditure as percent of GDP 1900–2050, with the medium scenario from 2007*

- Low-conflict scenario – conflict and military spending continue to fall to the low point after the decade following the Cold War.

It turns out, however, that the difference in scenarios is quite small as compared to the dramatic decline in costs from conflict that has taken place across the past century.

As we see in Figure I.8, the first part of the twentieth century was marked by the two huge world wars, reaching contemporaneous costs of almost 20% and almost 40% of GDP. Since then, there has been a dramatic reduction in military spending, albeit with some increases in the early stages of the Cold War and spikes for the first Gulf War and post-9/11.

Overall, it is possible to identify a very large peace dividend from no longer having to pay for guns as during World War II, World War I or the Korean War in 1952. Estimated as willingness to pay for avoiding expenditures like World War II, the benefit today to the world is about 26% (weighted) of current world consumption, or almost $10 trillion annually. The present discounted value of the whole peace dividend is about 3.7 times global GDP, with 3.9 times GDP for East Asia and 3.1 times GDP for North America.

These calculations are for the economic welfare loss alone. Adding in the human cost of the lives lost in battle (not counting civilian casualties), the annual, weighted global peace dividend rises from $10 trillion to $15 trillion. Clearly, it is worth paying a significant price to avoid the disastrous consequences of a return to general world conflict.

But overall, the message of a dramatically lower cost of conflict over the past half century and the coming 40 years is a strong one (Figure I.9).

Although not comparable with war in terms of its direct impact on human welfare, trade is an important driver of economic development, and it is now generally recognized that freer trade benefits all participants. In Chapter 9, the costs and opportunities of this are reviewed by Kym Anderson.

The present trend towards fewer restrictions on trade began with the Bretton Woods agreement after World War II. However, in 2004, typical tariffs on agricultural produce still stood at over 20%, while average import tariffs on manufactured goods for developing countries were 7.5%. Removing these barriers could have given a boost of at least $168 billion to the global economy, representing a 0.6% increase. Developing countries would have benefitted to a relatively greater extent than the current industrialized world. Notice also that these benefits are entirely static. It is likely the dynamic benefits would be many times greater, stemming from slightly higher growth rates because of acceleration in investment that would accompany a reduction in trade barriers.

In Figure I.10, we can see the welfare effects of price-distorting trade barriers. The "Low" and "High" scenarios that Anderson uses refer to

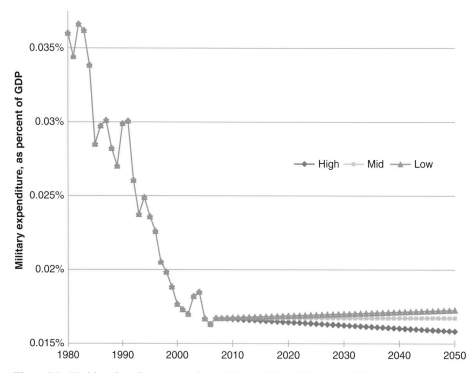

Figure I.9 *World-wide military expenditure/GDP: 1980–2050 (three different scenarios)*

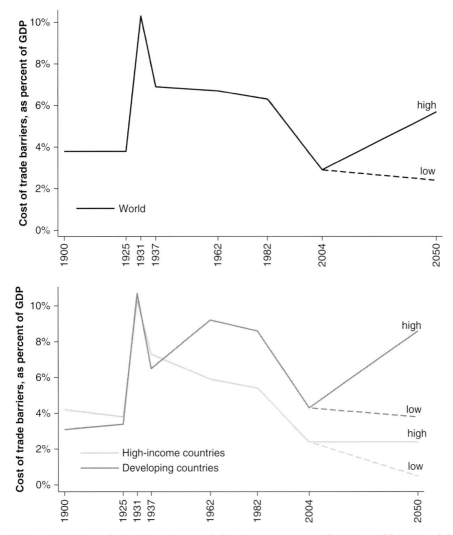

Figure I.10 *Cost of price-distorting trade barriers, as percent of GDP: world (top) and developing and high-income countries (bottom), 1900 to 2050. Note: "Low" and "High" scenarios refer to whether it is assumed that price distortions from trade barriers fall or rise between 2004 and 2050*

whether it is assumed that price distortions from trade barriers fall or rise between 2004 and 2050.

Greater liberalization, as proposed in the now-stalled Doha Round of World Trade Organization talks, could boost the economy further. If no further tariff cuts were made, it is quite likely that further agricultural protectionism would result, giving rise to an increase in developing country costs of more than 4 percentage points of GDP by 2050. The cost of 2.4% would remain for the developed world.

Conversely, in the scenario where greater liberalization was to occur, the cost to developing countries of trade barriers would fall slightly by half a percentage point, but nonetheless the world would be almost 5% richer than a continued Doha stall. In annual terms, this could be the difference by mid-century of $7.5 trillion. For the rich countries, it would be possible to see a further decrease of almost 2 percentage points of GDP towards 2050, resulting in almost no loss as a result of free trade.

These figures are for goods only, but the gains from removing barriers to trade in services could be considerably higher. It is also estimated that full, global, financial integration could permanently boost real consumption by 7.5%.

These sorts of increases can make a real difference to the lives of all people, and it is the poor who relatively have the most to gain. (Moreover, in another paper for the Copenhagen Consensus Center, Anderson has shown that the long-term, dynamic gain overwhelmingly benefits the developing world, even in absolute terms.)

While not a direct source of human misery in the same way as war, trade distortions seem to hold back many countries from realizing their full growth potential. Fundamentally, the cost of illiberal trade has come down dramatically since the Great Depression, and with smart policies that beneficial trend can be extended at least till 2050.

Providing adequate universal schooling is another challenge for many countries. In Chapter 5, Harry Patrinos and George Psacharopoulos estimate the economic costs of providing too little education, in terms of both productivity and equity across society.

In the prosperous countries of the West, rapid increases in literacy were achieved early in the twentieth century; in developing countries, similarly large gains were made in the increased provision of schooling from 1970 to 2000, with the biggest improvements in China. There is considerable continuing growth of education in developing countries, which still have a long way to go to catch up with the rich world. But this is a lengthy process: it typically takes somewhere between 35 and 80 years for a country to move from 10% to 90% net primary school enrollment. Even today, 23.6% of the world's population is still illiterate.

In the literature there are sharp disagreements on the relative importance of education to growth, and the greater part of the chapter discusses this in detail. Yet, all agree that the rate of return on education for individuals can be high, particularly at lower attainment levels, and especially in low-income countries, where highly educated individuals are more scarce.

The chapter also looks at how schooling not only improves economic performance, but also reduces inequality among members of society. Every country that has sustained high growth for long periods has put substantial effort into schooling; the challenge is to achieve this also in other, poorly performing developing countries. But education is not everything. In countries where people earn their living in traditional ways and new technologies are not readily taken up, the benefits of schooling are not fully realized.

Even in countries where education has been improving, girls are often disadvantaged relative to boys, and women may then suffer from lower social status, reduced earning power, and other discrimination in adult life.

If we are to evaluate the loss from inadequate education, one good measure is to see how much the world is losing from not having full literacy at different time points. The authors estimate that illiteracy costs 15.3 percentage points in GDP. They model illiteracy for countries with less than 5 years of schooling. By extrapolating illiteracy rates from 1950–2010 to 1900 and 2050 they find, as is evidenced in Figure I.11, that the global loss resulting from widespread illiteracy (around 70% in 1900) was 12.3% of GDP, dropping to 9% as midpoint of 1950–2010, and declining further to about 3.8% by 2050.

In Chapter 6, Joyce Jacobsen looks at the total economic cost of gender inequality. Participation in the workforce varies considerably from country to country, as does the ratio of women's hourly earnings to those of men. Yet, the overall and clear evidence is that women have participated much less in the workforce than men. With reasonable assumptions this means that the world has missed out in that GDP could be much larger, if the female productive segment had been better used.

In 1900, only 15% of the global workforce consisted of women and even in 2012, it was still a less-than-even 40%, probably trending towards 45% by mid-century. What is the loss of this underusage of women in the labor force? Jacobsen makes a maximal estimate by looking at how much more women would have contributed to GDP, had they participated in the workforce at the same rate as men and with the same pay. Deducted from this should be the value of forgone (and unpaid) household production from fewer housewives, as well as the increased cost of female education. With women constituting 40% of the global workforce

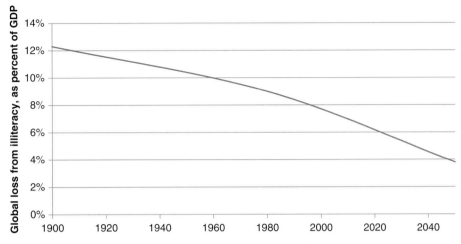

Figure I.11 *Global welfare loss from illiteracy, as percent of GDP*

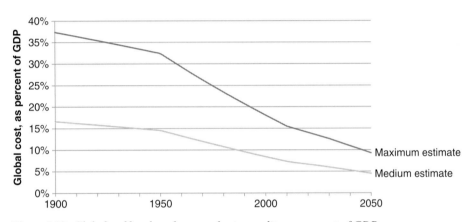

Figure I.12 *Global welfare loss from gender inequality, as percent of GDP*

in 2010, and earning only 60% as much as men, the loss to the economy is estimated at 15.5%, assuming the entire difference is due to discrimination.

The research acknowledges that part of the lower workforce participation may be ascribable to personal choices and not discrimination. In this medium estimate of gender inequality, the loss to the economy in 2010 is estimated at 7%.

Neither of these estimates takes into account other but equally important issues such as whether more equality would also mean more uncorrupt leaders (women are found to be less corrupt), fewer wars (female leaders would be less likely to go to war) and a quicker demographic transition (since formally employed women have fewer children).

Projecting forward to 2050, the more conservative, medium estimate still suggests a 4% loss to the world economy, totaling $6.4–9.7 trillion (for growth rates of 2.5% and 3.5%). Looking back towards the earlier part of the twentieth century, it would seem that the economic losses would have been very high; as late as after World War II, the economy lost over 15% of potential output, even if half the difference in labor market participation was due to personal choice.

In Figure I.12, we can see the decreasing trend of the global loss from gender inequality. Clearly, full gender equality would have significant additional benefits, although the extent of these is open to discussion.

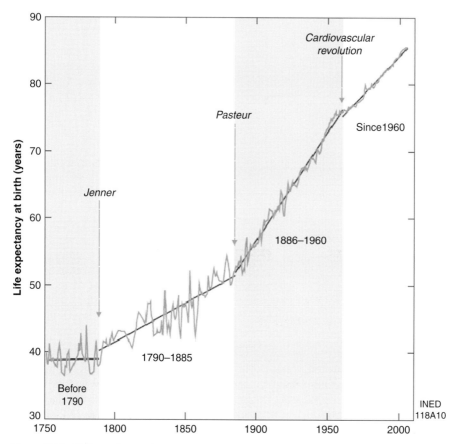

Figure I.13 *Highest observed national female life expectancies at a given moment in the world, 1750–2005. Note: Edward Anthony Jenner (1749–1823) was an English physician and scientist who was the pioneer of smallpox vaccine. Louis Pasteur (1822–95) was a French chemist and microbiologist who was one of the most important founders of medical microbiology.* Source: *Vallin and Meslé (2010)*

In Chapter 7, Dean T. Jamison, Prabhat Jha, Varun Malhotra, and Stéphane Verguet explore the twentieth century transformation of human health: its magnitude and value.

Although there was little change to life expectancy before the late eighteenth century, it is hard to overstate the magnitude of the improvement since then, as Figure I.13 shows.

The greatest improvements were in deaths of children under 5 years old, with mortality from infectious diseases falling much faster than for non-communicable diseases. Declines in low- and middle-income countries in the latter part of the twentieth century have been due to the rapid spread of technological advances from richer countries, where these same technologies had been drivers,

albeit at slower paces, of earlier increases in life expectancy. Income and education are also correlated with declining mortality, but direct causal links for all three factors are difficult to establish because of gaps in the data and the indirect effect of higher incomes on improved water supplies, transport, communications, and employment patterns, for example.

Incomes rose substantially in the twentieth century, but these do not account for much of the decline in mortality. Although higher incomes allow households to make some choices which help to reduce mortality of family members, the introduction of public health interventions such as smallpox vaccinations, quarantine for cases of infectious disease, or banning of smoking in public

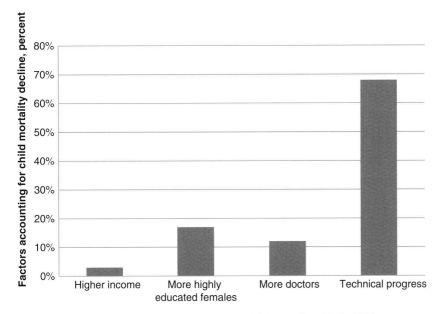

Figure I.14 *Factors accounting for decline in child mortality, 1970–2000*

places are often poorly correlated with income over-all. Thus technology (defined broadly as drugs, vaccines, diagnostics, treatment and prevention algorithms, and policies such as higher taxes on tobacco) appears to be the main driver of decreasing mortality (see Figure I.14).

Although death rates in some developing countries remain high, they are actually lower than those seen in Western countries a century or more ago. Childhood mortality in sub-Saharan Africa in 2008 was only a third of that in Liverpool in 1870, despite present-day Africans having a real per capita income just over half that of Liverpudlians in the late nineteenth century. In particular, vaccine-preventable deaths are much lower. For comparison, there were 10 million childhood deaths globally around 2001, rather than the 30 million there would have been if the death rates in Western countries at the beginning of the twentieth century had still applied. However, to put this in perspective, if global childhood death rates were the same as present-day England, the toll would be only 1 million across the world.

In the early twentieth century, an increasing knowledge of the causes of disease led to partially successful efforts to limit transmission. In the latter part of the century, because of the widespread use of vaccination, oral rehydration therapies, antibiotics, and malaria control interventions, much greater progress was made to reduce deaths. The probability of newborns dying before the age of 5 was still 23% in the early 1950s, but has fallen to just 6% in the current decade. This has largely come about because of the use of better technologies to control infectious diseases. In 1970, perhaps only 5% of infants were vaccinated against measles, tetanus, whooping cough, diphtheria, and polio. By 2000, 85% of children were being vaccinated, and it is estimated that this saves about 3 million lives each year. Diarrheal deaths have fallen by a similar number through the use of simple oral rehydration therapy, and the use of drugs can lower tuberculosis mortality rates from over 60% to 5% of cases.

Malaria remains an important contributor to mortality. However, it is estimated that between 13% and 33% of the overall decline in death rates over the period 1930–70 may have been due to malaria control and, more recently, the use of artemisinin in combination therapies has been shown to have a significant effect.

Major challenges still exist, with India alone losing over 2 million children in 2005, with nearly half of these deaths occurring in the first month of life. There is good evidence of lower death rates where vaccinations, treatment of acute respiratory infection in a medical facility, and use of oral rehydration therapy for diarrhea are used more widely. However, child mortality declines are likely to continue; even in Africa, mortality rates fell in the last decade of the twentieth century, despite increased malaria deaths, mother-to-child transmission of HIV, and economic stagnation. Current projections are that global child mortality (per live births) will fall from about 7.7% in 2000 to 3.1% in 2050.

However, there is a significant problem ahead. It is estimated that current smoking patterns will contribute to 1 billion deaths this century, mainly in low- and middle-income countries. This compares to about 100 million deaths in the twentieth century, mostly in high-income and Eastern European countries. Smoking currently directly causes 5–6 million deaths annually, about half of which are in low-income countries. About 70% of the 40 million worldwide deaths among adults over 30 are due to cancer and vascular and respiratory diseases, for all of which smoking is a contributory cause. Smoking also is a cause of tuberculosis death.

Lung cancer was a rare disease before World War II, but became common later in the West as the large increase in the incidence of smoking made possible by mass production manifested itself after a lag time

of about 30 years. China now has over 300 million smokers and India more than 120 million, and the full effects of this consumption have not yet been seen.

There have been large drops in the numbers of men smoking in high-income countries, and it has been found that cessation before middle age prevents more than 90% of the lung cancer mortality attributable to smoking. For those who do not stop, it seems that about half of all long-term smokers are killed by their addiction. Although about 80% of worldwide smoking deaths have been among men, this is because of the historical pattern of consumption; mortality risks for women are at least as high. Without significant increases in cessation (which is uncommon currently in low- and middle-income countries), total worldwide tobacco mortality will reach about 450 million over the first half of this century. Annual death rates will rise to about 10 million by about 2030, with some further increases expected.

Figure I.15 illustrates the total money metric value of years of life lost as percent of GDP for selected regions for the period 1900–2050. This dramatic decline is both a result of improved human health and economic growth.

In Chapter 8, Sue Horton and Richard Steckel explore the challenge of nutrition. Unfortunately, we do not have good data on nutrition for most regions across the past century. Instead the authors

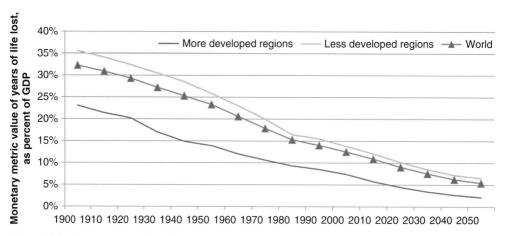

Figure I.15 *Money metric value of years of life lost (MMVYLL), selected regions, 1900–2050, as percent of GDP*

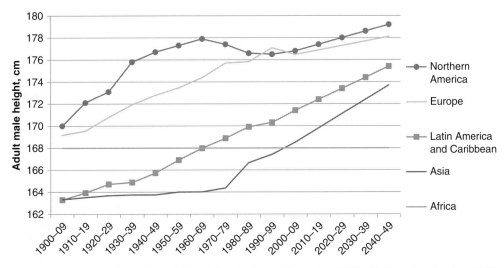

Figure I.16 *Estimated trends in adult male height (in cm) by region, 1900–2010, and projections 2010–2050*

use the well-known proxy of adult height, as it is a good indicator of long-term nutritional status.

Over the past century, we have seen increases in height and hence nutrition in most areas of the world, as is evident in Figure I.16. In North America height increased sharply in the first part of last century and then leveled off, Europe followed closely, whereas Latin America increased throughout the century but from a much lower level and Asia only beginning a sharp increase from a very low level towards the end of the century. Disappointingly, we have seen little or no development in African height over the past century. In the long run, it is assumed that all populations have similar genetic potential for height and hence if malnutrition was absent that all populations would trend towards a common upper height (as is evidenced in tall individuals from wealthy households across the world). It is thus clear that nutrition has dramatically improved throughout almost the entire world in the 150-year time-frame of this project.

The authors then use well-established empirical studies showing a clear connection between taller individuals and their income. Essentially, this is because taller individuals have experienced a better long-term nourishment and likely better physical and cognitive development. This relationship has not only been found in cross-section studies but also in longitudinal studies of nutritional interventions.

Notice, however, that the height proxy cannot take into account that better nourishment in adulthood can make you more productive (even if you're short from poor nutrition in your childhood) or that micronutrients in childhood may help cognitive development, independent of height. In this way, height is a conservative estimate of nutritional status.

From a range of empirical studies, the authors assume that populations with a median height of more than 178 cm (5 ft 10 in) have no loss of income. However, if the median height is lower, income is lower, and if the median height reaches just 170 cm (5 ft 7 in), studies indicate that you lose 22.5% of the income that would have been garnered by a taller and hence better-nourished population. It is assumed that below 170 cm, there is no extra wage penalty, just as there is no wage gain above 178 cm.

With this approach, the authors generate Figures I.17 and I.18 which demonstrate the loss from poor nutrition as a percentage of GNP, by geographic region and among developing/developed countries, and include projections ahead to 2050.

We can see that North America and Europe had a loss worth about 11% of GDP due to malnutrition in the early twentieth century, which then dropped steeply to the low levels found today. High levels continue in the developing world, but this is now dropping fast in Latin America and is expected to follow the same trend in Asia from 2020.

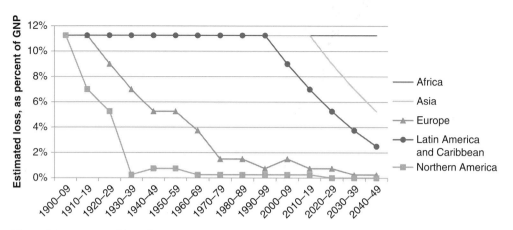

Figure I.17 *Estimated loss due to poor nutrition, geographic regions, 1900–2010, and projections 2010–2050, as percent of GNP*

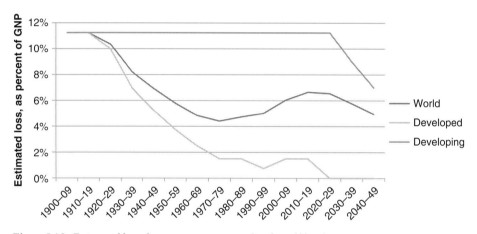

Figure I.18 *Estimated loss due to poor nutrition, developed/developing regions and world, 1900–2010, and projections 2010–2050, as percent of GNP*

Unfortunately, because of the stubborn low height in Africa, there is no expectation that the situation in Africa will improve by 2050. The "bulge" in the downwards-sloping world graph in Figure I.18 is due to the increasing weight of the developing world economy that still experiences losses of more than 11% of its GDP due to malnutrition.

Without the dramatic improvement in nutrition over the twentieth century, the welfare loss would have been about 8% of GDP. The average welfare loss of undernutrition in the first part of the twentieth century was more than 11% of GDP. Today, it is around 6% and by mid-century it will likely have been reduced to less than 5%.

In Chapter 10, Marc Jeuland and his colleagues analyze the impact of poor water and sanitation, which are associated with diseases that still cause 6–7% of deaths in developing countries.

Not surprisingly, most people want to have piped water and sewerage systems, but most of the health benefits can actually be realized using lower-cost interventions. Discerning the impact of improved water and sanitation is complicated because such improvements are accompanied by concurrent progress in healthcare and nutrition. In many cases, simple improvements such as chlorination or hand-washing significantly reduce the incidence of diarrhea, while access to piped water may make little difference if basic hygiene is not improved. This also means that improved access to water and sanitation cannot be the cause of the full or even a large part of the overall decrease in water- and sanitation-related deaths over the period.

A basic challenge turns out to be the very poor data on water and sanitation coverage stretching back before 1990, which means that in general the authors only make estimates from 1950–2050. Since most of the developed countries had already reaped almost all of the water and sanitation benefits by 1950, the analysis focuses on developing countries. Here, they estimate both the cost of mortality but also, and significantly for water acquisition, the cost of time spent in procuring water.

For the period 1950–2050, the authors first focus on four large developing countries – China, India, Brazil, and Nigeria – which account for more than half the total population of the developing world. These countries tell much of the water and sanitation story. The countries have all grown fast since 1990, but only China and Brazil have made big progress in provision of piped water and sewerage. India and Nigeria started from a much lower baseline and little progress has been made. While India may gradually overcome its problem by mid-century, excess mortality is likely to remain high in Nigeria. Already, the situation in India is better than in Nigeria, possibly because of better healthcare and more provision of simple water system improvements.

Fundamentally, the world has seen a dramatic reduction in the water- and sanitation-related death risk over the past 60 years and is likely to see even further reductions. The authors estimate the death rate per 1,000 in developing countries at 1.5 in 1950, reduced to 0.4 today and at 0.2 by mid-century. Time spent collecting water in the developing world has declined from 5 minutes per day per person in 1950, to about 2 ½ minutes today and likely will be reduced to just over 1 minute by mid-century.

This does not mean that water and sanitation is no longer a big issue. The deaths related to water and sanitation by 2050 will likely still be on the order of 1.7 million, mostly concentrated in sub-Saharan Africa, though down from 2.3 million today and 2.7 million in 1950. Likewise, today the developing world wastes 82 billion hours a year to procure water, though that number should be reduced to about 60 billion hours by mid-century.

The overall economic loss of lack of access to clean water and sanitation stemming from both mortality and time spent has in absolute terms remained significant across the period. It rose from a 1950 cost of $40 billion to a peak of about $60 billion in 1990. Since then it has declined, and will likely continue to do so till 2030 where the cost will be $45 billion and then rise somewhat to about $55 billion by 2050; although mortality and morbidity continue to fall, the value of time spent collecting water is steadily increasing because of higher incomes.

More importantly, though, the relative economic cost has declined dramatically over the period 1950–2050 for the developing world, as is evident in Figure I.19. Losses in 1950 were almost in the order of 2% of GDP, with mortality making up the vast majority of the losses. As more nations instituted better water and sanitation, mortality has declined precipitously, whereas the time loss has declined more slowly, making it constitute an increasing part of the ever smaller total loss.

The challenge of biodiversity is covered in Chapter 4 by Anil Markandya and Aline Chiabai. Although seemingly having less direct impact on human welfare, we clearly depend to a large extent on the Earth's natural resources. With the current high rate of species extinction, the – much-discussed – danger is that we lose valuable genetic resources and reduce ecosystem stability.

Markandya and Chiabai measure biodiversity via the well-developed concept of mean species abundance (MSA) as an indicator of overall ecosystem services. Essentially, MSA is an indicator of naturalness or biodiversity intactness. It is defined as the mean abundance of original species relative to their abundance in undisturbed ecosystems. An area with an MSA of 100% means a biodiversity that is similar to the natural situation, whereas an MSA of 0% means a completely disrupted ecosystem, with no original species remaining. They measure the MSA area as the area equivalent to undisturbed ecosystems – essentially if an area of 2,000 hectares has an MSA of 50%, it is seen as equivalent to an area of 1,000 hectares of undisturbed biome with an MSA of 100%.

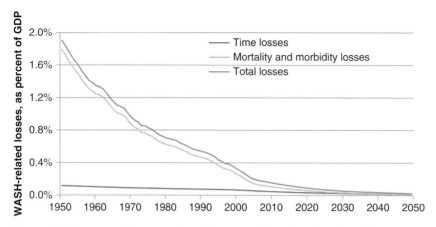

Figure I.19 *Base case "economic losses" associated with WASH-related diseases as percent of GDP for all developing regions (projections from 1950–2008 growth rates)*

The authors then used the estimates of a global biodiversity model providing MSA areas for the major biomes in the world – from tundra to tropical forests and deserts – in 1900, 2000, and 2050. This makes it possible to estimate what undisturbed biome equivalents the world had in those three representative years. Due to data limitations it is not possible to make a finer resolution of the world's biodiversity change over the period 1900–2050.

Overall, the world has lost significant biodiversity as humanity has encroached on many of the biomes. In total we have lost 21% in the period 1900–2000 and another 12% in 2000–2050, with a loss of 31% over the whole period.

In order to assess the total economic cost of these losses, the authors estimate the value of the reduction in MSA area for a number of main variables. Forests have value as forest products (e.g. wood, paper, and wood fuel) as well as non-wood products (like ferns, brazil nuts, maple syrup, as well as medicinal plants and bush meat). Forests also have cultural value as they are either used by humans (recreational value) or not used (e.g. the value of knowing-it-is-there for Westerners of having undisturbed rain forest in New Guinea). Finally, forests have value in that their loss means carbon dioxide emissions that have long-term negative global warming impacts.

On the other hand, most of the land converted (and hence the reduced MSA area) is converted to agriculture, which also provides a substantial benefit. This benefit is also included in the total estimate.

In total, the authors estimate that with mid-range estimates the world lost on average about 1% of GDP annually in the twentieth century because of biodiversity decline, as is evident in Figure I.20. This stems mainly from losses in temperate and especially tropical forests, whereas agricultural production contributes a benefit of almost 1.7% annually.

The authors then go on to estimate the benefits and losses of biodiversity in the period 2000–2050, taking the year 2000 as starting point. Here they find much reduced further losses in forests and likewise less conversion to agriculture, which is worth more nevertheless (because of higher food prices). In Figure I.21 we can see the total cost in terms of 2050 GDP to be a *benefit* of about 0.25 percentage point, composed of losses mostly from tropical forests and a significant benefit from increased agriculture.

The percentages in Figure I.21 are much smaller because they are part of a much larger GDP in 2050. However, if we look at the absolute cost, it is estimated with agricultural benefits to be a loss of $360 billion annually across the twentieth century (in 2000 US$). This loss continues into the twenty-first century (since the forests remain permanently lost), but we reduce biodiversity less in the first part of the twenty-first century, while the conversion to agriculture becomes more valuable, meaning that the total mid-range benefit is now $500 billion annually from 2000 to 2050 (in 2000 US$). Although this is pushing the numbers to their

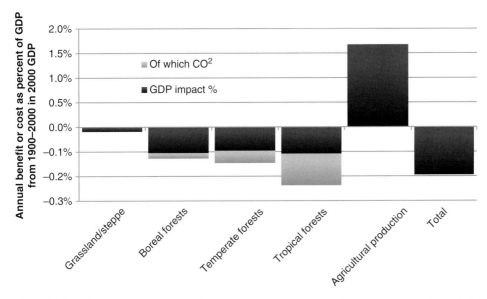

Figure I.20 *Relative annual economic benefits and loss as percent of 2000 GDP over the period 1900–2000 of biodiversity changes for various biomes (mid-range estimates)*

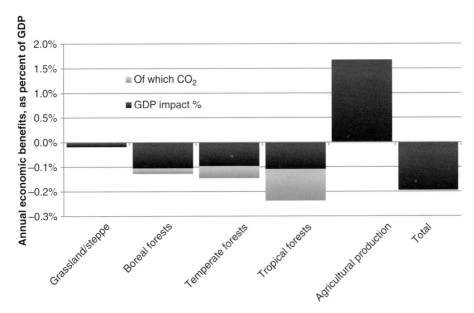

Figure I.21 *Relative annual economic benefits and loss as percent of 2050 GDP over the period 2000–2050 of biodiversity changes for various biomes (mid-range estimates, using 2000 as starting point)*

limit, the total benefit is $140 billion annually (from paying $360 billion in damages from the twentieth century, but receiving on average benefits of $500 billion in the twenty-first century).

In sum, there is a loss of biodiversity in both the twentieth century and first half of the twenty-first century, but this is compensated by gains in the agricultural sector. These gains promote the use of land for agriculture, but if the latter is intensive, it is not a sustainable solution in the long run. Also, the decrease in biodiversity levels in general will affect the agricultural sector at some point.

Summary

In some ways, this book represents a break from tradition for the Copenhagen Consensus Center. The think-tank undertakes research projects that inform governments, philanthropists and the public about the best ways to spend aid and development money by using cost–benefit analysis. All of our past projects – whose research has been published by Cambridge University Press – have focused on evaluating *solutions* to global challenges, rather than the *problems* themselves.

The Copenhagen Consensus 2004, 2008, and 2012 gathered expert panels of outstanding economists to deliver ranked lists of the most promising solutions to ten of the most pressing challenges facing the world. Around 60 leading economists and specialists in ten global challenges were involved in each project. The results of each project were published by Cambridge University Press, and will again be published from the 2012 Consensus, with new research and data delivering an up-to-date perspective on the smartest investments to respond to global challenges.

Consulta de San José 2007 (the Copenhagen Consensus for Latin America and the Caribbean) was a partnership with the Inter-American Development Bank. This project gathered highly esteemed economists to identify the projects that would best improve welfare in Latin America and the Caribbean.

Copenhagen Consensus United Nations brought together 24 United Nations ambassadors, including the Chinese, Indian, and American ambassadors, and set them the task of prioritizing limited resources along Copenhagen Consensus lines to improve efforts to mitigate the negative consequences of global challenges.

And the Copenhagen Consensus on Climate assembled an Expert Panel of five world-class economists, including three recipients of the Nobel Prize, to evaluate 21 research papers on different responses to climate change and to deliberate on which solutions would be most effective.

In 2011, RethinkHIV – funded by the Rush Foundation – gathered teams of economists and medical scientists to perform the first comprehensive, cost–benefit analysis of HIV/AIDS investment opportunities in sub-Saharan Africa.

Still, *The Twentieth-Century Scorecard* shares the same fundamental goal as those projects: to promote the use of fact-based economic science to identify the best spending priorities in any given area. It is very helpful to have a clear and unencumbered view of the scope of humanity's challenges.

One salient take-away point from these chapters is that sub-Saharan Africa remains the area experiencing the largest share of the world's afflictions. Despite long-term foreign aid programs, poverty, malnutrition, and disease are still the daily lot of many Africans and life expectancy is well below the global average. We need to prioritize policies that will reduce the widening welfare gap between the continent's citizens and the rest of the world.

The research presented here points to some salient lessons for policy-makers. The reduction of trade barriers, for example, would lead to an overwhelming boost to welfare everywhere, but especially in the developing world. Grasping these benefits is potentially one of this generation's greatest challenges. Trade barriers remain largely because further liberalization would redistribute jobs, income, and wealth in ways that governments fear would reduce their chances of remaining in power – and their own wealth in countries where corruption is rife. At a time of rising protectionist sentiment and with the Doha Round broken down, we are currently on a path to consigning millions more people to poverty needlessly.

Similarly, how we respond to climate change matters. As we see in Richard Tol's chapter, the negative effects are cruelly going to be worst in developing nations. Helping those nations adapt and build resilience must be at the forefront of any global warming response.

I believe that these analyses of very different human challenges are an important contribution to public discussion and debate. Overall this book showcases how humanity has solved substantial parts of many of its most challenging problems. When we look at the diagrams presented in this book and summarized here, we have seen problems decline often substantially in almost all areas in most of the period 1900–2050: this is true for water and sanitation, malnutrition, gender inequality, education, trade barriers, conflicts, air pollution, and diseases. Most of these reductions are in the order of 5–20% of GDP. The two environmental problems, climate change and biodiversity, are not clearly getting better. While climate change from 1900 to 2030 has contributed more and more to welfare (in the order of plus 1–2% of GDP) it is poised to be reduced going forward and will become a significant negative after the period considered in this book, towards the end of the century (in the order of minus 1–2% of GDP). Likewise biodiversity got worse in the twentieth century (in the order of minus 1% of GDP) while it may get slightly better in the twenty-first century (in the order of less than 1% of GDP). Of course, there are overlaps and synergies between these conditions. Some of the losses in the disease and education chapters are in fact attributable to nutrition as an underlying cause, for example. However it is difficult to estimate fully the amount of double-counting involved.

This matters because smart decisions, the goal of Copenhagen Consensus analysis, require a cool and rational approach to the world's big issues. It takes a level head to ask: "Where do we do the most good for the money?" Yet, often the world is portrayed as falling into a tailspin of epic destruction, where panic seems to be the only reasonable response. On TV and other mass media, it seems we are increasingly becoming guided by emotional appeals to respond to one catastrophe after another, with money often channeled to the issues that have the scariest pictures, the best PR agencies or proponents that scream the loudest. It is not likely that this offers the best way to do good.

Thus I hope that this book will help us keep our cool, so that we can look into the future, and resolutely ask: "Where can we do the most good first?" That is why I can summarize this book into a simple key message: things are getting better. Whether we look at air pollution or conflicts or education shortages, humanity made incredible strides over the last 100 years. That is not the same as saying that there are no problems. But by better understanding the real trajectory of the world's past, we are less likely to fall for panicky media messages. As we instead focus on the real shape of the biggest challenges facing humanity, it is my hope that we can better confront them.

Summaries

Summary of the Assessment Paper on Air Pollution: Global Damage Costs from 1900 to 2050

GUY HUTTON

Introduction

This chapter considers only air pollution of anthropogenic origin, since natural pollution events tend to be localized and relatively unimportant over the timescale covered. Indoor pollution can be traced back to the early use of fire for cooking and heating, and became an increasing problem as large-scale settlements developed. In present-day developing countries, the percentage of households burning solid fuels indoors ranges from 16% in Latin America and the Caribbean up to 77% in Africa. Man-made outdoor air pollution, on the other hand, only began to be a significant health issue with the Industrial Revolution in the eighteenth century.

Primary pollutants such as carbon monoxide or sulfur dioxide are released directly from engines or processes; ozone and particulate matter are among secondary pollutants formed by the reaction of primary pollutants. Polluted air can have direct impacts (on health, materials, and ecosystems) or less direct ones such as the formation of "acid rain" from sulfur dioxide, or population relocation. The major indirect effect of air pollution is the warming of the Earth's atmosphere by greenhouse gases emitted when fossil fuels are burned. This is included in another chapter in this Copenhagen Consensus project.

I estimate the damage caused by air pollution, but readers should bear in mind that this is a side effect of developments which have also had many positive benefits: permanent shelter, protection from cold, better food, and economic development.

There have been a number of economic studies done on outdoor or urban pollution. Damage cost studies tend to suffer from lack of direct comparability in terms of pollution components, impacts included and valuation approach, leading to widely differing costs of the health impacts. Cost–benefit analyses of alternative technology or policy options have also been done, with some efforts made by OECD members to quantify the benefits of different national policies, for example. For indoor air pollution, there are no damage cost studies, and only a few cost–benefit studies. There remain major gaps in our knowledge on global damage and trends, particularly for non-health impacts.

Methods

The aim in this chapter is to generate new estimates for the global damage costs of air pollution (anthropogenic only) between 1900 and 2050. Outdoor pollution – a mainly urban problem affecting industrialized countries, but increasingly in developing countries as well – and indoor pollution – affecting a high proportion of families in developing countries – are dealt with separately. Human health impacts of both indoor and outdoor pollution are included, while damage associated with aesthetics and buildings are estimated only for outdoor pollution, since these are the only data available. The effect of outdoor pollution on agriculture is estimated, as is the cost of time to collect biomass and other socio-economic factors on indoor pollution. Climate change, ecosystem impact, water resources, and acid rain are outside the scope of this chapter.

Our estimates are presented on a global basis, but also broken down by developed and developing countries. This separates regions where air pollution issues and the rate of population growth are very different. The 150-year timescale for this work presents some problems, since historical data on air pollution damage are incomplete and projections rely on estimates of unpredictable patterns of economic growth and policy measures. Overall, much of the available data have been published in a piecemeal way.

The damage estimates are based on the numbers of people exposed to pollution. Outdoor pollution affects primarily urban populations, but crop damage is estimated for the entire population; the population at risk from indoor pollution is that proportion using solid fuels. The comparative exposure levels over time are based on the development stages outlined by Mage: (1) industrial development, (2) emissions control, (3) stabilization of air quality, and (4) improvement of air quality. For example, in the USA, emissions of many pollutants increased from 1940 to 1970, and then fell back to 1940 levels by 1998, driven by regulations such as the Clean Air Act and federal motor vehicle emissions standards. Earlier in the century, pollutants such as sulfur dioxide and nitrogen oxides had shown a similar pattern of increase. Similar, steep reductions have been seen in the European Union and Japan, for example. A steady, but slower, rate of reduction in the developed world is expected, with air quality assumed to be 20% better than current levels by 2050.

In developing country cities, outdoor pollution has grown later, from a much lower baseline. I assume a gradual growth through the twentieth century, with continued increases beyond that due to economic growth, but offset by technology transfer. Generalizations are difficult, as some cities have already implemented controls and are experiencing declining pollution levels.

Solid fuel use is difficult to estimate, because of lack of data. I assume solid fuel use as 50% of developed country households in 1900, with a linear rate of decline until 2010, when a 5% rate is assumed. For developing countries, I assume a 95% use in 1900, falling to 67% in 2010, and then a faster drop after 2020 to 30% in 2050. Although total numbers living in urban areas is forecast to rise from 3.6 billion in 2010 to 6.6 billion in 2050, the population exposed to indoor air pollution is predicted to fall from 3.9 billion to 2.5 billion in 2050, as pollution control measures continue to take effect. If greater use is made of smokeless and more efficient biomass stoves in the developing world, exposure levels could be lower still.

Figure S.1 summarizes estimated patterns of population exposure over the period of study.

Health damage is assessed as premature mortality and the costs of higher morbidity (medical treatment and lost time due to sickness). Of the various alternative ways to value premature death, the established and widely used value of a statistical life (VSL) is used. There are a wide range of values reported from different studies, but I take a conservative figure of $3 million (deflated to 1990) for developed countries, which is based on elderly people being most at risk. For our sensitivity analysis, I take upper and lower bounds of $5 million and $1 million. The $3 million figure is used as a basis

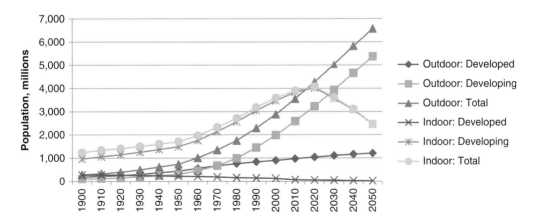

Figure S.1 *Total population exposed to air pollution*

to estimate the VSL for developing countries, adjusting based on comparative GDP with developed countries at official exchange rates. The average value comes to $685,000 (deflated to 1990) across middle- and low-income countries.

Medical costs vary widely depending on the severity of the condition, the type of care received, and the unit cost of treatment. I therefore derive an average cost estimate for a moderately severe case, assuming that 50% of patients visit an outpatient clinic at least once and 10% are admitted to hospital for an average of 5 days. Outpatient care is assumed to cost $70 in developed countries and $5 in developing countries; hospitalization is charged at $200 and $30 per bed-day respectively. These assumptions result in average costs per illness in 2010 of $159 in developed countries and $20 in developing countries, the latter likely to be a conservative estimate.

For time lost due to illness, I make a conservative assumption of 5 days away from productive activity per case. Other welfare losses are also taken into account – i.e. lost leisure time, missed education, etc. – and come to a conservative estimate of time valued at 30% of GDP per capita.

Material damage due to corrosion, soiling, or ozone damage to rubber and other polymers, for example, is assessed as cost per person in urban areas. Using the results of published studies, suggests a figure of $20 per person in developed countries, which is likely to be an underestimate. For developing countries, figures are somewhat lower, but fewer studies are available on which to base estimates. Adjustments are made from the available studies based on population exposed, relative pollution levels and economic levels (GDP per capita).

Natural resources can also suffer damage. Ozone is the most serious air pollution problem for agriculture and horticulture. For the USA, a number of studies have given costs in the range of $5–20 per capita per year. A similar range – with higher upper bounds – was found in a number of European countries. For this chapter, a figure of $20 per capita is used for developed countries and $5 for developing countries.

There are several other costs to be included. Time lost in gathering fuel and in cooking with inefficient stoves has to be allowed for, and for this I use an overall figure from a WHO study for non-OECD countries of $88 billion in 2000, adjusted for GDP and population size. The annual cost of visibility reductions to tourists and local residents is estimated as $10 per capita for urban populations of developed countries, with extrapolations to developing countries based on GDP per capita. Damage to ecosystems is valued at about $15 per capita, but this is not included in this chapter, as it is dealt with in another chapter for this Copenhagen Consensus project.

Lastly, I conducted sensitivity analysis, given a range of some important necessary assumptions. The two variables used for this are the economic value of life and the levels of historical and projected pollution.

Results

Total Damages

Our estimate of the total damages due to air pollution in 2010 is $3 trillion, or 5.6% of gross world product (GWP). The cost of outdoor pollution is shared equally by developed and developing countries, but the major burden of indoor pollution falls on the developing world. By 2050, the cost of air pollution is expected to fall to 4% of GWP.

Since 1900, developing countries have seen outdoor pollution costs fall from 5.2% of GDP, to a projected figure of 2.5% by 2050. The pattern in developing countries is very different, with a major growth in damages expected to stabilise at 2.8% of GDP in 2050. A cost of 7.7% of GDP for indoor air pollution in 1900 in developed countries has fallen rapidly to 0.3% today. For developing countries, indoor pollution has caused a high number of premature deaths, contributing to a cost of 42% of GDP in 1900, decreasing to 24% in 1950, 5.4% in 2010, and projected to drop further to 1.7% in 2050.

The costs of indoor and outdoor pollution remain similar until 2020, when cuts in indoor pollution make the costs of outdoor pollution dominate. Overall risks to health and premature deaths are expected to fall with time, but economic growth still leads to greater costs overall. Similarly, costs in developing countries are outstripping those in the developed world because of economic growth, even as risks decline. The result is still a per capita cost of $700–800 per capita by 2050, dominated by health costs and with outdoor air pollution accounting for two-thirds of these. The costs are inevitably borne largely by developing countries, where 85% of the global population lives.

Developing and Developed Countries

Damage costs in developing countries are continuing to escalate. This is largely driven by the numbers of premature deaths, which are declining as indoor pollution is reduced, but increasing with higher levels of outdoor pollution and urban population exposed. These countries are set to lose nearly $6 trillion by 2050, with the damage from outdoor pollution exceeding that of indoor pollution by 2040.

In developed countries, damage costs from indoor and outdoor pollution were similar at the beginning of the twentieth century, but have since diverged sharply, with outdoor pollution dominating. There is set to be a continuing decline in the number of deaths, but the lower proportional reductions in air pollution mean that rising real prices lead to a rising overall cost.

Contribution to Impacts

By far the largest contribution to the total damage from outdoor pollution in both developed and developing countries comes from the costs of mortality. In both cases, it represents over 80%

of the total, even in 1900, and rises slowly but steadily throughout the period studied. Health productivity, healthcare costs, crop production, material damage, and visibility are all quite minor contributors.

For indoor pollution in developed countries – which is much less of a problem than outdoor pollution – the costs are split between three main factors: premature mortality, health-related productivity loss, and healthcare costs. A little over 10% also comes from time to collect biomass, or equivalent costs of purchase. Damage costs from indoor pollution in developing countries, on the other hand, are dominated by excess mortality, which accounts for 85–90% of the total. This breakdown is quite stable over the whole time frame.

Sensitivity Analysis

Changing the baseline pollution figures to pessimistic ones makes a significant difference to the costs over the twentieth century, with costs in 1900 rising to 25% of GWP from a baseline figure of 20%. More optimistic assumptions make comparatively little difference, with the 1900 damage still amounting to more than 18% of GWP. By 2050, even with the most pessimistic assumptions, total damage is still only about 5% of GWP, supporting the confidence in the overall projected trends.

Given the dominance of mortality figures in the overall results, it is not surprising that changing the VSL assumption makes a large difference to the damage estimates, as shown in Figure S.2.

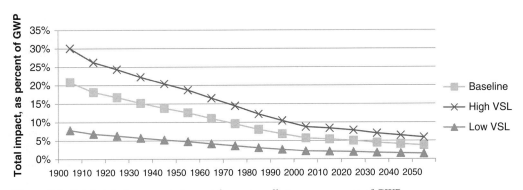

Figure S.2 *Total global economic impact from air pollution, as percent of GWP*

Discussion

Difficulties with collecting data for earlier periods and making projections to mid-century with any confidence have been real challenges for this study, and the estimates are, not surprisingly, imprecise. Even since 1990, when there have been many studies on the effect of air pollution, the evidence is incomplete, particularly for developing countries. Despite these caveats, the overall and continuing trend of declining damage costs (which continues to hold up in the sensitivity analysis) is encouraging for human development. However, the projected continued improvements depend on both the success of current and future policies and sustainable economic growth.

Costs are dominated by health issues, particularly mortality. This is partly due to the extensive literature in this area, making them easier to quantify. It is a possibility that other factors have been underestimated and that the total cost of damages could be significantly higher. Also, some non-health aspects of air pollution have been omitted as they are covered by other authors.

An equity analysis is outside the scope of this work, but one should remember that the burden of damage falls disproportionately on the poor, rural families, and some categories of urban workers. Particularly vulnerable groups include the elderly, those with existing respiratory health conditions, and women and children who are most subject to indoor (household) pollution. It is also important to note that comparisons between developed and developing countries in the same currency unit imply that pollution reduction measures are worth more in more prosperous countries. It is thus fairer to make comparisons based on percentage of GDP.

Finally, we should return to the issue of the double-edged nature of air pollution, it being an unwanted side effect of economic and technological developments which in other respects have increased incomes and living standards. Both governments and citizens have in practice been willing to trade off some health impacts against other gains in quality of life. Now, with freer trade and greater environmental knowledge, choices are available which could significantly increase or decrease our projected costs for damage from air pollution, depending on the development pathway followed.

Summary of the Assessment Paper on Armed Conflicts: The Economic Welfare Costs of Conflict

S. BROCK BLOMBERG AND GREGORY D. HESS

Introduction

Wars of various sorts have cast a long shadow over history. There are many theories which seek to explain international wars, civil conflict, and terrorist operations, generally based on the idea of leaders convincing followers to fight for a particular purpose, whether ostensibly noble (an ideology, religion, culture, or form of government) or not.

Leaders may or may not profit from conflicts, but the costs are largely borne by the men and women who fight, whose interests are by no means always reflected in those of their leaders. But, despite its inherent wastefulness, war is still with us and will certainly remain so throughout this century. Nevertheless, by better understanding the costs of war – by analyzing the waste – we may be able to build institutions which reduce the probability of future conflict.

In our chapter, we estimate the effect of military spending on economic activity and alternative consumption to consider how the balance of "Butter" and "Guns" would be affected by a return to more warlike times. We use standard economic theory to answer how much people would be prepared to pay to avoid a return to such times. The average person would be prepared to pay 8% – a significant tax – to avoid returning to a position of systemic conflict, which strongly suggests that domestic and international institutions can and should be designed to realize the benefits of peace.

Yet despite this, and even higher estimates from other researchers, conflicts continue to break out, for a variety of reasons. Studies have suggested on one hand that authoritarian regimes are more likely to engage in longer, riskier wars but that on the other hand democratic governments tend to use force to divert attention from domestic problems. Overall, the literature argues that the current generation's conflicts have ethnic or cultural tensions as their root cause, or have been due to increased changes brought on by democratization. However, though serious, these conflicts appear insignificant compared to previous generations' world wars.

Society has benefitted from the "peace dividend" experienced since the early 1990s, but there is still significant military spending which cuts into this. If one country increases its military spending, this typically results in neighboring countries following suit, at a significant cost to them all. Another limit placed on the peace dividend may arise from the break-up of large countries, resulting in an increase in regional conflicts.

Against this background, we estimate the "opportunity cost" of war by examining the returns from the peace dividend via the split of spending between "Guns" and "Butter" for different periods since 1900.

The World Economy from 1900 to the Present

Since the turn of the twentieth century, the world has become much richer (albeit unevenly so) at the same time as many more independent countries have emerged. In 1900, there were 57 countries; a hundred years later this had risen to 192. At the same time, the global population balance has changed enormously.

In general, the rate of economic growth slows as countries become more developed. But less-developed countries in Africa and Latin America have had periods of much slower growth than expected, which may be partly rooted in the higher level of conflict experienced. Overall, though, growth in the twentieth century has been much

greater than in any previous period. Based on the burst of global growth experienced over much of the new century's first decade, we expect growth in the twenty-first to be significantly higher again.

Conflicts in the Twentieth Century

Despite two world wars and many other conflicts, last century also showed a trend towards conflict resolution. Wars accounted for between 136.5 and 148.6 million deaths, but 78–90 million of these were in the two world wars. Since then, deaths have fallen considerably. Figure S.3 shows the pattern of military expenditure as percentage of global GDP, with World Wars I and II, the first Gulf War, and 9/11 marked in red.

There has been a dramatic reduction in military spending since World War II, with some increase during the Cold War, and a decline since 1991. But spending is still significant, and the decline may not continue, given the increases following the 9/11 attacks. Spending is dominated by a handful of countries, with the USA and UK alone making up more than 50% of the total, and spending in the USA has increased since 2001.

This has had some impact also on military expenditure in the highest-income countries, but most other countries have continued to enjoy a peace dividend. Looking at the issue of governance, we find that non-democratic states have had greater variation in their spending patterns, largely due to the outbreak of civil wars. Democracies, on the other hand, have seen a smoother decline but now tend to spend more than autocratic regimes. Breaking down the data by region, we see significant levels of military expenditure in the Middle East and North Africa, North America and Western Europe, with the peace dividend being enjoyed to a greater extent in other regions.

Analytical Methodology

Violent conflict involves significant human costs. We can estimate the economic costs, which are large; if we were also able to measure the non-economic costs, the total would rise considerably.

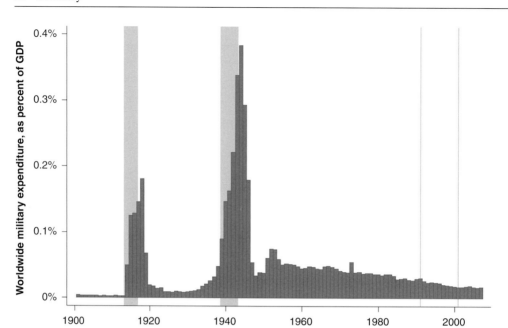

Figure S.3 *Worldwide military expenditure as percent of GDP, 1900–2007*

We use the simple Guns versus Butter trade-off popularized by Paul Samuelson in his 1973 textbook. A country has the possibility to produce various combinations of "Guns" and "Butter" and there are combinations which provide the average citizen with a given level of utility. All things being equal, a country is better off if they can consume more of each good, but the population may be willing to trade off Guns for Butter along a particular indifference curve (U). The curve which is just tangential to the production possibility frontier (connecting points $\bar{G}$ and $\bar{B}$ in Figure S.4) is optimal for society; it indicates combinations of Guns and Butter which the country can produce and which its society prefers to consume. Note also that, as the indifference curves move to the top right, they denote a result which is better for society.

Using this as a basis, we can estimate how much an average citizen would pay to consume his or her preferred combination of more Butter and less Guns (the pre-conflict curve above). This is a straightforward calculation which assumes there are no long-run growth costs or economic volatility costs of war. Neither does it include costs of

war from production reallocation, nor direct costs associated with the conflict itself and resultant loss of life. Because our estimated costs will be shown to be very large, the fact that these additional costs are omitted simply makes our conclusions stronger.

With these caveats in mind, we have estimated the ratio of military to total spending (Guns/Guns + Butter = g) for a number of contrasting periods – the 1944 spending peak, the height of the Korean War in 1952, the end of the Cold War in 1989, 2000 (just pre-9/11), and 2007. The average unweighted value of g, the military spending ratio, was 11.4% in 1944 and had fallen to 2.5% in 2007. If we weight the results according to GDP, then g reaches 33.2% in 1944. East Asia and the Pacific and North America have seen their military spending ratios decline the most since World War II, dominated by the United States, which has seen the biggest decline since the Korean War.

From these results, we can make welfare calculations, expressed as the fraction of consumption which would be forgone to avoid a return to the very high military spending ratios of World War II and the Korean War. The figures are

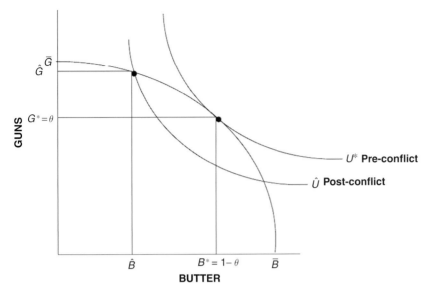

Figure S.4 *"Guns" vs. "Butter": How much would you pay?*

striking: the average East Asian economy would give up 38% of its current level of consumption to avoid this happening; North America and Western Europe would sacrifice 25% and 12% respectively. The unweighted average across all countries is 8%, but weighting by GDP increases that very significantly, to 26.2%, reflecting the very high expenditure by high-income countries during World War II.

If we consider the cost of conflict as a tax, we can calculate the total cost from figures for each country's consumption. For East Asia and the Pacific, the permanent annual peace dividend from the end of World War II is over US$500 billion, and for North America the figure is US$1.4 trillion. The present discounted value of the peace dividend, using a 5% discount rate and scaled by the current level of GDP, is 3.9 times GDP for East Asia and 3.1 for North America. Conflict, it turns out, can be quite expensive.

The Human Cost of War

To this point, we have considered only the welfare cost of lost consumption, but we cannot ignore the loss of human life in conflicts. Our approach to this is to calculate the present value of the consumption peace dividend with the increased survivorship inherent in fewer conflicts. In periods of conflict, not only do citizens consume too little Butter and too many Guns, they also value the future less and hence have a lower lifetime welfare.

To arrive at a value, we estimate from battle casualty figures from World War II that there was an enhanced global death rate of 1% during the war. Including this factor in our calculations, we find that all the previous costs based on consumption changes alone are increased by about 50%. The global annual post-World War II peace dividend (calculated on a weighted basis) without allowing for loss of life stands at over US$10 trillion; with increased mortality added, that rises to over US$15 trillion.

The additional cost of human losses may seem large, but in fact is quite conservative, since we do not take account of civilian deaths, which would roughly double the probability of premature loss of life. On the other hand, the nature of conflict is changing, with the use of robotics and deployment of drones, making human losses on a scale comparable to World War II unlikely in any future conflict. It is for reasons such as these that we

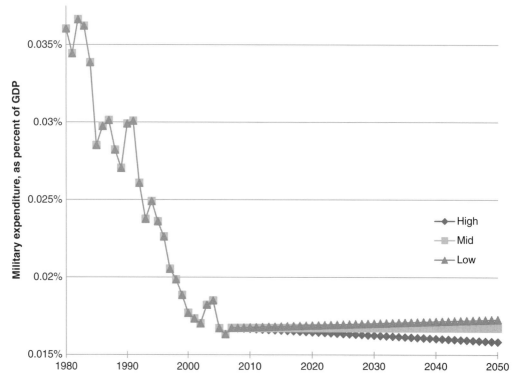

Figure S.5 *Worldwide military expenditure as percent of GDP, 1980–2050 (different conflict scenarios)*

have chosen to concentrate on losses of welfare due to lost consumption, which are less sensitive to these challenges.

2007–2050: Predicting the Peace Dividend?

In projecting forward, we use three scenarios:

- High-conflict scenario – conflict and military spending, due to the events following 9/11, continues to grow at the trend rate from 2000 to 2007.
- Medium-conflict scenario – conflict and military spending remain steady at the current ratios.
- Low-conflict scenario – conflict and military spending continue to fall to the low point after the decade following the Cold War.

Figure S.5 above shows the results. The three scenarios make little real difference in current circumstances and it would seem that the gains to peace have largely been achieved. Extending our

calculations, the future peace dividend is approximately 8%.

Conclusion

The world is now richer and has fewer conflicts, and military spending has been dramatically reduced. The peace dividend has been enormous, but the costs of war remain a large threat and investment in peace must therefore be at least as large.

The costs of war in terms of an opportunity cost to welfare are about 91% of GDP in present discounted terms. This is a welfare loss of US$9,250 per person (2007 dollars). Human costs, by our reckoning, add an additional US$4,760. The opportunity cost is similar to our previous estimate (US$10,449 per capita) made using a different approach. Calculating the human cost on the more conventional measure of disability-adjusted life years (DALYs) gives us a figure of US$3,900 per capita. Such comparisons, we believe, provide more support for our analysis.

Summary of the Assessment Paper on Climate Change: The Economic Impact of Climate Change in the Twentieth and Twenty-First Centuries

RICHARD S. J. TOL

Introduction

Climate is naturally variable and subject to a number of different cyclical changes, both short (over a period of years) and long (taking millennia). However, the term "climate change" is used here and more generally to mean the additional effect of so-called greenhouse gases (particularly carbon dioxide) added to the atmosphere by human activity. There are many papers which project the future impacts of climate change, but less is known about past impacts. However, such estimates would help to improve the models and so increase confidence in their use for future projections. This chapter uses a model to provide a "backcast" of past impacts, so generating hypotheses which can be tested against observational evidence.

Various effects of past climate change have been estimated, although no one has tried to produce an overall assessment. A significant amount of work has been done on the damage caused by natural disasters. The general conclusion is that upward trends are largely due to increases in the number of people and their wealth. Put simply, the major effect is that hurricanes, floods, droughts, etc. of any given size have tended to affect larger numbers of richer people with more extensive and expensive property.

Past changes in the climate have been found to have a significant effect on crop yields, albeit a small one compared to other agricultural trends. However, the observed impact can be either positive or negative, depending on the crop and location. There is little statistical evidence of any effect of increasing carbon dioxide concentrations, but direct experimental evidence shows that this in isolation has a positive effect on yield particularly if plants are well fertilized (for example, greenhouse crops are routinely grown using artificially boosted levels of carbon dioxide in the air).

Climate also affects health. There has been intense debate about the spread of malaria, although the general consensus is now that any climate effect may be small. The incidence of diarrhea is known to be sensitive to weather patterns, but there is little evidence for any link to changing patterns of climate. There is, however, direct evidence of negative effects of both heat and cold stress. A higher death rate among the elderly was a widely reported consequence of the 2003 European heatwave, while cold winter weather also regularly causes an increased number of deaths.

A related pattern is found for energy demand: more heating is needed in cold winters, and more cooling in hot summers. The few studies that have looked at long time periods, not surprisingly, conclude that warming would reduce energy demand in winter but increase it in summer. Depending on factors such as the current climate and the extent to which air conditioning and space heating is used, the net effect of warming could be either a higher or lower demand for energy. Likewise for the impact on water resources, studies on different catchment areas suggest that every river system responds differently to changes in precipitation and temperature.

Overall, researchers have found mixed effects of climate change on a range of variables, and none have aggregated these impacts to estimate the net impact. This chapter attempts to do just that using a specific model.

Starting Point: The Data and Model

Good data on population and income by country are available from 1960 to 2000. Prior to 1960, regional data are available, and I have assumed that national growth rates within regions are all the same. These data are used with a particular computer model of the climate, the Climate Framework for Uncertainty, Negotiation and Distribution (FUND) which covers the impacts of climate change at the national level. The model baseline is taken as 1895 and it runs from 1900 to 2100 in 5-year steps.

The impact module of the model covers the following areas: agriculture, forestry, sea level rise, disease and illness (cardiovascular disorders due to cold or heat stress, respiratory disorders, malaria, dengue fever, schistosomiasis, and diarrhea), energy consumption, water resources, unmanaged ecosystems, and storms (both tropical and others). This is not exhaustive, but there are no consistent quantitative data available for other factors.

Damage (due to climate change only) is expressed in dollars at market exchange rates. Damages are welfare losses expressed in income equivalents. That is, a $100 annual damage feels as if you had lost $100 of your annual income. Damage can be related to either the rate of temperature change (benchmarked at an annual rate of 0.04 °C) or the total extent of the change (benchmarked at 1.0 °C temperature rise since pre-industrial times). In this model, the damage due to the rate of temperature increase slowly fades, reflecting adaptation, while there is a continuing impact from higher average temperatures.

Climate change can have a range of effects, and all of these must be assigned a value. So, in the case of premature death, the value of a statistical life is set at 200 times the annual per capita income, which lies midway in the range observed. Similarly, sea level rise may force emigration, the value of which is set at three times per capita income. The loss of 1 square kilometer of dry land from rising sea level averaged $4 million in OECD countries in 1990 and is assumed to be proportional to GDP per square kilometer. A square kilometer of wetland is valued at $2 million.

Impacts in other categories such as agriculture, energy, and storm damage can be calculated directly. In the case of energy consumption, farming, and cardiovascular and respiratory disease, it is recognized that there is a climate optimum, where overall welfare is maximized. The impact of climate change may therefore be either positive or negative, depending on which side of the optimum a particular country begins at.

Population growth, economic growth, and technological progress all affect how vulnerable societies are to climate change, and the extent and direction of this varies from area to area. For example, water resources are expected to be more vulnerable as population rises and heat-related disorders will tend to increase with urbanization. On the other hand, energy supply is projected to become less vulnerable with technological progress, as is agriculture as economies grow.

Results

The model does not include any estimate of the impact of annual weather variability, but only takes account of climate change trends. There has been considerable variation in the recent past: the 1900s saw cooling, followed by three decades of warming, three decades of climate volatility and then warming once more from the 1970s to the turn of the century. The projected warming for the twenty-first century follows a smooth path. The overall effect is a rise in global mean surface air temperature of 3.5 °C from 1900 to 2100.

The economic impact of this pattern of temperature rise aggregated over the different sectors is summarized in Figure S.6.

Note that climate change has increased global welfare over the twentieth century and the impact is set to reach a maximum of about 1.5% of GDP by 2025 before falling steeply to a 1.2% loss by 2100. The equity-weighted impacts are more positive in the twentieth century, showing that poorer countries receive more benefit than the average, largely due to the positive impact of carbon dioxide on agriculture. However, the effect quickly becomes negative, and the equity-weighted economic loss amounts to 2.8% by 2100.

The impact on the different sectors varies enormously, and these are shown in Figure S.7. The impact of tropical storms and sea level rise are both small. There is a negative effect on water resources, but the overall impact is not more than 0.2% of GDP. Health impacts are mixed, depending on the extent of warming, demographics, and income (as a proxy for healthcare). This gives the complex pattern shown in Figure S.7 with positive (though falling) benefits through to the end of the twenty-first century.

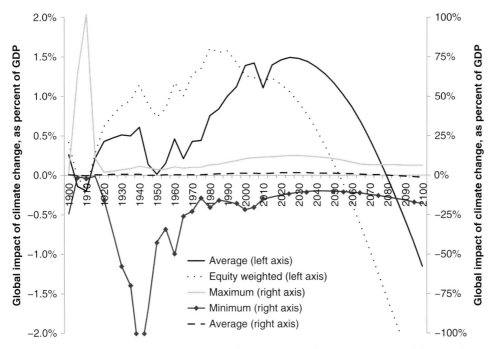

Figure S.6 *The global average, minimum, and maximum total economic impact of climate change in the twentieth and twenty-first centuries*

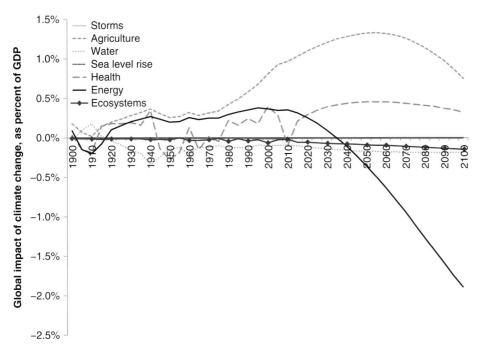

Figure S.7 *The global average economic impact of climate change by sector, as percent of GDP*

The biggest positive impact during the twentieth century is on agriculture, where the carbon dioxide fertilization effect greatly outweighs any other negative effects of rising temperatures. The positive impact is projected to peak at 1.3% of GDP by 2055, but to still stand at 0.8% of GDP at the end of the century. The impact on energy use is also positive through the twentieth century, largely due to the reduction in demand for heating. However, the annual savings of about 0.4% of GDP in the 1990s are soon offset by a rapidly rising demand for cooling, resulting in a large negative impact (1.9%) by 2100.

Figure S.6 also shows the maximum and minimum impact across countries, as well as the global mean. The large variations from the mean – by two orders of magnitude – reflect mainly differences in health outcomes in different countries during the rapid cooling in the 1900s and the rapid warming three decades later. In the twenty-first century, the range of impacts is much lower, but the average still hides considerable variation. China, for example, benefits most from twentieth century climate change because of positive effects from agriculture, energy use, and water resources. In contrast, every African country loses out over the century, with health impacts outweighing gains from agriculture.

Climate change has caused the premature deaths of a substantial number of people over the twentieth century, an average of over 7.5 million each year. According to the FUND model, the number of climate-change-related deaths in 2000 was 90,000. Projecting forward through the twenty-first century, cold-related cardiovascular deaths fall steadily, while those caused by heat rise rapidly. Deaths from respiratory disease also increase, but those due to malaria and diarrhea fall with improving healthcare as a consequence of economic growth. Since the 1900s, there has been a clear divide between rich, temperate countries which have seen positive impacts of climate change and the rest of the world, for which the consequences have been negative. This pattern is set to become more entrenched during the twenty-first century.

Conclusions

This study shows that past, moderate climate change brought net benefits, largely attributable to agriculture and reduced energy demand. However, for the twenty-first century, the impact on most countries, whether rich or poor, becomes negative and future climate change is therefore a cause for concern.

A comparison of the model output and observations allows some hypotheses on the future effects of climate change to be tested. Both the model and observation show impacts on human health to be more often negative than positive and the impact on energy use to be positive. The model projects a largely negative impact on water resources and a largely positive one for agriculture, but the actual evidence is more mixed in both cases. Climate variability is accounted for in the twentieth-century backcast, but not in the forecast. This suggests that the range of impacts projected for the twenty-first century has been underestimated. Overall, further work is needed with both FUND and other models to build confidence in their projections.

Summary of the Assessment Paper on Ecosystems and Biodiversity: Economic Loss of Ecosystem Services from 1900 to 2050

ANIL MARKANDYA AND ALINE CHIABAI

Introduction

Loss of biodiversity is an important issue, as it is estimated that species are becoming extinct at a rate two or three orders of magnitude greater than in geological times. This has important economic and social consequences, impacting, for example, the availability of traditional medicines and reducing the genetic diversity from which many modern pharmaceuticals are derived. However, measuring biodiversity is problematic, and its link to economic and social issues extremely complex.

Rather than tackle this complexity head-on, the Millennium Ecosystem Assessment (MEA) considers ecosystem services, grouped under the headings of provisioning, cultural, supporting, and regulating services. These services have themselves been facing major losses, with about 60% being degraded in the last 50 years, as 50% of wetlands, 40% of forests, and 35% of mangroves have been lost in a century.

Despite the complexity and the lack of full understanding, there is widespread agreement amongst ecologists that greater biodiversity tends to increase ecosystem stability, but this is not sufficient for us to place a value on biodiversity per se. In this study, we estimate the economic value of ecosystem services, and take account of the influence of biodiversity by using the so-called mean species abundance (MSA) approach. We estimate the total size and quality of the biomes (major habitat type) in different regions for 2000 and 1900 and then project forward to 2050, with calculations being based on MSA area. From this we estimate the value of services at these points in time. The data show significant losses in both periods.

Because it is difficult to know details of prices and economic conditions in 1900 and 2050, we have simplified the analysis in the following way. We estimate what the value of services in 2000 would have been if 1900 MSA areas had been available, and what they would be in 2050 if 2000 MSA areas still applied. To set against these figures, we also have to estimate the value of gains made by conversion of biomes to agricultural use, in order to arrive at overall estimates of impacts on ecosystem services at the different points in time.

Change in the MSA Area

A computer model of global biodiversity (GLOBIO3) was used to estimate the biodiversity impacts of various environmental drivers: climate change, habitat fragmentation, land-use change, infrastructures, and carbon and nitrogen cycles. In this model, the metric for biodiversity is the remaining mean species abundance (MSA) relative to the undisturbed environment. The MSA figures do not come from direct observation in each area, but from a meta-analysis of values from the literature on species abundance in virgin and disturbed areas. This enables the models to be used to calculate MSA values based on the cause/effect relationship for each driver over a range of biomes and regions.

Habitats are classified as belonging to one of seven different biomes: ice and tundra, grassland and steppe, scrubland and savanna, desert and boreal, temperate, and tropical forests. Although MSA areas are estimated for all biomes, limited data availability restricts our economic valuation to grassland/steppe and forest biomes only. The analysis also covers seven world regions: the OECD, Central and Latin America (CSAM), the Middle East and North Africa (MEA-NAFR), sub-Saharan Africa (SAFR), Russia and Central Asia (RUS-CASIA), South Asia (SASIA), and China (CHN).

The MSA area indicator we use takes account of both area and quality of ecosystems, which is related to their capacity to provide services. It also allows us to use a common unit of measurement – value per hectare – to enable comparison across all biomes and regions. In our analysis, we assume that the provision of ecosystem services is linearly related to the area of the ecosystem and the MSA value. We also assume values per hectare to be for ecosystem services in undisturbed habitats.

We have to recognize that there are certain limitations and uncertainties in our analysis. MSA area, for example, is based on data which exclude several biomes and regions and give equal weight to each hectare, whatever the species richness. But its main limitation is that it is based on mean values calculated over all species, rather than data for individual species. The model also does not include all drivers of biodiversity, and there is a degree of uncertainty for the data on climate, for example. On the other hand, this approach does enable us to assess the impact of MSA globally, and is used by the UNEP and OECD in their environmental analysis.

The OECD (Europe, USA, Canada, Australia, and New Zealand) is the region with the largest MSA area, while the distribution of MSA area across the world remains fairly constant over both periods. All biomes and regions showed a decrease in MSA area over the twentieth century. Regional losses were highest in SASIA (40%), followed by CSAM, CHN, and the OECD. Temperate forests showed the greatest loss (45%, mainly in the OECD) among biomes, with grassland/steppe (mainly OECD), scrubland and savanna (mainly SAFR), and tropical forests (mainly CSAM) following.

Further losses are projected for all regions during the first half of the twenty-first century. Losses are expected to be heaviest in SASIA, at 30%, with SAFR experiencing a further 18% decline, at almost double the rate of the previous 100 years. Scrubland and savanna will suffer the highest losses among biomes (22%, concentrated in SAFR), followed by temperate forests (18%, mainly in the OECD), grassland/steppe (16%, also mainly OECD), and tropical forests (12%, mainly in SAFR).

Overall estimated losses in MSA area are significant over both timescales: 21% in the twentieth century and 12% from 2000 to 2050, with SA and SAFR being most affected.

The Economic Impact

We assessed economic impact for the periods 1900–2000 and 2000–2050 by combining MSA data with monetary values of ecosystem services, estimated on a per-hectare basis. Losses in terms of present values were converted into annual economic flows on the assumption that ecosystem services will provide constant flow over time. This assessment was carried out for the biomes for which sufficient data were available: grasslands/steppe and boreal, temperate, and tropical forests. For forests, ecosystem services include wood and non-wood forest products, carbon and cultural services (recreation and passive use). For grassland/steppe, we estimated the impact on food supply, erosion prevention, conservation, recreation, and amenity.

Wood products from forests include roundwood, wood pulp, sawn wood, paper, and fuel; there is also a wide range of non-wood products, including various plants and animals for food, raw material for medicine, honey, and animal hides. The highest overall values are found for sub-Saharan African tropical forests ($111,000 ha^{-1}, in 2000 US$) and boreal forests in South Asia ($100,000 ha^{-1}), China

($89,000 ha^{-1}) and the OECD countries ($84,000/ha). Temperate forests generate much lower values.

The value of carbon sequestration is estimated by extrapolating known data on carbon capacity in certain countries to areas of forest in similar habitats in other countries, and valuing these on the basis of published ranges for the price of carbon. Tropical forests generally have the greatest carbon capacity and hence value for this service, although this is difficult to estimate with any degree of certainty because of the wide variation in sequestration capacity and the large range of carbon price values we use ($4–53 tonne^{-1} in 2000, rising to $13–179 tonne^{-1} in 2050). The value for carbon stocks in sub-Saharan African tropical forests, for example – which is the most valuable – is between $3,100 and $42,000 ha^{-1} in 2000.

Recreational and passive use values for forest are based on willingness-to-pay (WTP) studies, mainly in Europe and North America, with mean and median values being used as reference points for other regions. The highest values for passive use are found in the OECD and China (median values of $45,000 and $34,000 respectively in 2000). For recreational use, the greatest value is in China and South Asia (both with medians close to $15,000 ha^{-1} in 2000). Rates of increase vary considerably between regions between 2000 and 2050, depending on rates of forest loss and population growth.

Valuation of ecological services for grassland/steppe is based on assessments in Northern Europe, USA, Asia, and Africa. Because of the limited data available, we use income as the variable on which to base calculations for other countries, since grassland has a higher economic value in richer countries. The OECD and China have the highest values ($1,000 ha^{-1} median value in 2000), but these are much lower than for forest biomes. These values increase up to 2050, with Russia and Central Asia seeing the highest rate of increase.

The Economic Impact Related to a Loss of MSA Area

Economic impacts were, as a first step, calculated as the product of the present value per hectare for each biome and world region and the change in MSA areas for the two periods considered. Over the twentieth century, the highest losses were found in the OECD (30–38%), CSAM (11–22%), and SASIA (17–19%). Projected highest losses from 2000 to 2050 are in SAFR (27–29%), as well as the OECD (21–29%) and SASIA (17%). The greatest impact by biomes is on tropical forests in both periods.

In a second step, using these figures, we converted changes in natural capital into annual value flows at a 3% discount rate and set these against the expected annual benefit flows generated by agriculture. We assumed that the hectares of grassland and forest lost were used for farming. For the period 1900–2000, the benefits of agriculture on a global level mean that the overall impact ranges from break-even to a net loss of about 2% of 2000 GDP (lower- and upper-bound scenarios). SAFR and CSAM still both suffer significant losses over the century, while SASIA and China have a net benefit. Most of the losses come from forests, particularly tropical ones.

For the period to 2050, the inclusion of agriculture results in a global net benefit of 0.05–0.48% of GDP. However, SAFR and CSAM still experience a projected loss, mainly due to tropical forest loss, of respectively 1.2% and 1.5% of 2050 GDP in the upper-bound scenario. The importance of tropical forests in the overall picture is due to the combined effect of decreases in MSA and the high value per hectare.

Carbon losses are a significant contributor to the overall forest biome impacts. In SAFR, damage over the twentieth century ranges from 1.5% to 20% of country GDP. This falls to 0.1–2.0% of 2050 GDP in the first half of the twenty-first century, but this is largely due to expected economic growth; absolute losses are higher than over the previous 100 years. There are also large losses of forest products (both wood and non-wood), most probably because of the huge development of the forestry industry in recent decades. Boreal forests are under threat, particularly in OECD countries, China, and Russia, and losses as percentage of GDP are about the same as for tropical forests. Forest recreational activity losses are much smaller, but losses of passive use value have been significant over the twentieth century.

By far the greater losses come from forest biomes, but the split between particular environmental services not surprisingly varies considerably with the price of carbon. By way of illustration, Figures S.8 and S.9 show the breakdown for upper- and lower-bound scenarios for the period 2000–2050.

Conclusions

These results need to be viewed in the light of the limitations previously mentioned. Not all ecosystems are covered, biodiversity is covered only via the

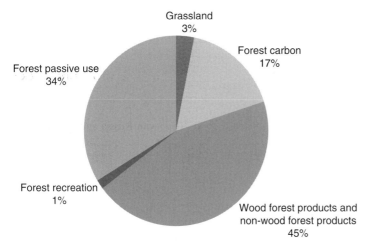

Figure S.8 *Economic loss registered by ecosystem services, 2000–2050, percent of total loss (lower-bound scenario)*

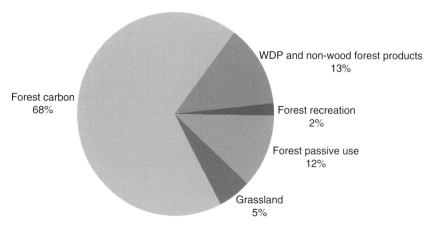

Figure S.9 *Economic loss registered by ecosystem services, 2000–2050, percent of total loss (upper-bound scenario)*

indirect measure of MSA, and losses during the twentieth century have been estimated on the basis of year 2000 prices.

Losses of natural capital over the twentieth century were substantial, in the range $20–45 trillion. Greatest losses occurred in the OECD, Central and South America, and South Asia. Expressing the losses as annual flows, we estimate a range of $603–1,300 billion, or 1.7–3.8% of 2000 GDP. However, in the lower-bound case, the benefit of agriculture effectively balances the loss, while for higher carbon prices, there is a net loss of $730

billion, or 2% of GDP. South Asia and China show a net gain even in the upper-bound case, while sub-Saharan Africa suffers the highest net loss in percentage terms.

Projecting from 2000 to 2050, we expect gross losses of $345–1,200 billion annually (0.9–3.2% of GDP). However, after allowing for agriculture, we find net gains of between $94 billion and $930 billion. Only Central and South America and sub-Saharan Africa show a net loss, and only in the upper-bound scenario. Overall, these results are heavily influenced by the price put on carbon.

Summary of the Assessment Paper on Education: The Income and Equity Loss of not Having a Faster Rate of Human Capital Accumulation

HARRY ANTHONY PATRINOS AND GEORGE PSACHAROPOULOS

Introduction

Education of a sort – for example philosophers teaching their students or masters training apprentices – has existed for millennia, but formal education is relatively recent. Some European universities were founded as long ago as the thirteenth century, but organized schooling of children started as late as the nineteenth century in England. Recognition of the role education plays in a

country's development occurred only in the early 1960s, when researchers at the University of Chicago developed the theory of human capital. In its original form, this drew parallels between expenditure on education and investment in equipment. An analysis of the discounted cash flows of costs and benefits allows the profitability of investment in human capital to be estimated, in the same way as a capital investment is assessed. The theory was later developed further, based on the idea that education not only improves the productivity of individuals, but also further increases national output by having a wider, more general effect on others.

But the difficulty lies in deciding how to provide the right amount and quality of education to create the greatest benefit for society; what economists call maximizing the social welfare. In this study, we consider the lost welfare due to too little education in terms of both efficiency (delivering higher productivity) and equity (distributing the benefits more equally). The welfare loss from inadequate education is measured via income loss. The effect of education on equity is measured via changes in the Gini coefficient[1] as seen in countries which have expanded their provision of education.

Here we use two comparative scenarios: the first in which countries follow their existing education policies and the second which considers the impact of following policies designed to improve productivity and equality. Real data are available for the period from 1950 to 2000, and estimates for the rest of the period are derived by backwards and forwards extrapolation.

Historical Perspective

There are few data available prior to 1950 (UNESCO was founded in 1946 but did not begin systematic collection of data until several years later). Prior to that, we have to rely on such evidence as censuses and the ability of people to sign their names in marriage registries, but it seems that literacy rates in many countries increased only slowly (and continue to do so in many developing countries). In the West rapid gains in literacy were made in the early part of the twentieth century, followed by a marked slowdown in more recent decades. This S-shaped pattern of data – an acceleration followed by a declining rate of improvement – is typical of educational development over time.

From 1970 to 2000 similar gains in the average number of years of schooling were found in developing regions, with the biggest gains in China and the smallest in South Asia. However, there has been only modest convergence in average years of schooling between the developing and industrialized worlds. Overall, the pace of world growth in human capital

accelerated in the second half of the twentieth century, with the average amount of schooling increasing at about 0.6–0.7 years per decade. This has been the rate of increase for the developed economies for the last 130 years (and this still continues) but the acceleration on a global basis is due to developing countries now investing to the same extent.

Currently, there are three clusters of educational development. This is high in the advanced economies of Europe, North America, and Central Asia (over 10 years of schooling), moderate in Latin America and the Middle East (around 8 years), and low in South Asia and sub-Saharan Africa (5–6 years). Development of high educational standards is a long-term affair; it takes between 35 and 80 years for a typical country to move from 10% to 90% net primary level enrollment.

Defining the Current Challenge

Despite the efforts of governments and international organizations, providing basic education for all children in developing countries remains a real challenge. The United Nations, UNESCO, UNICEF, the International Labor Office, and the World Bank all promote education as a basic human right and engine of growth. Education for All is an international initiative led by the above organizations but this has missed all its original target dates.

Over a quarter of primary-school-aged children in sub-Saharan Africa are not in school and more than a third of the adult population of South and West Asia remains illiterate. In 2007, there were 72 million children not at school, with a slow decline to 56 million projected by 2015. However, to put that in perspective, many children in poor countries (particularly in sub-Saharan Africa) do not start primary school until they are relatively old, but may well go on to complete this stage of their education. The total number of people who *never* go to school is therefore much lower than the figures suggest.

---

[1] The Gini coefficient is a widely used measure of relative equality, with a value of 0 representing total equality, and 1 maximum inequality.

There are two approaches used to estimate the effect of education on productivity: micro and macro. The micro route compares the benefits to individuals of additional education to the costs of providing it (giving the so-called "social rate of return"). Benefits are generally measured as the earnings differential between workers with different levels of education, and costs include the earnings forgone by those continuing in education, as well as the direct cost of provision. Other benefits, both direct and indirect, are ignored in most analyses. For example, those with better education may enjoy better health and there may be wider societal benefits by way of lower crime rates, reduced use of social services, etc.

Not surprisingly, such analyses show that the social returns are higher at lower levels of education and for lower-income countries, in a similar way that diminishing rates of return are found for capital investment. Rates of return range from over 20% for primary education in low-income groups to 10% for higher education in high-income groups.

Alternative macro analyses estimate the benefits for the economy as a whole. Although the figures are not identical, the early use of such approaches confirmed that the benefits of education are substantial; contributing 15% to the growth rate in the USA and 16% in Korea, for example. The 1980s saw the development of so-called endogenous growth theories, which take account of the overall impact of policies which promote, among other things, better education and do not just estimate rates of return to investments. This implies that "knowledge" is a public good with far-reaching benefits across society which increase growth beyond what classical theory would suggest. Of particular importance to the education challenge is the implication that there may be underinvestment in social capital formation, given its broader role as a public good.

The Extent of the Education Challenge

Governments and the global community are committed not simply to growth, but "growth with equity." This means that education must not just help to expand the economy, but that the benefits of economic growth should be shared across all sectors of society.

A range of metrics are used to assess the effect of education, but our central variable is the average number of years of schooling of the population aged 15 and over, which is the best summary available. A macro analysis also enables us to look at the effect of education on the population as a whole, rather than just the workforce, to find wider effects such as reduced birth rates or improved health.

However, not all schooling is of equal quality. There are some studies on the effect of education quality on economic growth; for example raising cognitive test scores by a given amount (one standard deviation) in a number of countries increased wages by a low of 5% in Ghana and a high of 48% in South Africa. Other studies relate literacy scores to labor productivity. However, there are no historical data available on education quality back to 1900. Political and geographic changes to countries, including the break-up of colonial territories and the Soviet Union, mean that we have to use regional averages when looking across the whole period.

An analysis of per capita income and years of schooling across 146 countries between 1950 and 2010 suggests that a minimum of 6 years of schooling is needed before the real benefits to the economy become obvious. However, another study showed a lower threshold; those developing countries where the average schooling was below about 2 years in 1960 showed a lower growth rate over the following 35 years. Other researchers found that a 10% increase in primary school enrollment increased economic growth by 0.27% annually.

Using the data available to date (complete from 1950 to the present day, partial prior to that) it is possible to look at the losses in global social welfare due to inadequate education from 1900 and project trends forward based on alternative policy scenarios. Before doing this, it is interesting to look at the case of just two countries: South Korea and Pakistan. Their per capita incomes were comparable in 1950, although Koreans averaged over 4 years of schooling to Pakistanis' 1½. By 2010, the educational attainment in Korea was nearly 12 years, equivalent to the average adult having completed secondary education, whereas in Pakistan it had not even reached 6 years, regarded as the minimum for literacy. Over this period, the per capita income in Korea grew 23-fold at constant prices (a 5.2% annual growth rate) while Pakistan's only grew by a factor of 3, equivalent to 1.8% annual growth. Much of this striking difference has been attributed to the gap in education.

We can estimate the welfare loss to Pakistan over the whole period from 1900 to 2050 by calculating what the per capita income would have been over this period if a different education policy had been in place. This is based on a figure of about 35% for the additional per capita GDP associated with each additional year of schooling (from our own calculations and the literature). The exact figures of course depend on the specific assumptions made, but our simulation indicates a current welfare loss in the range 10–20% of GDP, which persists to 2050. Alternative estimates produce figures in the same range.

Moving on to the global situation, we extrapolated the known data from the 1950–2010 period back to 1900 and forward to 2050 to give a mild S-curve typical of the known pattern in developed economies. Given that returns to primary education (the earlier part of the curve) are typically higher, we assumed a 30% rate of return for the 1900–1950 period and 20% from 2010 to 2050 (the actual rate for 1950 to 2010 is 28.5%). The global welfare loss in 2010 we then estimate to be in the range 15–29% of GDP, falling to 11–22% by 2050. These figures vary considerably between regions, reflecting such factors as the quality of education and the dynamism of the economy. Looking at the losses over time, we find somewhat counter-intuitively that returns to an additional year of education increase between 1950 and 2010. Endogenous growth theory may explain this; although individuals see a declining return with increasing years of education, the benefits from sharing knowledge across society continue to increase.

We have also been able to look at the effect on growth of spending more on education, for a varied group of 21 countries for which full data are available. On average, we find that investing an additional 1% of GDP in education could have boosted each country's growth rate by 3.3%.

Another aspect of the educational challenge is the cost of illiteracy. Since 6 years' schooling is generally found to be needed for adequate literacy, we looked at the case of countries having at some stage had less than 5 years' average schooling. Using the available data, we estimate that lack of literacy leads to a drop in per capita income of 15.3%.

We have also been able to compare years of schooling with Gini coefficients to assess the impact on social equity. Data for 114 countries between 1985 and 2005 show a decline in income inequality with better education. Each extra year of schooling on average reduces the Gini coefficient by 1.4 points, using the 0–100 scale used by the World Bank.

Inevitably, an analysis such as this can show trends but does not reveal all the detail. The actual situation in particular countries may not fit the general picture, as the case of Sri Lanka shows. The country has a highly educated workforce compared to its neighbors, but a dismal growth record, due to the political situation. In other countries, investment rates, trade policies, economic freedoms, and many other factors will influence growth independent of schooling.

Our figures are likely to be overestimates since they take account generally of wage-earners and not the self-employed. For poorer countries, for example in sub-Saharan Africa, education seems to bring few material benefits to farmers and other self-employed workers. The same is true for any countries where traditional technologies are used and new ones not readily taken up. In countries that limit shocks to the economy by controlling prices, there is little chance of the reallocation of resources which tends to increase the returns to human capital.

We also have to consider the resources needed to provide more schooling. Not only is there a direct cost, but the people needed as teachers and administrators could be doing other productive work, and this has to be subtracted from the calculated benefits of education. On the other hand, our figures may be underestimates because we have failed to take into account the wider impacts of education (what economists call externalities).

Conclusions

Taking all these factors into account, we have revised our estimates for the economic cost of poor education to give a set of conservative figures summarized in Table S.1.

Table S.1 Welfare loss due to low educational attainment

	Percent GDP loss from	
Year	One school year deficiency	Illiteracy
1900	10.3	12.3
1950	8.7	9.0
2010	8.7	9.0
2050	6.5	3.8

The global loss due to poor education is represented in Figure S.10.

Overall, we estimate that the average country would have increased its growth rate by about 1% by investing an additional percent of GDP in education. In addition to productivity improvements, better education reduces inequality. Every country that has sustained high growth for long periods has put substantial effort into schooling its citizens. The challenge that remains is that other developing countries are still not doing enough.

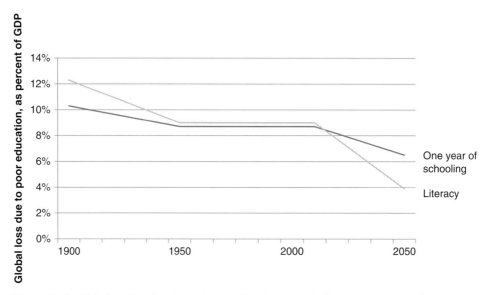

Figure S.10 *Global welfare loss from the world's education challenge, as percent of GDP*

Summary of the Assessment Paper on Gender Inequality: A Key Global Challenge – Reducing Losses due to Gender Inequality

JOYCE P. JACOBSEN

Introduction

Gender inequality continues to be a fact of life around the world. Women still earn less than men in the formal work sector, are more likely to live in poverty, are less likely to be employed, and do a larger share of work in the household. As well as these economic dimensions, women have a lower representation in politics and corporate life. On the social side, women are more likely to suffer from domestic violence and sexual assault. On the other hand, there are some social aspects of inequality which are less favorable to men; they are more prone to violence, imprisonment, and disability, and have a lower life expectancy. But we should also not forget that, in some societies (such as India and China), a proportion of female births is prevented and there are significantly more young men than women.

As well as the personal costs, the failure to allow individuals of different genders to have equal opportunities and develop to their full potential also represents a cost to society as a whole. In this chapter, I estimate the costs of gender inequality to society (as a percentage of GDP) for the period from 1900 and project the costs forward to 2050.

Historical Background

In 1893 New Zealand became the first country to extend voting rights to women, a key step in the push for equal treatment of women and men under the law. Universal suffrage became the norm in Western countries through the twentieth century, but other forms of official discrimination took longer to eliminate; for example, the US Equal Pay Act was only passed in 1963 and similar legislation was not in place in Japan until 1987.

Participation of women in the US labor force rose very significantly through the twentieth century and has now leveled out at 46%. This is currently a fairly typical figure for both high- and low-income countries (although interestingly the proportion is somewhat lower in middle-income countries); however, participation rates continue to vary significantly from country to country.

It seems reasonable to expect that higher levels of female education are necessary for higher labor market participation and earnings. However, from 1870 to 1950 women predominated over men in US secondary education, although they were less well represented at the tertiary level. A similar pattern of secondary schooling is seen today across most countries, with big differences in rates of university-level education. Thus education is not the fundamental precondition for formal employment.

The ratio of hourly earnings for women and men now stands at 0.79 in the USA, having risen fairly steadily since the 1980s. Some countries are higher (e.g. Sweden at 0.89 and Australia at 0.86) but others considerably lower (Canada 0.72 and Japan 0.52); there is no convergence. The question is to what extent these unequal outcomes are determined by unequal opportunities and also, what would have been the effect of equalizing opportunities over the twentieth century and how might a world of equal opportunities look in future?

The Extent of the Challenge

To start to look at what a gender-neutral world might look like today, let alone 110 years ago or 40 years in the future, we first need to decide whether to focus on equality of outcomes or opportunities. In a world where men and women received the same amount of education and training and had the same chances in life for economic, personal, and social advancement, their choices could still lead to significantly different outcomes by both occupation and earnings.

This also raises the question of how much of today's differential economic outcomes are due to free choice rather than to discrimination in education, hiring or pay. Nevertheless, by looking at the implications of total equality of outcomes, we can arrive at an absolute maximum value for the gains society could make by achieving gender equality. I only include the effect on GDP of changes in the labor market, because this is where we have systematic data, but other aspects of gender neutrality could also be important for altering economic outcomes.

There might be large gains, for example, from the increased participation of women in politics, where potentially less corrupt governments with a lower propensity to lead their countries into conflicts could lead to further direct economic benefits. The world might be very different in other ways as well if gender equality had already been achieved in 1900, possibly seeing lower birth rates and different working patterns for men. But this chapter is restricted for reasons of feasibility to the effects of changes in the labor market.

With this restricted focus, the costs of gender equality are the forgone gain which would have occurred if women had participated more fully in the formal work sector, along with sufficient education and training to allow them to be used to their full productive potential. The maximum gain from gender equality occurs if women work in the same sectors, for the same time, and for the same wage rate as men (assuming that pay rates for women rise rather than those for men falling). From this we have to subtract the estimated value of forgone unpaid household work and the cost of expanding education and training to provide the same standards for both genders. I also calculate a lower figure for each point across the time range, where women form a lower proportion of the formal workforce than men and receive somewhat lower earnings, to consider the outcome of the exercise of free choice as lowering GDP gains from equality of opportunity.

Calculating the Costs of Gender Differences at Work

The International Labor Organization estimates an average female participation in the paid workforce of 40%, the figure generally being lower in less developed countries and higher in the industrialized world. To some extent, this is because of women's greater responsibilities for unpaid work in the home. For richer nations, this is largely now a matter of free choice, but the situation is less clear in developing countries. Nevertheless, there is clear evidence that, as job opportunities expand and women's wages rise, there is a significant increase in the number of women choosing to work.

Generally, there has been a significant increase in the number of women in the workforce during the twentieth century. In part this has been due to the easing of restrictions on their participation, both formal (such as bars on employment of married women or bans on training for certain professions) and societal (the expectation by male family members that women would look after all the housework). When calculating the maximum cost of inequality, I assume that social inequality and discrimination causes the entire participation gap; for the medium cost calculation, I assume that half of the gap is due to free choice.

Based on surveys, I assume as a benchmark the current women's/men's pay ratio to be 60%. For the calculation based on complete equality, I assume pay for men and women is the same; for the medium calculation, half the pay gap is assumed to be due to personal preference.

If more women work in formal employment, this means that they do less household work, and the lost value of this must be taken into account. Childcare and growing food at home are important considerations in developing countries, but in the developed world much less so. Also, as households become more prosperous they are able to buy labor-saving devices such as washing machines to increase the efficiency of work in the home. Clearly, this is not an easy factor to allow for with any accuracy, but a recent study put the value of household production at between 12% and 62% of GDP. Other factors, including an allowance for unpaid work more broadly, could increase this even more. Taking all this into account, I take the net benefit of moving people from the unpaid sector into paid work to be 50% of the actual value of the paid work.

There is no longer an education gap in high-income countries, with young women actually receiving more secondary and even tertiary education than men in some countries. In the developing world there is still a significant gap in schooling although this varies widely between countries; the ratio of female to male primary enrollment in 2009 in Afghanistan was only 69%, while that in Mauritania was 108%. In all countries studied, women lag behind men in terms of on-the-job training and apprenticeships. Closing the gap is a necessary prerequisite for the achievement of equality, but this comes at a cost. Based on current expenditures, I assume that 10% of the additional GDP generated by more women in the workforce would need to be spent on education and training.

The Historical and Future Costs of Gender Inequality

Not all growth in the economy can be attributed to labor alone; there is also a capital element. In my calculations, I assume that the labor share is 70%. I use this and the factors I have already described as a basis for estimating the costs of two scenarios: one where the entire gap in workforce participation is due to discrimination and the other where 50% of it is down to personal choice. I assume that women comprised 15% of the global workforce in 1900,

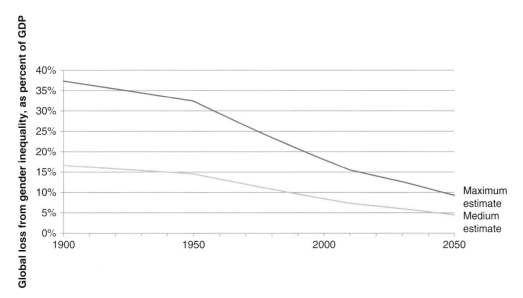

Figure S.11 *Global loss from gender inequality as percent of GDP in the given year, 1900 to 2050*

rising to 25% in 1950 and 40% in 2010. For the same years, the earnings ratios of women to men were 50%, 45%, and 60%. Projecting forward, I assume that women constitute 42% of the workforce in 2030 and 45% in 2050, with the earnings ratio standing at 65% and 70% respectively.

As an example, taking all these factors into account, the net cost of gender inequality to the world economy in 2010 is estimated to be a maximum of 15.5% of GDP (where it is all due to discrimination) or 7% if half is due to personal choice. A similar pair of estimates can be made for the costs of inequality based on the data available back to 1900 and the projections made to 2050. The results are summarized in Figure S.11.

Even if we assume that half the inequality in employment has been due to personal choice at all stages, the loss stayed at 15% or higher until after World War II, declining to 7% in 2010 and is projected still to be 4% of the world economy by 2050. Even using these more conservative estimates, the loss to the world economy currently is still twice the size of the entire global GDP in 1900, at $3.9 trillion. Projecting this forward to 2050, the 4% loss to the world economy would total between $6.4 trillion (assuming 2.5% annual growth) and $9.7 trillion (at a 3.5% growth rate).

Estimated losses for the early part of the twentieth century make the assumption that the labor market would have had the capacity to absorb a much greater number of women and that the 70% share of GDP from labor would have been the same. Both of these are feasible if progress towards gender equality had begun earlier than that. At the same time, if there had been demographic changes to factors such as marriage rates, household size, life expectancy, and child mortality, we would expect to see a better educated, more productive workforce. Given this, it is hard to envisage such changes reducing the total output per person and the estimates of losses in the early twentieth century could well be argued to be lower-bound figures.

This approach does not take account of all aspects of gender inequality, but most of these are less well studied and make a smaller contribution to the loss (although the costs to society may still be substantial). These other factors include access to land and other resources in the informal sector, domestic violence, sexual orientation, and the different disease burdens carried by men and women. However, the additional cost attributed to these in economic terms is relatively small.

This analysis can, of course be criticized both by those who consider the estimates too high and those who think they are too low. The point is that the costs of gender inequality are not zero, and neither are they unlimited. These figures should be considered as the starting point for a debate about how much of these costs we are willing to bear and how much we are willing to spend to reap the potential gains.

Summary of the Assessment Paper on Human Health: The Twentieth-Century Transformation of Human Health – Its Magnitude and Value

DEAN T. JAMISON, PRABHAT JHA, VARUN MALHOTRA, AND STÉPHANE VERGUET

Introduction

It is easy to forget that, not so very long ago, mortality was far higher, people suffered from frequent illness and malnutrition, and high fertility rates had debilitating consequences for women. Rapid increases in life expectancy began in the nineteenth century, accelerating from 1880 until 1960. In this chapter, we review the trends and analyze the reasons for declining mortality, particularly the improvements in health technology. We estimate the reducing number of years of life lost, and place a value on these, all relative to the idealized norm of the UN's projected mortality profile for Japan in 2050 (Japan is the country with the highest life expectancy).

The Magnitude and Origins of Mortality Decline

Although there was little change to life expectancy before the late eighteenth century, it is hard to overstate the magnitude of the improvement since then. The country with the highest life expectancy for much of the last century has been Japan. It showed a rapid improvement of 3.2 years per decade (see Figure S.12), but the rate of convergence is even more impressive, with life expectancy in India, for example, growing at 4.5 years per decade between 1960 and 2002.

The greatest improvements were in deaths of children under 5, with mortality from infectious diseases falling much faster than for non-communicable diseases. Declines in low- and middle-income countries in the latter part of the twentieth century have benefitted from the more rapid spread of technological advances from richer countries, where these same technologies had been drivers, albeit at slower paces, of earlier increases in life expectancy. Income and education are also correlated with declining mortality, but direct causal links for all three factors are difficult to establish because of gaps in the data and the indirect effect of higher incomes on improved water supplies, transport, communications, and employment patterns, for example.

Incomes rose substantially in the twentieth century, but these do not account for much of the mortality declines. Although higher incomes allow households to make some choices which help to reduce mortality of family members, the introduction of public health interventions such as smallpox vaccinations, quarantine for cases of infectious disease, or banning of smoking in public places are often poorly correlated with income overall. Thus technology (defined broadly as drugs, vaccines, diagnostics, treatment and prevention algorithms, and policies, such as higher taxes on tobacco) appears to be the main driver of decreasing mortality (see Figure S.13).

Quantifying the Impact

In this chapter, we make an estimate of the total number of years of life lost (YLL, relative to the projected 87.2-year life expectancy of a newborn in

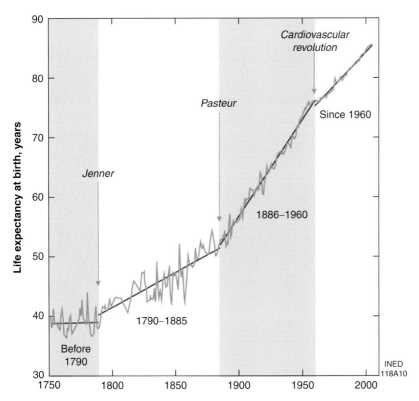

Figure S.12 *Highest observed national female life expectancies at a given moment in the world (1750–2005).* Source: *Vallin and Meslé (2010)*

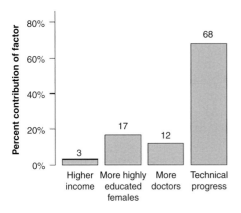

Figure S.13 *Factors accounting for decline in child mortality, all low- and middle-income countries, 1970–2000.* Source: *Jamison* et al. *(2012)*

Japan in 2050) over the period from 1900 to 2050 for a number of countries and regions: China, India, Japan, the USA, sub-Saharan Africa, the world, less developed regions, and more developed regions (as defined by the UN). For an illustration of different mortality profiles, see Figure S.14, which shows life expectancy as a function of age for Japanese born in 2050 and Mozambicans born in 1990.

In our study, we estimate two indicators for the countries and regions covered: the total number

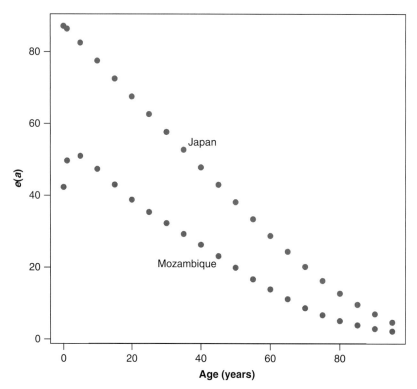

Figure S.14 *Life expectancy for Japanese newborns in 2050 and Mozambicans in 1990.* Source: *World Health Organization (2004), United Nations (2009)*

of YLL for infant deaths, and the number of YLL for deaths above the age of 5. We use published data on life expectancy at age 5, which varies from 31.8 in India in 1910 to 78.1 in Japan in 2005–7. In our base case of Japan in 2050, there are still excess lives lost for various reasons, but we subtract this figure from the estimates for all other times, countries, and regions to make our calculations. To arrive at a monetary value, a statistical life year is taken as being worth twice the per capita GDP.

As well as the general mortality rate for each country or region, there has been a series of what we might call "mortality shocks" during the twentieth century, including the 1918 flu pandemic, the two world wars, the Bengal famine of 1943, and the great Chinese famine of 1958–61. The Indian and Chinese shocks are dealt with at the country level; the others, as YLLs per capita at a world level, using published data sources. World War II, for example,

resulted in 71 million excess deaths, affecting a world population of 2,275 million (3.14 YLL per capita), while 29 million lives out of a population of 637 million were lost in the Chinese famine (3.03 YLL per capita).

Figure S.15 shows the ratio a of the value of YLL to lifetime income for different regions of the world. This illustrates the large cost of continued excess mortality in the less developed world, particularly in sub-Saharan Africa.

Accomplishments and Challenges

Here we use the statistical data gathered to consider two major health accomplishments of the twentieth century – much reduced infant mortality rates and smallpox eradication – plus an example of a remaining challenge: deaths attributable to tobacco. The challenge of AIDS has been extensively

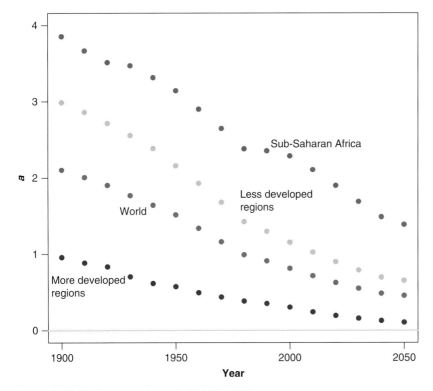

Figure S.15 *Ratio a over the period 1900–2050*

covered recently in a separate Copenhagen Consensus publication.

In high-income countries, 99% of children born today reach their fifth birthday, which is the consequence of a long process of mortality declines in children which started in the late nineteenth century. In low- and middle-income countries, infant mortality remains higher, but there has been much more rapid progress, particularly since the middle of last century. These declines in childhood mortality have driven the remarkable improvements in overall life expectancy over the twentieth century; crude death rates fell by nearly 80% and life expectancy at birth doubled to 66 years. Over the century, there were 5–6 billion deaths in total. Of these 2 billion were children under 5, far exceeding even the 200 million killed by war and famine.

Although death rates in some developing countries remain high, they are actually lower than those seen in Western countries a century or more ago. Childhood mortality in sub-Saharan Africa in 2008 was only a third of that in Liverpool in 1870,

despite present-day Africans having a real per capita income just over half that of Liverpudlians in the late nineteenth century. In particular, vaccine-preventable deaths are much lower. For comparison, there were 10 million childhood deaths globally around 2001, rather than the 30 million there would have been if the death rates in Western countries at the beginning of the twentieth century had still applied. However, to put this in perspective, if global childhood death rates were the same as present-day England, the toll would be only 1 million across the world.

In the early twentieth century, an increasing knowledge of the causes of disease led to partially successful efforts to limit transmission. In the latter part of the century, because of the widespread use of vaccination, oral rehydration therapies, antibiotics, and malaria control interventions, much greater progress was made to reduce deaths. The probability of newborns dying before the age of 5 was still 23% in the early 1950s, but has fallen to just 6% in the current decade, and this has largely come about because of the use of better technologies to control infectious diseases. In 1970, perhaps only 5% of infants were vaccinated against measles, tetanus, whooping cough, diphtheria, and polio. By 2000, 85% of children were being vaccinated, and it is estimated that this saves about 3 million lives each year. Diarrheal deaths have fallen by a similar number by the use of simple oral rehydration therapy, and use of drugs can lower tuberculosis mortality rates from over 60% to 5% of cases.

Malaria remains an important contributor to mortality. However, it is estimated that between 13% and 33% of the overall decline in death rates over the period 1930 to 1970 may have been due to malaria control and, more recently, the use of artemisinin combination therapies has been shown to have a big effect. However, therapies are mainly targeted at children, on the understanding that this is the group mainly affected. If recent findings from India that there are many more adult deaths from malaria than thought are generally true, then similar control strategies will have to be applied across the age range.

Nutrition and infection are also interlinked. Diets have undoubtedly improved substantially, but infectious diseases increase metabolic demands and so preventative strategies such as vaccination can reduce the level of severe malnutrition. Equally, maternal breastfeeding can protect against infection and reduce mortality, as can specific micronutrient interventions to reduce anemia and other deficiency diseases.

Major challenges still exist, with India alone having over 2 million childhood deaths in 2005, with nearly half occurring in the first month of life. There is good evidence of lower death rates where vaccinations, treatment of acute respiratory infection in a medical facility, and use of oral rehydration therapy for diarrhea are used more widely. However, child mortality declines are likely to continue; even in Africa, mortality rates fell in the last decade of the twentieth century, despite increased malaria deaths, mother-to-child transmission of HIV, and economic stagnation. Current projections are that global child mortality (per live births) will fall from about 7.7% in 2000 to 3.1% in 2050.

A second major accomplishment has been the eradication of smallpox, which at one time may have killed 1–3 million people a year worldwide. Widespread vaccination and better control of outbreaks led to substantial declines, built on by a successful WHO eradication campaign, which took only 12 years to achieve its goal in 1979. Crude attempts at vaccination which started as early as the tenth century in China were supplanted by more effective methods based on Jenner's work by the later nineteenth century. Vaccination spread widely during this period, including to low-income countries, an example of the early diffusion of technology.

The WHO eradication campaign increased coverage of routine vaccination, but also actively sought out cases of infection and vaccinated sufferers and people who had been in contact with them, to stop any spread of the disease (ring vaccination). The successful campaign cost $300 million over 12 years and avoided the need for continued routine vaccination, which cost the same amount in 1968 alone.

Other big challenges still remain. It is estimated that on current smoking patterns there will be 1 billion deaths attributable to smoking this century, mainly in low- and middle-income countries. This compares to about 100 million deaths in the twentieth century, mostly in high-income and Eastern European countries. Smoking currently directly causes 5–6 million deaths annually, about half of which are in low-income countries. About 70% of the 40 million worldwide deaths among adults over 30 are due to cancer and to vascular and respiratory diseases, for all of which smoking is a contributory cause. Smoking also is a cause of tuberculosis death.

Lung cancer was a rare disease before World War II, but became common later in the West as the large increase in incidence of smoking made possible by mass production manifested itself after a lag time of about 30 years. China now has over 300 million smokers and India more than 120 million, and the full effects of this consumption have not yet been seen.

There have been large drops in the numbers of men smoking in high-income countries, and it has been found that cessation before middle age prevents more than 90% of the lung cancer mortality attributable to smoking. For those who do not stop, it seems that about half of all long-term smokers are killed by their addiction. Although about 80% of worldwide smoking deaths have been among men, this is because of the historical pattern of consumption; mortality risks for women are at least as high. Without significant increases in cessation (which is uncommon currently in low- and middle-income countries), total worldwide tobacco mortality will reach about 450 million over the first half of this century. Annual death rates will rise to about 10 million by about 2030, with some further increases expected.

Cessation is the only answer. Halving the worldwide per capita consumption of tobacco by 2030 (which is what has happened in the UK in the last 30 years) would reduce deaths over the next few decades by 160–180 million. Halving the percentage of children who become prolonged smokers would have its greatest impact on mortality rates after 2050. Information campaigns, bans on public smoking, and other interventions all have their part to play, but taxation is the single most important factor.

Aggressive tax increases helped to halve cigarette consumption over 35 years in the UK and USA and 25 years in Canada, but the same reduction in France took only 15 years. Between 1990 and 2005, the inflation-adjusted price of cigarettes in France rose threefold. Tax revenues increased from €6 billion to €12 billion, while male lung cancer rates for 35–44-year-olds (a good indicator of recent smoking) fell sharply from 1997 onwards. An increase in global cigarette taxes of 10% would increase revenues by nearly 7%, and recent tax rises in such diverse countries as Poland, Mauritius, and Mexico have already resulted in lower consumption. The street price of cigarettes has been increased by 70% in numerous countries (and various US states) and wider application could save millions of lives.

Conclusion

Life expectancy during the twentieth century rose by about 3 months every year, largely through the development and widespread use of specific technologies, but what was the value and what are the future implications?

First, by any reasonable measure, the value of such health gains has been enormous.

Figure S.16 illustrates the total money metric value of years of life lost as percent of GDP for selected regions for the period 1900–2050. This is measured against Japan 2050 as baseline. The biggest decline has taken place in less developed regions where the ratio has fallen from 35% to 12% in the last century and expected to fall to 6.5% in 2050. The world as a whole has experienced a development bringing it from 32% to 5% in the same period. This is both a result of improved human health and economic growth.

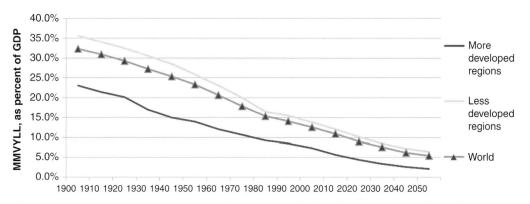

Figure S.16 *Money metric value of years of life lost (MMVYLL), selected regions, 1900–2050, as percent of GDP*

Second, ongoing investments are likely to make continuing improvements in child health. However, the costs of avoiding adult deaths are rising, partly due to the effects of smoking and HIV infection. Effective interventions, such as aggressive taxation of tobacco and long-term management of cardiovascular disease with low-cost combination pills, are perfectly feasible, but require more priority and focus.

Third, major institutions are central to health improvements. The major philanthropy of the Bill & Melinda Gates Foundation will continue to enable research on prevention and treatment of childhood diseases and infectious diseases, but similar efforts are needed for chronic conditions.

Finally, given the enormous returns on mortality and on human welfare from the twentieth century's investments in technology and its diffusion, traditional development aid would likely be better targeted towards operations research and research on chronic disease prevention and treatment. Such a shift is possible as affordability is increasing for effective interventions for child health and infectious diseases. These would become the responsibility of national governments and the major global health funds.

Summary of the Assessment Paper on Malnutrition: Global Economic Losses Attributable to Malnutrition 1900–2000 and Projections to 2050

SUE HORTON AND RICHARD H. STECKEL

Introduction

There is a strong two-way link between income and nutrition and in this chapter we focus on the beneficial effect of higher incomes. Although higher income can lead to more sedentary lifestyles, dietary imbalances such as overconsumption of fats and sugars, and increases in non-communicable diseases such as diabetes and cardiovascular disease, undernutrition remained a greater problem – particularly in developing countries – during the twentieth century. Higher incomes allow people to afford more and better food and enjoy improved sanitation and health. It also means that mothers are better educated and better able to care for themselves and ensure their babies are properly nourished. Individuals who are better nourished are more productive both in manual work (because they are stronger and have greater stamina) and non-manual work (because they have developed better cognitive skills, i.e. the capacity to learn and think).

During the twentieth century, nutrition improved considerably across much of the world and the most direct evidence we have for this is the increase in the average height of young adults. Evidence suggests that with few exceptions (e.g. pygmies) populations have a similar genetic potential as regards height, although that of individuals obviously varies. Better nutrition allows a greater proportion of people to reach their maximum potential stature. Although short periods of undernutrition can be partly compensated for when a better diet is available, chronic malnourishment can lead to stunting in adulthood (measured by height-for-age relative to international standards). There are good data available on increases in average height in various regions and this can be used to estimate productivity gains and hence economic effects. However, better nutrition in children also improves cognitive development and learning independently of height, although it is more difficult to measure these indirect benefits. The results in this chapter therefore underestimate the overall benefits of improved nutrition.

Evidence for a Link between Height and Earnings

It is not easy to find a reliable quantitative estimate of the effect of height on earnings because of the interrelated effects of nutrition, health, and education. Nevertheless, many studies have found that taller individuals earn more and that on average they have higher-status jobs. In this chapter, we use height as the best available proxy for nutrition.

It is quite plausible that better nutrition (measured via height data) should improve performance in both manual and non-manual work, and there is also direct evidence for this. A well-controlled trial in Guatemala using a nutritional supplement received in childhood showed a clear correlation with earnings of adult men once those children reached adulthood, and the biggest effect was when children below the age of 3 years received the supplement. A trial of iron supplements in Costa Rican infants was similarly positive.

Using historical data on height, combined with food availability, it was estimated that fully 30% of the increase in per capita income in the UK between 1790 and 1980 was due to improved nutrition. Nowadays in industrialized countries 80% of height variation is believed to be genetic, with only 20% determined by the environment, whereas in developing countries environmental effects (including nutrition) are likely to be much more important. But the effect is not the same across entire countries; in rural areas productivity from manual work will be strongly correlated with height, but in towns cognitive abilities will be more important.

Other factors may have indirect effects on wages. Better-fed, taller children are more likely to enter school earlier, to stay in education longer, and to perform better while in school. The study in Guatemala (previously mentioned) suggests that even in poor, rural communities it is the effect of

nutrition on cognitive ability which dominates the effect on physical development. It seems that nutrition influences productivity mainly via brains rather than brawn. Studies on twins in developed countries suggest that environmental factors (including nutrition) are twice as important as genetic make-up in determining height and intelligence.

Not surprisingly, the correlation between height and earnings at the national level becomes much smaller once people have excellent nutrition. So, studies show that, in a group of industrialized countries (the USA, UK, Germany, and Australia) the average height for adult men was 178 cm and each additional centimeter was found statistically to increase earnings by 0.55%. However, for a group of developing countries (Brazil, China, Côte d'Ivoire, Ghana, the Philippines, Tanzania, and Zimbabwe) adult male height averaged 170 cm but each additional centimeter led to a 4.5% increase in earnings.

Observed Trends and Projections

We have analyzed data covering about 30 countries from 1900 to 2010. Nineteen of the countries are European and the rest are in North and South America and Asia, but there are big gaps for Africa, Australia, and the Middle East. Measurements of female height over this period are less readily available, so we concentrated on adult males (for example, in some cases the best available information is for army conscripts). There are clear differences between countries representative of different regions and stages of development. Figure S.17 illustrates these,

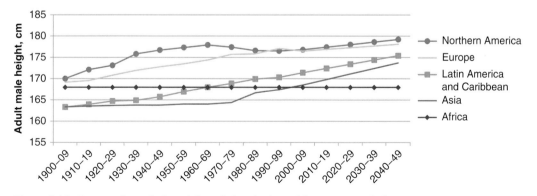

Figure S.17 *Estimated trends for adult male height (in cm) by region, including projections to 2050*

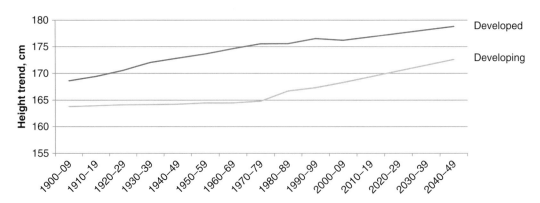

Figure S.18 *Estimated height trends (in cm) for developed and developing countries*

using informed guesses for trends in Africa and West Asia.

In 1900, men in Northern and Western Europe and North America had already reached an average height of 170 cm or more, and stature increased by about 1 cm per decade throughout the century. In Southern Europe, the average height was about 165 cm at the start of the twentieth century, but began to increase quickly after World War II. In South America, there were significant differences between the richer and poorer countries, with Brazil, for example, being similar to Spain but men being about 5 cm shorter in Bolivia. The tiger economies of Asia (Japan, Korea, and, somewhat later, China) began to expand rapidly from 1950 and showed height increases of up to 3 cm per decade at a time when per capita income was rising at 7% or more each year. However, the recent growth in the Indian economy has not yet resulted in significant adult height gains nationally.

These trends are based on weighted averages of country data where available, with a range of assumptions being made for regions where data are patchier. Western Asia (the Middle East) is assumed to follow a similar trend to Eastern Europe but delayed by 50 years. Very little information is available for Africa, but isolated studies are consistent with there being no significant change over the century. To highlight the difference between industrialized and developing countries, the regional information is aggregated and shown in Figure S.18.

In both figures, the height projections to 2050 are based on anticipated increases in life expectancy. There is a positive relationship between increased height and longevity, although of course the gains are relatively less marked in rich countries. The 5 cm differential between heights in developed and developing countries in 1900 widened to 10 cm in 1960 as rich countries grew faster. We expect the gap to narrow again by 2050, with height in Latin America only 3 cm less than in the West, and Asians generally being within 5 cm of inhabitants of the rich world. Unfortunately, there is no reason to expect any significant change in Africa.

The Economic and Human Costs of Undernutrition

The data can be used as a basis for modeling to estimate the total cost of undernutrition, not just by way of reduced productivity but also in terms of increased mortality. In a broad study across developing countries, it was found that birth length and growth in the first year of life were strongly related to adult height. We have therefore used measured adult height as an indicator both of height in early childhood and of child mortality risk. We should note that, although deaths in early childhood in the twentieth century have been primarily a developing-world problem, similarly high infant mortality rates

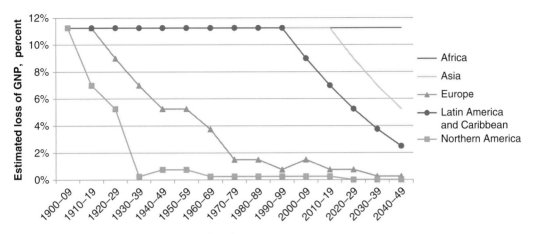

Figure S.19 *Estimated percent of GNP lost due to poor nutrition*

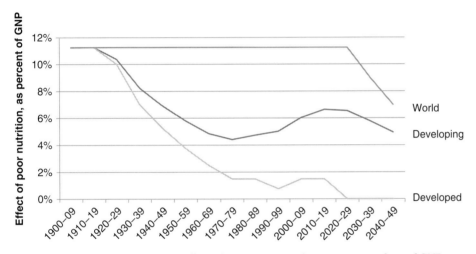

Figure S.20 *The global economic effect of poor nutrition shown as percent loss of GNP*

occurred in Western Europe and North America before 1900.

The overall economic cost of undernutrition is substantial, and regional trends are summarized in Figure S.19. This shows that nutrition improved rapidly in both North America and Europe from the early years of the twentieth century, whereas in other regions poor nutrition has resulted in an estimated 11% loss in GDP until the end of the twentieth century. By then, improvements became evident in Latin America. Similar improvements are projected to be found in Asia from 2020, but no improvement is expected in Africa even by 2050.

Figure S.20 summarizes the global situation. Economic losses averaged 8% over the twentieth century. Although they had declined from the early years of the century as nutritional status improved rapidly in Europe and North America, there was a reversal of the trend from the 1970s as the developing world economies increased their share of global GDP. As average heights increase in Latin America and Asia, it is expected that the net loss to the global economy will average 6% during the first half of the twenty-first century. These estimates are based on certain assumptions about the relationships between height and productivity and height and nutrition and so cannot be taken as definitive.

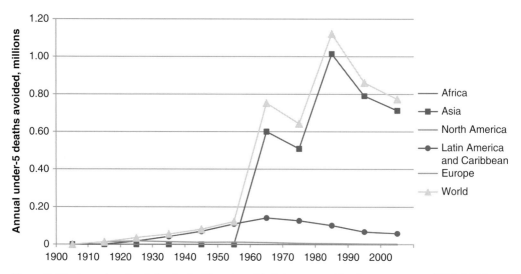

Figure S.21 *Annual under-5 deaths (millions) avoided due to nutrition improvements, 1900–2000*

Equally, we have assumed that the benefits of a better diet for women are similar to those for men; a reasonable view, but not one for which there is direct evidence.

Poor nutrition does not just reduce productivity; there is also a human cost. There is still a disturbingly high contribution to child mortality. Over the period from 1900 to 1970, undernutrition accounted for a quarter of early childhood deaths (not including the newborn) or on average 3–4 million deaths annually. By 2000, this had dropped to 15% of childhood deaths, but still approached 2 million each year. Figure S.21 shows the marked positive effect that improved nutrition has had. Note that there has been no improvement in either North America or Africa; in the first case because families were already well nourished, but in the case of Africa because diets have remained poor for the whole century.

These figures take account only of chronic malnutrition. We estimate that the additional effect of acute problems due to famines, crop failures, etc. raises the total deaths of under-5s due to undernutrition to about 1.7 million annually. Over the twentieth century, the main impact of improved nutrition in developing countries has been a reduction in infant and early childhood mortality. In contrast, the effect of dietary improvements in the rich world over the same period is primarily one of increased productivity and economic growth.

Conclusions

Our analysis suggests that undernutrition has caused a significant but slowly declining loss of global productivity, accounting for roughly 8% of global GDP during the twentieth century but set to decline to around 6% during the first half of the twenty-first. Poor diets in childhood reduce cognitive development, directly affecting both educational attainment and productivity. Undernutrition in adulthood leads to lower productivity in manual work.

The effect of nutrition overlaps to some extent with other factors. In particular, better-nourished children tend to stay at school longer, and education itself leads to direct gains in productivity. Similarly, both health and nutrition have an effect on infant mortality, with better-fed children having a higher capacity to survive infection.

Overall, we believe that our estimates for both productivity loss and increased mortality caused by undernutrition are conservative. Even so, our projection for 2050 is that it will still contribute a global economic loss of 5% and it is clear that there are very big regional variations.

Summary of the Assessment Paper on Trade Barriers: Costing Global Trade Barriers, 1900 to 2050

KYM ANDERSON

Introduction

Trade barriers represent a drag on the economies of both industrialized and developing countries, but there is much debate about the real cost. This chapter looks at changes in barriers over the twentieth century, using the best available data to get a precise estimate of the current situation, and then makes some projections to 2050. Most studies cover the economic effects of government restrictions on agricultural commodities and manufactured goods, but a true assessment also needs to take into account other costs, particularly those due to barriers and regulations affecting the market for services.

Writers as far back as the eighteenth century have recognized the economic and social benefits of free trade. Natural barriers to trade have fallen as the costs of transport and communication have plummeted, but governments continue to erect their own barriers in an attempt to protect specific sectors of their economies (although at a cost to their overall economies). Estimating the costs is not a trivial task and we keep it within manageable bounds by considering primarily trade in goods. At the same time, we need to recognize that free international movement of labor (that is, removal of restrictive immigration policies), capital, and services would make an even greater contribution to economic output, growth, and social welfare.

A Historical Perspective

Despite some prospect of negotiating more open trade between major trading nations from as early as the seventeenth century, it was only in 1846 that Britain, the dominant economy at the time, took unilateral action by repealing its Corn Laws. Although this example was not immediately followed by other European countries, Britain and France eventually signed the Cobden–Chevalier treaty in 1860. Significantly, this included a Most-Favoured Nation (MFN) clause, requiring each agreed bilateral tariff cut to be extended to the same goods imported from all other countries. By 1867, most other European countries, by concluding trade treaties with either Britain or France, automatically also signed up to this condition.

From this time until the outbreak of World War I (which led to a collapse of the system of trade agreements) the climate for trade was quite benign, and this was a period of relatively rapid economic growth. However, the United States entered into rather more restrictive agreements and so began the twentieth century with higher tariffs than most other rich countries. Post-war attempts to reintroduce a liberal trade regime were a failure, with no country being willing or able to take Britain's former place as the leader in global economic affairs. With the onset of recession in the late 1920s, the USA catalyzed a round of global beggar-thy-neighbor protectionist measures with the infamous Smoot–Hawley tariff regime in 1930. By 1932, the value of world trade had fallen by 40%. Countries tried to reduce their depression by discriminating in favor of their colonies, such that by 1939 protectionism was more entrenched than at the end of the previous century.

During World War II, Britain and the US became convinced that only binding multilateral rules would provide the liberalized world trade necessary for peace and congenial foreign relations. The Bretton Woods conference in 1944 laid the foundations for such a regime, as well as being the first step in setting up the International Monetary Fund and World Bank. Efforts to create an International Trade Organization at that time resulted only in the General Agreement on Tariffs and Trade (GATT). However, this allowed the progressive opening up of trade and eventually led to the inclusion of agriculture and services in negotiations and the setting up of the World Trade Organization (WTO) in 1995.

The Costs of Trade Distortion

Policies that distort trade include import taxes, export subsidies, and a range of so-called non-tariff barriers such as import quotas or bans. These together raise domestic prices compared to those at the border, with consumers paying more for their goods and producers competing with imports receiving higher prices than in a free market. The most common policy is to restrict imports via tariffs or other barriers. Production restrictions also are occasionally used, for example in the oil sector by OPEC since the mid-1970s. Less common is a policy to subsidize farm exports, as practiced by some rich countries particularly in the 1980s.

These various policies all have an impact on trade and the overall economy. However, they also affect production and consumption patterns as prices of competing products or substitutes are distorted. In the longer term, they may also alter investment and employment patterns across different sectors.

Estimating the global cost of these measures is possible for recent years using price distortion data from the Global Trade Analysis Project (GTAP) consortium as an input for one of a range of global economic models covering many separately identified individual countries, industries, and products. These models can also be used to make projections of the economic impact of various potential policies. However, for the earlier part of the twentieth century, detailed data are not available, so only relatively crude estimates of impacts can be made, using broader sectoral averages of tariff rates.

The contributions of various countries and sectors have to be weighted by their importance. For example, Europe and North America accounted for about two-thirds of global GDP and trade through most of the twentieth century, with Asia growing in importance since the mid-1970s. Agricultural commodities and manufactured goods account for the majority of total trade.

In the early 1900s, European tariffs on imports of manufactured goods were generally in the range 12–34%, while in the US they stood at 54%. These fell prior to World War I, but they rose in the late 1920s and early 1930s which contributed to the Great Depression. By the 1950s, however, import tariffs had fallen to about one-third of their peak two decades earlier. Among the larger developing regions, Latin America ran a highly protectionist policy regime compared to Europe and North America, while manufacturing tariffs in Asia were somewhat lower.

The situation was different with agriculture. Protection of domestic farmers in most advanced economies became widespread by the 1930s and, unlike for the manufacturing sector, this increased over the next half century. However, from the early 1980s, both high-income and developing countries began to lower their various barriers to trade in agricultural commodities. Nevertheless, barriers to free trade remain significant across both farm and manufacturing sectors.

Economic Effects of Trade Barriers

When trade is distorted, some producers may get a net benefit from higher domestic prices. However, there are many losers, with consumers having to pay higher prices and other firms unable to export as much as they could. This generates an overall loss of economic welfare. In 2004, the weighted average tariff on agricultural produce was 21.8% for developing countries compared to 22.3% in industrialized countries, while the equivalent figures for manufactured goods were 7.5% and 1.2%.

The overall loss of welfare can be estimated using the GTAP protection database for 2004, together with some additional data on agricultural distortions in developing countries. The economic effects were calculated using a World Bank model known as Linkage. Results from this are underestimates, because they do not take account of what are called dynamic gains – accelerated investment, greater productivity growth, etc. – made possible by free trade.

Removing the trade barriers in place in 2004 could have boosted the global economy by $168 billion a year, a total of 0.6%. But the benefit would not have been spread evenly: developing countries would have seen a 0.9% growth of their economies, compared to 0.5% for high-income countries. More than two-thirds of the cost of barriers is due to agricultural policies, and more than half of the cost to developing countries comes from their own policies.

Future Impacts

The cost of trade barriers in 2050 is estimated using three sets of assumptions: that policies remain the same, that policy becomes more liberal, or that there is a greater degree of protectionism. For the business-as-usual case, real incomes in developing countries are assumed to grow at an annual rate of 1.4%, and those in current high-income countries are assumed to grow at 0.5%, implying a global annual growth rate of 0.9%.

However, it is more likely that there will be some change, and the nature of this will be highly dependent on the outcome of the WTO Doha Round of negotiations. If the Doha Round was to be revived and agreement reached on the most comprehensive liberalization proposals made in 2008, recent reforms would be locked in and further phased opening would occur. This is projected to add a further 0.2% of annual growth to both developing and industrialized countries.

But in the case of a successful conclusion to the Doha Round, it would be reasonable to assume that a further round of liberalization would be implemented by 2050. For high-income countries, reform of the service and agriculture sectors could provide a further 0.2% annual growth, while for developing countries, potential gains are significantly higher at 0.4% to 2050.

On the other hand, if the Doha Round collapses, higher barriers could be imposed. Given the general consensus on the benefits of liberalized trade in the industrialized world, increased protectionism is unlikely to occur there to any great extent. However, in developing countries, rapid urbanization and marginalization of rural areas may lead to agricultural protectionism (as it did at a similar stage in the development of industrialized countries). Assuming a doubling of the distortion for this sector, the overall cost of trade barriers would rise from 1.4% to 1.8% by 2050, while for high-income countries they would remain at 0.5%. Contrast this with the scenario of increased liberalization, which would reduce these costs to 0.8% and 0.1% respectively.

For comparison, we can also estimate the benefits of reforms prior to 2004. For example, if the policies in place in 1980–4 had remained unchanged, the global economy would have been $233 billion smaller – a loss of 0.8% – and the cost would have been borne disproportionately by developing countries. These figures suggest the world moved about three-fifths of the way towards free markets for goods in this two-decade period. However, after the early years of the twentieth century, when trade barriers were relatively low, they rose during the 1930s and began falling after World War II only for manufactured imports. It took until the 1980s before trade barriers were lowered more broadly.

The Full Picture

This modeling does not take account of a range of other factors, including the impact of non-tariff barriers and distortions in the provision of services and finance. For example, barriers other than tariffs may at many times have had a greater impact than the tariffs themselves. They were used more widely than previously following the general lowering of tariffs via the Tokyo Round of GATT negotiations in 1979. Quantitative import restrictions, for example, were placed on textiles and clothing, cars, and steel, but they have now largely disappeared, at least in industrialized countries.

The costs of barriers to trade in services may be several times higher than those of barriers to goods, but there is a lack of good data to estimate those costs. Government regulation probably had a low impact in earlier years because of natural barriers such as transport costs, but a conservative estimate suggests that restrictions on trade in services added 40% to the total cost in 1982. The technical problems of trying to analyze the immensely complex web of tariffs by averaging we consider also to require an adjustment, rising to 50% from 2004 onwards.

Trade reform expands the market for financial services, contributing to their long-term stability. If there were to be full financial integration globally, allowing companies and individuals to borrow or save wherever they choose, it is estimated that real consumption would be permanently boosted by 7.5%. The lack of integration currently is thus a further cost to the economy.

Various other simplifications in the economic models contribute to the cost underestimation. In the real world, freer trade can subject monopolistic companies to competition and also lead to greater exploitation of economies of scale, both of which boost the welfare gains. Equally, more liberal markets can both improve product quality and increase variety, so boosting profit margins to a higher level than the increased volumes alone might suggest. Finally, the bureaucratic costs of administration, the traders' costs in trying to avoid barriers, and the costs of lobbying for protectionist policies must all be taken into account when considering the net benefits of liberalization.

Growth Promotion

Freer markets not only produce these above-estimated gains, but also promote economic growth. For example, more efficient companies may grow at the expense of others, multinationals may share more knowledge across countries, firms may relocate to other countries, and greater competition is likely to stimulate innovation. The extent of this growth dividend from trade liberalization is difficult to estimate, but it suggests that even the significant direct gains remain a lower-bound figure.

Overall Benefits of Liberalization

Leaving out the so-called dynamic gains from extra growth, we estimate the cost to the global economy of trade barriers decreased from 6.3% to 2.9% between 1982 and 2004. Assuming success in the Doha Round and continued reform thereafter, the cost reduces to 2.4% by 2050, with most of the continuing burden falling on developing countries (a cost of 3.8% to their economies). However, failure of Doha and a move back to protectionism would increase the cost to developing countries to 8.6%, so bringing them back to the situation in 1982. High-income countries would fare less badly but still be hurt, with the cost to their economies in 2050 rising from a possible 0.5% to 2.4%, which is about where it stood in 2004.

In summary, this historical analysis shows us that freer trade in goods and services would benefit the global economy substantially. Although significant gains have been made through policy reforms since World War II, more remains to be done, particularly for developing countries, which continue to bear the brunt of costs of barriers to international trade.

Summary of the Assessment Paper on Water and Sanitation: Economic Losses from Poor Water and Sanitation – Past, Present, and Future

MARC JEULAND, DAVID FUENTE, SEMRA ÖZDEMIR, MAURA ALLAIRE, AND DALE WHITTINGTON

Introduction

Diseases associated with poor water, sanitation, and hygiene (WASH) account for 6–7% of mortality in developing countries. Worldwide, in 2008, over 880 million people lacked access to improved water supplies, and 2.5 billion lived without adequate sanitation facilities. The economic costs associated with lack of coverage include health losses (due to mortality and morbidity) and losses associated with reduced productivity and inconvenience.

Potentially effective and low-cost WASH interventions are widely available; however, demand for many WASH interventions – including point-of-use water treatment, hygiene education, on-site sanitation – is surprisingly low. Household demand for piped water services is higher, but the costs of network services are also high. In this chapter we estimate the economic losses associated with diseases and time spent collecting water due to inadequate water and sanitation from 1950 to 2050, in all developing regions. Time costs associated with lack of sanitation have not been included. This chapter is the first global analysis of the economic losses associated with diseases and collection time resulting from poor water and sanitation over such a long time-frame.

Simulation Modeling Framework and Data, and Calibration

The main economic benefits of improved water and sanitation include better health, time savings, and improved aesthetics and convenience. We estimate the total economic loss as the sum of disease due to not having access to improved water and sanitation, and time forgone due to collection of water used for domestic purposes. As access to improved water and sanitation increases, the risk of mortality and illness from WASH-related diseases decreases, as does the time spent collecting water. Mortality, illness, and the distance households walk to collect water outside their home are also strongly associated with income.

The association between income, water and sanitation coverage, and WASH-related mortality is remarkably strong. For example, relatively high WASH-related mortality is associated with low piped-water coverage (Figure S.22). In addition, coverage with piped water and sewerage services increases rapidly as countries move from low GDP

per capita to middle-income status, after which coverage grows much more slowly. Interestingly, the kink in the relationship between piped coverage and income (at an annual household income of about US $4,000–5,000) nearly matches the kink in the relationship between GDP per capita and life expectancy in the Preston curve. Still, it is not easy to establish a causal link between income, improved water and sanitation coverage, and decreases in morbidity and mortality. Many changes occur simultaneously in countries with rapid economic development – such as improvements in healthcare, nutrition, and housing.

The relationships described above are analyzed at the country level. We create a simulation model to calculate the morbidity and mortality burden, and the time spent collecting water, associated with lack of coverage with water and sanitation services from 1950 to 2008. Then, projections of future GDP and population growth are used to estimate these costs from 2008 to 2050 for 126 countries included in the simulation model. The simulation model is calibrated based on regression analyses of cross-country, cross-sectional, and panel data.

Reductions in mortality risks are expressed in monetary terms by multiplying the mortality reductions for the population by the value of a statistical life (VSL). The VSL increases with income, as the willingness to pay for mortality risk reductions increases with income. Estimates of VSL in each country are based on average income of the bottom

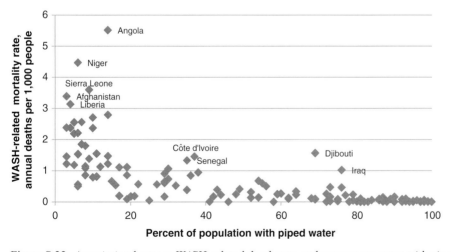

Figure S.22 *Association between WASH-related death rate and percent coverage with piped water in 2004*

80% of the population since upper-income house-holds are not as affected by diarrheal disease as the poor. These mortality benefit calculations are then added to estimates of the avoided morbidity burden. The reductions in morbidity are estimated as a fraction of mortality benefits. Economic losses due to morbidity are estimated to be 25% of the mortality cost of WASH-related disease.

We include both coverage with improved sanitation and piped water when developing the calibration for projecting WASH mortality since empirical data suggest that WASH mortality only approaches zero in countries with high piped water and sewerage coverage. We estimate that a 1% increase in piped water coverage or improved water coverage is associated with a decrease of 0.03 deaths per 1,000 people per year in WASH mortality. In addition, a 1-log increase in income is associated with a decline in WASH-related deaths of 0.3 per 1,000 per year (in other words, increasing income by a factor of about 2.7 decreases the death rate by about 0.3 per 1,000 per year). This is a significant decrease in relation to the range of global WASH mortality (0 to 5.5 deaths per 1,000). Coverage with improved sanitation is not significantly associated with the WASH-related death rate, perhaps due to high correlations with water coverage variables.

Average time to water source is available for a limited number of countries and years in several global surveys from the WHO, UNICEF, and MEASURE DHS. The opportunity cost of time is estimated as a fraction of the average GDP per capita among the bottom 80% of a country's income distribution. As income increases, collection time decreases and the opportunity cost of time rises. Time to water sources drops significantly as income and the opportunity cost of time increase. Analysis of collection time shows that a 1-log increase in GDP is associated with a decrease of roughly 1.3 minutes per trip.

Simulation Model Results

Coverage of Improved Water and Sanitation Services

Water and sanitation coverage expands across developing regions as incomes rise. In parallel with the rapid economic growth in East Asia, the Middle East, and Latin America, the increase in global coverage over the period for which data are available (1990–2008) is slightly faster than past and future predictions. China experienced the most dramatic expansion of piped water and sewerage. In contrast, sub-Saharan Africa (SSA) and South Asia (SA) have particularly low baseline and projected levels of coverage, which remain below 30% even in 2050. Furthermore, despite increases in coverage as a percentage of global population, the absolute number of people without piped water and sanitation is expected to increase until about 2030 due to population growth. Our projections suggest that 1.2 and 1.4 billion people in SSA and SA, respectively, could be without piped services in 2050.

WASH-Related Mortality

WASH-related death rates are estimated to be in decline over the entire study period, 1950–2050, as economic growth occurs and piped water and sanitation coverage expands. The average WASH-related mortality rate across developing countries has declined from an estimated 1.5 deaths per 1,000 in 1950 to 0.39 deaths per 1,000 in 2008. The declines projected for sub-Saharan Africa were smallest just as this region had the slowest economic growth and expansion of piped water and sanitation coverage. We predict that the average WASH-mortality rate across the developing world will decrease further to 0.22 by 2050, but this overall decrease is slowed by the persistence of high mortality rates among growing populations in sub-Saharan Africa. Based on sensitivity analysis, average mortality rates in 2050 could range from 0.3 to 0.34 deaths per 1,000, while total global WASH-related deaths could be between 1.0 million and 2.7 million per year.

It is unclear why WASH-related mortality rates in the WHO data for SSA are so much higher than for SA since both regions have low coverage of piped water and sewerage. These differences may be due to differences in per capita income, access to other health services, greater access to other improved (not piped) water and sanitation, or inconsistencies in the data. The number of WASH-related deaths in SSA is predicted to increase from a current level of

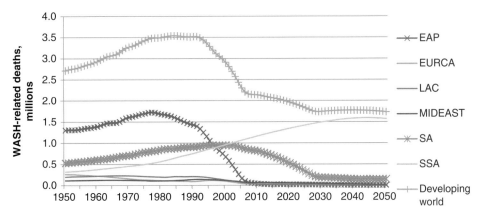

Figure S.23 *Predicted WASH-related deaths by region, 1950–2050*

1.2 to 1.6 million per year in 2050. Total WASH-related deaths in SSA are forecast to peak around 2045 once population growth slows sufficiently. As depicted in Figure S.23, only SSA experiences a future increase in total number of WASH-related deaths in the data. The only other region with a significant number of WASH-related deaths in the future is South Asia.

Predictions of average time to water

The average time to water across all developing regions falls from about 7 minutes in 1950 to just over 2 minutes in 2050 due to increased income and urbanization. However, SSA is again an exception – average time to water remains high (7 minutes) in 2050. While total time spent collecting water is declining in most regions, it could increase in the Middle East (until 2030) and SSA (beyond 2050) due to population growth. Globally, we estimate that aggregate water collection time peaked around 2003.

Economic Losses from Lack of Piped Water and Sanitation Services

Our analysis finds that WASH-related economic losses do not necessarily decrease with economic growth. Population growth, income, and WASH-mortality rate determine the magnitude of health and time losses. Due to rising incomes, the VSL and opportunity cost of time have increased in all world regions. If mortality rates and the VSL

remain unchanged, population growth will cause total economic losses due to poor WASH services to increase. However, economic growth has two conflicting effects on economic losses. First, economic growth increases infrastructure coverage and decreases mortality, decreasing economic losses. Second, economic growth increases the VSL or willingness-to-pay for mortality risk reductions, thereby increasing losses. Even if mortality rates decline, total WASH-related deaths can also increase due to rapid population growth. Health losses are estimated to increase during periods of rapid population growth in all world regions at various times over the study period. Similarly, time costs due to water collection also increase during periods of rising incomes and aggregate water collection time. We find that economic losses in most developing countries initially rise to a peak and then decline once mortality and time to water are sufficiently low.

Our base case estimations of economic losses by region are presented in Figure S.24. Health losses, depicted in panel A, peaked in most developing regions in the early 1980s or 1990s. Our simulations suggest that South Asia reached a peak in WASH-related health losses of about G-K$14 billion (in 1990 International Geary-Khamis dollars) near the end of the twentieth century. In contrast, WASH-related health losses for SSA only peak around 2050, at G-K$25 billion.

Trends for time costs, as shown in panel B, are dramatically different from health losses. The

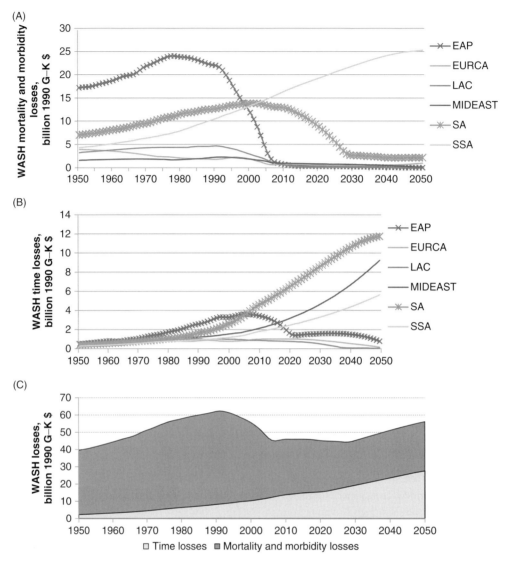

Figure S.24 *Base case "economic losses" associated with WASH: (A) health losses, by region; (B) time costs, by region; and (C) aggregate global losses*

average time to water source declines more slowly than mortality, and this decline is not always faster than the effects of increased opportunity cost and population growth. Time costs rise throughout the period in three regions – SSA, SA, and the Middle East. As a result, total economic losses could increase in the future, after a previous peak in the early 1990s (see Figure S.24, panel C). In addition, while health losses dominated WASH-related

economic losses in the past, when mortality rates were high, time costs will likely become relatively more important in the future.

It is useful to put these economic losses in per-spective by comparing them to the total regional GDP. We find that health and time costs have and are likely to continue to decline as a fraction of GDP, even as absolute losses increase. This is because population and economic growth also raise GDP, and at a faster rate than losses. WASH-related economic losses are predicted to decline to about 0.02% of developing world GDP in 2050, compared to about 2% of GDP in 1950 and 0.28% in 2008.

Discussion

To the best of our knowledge, this study is the first to quantify the economic costs of poor water and sanitation services over a long historical and future time-frame. The analysis provides a useful pro-spective on the scale of the global water and san-itation challenge and on the transition of countries as they follow different economic and demo-graphic growth paths. The study also highlights important data gaps and methodological chal-lenges. In general, WASH-related mortality declines over the study period, as average income rises. This is due to a negative association between coverage with piped water and sewerage and per capita WASH-related mortality, and the positive association between income and coverage with piped water and sewerage.

Perhaps counter-intuitively, our analysis finds that economic losses from WASH-related diseases do not necessarily decrease with economic growth. Economic losses due to WASH-related illnesses in most developing countries initially rise to a peak, and then decline once mortality is sufficiently low. The timing and size of the peak varies by country, and depends on a country's development trajectory and baseline mortality rate. In sub-Saharan Africa (SSA) and some countries of South Asia (SA), WASH-related mortality remains high over the timescale of our forecast, and economic losses

continue to increase. Our simulations indicate that the peak in health and time losses may not be reached before 2050 in SSA. This is in contrast to other regions. In SSA, average incomes are lower and mortality rates are much higher than in other regions, and demand remains low for preventative health improvements.

Thus, expected economic growth does not appear to be sufficient to correct the problem of rising future WASH-related mortality in SSA, and will also take some time in parts of SA. Societal pressure to invest in costly WASH infrastructure increases when the relative cost of WASH-related illness and time losses rises. People in less devel-oped countries are better able to afford piped water and sewer networks as their economies grow. Once WASH investments are made, the rate of increase in health and time losses slows, and is hypothesized to slow and eventually losses decline. The large expansion in piped networks in China and Latin America over the last decade was coupled by rap-idly growing income, increased demand, and a stronger public sector to provide services. Strong economic development often corrects the problem of WASH-related mortality, without the need for technological innovations.

Whenever economic development is successful, the problem of WASH-related mortality will likely be solved quickly from a historical perspective and without new technological breakthroughs. This is not to say, however, that such places will easily solve all of their water problems: this chapter has not considered issues of industrial pollution, cli-mate change, or water scarcity, for example. In addition, water and sanitation problems will likely persist in areas where economic development is slow and erratic.

CHAPTER
1

Air Pollution: Global Damage Costs from 1900 to 2050

GUY HUTTON

Introduction

Problem Identification

Air pollution is a problem as old as history itself. Air pollution can be defined broadly as the introduction of chemicals, particulate matter, or biological materials into the atmosphere that cause harm or discomfort to humans or other living organisms, or cause damage to the natural environment or built environment. Air pollution can be classified into anthropogenic and non-anthropogenic origin. The latter includes natural events such as wildfires, volcanic activity, and dust/sandstorms. This source of air pollution is not considered in this chapter as it is largely context-specific, and since the year 1900 is likely to be relatively unimportant compared with air pollution of anthropogenic origin.

Anthropogenic, or man-made, air pollution can be traced back to when humanity discovered how to make fire. While air pollution in those days was insignificant compared to the present time, burning biomass in enclosed spaces for space heating or for cooking purposes would have exposed humans to risk of respiratory diseases and injuries. As human populations became settled and increasingly burned

I would like to extend my sincere gratitude to the Copenhagen Consensus Center for their support and inputs to writing this chapter, and to two anonymous reviewers whose comments were valuable in improving a draft version of this chapter.
[1] For example, from European Space Agency (www.esa.int/esaEO/SEM340NKPZD_index_0.html), the North American Space Agency (www.nasa.gov/topics/earth/features/health-sapping.html), the US Environmental Protection Agency (www.epa.gov/oar/oaqps/montring.html), the European Environmental Agency (www.eea.europa.eu/maps/ozone/welcome), and the European Pollutant Release and Transfer Register (EPRTR) (prtr.ec.europa.eu/DiffuseSourcesAir.aspx).

biomass and fossil fuels (such as coal) indoors, the exposure to air pollution and its negative consequences rose significantly. Annex 1 shows the percentage of populations in developing countries burning solid fuels indoors, ranging from 16% of households in Latin America and the Caribbean and Central and Eastern European regions, to 74% in Southeast Asian and Western Pacific regions and 77% in Africa (Rehfuess *et al.* 2006).

Man-made outdoor air pollution, on the other hand, only became a health issue much more recently. The Industrial Revolution – which began in Great Britain and spread to the rest of Europe, the USA, and Japan in the eighteenth century – increased significantly the combustion of biomass and fossil fuels in urban centers, leading to dangerously high levels of air pollution. Pollutants can be classified as primary or secondary. Primary pollutants are directly emitted from a process, such as carbon monoxide gas from a motor vehicle exhaust or sulfur dioxide released from industrial processes. Secondary pollutants such as ozone (O_3) and particulate matter (PM) are not emitted directly, but form in the air when primary pollutants react or interact. Air pollution statistics in urban areas are available from various sources by country or by city, but not compiled globally. Air pollution maps and monitoring information are available from various internet sources.[1]

Air pollution's impacts are both direct and indirect. *Direct* impacts include health, damage of materials and ecosystems, and poor visibility. *Less direct* impacts include "acid rain" which results from chemicals being released into the atmosphere. Changes in human behavior also result from air pollution, such as inhabitants of heavily polluted urban areas relocating or tourists staying away from polluted cities. The main *indirect* impact is climate change. The biomass and fossil fuels that cause air pollution also have caused the warming of the

Earth's atmosphere resulting from the release of greenhouse gases (GHGs). Therefore, air pollution has many and diverse impacts. In this chapter, the most direct and measurable impacts are captured. The costs of climate change, water resource impact, biodiversity loss, and acid rain are assessed in other chapters.

In reading the findings of this chapter, careful interpretation is needed. Air pollution is double-edged. On the one hand, air pollution contributes to and is the result of "human development." Exposure to smoke from cooking and heating stoves happened as populations built themselves stable and permanent shelter and expanded the range of edible foodstuffs through various food preparation techniques, including cooking. Thus protection from excessive heat and severe cold, easier living conditions, and a better diet contributed to increased life expectancy. Exposure to outdoor air pollution several millennia later was a result of technological and economic development, which also brought about many improvements in standards of living and contributed to increased life expectancy. On the other hand, exposure to air pollution also damages peoples' health and the systems that support them. It is this latter aspect that this chapter focuses on. Therefore, while this chapter estimates the damage costs of air pollution, it should be kept in mind the various implications – and welfare effects – if humanity had followed a different or slower development path. In theory, mankind could have waited until "clean" technologies came along before expanding their use for mass production and consumption – however, this would have also stalled the economic development that has taken place, and the many benefits thereof.

Overview of Existing Research and Available Data

Economic assessments of outdoor and urban air pollution have been assessed in mainly country- or city-level studies. A number of economic impact studies, also known as damage cost studies, have valued the impacts on health, aesthetics, agriculture, buildings, and climate change. The data in these studies are selectively drawn on in this study, and fully referenced in the *Methods* section. A recent review

presents a summary of the health damage cost literature – totaling 17 studies (eight from OECD countries and nine from non-OECD countries) (Pervin *et al.* 2008). The review describes the heterogeneity of study methodologies (components of air pollution, economic impacts included, and valuation approach) and hence widely diverging cost per capita of air-pollution-related health impacts from less than 1 US dollar to US$2,000 per capita. This finding lends support to the conduct of a global study utilizing standard methods.

A second type of economic study is cost–benefit assessment, a technique that examines the economic performance of alternative technology options and/or policy measures to reduce air pollution. This literature has been reviewed previously (Voorhees *et al.* 2001; Hutton 2008; Larsen *et al.* 2008). In some OECD countries such as the USA (US Environmental Protection Agency 1999), the UK (UK Department for Environment Food and Rural Affairs 2006), and Japan (Kochi *et al.* 2001), there have been significant efforts to quantify the benefits of different national policy measures (US Environmental Protection Agency 2003). On climate change mitigation, several studies have examined the costs and benefits of GHG mitigation, including previous *Challenge Papers* of the Copenhagen Consensus Center. One of these papers explores the potential for a reduction in black carbon emissions to avert climate change (Montgomery *et al.* 2009). The paper concludes that introducing measures in China would achieve reductions in black carbon emissions at considerably lower cost than other world regions.

For indoor air pollution, there are fewer economic studies. There are no damage cost studies. However, there are a handful of cost–benefit studies. One study evaluates the costs and benefits of selected indoor air quality interventions for developing world regions, comparing improved biomass cook stoves with a switch to fuels less polluting for the indoor environment (Hutton *et al.* 2006a, 2007). At the country level, two studies examine the costs and benefits of efficient cook stoves implemented under a cooperation of the German government in Malawi (Habermehl 2008) and Uganda (Habermehl 2007).

Despite the cited studies, there remain major gaps in knowledge on overall global damage costs

Table 1.1 Damage costs included in this study

Impact	Outdoor Impact relevant	Outdoor Quantified in this study	Indoor Impact relevant	Indoor Quantified in this study
Human health – mortality	√	√	√	√
Human health – morbidity	√	√	√	√
Aesthetics (visibility)	√	√	√	
Buildings/non-organic materials	√	√	√	
Agriculture/timber	√	√		
Climate change[a]	√		√	
Ecosystems/biodiversity[a]	√			
Water resources for human use[a]	√			
Acid rain[a]	√			
Other socio-economic (time use)			√	√

[a] These impacts are covered in other chapters of this book.

for both indoor and outdoor air pollution, and the evolution of economic damages over time. Some non-health damages have still not been evaluated at the global level, such as the impacts of outdoor air pollution on crops, biodiversity, and visibility.

Methods

Aims

The aim of this chapter is to generate new estimates for the global damage costs of air pollution over a 150-year time period, from 1900 to 2050. The chapter focuses exclusively on air pollution of anthropogenic origin.

Scope

As is conventional practice, air pollution is split into outdoor air pollution and indoor air pollution, given that they involve different emission sources and vulnerable populations.

[2] Smoke generated from indoor sources can lead to a critical mass in densely populated areas and hence cause outdoor air pollution, and contributes to pollution caused by industrial areas and vehicle emissions. The reverse is also true: pollution from outdoor air can easily penetrate buildings and get trapped, hence causing indoor air pollution.

Outdoor air pollution is mainly a phenomenon of cities and towns, including peripheral urban areas and corridors where there is significant traffic and/or industrial activity. Outdoor air pollution remains a problem of developed countries as well as increasingly a problem of many developing countries.

Indoor air pollution results from burning of biomass and fossil fuels for the purposes of cooking and space heating. The free or low-cost availability of biomass, and the higher cost or limited availability of cleaner fuel options in rural areas (e.g. electricity, liquefied petroleum gas, or LPG), have meant that a major share (67%) of households in developing countries continue to use solid fuel (Rehfuess et al. 2006).

While there is unarguably some overlap between indoor and outdoor air pollution,[2] this study assesses them separately. At a global scale, this assumption is not expected to have a major impact on the precision of the results. The gathering and use of global epidemiological evidence by WHO and others explicitly avoids any possible double-counting of health impacts of these two sources of air pollution.

The various types of damage caused by air pollution were reviewed from the literature (Kochi et al. 2001). The damage costs that are relevant for each type of air pollution and those quantified in this chapter are shown in Table 1.1.

The damage costs associated with the human health impacts were included for both indoor and outdoor air pollution, due to their importance. While of relevance for indoor air pollution, the damages associated with aesthetics and buildings were only estimated for outdoor air pollution due to paucity of data for indoor air pollution. The main source of impact on the agricultural sector is from outdoor air pollution, which was estimated in this study. While of potential relevance, the climate change, ecosystem, water resource, and acid rain impacts of outdoor air pollution were not estimated in this study as they are included in the scope of other chapters. Other socio-economic impacts of indoor air pollution were included, in particular the time losses of collecting biomass fuels.

While the purpose of this chapter is to present overall global damage costs, it is also instructive to show a regional breakdown, given that the current size and the time trends vary between different countries and regions based on their level of development and policy environment. However, due to data constraints, it was most feasible to make a single distinction between developed and developing countries (see Table 1.2). The most constraining two factors in presenting damage costs for different world regions were (1) the lack of model input data on some key damage areas, in particular the non-health-related damages; and (2) the use of different regional classifications in the published literature for presenting air pollution damages, making it hard to extract the data to make damage cost estimates based on a single regional classification.

Table 1.2 Regional classification and populations

Classification	Countries/regions	Population (billion)		
		1900	2010	2050
Developing countries	Asia, Africa, Latin America and the Caribbean	1.02	5.72	8.15
Developed countries	Europe (including ex-USSR), USA, Canada, Australia, New Zealand, Japan	0.54	1.29	1.40

The time period indicated for this study presents problems due to the lack of global historical data on air pollution damages, as well as uncertainty of future projections 40 years ahead based on unpredictable patterns of economic growth and policy measures over that time period. Hence both geographical and time extrapolations are needed which generate significant uncertainty in the results.

An overview of the data available and the data missing is presented in Table 1.3. While several global databases are available, some key data sets providing a comprehensive overview of global damages are missing, thus requiring assumptions and extrapolation of data over time or across countries and regions. These data sources, and the approaches to filling the gaps, are described in the sections below.

Studies have shown damage costs to *other* countries produced by outdoor air pollution released by the emitting country. For example, in the ExternE project funded by the European Commission, Friedrich *et al.* show that more than half of the damage costs of pollutants released in Germany actually fall on other countries (Friedrich *et al.* 2001). However, the global nature of this study means that external damage costs of pollutants released by one country in another country are incorporated in the estimates, as far as the impacts have been captured by the estimation methodology.

Estimation Methodology Overview

Air pollution impacts are based on exposure to air pollution. For urban air pollution, the population at risk is the urban population, except for crop damages which are estimated on a total population basis. For indoor air pollution, the population at risk is calculated at the total population level, based on solid fuel use. Figure 1.1 provides an overview of the methodology for baseline assessment for the current year, and temporal extrapolation.

The assumptions on the relative exposure levels to the current time period are underpinning all intertemporal extrapolations. The comparative exposure levels over time of outdoor air pollution are assessed, based on the development stages

Table 1.3 Overview of data available for global damage cost study

Variable	Data available	Data not available
Coverage and exposure	• Published piecemeal data on pollutant emission and outdoor air quality in urban areas of developed and some developing countries • Global database on solid fuel use (WHO)	• Global compiled database on indoor and outdoor air quality indicators
Health benefits	• Global databases on deaths, cases, DALYs with regional and country breakdowns (1990–2010), and some projections made to 2020 for major categories of disease (WHO) • Global database on unit costs of health services in the period 2000–2010 (WHO, DCPP) • Piecemeal studies on the costs of treating selected diseases in selected countries • Value of life studies from developed countries from 1990 onwards, and few studies from developing countries	• Global updated databases on deaths, cases, DALYs with regional and country breakdowns (1900–1990 and 2010–2050) • Global compiled data on the health economic impacts of poor air quality • Global compiled data on the unit costs of treatment of air-pollution-related illnesses • Value of life in developing countries, and developed countries prior to 1990
Non-health benefits	• Published piecemeal data on economic damages of outdoor air pollution (mainly developed countries) • Global study on the benefits of reducing indoor air pollution in developing countries (WHO)	• Global compiled data on the economic non-health impacts of poor outdoor air quality (aesthetics, crops, buildings, materials, etc.) • Economic benefits of non-health effects of improving indoor air quality in developed countries
Other	• Global databases on historic, current and projected population size and economic product (e.g. GDP and GDP per capita) (CCC)	

CCC, provided by various United Nations agencies and adapted by the Copenhagen Consensus Center; DALY, disability-adjusted life year; DCPP, Disease Control Priorities Project; WHO, World Health Organization.

outlined by Mage (Mage *et al.* 1996): (1) industrial development, (2) emissions controls, (3) stabilization of air quality, and (4) improvement of air quality. Figure 1.2 shows the average evolution in urban air quality in both developed and developing countries. In developed countries, the exposure rises from 1900 to 1970, followed by a gradual decline in exposure as public health awareness increases and legislation is adopted to reduce emissions. For example, in the USA, emissions of polluting compounds rose from 1940 to 1970 and declined to 1940 levels in 1998 (see US Environmental Protection Agency 2000). The same study also reports reductions of 76% in particulate matter on the order of ~10 micrometers or less (PM_{10}) from 1940 to 1998. Levels of lead emissions also declined sharply from 1970 (220,000 tonnes) to 1990 (5,000 tonnes), after the Clean Air Act was passed in 1963 and the first

federal emissions standards for motor vehicles in 1965. Going back further, but with weaker data, the study estimates sulfur dioxide (SO_2) and volatile organic compound (VOC) emissions doubled from 1900 to 1940, while mono-nitrogen oxides (NO_x) increased by a factor of 2.5. In Europe, emissions reductions from 1990 to 2008 are reported by the European Environment Agency across 27 EU countries – the total reduction in SO_2 emissions for this period was 78%, nitrogen dioxide (NO_2) 39%, VOC 51%, and carbon monoxide (CO) 58%. From 2000 to 2008 PM_{10} declined by 8% and particulate matter on the order of ~2.5 micrometers or less ($PM_{2.5}$) by 13% (European Environment Agency 2010). In Japan, the 1967 law for environmental protection led to a reduction in SO_2 concentrations from 0.040 ppm in 1967 to 0.0050 ppm in 1992 (Kochi *et al.* 2001).

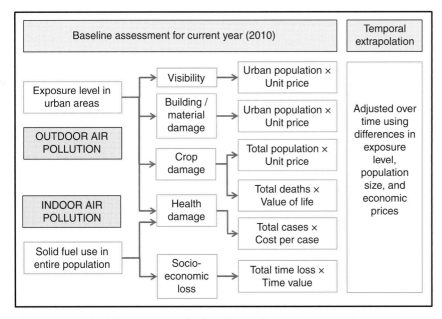

Figure 1.1 *Methodology overview for baseline and temporal extrapolation*

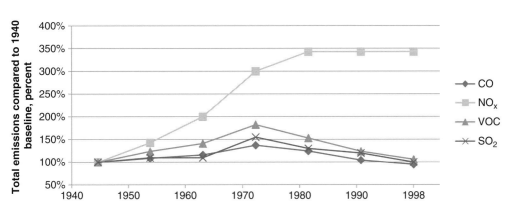

Figure 1.2 *Trends in emissions of nitrous oxides, carbon monoxide, sulfur dioxide, and volatile organic compounds in the USA from 1940 to 1998 (1940 = 100).* Source: *Environmental Protection Agency 2000*

After the year 2000, the exposure is expected to decline further in developed countries, but at a much slower rate than previously. By the year 2050, air quality across the developed world is assumed to be 20% improved over current levels based on the continued implementation of clean technologies and behavior change (e.g. reduced average distance traveled per person by car). The increasing proportion of the population living in urban areas will increase the population exposed to outdoor air pollution, even if pollution levels decline.

The evolution of urban air pollution in developing country cities is very different to that of developed countries. In 1900 it is assumed there are very few urban centers in the developing

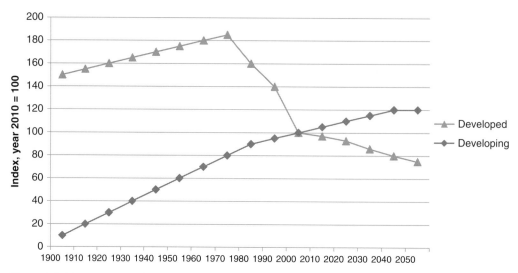

Figure 1.3 *Exposure to outdoor air pollution, evolution from 1900 to 2050 (year 2010 = index 100).* Source: *author's estimates*

world with serious air pollution related to burning of fossil fuels or biomass. A gradual growth is assumed from 1900 to 2000, with continued growth beyond 2000 due to economic growth, balanced by technology transfer. It is difficult to generalize across the entire developing world, given that some cities have already implemented air quality standards, and as a result are experiencing declining pollution levels (Figure 1.3). One study reports emissions in selected Asian cities, indicating a greater than 10% decline in PM_{10} and nitrogen dioxide (NO_2) concentrations, and an 80% reduction in SO_2 emissions (Clean Air Initiative for Asian Cities (CAI-Asia) Center 2010). The same report suggests declining PM_{10}, NO_2, and SO_2 levels across 243 cities of Asia.

Exposure to indoor air pollution is estimated using the rate of solid fuel use to reflect the exposure of populations to indoor air pollution (Figure 1.4). However, global monitoring of solid fuel use is a recent phenomenon, hence assumptions must be made for solid fuel use from 1900 until 1990. In developed countries, solid fuel use is

estimated at 50% in 1900 (Bruce *et al.* 2002)[3] with gradual and linear decline until 2010 when the rate is estimated at 5%. In developing countries, solid fuel use is assumed to be 95% in 1990, declining to 67% in 2010, and a faster decline after 2020 assuming successful implementation of ongoing and future clean cook stove and fuel switching programs to reach 30% in 2050.

Based on the urban population and the rate of solid fuel use, Figure 1.5 shows the total population exposed. Those living in urban centers is forecast to rise from 3.6 billion in 2010 to 6.6 billion in 2050. The severity of exposure is not reflected in these numbers. For urban areas, severity of air pollution of exposed populations is expected to decline in areas where pollution control measures are successfully implemented, and increase in urban centers where more fossil fuels are burned without accompanying pollution reduction measures. The global population exposed to indoor air pollution is predicted to decline from 3.9 billion in 2010 to 2.5 billion in 2050. If smokeless and more efficient biomass stoves are scaled up in the developing world, the exposure level will also decline, as well as the number exposed.

Given the high degree of uncertainty in all these assumptions, especially at the extremes of

---

[3] It is estimated the portion of global energy derived from biofuel was 50% in 1900.

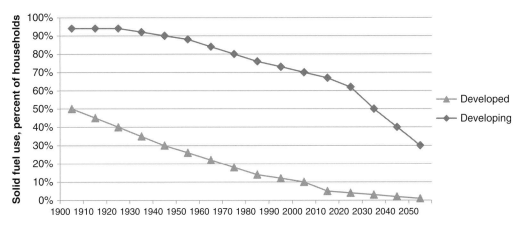

Figure 1.4 *Exposure to indoor air pollution: evolution of solid fuel use from 1900 to 2050, percent of household.* Source: *author's estimates; years 1990 to 2010 based on global statistics*

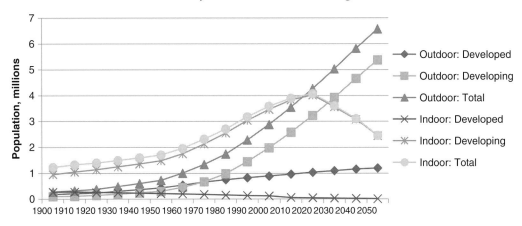

Figure 1.5 *Total population exposed to air pollution*

the 150-year time period covered in the study, sensitivity analysis explores high and low exposure levels (see later section).

Health Damage Estimation

Impacts Included

Two types of health impact are valued in the damage cost assessment:

- Premature mortality – costs of lives lost due to air pollution.
- Morbidity – costs of (1) medical treatment of air-pollution-related illnesses, and (2) lost time due to time spent sick.

Estimation Method

For outdoor air pollution, published studies focus on cities or parts of countries (Li *et al.* 2004; Stevens *et al.* 2005; Perez *et al.* 2009) as well as selected country examples (Seethaler 1999; US Environmental Protection Agency 1999; Zaim 1999; Kochi *et al.* 2001; Netalieva *et al.* 2005; UK Department for Environment Food and Rural Affairs 2006). Given the comparatively rich global data set on health impacts of air pollution, and the established methods for valuing health impacts in monetary units, this chapter makes a new set of calculations of health economic impact based on mortality and morbidity impacts and assigns unit cost values to each of these.

Available Health Impact Studies

The latest global burden of disease study is from the WHO, estimating deaths and disability-adjusted life year (DALYs) for the year 2004 (World Health Organization 2008). Data on deaths, cases, and DALYs are available for the early 1990s from Smith and Mehta (2003) for indoor air pollution in developing countries.

Methods for Valuing Health Impacts

Values are required for three variables to estimate health-related damage costs: cost of premature death, medical cost of an illness episode, and productive loss associated with an illness episode. For premature death, there are several alternative methods of valuation: (a) value of a statistical life, using estimates of values associated with a small change in the risk of death and multiplying up to estimate the value associated with saving one equivalent life; (b) human capital approach, which values the future net value contribution of individuals to society based income over their remaining working life; and (c) values obtained from life insurance companies or court cases where members of families are compensated for the death of an individual due to accident or injury.

The most established and widely used method for valuing life in economic studies is the value of a statistical life (VSL) method. Unlike the human capital approach and life insurance estimates, VSL is based on welfare theory, as it reflects the preferences and behavior of individuals. The human capital approach, on the other hand, which values a person according to their contribution to the economic wealth of society, does not take into account the intrinsic value of life and hence may undervalue life. Value of a life year (VOLY) is a more recently adopted technique, to give greater preference to saving lives of those with longer to live. However, there are several problems with VOLY (Krupnick *et al.* 2005). The lack of global data on age-specific premature mortality from air-pollution-related diseases supports the use of a single value of life, applied to all age groups equally.

There exists a rich literature, mainly from OECD countries, of VSL studies using different valuation techniques and different industries or population groups as the basis for the estimates. Several meta-analyses exist. Table 1.4 shows a number of these. For high-income countries, the mean or median estimates start at US$ 1,500,000 (1998 prices) from a review conducted by Mrozek and Taylor. However, more recent reviews tend towards US$5,000,000. In several of the studies in Table 1.4 that estimate both mean and median values from literature studies, the mean values are usually higher than median values, as the former are upward biased by a few very large willingness-to-pay responses. Also, different valuation methods give different VSL results. For example, wage risk studies tend to give higher VOSL values than studies that use contingent valuation (based on responses from interviews). Dionne and Lanoie compare meta-analysis results based on different types of study, and find that transportation studies on willingness to pay for risk reduction give a VSL on average 35% lower than all studies combined (comparing 8.3 versus 5.2 million Canadian Dollars) (Dionne and Lanoie 2002).

Given the wide variance between individual as well as meta-analytical studies and the differences observed between valuation techniques, choosing a single VSL for this current study is more a matter of judgment than scientific assessment. It is preferable to avoid choosing a VSL in the baseline analysis that risks overestimating the value of life. Based on the fact that the main population group likely to die prematurely from air pollution is the elderly, wage risk studies are not the appropriate basis for VSL estimates. Hence the lower estimates of the published meta-analyses should be used. Taking into account deflation to 1990 dollars, a VSL of US$3 million is chosen for developed countries. In the sensitivity analysis, a range of US$1 million (low value) to US$5 million (high value) is used.

For developing countries, in their review for the World Bank (Cropper and Sahin 2009) identified 16 studies that estimate VSL. Most of these studies are from middle-income countries. The authors conclude: "What is clear is that the developing country literature at this point is not sufficiently mature to provide estimates for individual countries. This suggests transferring estimates from countries where better studies exist to countries for which there are no empirical estimates of the VSL"

Table 1.4 VSL estimates from selected meta-analyses

Regional grouping	Price year	Type of average	Value in US$	Reference
High income	2005	Mean	4,271,000	Cropper and Sahin (2009)
Middle income	2005	Mean	709,000	
Low income	2005	Mean	180,000	
High income/Europe	2004	Mean	1,520,000 – 3,280,000	Alberini *et al.* (2006)
High income (wage risk)	1996	Median	5,630,000	Day (2007)
	1996	Mean	10,075,000	
High income	2002	Mean	2,500,000	Abelson (2003)
High income	2003	Mean	5,400,000	Kochi *et al.* (2006)
High income	1998	Mean	1,500,000 – 2,500,000	Mrozek and Taylor (2002)
High income/USA (wage risk)	2002	Median	7,000,000	Viscusi and Aldy (2003)
High income (stated preference)	2005	Mean	6,256,000	Braathen *et al.* (2009)
	2005	Median	2,814,000	
OECD countries	2005	Mean	9,523,000	Bellavance *et al.* (2007)
Wage risk	2005	Median	6,599,000	
USA (Environmental Protection Agency)	2003	Mean and median	5,500,000 – 7,500,000	Simon (2004)
Canada (road safety)	2000	Mean	5,528,000	Dionne and Lanoie (2002)
	2000	Median	3,996,000	

(p. 18). Hence the authors adopt the "benefits transfer" technique to estimate the VSL in developing countries, using a VSL from developed countries of US$5.4 million from Kochi *et al.* (2006). This value was adjusted using the proportional difference in GDP per capita between high-, middle- and low-income countries.[4] The mean VSL for middle-income countries was estimated at US$709,000 and for low-income countries it was US$180,000, in 2005 prices. This present study uses a similar method, transferring the value of US$3 million from developed countries – adjusted based on the GDP differential at official exchange rates and with an income elasticity of unity. This gives an average value of US$685,000 (at 1990 prices) for developing countries used in this present study.

The medical cost per case will vary between contexts depending in particular on (a) the type and severity of the condition; (b) the probability of seeking healthcare, the level and type of health facility visited, and the probability of being referred to a higher level of care; and (c) the unit costs per case treated. Given that the estimates are not based on country-specific inputs, it is necessary to make an estimate of a cost per average case of moderate severity ("moderate" being the most common medical complaint when medical advice is sought). For a moderate severity of a respiratory condition, the

[4] The latest World Bank classification of countries by income level uses gross national income in US dollars ($) from 2009, with the following thresholds: low income, $995 or less; middle income, $996–12,195; and high income, $12,196 or more. data.worldbank.org/about/country-classifications.

following assumptions are made to estimate an average unit cost (Hutton *et al.* 2006b):

- 50% of cases visit an outpatient clinic at the lowest level of care, and 20% of these require a follow-up visit
- 10% of cases visit an outpatient clinic at secondary level of care
- 10% of all patients are admitted for a hospital stay of an average 5 days
- In 2010, unit costs of outpatient care are US$70 in developed countries and US$5 in developing countries at the lowest level of care, and US$100 in developed countries and US$15 in developing countries for referral outpatient care. Unit costs of inpatient care are US$200 per bed day in developed countries and US$30 per bed day in developing countries.

Based on these rates of healthcare use and unit costs, the average cost per illness episode in 2010 equals US$159 in developed countries and US$20 in developing countries. The latter is a conservative estimate of likely costs per case in developing countries. For example, a study estimated the population is willing to pay US$44 in 1990 US$ for averting cases of lower respiratory infection in Mumbai, India (Lvovsky 1998). Unit costs in 2010 are adjusted to other time periods based on the proportional difference in GDP per capita compared to 2010.

The loss in economic value due to loss of productive time will depend on two main factors: (a) the time taken off productive activities by the sick person, and (b) the opportunity cost of that time, which depends, among other things, on the person's age, education level and the activity that could not be carried out due to sickness.

a) Respiratory illnesses vary in their severity, and the time to become well again and return to normal functioning will also depend on whether the right treatment was given. Some illness cases will last a short time – maximum 1 or 2 days – while the more severe cases may last for several weeks such as pneumonia, or be a permanent disability such as asthma, chronic obstructive pulmonary disease (COPD), and cancer. A conservative estimate of 5 days per case lost from productive

activities is used in this study, which is the same for all time periods (Hutton *et al.* 2006b).

b) Being an economic analysis, this study considers broader welfare implications of time lost from illness than just wage losses (for paid employees) or lost production time (e.g. for subsistence farmers). Hence, other activities than paid employment are considered in the assessment of opportunity cost of time. For one, leisure time is also valued by adults (Feather and Douglass Shaw 1999). Also, children of school age will miss education time, and these children – as well as children of 0–5 years – will require the care of a family member or other carer. Previous studies have commented that the value of time lost at the wage rate would overstate the actual losses, due to the substitutability of labor. A differential valuation of time of different age groups is not possible due to the lack of age breakdown of respiratory diseases at a global level. Therefore, to avoid overestimation, a more conservative value of time at the rate of 30% of the GDP per capita is used (Senhadji 2000).

Time Extrapolation of Available Data Sets

There are some but limited disease burden estimates before 1990, and projections after 2010. The problem inherent in using past and future values from other studies is that the methods and data sources may be different, hence leading to estimates that are inconsistent with the best current estimates for 2004. Therefore, disease burden estimates are scaled according to the average population exposure to main risk factors (see Figures 1.3 and 1.4 for outdoor air pollution exposure and for solid fuel use).

Building and Other Materials Damage Estimation

Impacts Included

Various impacts have been previously evaluated:

- Acid corrosion of stone, metals, and paints due to SO_2 and NO_X
- Ozone damage to polymeric materials, particularly natural rubbers

- Soiling of buildings and materials including both "utilitarian" and historic buildings and causes economic damages through cleaning and amenity costs
- Acid impacts on materials of cultural merit (including stone, fine art, and medieval stained glass).

The impacts included are limited to those impacts where there have been damage costs expressed in total terms for an identifiable population (typically at country level).

Estimation Method

From available studies, the cost per person in urban areas is calculated based on overall economic damages divided by the urban population.

Available Impact Studies

Lee *et al.* estimated annual damages to the UK of £170 to £345 million for impacts on surface coatings (paints) and elastomers and the cost of anti-ozonant protection used in rubber goods (Lee *et al.* 1996). The cost is equivalent to US$5–9 per capita per year in 1990 prices. Damage to rubber goods from ozone exposure in the UK was estimated at between £35 and £189 million, with a best estimate of £85 million per year, or US$2 per capita per year.

A series of studies from France, summarized in Rabl, estimated the air pollution contribution to damage of historical buildings at US$2.4 per person per year and to utilitarian buildings US$4 per person per year in 1990 (Rabl 1999), totaling US$7.4 per person per year in 2000 prices.

Some studies estimate cost savings of SO_2 control policies, such as in Budapest (US$50 per inhabitant) (Aunan *et al.* 1998), Prague (US$110 per inhabitant), and Stockholm (US$20 per inhabitant) (Kucera *et al.* 1993).

Based on the available studies, and taking account that the damages studied only cover part of the overall damages to buildings and materials, the damage cost used in this study is US$20 per capita per year in urban areas of developed countries. Based on the higher estimates found in the literature, this is likely to be an underestimate of average actual damages per person.

Fewer studies are available from developing countries. In Colombo, Sri Lanka, the average property damage cost due to air pollution is US$118 per year per household, or approximately US$20–25 per capita per year (Batagoda and Shanmuganathan 2004). From the same study, the average willingness to pay of the population to avoid property damage was estimated at US$5 per household per year, compared to US$14 to improve overall air quality.

Extrapolation of Available Data Set

The unit costs per person living in urban areas from country- or city-level studies are extrapolated to other countries, world regions, and time periods based on population exposed (based on the proportion of population living in urban areas), relative pollution level and economic levels (GDP per capita).

Natural Resources and Crop Damage Estimation

Impacts Included

Ozone is recognized as the most serious regional air pollution problem for the agricultural and horticulture sectors (Delucchi 2000). The impact of acid rain on natural resources and crops is the subject of a separate chapter.

Estimation Method

Studies in the literature on economic losses due to crop damages use either a mathematical approach (based on dose–response relationships from experimental studies) or they use an econometric model (based on observed changes in actual farm output due to a change in pollution). These estimates are extracted from studies and converted to average loss per capita per year, and are extrapolated to other time periods and geographical zones based on air pollution levels and economic level (GDP per capita).

Available Impact Studies

The US Environmental Protection Agency (1999) reports a total annual benefit to the US commercial timber sector of approximately $800 million and to grain crop producers of about $700 million in 2010 from improved yields due to ozone reductions as a result of the 1990 Clean Air Act Amendments (CAAA) (Chestnut and Mills 2005). Other studies have shown significantly greater impacts. Several studies were published during the 1990s on losses to US agriculture due to ozone. Losses due to vehicular pollution alone were estimated at between US$2 billion and US$3.9 billion by Murphy *et al.* (1999), between US$2.6 and US$ 5.3 billion by Delucchi *et al.* (1996) in 1990, while US$1.2 billion was estimated by Muller and Mendolsohn (2007). Hence, the cost in the USA ranges from US$5 to US $20 per capita per year.

European countries have also been the focus of other crop loss studies. In Hungary, as much as US $716 million losses due to ozone-induced crop losses, or US$100 per capita (Aunan *et al.* 1998). The PESETA[5] study estimated crop losses of €6.7 billion across 47 European countries, or €12 per capita (US$16 per capita) (Ciscar *et al.* 2009). A UNECE study estimated £4.3 billion (US$6.8 billion) across 36 European countries, or US$12 per capita, in 1990 (Holland *et al.* 2002). A cost–benefit analysis carried out under the Clean Air For Europe (CAFE) programme estimates damage costs in EU countries in the year 2000 for crop damages (€2.8 billion) and materials (€1.1 billion), equal to €8 per capita, or US$11 (Pye and Watkiss 2005). A study from the mid-1980s in the Netherlands estimated crop losses at US$320 million per year, or US$22 per capita (van der Eerden *et al.* 1988). Therefore, adjusting to 1990 dollars, this study uses US$20 per capita for developed regions, and US$5 per capita for developing countries.

Other Socio-Economic Damage Estimation

Impacts Included

The time losses from collecting biomass and the time spent cooking with inefficient and polluting stoves or fuel are valued in this study.

Estimation Method and Available Study

A global study was conducted by the WHO in 2006 which estimated the health, environmental, and time

gains from measures to reduce exposure to indoor air pollution (Hutton *et al.* 2006a). The study covered only non-OECD countries. The value of the time lost per year of US$88 billion is used for developing countries for the year 2000, and also extrapolated to non-OECD countries adjusting for population sizes, economic prices (GDP per capita) and rates of solid fuel use.

Visibility Damage Estimation

Impacts Included

Particulate matter in the air absorbs and scatters light as it passes through the atmosphere, reducing the clarity of viewed objects and visual range. Analyses of visibility often use a measure of haziness called the "Deciview." Visibility conditions directly affect people's enjoyment of a variety of daily activities. Individuals value visibility where they live and work, where they go for recreation, and at sites of unique aesthetic value such as national parks.

Estimation Method and Available Impact Studies

This study identifies economic impact studies in the literature and extrapolates them across time and geographical location. Economic studies have estimated monetary values held by the visitors to facilities (such as historical monuments or national parks) and of the general public in their place of abode for changes in visibility. Most work has been conducted in the USA. For example, the estimate of the total annual value for visibility improvement at all national parks and wilderness areas is about US$3 billion (Chestnut and Mills 2005). Adding to this value the WTP estimates of households for visibility improvements in locations where they live brings the total value of related Title IV (also known as the acid rain program) visibility improvements to about US$5 billion, or US$17 per capita. A comprehensive damage cost study from the US estimates visibility as having a value of US$2.7 billion annually (Muller and Mendolsohn 2007), or US$10 per capita. Delucchi estimates visibility losses at between US$5 and US$37 billion per year, or US$20–150

---

[5] Projection of Economic impacts of climate change in Sectors of the European Union based on bottom–up analysis.

Table 1.5 Ecological impacts with identifiable human service flows

Pollution source	Causal pathway of impact	Activity impacted
Acidification (H₂SO₄, HNO₃)	High-elevation forest acidification resulting in dieback	Forest aesthetics
	Freshwater acidification resulting in aquatic organism (e.g. fish) population decline	Recreational fishing
	Changes in biological diversity and species mix in terrestrial and aquatic systems	Existence value for maintenance of biological diversity
Nitrogen saturation and eutrophication (NOₓ)	Freshwater acidification resulting in aquatic organism (e.g. fish) population decline	Recreational fishing
	Estuarine eutrophication causing oxygen depletion and changes in nutrient cycling	Recreational and commercial fishing
	Changes in biological diversity and species mix in terrestrial and aquatic systems	Existence value for maintenance of biological diversity
Toxics deposition (mercury, dioxin)	Terrestrial bioaccumulation of mercury and dioxin	Hunting, wildlife aesthetics
	Aquatic bioaccumulation of mercury and dioxin	Recreational and commercial fishing
	Changes in biological diversity and species mix in terrestrial and aquatic systems	Existence value for maintenance of biological diversity
Tropospheric ozone (O₃)	Terrestrial plant foliar damage causing lower productivity	Commercial timber productivity and reduced competitiveness, forest aesthetics, existence value
Multiple pollutant stress	Ecosystem deterioration resulting in visual effects habitat loss, and changes in biological diversity and species mix caused by synergistic action of several pollutants	Ecosystem aesthetics, and ecosystem existence value

Source: US Environmental Protection Agency (1999).

per capita per year (Delucchi 2000), and in a later paper US$8–31 billion (Delucchi *et al.* 2002).

This study uses an estimate of US$10 per capita per year for loss of visibility in developed countries, applied to the urban populations where the major loss of visibility takes place. This value is extrapolated to developing countries adjusting by differences in GDP per capita. Extrapolations are made over time adjusting for economic prices (GDP per capita), population size, and pollution levels.

Ecosystems

Damage costs to ecosystems are estimated in another chapter, so estimates are not included within this chapter. Table 1.5 presents a range of different impacts on ecosystems identified by the US Environmental Protection Agency (EPA). A study produced by the EPA estimated annual economic losses avoided from implementing the Clean Air Act by 2010, which included: estuarine ecosystems (US$2.7 billion), acidification of freshwater fisheries (US$88 million), aesthetics of two selected forests (US$250 million), timber production losses (US$600 million), and net surplus on crop production (US$1.1 billion) (US Environmental Protection Agency 1999). With a population of 312 million in 2010, this gives a benefit of US$15 per capita per year. As these figures reflect damages avoided from a partial reduction in emissions, the total damages are likely to be considerably more than these figures.

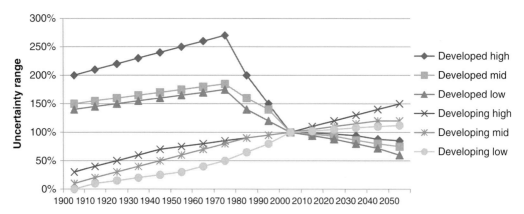

Figure 1.6 *Uncertainty range tested in pollution exposure in urban centers*

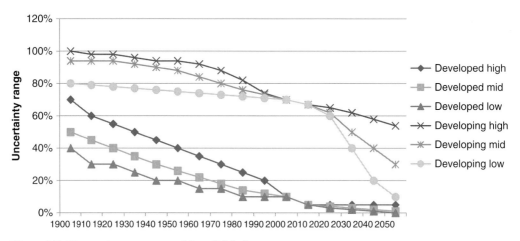

Figure 1.7 *Uncertainty range tested in solid fuel use*

Sensitivity Analysis

While this study has used a number of assumptions, the sensitivity analysis focuses on two single variables that are expected to influence the results. These are (a) the economic value of life and (b) the historical and projected pollution levels. The latter leads to changes in estimates in the years before and after the baseline, but no changes in the actual baseline years. For both these variables, high and low values are used. The ranges on the pollution level variables are shown in Figure 1.6 (outdoor air pollution) and Figure 1.7 (indoor air pollution). For VSL, a low value of US$1 million and a high value of US$5 million are used for the year 2010 in developed countries. For developing countries, a low value of

US$228,560 and a high value of US$1,142,800 are used for the year 2010. For pollution levels, high and low assumptions are used to provide a range around the baseline assumptions from 1900 to 1990 and from 2020 to 2050. For other variables such as healthcare unit costs, GDP values, population sizes, and health impacts (deaths and cases), there is less uncertainty in their values and hence they are not tested in the sensitivity analysis.

Results

Total Damages

This study estimates the total damage costs of air pollution to be US$3 trillion in 2010, or 5.6% of

Table 1.6 Evolution of air pollution damage costs over time: absolute (US$ billion, 1990 prices) and as percent of GDP

	1900		1950		2010		2030		2050	
Impact	Cost	%GDP	Cost	%GDP	Cost	%GDP	Cost	%GDP	Cost	%GDP
Outdoor air										
Developed	69	5.2%	238	6.1%	828	3.1%	1,113	2.8%	1,521	2.5%
Developing	2	0.3%	26	1.8%	644	2.4%	1,515	2.5%	3,681	2.8%
Total	71	3.6%	265	5.0%	1,472	2.7%	2,628	2.6%	5,202	2.7%
Indoor air										
Developed	103	7.7%	102	2.6%	87	0.3%	74	0.2%	36	0.1%
Developing	272	42.4%	347	23.9%	1,467	5.4%	1,933	3.2%	2,259	1.7%
Total	375	19.0%	449	8.4%	1,554	2.9%	2,007	2.0%	2,295	1.2%
Total air										
Developed	172	12.9%	340	8.8%	915	3.4%	1,187	3.0%	1,558	2.6%
Developing	274	42.7%	373	25.8%	2,111	7.8%	3,448	5.8%	5,940	4.5%
Total	446	22.6%	713	13.4%	3,026	5.6%	4,635	4.6%	7,498	3.9%

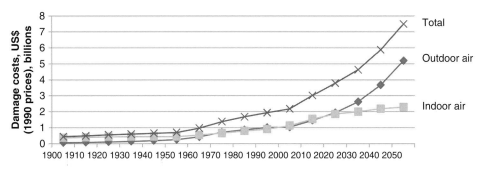

Figure 1.8 *Global damage costs from air pollution, outdoor versus indoor (US$, 1990 prices)*

gross world product (GWP). Table 1.6 shows the evolution over time at five time points. At present, in 2010, the damages are shared equally between developed and developing countries for outdoor air, but for indoor air the major share of damages falls on developing countries. Over the next 40 years, the relative impact of overall air pollution damages is expected to fall to under 4% of GWP by 2050.

Since the start of the last century, damage costs to developed countries of outdoor air pollution have been falling from 5.2% of GDP, predicted to be 2.5% of GDP in 2050. Developing countries on the other hand have seen a major growth in damages

due to outdoor air pollution, stabilizing at 2.8% of GDP in 2050.

Damages due to indoor air pollution started high for developed countries in 1900 at 7.7% of GDP, falling rapidly to 2.6% in 1950 and 0.3% in 2010 as households switched from solid fuels to kerosene, electricity, and gas. In developing countries, a high number of deaths due to indoor air pollution led to very high economic losses at 42% of GDP, falling to 24% in 1950, 5.4% in 2010, and falling further to 1.7% in 2050 as solid fuels are phased out.

Figure 1.8 shows the growth in damage costs in billion US dollars (at constant 1990 prices). It can

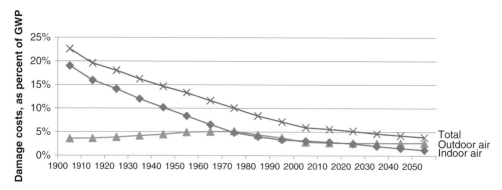

Figure 1.9 *Global damage costs from air pollution, outdoor versus indoor, as percent of GWP*

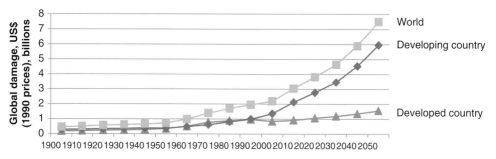

Figure 1.10 *Global damage costs from air pollution (US$ 1990 prices)*

be seen that indoor and outdoor air had similar costs globally until 2020, when declining deaths from indoor air pollution are expected to be halved from 1.7 million to 0.8 million annually, and outdoor air pollution deaths are expected to increase in the developing world. While overall health risks and deaths from air pollution are expected to fall over time, the growth in economic costs seen in the figure is due to the higher relative prices that economic growth gives rise to, especially in the developing world.

Figure 1.9 shows the declining damage costs as a proportion of GWP for both indoor air and outdoor air pollution. For indoor air pollution, the damages have been decreasing substantially since 1900, while for outdoor air pollution the decline has been mainly since 1970. After around 2020, outdoor air will have higher damage costs than indoor air, reversing the trend of the past century.

Figure 1.10 shows that the damage costs from air pollution are significantly increasing in developing countries, compared to developed countries. The

rise is almost totally from rising real prices (i.e. economic growth) in the developing world.

Figure 1.11 shows the convergence of developing with developed countries of overall air pollution damage costs, when expressed as a proportion of GDP. From a global average of close to 23% of GWP, the damage costs have fallen to little over 4% of GWP.

Table 1.7 shows the per capita costs for selected time points. Despite the overall declining levels of pollution, the per capita costs are rising over time. This phenomenon is largely due to rising real prices resulting from continued economic growth. By 2050, the total damage cost is between US$700 and US$800 per capita per year. The greater part of overall damage costs are incurred in the developing world due to 85% of the global population being located in countries defined by this study as belonging to the developing country region. As shown in Table 1.7, the overall damage costs are dominated by health costs, and of these, health damage costs from outdoor air exceed indoor air

Table 1.7 Per capita damage costs of air pollution (US$, 1990 prices)

Variable	1900	1950	2000	2010	2050
Health impacts of outdoor air					
Developed country	111	258	510	585	999
Developing country	2	14	64	101	408
World	40	94	153	190	495
Non-health impacts of outdoor air					
Developed country	16	29	49	56	90
Developing country	0	2	7	11	44
World	6	11	16	20	50
Health impacts of indoor air					
Developed country	167	108	104	60	23
Developing country	243	187	183	234	253
World	217	161	167	202	219
Non-health impacts of indoor air					
Developed country	23	15	14	8	3
Developing country	24	18	18	23	24
World	23	17	17	20	21
Outdoor and indoor air					
Developed country	317	410	677	709	1,116
Developing country	269	220	273	369	729
World	285	283	353	431	786

pollution by more than two times. The disaggregated findings are presented further below.

Outdoor Air Pollution

Figure 1.12 shows the converging damage costs of developing countries with developed countries, as a % of GDP. Starting at under 0.5% of GDP in 1900, damage costs have grown to almost 3% of GDP in developing countries. In developed countries, damage costs have been falling since 1970 in developed countries, from over 6% of GDP to the current levels of 3.5% of GDP.

Indoor air pollution

Figure 1.13 shows falling damage costs associated with indoor air pollution, due to gradually falling rates of solid fuel use since 1900. In developed countries, damages of below 3% of GDP were achieved as early as the 1950s, whereas for developing countries, damage costs of 3% are expected to be achieved by 2050 – assuming continued declines in solid fuel use.

Developing Countries

Figure 1.14 shows the damage costs in developing countries are increasing significantly due to outdoor air pollution, while the growth is smaller from indoor air pollution. The results are largely being driven by the number of deaths, which are increasing from outdoor air pollution and decreasing from

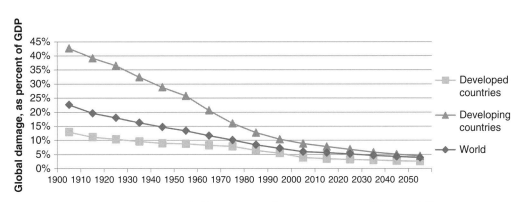

Figure 1.11 *Global damage costs of all-cause air pollution, as percent of GDP and GWP*

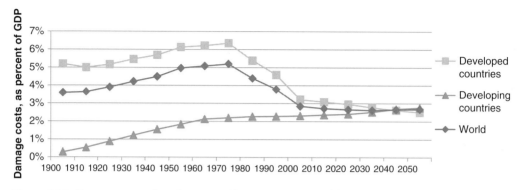

Figure 1.12 *Damage costs of outdoor air pollution, as percent of GDP*

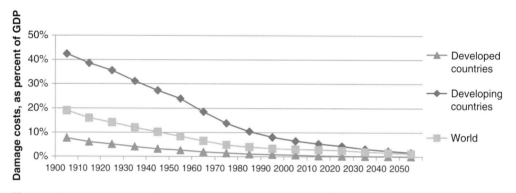

Figure 1.13 *Damage costs of indoor air pollution, as percent of GDP*

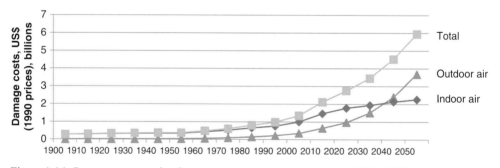

Figure 1.14 *Damage costs to developing countries from air pollution (US$, 1990 prices)*

indoor air pollution. By 2050, almost US$6 trillion will be lost from air pollution.

Figure 1.15 shows the drastic fall in damage costs from indoor air pollution from 1900 to 2050, while there is an increasing trend for damage costs from outdoor air pollution. After 2040, and at projected indoor and outdoor air pollution paths in developing countries, the deaths and damage costs from outdoor air pollution will exceed indoor air pollution.

Developed Countries

Figure 1.16 shows that from similar damage costs in 1900, there is now a wide divergence in damage

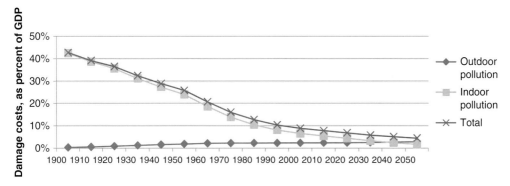

Figure 1.15 *Damage costs of air pollution in developing countries, as percent of GDP*

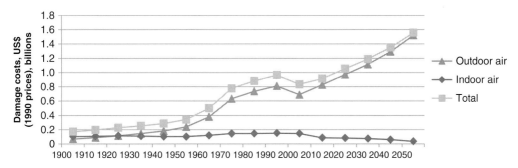

Figure 1.16 *Damage costs to developed countries from air pollution, (US$, 1990 prices)*

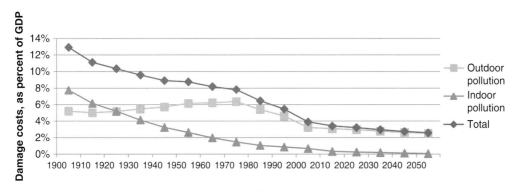

Figure 1.17 *Damage costs of air pollution in developed countries, as percent of GDP*

costs between indoor and outdoor air pollution. There is an apparent dip in damage costs between 1990 and 2010 due to the continued large fall in the number of deaths from 1990 to 2000, after which the marginal rate of decline in deaths falls (due to lower proportional declines in air pollution). The growth of damage costs after 2000 is due to the

increase in real prices (from economic growth) outstripping the continued decline in the number of deaths.

Figure 1.17 shows a gradually declining trend in air pollution damage costs as a proportion of GDP in developed countries, from 13% in 1900 to 2.5% in 2050. This declining trend is being driven by

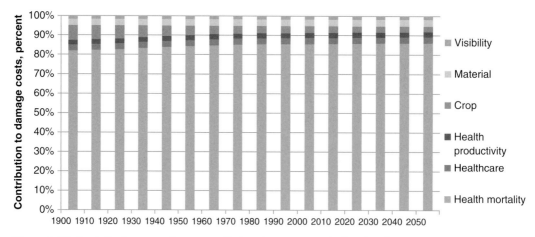

Figure 1.18 *Contribution to outdoor air pollution damage costs in developed countries*

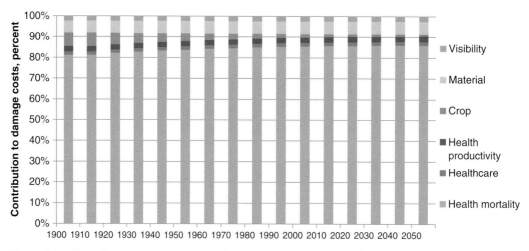

Figure 1.19 *Contribution to outdoor air pollution damage costs in developing countries*

reductions in solid fuel use – and the associated reductions in health damage costs. However, these reductions are accompanied by a gradual increase in damage costs from outdoor air pollution rising from 1900 to 1970, followed by a rapid decline to below 5% of GDP from 1990 onwards.

Contribution to Impacts

Figures 1.18 and 1.19 show that for both developed and developing countries the major contributor to overall damage costs of outdoor air pollution is mortality cost, accounting for over 80% of overall

damages. Making up the remaining costs are health productivity, healthcare costs, crop production, material damages, and visibility.

Figure 1.20 shows that the overall damage costs of indoor air pollution in developed countries are shared between premature mortality, health-related productivity, and healthcare costs. A smaller share, a little over 10%, is contributed by access time to collect biomass (or equivalent cost if purchased).

Figure 1.21 shows that the mortality cost is the major contributor in developing countries, at 85–90% of overall damage cost. Collection time

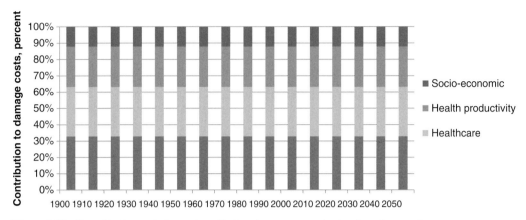

Figure 1.20 *Contribution to indoor air pollution damage costs in developed countries*

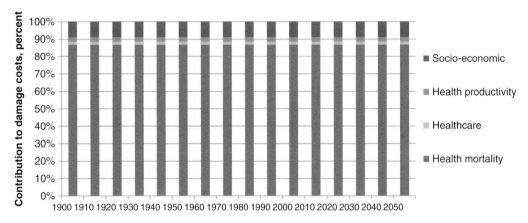

Figure 1.21 *Contribution to indoor air pollution damage costs in developing countries*

losses account for almost 10% of overall solid fuel use losses, a proportion which is stable over time.

Sensitivity Analysis

The sensitivity analysis made adjustments to the pollution levels used in the baseline analysis. Figure 1.22 shows the variation in overall damage costs under pessimistic (top line) and optimistic (bottom line) pollution scenarios, as a percent of GWP. Under high pollution levels, the damage costs reach little over 25% of GWP in 1900, while under low pollution levels the damage cost remains over 18% of GWP. In 2050, even under pessimistic assumptions, the total damage cost is around 5% of GWP. In conclusion, although quite significant

adjustments were made to the pollution levels, the impact on the overall results is not major. Hence the results are sensitive to the assumptions on pollution levels, but do not change the results by any order of magnitude. Hence, a stable or continued declining trend in global losses is confirmed by this analysis.

Figure 1.23 shows the influence of high and low value of statistical lives (VSL) on the global damage costs of air pollution. Given that the value of premature deaths accounted for at least 80% of total damage costs for all time periods of the analysis, the alternative VSL values chosen had a major impact on the results. The high VSL value of US$5 million per death in developed countries in 2010 leads to almost twice the damage costs at 8.4% of GWP in 2010 compared to 5.4% in the baseline. Likewise,

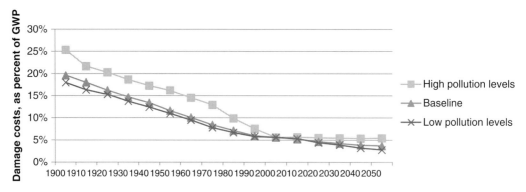

Figure 1.22 *Variation in pollution exposure and resulting impact on baseline estimates of air pollution damage costs, developed and developing countries combined, as percent of GWP*

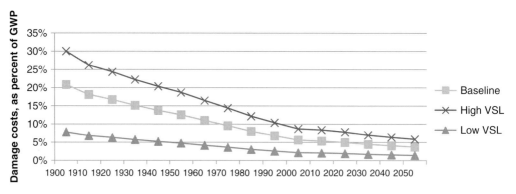

Figure 1.23 *Variation in value of life and resulting impact on baseline estimates of air pollution damage costs, developed and developing countries combined, as percent of GWP*

the low VSL value of US$1 million lead to a major cut in damage costs to 2.1% of GWP. Hence the choice of VSL is critical to the size of impact and the resulting conclusions.

Discussion

This study has faced several challenges in estimating the global damage costs of air pollution from 1900 to 2050. Even since 1990, when many scientific articles on damage costs of air pollution have been published, there is a lack of evidence, especially studies from developing countries, to estimate global health and non-health damages from air pollution. The resulting estimates are not precise. Prior to 1990, and post 2010, this study faced many challenges in estimating input values within

the damage cost function. Hence, both geographical and temporal extrapolation of available research studies has lead to some weaknesses in the results. Using best available extrapolation techniques of damage functions and expert judgment, this study gives a global overview on relative size of damage costs for two main causes of air pollution – indoor and outdoor – and two categories of country – developed and developing. One-way sensitivity analysis on important determining variables – pollution levels and value of life – has indicated a probable range of global damage costs between 2.1% to 8.4% of GWP in 2010. In 1900, the damage costs ranged between 8% and 30% of GWP; with a decline to between 1.5% and 6% of GWP in 2050. Hence, the overall and continuing trend of declining global damage costs is encouraging from a human development perspective. However, it is important to bear in mind that the projected reductions in damage costs (as percent of GWP) beyond 2010 depend on the success of current and future policies to reduce exposure to air pollution in both urban and indoor environments. The estimates of future pollution exposure assume appropriate policies are pursued and implemented, supported by sustainable economic growth which increases the available funds for households, governments and private sector to make the necessary investments in pollution abatement technologies, different fuels and measures to reduce exposure.

The health damage costs account for a large proportion of overall damage costs. This is partly because health damages are easier to quantify due to the availability of global data on burden of disease. Other non-health benefits are likely to have been significantly underestimated. First, few economic data exist on the non-health impacts that were included such as crop and material damage. It is indeed possible that the unit cost estimates that were chosen are very conservative estimates, and hence damage costs could be significantly higher. Second, some non-health impacts were omitted as they have been included in other chapters.

In interpreting the overall damages, it should be noted whom the health impacts fall on. Air pollution generally affects those most vulnerable to poor air quality such as those with underlying (respiratory) health conditions, the elderly and the young. Some types of worker are also more exposed to urban air pollution than others, being located in the outdoor environment, such as street sellers and construction workers. Poor and rural families are more likely to use solid fuel for cooking or for indoor heating, and not have access to improved stoves, than richer households. Women and (young) children are most exposed to indoor air pollution, as the home is where their lives are based. Also, those who are poorer are less able to take avertive measures to protect themselves from air pollution (such as using an air conditioning in homes or in a car in cities), and these same low-income groups are least able to afford adequate medical care when they fall sick. Hence, while it was not within the scope of this chapter to perform an equity analysis, it is important to be aware of whom these impacts most fall on.

The distinction between developed and developing regions has been instructive – indicating different air pollution exposure patterns and different strength of trends over time. However, the economic analysis has also given different values to the physical impacts felt by those living in developed compared to developing countries. Such an approach is justified from the perspective of national or regional policymakers who need to make decisions based on a comparison of the actual costs and benefits of different policy choices. For example, if national policy from developing countries used evidence based on an average world price for medical cost savings or deaths averted, they would be misled into allocating too many resources to a pollution reduction activity, as the actual gains would be lower. On the other hand, when damage costs from developed and developing regions are compared in the same currency unit, but based on different underlying prices, the implicit assumption is that pollution reduction measures are worth more to those in developed countries. This is clearly wrong from a global equity perspective. Hence, when considering the global allocation of pollution control resources, it is fairer to compare damage costs between developed and developing countries as a percentage of GDP (e.g. Figure 1.11) rather than in currency units (e.g. Figure 1.10). Importantly, globally available resources – such as the Green Climate Fund – should be allocated to where consumers have least ability to pay for pollution control measures, and/or countries where the private sector is least likely to invest their funds. In particular, where the private sector is willing to invest, it is important to avoid "crowding out" private investment potential with public subsidies, the latter which could be used more efficiently elsewhere.

As was mentioned in the introduction, air pollution is double-edged. Economic growth has unarguably led to increased levels of income and improved standards of living, while this economic growth has been possible because of longer life expectancies and technological progress such as the combustion engine and industrial development, which compromise air quality. Governments and citizens alike, while they may not have been fully aware of the health and other impacts of air pollution, have been shown to be willing to trade off the health of the population for other gains in quality of life. These decisions have been made without the offer of cleaner technologies, nor (often) the ability to choose a different paradigm of economic growth. However, in the latter part of the twentieth century, greater environmental knowledge combined with technological development and freer trade regimes – which have themselves enabled the multinational private sector to reach almost every household on the planet – have together given rise to many new possibilities for sustainable living. The damage costs of air pollution in the coming decades could be significantly more or significantly less than those presented here, depending on which development pathway is chosen. This is a decision that needs to be made collectively, based on developments in science and technology, improved delivery mechanisms for green technology, and sustainability concerns placed at the center of economic planning.

References

Abelson, B. (2003) The value of life and health for public policy. *The Economic Record* **79**: S2–S13.

Alberini, A., A. Hunt, and A. Markandya (2006) Willingness to pay to reduce mortality risks: evidence from a three-country contingent valuation study. *Environmental and Resource Economics* **33**: 251–264.

Aunan, K., G. Patzay, H. Asbjorn Aaheim, and H. Martin Seip (1998) Health and environmental benefits from air pollution reductions in Hungary. *Science of the Total Environment* **212**: 245–268.

Batagoda, B. and G. Shanmuganathan (2004) Valuation of property damages from urban air pollution: a case study of Colombo, Sri Lanka. Available at: http://cleanairinitiative.org/portal/sites/

Bellavance, F., G. Dionne, and M. Lebeau (2007) The value of a statistical life: a meta-analysis with a mixed effects regression model. *Journal of Health Economics* **28**: 444–464.

Braathen, N., H. Lindhjem, and S. Navrud (2009) *Valuing Lives Saved from Environmental, Transport and Health Policies: A Meta-analysis of Stated Preference Studies*. Paris: OECD.

Bruce, N., R. Perez-Padilla, and R. Albalak (2002). *The Health Effects of Indoor Air Pollution in Developing Countries*. Geneva: WHO.

Chestnut, L. and D. Mills (2005) A fresh look at the benefits and costs of the US acid rain program. *Journal of Environmental Management* **77**: 252–266.

Ciscar, J.-C., Ǎ. Iglesias, L.Feyen *et al.* (2009) *Climate change impacts in Europe: final report of the PESETA research project*. Seville, Spain: European Commission Joint Research Centre.

Clean Air Initiative for Asian Cities (CAI-Asia) Center (2010) *Air Quality in Asia: Status and Trends*. Metro Manila, Philippines.

Cropper, M. and S. Sahin (2009) *Valuing Mortality and Morbidity in the Context of Disaster Risks*. New York: World Bank.

Day, B. (2007) *A Meta-Analysis of Wage-Risk Estimates of the Value of Statistical Life*. Norwich, UK: Centre for Social and Economic Research on the Global Environment.

Delucchi, M. (2000) Environmental externalities of motor vehicle use in the US. *Journal of Transport Economics and Policy* **34**: 135–168.

Delucchi, M., J. Murphy, J. Kim, and D. McCubbin (1996) The cost of crop damage caused by ozone air pollution from vehicles. Berkeley, CA: Institute of Transportation Studies.

Delucchi, M., J. Murphy, and D. McCubbin (2002) The health and visibility cost of air pollution: a comparison of estimation methods. *Journal of Environmental Management* **64**: 139–152.

Dionne, G. and P. Lanoie (2002) *How to Make a Public Choice about the Value of a Statistical Life: The Case of Road Safety*. Montreal: HEC.

European Environment Agency (2010) European Union Emission Inventory Report 1990–2008 under the UNECE Convention on Long-Range Transboundary Air Pollution (LRTAP). EEA Technical Report No. 7/2010.

Feather, P. and W. Douglass Shaw (1999) Estimating the cost of leisure time for recreation demand models. *Journal of Environmental Economics and Management* **38**: 49–65.

Friedrich, R., A. Rabl, and J. Spadaro (2001) Quantifying the costs of air pollution: the ExternE project of the EC. *Pollution Atmosphérique* Special Issue: 77–104.

Habermehl, H. (2007) Economic evaluation of the improved household cooking stove dissemination programme in Uganda. Available at: www. gtz.de/de/dokumente/

(2008) Costs and benefits of efficient institutional cook stoves in Malawi. Available at: www.gtz.de/de/dokumente/

Holland, M., G. Mills, F. Hayes, *et al.* (2002) *Economic Assessment of Crop Yield Losses from Ozone Exposure.* Geneva: UNECE International Cooperative Programme on Vegetation.

Hutton, G. (2008) Economic evaluation of environmental health interventions to support decision making. *Environmental Health Insights* **2**: 137–155.

Hutton, G., E. Rehfuess, F. Tediosi, and S. Weiss (2006a) *Evaluation of the Costs and Benefits of Household Energy and Health Interventions at Global and Regional Levels.* Geneva: WHO.

(2006b) *Global Cost-Benefit Analysis of Household Energy and Health Interventions.* Geneva: Department for the Protection of the Human Environment, WHO.

Hutton, G., E. Rehfuess, and F. Tediosi (2007) Evaluation of the costs and benefits of interventions to reduce indoor air pollution. *Energy for Sustainable Development* **11**: 34–43.

Kochi, I., B. Hubbell, and R. Kramer (2006) An empirical Bayes approach to combining and comparing estimates of the value of a statistical life for environmental policy analysis. *Environmental and Resource Economics* **34**: 385–406.

Kochi, I., S. Matsuoka, M. A. Memon, and H. Shirakawa (2001) Cost benefit analysis of the sulfur dioxide emissions control policy in Japan. *Environmental Economics and Policy Studies* **4**: 219–233.

Kucera, V., J. Henriksen, D. Knotkova, and C. Sjöström (1993) Model for calculations of corrosion costs caused by air pollution and its application in three cities. In: J. M. Costa, and A. D. Mercer (eds.), *Progress in the Understanding and Prevention of Corrosion.* London: Institute of Materials.

Larsen, B., G. Hutton, and N. Khanna (2008) *Air Pollution* Copenhagen Consensus 2008 Challenge Paper. Copenhagen Business School.

Lee, D., M. Holland, and N. Falla (1996) The potential impact of ozone on materials. *Atmospheric Environment* **30**: 1053–1065.

Li, J., S. Guttikunda, G. Carmichael, *et al.* (2004) Quantifying the human health benefits of curbing air pollution in Shanghai. *Journal of Environmental Management* **70**: 49–62.

Lvovsky, K. (1998) Economic costs of air pollution with special reference to India. *National Conference on Health and Environment*, Delhi, India, July 7–9, 1998.

Mage, D., G. Ozolins, P. Peterson, *et al.* (1996) Urban air pollution in megacities of the world. *Atmospheric Environment* **30**: 681–686.

Montgomery, W., R. Baron, and S. Tuladhar (2009) *An Analysis of Black Carbon Mitigation as a Response to Climate Change.* Copenhagen Consensus Center.

Mrozek, J. and L. Taylor (2002) What determines the value of life? A meta-analysis. *Journal of Policy Analysis and Management* **21**: 253–270.

Muller, N. and R. Mendolsohn (2007) Measuring the damages of air pollution in the United States. *Journal of Environmental Economics and Management* **54**: 1–14.

Murphy, J., M. Delucchi, D. McCubbin, and H. Kim (1999) The cost of crop damage caused by ozone air pollution from motor vehicles. *Journal of Environmental Management* **55**: 273–289.

Netalieva, I., J. Wesseler, and W. J. Heijman (2005) Health costs caused by oil extraction emissions and the benefits from abatement: the case of Kazakhstan. *Energy Policy* **33**: 1169–1177.

Perez, L., J. Sunyer, and N. Kunzli (2009) Estimating the health and economic benefits associated with reducing air pollution in the Barcelona metropolitan area (Spain). *Gaceta Sanitaria* **23**: 287–294.

Pervin, T., U.-G. Gerdtham, and C. Lyttkens (2008) Societal costs of air pollution-related health hazards: a review of methods and results. *Cost Effectiveness and Resource Allocation* 6 Article 19.

Pye, S. and P. Watkiss (2005) *Clean Air for Europe (CAFE) Programme Cost–Benefit Analysis: Baseline Analysis 2000 to 2020*, Study conducted by AEA Technology Environment for the European Commission, DG Environment.

Rabl, A. (1999) Air pollution and buildings: an estimation of damage costs in France. *Environmental Impact Assessment Review* **19**: 361–385.

Rehfuess, E., S. Mehta, and A. Prüss-Üstün (2006) Assessing household solid fuel use: multiple implications for the Millennium Development Goals. *Environmental Health Perspectives* **114**: 373–378.

Seethaler, R. (1999) *Health Costs due to Road Traffic-Related Air Pollution: An Impact Assessment Project of Austria, France and Switzerland: Synthesis Report.* Geneva: WHO Regional Office for Europe.

Senhadji, A. (2000) Sources of economic growth: an extensive accounting exercise. *IMF Staff Papers* **47**: 129–158.

Simon, N. (2004) *Value of Statistical Life Analysis and Environmental Policy: A White Paper.* Washington, DC: US Environmental Protection Agency.

Smith, K. and S. Mehta (2003). The burden of disease from indoor air pollution in developing countries: comparison of estimates. *International Journal of Hygiene and Environmental Health* **206**: 279–289.

Stevens, G., A. Wilson, and J. Hammitt (2005) A benefit–cost analysis of retrofitting diesel vehicles with particulate filters in the Mexico City metropolitan area. *Risk Analysis* **25**: 883–899.

UK Department for Environment, Food and Rural Affairs (2006) *Economic Analysis to Inform the Air Quality Strategy Review Consultation: Third Report of the Interdepartmental Group on Costs and Benefits*. London: Department for Environment, Food and Rural Affairs (DEFRA).

US Environmental Protection Agency (1999) *The Benefits and Costs of the Clean Air Act: 1990 to 2010*. www.epa.gov/oar/sect812.

US Environmental Protection Agency (2000) *National Air Pollution Emission Trends 1990–1998*. Washington, DC: Office of Air Quality Planning and Standards, US Environmental Protection Agency.

US Environmental Protection Agency (2003) *Benefits and Costs of the Clean Air Act: Second Prospective Study – 1990 to 2020*. www.epa.gov/air/sect812/index.html.

van der Eerden, L., A. Tonneijck, and J. Wijnands (1988) Crop loss due to air pollution in The Netherlands. *Environmental Pollution* **53**: 365–376.

Viscusi, W. and J. Aldy (2003) The value of a statistical life: a critical review of market estimates throughout the world. *Journal of Risk and Uncertainty* **27**: 5–76.

Voorhees, A., R. Sakai, S. Araki, H. Sato, and A. Otsu (2001) Cost-benefit analysis methods for assessing air pollution control programs in urban environments: a review. *Environmental Health and Preventive Medicine* **6**: 63–73.

World Health Organization (2008) *The Global Burden of Disease: 2004 Update*. Geneva: WHO.

Zaim, K. (1999) Modified GDP through health cost analysis of air pollution: the case of Turkey. *Environmental Management* **23**: 271–277.

Annex 1.1

Table A1.1 Percent of population using solid fuels, by country and WHO region

Region/country	Percentage	Region/country	Percentage	Region/country	Percentage
Africa	77	Colombia	15	Hungary	<5
Algeria	<5	Costa Rica	23	Kazakhstan	5
Angola	>95	Cuba	<5	Kyrgyzstan	76
Benin	95	Dominican Republic	14	Latvia	10
Botswana	65	Ecuador	<5	Lithuania	<5
Burkina Faso	>95	El Salvador	33	Poland	<5
Burundi	>95	Grenada	48	Republic of Moldova	63
Cameroon	83	Guatemala	62	Romania	23
Cape Verde	36	Guyana	59	Serbia and Montenegro	ND
Central African Republic	>95	Haiti	>95	Slovakia	<5
Chad	>95	Honduras	57	Tajikistan	75
Comoros	76	Jamaica	45	Macedonia	30
Congo	84	Mexico	12	Turkey	11
Côte d'Ivoire	74	Nicaragua	58	Turkmenistan	<5
Democratic Republic of the Congo	>95	Panama	33	Ukraine	6
Equatorial Guinea	ND	Paraguay	58	Uzbekistan	72
Eritrea	80	Peru	33	Russian Federation	7
Ethiopia	>95	Saint Kitts and Nevis	<5	**Southeast Asia**	74
Gabon	28	Saint Lucia	63	Indonesia	72
Gambia	>95	St Vincent and the Grenadines	31	Sri Lanka	67
Ghana	88	Suriname	ND	Thailand	72
Guinea	>95	Trinidad and Tobago	8	Bangladesh	88
Guinea-Bissau	95	Uruguay	<5	Bhutan	ND
Kenya	81	Venezuela	5	India	74
Lesotho	83	**Eastern Mediterranean**	36	Korea, Democratic People's Republic of	ND
Liberia	ND	Afghanistan	>95	Maldives	ND
Madagascar	>95	Bahrain	<5	Myanmar	95
Malawi	>95	Cyprus	<5	Nepal	80
Mali	>95	Djibouti	6	Timor–Leste	ND
Mauritania	65	Egypt	<5	Western Pacific	74

Table A1.1 (cont.)

Mauritius	<5	Iran, Islamic Republic of	<5	Cambodia	>95
Mozambique	80	Iraq	<5	China	80
Namibia	63	Jordan	<5	Cook Islands	ND
Niger	>95	Kuwait	<5	Fiji	40
Nigeria	67	Lebanon	<5	Kiribati	ND
Rwanda	>95	Libyan Arab Jamahiriya	<5	Korea, Republic of	<5
São Tome and Principé	ND	Morocco	5	Lao People's Democratic Republic	>95
Senegal	41	Oman	<5	Malaysia	<5
Seychelles	<5	Pakistan	72	Marshall Islands	ND
Sierra Leone	92	Qatar	<5	Micronesia, Federated States of	ND
South Africa	18	Saudi Arabia	<5	Mongolia	51
Swaziland	68	Somalia	ND	Nauru	ND
Togo	76	Sudan	>95	Niue	ND
United Republic of Tanzania	>95	Syrian Arab Republic	32	Palau	ND
Uganda	>95	Tunisia	5	Papua new Guinea	90
Zambia	85	United Arab Emirates	<5	Philippines	47
Zimbabwe	73	Yemen	42	Samoa	70
Latin America and the Caribbean	16	**Central and Eastern Europe**	16	Singapore	<5
Antigua and Barbuda	46	Albania	50	Solomon Islands	95
Argentina	<5	Armenia	26	Tonga	56
Bahamas	<5	Azerbaijan	49	Tuvalu	ND
Barbados	<5	Belarus	19	Vanuatu	79
Belize	43	Bosnia and Herzegovina	51	Viet Nam	70
Bolivia	25	Bulgaria	17		
Brazil	12	Estonia	15		
Chile	<5	Georgia	42	World	52

ND, no data. For a more detailed explanation of WHO regions and epidemiologic sub-regions based on mortality strata, see WHO (2008).
Source: Rehfuess *et al.* (2006). Reproduced with permission from Environmental Health Perspectives.

Armed Conflicts: The Economic Welfare Costs of Conflict

S. BROCK BLOMBERG AND GREGORY D. HESS

Introduction

Conflicts, of various sizes and purported purposes, cast a long and dark shadow on the lives of many and on the histories of nations and peoples. Theories of conflict abound – for wars between nations, internal civil conflicts, and terrorist operations – primarily based on national or group leaders convincing followers to take up a fight for some purpose, noble (to advance an idea, a religion, a culture, a form of government) or otherwise (to appropriate). While leaders, on occasion, do profit from conflict, they do so less often than they might ever imagine. Indeed, leaders, depending on institutional constraints, can separate the spoils of war (land, resources) from the dim costs of war.

The men and women who conduct the battles, however, can seldom avoid the costs of war, and so are fully saddled with the loss of life, limb, loved ones, livelihood, and way of life. Nor are the soldiers' interests fully reflected in the interests of those who make the decision to initiate, continue or to change the course of battle. In his famous letter to his World War I commanding officer, Lt. Siegfried Sassoon of the Royal Welch Fusiliers, wrote:

I believe that the war upon which I entered as a war of defence and liberation has now become a war of agression [sic] and conquest. ... I have seen and endured the sufferings of the troops and I can no longer be a party to prolonging these sufferings for ends which I believe to be evil and unjust. I am not protesting against the conduct of the war, but against the political errors and insincerities for which the fighting men are being sacrificed. On behalf of those who are suffering now, I make this protest against the deception which is being practised upon them; also I believe it may help to destroy the callous complacency with which the majority of those at home regard the continuance of agonies

which they do not share and which they have not enough imagination to realise. July, 1917

Despite the inherent wastefulness of conflict, we continue to observe it in all its infinite manifestations. And there should be no doubt that we will certainly continue to observe it throughout this century. As he remarked in his speech in accepting the 2009 Nobel Prize for Peace, US President Barack Obama stated "We must begin by acknowledging the hard truth: we will not eradicate violent conflicts in our lifetimes," and that "There will be times when nations – acting individually or in concert – will find the use of force not only necessary but morally justified."

Violent conflict is thus wasteful and inevitable – a cheerless combination. But this odd coupling, perhaps surprisingly, may help us to understand how to create a less violent world. Indeed, the key to reversing the inevitability of violent conflict may lie in our better understanding and coming to grips with its wastefulness. In other words, by better understanding the costs of war we may be able to chip away at the existence of conflicts, and build institutions to better insure against their return.

In our chapter, we will provide an empirical analysis of data to better understand the effect of conflict, as measured by military spending, on economic activity and the consumption alternatives that a society faces. In other words, how would the present-day mix of Butter and Guns consumed by a society change if we were to return to a more warlike time in history. We will then use standard economic theory to answer the question "How much would you pay to consume the current level of Guns and Butter rather than consume the level required to sustain a more violent environment that we experienced in the

This chapter was prepared for the Copenhagen Consensus Center. We would like to thank Ashvin Ghandi for his research assistance.

past?" Our answer is that an average person would permanently pay no less than 8% of their current consumption to avoid returning to such a systemic conflict world such as we saw in World War II. That violent, systemic conflict is such a large tax leads us to believe that domestic and international institutions can and should be better designed to realize the benefits to peace.

The literature on the economics of war rests on the shoulders of the founders of modern economics: Keynes (1919), Pigou (1940), Meade (1940), and Robbins (1942), examined the nature and effects of World Wars I and II in times when tremendous, costly international conflict was the unfortunate reality.[1] Since then, as computing power and econometric techniques have progressed, economists have continued to beg the question "How costly is war?" Barro (2009) determined that "society would willingly reduce GDP by around 20 percent each year to eliminate rare disasters" (p. 244). Blomberg and Hess (2012) look specifically at the welfare costs to consumption of war between 1950 and 2004 and estimate that those countries who have

been engaged in conflict would have been willing to forfeit 9% of their current level of consumption, on average, to avoid war. This is likely a conservative estimate for those countries, since it accounts only for costs to consumption and ignores many of the more difficult to quantify costs to war. Using a similar type of analysis, Bozzoli *et al.* (2011) find large and long-lasting costs of conflict.

If war has long been studied and found to be highly costly, why then does conflict persist? Kaysen's (1990) response is that "cultures change much more slowly than technologies and institutions" (p. 62), and thus even if wars are exceedingly harmful, they are not yet "subrationally unthinkable." Others examine the structural elements, such as regime type, that affect the probability of war. Mesquita and Siverson (1995) examined international wars between 1816 and 1975 and found that war is often a political liability to democratically elected leaders, and thus authoritarian leaders will be inclined to longer, more risky wars than are democratic ones. Garfinkel (1994) found that political competition and electoral uncertainty in a democratic nation can foster cooperation between that nation and others, thus reducing military spending and the number and severity of conflicts.

On the other hand, Gelpi (1997) finds that the data for international crises between 1948 and 1982 indicate that it is democratic, not authoritarian, regimes that use force to divert attention away from domestic problems, since authoritarians have greater capability to deal with or repress domestic unrest. Smith (1996) makes the argument that under a democratic system, when politicians believe elections can be positively affected by adventurous foreign exploits, military action becomes more probable. Further, Hess and Orphanides (1995, 2001a, 2001b) show, theoretically and through the use of data for the United States during the Cold War, that even in a democratic state with rational voters and informational symmetry, a leader might initiate a war in times of economic or other hardship to increase his probability of re-election.[2] Hess and Orphanides' analysis is affirmed by DeRouen (1995), which used empirical evidence from 1949 to 1984 in the United States to determine that public approval provides an indirect link between the economy and the use of force.[3]

---

[1] Research on the effects of the world wars continued well past the signing of treaties. For example, Braun and McGrattan (1993) documented the effects World War II had on Britain and the United States and found that war did, in fact, crowd out private investment and consumption.

[2] Not all analyses are in line with that of Hess and Orphanides, however. The model presented in Richards *et al.* (1993) implies, ironically, that competent leaders are generally more inclined than incompetent ones to use diversionary force. Levy (1989) called into question the proposition that politicians definitively use conflict as a means of scapegoating, arguing that such a relationship might be coincidental as opposed to causal. Lian and Oneal (1993) examined the effect of military action on presidential approval ratings, finding that even for important, well-publicized cases, military action never yielded more than a 3% change in popularity.

[3] If poor economic conditions cause leaders to be more likely to start wars, and wars are themselves harmful to the economy, it begs the question: does a "poverty–conflict trap" exist? Using a Markov probability model on data from 152 countries between 1950 and 1992, Blomberg and Hess (2002) found that recessions increase the probability of external and internal conflict (the latter is even more significantly increased when external conflict also exists), which both increase the probability of a recession – evidence indicating that such a trap exists. Further, Blomberg *et al.* (2006) determined that a poverty–conflict nexus is most likely to occur in economies with selfish leaders and small returns to capital.

Some papers even found that a democratic constituency's attempts to punish executives for military adventurism might actually exacerbate the problem. Downs and Rocke (1994) found that this would lead to unwarranted punishing of some executives genuinely acting in the interest of their constituency and to some amount of "gambling for resurrection" – where executives already in a costly conflict choose to unnecessarily perpetuate said conflict, gambling on the chance that the situation might improve and allow them to avoid punishment. Richards *et al.* (1993) similarly found that incompetent leaders will be inclined to use diversionary force if they are sufficiently risk-accepting.

In short, the literature argues that the current generation's conflicts have arisen out of ethnic or cultural tensions, or due to increasing changes brought by democratization. These challenges pale in comparison to those brought by previous generations' world wars and the Cold War. In other words, though conflict remains a serious problem, the cost of war has fallen due to the "peace dividend" experienced since the early 1990s.

However, though wars today are nowhere near the size of the world wars, there is still significant military spending cutting into this peace dividend. Davoodi *et al.* (2001) confirmed the existence of such dividends as world conflict decreased;[4] further, they found that decreases (increases) in military spending are a public good (bad) as it typically results in neighboring countries following suit in decreasing (increasing) military spending. Hartley and Russett (1992) also found that military spending had externalities in the Cold War – public opinion in the United States affected military spending less than did changes in Soviet's military spending. Alesina and Spolaore (2006) provide another explanation for why the peace dividend is limited: decreases in conflict lead to the break-up of larger countries, and such a break-up is liable to lead to an increase in regional conflict.

The purpose of our chapter is to estimate the "opportunity cost" of war on economic welfare. We will do this by examining the returns from the peace dividend during very different periods of world-wide conflict during the period since 1900. We will then use these returns to compare them to estimates on the welfare cost of conflict. Rather than use the method

we deployed in Blomberg and Hess (2012) to calculate the costs of war, which employed assumptions about the effect of conflict on the long-run level of economic well-being, we use an alternative approach that looks at the composition of spending between Guns (military spending) and Butter (private consumption). We find that society has benefitted enormously by the decline in conflict and military spending since the end of World War II and the Korean War. This suggests that while there has been a significant decrease in the welfare cost of war, we must remain ever vigilant and guarded against the potential for the return of larger-scale conflict. A prudent society should thus aim for better institutional peace and the peaceful resolution of areas of disagreement.

The World Economy from 1900 to the Present

At the turn of the twentieth century, the global economy was a significantly different place than it is today. First, the world has become richer, although, admittedly, the pace of development has been very uneven. Second, there are a lot more countries. Let's investigate this second point first. According to the US State Department, the world comprised 57 countries in 1900 and has grown to 192 countries by 2000.[5] The population of the global economy has also experienced a dynamic evolution. In 1900, there were 467 million Chinese, 325 million Europeans, 178 million in the Americas and 13.5 in Africa. Now there are more people living in the United States and Africa than people residing in Europe.

What has this change meant for the economic outcomes for these groups? Figure 2.1 plots the growth in world GDP during the twentieth century, relative to previous centuries, as estimated by Delong (1988).[6]

---

[4] Davoodi *et al.* (2001) attribute 66%, 26%, and 11% of decline in military spending to easing of international tensions, easing of regional tensions, and participation in IMF-supported adjustment programs.

[5] See   www.ppionline.org/ndol/print.cfm?contentid=252023.

[6] As Delong (1988) states, "Angus Maddison (1995) has constructed estimates of real GDP per capita for the world from 1820 to 2008. His estimates are best thought of as Laspeyres purchasing power parity estimates in 1990 international dollars. That is, they: Compare income levels across

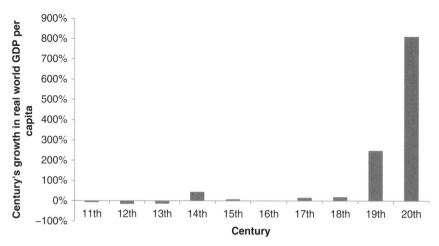

Figure 2.1 *Growth in real world GDP per capita, 1000–present. Note: All figures in this chapter are from Maddison (www.ggdc.net/maddison/oriindex.htm) and are in Geary–Khamis 1990 dollars*

The figure demonstrates that the global economy began to take shape during the nineteenth century after a millennium of stagnation. Economic growth increased by 200% during the nineteenth century, such that the average GDP per person in 1900 (in 1990 dollars) was $1,262. The distribution of wealth was heavily influenced by the British empire: indeed, the top 10th percentile of countries with per capita GDP above $4,000 (1990 $US) were the United Kingdom, the United States, and Australia.

Figure 2.1 demonstrates the first point: namely, the significant economic gains of the twentieth century that took place as growth rose again by an additional 843%. However, the rate of economic transformation was decidedly uneven. As nations splintered, as witnessed by the country coverage of our data set increasing from 39 to 164 countries, the

dispersion of GDP per capita increased. By the end of the twentieth century, approximately one-quarter of the countries in the sample had not reached the average world GDP per person in 1900. Moreover, approximately one-half of the countries had not reached the income level that the four richest countries obtained in 1900.

The influence of the British empire was less obvious by the year 2000, as countries from many different regions joined the top 10th percentile. While the rich were primarily concentrated in Europe, countries from Asia (Japan and Singapore) joined the club. By contrast, many countries in Latin America and Africa have lost ground. As the data are sparser before World War II, we provide a regional breakdown of the growth over time in Table 2.1.

On an individual country level, world growth and world growth on a per capita basis appear to be falling in each successive decade. This may be consistent with the predictions of the Solow growth model (Solow 1956). As countries approach their long-run equilibrium steady state, growth due to capital deepening vanishes, and all growth is brought about through technological innovation. This is also consistent with the fact that less developed countries tend to grow faster than more developed countries and that Asia has grown faster than both Europe and North America.

There are a few areas, however, that cannot be so easily understood using a simple Solow growth

countries not using current exchange rates, but instead trying to change one currency into another at rates that keep purchasing power constant ('purchasing power parity'); Value goods in relative terms using the prices found in a country in the middle of the world distribution of income ('international'); Calculate a value for 1990 GDP per capita in the United States equal to U.S. current-dollar GDP per capita in 1990 ('1990 dollars'); Do not take explicit account of the benefits of the introduction of new goods and new types of goods, but instead calculate GDP per capita in the past by valuing the commodities produced in the past at recent prices – and not making any correction for the restricted range of choice enforced by limited production possibilities ('Laspeyres')."

Table 2.1 GDP growth and growth per capita 1950–2010: selected groupings

Century	World	More developed	Less developed	Africa	Asia	Europe	Latin America	North America
GDP growth								
1950s	4.34%	4.23%	4.61%	3.84%	5.07%	4.34%	4.94%	3.79%
1960s	5.04%	5.20%	4.64%	4.62%	5.86%	4.97%	5.25%	4.48%
1970s	4.14%	3.55%	5.60%	4.39%	5.52%	3.36%	5.73%	3.35%
1980s	3.08%	2.59%	4.10%	2.54%	4.85%	2.00%	1.85%	3.05%
1990s	2.80%	1.64%	4.75%	2.46%	4.63%	0.48%	2.89%	3.06%
2000s	4.27%	2.56%	6.37%	4.85%	6.17%	3.06%	3.56%	2.31%
Growth per capita								
1950s	2.60%	2.50%	2.88%	2.11%	3.33%	2.61%	3.21%	2.06%
1960s	3.31%	3.47%	2.91%	2.88%	4.12%	3.23%	3.52%	2.75%
1970s	2.40%	1.81%	3.86%	2.65%	3.78%	1.63%	3.99%	1.62%
1980s	1.35%	0.86%	2.36%	0.81%	3.12%	0.26%	0.12%	1.32%
1990s	1.06%	−0.09%	3.01%	0.73%	2.90%	−1.25%	1.16%	1.33%
2000s	2.54%	0.83%	4.64%	3.12%	4.43%	1.33%	1.82%	0.58%

All figures are from Maddison (www.ggdc.net/maddison/oriindex.htm) and are in Geary–Khamis 1990 dollars.

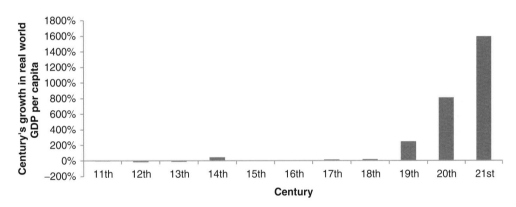

Figure 2.2 *Growth in real world GDP per capita, estimate*

framework. Why have Africa and Latin America had periods of growth lower than Asia and not significantly different (in fact lower than) North America? One answer to this question may be that these regions (specifically Africa) have experienced significantly more conflict than seen in the developed world. Our chapter seeks to address this point during the empirical analysis.

It is also interesting to note that for the majority of the decade of the 2000s, there has been a burst of global growth. This is true for every region to include Africa and Latin America. This is one reason that many investors are now paying more attention to the economic BRICs (Brazil, Russia, India, China) and other emerging market economies. Figure 2.2 plots the expected growth during the

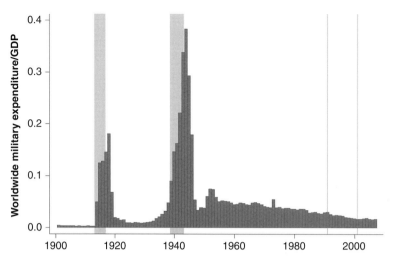

Figure 2.3 *Worldwide military expenditure as percent of GDP, 1900–2007*

twenty-first century if the first eight years of this century's growth were to be duplicated throughout the remainder of time. As you can see, growth in the twenty-first century should continue to dwarf that obtained in previous centuries.

Conflicts in the Twentieth Century

Over the past century, there have been two world wars, and innumerable civil and foreign conflicts. The scope of countries involved in mutual conflict has never been higher. Remarkably, however, there has also been a trend toward more conflict resolution during the same period in question. Milton Leitenberg (2006) did an intensive study of conflict during the 1900s and found that wars accounted for 136.5 to 148.6 million deaths. Leitenberg (2006) also showed that the majority of these losses occurred in the first part of the twentieth century, as World War I and World War II accounted for between 78 and 90 million deaths. Indeed, Leitenberg (2006) estimates that since the end of World War II, approximately 27% of the fatalities from conflict for the century have occurred with 41 million lives lost. In short, deaths in conflict have fallen since the end of the second, and hopefully last, world war.

One way to see this is to consider the peace dividend which occurs at the end of major conflicts – we denote in red World Wars I and II, Persian Gulf I

and September 11, 2001. We examine this by looking at the cost of maintaining a military at the expense of private consumption. Figure 2.3 shows spending on the military as a percentage of GDP since 1900.

Worldwide military spending has two obvious peaks – in World War I and World War II – as spending due to the war effort spiked to nearly 40% of GDP. Subsequently, there has been a dramatic shift and trend downward. However, it has not fallen to zero. Figure 2.4 highlights the time period since 1980. Notice that there has been an uptick in spending during the Cold War, and an associated decline since 1991. There is reason to be concerned that this decline will not continue, as there has been an increase in spending in response to the 9/11 terrorist attacks.

While there are many countries that devote a significant portion of their budget to defense, a handful of countries dominate world wide military expenditure. In fact, two countries, the United States and the United Kingdom, make up greater than 50% of spending. Figure 2.5 plots military expenditure as a percentage of GDP of the highest spending country – the United States.

Figure 2.5 shows similar trends as seen in Figure 2.4. The United States has enjoyed a peace dividend since the end of the Cold War, but recently has seen an increase in spending since 9/11, primarily associated with the subsequent "War on Terror."

How has the most recent US foreign policy affected the rest of the world? To investigate this,

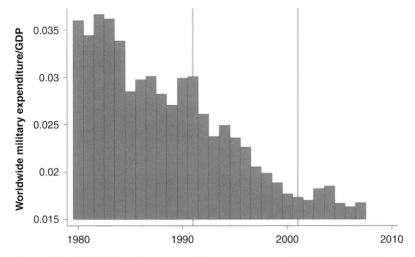

Figure 2.4 *Worldwide military expenditure as percent of GDP, 1980–2007*

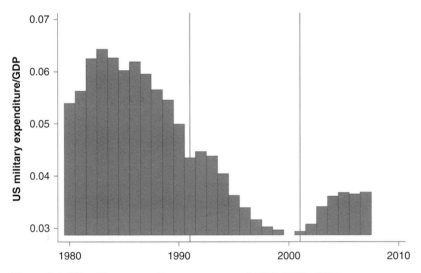

Figure 2.5 *US military expenditure as percent of GDP, 1980–2007*

we parse the data by a number of groupings. The short answer to the question is that most countries continue to enjoy a peace dividend, though defense spending remains a significant portion of their economic activities. Figure 2.6 plots the dynamics of military spending by the various income groups defined by the World Bank. In each and every grouping, countries have enjoyed a peace dividend after the end of the Cold War. However, it appears that the highest income group has been most affected by the events following 9/11.

Figure 2.7 plots the data over the same time period to investigate the extent to which these dynamics are explained by democratization. As was noted in the Introduction, many authors conjecture that these factors explain much of the conflict seen since World War II. Figure 2.7 shows that there are significant differences between these two groups. Non-democracies have seen more variation in their spending patterns. Spending rose drastically during various civil wars but has quieted in the most recent period. At this same time, democracies have seen a

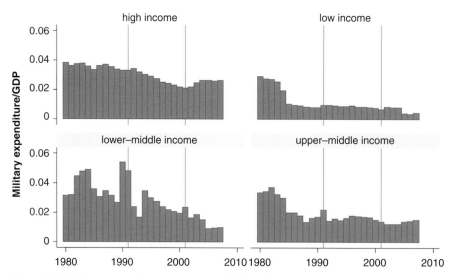

Figure 2.6 *Military expenditure as percent of GDP, by income group*

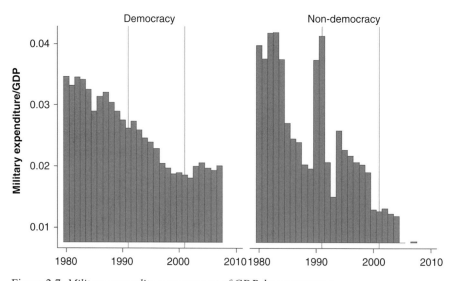

Figure 2.7 *Military expenditure as percent of GDP, by governance*

smoother transition but have had a more persistent pattern of spending.

Figure 2.8 parses the data by region. We employ the standard World Bank definitions. It is easy to see the significant spending levels in the Middle East and North Africa, North America, and Western Europe. By contrast, in other regions, there has been less spending devoted to the military. It is also easy to see the peace dividend in the recent era, although it

appears that North America and West Europe are the areas that have continued to see higher levels of military spending since 9/11.

These figures appear to show a consistent story. There has been a peace dividend enjoyed by most individuals since World War II and this dividend has increased since the end of the Cold War. The notable exceptions are countries affected by the ensuing events of 9/11. These events include targeted terrorist

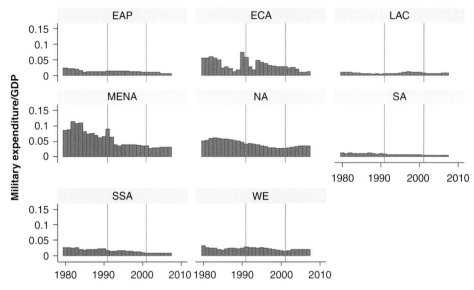

Figure 2.8 *Military expenditure as percent of GDP, by region. EAP, East Asia and the Pacific; MENA, Middle East and North Africa; LAC, Latin America and the Caribbean; NA, North America; ECE, East and Central Europe; SA, South Asia; SSA, sub-Saharan Africa; WE, is Western Europe*

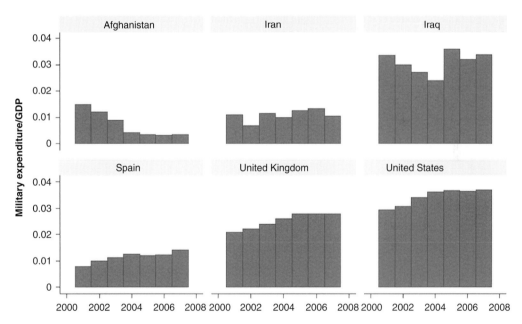

Figure 2.9 *Military expenditure as percent of GDP since 9/11: selected countries*

attacks in rich democracies, in Western Europe and North America, and parts of the Middle East.

Figure 2.9 plots spending in many of these countries since 2001. The graphs include data for

countries that have experienced high-profile attacks such as the United States, the United Kingdom, and Spain. Also included are countries that have been strategically impacted by these events – Iran, Iraq, and Afghanistan. In each of these cases there has been an increase in military spending. However, none of these patterns have been very dramatic, certainly as compared to spending patterns during the world wars. In short, the preliminary data analysis suggests that there has been a significant decrease in military spending and an increase in peace throughout the twentieth century.

Analytical Methodology

Violent conflict involves significant human costs. A component of these human costs is economic in that conflict affects resource allocations and measurable economic living standards. In general, economists are reasonably good at measuring the economic costs of activities while, admittedly, they are not very good at measuring their non-economic costs. Indeed, while we cannot directly calculate them, we acknowledge them, and note that this omission only strengthens our argument. We will demonstrate with our empirical analysis that the economic cost of violent conflict is large; hence, given all the costs we do not measure, the true total cost of war must be very large.

As stated earlier, the work by Barro (2009), Blomberg and Hess (2012) and Bozzoli *et al.* (2011)

investigate the economic growth and uncertainty affects from conflict. We refer the reader to each for a more formal explanation. Measuring such effects, however, while informative require the researcher to understand and parameterize the short-run and long-run effects of conflict on growth. Sometimes these can be difficult to disentangle. Despite their various parametric statistical approaches, there is broad agreement that war has negative economic growth effects, with various levels of short-run and long-run consequences.

To build on this work, however, one can consider other economic costs associated with conflict and the effects stemming from the required associated expenditures on military goods. The easiest presentation for these calculations is the simple Guns versus Butter trade-off popularized in the textbook *Economics* authored by Paul Samuelson (1973). Conflict entails military expenditures, and this reallocates a country away from private consumption opportunities.

Figure 2.10 illustrates our methodology. On the vertical axis, we measure the amount of Guns consumed and produced by a country and on the horizontal axis we measure the amount of Butter, i.e. private consumption, consumed and produced by society. The bowed-out production possibility frontier, connected from points $\bar{G}$ and $\bar{B}$, denotes a

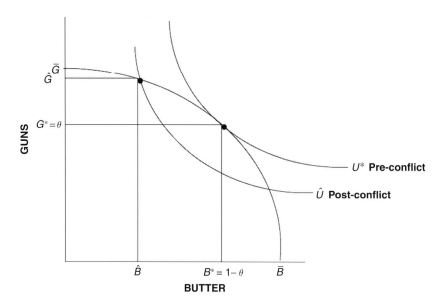

Figure 2.10 *Guns vs. Butter: How much would you pay?*

country's ability to produce combinations of Guns and Butter. The bowed-inward country indifference curves demonstrate combinations of Guns and Butter that provide the average citizen in a country a given level of utility. Everything else equal, a country is better off if they can consume more of each good; however, they are willing to trade off Guns for Butter along a given indifference curve. As a final point, note that as indifference curves move in the north-east direction, they denote higher levels of utility since they allow citizens to consume more of each good.

With respect to our analysis, the indifference curve that is just tangent to the production possibility frontier is optimal for society. It indicates combinations of Guns and Butter that a country can produce and that a country prefers to consume. Indeed, a country cannot obtain a higher level of utility with any other combination of Guns and Butter given what it can produce. For example, a country that consumes the bundle (G^*, B^*) is at an optimum point. By contrast, were the country to consume a bundle $(\hat{G}, \hat{B})$, the country would achieve a lower level of utility and hence would be at a sub-optimal point.

Interestingly, we can calculate how much worse off a country is made if it consumes this inferior bundle of goods. To keep matters simple, let's assume that a country gains utility from consuming Guns and Butter as follows:

$$U(C) = G^\theta B^{1-\theta} \qquad (2.1)$$

where θ is a parameter of the utility function. Utility functions such as these are called Cobb–Douglas, and they have the added benefit that the parameter θ can be shown to be identified through the optimal fraction of expenditures on Guns vis-à-vis the total consumption on Guns and Butter, $X = G + B$: namely, $\theta = G/X$ and $1 - \theta = B/X$, evaluated at the optimal bundle.

In order to demonstrate how the world has benefitted from the cessation of periods of heightened conflict, we ask ourselves the following question – how much would a representative citizen pay to consume his or her preferred consumption bundle of more Butter and less Guns, denoted in Figure 2.10 with a *, as compared to the inferior combination of more Guns and less Butter, denoted with a hat, ^? Using expression (2.1), the answer to this question can be expressed in the following equation where τ is

the fraction of current private consumption, Butter, one would be willing to give up in order not to return to a more militarized world. The value of τ can be determined from the following equation

$$G * \theta[(1 + \tau)B*]1 - \theta = \hat{G}\theta\hat{B}1 - \theta \qquad (2.2)$$

Solving for τ we get that :

$$\tau = \left[\hat{B}/B^*\right]\left[\hat{G}/G^*\right]^{\theta/(1-\theta)} - 1 \qquad (2.3)$$

Following our earlier discussion, and as shown in the diagram, we can easily measure θ using the optimal expenditure share expressions $\theta = G^*/(B + G^*)$, and $1 - \theta = B^*/(B + G^*)$. Moreover, by assuming that overall economic activity is not affected by war, even if the composition of consumption is affected, we are implicitly assuming that $= X^*$ so that

$$\tau = [1 - \hat{g}]/[1 - g*][\hat{g}/g*]^{g*/(1-g*)} - 1 \qquad (2.4)$$

where $g = G/X$ and $\theta = g^*$.

Our calculation is simple and straightforward. It assumes that there are no long-run growth costs or long-run economic volatility costs of war. Moreover, it assumes that the reallocation costs of war are fully embodied in consumption and we do not include the costs of war from production reallocation. Moreover, if conflicts utilize resources that are not fully reported in GDP statistics on military spending, we will likely be underestimating the costs of conflict. Finally, this calculation also omits costs associated with conflict and the loss of life, which we will discuss below. Taken together, our omission of these costs goes to make our conclusion stronger: namely, even when omitting many costs of conflict, the cost remains very high.

Despite these caveats, which tend to bias down our simple welfare measure of conflict, in Table 2.2 we present the measures of G/X, g, for a number of key time periods in the data: namely, during the peak of spending in 1944, the height of the Korean War in 1952, the end of the Cold War in 1989, the period just before 9/11 in 2000, and the last period of the data sample, 2007. The table has two key results. First, the military spending ratios have fallen from the peak of World War II for the total and most sub-groups. Indeed, the average ratio (un-weighted) of g, G/X, in 1944 was 11.4%, and this ratio has fallen to 2.5%

Table 2.2 *G/X* (g) ratio in various years, grouped by region, income, and governance

Grouping	G/X(g): ratio of Guns to the sum of Guns and Butter				
	1944	1952	1989	2000	2007
EAP	0.408	0.032	0.042	0.023	0.026
ECE	0.024	0.033	0.041	0.026	0.015
LAC	0.016	0.022	0.015	0.011	0.01
MENA		0.046	0.118	0.101	0.07
NA	0.336	0.148	0.054	0.028	0.038
SA		0.024	0.012	0.015	0.007
SSA		0.011	0.036	0.027	0.02
WE	0.154	0.044	0.039	0.025	0.033
High income	0.227	0.057	0.055	0.057	0.048
Low income	0.009	0.035	0.032	0.023	0.015
Lower–middle income	0.01	0.013	0.053	0.026	0.014
Upper–middle income	0.023	0.033	0.055	0.042	0.04
Democracy	0.188	0.046	0.031	0.021	0.019
Non-democracy	0.081	0.029	0.056	0.046	0.035
Average (unweighted)	0.114	0.037	0.046	0.033	0.025
Average (weighted)	0.332	0.094	0.041	0.029	0.027

EAP, East Asia and the Pacific; MENA, Middle East and North Africa; LAC, Latin America and the Caribbean; NA, North America; ECE, East and Central Europe; SA, South Asia; SSA, sub-Saharan Africa; and WE, is Western Europe.

in 2007. Note that if we weight these spending ratios by the country's size of GDP, then the weighted ratio of g was 33.2% in 1944. Second, East Asia and the Pacific and North America have military spending ratios that, on average, have declined the most since World War II. Moreover, the ratio for North America, which is dominated in the data by the United States, has declined the most since the Korean War.

Table 2.3 presents some welfare calculations based on the data presented in Table 2.2. The first two columns report that fraction of current consumption that would be willingly forgone in 2007 in

order not to return to a mix of spending on military and private consumption that was consumed at the peak of World War II (1944) and the Korean War (1952). Columns (3) and (4) report the value in 2007 US$ (billions) of the willingness to pay as measured by $\tau \times B$. Columns (5) and (6) express this as a present discounted value scaled by each country's 2007 level of GDP.[7]

The results in Table 2.3 are striking. Beginning with the reported values of τ in columns (1) and (2), we see that the average East Asian economy would give up 38% of their current level of consumption so as not to return to the level of military spending associated with the peak of World War II.[8] Other regions, in particular North America and Western Europe, would also be willing to pay dearly not to return to that prior level of consumption allocation – 25% and 12%, respectively. The tax would also be higher for countries that are currently higher income and democracies. On average, as indicated in the row

[7] We calculate the present discounted value using a discount factor of 0.95 which is equivalent to a discount rate of approximately 5% per year.
[8] While this number may seem high, recall that the war in the Pacific during World War II had significant impacts on countries such as Japan and the Philippines.

Table 2.3 Tax, dividends, and present value of peace in various years grouped by region, income, and governance

			Peace dividends			
			$\tau \times B$ (billions 2007 US$)		PV($\tau \times B$) / GDP (percent of GDP)	
	Tax (τ)					
Grouping	1944	1952	1944 Div	1952 Div	1944 PV	1952 PV
EAP	−0.381	−0.011	546.20	28.24	3.91	0.11
ECE	−0.003	−0.002	0.89	1.21	0.04	0.03
LAC	−0.004	−0.006	1.33	2.09	0.05	0.07
MENA	.	−0.011		2.19		0.18
NA	−0.252	−0.071	1,441.10	434.56	3.11	0.85
SA	.	−0.014		5.24		0.20
SSA	−0.002	−		0.11		0.01
WE	−0.127	−0.008	149.13	5.55	1.21	0.07
High income	−0.177	−0.016	430.64	58.58	1.98	0.20
Low income	−0.002	−0.019	0.03	42.04	0.03	0.20
Lower–middle income	−0.004	−0.003	0.73	0.66	0.05	0.05
Upper–middle income	−0.005	−0.008	1.87	3.79	0.05	0.10
Democracy	−0.124	−0.015	199.45	29.33	0.94	0.13
Non-democracy	−0.052	−0.008	0.48	34.31	0.02	0.17
Total (unweighted)	−0.082	−0.012	3,332.07	446.99	91.94	0.12
Total (weighted)	−0.262	−0.036	10,735.84	1,465.40	369.95	0.51

labeled Total unweighted, countries would be willing to forgo 8% of their current level of consumption to live in a more peaceful world.[9] Note that if we weight each country's values of τ by GDP, we get a much higher average cost of war, namely, 26.2%. This, of course, reflects the fact that many larger and higher-income countries had high levels of military spending during World War II.

As shown in column (2), however, the peace dividend calculated since the peak of the Korean War is smaller, averaging just over 1% of current consumption for the average country. Of course, the peace dividend is much higher for North America, as they played a large role in the Korean conflict.

While considering the cost of conflict as a tax (or, its mirror image, which is the dividend from peace), it is also useful to come up with a dollar measure for the costs of conflict. In the remaining columns of

Table 2.3 we present dollar measures of this tax. In column (3), we present measures for the peace dividend by multiplying the tax, τ, by the 2007 US $ measure of a country's consumption, B. In current dollar terms, the permanent peace dividend from the end of World War II for East Asia and the Pacific is over US$500 billion per year, and over US$1.4 trillion per year for North America. Moving to column (5), the present discounted value of these permanent costs, discounted at 5% per year and scaled by the current level of GDP, is 3.9 for East Asia and 3.1 for North America. In other words, the full value of the peace dividend is equal to

[9] Note that since the value of θ is low due to the low level of $g = G/X$ in 2007, the value of τ is approximately equal to the decline in military spending. This can be seen in equation (2.4) since as $\theta \to 0$, $\tau \approx g^* - \hat{g}$.

somewhere over three times their current level of GDP. Peace, it turns out, can be quite expensive.

The calculations for the peace dividend, following the end of the Korean War, are correspondingly smaller than those for World War II. In current dollar terms, the permanent peace dividend from the end of the Korean War for East Asia and the Pacific is over US$28 billion per year, and over US$430 billion per year for North America. As shown in column (6), the present discounted value of these permanent costs, discounted at 5% per year and scaled by the current level of GDP, is 0.113 for East Asia and 0.845 for North America. In other words, the full value of peace dividend for North America is equal to just under the current level of GDP.

The Human Cost of War

To this point our methodology has concentrated on calculating the cost of war by finding the welfare cost of lost consumption of private goods due to war. Another cost of war that should not be ignored, separate from the cost of increased military spending, is the costly loss of human lives associated with conflict. While there are a variety of approaches to including such costs, our experiment has been to compare periods of extreme conflict, an approach that is more consistent with our methodology would be similar to what was done in Blanchard (1985). In his chapter, to calculate debt costs, Blanchard included the mortality rate in the subjective rate of time preference in order to show that finite horizons lower long-run welfare and hence affect long-term decision-making. Below, we employ a modification of his approach in order to calculate the present value of the consumption peace dividend with increased survivorship. In essence, Blanchard (1985) demonstrates that a rise in the probability of death, p, lowers the discount factor for valuing future welfare in an additive fashion. Therefore, if we value the future welfare with a discount factor of β, $0 < \beta < 1$, then if conflict raises the probability of death by p, then the

value we place on future welfare receives a lower discount factor, $\beta - p$.

To incorporate the cost of higher deaths associated with war, and following our earlier calculation based on equation (2.2), we now have the following equation:

$$
\begin{aligned}
&\sum_{t=0}^{\infty} \beta^t \left\{ G^{*\theta} \left[(1 + \tau) B^* \right]^{1 - \theta} \right\} \\
&= \sum_{t=0}^{\infty} (\beta - p)^t \left\{ \hat{G}^\theta \hat{B}^{1 - \theta} \right\}
\end{aligned}
\tag{2.5}
$$

Ignoring τ for the moment, the left-hand side of (2.5) is the discounted present value of welfare for the optimal level of consumption at reduced levels of conflict and military spending. The right-hand side, by contrast, is the discounted present value of welfare when the mix between Guns and Butter is not ideal. Much like before, τ is the fraction of current private consumption, Butter, one would be willing to give up in order not to return to a more militarized world that is associated with shorter life spans and which places less value on future utility. As before, we can solve for τ. Note that higher levels of conflict have two distinct costs: first, in each period citizens consume too little Butter and too many Guns. Second, citizens value the future less and hence have lower lifetime welfare.

Solving for τ from (2.5), and following the steps used in (2.4), we obtain that:

$$
\begin{aligned}
\tau = &\left[(1 - \beta) / (1 - \beta + p) \right]^{1/(1 - g*)} \\
&\times \left[1 - \hat{g} \right] / \left[1 - g* \right] \left[\hat{g}/g* \right]^{g*/(1 - g*)} - 1
\end{aligned}
\tag{2.6}
$$

Note the role of p in the first term in square brackets reflects how the additional costs of war from shorter life spans makes that value for τ, which is negative, more negative.[10]

To see how an increase in the probability of death associated with war affects the willingness to pay for peace, let's reconsider the costs of war for the weighted GDP case where we compare the Guns and Butter consumption bundle in World War II with that for 2007. Recall from the bottom row of Table 2.3 that the original value of τ for this case, not including the cost of war from shorter lifetimes, is $\tau = -0.262$.

---

[10] It is straightforward to show that the approximate change in τ brought about by a small change in the probability of death is equal to $\Delta \tau = - (1 + \tau)[(1 - \beta)(1 - \theta)]^{-1} \Delta p$. This is simply the first derivative of (2.5) evaluated at $p = 0$.

To calculate the new value of τ using expression (2.6), we will need to specify p and β. To calibrate the value of p from World War II, we note that work by Leitenberg (2006) suggests that there were 25 million battle deaths from World War II on a base population of approximately 2.5 billion at that time, suggesting an enhanced death rate of $p = 1\%$ throughout the world during the war. As before, we continue to use the standard value of $\beta = 0.95$ which implies a discount rate of about 5% per year. Plugging these values of p and β into expression (2.6), we obtain a new value of τ, $\tau = -0.388$, which is approximately 50% higher than the original value reported in the bottom row of Table 2.3. Indeed, by including the human costs associated with a higher probability of death associated with World War II, all the calculations for the Total (weighted) case based on a comparison to spending in 1944 would rise by about 50%. For example, by including the costs of war for shorter lifetimes, the per-period worldwide peace dividend rises from over US$10 trillion (2007 dollars) to over US$15 trillion. This example is very illustrative – our baseline peace dividend is large. However, incorporating the increased chance of the loss of life from conflict makes it larger by half.

The magnitude of the increased welfare cost due to human losses may appear to be large at 50%. There are several caveats. First, our experiment may provide a very conservative estimate on the human cost as we employ the number of military deaths and exclude civilian deaths in our calculation of the probability of death. If we include civilian deaths then the likelihood of death increases by approximately 2 percentage points. Second, our experiment may provide an estimate that is less conservative because it compares a conflict that was very human personnel-intensive to the current scenario which due to peace and technology is less human personnel-intensive. In fact, due to the changes brought to the battlefield by robotics and drones, it is unlikely that the human/personnel cost of war will be comparable again in history. For these reasons and others, we have chosen to concentrate the thrust of our arguments and our calculations on the welfare cost due to lost consumption which we believe is less sensitive to the challenges inherent in calculating costs.

2007 to 2050: Predicting the Peace Dividend?

In our final section, we use our historical estimates to predict future peace dividends. We allow for three different scenarios: a high-conflict, a medium-conflict and a low-conflict future. We use recent history to best approximate the future possibilities. We find that in each of our scenarios, the welfare benefit of peace is highly significant relative to the conflicts experienced in the world wars of the twentieth century. Moreover, there is little evidence to suggest that these dividends will vary greatly in the future. In other words, we predict that there appears to be little deviation from the current scenario relative to the future.

We construct the three scenarios presuming that either:

- High-conflict scenario – conflict and military spending, due to the events following 9/11, continues to grow at the trend rate from 2000 to 2007
- Medium-conflict scenario – conflict and military spending remains steady at the current ratios
- Low-conflict scenario – conflict and military spending continue to fall to the low point after the decade following the end of the Cold War.

Figure 2.11 plots the result from this experiment as it depicts the G/Y ratio from 1980 to 2050. Notice there is little difference in the gains to peace between the high-conflict, medium-conflict, and low-conflict scenarios – note that the figure is similar for G/X.[11] A simple interpretation is that the gains to peace have largely been reaped as the world has less globally driven nation–state conflict as compared to the World War II era. If we were to extend our calculations, we find that the range of values for the peace dividend is somewhere between 7.9% and 8.1%.

[11] Alternatively, we could depict the G/Y ratio over a longer time period similar to what was shown in Figure 2.3. However, the various scenarios would be visually indistinguishable in such a figure given the increased size of the vertical scale to depict spending associated with world wars. Hence, we choose to depict the more recent time period and extend it into the future.

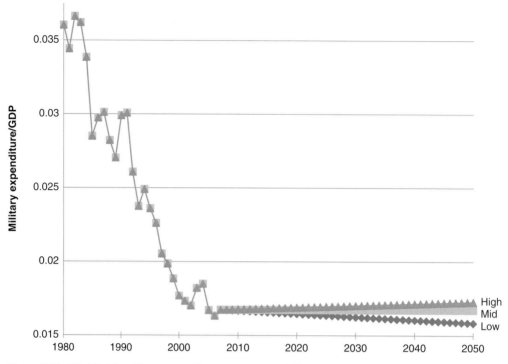

Figure 2.11 *Worldwide military expenditure as percent of GDP, 1980–2050, different conflict scenarios*

Conclusion

The world is now richer, and it has fewer conflicts. Military spending has also been dramatically reduced, particularly since the second half of the twentieth century. The consumption welfare benefits from not returning to a prior age of grand-scale conflict are large, though these costs have been falling. To continue to secure these enormous benefits from peace, society must be willing to allocate sufficient resources to maintain it. The costs of war are ever-present and large. The investment in peace must remain at least as large.

Our approach has been to estimate the cost of war in terms of an opportunity cost to welfare. In doing so, we present many calculations that may serve as a guide to those interested in public policy alternatives. We find that the opportunity cost in terms of lost "Butter" amounts to approximately 91% of GDP in present discounted terms. This adds up to a loss in welfare of US$9,520 per person in 2007 dollars. When we include human costs, we estimate the loss

to be 50% greater, or an additional US$4,760 per person.

Alternatively, it may be useful to compare our approach to previous studies as a final robustness check of our methodology. Table 2.4 presents a comparative summary of analyses on aspects of the costs of conflict, which can be useful for benchmarking our findings to others in the literature. The first column describes the name, year, publication and author of the studies. The second column presents the econometric technique and the third column presents the types of conflicts considered in the study. The fourth column presents the "bottom-line" economic cost estimate from the study with the final column including a "human cost" estimate.

The results from our chapter are given in the fifth panel down from the top of Table 2.4. The results seen in column (4) demonstrate that the opportunity cost estimate from our chapter is similar to our previous estimate of US$10,449 per capita. Attempting to compare this estimate to others in the literature is quite difficult as most of the other estimates are given

Table 2.4 Summary of results in current and previous studies

Study	Estimation strategy	Conflicts considered	Cost of conflict	Human cost
Blomberg and Hess (2002) The temporal links between conflict and economic activity. *Journal of Conflict Resolution* **46**.	Markov-switching model (GDP loss)	Civil war, external war	2% reduction in GDP per conflict or US$204 per capita per conflict	N/A
Barro (2009) Rare disasters, asset prices, and welfare costs. *American Economic Review* **99**.	Calibration (GDP loss)	Internal conflict, external conflict	1.5% reduction in GDP per year or US$153 per capita per conflict	N/A
Rose and Blomberg (2010) Total Economic Consequences of Terrorist Attacks: Insights from 9/11. *Peace Economics, Peace Science, and Public Policy* 16.	Structural VAR model (GDP loss)	9/11	0.48% reduction in GDP per capita or US$48.96 per capita	N/A
Blomberg and Hess (2012) The economic welfare cost of conflict: an empirical assessment. *Oxford Handbook of Peace and Conflict*.	Calibration (consumption loss)	Civil war, external war, terrorism	US$224 per capita per conflict	N/A
Current analysis	Opportunity cost of war (consumption loss)	World War I, World War II	Welfare loss of US$9,520 per capita	Additional $4,760 per capita
Disability-adjusted life year (DALY)	–	–	–	Additional $3,900 per capita

as the cost of conflict for a particular country in a particular year. Still, this value is obtainable from our previous study (US$224 per capita) and is quite similar to that found in Barro (2009) (US$153 per capita) and our 2002 study (US$204 per capita). The cost when considering only 9/11 is not surprisingly significantly smaller at US$49 as shown in Rose and Blomberg (2010). Hence, we believe our estimates are consistent with what has been previously found both by other authors and our own work.

One significant difference in this chapter is the inclusion of the "human cost" of conflict which was not considered in any of the previous analyses. As stated previously, we adopt an approach first employed by Blanchard (1985) and estimate the human cost to increase the economic cost by 50% or US$4,760 per capita. Again, it may be useful to consider how this estimate differs from a more conventional measure. As a baseline, consider the approach of calculating the loss of life using

disability-adjusted life years (DALYs), which we also provide in Table 2.4. To make the comparison as straightforward as possible, we examine a DALY measure for the lives lost during the most costly period (World War II) relative to the present and beyond. During the war, life expectancy was 65 and the average age of military personnel was 26 making the average number of years lost 39 years. We multiply this by average income and the number of lives lost in World War II relative to population. This conventional approach increases the economic cost by 40% or US$3,900 per capita. Again, this is similar to what our opportunity cost approach yields. The sturdiness of our measure, we believe, provides more support for our analysis.

References

Alesina, A. and E. Spolaore (2006) Conflict, defense spending, and the number of Nations. *European Economic Review* **50**: 91–120.

Barro, R. J. (2009) Rare disasters, asset prices, and welfare costs. *American Economic Review* **99**: 243–264.

Blanchard, O. J. (1985) Debts, deficits, and finite horizons. *Journal of Political Economy* **93**: 223–247.

Blomberg, S. B. and G. Hess (2002) The temporal links between conflict and economic activity. *Journal of Conflict Resolution* **46**: 74–90.

(2012) The economic welfare cost: an empirical assessment. In: M. R. Garfinkel and S. Skaperdas (eds.), *Oxford Handbook of Peace and Conflict*. Oxford: Oxford University Press.

Blomberg, S. B., G. Hess, and A. Orphanides (2004) The macroeconomic consequences of terrorism. *Journal of Monetary Economics* **51**: 1007–1032.

Blomberg, S. B., G. Hess, and S. Thacker (2006) Is there evidence of a poverty–conflict trap? *Economics and Politics* **18**: 237–267.

Bozzoli, C., T. Brück, and O. J. de Groot (2012) How many bucks in a bang: on the estimation of the economic costs of conflict. In: M. R. Garfinkel and S. Skaperdas (eds.), *Oxford Handbook of Peace and Conflict*. Oxford: Oxford University Press.

Braun, R. A. and E. McGrattan (1993) The Macroeconomics of war and peace. *National Bureau of Economic Research Macroeconomics Annual* **8**: 197–258.

Bueno de Mesquita, B. and R. M. Siverson (1995) War and the survival of political leaders: a comparative study of regime types and political accountability. *American Political Science Review* **89**: 841–855.

Davoodi, H., B. Clements, J. Schiff, and P. Debaere (2001) Military spending, the peace dividend, and fiscal adjustment. *IMF Staff Papers* **48**: 290–316.

DeLong, J. B. (1988) Productivity growth, convergence, and welfare: comment. *American Economic Review* **78**: 1138–1154.

DeRouen, K. R. (1995) The indirect link: politics, the economy, and the use of force. *Journal of Conflict Resolution* **39**: 671–695.

Downs, G. W. and D. M. Rocke (1994) Conflict, agency, and gambling for resurrection: the principle–agent model goes to war. *American Journal of Political Science* **38**: 362–380.

Garfinkel, M. R. (1994) Domestic politics and international conflict. *American Economic Review* **84**: 1294–1309.

Gelpi, C. (1997) Democratic diversions: governmental structure and the externalization of domestic conflict. *Journal of Conflict Resolution* **41**: 255–282.

Hartley, T. and B. Russett (1992) Public opinion and the common defense: who governs military spending in the United States? *American Political Science Review* **86**: 905–915.

Hess, G. D. and A. Orphanides (1995) War politics: an economic, rational voter framework. *American Economic Review* **85**: 828–846.

(2001a) Economic Conditions, Elections, and the Magnitude of Foreign Conflicts. *The Journal of Public Economics* **80**, (April 2001): pp. 121–40.

(2001b) War and democracy. *Journal of Political Economy* **109**: 776–810.

Kaysen, K. (1990) Is war obsolete? *International Security* **14**: 42–64.

Keynes, J. M. (1919) *The Economic Consequences of the Peace*. London: Macmillan.

Leitenberg, M. (2006) *Deaths in Wars and Conflicts of the 20th Century*. Ithaca, NY: Cornell University Press.

Levy, J. S. (1989) The diversionary theory of war: a critique. In: M. Midlarsky (ed.), *The Handbook of War Studies*. New York: Unwin-Hyman.

Lian, B. and J. Oneal (1993) Presidents, the use of military force, and public opinion. *Journal of Conflict Resolution* **37**: 277–300.

Maddison, A. (1995) *Monitoring the World Economy, 1820–1990*. Paris: OECD.

Meade, J. E. (1940) *The Economic Basis of a Durable Peace*. New York: Oxford University Press.

Pigou, A. C. (1940) *The Political Economy of War*. London: Macmillan.

Richards, D., T. C. Morgan, R. Wilson, V. Schwebach, and G. Young (1993) Good times, bad times and the diversionary use of force: a tale of some not-so-free agents. *Journal of Conflict Resolution* **37**: 504–535.

Robbins, L. (1942) *The Economic Causes of War*. London: Jonathan Cape.

Rose, A. and S. B. Blomberg (2010) Total economic impacts of a terrorist attack: insights from 9/11. *Peace Economics, Peace Science, and Public Policy*, 16, Article 2.

Samuelson, P. (1973) *Economics*. New York: McGraw-Hill.

Smith, A. (1996) Diversionary foreign policy in democratic systems. *International Studies Quarterly* **40**: 133–153.

Solow, R. (1956) A contribution to the theory of economic growth. *Quarterly Journal of Economics* **70**: 65–94.

Climate Change: The Economic Impact of Climate Change in the Twentieth and Twenty-First Centuries

RICHARD S. J. TOL

Introduction

There is a substantial literature about the future impacts of climate change (Nordhaus 1991; Cline 1992b; Fankhauser 1995; Mendelsohn *et al.* 2000; Tol 2002a); see Tol (2009b) for an overview. Less is known, however, about the impacts of climate change in the past. While there is no immediate policy relevance of estimates of past effects – as liability is yet to be established (Tol and Verheyen 2004) – such estimates would serve to validate models of future impacts – and thus help to improve these models and build confidence. In this chapter, I turn this question on its head. I use a model to backcast past impacts, thus generating hypotheses to be tested against observations.

Unfortunately, there are no direct observations of the economic impact of past climate change. Note that the cause of climate change, past or future, is irrelevant for its impacts. There are, however, some studies that estimate particular aspects of the impact of past climate change, typically focussing on bio-physical impacts.

The literature on natural disasters is perhaps most advanced (Changnon and Changnon 1992; Changnon and Changnon Jr. 1998; Changnon 2003; Pielke 2005; Pielke *et al.* 2008; Barredo 2009; Neumayer and Barthel 2011; Ryan 2011). These studies typically conclude that trends in the damage done by natural disasters are largely, if not entirely, the result of increases in the number of people and their wealth. It should be noted, though, that these studies rely on ad hoc normalization rather than multiple regression (Toya and Skidmore 2007).

Estimates of the impact of past climate change on crop yields generally find a significant effect, but one that is small relative to other trends in agriculture; impacts are positive or negative depending on crop and location (Myneni *et al.* 1997; Nicholls 1997; Lobell and Asner 2003; Lobell *et al.* 2005; Tao *et al.* 2006; Lobell and Field 2007; Holmer 2008; Tao *et al.* 2008; Twine and Kucharik 2009; Zhang *et al.* 2010; Lobell *et al.* 2011). Carbon dioxide concentrations vary little over space and only slowly over time, so there is little statistical evidence of its impact on crop yields. Experimental evidence, however, points to a positive impact (Long *et al.* 2006).

The impact of past climate change on malaria has also been the subject of intense debate (Loevinsohn 1994; Hay *et al.* 2002a, 2002b; Small *et al.* 2003; Craig *et al.* 2004; Thomas 2004; Byass 2008; Chaves and Koenraadt 2010; Gething *et al.* 2010). Overall, there is agreement that climate change is not the main driver of the spread of malaria; some people argue it has a small effect while others argue the effect is negligible. The story is the same for diarrhea – another big killer that is sensitive to weather and climate – but there is less evidence (Lloyd *et al.* 2007). There is empirical evidence for negative health impacts of both heat and cold stress (Martens 1998; D'Ippoliti *et al.* 2010; McMichael and Dear 2010). The net impact is different across space (EUROWINTER Group 1997) and over time (Carson *et al.* 2006; Davis *et al.* 2002, 2003).

Empirical research into the effect of climate change on energy demand resembles that of heat and cold stress: there are many case studies (Henley and Peirson 1998; Pardo *et al.* 2002; Moral-Carcedo and Vicens-Otero 2005; Giannakopoulos

I am grateful to the Copenhagen Consensus Center and the EU ClimateCost project for financially supporting this research. Two anonymous referees had excellent comments.

and Psiloglou 2006; Sailor and Munoz 1997), but few multi-country studies (Bessec and Fouquau 2008) and few studies that cover a longer time period (Considine 2000; Hekkenberg *et al.* 2009). The latter studies are, of course, best suited for the detection of structural patterns that would allow extrapolation into the future. These studies find that warming would lead to a decrease of energy demand in winter and an increase of energy demand in summer. The relative magnitude of these two opposite effects depends on socio-economic circumstances and the climatic starting point.

Statistical analyses of climate and water resources are typically done for single river basins. There are a few studies that cover a wider area (Lins and Slack 1999; Lindstroem and Bergstroem 2004; Kundzewicz *et al.* 2005; Svensson *et al.* 2005). These studies typically conclude that every river responds differently to changes in precipitation and temperature.

In sum, the empirical literature on the impacts of climate change finds mixed effects. Unfortunately, none of these studies aggregates the impacts, so that it is difficult to say whether past climate change was positive or negative. Below, I will use a model, FUND, to answer that question.

The chapter proceeds as follows. The next section presents the data and the model and the following section discusses the results. Then comes the final concluding section, paying particular attention to the testable hypotheses that emerge from this chapter.

Data and Model

Data

National data on population and income for 1960–2000 are taken from EarthTrends by the World Resources Institute (http://earthtrends.wri.org/). For 1900–1960, regional data are from Maddison

(1995). I assumed equal national growth rates within regions. I used HadCRUT3 for the global mean temperature (http://earthtrends.wri.org/) and carbon dioxide concentration from CDIAC (http://cdiac.ornl.gov/trends/co2/contents.htm).

Model

I use the Climate Framework for Uncertainty, Negotiation, and Distribution (FUND), v. 3.6 in its national resolution. The continental version of FUND is a fully integrated model, including scenarios of population, economy, energy use, and emissions; a carbon cycle and simple climate model; and a range of impact models. The national version of FUND (Link and Tol 2011) only covers the impacts of climate change – while population etc. are as observed for the twentieth century and exogenous for the twenty-first century.

Version 3.6n of FUND corresponds to v. 1.6 (Tol *et al.* 1999; Tol 2001, 2002c) except for the impact module (Tol 2002a, 2002b; Link and Tol 2004; Narita *et al.* 2009, 2010) and carbon cycle feedbacks (Tol 2009a).[1]

The model runs from 1900 to 2100 in time steps of 5 years. The model is initialized for 1895.

The climate impact module (Tol 2002a, 2002b) includes the following categories: agriculture, forestry, sea level rise, cardiovascular and respiratory disorders related to cold and heat stress, malaria, dengue fever, schistosomiasis, diarrhea, energy consumption, water resources, unmanaged ecosystems, and tropical and extratropical storms. This list of impacts is not exhaustive, but other impacts have yet to be consistently quantified and monetized at the global scale. Climate change related damages can be attributed to either the rate of change (i.e. the annual change in temperature, benchmarked at 0.04 °C per year) or the level of change (i.e. the temperature change since pre-industrial times, benchmarked at 1.0 °C). Sectors impacted by climate change also change for other reasons, but the impacts shown below are the impacts of climate change only. Impacts are impacts on welfare, expressed in dollars at market exchange rates. Damages from the rate of temperature change slowly fade, reflecting adaptation (Tol 2002b).

---

[1] A full list of papers and the technical documentation for the model can be found online at www.fund-model.org/. The model code for this chapter is at: http://dvn.iq.harvard.edu/dvn/dv/rtol

People can die prematurely due to climate change, or they can migrate because of sea level rise. Like all impacts of climate change, these effects are monetized. The value of a statistical life is set to be 200 times the annual per capita income. The resulting value of a statistical life lies in the middle of the observed range of values in the literature (Cline 1992a). The value of emigration is set to be three times the per capita income (Tol 1995). Losses of dryland and wetlands due to sea level rise are modeled explicitly. The monetary value of a loss of 1 square kilometer of dryland was on average US$4 million in OECD countries in 1990 (Fankhauser 1994). Dryland value is assumed to be proportional to GDP per square kilometer. Wetland losses are valued at US$2 million per square kilometer on average in the OECD in 1990 (Fankhauser 1994). The wetland value is assumed to have logistic relation to per capita income. Coastal protection is based on cost–benefit analysis, including the value of additional wetland lost due to the construction of dikes and subsequent coastal squeeze.

Other impact categories, such as agriculture, forestry, energy, water, storm damage, and ecosystems, are directly expressed in monetary values without an intermediate layer of impacts measured in their "natural" units (Tol 2002a). Impacts of climate change on energy consumption, agriculture, and cardiovascular and respiratory diseases explicitly recognize that there is a climatic optimum, in which welfare is maximum. The location of the optimum is determined by a variety of factors, including physiology, infrastructure, and behavior. Impacts are positive or negative depending on whether the actual climate conditions are moving closer to or away from the optimum climate. Impacts are larger if the initial climate conditions are further away from the optimum climate. The optimum climate is of importance with regard to the potential impacts. The actual impacts lag behind the potential impacts, depending on the speed of adaptation. The impacts of not being fully adapted to new climate conditions are always negative (Tol 2002b).

The impacts of climate change on coastal zones, forestry, tropical and extratropical storm damage, unmanaged ecosystems, water resources, diarrhea,

malaria, dengue fever, and schistosomiasis are modeled as simple power functions. Impacts are either negative or positive, and they do not change sign (Tol 2002b).

Vulnerability to climate change changes with population growth, economic growth, and technological progress (Yohe and Tol 2002). Some systems are expected to become more vulnerable, such as water resources (with population growth), heat-related disorders (with urbanization), and ecosystems and health (with higher per capita incomes). Other systems such as energy consumption (with technological progress), agriculture (with economic growth), and vector- and water-borne diseases (with improved health care) are projected to become less vulnerable at least over the long term (Tol 2002b). The income elasticities (Tol 2002b) are estimated from cross-sectional data or taken from the literature.

Heat and cold stress are assumed to have an effect only on the elderly, non-reproductive population. In contrast, the other sources of mortality also affect the number of births. Heat stress only affects the urban population (because of the urban heat island effect and the combination of poverty, isolation and crime). The share of the urban population among the total population is based on the World Resources Databases (http://earthtrends.wri.org). It is extrapolated based on the statistical relationship between urbanization and per capita income, which are estimated from a cross-section of countries in 1995.

Results

Figure 3.1 shows the global mean surface air temperature and the rate of change. Temperature is averaged over 5 years, that is, the value for, say, 1900 is the average of 1898–1902. Averaging is needed because the impact model is designed with smooth trajectories of warming in mind. The model does not estimate the impact of annual weather variability; rather, it estimates the impact of secular climate change. The first decade of the twentieth century saw cooling, followed by three decades of warming, three decades of volatility, and three decades of warming. The projected warming for the twenty-first century is smooth.

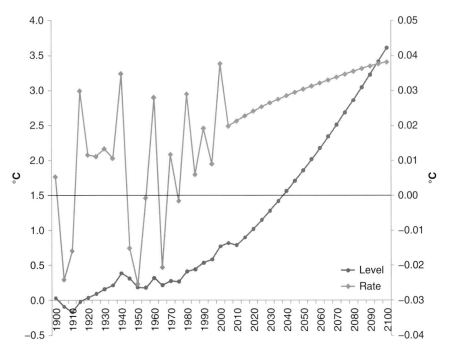

Figure 3.1 *The level of the (5-year running average) global mean surface air temperature and the rate of change in the twentieth and twenty-first centuries*

Figure 3.2 shows the economic impact of climate change, aggregated over countries and over sectors. Note that the results are welfare impacts, rather than changes in economic activity. In the twentieth century, the impact is small but positive. Climate change increased welfare by the equivalent of a 0.5% increase in income for the first half of the twentieth century. After 1950, impacts became more positive, edging up to 1.4% of GDP by 2000. However, impacts roughly stabilize after that, reaching their maximum at 1.5% of GDP in 2025 and then precipitously fall to reach −1.2% of GDP in 2100.

Figure 3.3 shows the global economic impact of climate change by sector (see Figure 3.2 for the total). The top panel shows the impact over time, the bottom panel shows the impact as a function of temperature (cf. Figure 3.1). The impact of climate change through tropical storms is small, in line with

the statistical analyses referred to in the introduction. The impact of sea level rise is small too, because sea level rose by only 12 cm over the course of the twentieth century. In the twenty-first century, sea level rise is 61 cm but coastal protection keeps the impacts in check.

The aggregate impact of global warming on water resources is negative. The relationship to accumulative warming is roughly linear in temperature in the first half of the twentieth century, but the negative effect is alleviated by improved water use efficiency and economic growth in the second half of the twentieth century and the twenty-first century.[2] Impacts are about −0.1% of GDP in 2000 and edge up to −0.2% of GDP. Although the overall impact is negative, national impacts are mixed with some countries benefitting in some periods. Qualitatively, therefore, the model is not inconsistent with the empirical literature reviewed in the introduction.

The health impact of climate change is mixed. Generally speaking, cooling brings net benefits, moderate warming brings both benefits and damages, while larger warming brings net damages.

---

[2] Water is a necessary good. The assumed income elasticity is 0.85, that is, a 10 % increase in per capita income leads to an 8.5% increase in the per capita value of water.

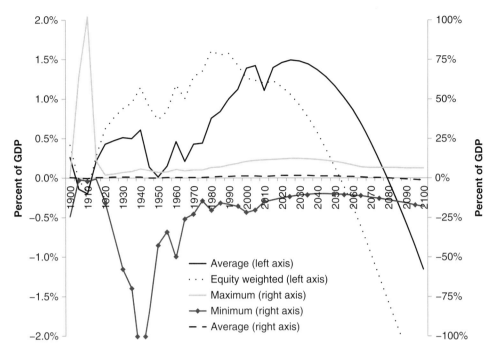

Figure 3.2 *The global average, minimum, and maximum total economic impact of climate change in the twentieth and twenty-first centuries*

This is because FUND has a number of health impacts, some related to cold and some to heat – see below – and some related to the level of climate change and others to its rate. Furthermore, health impacts depend on the age structure of the population and income (a proxy for healthcare), while the value also depends on income. The result is the complex pattern shown in Figure 3.3. By the end of the twentieth century, the impact is clearly positive, equivalent to an income gain of 0.4%. Impacts continue to increase slightly till 2055 and then begin to fall to reach 0.3% in 2100.

The impact of global warming on energy consumption is positive during the twentieth century. While the demand for cooling in summer increased, this is more than offset by the reduction in the demand for heating in winter. Towards the end of the twentieth century, the annual savings on energy amount to almost 0.4% of GDP. The national impacts are mixed, with losses and gains in different places and times, qualitatively corresponding to the literature surveyed above. After 2010, however, the demand for cooling starts to rise rapidly while

the reduction in demand for heating levels off. The result is a large negative impact, reaching −1.9% of GDP by 2100.

Agriculture is the biggest positive impact in the twentieth century, approaching 0.8% of GDP by 2000. This is entirely due to carbon dioxide fertilization, which makes crops grow faster and more water efficient. The impact of climate change (temperature, precipitation, cloud cover, wind, etc.) is actually negative, reaching −0.3% in 2000. Because carbon dioxide fertilization is the dominant effect, impacts are positive for all countries and periods. This is in contrast to the empirical literature reviewed in the introduction – although it should be noted that that literature is limited to crop yields while the results here are for agricultural production. Impacts continue to increase to 1.3% in 2055. After that, impacts begin to fall as carbon dioxide fertilization begins to saturate and the negative impacts of warming grow larger. By 2100, however, impacts are still positive (0.8% of GDP).

Figure 3.2 shows world aggregate economic impact, which ranges between −0.2% and 1.4% of

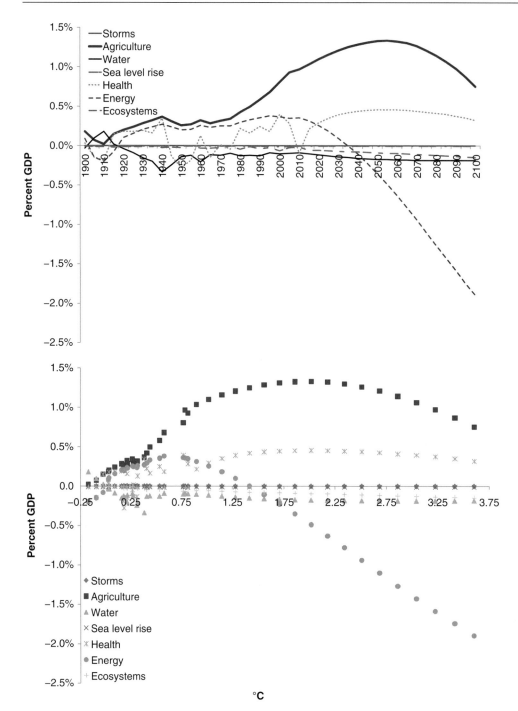

Figure 3.3 *The global average sectoral economic impact of climate change in the twentieth and twenty-first centuries as a function of time and temperature*

Figure 3.4 *The net total economic impact of climate change by nation averaged over the twentieth century, ranked from highest to lowest*

GDP in the twentieth century and between −1.2% and 1.4% of GDP in the twenty-first century. Figure 3.2 also shows the maximum and minimum impact across countries.[3] The range is large with high positive impacts (~100%) for the rapid cooling around 1910 and high negative impacts (~−120%) for the rapid warming around 1940 – health is the main driver of these large impacts (see below). Overall, the maximum and minimum are two orders of magnitude larger (in absolute terms) than the average. In the twenty-first century, the range of impacts is much narrower. Nonetheless, a lot of variation is hidden by the mean. In 2100, for instance, impacts range from −18% to +6% of GDP – roughly an order of magnitude larger than the mean. This suggests that the variability of the climate in the twentieth century drives the distribution of impacts across countries.

Figure 3.2 further shows the equity-weighted impacts.[4] These are more positive in the twentieth century than the non-weighted average, indicating that poorer countries see greater benefits than richer countries – primarily due to carbon dioxide

fertilization of agriculture. However, the gap begins to close in 1980 – the maximum impact of climate change occurs 45 years earlier when equity weighted. The equity-weighted impacts fall rapidly to reach −2.8% in 2100.

Figure 3.4 highlights the differences between countries. It shows the average impact over the century for each of the 207 countries in the model, which ranges from a negative 19% (Timor Leste) to a positive 6.0% (China). Figure 3.5 shows the same information on the map. Figure 3.5 also shows the impact for the years 1900, 1950, 2000, 2050, and 2100.

A number of countries stand out. China benefits most from climate change on average across the twentieth century. Agriculture is a big positive, followed by energy use and water resources. Haiti

[3] Note that Figure 3.2 shows the worst-off and best-off countries at each point in time, rather than the worst-off and best-off countries averaged over the centuries.

[4] National impacts are weighted with the ratio of world average per capita income and national per capita income. This corresponds to a logarithmic function for individual utility and utilitarian social welfare (Fankhauser *et al.* 1997).

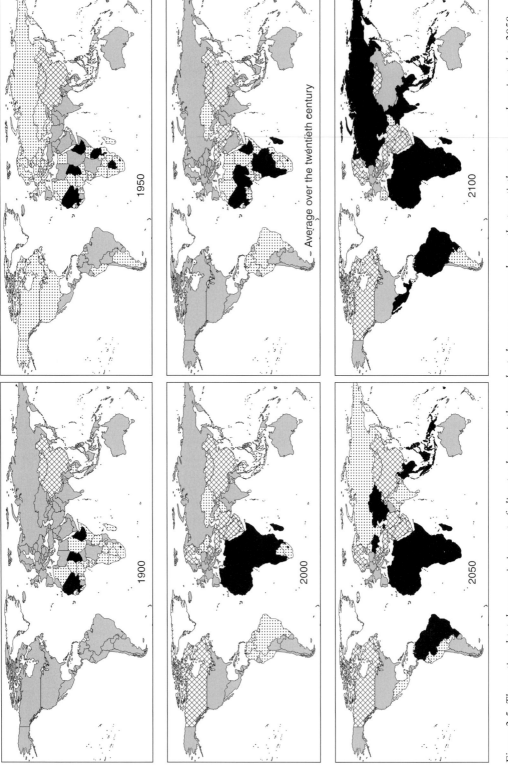

Figure 3.5 *The national total economic impact of climate change in three selected years, averaged over the twentieth century, and projected to 2050 and 2100*

is the second biggest beneficiary. This is entirely due to the positive effects of carbon dioxide fertilization on agriculture. Averaged over the twentieth century, each African nation loses out. In the first half of the century, however, there are both winners and losers. The main positive factor is the large impact on agriculture. Negative impacts on health outweigh agriculture in the second half of the twentieth century.

Timor Leste is hurt most by climate change on average across the twentieth century. This is largely due to the impacts of climate change on poverty-related health problems, particularly diarrhea and malaria. Bangladesh is the most vulnerable country outside of Africa. It sees relatively large negative impacts on its health, coastal zone, and water resources – which are larger than the positive impacts on agriculture and energy use. Russia also stands out. Although there are large damages due to a climate-change-induced increase in water scarcity, this is more than offset by benefits for energy use, agriculture and human health.

Figure 3.6 shows the world aggregate health impacts per disease. The total number of premature deaths roughly traces the global mean temperature (cf. Figure 3.1). The temperature impact on cardiovascular deaths is modeled as a process of acclimatization, so that the effect does not manifest itself during cooling-after-warming (1945, 1975, 2010). Winter cold dominates summer heat as a health problem. Warming has a negative (positive) impact on respiratory disorders, malaria, dengue fever, and diarrhea (schistomiasis), and the pattern in Figure 3.6 follows (mirrors) that in Figure 3.1. Climate change has caused the premature deaths of a substantial number of people over the twentieth century – on average 7.5 per million per year. In 2000, according to FUND, 90,000 people died because of climate change. This estimate is roughly equal to the one by Campbell-Lendrum and Woodruff (2006). In the twenty-first century, avoided cold-related cardiovascular deaths increase steadily whereas heat-related cardiovascular deaths increase rapidly. Respiratory deaths increase too,

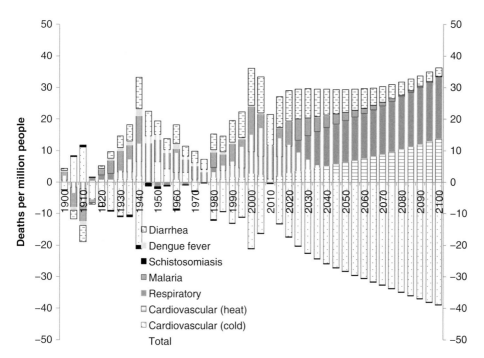

Figure 3.6 *The global average impact of climate change on mortality by cause of death; the white insets denote total mortality*

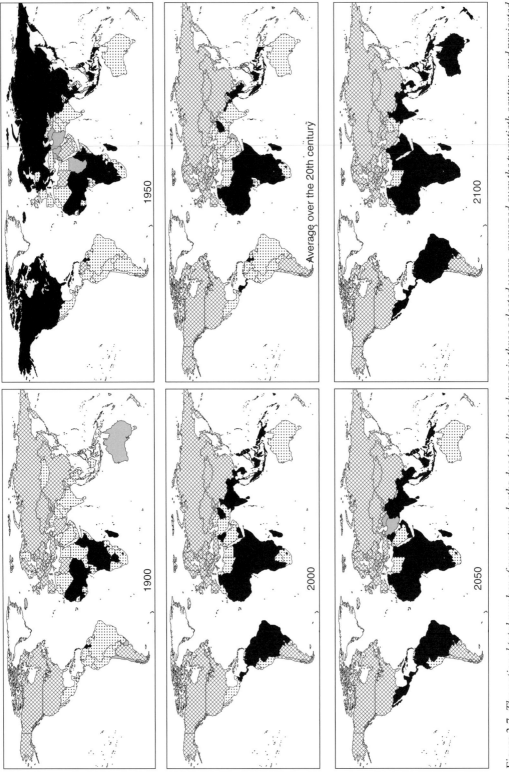

Figure 3.7 The national total number of premature deaths due to climate change in three selected years, averaged over the twentieth century, and projected to 2050 and 2100

but malaria and diarrhea fall with economic growth and the concomitant improvement in health care.

Figure 3.7 shows the aggregate health impact per country for selected years and averaged over the century. In 1900 and 2000, there are positive impacts in the richer and cooler countries, and negative impacts in poorer and hotter countries. In 1950, negative impacts are widespread. Averaged over the century, there is a clear divide. Rich countries with temperate climates see positive impacts of climate change on health; other countries see negative impacts. This pattern becomes more entrenched in the twenty-first century.

Discussion and Conclusion

Previous studies have found that moderate, future climate change would bring net benefits (Tol 2009b). This study finds that past, moderate climate change brought net benefits. This is no surprise as the current study infrapolates from previous work. Carbon dioxide fertilization of crops and reduced energy demand for heating are the main positive impacts. Climate change had a negative effect on water resources and (by and large) human health. Most rich and most poor countries benefitted from climate change until 1980, but after that the trend is negative for poor countries and positive for rich countries. In the twenty-first century, impacts turn negative in most countries, rich and poor. Future climate change is a reason for concern.

A number of testable hypotheses arise from these results. Energy demand and agricultural production are relatively well understood. While statistical analyses have focused on recent decades for which data are excellent, it should be feasible to use older data to test the impact of climate change. The same should be possible for water resources in at least some parts of the world. For health, data availability would allow for selected case studies only. Care should be taken that like is compared with like. For example, FUND considers agricultural production while empirical studies tend to focus on crop yields.

I briefly reviewed the empirical literature above (pp. 117–118). Not surprisingly as FUND is calibrated to that literature, the model backcasts are roughly in line with the data. The impact of climate change on tropical cyclone damages is small in both model and observations. The impact on human health varies but is more often negative than positive in both model and observations. The impact on water resources is predominantly negative in the model, while the observations suggest a mixed impact. The impact on agriculture is predominantly positive in the model, while the observations suggest a mixed impact. The impact on energy use in positive in both model and observations. Note, however, that a direct comparison between the model results and the empirical results is not possible, because coverage and scope are different, and the empirical studies focus on different indicators.

The results for the twentieth and twenty-first century were derived with the same model, and impact patterns are therefore similar. However, the spread of impacts is larger in the twentieth century than in the twenty-first century. This is because climate variability is considered in the twentieth century but not in the twenty-first. This would suggest that the spread of the impacts is underestimated for the twenty-first century. This result affects not only FUND, but all models of the economic impact of climate change.

The exercise presented here should be repeated with other models of the impact of climate change. Surveys and meta-analyses of the empirical literature on the impact of climate change should be conducted to created indicators that can be directly compared to the model results. This is needed to build confidence in the models that are used to assess the magnitude of the problem of climate change.

References

Barredo, J. I. (2009) Normalised flood losses in Europe: 1970–2006. *Natural Hazards and Earth System Science* **9**: 97–104.

Bessec, M. and J. Fouquau (2008) The non-linear link between electricity consumption and temperature in Europe: a threshold panel approach. *Energy Economics* **30**: 2705–2721.

Byass, P. (2008) Making sense of long-term changes in malaria. *The Lancet* **372**: 1523–1525.

Campbell-Lendrum, D. and R. Woodruff (2006) Comparative risk assessment of the burden of disease from climate change. *Environmental Health Perspectives* **114**: 1935–1941.

Carson, C., S. Hajat, B. Armstrong, and P. Wilkinson (2006) Declining vulnerability to temperature-related mortality in London over the twentieth century. *American Journal of Epidemiology* **164**: 7–14.

Changnon, D. and S. A. Changnon Jr. (1998) Evaluation of weather catastrophe data for use in climate change investigations. *Climatic Change* **38**: 435–445.

Changnon, S. A. (2003) Shifting economic impacts from weather extremes in the United States: a result of societal changes, not global warming. *Natural Hazards* **29**: 273–290.

Changnon, S. A. and J. M. Changnon (1992) Temporal fluctuations in weather disasters: 1950–1989. *Climatic Change* **22**: 191–208.

Chaves, L. F. and C. J. M. Koenraadt (2010) Climate change and highland malaria: fresh air for a hot debate. *Quarterly Review of Biology* **85**: 27–55.

Cline, W. R. (1992a) *Global Warming: The Benefits of Emission Abatement*. Paris: OECD.

(1992b) *The Economics of Global Warming*. Washington, DC: Institute for International Economics.

Considine, T. J. (2000) The impacts of weather variations on energy demand and carbon emissions. *Resource and Energy Economics* **22**: 295–314.

Craig, M. H., I. Kleinschmidt, J. B. Nawn, D. le Sueur, and B. L. Sharp (2004) Exploring 30 years of malaria case data in KwaZulu-Natal, South Africa: Part I. The impact of climatic factors. *Tropical Medicine and International Health* **9**: 1247–1257.

D'Ippoliti, D., P. Michelozzi, C. Marino, *et al.* (2010) The impact of heat waves on mortality in nine European cities: Results from the EuroHEAT project. *Environmental Health: A Global Access Science Source* **9**, Article 1.

Davis, R. E., P. C. Knappenberger, W. M. Novicoff, and P. J. Michaels (2002) Decadal changes in heat-related human mortality in the eastern United States. *Climate Research* **22**: 175–184.

(2003) Decadal changes in summer mortality in U.S. cities. *International Journal of Biometeorology* **47**: 166–175.

EUROWINTER Group (1997) Cold exposure and winter mortality from ischaemic heart disease, cerebrovascular disease, respiratory disease, and all causes in warm and cold regions of Europe. *The Lancet*, **349**: 1341–1346.

Fankhauser, S. (1994) Protection vs. retreat: the economic costs of sea level rise. *Environment and Planning A* **27**: 299–319.

(1995) *Valuing Climate Change: The Economics of the Greenhouse*. London: Earthscan.

Fankhauser, S., R. S. J. Tol, and D. W. Pearce (1997) The aggregation of climate change damages: a welfare theoretic approach. *Environmental and Resource Economics* **10**: 249–266.

Gething, P. W., D. L. Smith, A. P. Patil, *et al.* (2010) Climate change and the global malaria recession. *Nature* **465**: 342–345.

Giannakopoulos, C. and B. E. Psiloglou (2006) Trends in energy load demand for Athens, Greece: weather and non-weather related factors. *Climate Research* **31**: 97–108.

Hay, S. I., J. Cox, D. J. Rogers, *et al.* (2002a) Climate change and the resurgence of malaria in the East African highlands. *Nature* **415**: 905–909.

Hay, S. I., D. J. Rogers, S. E. Randolph, *et al.* (2002b) Hot topic or hot air? Climate change and malaria resurgence in East African highlands. *Trends in Parasitology* **18**: 530–534.

Hekkenberg, M., R. M. J. Benders, H. C. Moll, and A. J. M. Schoot Uiterkamp (2009) Indications for a changing electricity demand pattern: the temperature dependence of electricity demand in the Netherlands. *Energy Policy* **37**: 1542–1551.

Henley, A. and J. Peirson (1998) Residential energy demand and the interaction of price and temperature: British experimental evidence. *Energy Economics* **20**: 157–171.

Holmer, B. (2008) Fluctuations of winter wheat yields in relation to length of winter in Sweden 1866 to 2006. *Climate Research* **36**: 241–252.

Kundzewicz, Z. W., D. Graczyk, T. Maurer, *et al.* (2005) Trend detection in river flow series: Part I. Annual maximum flow. *Hydrological Sciences Journal* **50**: 79–100.

Lindstroem, G. and S. Bergstroem (2004) Runoff trends in Sweden 1807–2002. *Hydrological Sciences Journal* **49**: 69–84.

Link, P. M. and R. S. J. Tol (2004) Possible economic impacts of a shutdown of the thermohaline circulation: an application of FUND. *Portuguese Economic Journal* **3**: 99–114.

(2011) The economic impact of a shutdown of the thermohaline circulation: an application of FUND. *Climatic Change* **104**: 287–304.

Lins, H. F. and J. R. Slack (1999) Streamflow trends in the United States. *Geophysical Research Letters* **26**: 227–230.

Lloyd, S. J., R. S. Kovats, and B. G. Armstrong (2007) Global diarrhoea morbidity, weather and climate. *Climate Research* **34**: 119–127.

Lobell, D. B. and G. P. Asner (2003) Climate and management contributions to recent trends in U.S. agricultural yields. *Science* **299**: 1032.

Lobell, D. B. and C. B. Field (2007) Global scale climate–crop yield relationships and the impacts of recent warming. *Environmental Research Letters* 2, Article 1.

Lobell, D. B., J. I. Ortiz-Monasterio, G. P. Asner, *et al.* (2005) Analysis of wheat yield and climatic trends in Mexico. *Field Crops Research* **94**: 250–256.

Lobell, D. B., W. Schlenker, and J. Costa-Roberts (2011) Climate trends and global crop production since 1980. *Science* **333**: 616–620.

Loevinsohn, M. E. (1994) Climatic warming and increased malaria incidence in Rwanda. *The Lancet*, **343**: 714–718.

Long, S. P., E. A. Ainsworth, A. D. B. Leakey, J. Noesberger, and D. R. Ort (2006) Food for thought: lower-than-expected crop yield stimulation with rising CO_2 concentrations. *Science* **312**: 1918–1921.

Maddison, A. (1995) *Monitoring the World Economy 1820–1992*. Paris: OECD.

Martens, W. J. M. (1998) Climate change, thermal stress and mortality changes. *Social Science and Medicine* **46**: 331–344.

McMichael, A. J. and K. B. G. Dear (2010) Climate change: heat, health, and longer horizons. *Proceedings of the National Academy of Sciences of the USA* **107**: 9483–9484.

Mendelsohn, R. O., W. N. Morrison, M. E. Schlesinger, and N. G. Andronova (2000) Country-specific market impacts of climate change. *Climatic Change* **45**: 553–569.

Moral-Carcedo, J. and J. Vicens-Otero (2005) Modelling the non-linear response of Spanish electricity demand to temperature variations. *Energy Economics* **27**: 477–494.

Myneni, R. B., C. D. Keeling, C. J. Tucker, G. Asrar, and R. R. Nemani (1997) Increased plant growth in the northern high latitudes from 1981 to 1991. *Nature* **386**: 698–702.

Narita, D., D. Anthoff, and R. S. J. Tol (2009) Damage costs of climate change through intensification of tropical cyclone activities: an application of FUND. *Climate Research* **39**: 87–97.

(2010) Economic costs of extratropical storms under climate change: an application of FUND.

Journal of Environmental Planning and Management **53**: 371–384.

Neumayer, E. and F. Barthel (2011) Normalizing economic loss from natural disasters: a global analysis. *Global Environmental Change* **21**:. 13–24.

Nicholls, N. (1997) Increased Australian wheat yield due to recent climate trends. *Nature* **387**: 484–485.

Nordhaus, W. D. (1991) To slow or not to slow: the economics of the greenhouse effect. *Economic Journal* **101**: 920–937.

Pardo, A., V. Meneu, and E. Valor (2002) Temperature and seasonality influences on Spanish electricity load. *Energy Economics* **24**: 55–70.

Pielke, J. (2005) Are there trends in hurricane destruction? *Nature* **438**, Article E11.

Pielke, R. A., J. Gratz, C. W. Landsea, *et al.* (2008) Normalized hurricane damage in the United States: 1900–2005. *Natural Hazards Review* **9**: 29–42.

Ryan, P. C., R. A. Pielke Jr., and K. J. McAneny (2011). Emergence timescales for detection of anthropogenic climate change in US tropical cyclone loss data. *Environmental Research Letters* **6**, Article 014003.

Sailor, D. J. and J. R. Munoz (1997) Sensitivity of electricity and natural gas consumption to climate in the U.S.A.: methodology and results for eight states. *Energy* **22**: 987–998.

Small, J., S. J. Goetz, and S. I. Hay (2003) Climatic suitability for malaria transmission in Africa, 1911–1995. *Proceedings of the National Academy of Sciences of the USA* **100**: 15 341–15 345.

Svensson, C., Z. W. Kundzewicz, and T. Maurer (2005) Trend detection in river flow series: Part II. Flood and low-flow index series. *Hydrological Sciences Journal* **50**: 811–824.

Tao, F., M. Yokozawa, Y. Xu, Y. Hayashi, and Z. Zhang (2006) Climate changes and trends in phenology and yields of field crops in China, 1981–2000. *Agricultural and Forest Meteorology* **138**: 82–92.

Tao, F., M. Yokozawa, J. Liu, and Z. Zhang (2008) Climate–crop yield relationships at provincial scales in China and the impacts of recent climate trends. *Climate Research* **38**: 83–94.

Thomas, C. (2004) A changed climate in Africa? *Nature* **427**: 690–691.

Tol, R. S. J. (1995) The damage costs of climate change toward more comprehensive calculations. *Environmental and Resource Economics* **5**: 353–374.

(2001) Equitable cost–Benefit analysis of climate change. *Ecological Economics* **36**: 71–85.

(2002a) Estimates of the damage costs of climate change: Part I. Benchmark estimates. *Environmental and Resource Economics* **21**: 47–73.

(2002b) Estimates of the damage costs of climate change: Part II. Dynamic estimates. *Environmental and Resource Economics* **21**: 135–160.

(2002c) Welfare specifications and optimal control of climate change: an application of FUND. *Energy Economics* **24**: 367–376.

(2009a) *Climate Feedbacks on the Terrestrial Biosphere and the Economics of Climate Policy: An Application of FUND*, Working Paper No. 288. Dublin: Economic and Social Research Institute.

(2009b) The economic effects of climate change. *Journal of Economic Perspectives* **23**: 29–51.

Tol, R. S. J. and R. Verheyen (2004) State responsibility and compensation for climate change damages: a legal and economic assessment. *Energy Policy* **32**: 1109–1130.

Tol, R. S. J., T. E. Downing, and N. Eyre (1999) *The Marginal Costs of Radiatively-Active Gases* Working paper No. 99/32. Amsterdam: Institute for Environmental Studies Vrije Universiteit.

Toya, H. and M. Skidmore (2007) Economic Development and the Impacts of Natural Disasters. *Economics Letters* **94**: 20–25.

Twine, T. E. and C. J. Kucharik (2009) Climate impacts on net primary productivity trends in natural and managed ecosystems of the central and eastern United States. *Agricultural and Forest Meteorology* **149**: 2143–2161.

Yohe, G. W. and R. S. J. Tol (2002) Indicators for social and economic coping capacity: moving towards a working definition of adaptive capacity. *Global Environmental Change* **12**: 25–40.

Zhang, T., J. Zhu, and R. Wassmann (2010) Responses of rice yields to recent climate change in China: an empirical assessment based on long-term observations at different spatial scales (1981–2005). *Agricultural and Forest Meteorology* **150**: 1128–1137.

CHAPTER 4

Ecosystems and Biodiversity: Economic Loss of Ecosystem Services from 1900 to 2050

ANIL MARKANDYA AND ALINE CHIABAI

Introduction

Much has been written and said on the loss of bio-diversity that we have been experiencing in recent decades. Species are estimated to be going extinct at rates 100 to 1000 times faster than in geological times (Pimm *et al.* 1995). Moreover there is reason to believe that these extinctions are associated with economic and social losses. For example, between 1981 and 2006, 47% percent of cancer drugs and 34% of all "small molecule new chemical entities" (NCE) for all disease categories were natural products or derived directly from them (Newman and Cragg 2007). In some countries in Asia and Africa 80% of the population relies on traditional medi-cine (including herbal medicine) for primary healthcare (www.who.int/mediacentre/factsheets/fs134/en/index.html). As extinctions continue the availability of some of these medicines may be reduced and new drug developments may well be curtailed. Yet, while we have a number of pieces of anecdotal evidence of this nature, and there are several studies that look at the value of bio-diversity in specific contexts, no one has estimated the global value of the loss of biodiversity as such.[1] This is because the links between biodiversity and biological systems and the economic and social val-ues that they support are extremely complex. Even the measurement of biodiversity is problematic, with a multidimensional metric being regarded as appro-priate (Purvis and Hector 2000; Mace *et al.* 2003), but with further work being considered necessary to define the appropriate combination.

For this reason the focus, initiated by the Millennium Ecosystem Assessment (MEA 2005), has been on measuring ecosystem services, which are derived from complex biophysical systems. The MEA defines ecosystem services under four headings: provisioning, regulating, cultural, and supporting and under each there are a number of sub-categories. Table 4.1 summarizes the main eco-system services that the MEA has listed.

The first thing to note is that services from eco-systems have also been facing major losses. During the last century the planet has lost 50% of its wet-lands, 40% of its forests, and 35% of its mangroves. Around 60% of global ecosystem services have been degraded in just 50 years (ten Brink 2011).

While working at the ecosystem level makes things somewhat easier it is of critical importance to understand the causes of this loss of services and the links between losses of biodiversity and the loss of ecosystem services. Indeed this is a major field of research for ecologists in which one thesis that has been developed over a long period is that more diverse ecosystems are more stable and less subject to malfunction (Tilman and Downing 1994; McCann 2000; Haines-Young and Potschin 2010). Evidence in support of this has been provided from a range of natural and synthesized ecosystems, but the evidence also points to more complex rela-tionships, in particular to the fact that the functions of ecosystems are determined more by the functional characteristics of the component organisms rather than the number of species (Grime 1997). Overall, however, many ecologists would agree with the statement that "diversity can be expected, on aver-age, to give rise to ecosystem stability" (McCann 2000, p. 232).

The authors wish to thank two anonymous referees who have provided a lot of useful advice and guidance. We also thank Ben ten Brink and Michel Jeuken from the Environmental Assessment Agency of the Netherlands (PBL) for providing the MSA data and advice on its construction. All errors and omissions are of course ours alone.

[1] For a brief review see ten Brink (2011), Chapter 5.4.

Table 4.1 Types of ecosystem services

Provisioning services	Regulating services
• Food and fiber	• Air quality maintenance
• Fuel	• Climate regulation (e.g. temperature and precipitation, carbon storage)
• Biochemicals, natural medicines, and pharmaceuticals	• Water regulation (e.g. flood prevention, timing and magnitude of runoff, aquifer recharge)
• Ornamental resources	• Erosion control
• Fresh water	• Water purification and waste management
Cultural services	• Regulation of human diseases
• Cultural diversity, spiritual and religious values, educational values, inspiration, aesthetic values, social relations, sense of place and identity	• Biological control (e.g. loss of natural predators of pests)
• Cultural heritage values	• Pollination
• Recreation and ecotourism	• Storm protection (damage by hurricanes or large waves)
Supporting services	• Fire resistance (change of vegetation cover leading to increased fire susceptibility)
• Primary production	• Avalanche protection
• Nutrient cycling	• Other (loss of indicator species)
• Soil formation	

Source: MEA (2005).

To sum up, the current state of knowledge on the links between biodiversity and ecosystem services is still a topic of research and while some clear lines are emerging, they are not strong enough to

[2] Theoretical models of the economic values attached to biodiversity have been developed. See for example Brock and Xepapadeas (2003). Such models draw simple links between harvesting rates, system biodiversity, and overall system value. As yet, however, they are not supported by empirical estimates that could be used to apply the methods to derive these system values.

allow a formal modeling to be carried out at a level that would produce credible estimates of the global value of biodiversity. The latter therefore remains a topic for research.[2]

Since the objective of this study is to obtain estimates of changes in the economic values of services from natural systems at the global level we have, of necessity, gone for ecosystem function valuation, recognizing that there is a complex link between changes in such values and the changes in the measures of biodiversity (defined appropriately). However, our ecosystem methodology does take into account the quality of an ecosystem and the services it produces, based on the species abundance within it. This is derived from the mean species abundance (MSA) approach, which is explained more fully in the next section. To some extent, therefore, the study does build on the linkages between the biodiversity of a biome and its ecosystem functions.

Specifically, this chapter examines the changes of key ecosystem services between 1900 and 2000, the estimated changes between 2000 and 2050 under some projected scenarios, and attempts to value these changes in monetary terms. Note that not all the services listed in Table 4.1 will be valued. Limitations of data restrict us to a few of the key ones and to that extent the exercise is incomplete and an underestimate of the changes in services.

The approach taken in the study is as follows. First, an estimate is made of the range of ecosystem services that are being derived from the different biomes in the different regions of the world in 2000. These calculations are based on recent research that has been addressing exactly that question – i.e. the links between the level of services and the quantity and quality of the biomes. Second, an estimate is made of what the quantity and quality of these biomes were in 1900 and 2000 and what they will be in 2050, assuming current economic and environmental trends continue. Third, the values of ecosystem services are estimated for the years 2000 and 2050, given the quality and quantity of the biomes. The estimates of the quality and quantity of the biomes are based on the work of GLOBIO team (see below, p. 133), which has estimated the combination of quantity and quality in terms of "mean species abundance (MSA) area." This concept is elaborated further in the next section. The data show significant losses between 1900 and 2000, and a mixture of expected losses and gains between 2000 and 2050.

The analysis is therefore carried out for the two time-frames: 1900–2000 and 2000–2050. Given the difficulties in knowing the prices and economic conditions in 1900 in adequate detail, the estimates are based on the following mental experiment. First we estimate what would have been the value of the services in 2000 with the 1900 MSA areas had they been available in 2000, and second we estimate what would have been the value of the ecosystem services in 2050 if the 2000 MSA areas had been available in 2050. The difference between the 1900 and 2000 values is then the gain we would have had in 2000, if the 1900 levels of services had been available. Likewise the difference between the 2000 and the 2050 levels tells us what we have lost (or gained) by 2050 as a result of the change in services between 2000 and 2050. Both calculations make the simplifying assumption that the changes are marginal and that the unit value of areas does not change as a result. Given the limited data it is difficult to do anything else.

The next step in the overall assessment is to value the gains that have been made by the conversion of the biomes with significant ecosystem benefits to agricultural use. The net benefits of agriculture from the land that has been converted to that use from forest clearance or grassland modification are then subtracted from the losses due to biodiversity as a result of the loss of MSA areas. The resulting figures show the net losses or gains in 2000 and in 2050 under the thought-experiment of what would have been the situation had we not suffered any change of biomes during the twentieth century and the first half of the twenty-first century. We conclude with some reflections on the results, what messages can be drawn from them and where we should not extend ourselves beyond what the data can reveal.

Change in MSA Area

The Model

The Global Biodiversity Model GLOBIO3 is used to assess the impacts of human activities on biodiversity in different biomes and world regions (Alkemade *et al.* 2006). The model links environmental drivers

and biodiversity impacts using cause–effect relationships derived from the literature. The impacts are driven by climate change, fragmentation, land-use change, infrastructures, and carbon and nitrogen cycles. The GLOBIO3 model is linked to the IMAGE 2.4 model, as changes in drivers are assessed using the latter, which is an Integrated Model to Assess the Global Environment (Bouwman *et al.* 2006) quantifying the impacts of human activities on natural environment and reflecting social, economic and technological features in the society.

In this model biodiversity is analyzed as "the remaining mean species abundance (MSA) of original species, relative to their abundance in pristine or primary vegetation, which are assumed to be not disturbed by human activities for a prolonged period" (Alkemade *et al.* 2009, p. 375). The peculiarity of MSA is related to the fact that it is not built on actual observations in the study area, but on the relations between pressures or drivers and impacts on species abundance. For each pressure under analysis a meta-analysis is first carried out to put in relation the MSA values with a number of drivers. The MSA values used in the meta-analysis are constructed from indicators taken from the literature, and specifically the abundance of different species (number of individuals per species, density, or cover) registered in primary vegetation areas (natural or relatively untouched) and the abundance of species in disturbed environments. The MSA indicator as dependent variable in the meta-analysis is constructed by dividing the latter number by the former.

The MSA values are calculated for each of the above mentioned drivers taking into account the cause–effect relationships for each driver as estimated in the meta-analysis. As the IMAGE model uses the area of land as an input, the MSA value of a geographical region is calculated as the area-weighted mean of MSA values for each region. The GLOBIO3 model is then used to assess the expected impacts of the selected drivers on MSA in a number of world regions and future scenarios, as well as the impacts of specific predefined policy measures. For the purpose of this study we used the first set of the results provided by GLOBIO3 model related to the estimated changes in MSA areas over the period 1900–2050 for a number of biomes and world regions. Biomes refer to ecosystems with similar climatic conditions and are characterized by specific features related to plants and leaves. A biome can be defined as a major habitat type. The classification used for this study refers to seven different biomes, namely: ice and tundra, grassland/steppe, scrubland and savanna, desert, and boreal, temperate, and tropical forests. Projections of MSA areas are shown for all the seven biomes, while the economic valuation is presented only for grassland/steppe and the forest biomes. This choice is related to the limited availability of valuation studies and monetary estimates in many biomes. Seven world regions are analyzed as listed in Table 4.2 below.

For the purpose of this study we decided to use the MSA area indicator for the physical impacts as it is built on the product of the area of the residual ecosystem and its quality in terms of species abundance. The measure therefore takes into account a quality dimension of the ecosystem which is related to its capacity to provide ecosystem services. In one of our previous studies (Chiabai *et al.* 2011), we used directly the change in hectares over time, as we wanted to estimate the impacts of changes in forest areas in different biomes, so that we multiplied the projected variation in area by the monetary values, calculated on a per hectare basis, for a set of ecosystem services provided by those

Table 4.2 World regions

OECD	Western and Eastern Europe, Western offshoots (Australia, Canada, New Zealand, USA)
CSAM	Central and Latin America
MEA-NAFR	Middle East and North Africa
SAFR	Sub-Saharan Africa
RUS-CASIA	Russia and Central Asia
SASIA	South Asia
CHN	China

[3] We acknowledge that the adjustment for changes in biodiversity is relatively simple in the GLOBIO assessment but given the generally clear link between some indicators of biodiversity and the quality and quantity of ecosystem services we felt justified in using the MSA measure as the one to which ecosystem service calculations should be applied.

biomes. In this study, we decided to use the variation in MSA area indicator instead of the area directly, for two reasons. First, this indicator is expressed in terms of area, and it incorporates the impact on biodiversity. The economic impact is assessed through the impact on ecosystem services, which are expected to decrease as a consequence of the pressure on the natural environment, as discussed in the introduction. A common unit of measurement has to be used for this assessment and monetary values are usually provided in terms of values per hectare, which allows for comparisons across different ecosystem services. This is the reason why we need an indicator based on the area on the physical side as well. Second, the use of MSA area instead of the simple area allows us to integrate in the assessment the fact that biodiversity loss is causing a degradation of the ecosystem which in turns reflects a decrease in the provision of ecosystem services.[3]

Two main underlying assumptions are made in this regard. The first is that the provision of ecosystem services is linearly related to the area of the ecosystem and to the magnitude of the biodiversity indicator, the MSA area. The second assumption is that the estimated monetary values per hectare refer to ecosystem services provided in undisturbed environmental conditions.

According to this approach, the following formulation is used to calculate the expected economic impacts associated with a degradation of the ecosystems and related loss of ecosystem services:

$$I = V_h \times \Delta h \times Q \tag{4.1}$$

where I is the estimated economic impact, V_h is the value per hectare of the ecosystem service, Δh is the change in hectares, and Q is the quality of the ecosystem measured as species abundance. The variation in the MSA area indicator, assessed through GLOBIO3, is the combination between the area of the remaining ecosystem and its quality.

Limitations and Uncertainties

GLOBIO3 presents a number of limitations related to the construction of the MSA indicator, the drivers estimated through IMAGE 2.4, and in general to the set of data used.

The MSA area indicator is a pressure-based indicator taking into account the relationship between pressures and species abundance. This relationship has been built on a literature review process in order to construct a meta-analysis, which however includes only a limited set of studies taken from a sample that excludes several biomes, species, and geographical regions. Furthermore, the MSA indicator is constructed by giving equal weight to each hectare, while areas with higher species richness should be assigned a higher weight. In addition this indicator takes into account the change in the number of species but this is an imperfect measure as it does not represent entirely the biodiversity loss (see earlier discussion on the measurement of biodiversity).

However, the most important limitation of this indicator is probably related to the fact that it is not built on individual species, but it is based on the mean calculated over all the species. In this sense "it represents the average response of the total set of species belonging to the ecosystem" (Alkemade et al. 2009, p. 375). This is a major limitation as averages do not take into account the functional relationship between the different elements of an ecosystem and cannot therefore properly assess the health of an ecosystem. As stated in Villa and McLeod (2002, p. 341), "it would be inappropriate to use averages to evaluate the health of an organism on the basis of functionality indicators for its vital organs. Even if the exact dynamics of the interaction are not known, a conservative indicator should be drastically influenced by the fact that even just one is very dysfunctional or subjected to high risk."

Another limitation of the GLOBIO3 model relates to the drivers of biodiversity loss included in the model. Some of them are not considered, such as the impact of augmented carbon dioxide concentration in the atmosphere, increased forest fires, extreme events, and pollution. Lastly, uncertainty also arises from the quality of the data used in the model, related for example to the measurements and forecasts for climate, and the availability of data and maps for agricultural land, forest areas, and infrastructures.

On the other hand, the advantage of this model is that it allows us to assess the impact of MSA on a worldwide basis, which is quite difficult (and controversial) at the current stage considering the lack of quantitative data on global species trends. The results of the GLOBIO3 model have been used in many assessment reports (e.g. UNEP's Global Environment Outlooks, CBD's Global Biodiversity Outlook 2, and the OECD Environmental Outlook). The Convention on Biological Diversity (CBD) accepted the MSA indicator to evaluate the achievement of the 2010 target about the reduction of biodiversity loss at global, regional and national levels.

Projections of MSA Areas

Tables 4.3–4.8 present the main results in terms of MSA area in year 1900, 2000, 2050, and the projected change over those periods. Results are reported per world region and in terms of biomes.

In all the three time-frames, the largest MSA area is recorded for desert, boreal forests, and scrubland and savanna. The world region with the largest MSA area is the OECD (Western and Eastern Europe, US, Canada, Australia and New Zealand). The relative contribution of each biome type within each world region differs in the three periods considered, depending on the shifts recorded over time between type of biome and land use.

The distribution of MSA area by world region remains fairly constant over the two periods 1900–2000 and 2000–2050. In terms of overall losses in the period 1900–2000, it appears from Table 4.6 that the highest loss was recorded for South Asia (SASIA) (40% loss on 1900 levels), followed by Central and South America (CSAM), China (CHN), and the OECD region. In terms of biomes, temperate forests have recorded the highest loss (45% loss on 1900 levels, mainly registered in OECD region), followed by grassland/steppe (mainly in OECD region), scrubland and savanna (mainly in sub-Saharan Africa, SAFR), and tropical forests (mainly in Central and South America, CSAM). These have been the most affected biomes in the period 1900–2000.

Table 4.7 shows the changes in MSA area over the period 2000–2050. South Asia (SASIA) is expected to lose another 30% of MSA area in 50 years, in addition to the 40% loss registered in the previous period over 100 years. Sub-Saharan Africa, (SAFR) will also see a further considerable decrease in MSA area, registering a loss of 18%, comparable to that of

Table 4.3 MSA area by biome and world region, year 1900 (1000 ha)

Biome	OECD	CSAM	MEA-NAFR	SAFR	RUS-CASIA	SASIA	CHN	Total	Percent of total
Ice and tundra	423,734	20,183	0	0	290,684	11,794	178,340	924,735	7.8%
Grassland and steppe	560,128	166,240	105,941	191,707	271,132	64,086	292,332	1,651,566	13.9%
Scrubland and savanna	363,089	454,955	30,511	1,044,123	0	276,279	286	2,169,243	18.3%
Boreal forests	725,526	22,944	0	0	1,160,247	10,150	119,542	2,038,410	17.2%
Temperate forests	620,356	145,706	0	32,704	133,330	63,087	185,196	1,180,380	10.0%
Tropical forests	32,809	909,390	0	354,737	0	338,356	3,770	1,639,062	13.8%
Desert	394,271	21,061	898,727	591,297	121,686	89,565	140,179	2,256,785	19.0%
Total	**3,119,914**	**1,740,480**	**1,035,179**	**2,214,567**	**1,977,079**	**853,318**	**919,645**	**11,860,181**	
Percent of total	26.3%	14.7%	8.7%	18.7%	16.7%	7.2%	7.8%		100.0%

For definitions of regions, see Table 4.2.

Table 4.4 MSA area by biome and world region, year 2000 (1000 ha)

Biome	OECD	CSAM	MEA-NAFR	SAFR	RUS-CASIA	SASIA	CHN	Total	Percent of total
Ice and tundra	405,576	16,983	0	0	279,055	10,167	158,638	870,420	9.3%
Grassland and steppe	385,470	131,285	72,466	145,425	212,944	37,588	215,643	1,200,822	12.9%
Scrubland and savanna	291,855	319,427	17,046	809,263	0	157,025	169	1,594,784	17.1%
Boreal forests	606,849	18,882	0	0	989,207	6,672	84,347	1,705,957	18.3%
Temperate forests	341,601	63,364	0	21,466	91,490	29,761	105,763	653,445	7.0%
Tropical forests	19,219	717,571	0	278,665	0	204,996	2,191	1,222,642	13.1%
Desert	351,629	17,156	848,938	546,730	118,892	66,693	130,857	2,080,896	22.3%
Total	**2,402,199**	**1,284,667**	**938,450**	**1,801,548**	**1,691,589**	**512,904**	**697,609**	**9,328,965**	
Percent of total	25.7%	13.8%	10.1%	19.3%	18.1%	5.5%	7.5%		100.0%

For definitions of regions, see Table 4.2.

Table 4.5 MSA area by biome and world region, year 2050 (1000 ha)

Biome	OECD	CSAM	MEA-NAFR	SAFR	RUS-CASIA	SASIA	CHN	Total	Percent of total
Ice and tundra	381,614	15,041	0	0	258,109	8,684	146,299	809,748	9.9%
Grassland and steppe	322,192	116,629	65,597	114,110	175,338	20,193	191,473	1,005,532	12.3%
Scrubland and savanna	245,209	276,781	14,773	611,574	0	92,045	130	1,240,512	15.2%
Boreal forests	549,979	16,580	0	0	911,206	4,593	72,567	1,554,924	19.0%
Temperate forests	289,280	53,888	0	11,839	74,035	17,671	85,989	532,702	6.5%
Tropical forests	17,321	669,493	0	219,830	0	169,682	1,755	1,078,081	13.2%
Desert	313,272	15,496	818,883	515,059	109,103	44,309	125,653	1,941,774	23.8%
Total	**2,118,867**	**1,163,909**	**899,253**	**1,472,412**	**1,527,791**	**357,177**	**623,864**	**8,163,273**	
Percent of total	26.0%	14.3%	11.0%	18.0%	18.7%	4.4%	7.6%		100.0%

For definitions of regions, see Table 4.2.

Table 4.6 Changes in MSA area by biome and world region, period 1900–2000 (1000 ha)

Biome	OECD	CSAM	MEA-NAFR	SAFR	RUS-CASIA	SASIA	CHN	Total	Percent of 1900 levels
Ice and tundra	−18,158	−3,200	0	0	−11,629	−1,627	−19,701	−54,316	−5.9%
Grassland and steppe	−174,658	−34,955	−33,475	−46,282	−58,187	−26,498	−76,689	−450,744	−27.3%
Scrubland and savanna	−71,234	−135,528	−13,465	−234,860	0	−119,254	−118	−574,459	−26.5%
Boreal forests	−118,677	−4,062	0	0	−171,040	−3,478	−35,195	−332,452	−16.3%
Temperate forests	−278,755	−82,342	0	−11,238	−41,840	−33,326	−79,433	−526,934	−44.6%
Tropical forests	−13,590	−191,819	0	−76,072	0	−133,360	−1,579	−416,421	−25.4%
Desert	−42,642	−3,905	−49,790	−44,567	−2,793	−22,872	−9,321	−175,890	−7.8%
Total	**−717,715**	**−455,812**	**−96,729**	**−413,019**	**−285,489**	**−340,414**	**−222,036**	**−2,531,216**	
Percent of 1900 levels	−23.0%	−26.2%	−9.3%	−18.7%	−14.4%	−39.9%	−24.1%		−21.3%

For definitions of regions, see Table 4.2.

Table 4.7 Changes in MSA area by biome and world region, period 2000–2050 (1000 ha)

Biome	OECD	CSAM	MEA-NAFR	SAFR	RUS-CASIA	SASIA	CHN	Total	Percent of 2000 levels
Ice and tundra	−23,962	−1,942	0	0	−20,946	−1,483	−12,339	−60,672	−7.0%
Grassland and steppe	−63,278	−14,656	−6,869	−31,315	−37,606	−17,395	−24,171	−195,289	−16.3%
Scrubland and savanna	−46,646	−42,645	−2,273	−197,689	0	−64,980	−39	−354,272	−22.2%
Boreal forests	−56,870	−2,302	0	0	−78,001	−2,079	−11,780	−151,033	−8.9%
Temperate forests	−52,321	−9,476	0	−9,627	−17,456	−12,091	−19,775	−120,744	−18.5%
Tropical forests	−1,897	−48,078	0	−58,835	0	−35,314	−436	−144,560	−11.8%
Desert	−38,357	−1,660	−30,055	−31,671	−9,790	−22,385	−5,205	−139,122	−6.7%
Total	**−283,332**	**−120,759**	**−39,197**	**−329,137**	**−163,798**	**−155,726**	**−73,745**	**−1,165,693**	
Percent of 2000 levels	−11.8%	−9.4%	−4.2%	−18.3%	−9.7%	−30.4%	−10.6%		−12.5%

For definitions of regions, see Table 4.2.

the previous period but referring to 50 years only. In the other regions the decrease in MSA area is expected to be smaller but follows the same trend registered in the previous period. If we look at the most affected biomes, the period 2000–2050 will see the highest loss in scrubland and savanna (22%, mainly in sub-Saharan Africa SAFR), followed by temperate forests (18%, mainly in the OECD region), grassland/steppe (16%, mainly in the OECD region) and tropical forests (12%, mainly in sub-Saharan Africa, SAFR).

There is a shift registered in the type of biome affected over time, due to the combination of the different pressures in terms of land-use change, infrastructures, climate change, fragmentation, etc. While in the period 1900–2000 the most affected biome is temperate forest (the OECD region having the highest loss), in the period 2000–2050 the most vulnerable biome turns out to be scrubland and savanna (with the highest decrease in sub-Saharan Africa). Overall, the estimated loss of MSA area is significant (21% in 1900–2000 and 12% in 2000–2050, with a total loss of 31% over the whole period), and the most affected regions are South Asia and sub-Saharan Africa (Table 4.8).

The Economic Impact

The methodological approach adopted to estimate the economic loss associated with a loss of MSA area is largely based on the study of Chiabai et al. (2011). The economic impact is assessed through the loss of ecosystem services engendered by a degradation of the ecosystem, this latter being measured in terms of loss of MSA area.

Ecosystem services have been valued in the literature using a broad set of methodologies, ranging from market to non-market techniques, depending on the type of benefits considered. In this study we use a combination of methods, following the framework developed in Chiabai et al. (2011) and adapting it to the specific context under analysis. Monetary values are available in different metrics,

Table 4.8 Changes in MSA area by biome and world region, period 1900–2050 (1000 ha)

Biome	OECD	CSAM	MEA-NAFR	SAFR	RUS-CASIA	SASIA	CHN	Total	Percent of total
Ice and tundra	−42,120	−5,143	0	0	−32,575	−3,110	−32,041	−114,988	−12.4%
Grassland and steppe	−237,937	−49,611	−40,343	−77,596	−95,793	−43,893	−100,859	−646,033	−39.1%
Scrubland and savanna	−117,880	−178,173	−15,738	−432,549	0	−184,234	−157	−928,731	−42.8%
Boreal forests	−175,548	−6,364	0	0	−249,041	−5,557	−46,975	−483,485	−23.7%
Temperate forests	−331,076	−91,818	0	−20,865	−59,296	−45,416	−99,207	−647,678	−54.9%
Tropical forests	−15,487	−239,897	0	−134,907	0	−168,674	−2,015	−560,981	−34.2%
Desert	−80,999	−5,565	−79,845	−76,238	−12,583	−45,256	−14,526	−315,012	−14.0%
Total	**−1,001,047**	**−576,571**	**−135,926**	**−742,155**	**−449,287**	**−496,141**	**−295,781**	**−3,696,908**	
Percent of 1900 levels	−32.1%	−33.1%	−13.1%	−33.5%	−22.7%	−58.1%	−32.2%		−31.2%

For definitions of regions, see Table 4.2.

but for comparability purposes we refer to values per hectare. The economic impact is estimated over two periods of time, 1900–2000 and 2000–2050, for which MSA data were available in terms of point estimates in time. We use therefore MSA data for the years 1900, 2000, and 2050, and we combine them with monetary values of ecosystem services (present value), estimated on a per hectare basis. Basically, first we estimate the loss in terms of present values, and second we convert these latter into annual economic flows using the formula of perpetual revenue under the assumption of constant flows over time. It was not possible to estimate annual flows independently, due to the huge amount of data and information necessary for this purpose, both on the physical and economic side, in terms of MSA data, quantitative flows of ecosystem services and monetary values per year. Present values are however very important as they refer to the existing natural capital and changes in the latter show the actual depletion of natural resources. Natural capital includes natural resources (e.g. trees, fish, minerals), land, and ecosystems, which provide flows of

environmental goods and services to human being. An adequate natural capital has to be maintained over time to generate sufficient flows of ecosystem services in a condition of long-term sustainability. If this is not preserved, then its ability to generate perpetual flows is compromised.

The economic impact (loss or gain) is estimated in year 2000 and in year 2050 for the two time-frames. Original economic values are taken from the literature and standardized to the year 2000 to build a baseline scenario. These values are projected in a second step in year 2050 following different assumptions and methods according to the type of ecosystem services analyzed; and for the year 1900 based on the assumption that the 1900 levels of services are available in 2000. In this way we have point estimates in the time-frame 1900–2050. It was not possible to present the analysis for year 1900 or for 1950 with the economic and social conditions that prevailed in that year, for two main reasons. First, original monetary estimates of ecosystem services are not available for those years. Second, the value transfer back to 1900 or 1950 was not feasible for some ecosystem services, such as carbon and timber, due to insufficient and inadequate economic statistics. An assessment back to 1900 would indeed require an extrapolation for constructing new estimates beyond the known trends with insufficient data, resulting in too much uncertainty.

The analysis of the economic impact is carried out for the following biomes, for which economic data were available: grasslands/steppe, and boreal, temperate, and tropical forests. The ecosystem service analyzed in the forest biomes include wood and non-wood forests products, carbon, and cultural services (recreational and passive use). As regards grasslands/steppe, we estimated the impact on food provisioning, erosion prevention, conservation, recreation, and amenity. The choice of these ecosystem services is mainly based on the availability of physical data and monetary estimates.

The specific methods used for each ecosystem service and biome, underlying assumptions and methodological limitations are discussed below, together with the results presented in terms of values per hectare for the two years 2000 and 2050. The economic impacts are estimated based on the three calculations for these two years.

Forests

Wood and Non-Wood Forest Products

Wood forests products (WFPs) are estimated taking into account seven economic sectors, including industrial roundwood, wood pulp, recovered paper, sawnwood, wood-based panels, paper and paper board, and wood fuel. Non-wood forest products (NWFPs) include goods and services of biological origin derived from the forest, as defined by FAO (1999) (Table 4.9).

The estimation process differs for WFP and NWFP. For the former we used an approximation of the stumpage price (the value of standing trees),[4] calculated by taking into account export/import values and quantities, and domestic production for

[4] Stumpage is the value paid by a contractor to the landowner for the standing trees in a designated harvest area. The contractor assumes the right to harvest the trees, under specific requirements concerning the timing of harvest or the conservation of the area.

Table 4.9 Non-wood forest products

Plant products	Animal products
Food	Living animals
Fodder	Hides, skins, and trophies
Raw material for medicine and aromatic products	Wild honey and beeswax
Raw material for colorants and dyes	Bushmeat
Raw material for utensils, crafts, and construction	Other edible animal products
Ornamental plants	
Exudates	
Other plant products	

Source: FAOSTAT and FAO/FRA 2005. Adapted from Chiabai *et al.* (2011).

year 2000 (http://faostat.fao.org/site/626/default.aspx#ancor), finally adjusted for net profit (Bolt *et al.* 2002). The assessment is made at the country level using the bottom–up approach followed in Chiabai *et al.* (2011). The calculation has been however adjusted to take into account also import values/quantities besides export values/quantities:

$$V_{i,j} = \left[VIE_{i,j} \times \frac{QP_{i,j}}{QIE_{i,j}} \right] \times p_i \qquad (4.2)$$

where $V_{i,j}$ represents the annual value of WFPs by country i and product j, $VIE_{i,j}$ is the average of the annual import and export values, $QP_{i,j}$ is the annual domestic production quantity, $QIE_{i,j}$ is the average of annual import and export quantities, and p is the profit rate. We took as reference the year 2000 and we computed all the values in US$ as of 2000. These values are aggregated across countries and divided by the forest area designated to timber production in each country and forest biome in 2000, using a weighted mean. According to this approach, we are assuming a constant productivity factor for each forest hectare. This is a limitation of the estimates, as productivity is actually influenced by the type of forest. The lack of economic data (export and import values and quantities, profit rates) by forest type for each country compelled us to make this simplifying assumption.

As regards NWFPs, these can be plants or animals, the former including for example medicinal or aromatic plants, ornamental plants, raw material for utensils, colorants, and dyes, and the second referring to hides, skins, trophies, wild honey, bushmeat, etc. These are estimated using information from FAO, which provide export values of the total removals of these products by country. Export values are aggregated by region and divided by the total forest area to get an annual value per hectare. These NWFPs play an important role for indigenous people in developing countries; however their contribution to the economy is very low, compared to timber and other WFPs.

For both WFPs and NWFPs, values estimated for year 2000 are assumed to be constant over time.[5] Considering that the natural capital is generating flows of ES year after year, and that the flows can be translated into monetary terms, we can convert the latter into a present value, using the following formulation:

$$PV_i = \sum_{t=1}^{T} \frac{[(V_i)]_t}{(1+d)^t} \tag{4.3}$$

where PV_i is the present value per hectare of WFPs and NWFPs for country i calculated for the baseline year 2000, V_i is the annual value per hectare, and d is the discount rate. As V_i is constant over time the formulation is simplified by dividing this value by the discount rate. A 3% rate is used for this calculation. It is assumed that flows of WFP and NWFP will continue over time constantly (i.e. that the use of the resource is broadly sustainable). Table 4.10 reports the present values per hectare generated by WFPs and NWFPs in the baseline year 2000. We do not differentiate between the two categories as NWFPs provide a very low contribution to the total present value, ranging from 0.02% to a maximum of 1.93%, as estimated in Chiabai *et al.* (2011). These values can be used also for the projections in year 2050, as no increase in real prices for timber is expected globally in the long run, as discussed in Chiabai *et al.* (2011) and Clark (2001).

The highest values are registered for tropical forests in sub-Saharan Africa (SAFR), and boreal forests in South Asia (SASIA) and China (CHN) regions. Temperate forests generate much lower

Table 4.10 Present values for WFPs and NWFPs (2000 US$/ha)

World regions	Forest biomes		
	Boreal	Temperate	Tropical
OECD	83,738	29,980	5,711
CSAM	24,343	159	36,115
MEA-NAFR	–	–	–
SAFR	–	714	111,214
RUS-CASIA	9,258	4,733	–
SASIA	100,559	5,689	47,002
CHN	89,177	19,123	1,678

For definitions of regions, see Table 4.2.

values. According to these estimates, tropical and boreal forests generate much higher economic values than temperate forests. As discussed in detail in Chiabai *et al.* (2011), values per hectare for WFPs are overestimated as we presume that timber removal occurs only in plantations, while in reality it takes place also in primary forests. Illegal harvesting is not considered in our calculations due to lack of reliable data on its dimension.

Carbon

The estimation process is based on the quantitative assessment of the biomass carbon capacity by forest type and country, and consequently the calculation of a price of carbon stocked per hectare, following the approach suggested in Chiabai *et al.* (2011). The carbon capacity is taken from the literature, and basically from two studies, Myneni *et al.* (2001) and Gibbs (2007). These studies make use of the biome average approach to calculate the average carbon capacity in different forest biomes. The approach is based on direct estimates of the existing forest biomass (Reichle 1981; Olson *et al.* 1983), complemented by the analysis of forest inventories archived by the FAO (Gibbs 2007). The advantage of this method is related to the availability of these figures at a global scale, but the limitation is due to

---

[5] This assumption was corroborated by an analysis of the timber prices and associated rents in the World Bank database (Bolt *et al.* 2002). See Chiabai *et al.* (2011).

Table 4.11 Present values for carbon stocks in year 2000 (2000 US$/ha)

| World region | Forest biomes | | | | | |
| | Boreal | | Temperate | | Tropical | |
	LB	UB	LB	UB	LB	UB
OECD	593	7,858	828	10,974	1,547	20,502
CSAM	270	3,575	748	9,912	2,658	35,221
MEA-NAFR	–	–	–	–	–	–
SAFR	–	–	943	12,490	3,174	42,055
RUS-CASIA	598	7,922	773	10,238	–	–
SASIA	943	12,490	1,804	23,908	2,515	33,328
CHN	409	5,419	409	5,419	1,523	20,186

LB, lower bound; UB, upper bound. LB = US$4 per tonne of CO_2. UB = US$53 per tonne of CO_2.
For definitions of regions, see Table 4.2.

inadequate sampling at national level, so that the data cover only specific locations while important portions of the forest are not taken into account.

In our estimates we used the data available at country level, and we assumed the same carbon capacity for the regions not covered by the two studies when located in the same geographical area and covered by the same type of forest. The countries included in the two studies are Canada, Northern America, China, Japan, Russia, Finland, Sweden, Eurasia, South Eastern Asia, Brazilian Amazon, Latin America, sub-Saharan Africa, and tropical Asia. According to Myneni *et al.* (2001), forest carbon capacity ranges from an average of 25.77 tC ha^{-1} in China to an average of 59.4 tC ha^{-1} in some European countries such as Austria, Belgium, Croatia, Czech Republic, Denmark, France, Germany, Greece, Italy, Netherlands, Norway, Poland, Portugal, Slovenia, Spain, Switzerland, Turkey, and the United Kingdom. Gibbs *et al.* (2007) provide estimates of carbon capacity for tropical forests in different countries making reference to a number of studies (Brown 1997; Houghton 1999; DeFries *et al.* 2002; Achard *et al.* 2004; IPCC 2006; Gibbs and Brown 2007a, 2007b), according to which carbon capacity ranges from 17 tC ha^{-1} in sub-Saharan Africa tropical dry forests to 250 tC ha^{-1} in Asian tropical equatorial forests.

The second step consists of using estimated prices per ton of CO_2, converting them into prices

per tonne of carbon (1 ton carbon ≈ 3.66 tons CO_2) and calculating the present value of carbon stocked in forests, multiplying the price per tC by the carbon capacity. The price per tonne of CO_2 is taken from Markandya *et al.* (2010), who provide values ranging from US$4 to US$53 per tonne of CO_2 for year 2000, and US$13–179 for year 2050. Tables 4.11 and 4.12 report present values for carbon stocks for the years 2000 and 2050, in 2000 US$.

Tropical forests register in general the highest values, specifically in sub-Saharan Africa (SAFR), Central and South America (CSAM), and South Asia (SASIA), which depends on the high capacity of carbon capacity in this forest biome. A limitation of these estimates is that we have not considered different land uses, which is a main factor of variation in carbon sequestration capacity, as well as altitude, slope, and similar features related to the type of land and soil, due to the lack of data at a global scale.

Cultural Services

Forest cultural services comprise recreational and passive use values, which are estimated using meta-analysis, value transfer, and scaling-up techniques as performed in Chiabai *et al.* (2011). The meta-regression function used to estimate these values takes the following form:

$$V = f(S, I) \tag{4.4}$$

Table 4.12 Present values for carbon stocks in year 2050 (2000 US$/ha)

	Forest biomes					
	Boreal		Temperate		Tropical	
World region	LB	UB	LB	UB	LB	UB
OECD	1,927	26,539	2,692	37,062	5,029	69,242
CSAM	877	12,073	2,431	33,477	8,639	118,954
MEA-NAFR	–	–	–	–	–	–
SAFR	–	–	3,064	42,184	10,315	142,034
RUS-CASIA	1,943	26,756	2,511	34,578	–	–
SASIA	3,064	42,184	5,864	80,747	8,175	112,562
CHN	1,329	18,301	1,329	18,301	4,951	68,176

LB, lower bound; UB, upper bound. LB = US$13 per tonne of CO_2. UB = US$179 per tonne of CO_2.
For definitions of regions, see Table 4.2.

where V is the annual value (recreational or passive use, based on willingness to pay, WTP), S and I are explanatory variables, the first representing the forest-related features, such as forest area and forest type, and I includes socio-economic variables such as income per capita and population of the country. We used the β coefficients (which give the sensitivity of the annual estimated values to changes in the explanatory variables) estimated in Chiabai *et al.* (2011) to carry out a value transfer from the study sites to the policy sites, and scaling up from national to regional level. The coefficients on income are in the range of 0.63 for recreational values and 0.75 for passive use, while the coefficients on forest size are −0.43 for recreation and −0.39 for passive use. For the latter population is also significant and positive, with a coefficient of 0.64.

The value transfer and scaling-up is performed using the following equation:

$$V_p = V_s^* \left(\frac{P_p}{P_s}\right)^\delta \left(\frac{S_p}{S_s}\right)^\sigma \left(\frac{I_p}{I_s}\right)^\gamma \qquad (4.5)$$

where V_s^* is the average annual value for the world region having original or study site values (taken from the literature), V_p is the value we would like to estimate which refers to world regions for which no original value exists (policy sites), P is the population of the country, I the country GDP per capita (adjusted for the purchasing power parity, World Bank World Development Indicators), and S is the forest size designed to recreation or conservation (ftp://ftp.fao.org/docrep/fao/008/A0400E/A0400E00.pdf).

Most of the studies for recreation and passive use (based on stated and revealed preferences) are from Europe and North America. Mean and median WTP for these regions are therefore used as reference values to carry out the value transfer. All the original values from Chiabai *et al.* (2011) have been re-estimated using the world regions and forest biomes analyzed in the current study. The original values represent annual flows in terms US$ per hectare per year. These have been transformed into present values using a 3% discount rate assuming perpetual constant flows generated by the forests (see equation (4.3)). Values are finally projected from 2000 to 2050 using the coefficients estimated in the meta-regression mentioned above.

Tables 4.13–4.16 show the estimated present values in year 2000 and 2050, both presented in 2000 US$. The highest values for passive use are estimated for OECD region and China (CHN), while the highest recreational values are registered respectively in China (CHN) and South Asia (SASIA). Values are obviously increasing between 2000 and 2050 but the rate of increase differs considerably between world regions, ranging from 1.9 to 4.2 increase for passive use values, and from 1.6 to 3 for recreational values. This can be explained mainly by the depletion and

Table 4.13 Value-transfer results: present values for passive use in year 2000 (2000 US$/ha)

World region	Mean	Median	Maximum	Minimum
OECD	53,203	44,712	148,296	16,678
CSAM	20,175	16,955	56,234	6,324
MEA-NAFR	–	–	–	–
SAFR	24,976	20,990	69,617	7,829
RUS-CASIA	8,307	6,981	23,155	2,604
SASIA	18,135	15,241	50,549	5,685
CHN	40,255	33,830	112,204	12,619

For definitions of regions, see Table 4.2.

Table 4.14 Value-transfer results: present values for passive use in year 2050 (2000 US$/ha)

World region	Mean	Median	Maximum	Minimum
OECD	104,531	87,848	291,365	32,768
CSAM	45,678	38,388	127,321	14,319
MEA-NAFR	–	–	–	–
SAFR	95,854	80,556	267,179	30,048
RUS-CASIA	27,096	22,771	75,525	8,494
SASIA	76,666	64,430	213,695	24,033
CHN	158,131	132,894	440,768	49,571

For definitions of regions, see Table 4.2.

Table 4.15 Value-transfer results: present values for recreation in year 2000 (2000 US$/ha)

World region	Mean	Median	Maximum	Minimum
OECD	39,837	9,396	212,509	203
CSAM	6,138	1,448	32,746	31
MEA-NAFR	–	–	–	–
SAFR	16,764	3,954	89,425	86
RUS-CASIA	2,568	606	13,700	13
SASIA	61,859	14,591	329,990	316
CHN	62,421	14,723	332,986	319

For definitions of regions, see Table 4.2.

Table 4.16 Value-transfer results: present value for recreation in year 2050 (2000 US$/ha)

World region	Mean	Median	Maximum	Minimum
OECD	65,461	15,440	349,204	334
CSAM	10,721	2,529	57,190	55
MEA-NAFR	–	–	–	–
SAFR	34,782	8,204	185,547	178
RUS-CASIA	7,532	1,777	40,179	38
SASIA	166,777	39,337	889,672	851
CHN	190,657	44,970	1,017,060	973

For definitions of regions, see Table 4.2.

degradation of forests, consistently with the "diminishing marginal utility" theory according to which the first unit of a good provides the consumer with a higher utility than the successive units. Therefore, if the good becomes scarcer, then its value is boosted up. In addition, the estimates in 2050 depend on the projected population and GDP increase, which are expected to rise differently country by country.

Grassland and Steppe

The values of ecosystem services in grassland are estimated using the database values and the

[6] Contingent valuation and choice experiments have been used for recreational values of grasslands and wildlife conservation, hedonic pricing has been used for the amenity value, and the net factor income and market prices have been used to estimate food provisioning (Hussain *et al.* 2011).

coefficients of the meta-regression function as calculated in Hussain *et al.* (2011). The following ecosystem service categories are valued within this biome: food provisioning, recreation and amenity, erosion prevention, and conservation. The countries considered in the assessment include Northern Europe, United States, Asia, and Africa. The limitation of this approach is that we can estimate an overall value of ecosystem services provided by grassland, while we cannot provide values for any specific ecosystem service. The meta-regression function takes the following form:

$$V = f(S, R, A, I) \tag{4.6}$$

where V is the annual value of ecosystem services provided by grasslands from the existing case studies,[6] S is the grassland area within 50-km radius of the study site, R is the length of roads within 50-km radius of the study site, A is an accessibility index, I is the country GDP per capita (measured in purchasing power parity, PPP).

The results of the meta-regression show that the estimated coefficients have the expected signs, but only one variable is significant, namely the accessibility index, which indicates that grasslands with higher accessibility have a higher value. Income has a positive sign, which means that grasslands located in richer countries have higher economic value. The grassland area is negative, which is due to a substitution effect influencing negatively its value. Finally, the existence of roads impacts negatively the value of the grassland ecosystem services, which is due to a fragmentation effect as discussed in Hussain *et al.* (2011).

Due to the limitation of data in this context, we used the coefficients on income only, being of the expected sign, to transfer the ecosystem services grassland values from the original case study sites to policy sites, using the following equation:

$$V_i = V_s^* \left(\frac{I_i}{I_s} \right)^\gamma \qquad (4.7)$$

where V_i is the annual estimated value for grassland in the world region i, V_s^* is the annual mean or median value observed in the original case studies described in Hussain *et al.* (2011), and I is the GDP per capita adjusted using PPP. Original values estimated in Hussain *et al.* (2011) are annual values and

have been converted into present values using a 3% discount rate. Values are finally projected to year 2050 using the following equation:

$$V_{i,T_1} = V_{i,T_0} \left(\frac{I_{i,T_1}}{I_{i,T_0}} \right)^\gamma \qquad (4.8)$$

where V_{i,T_0} is the value for the world region i in year 2000, V_{i,T_1} is the value projected to year 2050, T_0 is the baseline 2000 year and T_1 is the projection year 2050. Results are presented in Tables 4.17 and 4.18 below. The highest values are registered for OECD region, China (CHN), and Russia and Central Asia (RUS-CASIA).

The rate of increase from year 2000 to year 2050 ranges from 1.9 (for China) to 3.6 (for Russia).

The Economic Impact Related to a Loss of MSA Area

The economic impact associated with a decrease in the MSA area decrease is calculated for two periods of time, 1900–2000 and 2000–2050, taking into account both changes in present values and in annual economic flows, by world region and biome. The variation in the present value is related to the change in the natural capital (represented in this study by the four biomes types), and is calculated by multiplying the estimated present values per hectare (for each ecosystem services in each biome and each world

Table 4.17 Value-transfer results for grassland ecosystem services, stock values in year 2000 (2000 US$/ha)

World region	Mean	Median
OECD	5,930	1,027
CSAM	2,969	514
MEA-NAFR	2,139	370
SAFR	1,126	195
RUS-CASIA	3,231	559
SASIA	2,381	412
CHN	5,806	1,005

For definitions of regions, see Table 4.2.

Table 4.18 Value-transfer results for grassland ecosystem services, stock values in year 2050 (2000 US$/ha)

World region	Mean	Median
OECD	17,015	2,945
CSAM	6,124	1,060
MEA-NAFR	6,646	1,151
SAFR	3,024	524
RUS-CASIA	11,914	2,062
SASIA	5,105	884
CHN	11,253	1,948

For definitions of regions, see Table 4.2.

region) by the projected change in MSA areas for the two periods under analysis. For WFP and forest cultural services, we used the forest area designated respectively to plantations, recreation and conservation available from FAO data for year 2005. Due to data limitation, forest land uses are assumed to be constant from 1900 to 2050, which is a simplifying assumption.

Gross Economic Impact on Natural Capital

The changes in the present value or natural capital for the two periods are presented in Tables 4.19 and 4.20. Gross losses are reported in US$2000 separately for the two periods, 1900–2000 and 2000–2050. The highest losses in the period 1900–2000 are registered in OECD region, Central and South America (CSAM), and South Asia (SASIA), while in the period 2000–2050 the expected losses are greatest for sub-Saharan Africa (SAFR), besides the OECD region and South Asia. As regards the type of biome concerned, the greatest impact is estimated for tropical forests in both periods. In general forests are most affected than grassland and steppe. Annex 4.1 reports the changes in present value for the four forest ecosystem services, carbon, WFP and NWFP, recreation, and passive use, by forest type and world region.

Figures 4.1–4.4 show the percent share of the total loss by geographical region in the upper- and lower-bound scenarios. In the period 1900–2000, the highest share of loss is for the OECD, followed by Central/South America (CSAM) and South Asia (SASIA) for the upper-bound scenario, while in the lower-bound scenario OECD region is followed by South Asia (SASIA) and China (CHN) (the precise ranking depending on the value of carbon). In the period 2000–2050, sub-Saharan Africa shows an increase in the expected economic loss and is ranked in the first place in the upper-bound scenario. The OECD region is still among the highest affected, but with a lower share of total losses, followed by

Central/South America (in the upper-bound scenario).

Net Economic Impacts on Annual Flows Provided by Ecosystem Services Taking Account of Agricultural Benefits

In this section the changes in values of natural capital as estimated above are converted into annual flows using the conventional 3% discount rate (see equation (4.3)) and compared with the expected flows of benefits generated by agricultural production.[7] Basically, we assume that the hectares lost in grassland and forests are converted into agricultural land and the associated economic benefits are calculated as follows:

$$AgB_i = GDPA_i \left(\frac{\Delta MSAarea_i}{Ag_i} \right) \qquad (4.10)$$

where AgB_i represents the expected benefits from agricultural production in world region i, $GDPA_i$ is the GDP in the agricultural sector, $\Delta MSAarea$ is the registered variation in the MSA area in forests and grassland, and AG_i is the area designated to agriculture in each world region. The formula is calculated for both year 2000 and 2050 (Bakkes and Bosch 2008).

Tables 4.21 and 4.22 present the final results related to changes in annual gross flows in the periods 1900–2000 and 2000–2050, expected benefits from the agricultural sector and net economic losses or gains in terms of 2000 and 2050 GDP.

The loss in MSA area always generates an annual economic loss due to a reduced provision of ecosystem services. However, when account is taken of the agricultural benefits these losses can be offset in some regions. Results in Table 4.21 show an impact at worldwide level ranging from a net benefit of 0.03% to a net loss of −2.0% of 2000 GDP. The world region reporting the highest loss in the period 1900–2000 is sub-Saharan Africa (SAFR), with up to 32% loss of 2000 GDP, mainly in tropical forests. Central and South America (CSAM) follow, with a 6.2% net loss in the upper-bound scenario. South Asia (SASIA) and China (CHN) report a net benefit, while the other regions show mixed results ranging from a benefit in the lower-bound scenario to a loss in the upper-bound scenario. As regards the specific biomes analyzed, the highest economic loss

---

[7] The conversion of carbon stock values to flows is an artificial construct as in fact the carbon stock does not represent a present value of a sequence of flows. Rather the flow associated with a given carbon stock gives us an annuity that would result to someone who had securitized that capital value of the carbon.

Table 4.19 Change in present values due to MSA area loss 1900–2000 (billion 2000 US$)

Biome	OECD		CSAM		MEA-NAFR		SAFR		RUS-CASIA		SASIA		CHN		Total	
	LB	UB	LB	UB	LB	UB	LB	UB	LB	UB	LB	UB	LB	UB	LB	UB
Grassland/steppe	−179	−1,036	−18	−104	−12	−72	−9	−52	−33	−188	−11	−63	−77	−445	−339	−1,960
Boreal forests	−3,270	−4,433	−25	−43	0	0	0	0	−1,114	−2,446	−139	−183	−1,873	−2,076	−6,421	−9,181
Temperate forests	−4,043	−7,578	−304	−1,151	0	0	−57	−199	−179	−595	−264	−1,041	−1,000	−1,457	−5,847	−12,022
Tropical forests	−121	−413	−1,935	−8,395	0	0	−2,379	−5,424	0	0	−3,054	−7,326	−6	−36	−7,495	−21,595
Total	**−7,612**	**−13,460**	**−2,283**	**−9,693**	**−12**	**−72**	**−2,444**	**−5,676**	**−1,326**	**−3,229**	**−3,468**	**−8,614**	**−2,956**	**−4,015**	**−20,101**	**−44,757**
Percent of total	−38%	−30%	−11%	−22%	−0.1%	−0.2%	−12%	−13%	−7%	−7%	−17%	−19%	−15%	−9%		

LB, lower bound; UB, upper bound. LB = US$4 per tonne of CO_2, and median values for grasslands, forest recreation, and passive use. UB = US$53 per tonne of CO_2, and mean values for grasslands, forest recreation, and passive use.

For definitions of regions, see Table 4.2.

Table 4.20 Change in present values due to MSA area loss 2000–2050 (billion 2000 US$)

Biome	OECD		CSAM		MEA-NAFR		SAFR		RUS-CASIA		SASIA		CHN		Total	
	LB	UB	LB	UB	LB	UB	LB	UB	LB	UB	LB	UB	LB	UB	LB	UB
Grassland/ steppe	−186	−1,077	−16	−90	−8	−46	−16	−95	−78	−448	−15	−89	−47	−272	−366	−2,116
Boreal forests	−1,978	−3,636	−24	−55	0	0	0	0	−788	−2,833	−115	−205	−674	−902	−3,578	−7,631
Temperate forests	−1,165	−3,200	−85	−400	0	0	−174	−586	−144	−729	−304	−1,263	−327	−711	−2,200	−6,890
Tropical forests	−35	−165	−946	−6,356	0	0	−2,903	−10,869	0	0	−1,474	−5,317	−4	−33	−5,362	−22,740
Total	**−3,365**	**−8,078**	**−1,071**	**−6,901**	**−8**	**−46**	**−3,093**	**−11,549**	**−1,010**	**−4,010**	**−1,908**	**−6,875**	**−1,052**	**−1,918**	**−11,506**	**−39,377**
Percent of total	**−29%**	**−21%**	**−9%**	**−18%**	**−0.1%**	**−0.1%**	**−27%**	**−29%**	**−9%**	**−10%**	**−17%**	**−17%**	**−9%**	**−5%**		

LB, lower bound; UB, upper bound. LB = US$13 per tonne of CO_2, and median values for grasslands, forest recreation, and passive use. UB = US$179 per tonne of CO_2, and mean values for grasslands, forest recreation, and passive use.
For definitions of regions, see Table 4.2.

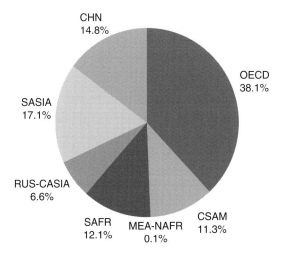

Figure 4.1 *Gross economic loss by region, 1900–2000 (lower-bound scenario)*

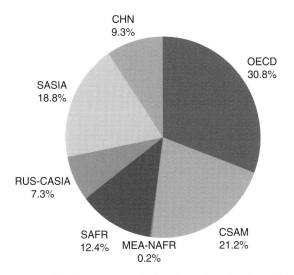

Figure 4.2 *Gross economic loss by region, 1900–2000 (upper-bound scenario)*

is estimated in tropical forests, followed by temperate and boreal forests, while grasslands are much less impacted.

Table 4.22 presents the results for the period 2000–2050, showing a net benefit at a global scale ranging from 0.05% to 0.48% of 2050 GDP. Sub-Saharan Africa (SAFR) and Central and South America (CSAM) are the most impacted geographical regions and report a loss in the upper-bound scenario of respectively 1.2% and 1.5% of 2050 GDP, mainly registered in tropical forests.

We report here below a brief analysis of the changes in annual gross flows for the forest ecosystem services, which can explain some of these trends (i.e. without accounting for the agricultural benefits). Results by world regions sometimes differ from those obtained in Chiabai *et al.* (2011), which is related to the different geographical aggregation used in the two studies. The large impact in all ecosystem services expected in tropical forests, as discussed here below, can be explained by the combined effect of a decrease in MSA area (12% from 2000 to 2050, as

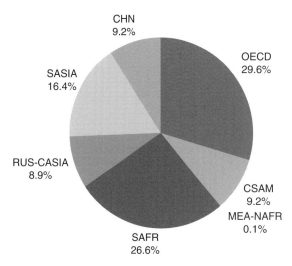

Figure 4.3 *Gross economic loss by region, 2000–2050 (lower-bound scenario)*

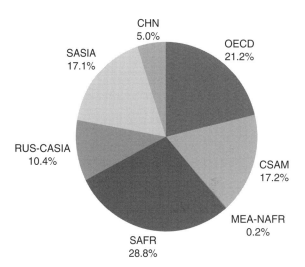

Figure 4.4 *Gross economic loss by region, 2000–2050 (upper-bound scenario)*

shown in Table 4.7) and high economic values per hectare.

Carbon in Forests

As regards carbon, sub-Saharan Africa (SAFR) is the most impacted region with a damage ranging from 1.5% to 20% of the country 2000 GDP in the period 1900–2000 (Table 4.23), and from 0.1% to 2% of the 2050 GDP in the period 2000–2050

(Table 4.24). Central and South America (CSAM) follows with a lower percent of damage. The much lower proportion of damages expected by 2050 is due to the fact that the loss is measured in 2050 GDP, which is expected to increase considerably in all countries. In absolute terms, however, economic losses related to carbon in SAFR in the next 50 years are twice as high as in the previous 100 years, and are almost the same in the other world regions. In SAFR and CSAM the loss is mainly

Table 4.21 Change in annual values due to MSA area loss 1900–2000, discount 3% (billion 2000 US$)

Biome	OECD		CSAM		MEA-NAFR		SAFR		RUS-CASIA		SASIA		CHN		Total			Percent of 2000 GDP	
	LB	UB	LB	UB	LB	UB	LB	UB	LB	UB	LB	UB	LB	UB	LB	mid range	UB	LB	UB
Grassland/steppe	−5.4	−31	−0.5	−3.1	−0.4	−2	−0.3	−1.6	−1.0	−5.6	−0.3	−1.9	−2.3	−13	−10	−34	−59	−0.05%	−0.27%
Boreal forests	−98	−133	−0.8	−1.3	0	0	0	0	−33	−73	−4.2	−5.5	−56	−62	−193	−234	−275	−0.5%	−0.8%
Temperate forests	−121	−227	−9.1	−35	0	0	−2	−6	−5.4	−17.8	−7.9	−31	−30	−44	−175	−268	−361	−0.5%	−1.0%
Tropical forests	−3.6	−12.4	−58	−252	0	0	−71	−163	0	0	−92	−220	−0.2	−1.1	−225	−436	−648	−0.6%	−1.8%
Total flow loss	**−228**	**−404**	**−68**	**−291**	**−0.4**	**−2.1**	**−73**	**−170**	**−40**	**−97**	**−104**	**−258**	**−89**	**−120**	**−603**	**−973**	**−1,343**	**−1.7%**	**−3.8%**
Benefit agricultural production	**404**		**101**		**2.8**		**11.3**		**49**		**752**		**169**		**614**			1.7%	2.9%
Net loss or benefit	175.3	−0.2	32.6	−189.7	2.5	0.7	−62.0	−159.0	9.0	−48.1	468.5	314.1	78.6	46.8	10.9	−358.9	−728.8		
Percent of 2000 GDP	1.0%	−0.001%	1.1%	−6.2%	0.5%	0.1%	−12.6%	−32.4%	0.7%	−3.7%	11.5%	7.7%	1.6%	1.0%	0.03%	−1.0%	−2.0%		

LB, lower bound; UB, upper bound. LB = US$4 per tonne of CO_2, and median values for grasslands, forest recreation, and passive use. UB = US$53 per tonne of CO_2, and mean values for grasslands, forest recreation, and passive use.

For definitions of regions, see Table 4.2.

Table 4.22 Change in annual values due to MSA area loss 2000–2050, discount 3% (billion 2000 US$)

Biome	OECD		CSAM		MEA-NAFR		SAFR		RUS-CASIA		SASIA		CHN		Total			Percent of 2050 GDP	
	LB	UB	LB	UB	LB	UB	LB	UB	LB	UB	LB	UB	LB	UB	LB	mid range	UB	LB	UB
Grassland/steppe	-5.6	-32	-0.5	-2.7	-0.2	-1	-0.5	-2.8	-2.3	-13.4	-0.5	-2.7	-1.4	-8	-11	-37	-63	-0.01%	-0.03%
Boreal forests	-59	-109	-0.7	-1.6	0	0	0	0	-24	-85	-3.4	-6.2	-20	-27	-107	-168	-229	-0.05%	-0.12%
Temperate forests	-35	-96	-2.6	-12	0	0	-5	-18	-4.3	-21.9	-9.1	-38	-10	-21	-66	-136	-207	-0.03%	-0.1%
Tropical forests	-1.0	-5.0	-28	-191	0	0	-87	-326	0	0	-44	-160	-0.1	-1.0	-161	-422	-682	-0.1%	-0.3%
Total flow loss	**-101**	**-242**	**-32**	**-207**	**-0.2**	**-1.4**	**-93**	**-346**	**-30**	**-120**	**-57**	**-206**	**-32**	**-58**	**-345**	**-763**	**-1,181**	**-0.2%**	**-0.6%**
Benefit agricultural production	**399**		**62**		**2.9**		**182**		**129**		**945**		**272**		**1,276**			**0.7%**	**0.5%**
Net loss or benefit	298.0	156.6	29.7	-145.2	2.7	1.5	88.9	-164.8	99.2	9.1	887.4	738.4	240.9	214.9	930.5	512.4	94.4		
Percent of 2050 GDP	0.4%	0.2%	0.3%	-1.5%	0.04%	0.02%	0.6%	-1.2%	1.2%	0.1%	2.4%	2.0%	0.5%	0.5%	0.48%	0.26%	0.05%		

LB, lower bound; UB, upper bound. LB = US$13 per tonne of CO_2, and median values for grasslands, forest recreation, and passive use. UB = US$179 per tonne of CO_2, and mean values for grasslands, forest recreation, and passive use.
For definitions of regions, see Table 4.2.

Table 4.23 Change in annual values for carbon in forests 1900–2000, discount 3% (billion 2000 US$)

Biome	OECD		CSAM		MEA-NAFR		SAFR		RUS-CASIA		SASIA		CHN		Total		Percent of 2000 GDP	
	LB	UB	LB	UB	LB	UB	LB	UB	LB	UB	LB	UB	LB	UB	LB	UB	LB	UB
Boreal forests	-2	-28	-0.03	-0.4	0		0	0	-3	-41	-0.1	-1.3	-0.4	-6	-6	-76	-0.02%	-0.2%
Temperate forests	-7	-92	-1.8	-24	0		-0.3	-4	-1.0	-12.9	-1.8	-24	-1	-13	-13	-170	-0.03%	-0.5%
Tropical forests	-0.6	-8.4	-15	-203	0		-7	-96	0	0	-10	-133	-0.1	-1.0	-33	-441	-0.1%	-1%
Total flow loss	**-10**	**-128**	**-17**	**-228**	**0**		**-8**	**-100**	**-4**	**-54**	**-12**	**-159**	**-1**	**-20**	**-52**	**-688**		
GDP 2000 US$	17,713		3,067		515		491		1,288		4,079		4,851		36,688			
Percent of 2000 GDP	**-0.1%**	**-0.7%**	**-0.6%**	**-7%**	**0%**		**-1.5%**	**-20%**	**-0.3%**	**-4.2%**	**-0.3%**	**-3.9%**	**-0.03%**	**-0.4%**	**-0.1%**	**-1.9%**		

LB, lower bound; UB, upper bound. LB = US$4 per tonne of CO_2. UB = US$53 per tonne of CO_2.
For definitions of regions, see Table 4.2.

Table 4.24 Change in annual values for carbon in forests 2000–2050, discount 3% (billion 2000 US$)

Biome	OECD		CSAM		MEA-NAFR		SAFR		RUS-CASIA		SASIA		CHN		Total		Percent of 2050 GDP	
	LB	UB	LB	UB	LB	UB	LB	UB	LB	UB	LB	UB	LB	UB	LB	UB	LB	UB
Boreal forests	−3	−45	−0.1	−0.8	0	0	0	0	−5	−63	−0.2	−2.6	0	−6	−9	−118	−0.004%	−0.1%
Temperate forests	−4	−58	−0.7	−10	0		−1	−12	−1.3	−18.1	−2.1	−29	−1	−11	−10	−138	−0.01%	−0.1%
Tropical forests	−0.3	−3.9	−12	−172	0		−18	−251	0	0	−9	−119	−0.1	−0.9	−40	−546	−0.02%	−0.3%
Total flow loss	−8	−107	−13	−182	0		−19	−263	−6	−81	−11	−151	−1	−18	−58	−802		
GDP 2050 US$	74,176		9,906		6,437		13,962		8,602		37,234		45,171		195,489			
Percent of 2050 GDP	−0.01%	−0.1%	−0.1%	−1.8%	0%		−0.1%	−2%	−0.1%	−0.9%	−0.03%	−0.4%	−0.003%	−0.04%	−0.03%	−0.4%		

LB, lower bound; UB, upper bound. LB = US$13 per tonne of CO_2. UB = US$179 per tonne of CO_2.
For definitions of regions, see Table 4.2.

Table 4.25 Change in annual values for WFP and NWFP 1900–2000, discount 3% (billion 2000 US$)

Biome	OECD	CSAM	MEA-NAFR	SAFR	RUS-CASIA	SASIA	CHN	Total	Percent of 2000 GDP
Boreal forests	−74	−0.4	0	0	−25	−3.6	−55	−157	−0.4%
Temperate forests	−62	0.0	0	−0.1	−3.2	−2.0	−26	−94	−0.3%
Tropical forests	−0.4	−26	0	−55	0	−65	−0.05	−147	−0.4%
Total flow loss	**−136**	**−26**	**0**	**−55**	**−28**	**−71**	**−81**	**−398**	
GDP 2000 US$	17,713	3,067	515	491	1,288	4,079	4,851	36,688	
Percent of 2000 GDP	**−0.8%**	**−0.9%**	**0%**	**−11%**	**−2.2%**	**−1.7%**	**−1.7%**	**−1.1%**	

For definitions of regions, see Table 4.2.

Table 4.26 Change in annual values for WFP and NWFP 2000–2050, discount 3% (billion 2000 US$)

Biome	OECD	CSAM	MEA-NAFR	SAFR	RUS-CASIA	SASIA	CHN	Total	Percent of 2000 GDP
Boreal forests	−35	−0.2	0	0	−11	−2.2	−18	−67	−0.03%
Temperate forests	−12	−0.01	0	−0.04	−1.3	−0.7	−7	−20	−0.01%
Tropical forests	−0.1	−6	0	−43	0	−17	0.0	−66	−0.03%
Total flow loss	**−47**	**−7**	**0**	**−43**	**−13**	**−20**	**−25**	**−154**	
GDP 2000 US$	74,176	9,906	6,437	13,962	8,602	37,234	45,171	195,489	
Percent of 2000 GDP	**−0.1%**	**−0.1%**	**0%**	**−0.3%**	**−0.1%**	**−0.1%**	**−0.06%**	**−0.1%**	

For definitions of regions, see Table 4.2.

registered in tropical forests. Overall the highest loss is expected in tropical forests, due to their larger carbon capacity.

Wood Forest Products and Non-Wood Forest Products

Sub-Saharan Africa (SAFR) shows the highest loss also for WFP and NWFP in both periods (11% of the 2000 GDP and 0.3% of 2050 GDP), mostly in tropical forests (Table 4.25 and 4.26). This high loss might be due to the huge development of the forestry industry in these last decades, as extensively explained in Chiabai *et al.* (2011). From 1980 to 2000 in South Africa this sector has seen an increase in sales of up to 1460% (Chamshama and Nwonwu 2004).

As regards the type of biome, boreal and tropical forests record the same loss in percent of the GDP.

Boreal forests are in danger particularly in OECD region, China (CHN) and Russia (RUS-CASIA) in both periods.

Forest Recreational Activities

Forest recreation shows much lower losses, but sub-Saharan Africa is still the region having the largest economic damage in the period 1900–2000, registered for tropical forests (Table 4.27). Overall, however, temperate forest is the biome most affected, due to the extent of recreational activities registered in this forest type. As regards the period 2000–2050, Central and South America (CSAM) and Russia (RUS-CASIA) are expected to support the highest cost for decreased recreation, respectively in tropical and boreal forests (Table 4.28). Regardless of specific regions, the highest loss is expected in boreal forests.

Table 4.27 Change in annual values for forest recreation 1900–2000, discount 3% (billion 2000 US$)

Biome	OECD		CSAM		MEA-NAFR		SAFR		RUS-CASIA		SASIA		CHN		Total		Percent of 2000 GDP	
	LB	UB	LB	UB	LB	UB	LB	UB	LB	UB	LB	UB	LB	UB	LB	UB	LB	UB
Boreal forests	-2	-7	-0.02	-0.1	0	0	0	0	-0.5	-2	-0.01	-0.1	-0.2	-1	-2	-10	-0.01%	-0.03%
Temperate forests	-4	-16	-0.5	-2	0	0	-0.05	-0.2	-0.1	-0.5	-0.1	-1	-0.4	-2	-5	-21	-0.01%	-0.1%
Tropical forests	-0.2	-0.8	-1	-4	0	0	-0.3	-1	0	0	-1	-2	-0.01	-0.04	-2	-9	-0.01%	-0.02%
Total flow loss	**-5**	**-23**	**-2**	**-6**	**0**		**-0.4**	**-1**	**-1**	**-2**	**-1**	**-3**	**-1**	**-3**	**-9**	**-39**		
GDP 2000 US$	17,713		3,067		515		491		1,288		4,079		4,851		36,688			
Percent of 2000 GDP	**-0.03%**	**-0.1%**	**-0.05%**	**-0.2%**	**0%**		**-0.1%**	**-0.3%**	**-0.04%**	**-0.2%**	**-0.02%**	**-0.1%**	**-0.01%**	**-0.1%**	**-0.03%**	**-0.1%**		

LB, lower bound, median values; UB, upper bound, mean values.
For definitions of regions, see Table 4.2.

Table 4.28 Change in annual values for forest recreation 2000–2050, discount 3% (billion 2000 US$)

Biome	OECD		CSAM		MEA-NAFR		SAFR		RUS-CASIA		SASIA		CHN		Total		Percent of 2050 GDP	
	LB	UB	LB	UB	LB	UB	LB	UB	LB	UB	LB	UB	LB	UB	LB	UB	LB	UB
Boreal forests	−1.2	−5.3	−0.02	−0.1	0	0	0	0	−0.6	−2.6	−0.02	−0.1	−0.2	−0.8	−2.1	−8.9	−0.001%	−0.005%
Temperate forests	−1.1	−4.8	−0.1	−0.4	0	0	−0.1	−0.3	−0.1	−0.6	−0.1	−0.6	−0.3	−1.4	−1.9	−8.1	−0.001%	−0.004%
Tropical forests	−0.04	−0.2	−0.5	−2	0	0	−0.5	−2.1	0	0	−0.4	−1.7	−0.01	−0.03	−1.4	−6.0	−0.001%	−0.003%
Total flow loss	**−2.4**	**−10.3**	**−0.6**	**−2.4**	**0**		**−0.6**	**−2.4**	**−0.7**	**−3.2**	**−0.6**	**−2.4**	**−0.5**	**−2.2**	**−5.4**	**−22.9**		
GDP 2050 US$	74,176		9,906		6,437		13,962		8,602		37,234		45,171		195,489			
Percent of 2050 GDP	**−0.003%**	**−0.01%**	**−0.01%**	**−0.02%**	**0%**		**−0.004%**	**−0.02%**	**−0.01%**	**−0.04%**	**−0.002%**	**−0.01%**	**−0.001%**	**−0.005%**	**−0.003%**	**−0.01%**		

LB, lower bound, media values; UB, upper bound, mean values.
For definitions of regions, see Table 4.2.

Forest Passive Use

In relation to forest passive use, sub-Saharan Africa is again the most affected region in both periods, mainly in tropical forests having the highest passive use values (Table 4.29 and 4.30). In terms of biomes, however, the greatest impact is recorded in temperate forests in the period 1900–2000 and in tropical forests in 2000–2050. It can be noticed that in the first period, the high impact in sub-Saharan Africa is partially attributable to the very low GDP of the region. In the next period (2000–2050), the weight of SAFR decreases but still remains important, which is due to the high absolute loss expected in tropical forests in this region (US$26 to US$31 billion 2000 US$, the largest registered impact).

Distribution of the Impact by Ecosystem Services

Finally, we analyze how the damage is distributed between ecosystem service in both periods of time. It was not possible to disentangle the impacts on each ecosystem service provided by grassland, as the economic values used for this particular biome refer to the overall set of services provided. Figures 4.5 and 4.6 summarize the losses for the period 1900–2000, while Figures 4.7 and 4.8 refer to the next period 2000–2050. Losses are reported in terms of percent over the total gross damage, not taking into account the benefits registered in the agricultural sector. There is a big difference between the two scenarios, especially as regards the share between carbon and WFP/NWFP. This discrepancy is largely attributable to the range of carbon prices used, varying from US$4 to US$53 per tonne of CO_2 in the period 1900–2000, and from US$13 to US$179 in 2000–2050.

In the first scenario (using lower-bound values of ecosystem services), in both periods, WFP and NWFP are the most affected by the loss in MSA area, followed by forest passive use and carbon. On the other side, grassland ecosystem services register a much lower damage, as well as recreational activities in forests.

In the second scenario (using upper-bound values of ecosystem services) in both periods carbon in forests largely dominates attaining 51% and 68% of

the total impact; WFP/NWFP and forest passive use follow. Again, grassland services and forest recreation are the less impacted.

Conclusions

The analysis presented here provides a partial value of the losses of ecosystem services between 1900 and 2000, and between 2000 and 2050. These losses reflect in part the loss of biodiversity between these dates, captured through the use of the measure of mean species abundance (MSA). Before reviewing the main results it is important to note that the comparisons need to be qualified in a number of respects. First, not all ecosystem services are covered. Data limitations only allow us to look at carbon, recreation passive use, and wood and non-wood services derived from forests, and ecosystem services derived from grasslands. Second, while the links between biodiversity and ecosystem services are partly captured through the use of MSA, this measure has several limitations, which have been noted. Third, the comparison between the ecosystem services in 1900 and 2000 is based on the thought-experiment that assumes the level of ecosystem services of 1900 to be available in 2000 at the prices for these services that actually prevailed in 2000. It is impossible to estimate actual values in 1900 based on socio-economic conditions that prevailed then, as the data are simply not available. As far as the comparison between 2000 and 2050 is concerned, the 2050 levels of services are valued at 2050 projected prices, and so in this respect the second comparison is more complete than that between 1900 and 2000.

Turning to the results we find significant gross losses in ecosystem services between both dates. The gross loss of natural capital between 1900 and 2000 is estimated at between US$20 trillion and US$45 trillion, which range from around 54% to over 100% of the GDP of 2000. Of course it is important to note that the loss is a capital loss and the GDP figure is a flow, so the former can be much greater than the latter. In terms of regions, the greatest losses occurred in the OECD region, followed by Central and South America and South Asia. In terms of biomes the most important sources of losses were

Table 4.29 Change in annual values for forest passive use 1900–2000, discount 3% (billion 2000 US$)

Biome	OECD		CSAM		MEA-NAFR		SAFR		RUS-CASIA		SASIA		CHN		Total		Percent of 2050 GDP	
	LB	UB	LB	UB	LB	UB	LB	UB	LB	UB	LB	UB	LB	UB	LB	UB	LB	UB
Boreal forests	−21	−25	−0.3	−0.4	0	0	0	0	−5	−6	−0.4	−0.5	−1	−1	−27	−32	−0.1%	−0.1%
Temperate forests	−49	−58	−6.8	−8	0	0	−1	−2	−1.1	−1.4	−4.0	−5	−2	−3	−64	−76	−0.2%	−0.2%
Tropical forests	−2.4	−2.8	−16	−19	0	0	−9	−10	0	0	−16	−19	−0.04	−0.1	−43	−51	−0.1%	−0.1%
Total flow loss	**−72**	**−85**	**−23**	**−27**	**0**		**−10**	**−12**	**−6**	**−7**	**−20**	**−24**	**−3**	**−4**	**−134**	**−160**		
GDP 2050 US$	17,713		3,067		515		491		1,288		4,079		4,851		36,688			
Percent of 2050 GDP	**−0.4%**	**−0.5%**	**−0.7%**	**−0.9%**	**0%**		**−2%**	**−2.4%**	**−0.45%**	**−0.54%**	**−0.5%**	**−0.6%**	**−0.07%**	**−0.1%**	**−0.37%**	**−0.44%**		

LB, lower bound, median values; UB, upper bound, mean values.
For definitions of regions, see Table 4.2.

Table 4.30 Change in annual values for forest passive use 2000–2050, discount 3% (billion 2000 US$)

Biome	OECD		CSAM		MEA-NAFR		SAFR		RUS-CASIA		SASIA		CHN		Total		Percent of 2050 GDP	
	LB	UB	LB	UB	LB	UB	LB	UB	LB	UB	LB	UB	LB	UB	LB	UB	LB	UB
Boreal forests	−20	−23	−0.4	−0.5	0	0	0	0	−7	−8	−1.1	−1.3	−1	−2	−29	−35	−0.01%	−0.02%
Temperate forests	−18	−21	−1.8	−2	0	0	−4	−5	−1.6	−1.9	−6.1	−7	−2	−3	−34	−40	−0.02%	−0.02%
Tropical forests	−0.7	−0.8	−9	−11	0	0	−26	−31	0	0	−18	−21	−0.0	−0.1	−53	−63	−0.03%	−0.03%
Total flow loss	**−38**	**−45**	**−11**	**−13**	**0**	**0**	**−30**	**−36**	**−9**	**−10**	**−25**	**−30**	**−3**	**−4**	**−116**	**−138**		
GDP 2050 US$	74,176		9,906		6,437		13,962		8,602		37,234		45,171		195,489			
Percent of 2050 GDP	**−0.1%**	**−0.1%**	**−0.1%**	**−0.1%**	**0%**		**−0.2%**	**−0.3%**	**−0.1%**	**−0.1%**	**−0.1%**	**−0.1%**	**−0.01%**	**−0.01%**	**−0.06%**	**−0.07%**		

LB, lower bound, median values; UB, upper bound, mean values.
For definitions of regions, see Table 4.2.

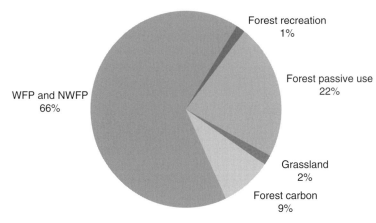

Figure 4.5 *Economic loss registered by ecosystem services, 1900–2000, percent of total loss (lower-bound scenario)*

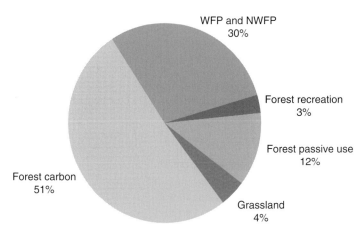

Figure 4.6 *Economic loss registered by ecosystem services, 1900–2000, percent of total loss (upper-bound scenario)*

the tropical forests, followed by temperate forests. Grassland losses contributed a small share of the total.

If one compares the losses in terms of flows, the total loss between 1900 and 2000 was between US$603 billion and US$1.3 trillion, which is around 1.7% and 3.8% of the GDP of 2000. However, against this loss we also have to account for the gain made by the conversion of forest and grassland to agriculture. This gain more or less cancels out the loss in the case of the lower-bound figure. Only if the upper-bound figure is valid is there a net loss, which is then about US$730 billion,

or 2% of the 2000 GDP. It is also important to note that there are major differences in the net loss by region. In particular, sub-Saharan Africa suffers a net loss of 13%–32% of its 2000 GDP. The other regions all show a gain if we take the lower-bound figure for their losses of ecosystem services and in two regions (South Asia and China) the net figure is a gain even in the case of the upper bound of the losses.

Looking at the comparison between 2000 and 2050, we find similar overall results but with some notable differences. In terms of the natural capital the losses range from US$11 trillion to US$39 trillion,

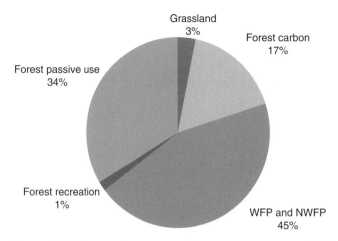

Figure 4.7 *Economic loss registered by ecosystem services, 2000–2050, percent of total loss (lower-bound scenario)*

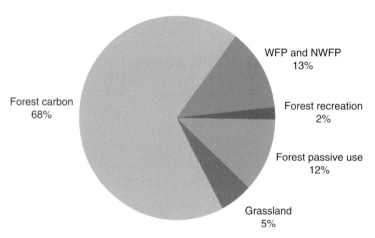

Figure 4.8 *Economic loss registered by ecosystem services, 2000–2050, percent of total loss (upper-bound scenario)*

with the greatest losses expected in sub-Saharan Africa, the OECD, and South Asia. In terms of biomes, the most affected is tropical forests followed by boreal forests. In terms of flows, gross losses are between US$345 billion and US$1.2 trillion, representing between 0.9% and 3.2% of the GDP of 2000. In terms of net changes, however, after allowing for agricultural gains, we estimate a gain of between US$94 billion and US$930 billion. The only regions to show a net loss are Central and South America and sub-Saharan Africa, but only with the upper bound of the gross loss figure.

The ecosystem services that contribute most to human well-being and to which we are most vulnerable when they are lost depend mainly on the valuations put on carbon. At a low value for carbon the main contributors are wood forest products, passive use of forests, and carbon, in that order. At a high value of carbon the order changes, with carbon being the largest, followed by forest products and passive use.

As already noted, the results here are a partial valuation of ecosystem services and it is possible that a more complete coverage would give a higher gross loss as well as a greater net loss. More work is needed to establish the extent to which this is the case. More work is also needed to understand better the links between biodiversity and the ecosystem services that have been the main focus of this assessment.

References

Achard, F., H. D. Eva, P. Mayaux, H.-J. Stibig, and A. Belward (2004) Improved estimates of net carbon emissions from land cover change in the tropics for the 1990s. *Global Biogeochemical Cycles* **18**. DOI: 10.1029/2003GB002142.

Alkemade, R., M. Blackens, R. Bobbin, *et al.* (2006) GLOBIO 3: framework for the assessment of global biodiversity. In: A. F. Bouwman, T. Kram, and K. Klein (eds.), *MNP: Integrated Modelling of Environmental Change – An Overview of IMAGE 2.4. NEAA/MNP*. Bilthoven, The Netherlands: Netherlands Environmental Assessment Agency.

Alkemade, R., M. Oorschot, L. Miles, *et al.* (2009) GLOBIO 3: a framework to investigate options for reducing global terrestrial biodiversity loss. *Ecosystem* **12**: 374–390.

Bakkes, J. A. and P. R. Bosch (eds.) (2008) *Background Report to the OECD Environmental Outlook to 2030: Overviews, Details, and Methodology of Model-Based Analysis.* Bilthoven, The Netherlands: Netherlands Environmental Assessment Agency.

Bolt, K., M. Matete, and M. Clemens (2002) *Manual for Calculating Adjusted Net Savings.* New York: Environment Department, World Bank.

Bouwman, A. F., T. Kram, and K. Klein (eds.) (2006) *MNP: Integrated Modelling of Global Environmental Change – An Overview of IMAGE 2.4.* Bilthoven, The Netherlands: Netherlands Environmental Assessment Agency.

Brock, W. A. and A. Xepapadeas (2003) Valuing biodiversity from an economic perspective: a unified economic, ecological, and genetic approach. *American Economic Review* **93**: 1597–1614.

Brown, S. (1997) *Estimating Biomass and Biomass Change of Tropical Forests: A Primer*, Forestry Paper No. 134 Rome: FAO.

Chamshama, S. A. O. and F. Nwonwu (2004) *Case Studies on Forest Plantations in Africa.* Nairobi: AFORNET/KSLA/FAO.

Chiabai, A., C. Travisi, A. Markandya, H. Ding, and P. A. L. D. Nunes (2011) Economic assessment of forest ecosystem services losses: cost of policy inaction. *Environmental and Resource Economics* **3**: 405–455.

Clark, J. (2001) The global wood market, prices and plantation investment: an examination drawing on the Australian experience. *Environmental Conservation* **28**: 53–64.

DeFries, R. S., R. A. Houghton, M. C. Hansen *et al.* (2002) Carbon emissions from tropical deforestation and regrowth based on satellite observations for the 1980s and 1990s. *Proceedings of the National Academy of Sciences of the USA* **99**: 14 256–14 261.

FAO (1999) *State of the World's Forests*, 3rd edn. Rome: FAO. www.fao.org/forestry/FO/SOFO/SOFO99/sofo99-e.stm

Gibbs, H. K. and S. Brown (2007a) Geographical distribution of woody biomass carbon stocks in tropical Africa: an updated database for 2000. Available at: http://cdiac.ornl.gov/epubs/ndp/ndp0555/ndp05b.html from the Carbon Dioxide Information Center, Oak Ridge National Laboratory, Oak Ridge, TN.

  (2007b) Geographical distribution of biomass carbon in tropical southeast Asian forests: an updated database for 2000. Available at: http://cdiac.ornl.gov/epubs/ndp/ndp068/ndp068b.html from the Carbon Dioxide Information Center, Oak Ridge National Laboratory, Oak Ridge, TN.

Gibbs, H. K., S. Brown, J. O. Niles, and J. A. Foley (2007) Monitoring and estimating tropical forest carbon stocks: making REDD a reality. *Environmental Research Letters* **2**, Article 045023.

Grime, J. P. (1997) Biodiversity and ecosystem function: the debate deepens. *Science* **277**: 1260–1261.

Haines-Young, R. and M. Potschin (2010) The links between biodiversity, ecosystem services and human well-being. In: D. Raffaelli and C. Frid (eds.), *Ecosystem Ecology: A New Synthesis.* Cambridge: Cambridge University Press.

Houghton, R. A. (1999) The annual net flux of carbon to the atmosphere from changes in land use 1850–1990. *Tellus B* **51**: 298–313.

Hussain, S. S., A. McVittie, L. Brander, *et al.* (2011) *The Economics of Ecosystems and Biodiversity: The Quantitative Assessment*, Draft Final Report to the United Nations Environment Programme.

IPCC (2006) *IPCC Guidelines for National Greenhouse Gas Inventories.* Prepared by the National Greenhouse Gas Inventories Programme, eds. H. S. Eggleston, L. Buendia, K. Miwa, T. Ngara, and K Tanabe. Kobe, Japan: Institute For Global Environmental Strategies.

Mace, G. M., J. L. Gittleman, and A. Purvis (2003) Preserving the tree of life. *Science* **300**: 1707–1709.

Markandya, A., A. Bigano, and R. Porchia (eds.) (2010) *The Social Cost of Electricity: Scenarios and Policy Implications.* Cheltenham, UK: Edward Elgar.

McCann, K. S. (2000) The diversity–stability debate. *Nature* **405**: 228–233.

MEA (2005) *Millennium Ecosystem Assessment Ecosystems and Human Wellbeing: Current State and Trends.* Washington, DC: Island Press.

Myneni, R. B., J. Dong, C. J. Tucker, *et al.* (2001) A large carbon sink in the woody biomass of northern forests. *Proceedings of the National Academy of Sciences of the USA* **98**: 14 784–14 789.

Newman, D. J. and G. M. Cragg (2007) Natural products as sources of new drugs over the last 25 years. *Journal of Natural Products* **70**: 461–477.

Olson, J. S., J. A. Watts, and L. J. Allison (1983) *Carbon in Live Vegetation of Major World Ecosystems.* Oak Ridge, TN: Oak Ridge National Laboratory.

Pimm, S. L., G. J. Russel, J. L. Gittleman, and T. M. Brooks (1995) The future of biodiversity. *Science* **269**: 347–350.

Purvis, A. and A. Hector (2000) Getting the measure of biodiversity. *Nature* **405**: 212–219.

Reichle, D. E. (Ed.) (1981) *Dynamic Properties of Forest Ecosystems.* Cambridge: Cambridge University Press.

Ten Brink, P. (ed.) (2011) *The Economics of Ecosystems and Biodiversity in National and International Policy Making.* London: Earthscan.

Tilman, D. and J. A. Downing (1994) Biodiversity and stability in grasslands. *Nature* **367**: 363–365.

Villa, F. and E. McLeod (2002) Environmental vulnerability indicators for environmental planning and decision-making: guidelines and applications. *Environmental Management* **29**: 335–348.

Annex 4.1

Table A4.1 Change in present values for carbon 1900–2000 (billion 2000 US$)

Biome	OECD		CSAM		MEA-NAFR		SAFR		RUS-CASIA		SASIA		CHN		Total	
	LB	UB	LB	UB	LB	UB	LB	UB	LB	UB	LB	UB	LB	UB	LB	UB
Boreal forests	−70	−933	−1	−15	0		0	0	−102	−1,355	−3	−43	−14	−191	−191	−2,536
Temperate forests	−231	−3,059	−62	−816	0		−11	−140	−32	−428	−60	−797	−32	−430	−428	−5,671
Tropical forests	−21	−279	−510	−6,756	0		−241	−3,199	0	0	−335	−4,445	−2	−32	−1,110	−14,710
Total	−322	−4,270	−573	−7,587	0		−252	−3,340	−135	−1,783	−399	−5,285	−49	−653	−1,730	−22,918
Percent of total	−19%		−33%		0%		−15%		−8%		−23%		−3%			

Table A4.2 Change in present values for carbon 2000–2050 (billion 2000 US$)

Biome	OECD		CSAM		MEA-NAFR		SAFR		RUS-CASIA		SASIA		CHN		Total	
	LB	UB	LB	UB	LB	UB	LB	UB	LB	UB	LB	UB	LB	UB	LB	UB
Boreal forests	−110	−1,509	−2	−28	0		0	0	−152	−2,087	−6	−88	−16	−216	−285	−3,927
Temperate forests	−141	−1,939	−23	−317	0		−29	−406	−44	−604	−71	−976	−26	−362	−334	−4,604
Tropical forests	−10	−131	−415	−5,719	0		−607	−8,357	0	0	−289	−3,975	−2	−30	−1,323	−18,212
Total	−260	−3,580	−440	−6,064	0		−636	−8,763	−195	−2,691	−366	−5,039	−44	−607	−1,942	−26,743
Percent of total	−13%		−23%		0%		−33%		−10%		−19%		−2%			

Table A4.3 Change in present values for WFP and NWFP 1900–2000 (billion 2000 US$)

Biome	OECD	CSAM	MEA-NAFR	SAFR	RUS-CASIA	SASIA	CHN	Total
Boreal forests	−2,456	−12	0	0	−840	−121	−1,820	−5,249
Temperate forests	−2,065	−2	0	−2	−105	−66	−881	−3,120
Tropical forests	−14	−864	0	−1,838	0	−2,166	−2	−4,883
Total	−4,535	−878	0	−1,840	−945	−2,352	−2,703	−13,253
Percent of total	−34%	−7%	0%	−14%	−7%	−18%	−20%	

Table A4.4 Change in present values for WFP and NWFP 2000–2050 (billion 2000 US$)

Biome	OECD	CSAM	MEA-NAFR	SAFR	RUS-CASIA	SASIA	CHN	Total
Boreal forests	−1,177	−7	0	0	−383	−72	−609	−2,248
Temperate forests	−388	−0.2	0	−1.5	−44	−24	−219	−676
Tropical forests	−2	−217	0	−1,421	0	−574	−0.4	−2,214
Total	−1,566	−224	0	−1,423	−427	−670	−829	−5,138
Percent of total	−30%	−4%	0%	−28%	−8%	−13%	−16%	

Table A4.5 Change in present values for recreation 1900–2000 (billion 2000 US$)

Biome	OECD		CSAM		MEA-NAFR		SAFR		RUS-CASIA		SASIA		CHN		Total	
	LB	UB	LB	UB	LB	UB	LB	UB	LB	UB	LB	UB	LB	UB	LB	UB
Boreal forests	−52	−223	−1	−3	0		0	0	−15	−65	−0.5	−2	−6.2	−26	−75	−319
Temperate forests	−123	−523	−15	−64	0		−2	−6	−4	−16	−5	−20	−14	−59	−162	−688
Tropical forests	−6	−25	−35	−149	0		−10	−43	0	0	−19	−80	−0.3	−1	−71	−299
Total	−182	−771	−51	−216	0		−12	−50	−19	−80	−24	−103	−21	−87	−308	−1,306
Percent of total	−	59%	−	17%	0%		−	4%	−	6%	−	8%	−	7%		

Table A4.6 Change in present values for recreation 2000–2050 (billion 2000 US$)

Biome	OECD		CSAM		MEA-NAFR		SAFR		RUS-CASIA		SASIA		CHN		Total	
	LB	UB	LB	UB	LB	UB	LB	UB	LB	UB	LB	UB	LB	UB	LB	UB
Boreal forests	−41	−175	−1	−3	0		0	0	−20	−86	−1	−3	−6	−27	−70	−295
Temperate forests	−38	−161	−3	−13	0		−3	−11	−5	−19	−5	−20	−11	−45	−64	−270
Tropical forests	−1	−6	−15	−65	0		−16	−69	0	0	−14	−57	−0	−1	−47	−199
Total	−81	−342	−19	−81	0		−19	−81	−25	−106	−19	−80	−17	−73	−180	−763
Percent of total	−	45%	−	11%	0%		−	11%	−	14%	−	11%	−	10%		

Table A4.7 Change in present values for passive use 1900–2000 (billion 2000 US$)

Biome	OECD LB	OECD UB	CSAM LB	CSAM UB	MEA-NAFR LB	MEA-NAFR UB	SAFR LB	SAFR UB	RUS-CASIA LB	RUS-CASIA UB	SASIA LB	SASIA UB	CHN LB	CHN UB	Total LB	Total UB
Boreal forests	-691	-822	-11	-13	0		0	0	-156	-186	-14	-17	-32	-38	-905	-1,077
Temperate forests	-1,623	-1,932	-226	-269	0		-43	-51	-38	-46	-133	-159	-73	-86	-2,137	-2,542
Tropical forests	-79	-94	-527	-627	0		-289	-344	0	0	-534	-636	-1.4	-1.7	-1,431	-1,702
Total	-2,394	-2,848	-764	-909	0		-332	-395	-195	-232	-682	-811	-106	-126	-4,472	-5,321
Percent of total	-54%		-17%		0%		-7%		-4%		-15%		-2.4%			

Table A4.8 Change in present values for passive use 2000–2050 (billion 2000 US$)

Biome	OECD		CSAM		MEA-NAFR		SAFR		RUS-CASIA		SASIA		CHN		Total	
	LB	UB	LB	UB	LB	UB	LB	UB	LB	UB	LB	UB	LB	UB	LB	UB
Boreal forests	−651	−774	−14	−17	0		0	0	−233	−277	−35	−42	−42	−50	−975	−1,161
Temperate forests	−599	−712	−59	−70	0		−140	−167	−52	−62	−205	−244	−71	−84	−1,126	−1,340
Tropical forests	−22	−26	−299	−356	0		−858	−1,021	0	0	−598	−711	−2	−2	−1,778	−2,116
Total	−1,271	−1,512	−372	−443	0		−999	−1,188	−285	−339	−838	−997	−115	−137	−3,879	−4,616
Percent of total	−33%		−10%		0%		−26%		−7%		−22%		−3%			

Education: The Income and Equity Loss of not Having a Faster Rate of Human Capital Accumulation

HARRY ANTHONY PATRINOS AND
GEORGE PSACHAROPOULOS

Introduction

Formal education is a relatively recent institution in the history of mankind, dating back a mere two centuries. The recognition that education relates to a country's development is even more recent, dating back just a few decades. Non-formal education of course existed since time immemorial in the form of philosopher–student or master–apprentice relationships, and some European universities date back to the thirteenth century. But organized schooling where children of a certain age were obliged to attend school started as late as the nineteenth century in England.

The link between education and economic development was identified by the so-called "Human Capital School" originating at the University of Chicago in the early 1960s (Schultz 1961a; Becker 1964). According to early versions of human capital theory, expenditure on education is an investment with many similarities to investment in machines. National resources are used while the student is in school, in the form of direct outlays to education and forgone labor earnings. But later in life more-educated workers contribute more to national output than less-educated workers. The discounted difference between the cost and benefit flows related to education can lead to estimates of the profitability of investment in human capital.

This basic idea was expanded in the 1980s and 1990s to include predictions of the so-called new growth theory postulating that education, beyond enhancing an individual's productivity, also has an efficiency-boosting "external" effect on others, thus further enhancing national output (Romer 1986, 1990; Lucas 1988). A flood of empirical research has followed attempting to estimate the effect of education on economic growth (see, for example, Barro 1991; Mankiw *et al.* 1992; Benhabib and Spiegel 1994, 2005; McMahon 1999).

Throughout the short history of formal education it has been a perennial challenge as to how to provide the quantity and type of education that would maximize social welfare. In this chapter we define the welfare loss related to education in terms of efficiency and equity. Given the lack of a global utility function, welfare loss in this chapter really means loss of income. The efficiency component is estimated as a counterfactual of higher per capita income or its growth had educational development proceeded faster than indicated in the historical data. The equity component is estimated by the change in the Gini inequality index had countries followed more expansive education policies.[1]

Our estimates of the loss associated with education spanning 1900 to 2050 are based on a comparison of two scenarios: (1) an inertia scenario in which countries follow existing education policies and (2) a challenge scenario in which countries would have followed more efficiency- and equity-oriented education policies.

Backward and forward extrapolation of the welfare loss is based on coefficients regarding the

We thank Emilio Porta, Kevin Macdonald, and Martin Schlotter for assisting us in constructing the database, and two anonymous reviewers whose comments on a draft of this chapter led to significant improvements in content and exposition. We thank Kasper Thede Anderskov and Bjørn Lomborg for useful questions and guidance. All errors remain our own and the views expressed here are those of the authors and should not be attributed to the World Bank Group.

[1] The Gini coefficient is a widely used measure of relative equality, with a value of 0 representing total equality, and 1 maximum inequality.

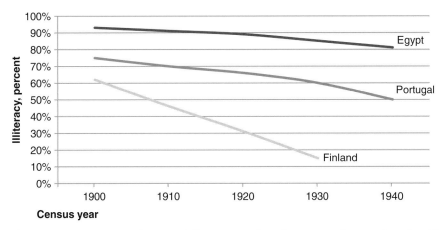

Figure 5.1 *Progress in reduction of illiteracy in selected countries.* Source: *Based on UNESCO (1953)*

contribution of education to economic growth and equity in the "actual" or "data-known" period 1950 to 2000 from new estimates and the empirical literature on the subjects and, of course, assumptions regarding the application of such coefficients beyond the range of actual data. Given the highly aggregate nature of this exercise, high and low estimates are given.

The coefficients linking education to economic growth are derived from two subsets of the economics of education literature: (1) micro estimates of the social rates of return to investment at different levels of education and (2) macro estimates of the contribution of education to economic growth. The data come from historical national accounts statistics and a variety of education databases.

The following section provides a bird's-eye view of world educational development in the period 1900 to the present. Section 3 defines the education challenge. Section 4 provides a brief review of empirical findings regarding the contribution of education to economic growth and equity. Section 5 presents the methodology used in this chapter for assessing the macro effect of one additional year of schooling on per capita income and applies it at the world, regional, and individual country scales. Section 6 assesses the effect of illiteracy on per capita income. Section 7 estimates the effect of education on equity. Section 8 discusses several caveats associated with this study. The final section gives our best

estimate of the size and evolution over time of the welfare loss related to education.

Historical Perspective

Education statistics prior to 1950 are spotty. The first systematic collection of school enrollment statistics started well after the foundation of UNESCO in 1946. From the ability of people to sign their name in marriage registries in England and a few other countries, as well as from population censuses, we know that the extent and progress of literacy was very slow early in the twentieth century (Figure 5.1).

The slow build-up of human capital since 1900 in developing countries and the deceleration of human capital formation in Western countries since 1960 is shown in Table 5.1 and Figure 5.2. Such a pattern suggests an *S*-shaped trend over time in educational development, a theme that we will return to later in this chapter.

The pattern in Table 5.1 shows that between 1970 and 2000, average years of schooling rose by similar amounts across all regions at about 2–3 years of schooling. The biggest increases are in China and the smallest in South Asia. Other than China and Other Asia, there is only modest convergence in average years of schooling between developed and developing worlds. The pace of world growth in human capital accelerated in the second half of the twentieth century. Since 1950,

Table 5.1 Mean years of schooling and illiteracy rates (percent), 1870–2000

Year		Africa	Japan, Korea, Taiwan	Latin America	Eastern Europe	Europe and offshoots	China	South Asia	Other Asia	World mean
1870	School years	0.13	0.63	0.59	0.83	3.02	1.00	0.03	0.25	1.0
	Illiteracy	96.5	82.9	86.0	79.1	37.2	82.3	99.3	94.6	78.9
1910	School years	0.27	2.41	1.28	1.61	5.00	1.26	0.27	0.50	1.8
	Illiteracy	93.8	46.2	71.8	67.8	16.1	78.6	94.6	89.6	67.0
1950	School years	0.79	6.31	2.81	5.05	7.22	1.65	0.88	1.43	3.2
	Illiteracy	85.2	13.2	44.7	12.1	4.5	73.8	83.9	73.4	51.2
1970	School years	1.71	8.78	4.13	7.65	9.06	3.33	2.25	3.35	4.7
	Illiteracy	70.5	4.1	32.7	7.0	1.7	50.9	66.9	46.4	39.1
1980	School years	2.37	9.58	4.89	8.02	9.83	4.55	2.91	4.35	5.3
	Illiteracy	60.4	2.0	26.6	6.6	1.6	37.1	60.1	34.5	33.3
1990	School years	3.18	10.29	6.22	9.47	10.50	5.66	3.31	5.57	6.1
	Illiteracy	50.2	1.2	18.4	6.9	1.7	26.0	54.3	21.1	27.7
2000	School years	4.02	10.98	6.94	9.86	10.99	6.64	4.02	6.52	6.7
	Illiteracy	39.5	1.3	14.5	5.5	1.8	19.7	48.3	15.3	23.6

Source: Based on Morrisson and Murtin (2007, Table 2).

world years of schooling have increased relatively steadily at a rate of 0.6 to 0.7 years per decade. Before 1950, only Europe, North America, and the OECD countries of Asia maintained that pace of schooling increase. That means that the current developing countries are adding human capital at a pace comparable to that of the current developed countries. The recent acceleration of world human capital development is due to developing countries investing at the pace of developed economies. The developed economies have not slowed their pace, adding about 0.7 years of schooling per decade for the last 130 years.

More comprehensive education data exist for the period 1950–2010 in 5-year intervals referring to 146 countries (Table 5.2). Pooling together such data for the whole period, world educational development (measured by the mean years of schooling

of the population aged 15-plus) evolved as shown in Figure 5.3.

There are three clusters of educational development: (1) high in the advanced economies of Europe, North America and Central Asia; (2) moderate in Latin America and the Middle East; and (3) low in South Asia and sub-Saharan Africa.

Building human capital stock is a long-term affair. For a typical country it takes 35–80 years to make a transition from 10% net primary enrollment to 90% (Wils 2003; Wils and O'Connor 2003a). Education transition follows an *S*-shaped curve due to the diminishing speed of increases in attainment over time, and the fact that there is only so much education one can attain in terms of years of schooling (Meyer *et al.* 1992). After all, compulsory schooling is set, and most graduate programs are for a specified length.

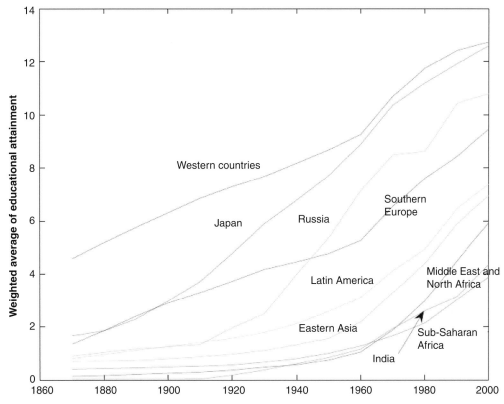

Figure 5.2 *Historical progress in building human capital stock (weighted average of educational attainment by geographical area).* Source: *Morrisson and Murtin (2008, Figure 14). Note: Country grouping as in original*

Defining the Challenge

Governments and international organizations alike have been trying hard to improve educational development over the past 50 years or so. Yet, such efforts have proved to be a real challenge in developing countries regarding basic education. The United Nations, UNESCO, UNICEF, the International Labor Office and the World Bank have all been promoting education as a basic human right and growth engine.[2] Target years for achieving "education for all" have been set and reset because the targets have been missed. According to the latest statistics more than one in four primary-school-age children are out of school in sub-Saharan Africa, and in South and West Asia more than one-third of the adult population are illiterate (UNESCO

2010). And, as shown in Figure 5.4, the outlook does not seem very promising. Many primary-school-age children in poor countries, and in most of sub-Saharan Africa, are not in school because they start at a late age. Some of those who start at a late age may well finish primary school, so while at any point in time one out of four children of primary school age are not in school the fraction who *never* go to school is much lower.

Table 5.2 Mean years of schooling of the population by region, 1950–2010

Year	Advanced economies	East Asia and Pacific	Europe and Central Asia	Latin America and Caribbean	Middle East and North Africa	South Asia	Sub Saharan Africa	World mean
1950	5.9	2.8	5.0	3.1	1.5	1.5	1.1	3.1
1955	6.2	3.1	5.3	3.3	1.8	1.6	1.3	3.3
1960	6.5	3.4	5.8	3.6	2.0	1.7	1.4	3.6
1965	6.9	3.8	6.2	4.0	2.4	1.9	1.6	3.9
1970	7.3	4.3	6.8	4.5	2.9	2.3	2.0	4.4
1975	7.9	4.9	7.4	4.9	3.5	2.6	2.4	4.9
1980	8.4	5.6	8.0	5.6	4.2	2.9	2.8	5.4
1985	8.7	6.0	8.5	6.1	4.9	3.3	3.3	6.0
1990	9.1	6.4	8.9	6.6	5.6	3.7	3.9	6.4
1995	9.5	7.0	9.5	7.0	6.2	4.0	4.3	6.9
2000	9.9	7.4	9.8	7.4	6.8	4.4	4.7	7.3
2005	10.3	7.9	10.1	7.9	7.3	5.0	5.1	7.7
2010	10.6	8.3	10.2	8.4	7.8	5.6	5.5	8.1
World mean	8.2	5.5	7.8	5.6	4.4	3.1	3.0	5.5

Source: Based on Barro and Lee (2010b).

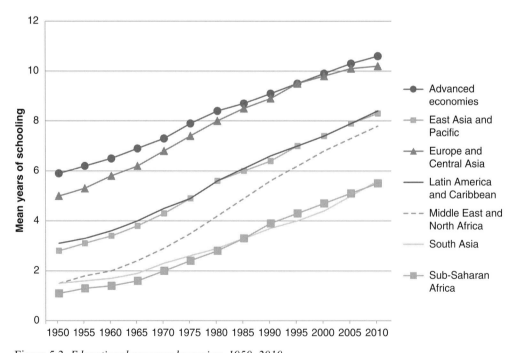

Figure 5.3 *Educational progress by region, 1950–2010*

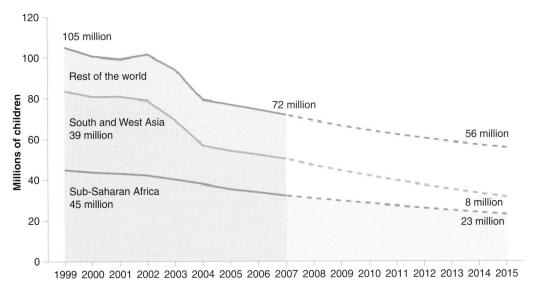

Figure 5.4 *Out-of-school trend and projection to 2015 (millions of children).* Source: *UNESCO (2010, Figure 2.8)*

Review of the Analytical Literature

Empirical applications on the effect of education in promoting efficiency have followed two grand analytical routes: micro and macro. The micro literature focused on estimating the so-called "social rate of return to investment in education." This measure compares the benefits of having more education to the costs of obtaining that education. The benefits are typically measured by the earnings difference between more and less educated workers, that under competitive conditions approximates the productivity differential between the two kinds of workers. The costs consist of direct private and public expenditure on schooling, plus the forgone earnings of those who are in school rather than working.

Estimates of social returns to education, as commonly found in the literature, ignore non-income benefits of education (for example, improved health) and the possibility of positive externalities from education, such as productivity spillovers, lower crime, reduced use of social services, increased civic participation, and so on.

The private rate of return to an investment in a given level of education in such a case can be estimated by finding the rate of discount (r) that equalizes the stream of discounted benefits to the stream of costs at a given point in time. In the case of university education lasting 5 years, for example, the formula is:

$$\sum_{t=1}^{42} \frac{(W_u - W_s)_t}{(1+r)^t} = \sum_{t=1}^{5} (W_s + C_u)_t (1+r)^t$$

(5.1)

where $(W_u - W_s)$ is the earnings differential between a university graduate (subscript u) and a secondary school graduate (subscript s, the control group); C_u represents the direct costs of university education (tuition, fees, books), and W_s denotes the student's forgone earnings or indirect costs.

Typical results of rate of return applications are reported in Table 5.3 showing that the returns are higher when investment takes place at the lower level of education, especially in low-income countries. This well-documented pattern is due to diminishing returns as investment in human capital ascends by level of education, similar to the diminishing returns on investment in physical capital. In addition, the returns to education are higher in developing countries because of the scarcity of human capital in those countries relative to industrial countries.

Table 5.3 Social returns to investment in education by level and per capita income group (percent)

Per capita income group	Educational level		
	Primary	Secondary	Higher
Low income	21.3	15.7	11.2
Middle income	18.8	12.9	11.3
High income	13.4	10.3	9.5
World average	18.9	13.1	10.8

Source: Based on Psacharopoulos and Patrinos (2004, Table 2).

Table 5.4 Macro-estimated returns to 1 additional year of schooling

Effect	Source
No significant effect of years of schooling on economic growth	Benhabib and Spiegel (1994)
Each additional year of schooling attainment in a country is associated with about 30% higher GDP per capita	Heckman and Klenow (1997)
A 1-year increase in the average years of schooling of the labor force raises output per worker between 5% and 15%	Topel (1999)
A 1-year increase of years of schooling associated with 0.30% per year faster growth	Bils and Klenow (2000)
Macro-estimated rate of return to schooling between 18% and 30%	Krueger and Lindahl (2001)
A 1-year increase in average education raises per capita income between 3% and 6%	Bassanini and Scarpetta (2001)
A 1-year increase in the mean years of schooling is associated with a rise in per capita income by 3%-6%, or a higher growth rate of 1 percentage point	Sianesi and van Reenen (2003)
No evidence of wide social returns to education based on cross-country regressions	Pritchett (2006)
Macro-estimated rate of return to schooling 27%	de la Fuente and Doménech (2006)
Macro-estimated rate of return to schooling between 9.0% and 12.3%	Cohen and Soto (2007)
Macro returns to years of schooling 36.9%, or each year of schooling is statistically significantly associated with a long-run growth rate that is 0.58 percentage points higher	Hanushek and Woessmann (2008)
Controlling for physical capital stock, the rate of return to the average year of schooling is 12.1%	Barro and Lee (2010)

An alternative methodology is the so-called "Mincerian earnings function" used mainly to estimate the private returns to education (Mincer 1974):

$$\text{Ln}(Y_i) = f(S_i, Z_i) \tag{5.2}$$

where Y refers to the earnings of person i, S to the number of years of schooling, and Z to a battery of other individual characteristics. The property of this semi-logarithmic expression is that the regression coefficient of the years of schooling can be interpreted as the rate of return to investment in education.

Such a function has also been applied in a macro context where Y refers to per capita income or output per worker in country i and S to the mean years of schooling of the population or the workforce. The enrollment ratio at different levels of education has also been used in lieu of years of schooling as an independent variable. Table 5.4 gives typical results of the application of such a function fitted to pooled cross-country-time data.

Another methodological line of estimating the contribution of education to economic growth has been instigated by the work of Solow (1956, 1957) who added technical change (T) as an independent variable in an aggregate production function, along with the traditional factors of production physical capital (K_p) and labor input (L) in order to explain output (Y). Omitting time subscripts for expository simplicity, the Solow function takes the form

$$Y = f(L, K_p, K_n) \tag{5.3}$$

Schultz (1961a,b) challenged Solow's formulation and added education as a determining factor of income. A stream of empirical research followed

along two alternative measures of the education input: "Schultz-type" and "Denison-type" growth accounting.

In Schultz-type accounting, human capital (K_h) is added as an independent variable in the production function, along with physical capital (K_p) and the number of people employed:

$$Y = f(L, K_p, K_h) \qquad (5.4)$$

Differentiating with respect to time as to get the growth rate of output (g_y), and making elementary substitutions, one gets the estimating expression:

$$g_y = s_l \cdot g_l + \frac{I_p}{Y} r_p + \frac{I_h}{Y} r_h \qquad (5.5)$$

where s_l is the share of labor in national income, g_l the rate of growth of the labor force, I is the investment in physical (p) or human (h) capital, and r the rate of return on the respective investment. Therefore, r_p and r_h correspond to the return on physical and human capital. Note that r_h corresponds to the coefficient of schooling in our estimates, namely equation (5.2), though r_h in Schultz's model corresponds to the social rate of return while the coefficient on S gives the private rate of return.

In Denison's formulation, instead of adding human capital in monetary terms, the labor force (L) is split up by level of education, say L_0, L_1, L_2, and L_3, to denote those whose highest qualification is no schooling, primary, secondary, and higher education:

$$Y = f(K_p, L_0, L_1, L_2, L_3) \qquad (5.6)$$

Differentiating with respect to time, growth accounting takes the form:

$$g_y = s_{10} \cdot g_{10} + s_{11} \cdot g_{11} + s_{12} \cdot g_{12} + s_{13} \cdot g_{13} + \frac{I_p}{Y} r_p \qquad (5.7)$$

where s_i stands for the wage share of labor with the ith qualification in national income, and g_i for the rate of growth of workers with that qualification.

Typical results from the early literature on the macro contribution of education to economic growth based on "Schultz-type" and "Denison-type" growth accounting are presented in Table 5.5. The results show consistency with the micro literature in the sense that the effect of education on growth is substantial.

The 1980s experienced the appearance of endogenous growth theory (Lucas 1988; Romer 1990). In the formulation of Lucas and Romer, beyond a

Table 5.5 The contribution of education to economic growth in the early literature

Country	Contribution of education to the economic growth rate (percent)[a]
Belgium	14.0
Canada	25.0
Korea	16.0
UK	12.0
USA	15.0

[a] Estimates are based on within-country growth accounting using Schultz (1961b) and Denison (1967) methodologies
Source: Psacharopoulos (1984).

measure of human capital that is actually used by different firms in the economy (K_h), S years output also depends on the average level of human capital ($\overline{K}h$). In addition, human capital is endogenous, rather than exogenous, in the system; that is, human capital is produced by using resources:

$$Y = \overline{K}_h f(K_h, L) \qquad (5.8)$$

$$K_h = f(Y, \overline{K}_h) \qquad (5.9)$$

The dramatic theoretical implications of endogenous growth theories is that output is no longer constrained by the constant-returns-to-scale property of the Solow production function, and that "knowledge" (proxied by $\overline{K}_h$) becomes a kind of public good that spills over into the economy as an externality, allowing output to grow beyond the measurable inputs. Another, equally important, implication of this model is that, by virtue of the average stock of human capital being a public good, there might be social underinvestment in human capital formation. This implication is very relevant to the education challenge topic of this chapter.

Empirical applications of the new growth theory are relatively recent, diverse, and not easily summarized. Although some studies have reported a high impact of education on growth, others have argued that there is little or nothing to be learned from the empirical growth literature (for example, Topel 1999; Banerjee and Dufflo 2005; Durlauf, *et al.* 2005; Pritchett 2006).

The inconsistency between micro and newer macro evidence on the returns to education has occupied the literature for a long time (for example, Krueger and Lindahl 2001; Sianesi and van Reenen 2003). The main reason for such inconsistency is that countries differ in many other respects that cannot easily be measured and controlled for in cross-country regressions, whereas within-country micro data automatically control for such factors.

Estimating the Challenge

"Growth with equity" is a contemporary development goal espoused by governments and international organizations (for example, World Bank 2005). In theoretical terms one can assume that social welfare (*SW*) consists of two components: efficiency (*EF*) and equity (*EQ*), as in the following social welfare function:

$$SW = f(EF, EQ) \qquad (5.10)$$

This function could be specified as:

$$SW = (Y/P)^{\alpha} (1 - GINI)^{\beta} \qquad (5.11)$$

where (*Y/P*) is per capita income, *GINI* is the common inequality index and α and β the value of the weights one puts at the efficiency and equity components. Assigning such weights implies a value-judgment that is best left to voters and politicians. The education challenge in this framework is how particular education policies (for example, greater coverage of primary education) are conducive or not to changing the values of per capita income and income distribution in a way that promotes social welfare.[3]

Data and Sources

The following data were used in our simulations:

- Historical national accounts data from Maddison (2010)
- Investment in education data from the World Bank on line indicators (EdStats)
- Education data from Barro and Lee (2010) and World Bank indicators

- Micro returns to education from Psacharopoulos and Patrinos (2004)
- Gini coefficients from the World Bank indicators.

Although all measures of education are used in this chapter, our central education variable is the average years of schooling of the population aged 15-plus. This choice is dictated both by the availability of a solid comparable database spanning 60 years (1950–2010), and the fact that this measure is a summary of educational development encompassing all levels (Barro and Lee 2010). This measure of education also links to an extensive body of recent theoretical and empirical economic growth literature from which we can borrow parameters or compare our estimates. It also happens that the educational level of the population, rather than the workforce, is more appropriate in a macro analysis of this kind in order to catch the wider or external effects of education on per capita income, for example, by lowering fertility or improving health conditions of the population at large.

It should be mentioned at the outset that years of schooling sometimes or often masks the quality of schooling; for example, 4 years of education in Finland does not equal 4 years of schooling in Colombia. Hanushek and Woessmann (2008) have shown that education quality affects economic growth. Increases in wages from a one-standard-deviation increase in cognitive test scores range from a low 5% in Ghana (Jolliffe 1998) to a high of 48% in South Africa (Moll 1998). In South Africa, Gustafsson *et al.* (2011) using a grade- and race-specific educational quality measure in a Mincerian earnings function, find that an improvement of 1.07 standard deviations in the quality measure for adults aged 20 to 29 results in an income improvement of 30%. Hanushek and Kimko (2000) found that a one-standard deviation change in labor force quality is associated with a nearly 1 percentage point higher economic growth rate. Coulombe *et al.* (2004) report that a 1% higher literacy score raises labor productivity by 2.5%. However, there are no historical data back to 1900 on education quality to use in our analysis.

In addition to the spottiness of the historical data, there are many new countries in the known data period that did not exist before 1950 (for example, break-ups of colonial territories), and many others

---

[3] For an application of this framework to an actual country case, see Psacharopoulos (1977).

that did not exist before 1990 (for example, the offshoots of the former Soviet Union), thus limiting the number of education–income observations. For all the above reasons we opted to work with regional averages in the simulations and projections. Of course we report illustrative individual country stories when sufficient data are available.

Efficiency and Equity Links

Figure 5.5 plots 1,596 pairs of observations of per capita income and years of schooling in 146 countries between 1950 and 2010. Treating the oil-rich countries in the upper left quadrant as outliers, the shape of the income–education relationship seems to illustrate a threshold level of 6 years of schooling as a necessary condition for the returns to schooling to manifest. In the new growth literature Azariadis and Drazen (1990) were the first to suggest what educators (Anderson and Bowman 1963) and economic historians (Easterlin 1981) had been saying for a long time: that there might be a threshold in terms of human capital accumulation before a country can reap growth benefits. In their words: "once … the stock of knowledge surpass[es] certain critical values, aggregate production possibilities may expand especially rapidly" (Azariadis and Drazen 1990). Benhabib and Spiegel (2005) identified an even lower threshold of human capital. Unless nations had a critical value of about 2 years of schooling in

1960 they achieved lower growth rates over the next 35 years relative to the comparators. Sala-I-Martin et al. (2004) found that a 10 percentage point increase of the primary school enrollment rate is associated with a 0.27 percentage point increase of the growth rate.

Methodology

The welfare loss associated with more or less education is obtained in three steps:

Step 1. A link is established between education and income by fitting a semi-logarithmic "Mincerian" macro function:

$$\ln(Y_{it}) = a + b\,S_{it} \tag{5.12}$$

to data on per capita income (Y) and years of schooling (S) in country i in year t. The b coefficient in this function can be loosely interpreted as a macro return to investment in 1 extra year of schooling (Mincer 1974).

Step 2. Predicted values of income ($\hat{Y}$) are obtained by applying the a and b coefficients of the above function to assumed values of years of schooling ($\hat{S}$):

$$\hat{Y} = e^{(a+b\hat{S})} \tag{5.13}$$

where e is the base of the natural logarithms.

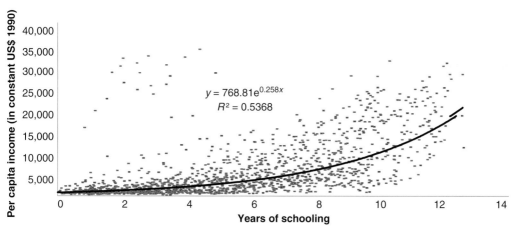

Figure 5.5 *The relationship between years of schooling and per capita income, 1950–2010 (based on pooled country–year data)*

Step 3. The welfare loss is defined as the percent increase of the base per capita income had the country a higher level of educational attainment:

$$\text{Welfare loss} = \left[\left(\hat{Y} - Y \right)/Y \right]/100 \quad (5.14)$$

Data Periods

There are three distinct data periods in the 150-year time-span considered in this chapter, as shown in Figure 5.6:

1. The period 1950–2010 refers to actual data on income and education available in our database
2. The period 1900–1950 contains a mix of actual data and estimated data, as, for example, many countries in the data set did not exist in that period

3. The period 2010–2050 contains only assumed or estimated data based on the known trends in the 1950 to 2010 period or assumptions

An Illustrative Case

Before applying our methodology on a world scale, it should be useful to illustrate it by comparing only two countries' record regarding education and economic growth: South Korea and Pakistan. Table 5.6 contrasts the educational and economic history of the two countries in the "known" 1950–2010 period. Both countries started with more or less the same per capita income in 1950, but Korea had a considerable advantage in years of schooling relative to Pakistan. By 2010 Korea's level of educational development reached nearly 12 years of schooling, equivalent to the average adult having completed secondary schooling, whereas Pakistan's educational development has not yet reached 6 years of schooling – a minimum for literacy. Since 1950 the income difference grew dramatically in favor of Korea. In constant prices Korea's per capita income grew 23-fold versus Pakistan's threefold growth, corresponding to a 5.2% versus 1.8% rate of economic growth. Many analysts have attributed much of the differential economic performance of Korea and Pakistan to the difference in the countries' educational development (Easterlin 1981; World Bank 1993).

Table 5.6 Comparison of Korea and Pakistan

Country	Years of schooling (15+ years old) 1950	Years of schooling (15+ years old) 2010	Per capita income (1990 constant $) 1950	Per capita income (1990 constant $) 2010	Economic growth rate (%)
Pakistan	1.0	5.6	643	2,239	1.8
South Korea	4.5	11.8	854	19,614	5.2

Source: Years of schooling from Barro-Lee (2010); per capita income from Maddison (2010)

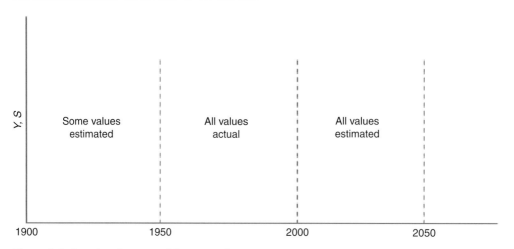

Figure 5.6 *Actual and estimated data periods*

It may take a decade for a country to increase the mean level of education attainment of the population by one year, as shown in Figure 5.7. It also depicts the S-shaped path countries follow in their educational development history. That is, progress is slow in the beginning, then it accelerates, and eventually it slows down.

In order to establish what Pakistan's per capita income would have been in the period 1900–2050 had it followed a different education policy, we must first establish a relationship between education and income. In this illustrative example such a relationship is obtained by fitting a Mincerian function using per capita income (Y) and years of schooling (S) circa 2009 in 128 countries:

$$\ln Y = 5.805 + 0.351\,S, \quad R^2 = 0.62, N = 128$$
$$(t = 14.4)$$
$$(5.15)$$

Variants of the above Mincer macro function using per capita income as the dependent variable in cross-country data have been fitted by Krueger and Lindahl (2001), Heckman and Klenow (1997), and Hanushek and Woessmann (2008). Our estimate of a 35% "return" to 1 additional year of schooling is nearly identical to theirs. After fitting such a function, Heckman and Klenow (1997) concluded that:

> *each additional year of schooling attainment in a country is associated with about 30% higher GDP per capita, whether one looks at 1990, 1985 or 1960 … The macro-Mincer coefficients … are consistent with large positive external productivity gains to economy-wide schooling attainment.*

Barro and Lee (2010), among many others, have fitted the same function using output per worker (rather than per capita income) as the dependent variable and adding a measure of physical capital stock as an independent variable. Since their estimate of the b coefficient is about one-half of ours, we adopted a 50% reduction of our estimated welfare loss as a lower bound. Table 5.7 and Figure 5.8

Table 5.7 Pakistan: Welfare loss as percent of per capita income

Year	Enhanced years of schooling	Per capita income (constant 1990 $) Actual	Per capita income (constant 1990 $) Simulated	Welfare loss (%) Lower bound	Welfare loss (%) Upper bound
1900	0.2	264	354	17.1	34.2
1950	3.0	643	947	23.6	47.2
2010	6.0	2,239	2,714	10.6	21.2
2050	8.0	4,570	5,475	9.9	19.8

Notes: Col. (2), hypothetical years of schooling used in the simulation; Col. (3), actual or projected per capita income given the 1950–2010 growth rate; Col. (4), estimate value based on equation (5.15) and Col. (2);. Col. 5 = (Col. 6) / 2; Col. (6) = [Col. 4 − Col. 3] / Col. 3)100.
Source: Based on equation (5.15), Table 5.6, and assumed enhanced years of schooling.

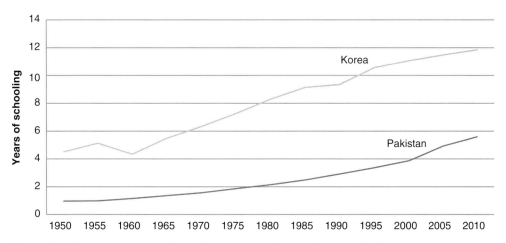

Figure 5.7 *Mean years of schooling of the adult population, Korea and Pakistan*

present estimates the welfare loss in terms of potentially higher per capita income had Pakistan a higher level of educational attainment as indicated in column (2), Table 5.7.

Alternative Pakistan Simulation

The Mincerian function was fitted to just the time-series observations for Pakistan, 1950–2010. The number of observations is only 13 because the education data are available in 5-year periods (see Table 5.8):

$$LnY = 6.319 + 0.290\,S, \quad R^2 = 0.89, N = 13$$
$$(t = 9.41)$$

(5.16)

The results are largely consistent with the 13 percent micro-estimated social rate of return to investment in primary education in Pakistan in 1975 (Psacharopoulos 1984, table A-1).

Table 5.8 Alternative Pakistan simulation using-time series

Schooling/loss	1900	1950	2010	2050
Inertia S	0.1	0.9	5.6	7.0
Enhanced S	1.3	1.9	6.6	7.8
Upper bound loss (%)	42.0	34.0	34.0	26.0
Lower bound loss (%)	21.0	17.0	17.0	13.0

World Estimates

The macro Mincerian function was fitted to pooled country–year data for the period 1950–2010 for which we have on average 11 actual observations on the mean years of schooling of the population 15-plus years and per capita income:

$$LnY = 6.645 + 0.258\,S, \quad R^2 = 0.57, N = 1596$$
$$(t = 42.98)$$

(5.17)

Predicted values of per capita income were estimated under assumed years of schooling and returns to education for the 1900–1950 and 2010–2050 periods for which no data exist. The assumed inertia values of half-year of mean world years of schooling for 1900 and 10 years for 2050 were obtained by extrapolating backward and forward the actual 1950–2010 trend shown in Figure 5.9 to fit a mild S-curve, as suggested by the historical data reviewed earlier. The enhanced schooling values were assumed to be just 1 extra year of schooling relative to the inertia values (Table 5.9).

Given the fact the low levels of S correspond mostly to primary education and the later years to post-compulsory education, it was assumed that the known period returns to education of 28.5%, would be 30% in the period 1900–1950 and 20% in the period 2010–2050. Most of the education increase of education in the early period must have been that

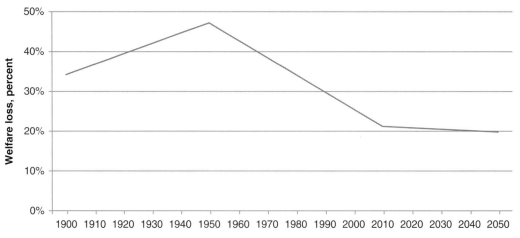

Figure 5.8 *Welfare loss associated with not having 1 additional year of schooling, Pakistan (upper bound)*

of farmers, and our early returns assumption is consistent with Jamison and Lau's (1982) findings on the effect of farmers' education on agricultural productivity.

Regional Estimates

The years of schooling coefficient of fitting the basic Mincerian function (equation 5.12) within regional groups of countries is reported in Table 5.10. This is the upper bound of what countries might have lost in the period of known actual data by not having 1 more year of schooling. East Asia and the Pacific that includes many dynamic economies in the period 1950–2010 exhibit the highest loss, whereas Latin America and sub-Saharan Africa the least. Such a pattern might be

due to two reasons. First, it is a well-known fact that the Mincerian function underestimates the returns to primary education; that is, the level of education most relevant to these countries (Psacharopoulos 1994). Second, the inferior education quality in Latin America and sub-Saharan Africa relative to other countries could be depressing returns in those regions. Also, it could be due to the fact that education is worth so much more in East Asia,

Table 5.9 Welfare loss associated with not having 1 additional year of schooling, world

			Welfare loss (%)	
Year	Inertia S	Enhanced S	Lower bound	Upper bound
1900	0.5	1.5	17.5	35.0
1950	2.7	3.7	14.7	29.4
2010	8.0	9.0	14.7	29.4
2050	10.0	11.0	11.1	22.1

Note: Enhanced S = Inertia S + 1.

Table 5.10 The welfare loss of not having 1 additional year of schooling, by region, 1950–2010

Country group	Welfare loss (% per capita income)
Advanced economies	20.2
East Asia and Pacific	34.3
Europe and Central Asia	22.8
Latin America and Caribbean	16.1
Middle East and N. Africa	14.5
South Asia	21.0
Sub-Saharan Africa	17.0
World	**25.8**

Note: *When multiplied by 100 the education coefficient measures the percent increase of per capita income associated with 1 extra year of schooling; all coefficients are statistically significant at the 1% probability level or better.*

Source: Equation (5.12) fitted within regional groups of countries.

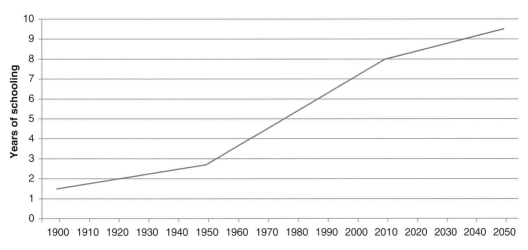

Figure 5.9 *Actual and assumed years of schooling of world population*

especially the fast-growing "tigers," that any deviation from the optimum shows larger relative losses. The fact that income loss differs between regions could be due to differences regarding economic institutions or access to capital.

Yearly Estimates

Mincerian macro regressions were fitted within each year. As shown in Table 5.11 and Figure 5.10

Table 5.11 Trend over time of the returns to education

Year	Returns (%)
1950	24.9
1955	25.6
1960	25.7
1965	27.3
1970	27.0
1975	27.3
1980	27.9
1985	30.7
1990	31.8
1995	30.9
2000	32.8
2005	34.4
2010	36.3
Overall	**25.8**

the macro returns to schooling seem to increase over time, a trend that might be counter-intuitive given expected diminishing returns to investment in education as the stock of human capital rises. But the new growth theory provides some clues for this pattern. According to Azariadis and Drazen (1990) cited earlier, there is a threshold level of schooling after which returns increase significantly. As more and more people achieve higher levels of schooling, and since schooling attainment is not infinite (see S-shape above), relative earnings tend to decline, and the individual rate of return will decrease, as predicted by classical economic theory. The point here is that increased schooling does not increase inequality, and may in fact contribute to its decline. The steady increase in schooling demonstrated in Table 5.1 should result in falling inequality in the world over time, but not necessarily a falling gap between developed and developing countries because of the lack of convergence in schooling across rich and poor countries, as demonstrated in the recent growth literature.

However, at the country level, higher levels of schooling for a larger proportion of the population lead to spillover effects, as more people are able to learn and share knowledge. Thus it is not odd to see declining individual returns to schooling while social returns continue to rise. Individual returns to schooling at early stages of development, when only a fraction of the population is educated, could reflect "rents" as educated individuals are able to

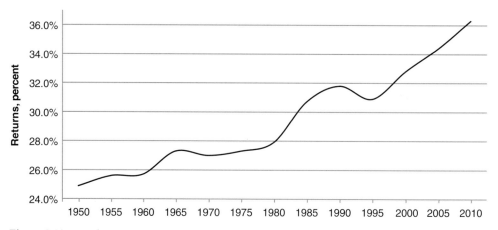

Figure 5.10 *Trend over time of the returns to education*

Table 5.12 Growth accounting simulation of the welfare loss

Country	r Overall social r, full method average (%)	(I_e/Y) Inertia education expend. as % of GDP (%)	$r*(I_e/Y)$ Inertia education contribution growth points	Enhanced education contribution growth points if $(I_e/Y) + 1$	Enhanced– inertia inertia difference in growth points	Actual inertia growth rate	Enhanced to inertia growth rate (%)
(1)	(2)	(3)	(4)	(5)	(6)	(7)	(8)
Argentina	7.7	4.6	0.35	0.43	0.08	4.1	1.9
Brazil	20.7	4.0	0.83	1.04	0.21	2.9	7.1
Chile	11.1	3.9	0.43	0.54	0.11	5.3	2.1
China	12.9	2.5	0.32	0.45	0.13	8.0	1.6
Colombia	15.1	3.1	0.47	0.62	0.15	3.2	4.7
Ecuador	12.4	1.3	0.16	0.29	0.12	2.0	6.2
Ethiopia	13.7	3.9	0.54	0.67	0.14	5.3	2.6
Ghana	15.8	4.7	0.74	0.90	0.16	4.8	3.3
Israel	10.0	6.6	0.66	0.76	0.10	4.3	2.3
Japan	8.4	3.7	0.31	0.39	0.08	1.2	7.0
Malawi	13.8	4.1	0.57	0.70	0.14	3.9	3.5
Mexico	12.5	4.9	0.61	0.74	0.13	2.9	4.3
Nepal	11.0	3.0	0.33	0.44	0.11	4.0	2.7
Paraguay	14.6	5.3	0.77	0.92	0.15	2.7	5.4
Philippines	10.9	3.5	0.38	0.49	0.11	3.8	2.9
Singapore	13.6	3.1	0.42	0.56	0.14	6.1	2.2
Spain	9.8	4.3	0.42	0.52	0.10	2.9	3.4
Uganda	35.5	2.5	0.89	1.24	0.36	6.3	5.6
United Kingdom	7.5	4.6	0.35	0.42	0.08	2.4	3.1
Venezuela	13.3	3.0	0.40	0.53	0.13	3.1	4.3
Vietnam	8.1	2.9	0.23	0.31	0.08	7.3	1.1
World mean	**13.9**	**4.0**	**0.55**	**0.69**	**0.14**	**4.0**	**3.3**

Notes: Col. (2) from Psacharopoulos and Patrinos (2004), average of social rates of return, full method; Col. (3) from World Bank indicators; Col. (4) = (Col. 2) × (Col. 3)/100; Col. (5) re-estimation based on a 1 percentage point increase in education expenditure; Col. 6 = (Col. 5) – (Col. 4); Col. (7) from Maddison (2010); Col. (8) = (Col. 6 / Col. 7) × 100.
Source: Based on the estimated education term of equation (5.5).

extract surplus earnings. As education rises, rents are eliminated and returns seem to decrease, while for society the more educated population contributes to more social learning and thus higher social returns.

Welfare Loss Using Growth Accounting

Estimates of the welfare loss in terms of a potentially higher growth rate in the growth rate in 21 countries using the Schultz methodology described above (equation 5.5) are presented in Table 5.12. The countries were selected on the criterion that social returns to education were available for all levels of education using the most reliable "full-method" estimation (equation 5.1, above). The education policy variable is the share of the GDP allocated to education. The simulation is based on a hypothetical increase in such share by 1 percentage point. As previous micro evidence has indicated, there exists extensive variation of the returns across countries. In our macro analysis, such returns are averaged out in order to arrive at a global estimate of the welfare loss. Moreover, we use a higher-bound estimate in making the predictions.

The results show that educational development, measured as the effort a country puts on education, amounts to just over 0.5 percentage point to a country's economic growth rate. Or, a country's growth rate could have been 3.3 % higher had the country invested one extra percentage point of the GDP to education.

The Welfare Loss of Illiteracy

The simulations presented above were based on 1 extra year of schooling relative to the countries' historical and inertia-projected educational attainment. We now ask the question: what is the welfare cost of illiteracy? This is estimated as the effect of some countries at some point in their history having less than 5 years of schooling on average.[4]

In order to do this simulation we assigned to countries in this category 5 years of schooling and fitted again the main Mincerian function (equation 5.17, above):

$$\text{Ln} Y = 5.530 + 0.381\,\hat{S}, \quad R^2 = 0.46, N = 1596$$
$$(t = 37.2)$$
$$(5.18)$$

The 38.1% return to years of schooling in the above function is of course exaggerated because of the artificial assignment of extra human capital to countries in the past were below the literacy level. Subtracting from this coefficient the 25.8% return

[4] About one half of the observations belong to this category.

of the base equation (5.17), above, we obtain a net return of 15.3% due to literacy. Or, the welfare loss associated with illiteracy is equivalent to a 15.3% drop in per capita income. Note that this result is especially robust in the sense that, by comparing the base to the "literacy-for-all" function we net out or hold constant differences between countries in the physical capital stock and many other unobservables that affect per capita income. Gustafsson *et al.* (2011) report that in South Africa an increase of literacy from 21% to 50% on the PIRLS (Progress in International Reading Literacy Study) scale, GDP per capita would be around 23% higher.

Equity Links

In our database we could match Gini coefficients and mean years of schooling for 114 country cases in the 1985 to 2005 period. Figure 5.11 shows that income inequality declines with increasing levels of schooling. One extra year of schooling is associated with a reduction of the Gini index by 1.4 points (on the World Bank scale measuring the Gini index from 0–100, rather than 0–1):

$$\text{Gini} = 52.088 - 1.351\,S, \quad R^2 = 0.10, N = 114$$
$$(t = 3.5)$$
$$(5.19)$$

Caveats

The results reported above are subject to several qualifications necessitated by the overly aggregate nature of the exercise spanning 146 countries and one and a half centuries. Cross-country regressions tacitly assume that all countries are on the same production frontier. Yet this is hardly the case (Klenow and Rodriguez-Clare 1997). The classic counterfactual is that of comparing Sri Lanka and other South Asian countries. Sri Lanka has a highly educated labor force relative to its neighbors, yet its economic growth record has been dismal. The reason for such bad economic performance has not been the lack of education; rather the political environment that has dampened incentives and opportunities for human capital to release its productivity (Bruton 1996; Lal and Myint 1996). Also, variables

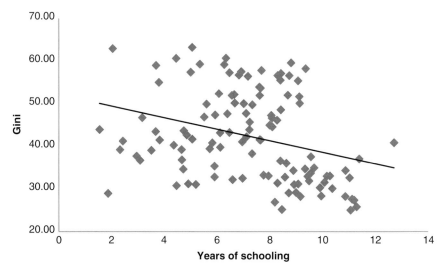

Figure 5.11 *The relationship between years of schooling and income inequality, 1950–2010 (based on country–year pooled data)*

used in typical macro growth regressions do not capture cross-country variation in growth of labor force participation or hours of work (Stokey 1994).

Estimates of the returns to education are typically based only on wage-earners and do not include the self-employed. This is due to the fact most household surveys do not collect income data for the self-employed, or at least not at the individual level. There are two problems with this. First, there is sample selection bias. Second, many studies have shown that the returns to education among the self-employed are lower than those of wage-earners. Indeed, this is particularly true of sub-Saharan Africa, where there is little evidence of returns to education to farmers and other self-employed workers. Thus, these estimates of the benefits of education are likely to overestimate the true benefits (Jolliffe 1998).

Countries also differ in many other aspects than those measured by the physical and human capital stock, for example, a different culture and discipline towards study and work; quality of schooling; quality of institutions; quality of policy-making; openness of economy; democracy; civil rights; and economic freedoms. There are many other "causal" variables that are likely to have a positive effect on growth and also likely to be positively correlated with the error term, such as investment rates, trade policies, colonial history, monetary policies, and restrictions on markets.

Such omitted variables can lead to large margins of error in accounting for differences in the economic growth path between countries.

Even if other inputs in production are held fixed, countries that limit the scope for using human capital should generate low estimates of the social returns to schooling. There will only be a return to human capital when there is disequilibrium due to shocks caused by technology, prices, or other factors that require a reallocation of resources (Schultz 1975). Countries that limit shocks by setting input or output prices centrally, or countries that use traditional technologies that do not change, will have limited returns to human capital. The former reason is why returns to schooling doubled following the transition to market (Fleisher *et al.* 2005), while the second is why returns to schooling are larger off-farm than on-farm in countries with traditional agricultural methods (Fafschamps and Quisumbing 1999; Godoy *et al.* 2005). Countries with bad institutions that create returns to corrupt actions will have human capital diverted to non-productive expropriation of the returns of entrepreneurs rather than productive innovation (Murphy *et al.* 1991, 1993). That suggests that the economic environment is critical to the return to an additional year of schooling.

One possibility running in the opposite direction that might be that our estimates are underestimates of the real impact of education is the existence of externalities. However, there is no clear evidence in the literature on the existence or magnitude of such externalities (Banerjee and Duflo 2005; Lange and Topel 2006; Pritchett 2006).

The most plausible argument for large positive social returns is from agglomeration economies where all firms in a locality become more productive because of an atypically high density of educated people. This argument makes the most sense in an industrialized economy rather than in the developing economies that have been our focus.

Because of liquidity constraints in developing countries poor children spend less time in school when their families get an unforecastable negative income shock from weather, unemployment due to national business cycles or localized job loss, or currency crises. However, it is unclear if transitory shocks that reduce current schooling result in a permanently lower level of schooling completed.

Another issue is the resource cost of "fixing" the challenge. In the case of education, a very large amount of resources would have to be used to provide an additional 1–2 years of schooling or, alternatively, ensure that everyone has enough years of schooling to be literate, and this cost needs to be subtracted from the welfare gains associated with such an increase in the years of schooling of the population. Put another way, the welfare loss of having low levels of schooling is offset, at least to some extent, by the actual uses made of the resources that would have to be devoted to avoid those low levels of schooling.

If, as is likely, the marginal cost of schooling is increasing in years of schooling, then the cost of adding an additional year of schooling will be greater than the average cost of attaining the current level of schooling. Rising marginal cost of schooling mean that estimates of current marginal returns to schooling will overstate the returns to further increases in schooling attainment.

Conclusion

In order to provide a best and conservative indication of the welfare loss associated with one extra year of schooling we adjusted the lower-bound estimates

Table 5.13 Welfare loss in terms of lower per capita income because of low educational attainment

Year	Percent GDP loss from	
	One school year deficiency	Illiteracy
1900	10.3	12.3
1950	8.7	9.0
2010	8.7	9.0
2050	6.5	3.8

presented in Table 5.9, above, by 41%. This adjustment is based on the difference between private and social returns to primary education, as in Psacharopoulos and Patrinos (2004) (Table 5.2). Making a similar adjustment to the gross loss associated with literacy we obtain a 9% net loss on average during the 1950–2010 period on which this estimate is based. As indicated in the last column of Table 5.1, world illiteracy has been falling by about three percentage points per decade. Based on linear interpolation and extrapolation of the historical data, the 9% central loss estimate has been adjusted upwards and downwards to obtain values for 1900 and 2050, respectively. Table 5.13 shows our best estimates of the welfare loss associated with a lower level of educational attainment over one and a half centuries.

Our lower-bound estimate of the global loss in terms of a lower or potentially higher per capita income, had countries a higher level of educational attainment by 1 schooling year, is depicted in Figure 5.12. Such losses range from 7% to 10% over the 150-year period. The loss from illiteracy ranges from about 4% to 12%.

Based on our growth accounting results, the welfare or income loss amounts to about 1 percentage point of the average country's growth rate had the countries not invested 1 percentage point more of their GDP on education. In addition to the above efficiency effects, one additional year of schooling is associated with a reduction of inequality by 1.4 points on the Gini scale.

Investments in the health, knowledge, and skills of the people – human capital – are as important as investments in the more visible, physical capital of the country. Every country that sustained high growth for long periods put substantial effort into schooling its citizens and deepening its human

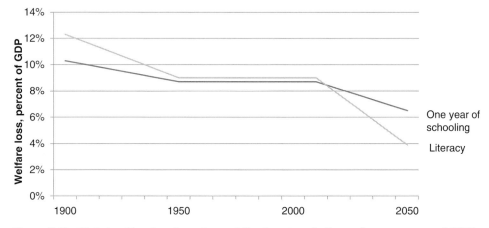

Figure 5.12 *Global welfare loss from the world's education challenge (loss as percent of GDP)*

capital. Conversely, considerable evidence suggests that other developing countries are not doing enough (Commission on Growth and Human Development 2008). This is the remaining challenge.

References

Azariadis, C. and A. Drazen (1990) Threshold externalities in economic development. *Quarterly Journal of Economics* **105**: 501–526.

Banerjee, A. and E. Duflo (2005) Growth theory through the lens of development economics. In: P. Aghion and S. Durlauf (eds.), *Handbook of Economic Growth*. Amsterdam: North Holland.

Barro, R. J. (1991) Economic growth in a cross-section of countries. *Quarterly Journal of Economics* **106**: 407–444.

Barro, R. J. and J-W. Lee (1993) International comparisons of educational attainment. *Journal of Monetary Economics* **323**: 363–394.

Barro, R. J. and J-W. Lee (2010b) *Educational Attainment Database*, v.2.0, 07/10, http://www.barrolee.com.

Barro, R. J. and X. Sala-i-Martin (1995) *Economic Growth*. New York: McGraw Hill.

(1997) *Determinants of Economic Growth: A Cross-Section Empirical Study*. Cambridge, MA: MIT Press.

(2010) *A New Data Set of Educational Attainment in the World, 1950–2010*, Working Paper No. 15 902. Cambridge, MA: National Bureau for Economic Research.

Bassanini, A. and S. Scarpetta (2001) The driving forces of economic growth: panel data evidence from OECD countries. *OECD Economic Studies* **33**: 9–56.

Becker, G. S. (1964) *Human Capital*. New York: Columbia University Press.

Benhabib, J. and M. Spiegel (1994) The role of human capital in economic development: evidence from aggregate cross-country data. *Journal of Monetary Economics* **34**: 143–174.

(2005) Human capital and technology diffusion. In: P. Aghion and S. Durlauf (eds.), *Handbook of Economic Growth*. Amsterdam: North Holland.

Bils, M. and P. Klenow (2000) Does schooling cause growth? *American Economic Review* **90**: 1160–1183.

Bowman, M. J. and C. A. Anderson (1963) Concerning the role of education in development. In: C. Geertz (ed.), *Old Societies and New States*. Glencoe, IL: Free Press.

Bruton, H. J. (1996) *The Political Economy of Poverty, Equity and Growth: Sri Lanka and Malaysia*. Oxford: Oxford University Press.

Cohen, D. and M. Soto (2007) Growth and human capital: good data, good results. *Journal of Economic Growth* **12**: 51–76.

Commission on Growth and Human Development (2008) *The Growth Report: Strategies for Sustained Growth and Inclusive Development*. New York: World Bank.

Coulombe, S., J-F. Tremblay, and S. Marchand (2004) *Literacy Scores, Human Capital and Growth across 14 OECD Countries*. Ottawa: Statistics Canada.

de la Fuente, A. and R. Doménech (2006) Human capital in growth regressions: how much difference does data quality make? *Journal of the European Economic Association* **4**: 1–36.

Denison, E. F. (1967) *Why Do Growth Rates Differ?* Washington, DC: Brookings Institution.

Durlauf, S., P. A. Johnson and J. Temple (2005) Growth econometrics. In: P. Aghion and S. Durlauf (eds.), *Handbook of Economic Growth*. Amsterdam: North Holland.

Easterlin, R. (1981) Why isn't the whole world developed? *Journal of Economic History* **41**: 1–19.

Fafchamps, M. and A. Quisumbing (1999) Human capital, productivity, and labor allocation in rural Pakistan. *Journal of Human Resources* **34**: 369–406.

Fleisher, B. M., K. Sabirianova, and X. Wang (2005) Returns to skills and the speed of reforms: evidence from Central and Eastern Europe, China and Russia. *Journal of Comparative Economics* **33**: 351–370.

Gemmell, N. (1996) Evaluating the impacts of human capital stock and accumulation on economic growth: some new evidence. *Economica* **58**: 9–28.

Glaeser, E. L. (1994) Why does schooling generate economic growth? *Economics Letters* **44**: 333–337.

Godoy, R., D. S. Karlan, S. Rabindran, and T. Huanca (2005). Do modern forms of human capital matter in primitive economies? Comparative evidence from Bolivia. *Economics of Education Review* **24**: 45–53.

Gustafsson, M., S. Van der Berg, D. L. Shepherd, and J. W. Burger (2011) The costs of illiteracy in South Africa. *Development Economics eJournal* **3**, Article 1.

Gylfason, T. and G. Zoega (2003) Education social equality and economic growth: a view of the landscape. *CESifo Economic Studies* **49**: 557–579.

Hanushek, E. and D. Kimko (2000) Schooling, labor-force quality, and the growth of nations. *American Economic Review* **90**: 1184–1208.

Hanushek, E. A., and L. Woessmann (2008) The role of cognitive skills in economic development. *Journal of Economic Literature*, **46**: 607–668.

Heckman, J. and P. Klenow (1997) *Human Capital Policy*. Chicago, IL: University of Chicago. Available at: http://klenow.com/HumanCapital.pdf.

Jamison, D. T. and L. Lau (1982) *Farmer Education and Farm Efficiency*. Baltimore, MD: Johns Hopkins University Press.

Jolliffe, D. (1998) Skills, schooling, and household income in Ghana. *World Bank Economic Review* **12**: 81–104.

Klenow, P. and A. Rodriguez-Clare (1997) The neo-classical revival in growth economics: has it gone too far? In: B. Bernanke and J. Rotemberg (eds.), *NBER Macroeconomics Annual*. Cambridge, MA: MIT Press.

Krueger, A. B. and M. Lindahl (2001) Education for growth: why and for whom? *Journal of Economic Literature* **39**: 1101–1136.

Lal, D. and H. L. Myint (1996) *The Political Economy of Poverty, Equity and Growth: A Comparative Study*. Oxford: Clarendon Press.

Lange, F. and R. Topel (2006) The social value of education and human capital. In: E. Hanushek and F. Welch (eds.), *Handbook of the Economics of Education*, vol.**1**. Amsterdam: North Holland.

Lucas, R. (1988) On the mechanics of economic development. *Journal of Monetary Economics* **22**: 3–42.

Maddison, A. (2010) *Historical Statistics of the World Economy: 1–2008 AD*. Available at: http://www.ggdc.net/Maddison/Historical_Statistics/horizontal-file_02-2010.xls.

Mankiw, N. G., D. Romer, and D. M. Weil (1992) A contribution to the empirics of economic growth. *Quarterly Journal of Economics* **107**: 407–437.

McMahon, W. W. (1999) *Education and Development: Measuring the Social Benefits*. Oxford: Oxford University Press.

Meyer, J. W., F. O. Ramírez, and Y. N. Soysal (1992) World expansion of mass education, 1870–1980. *Sociology of Education* **65**: 128–149.

Mincer, J. (1974) *Schooling, Experience and Earnings*. New York: Columbia University Press.

Moll, P. G. (1998) Primary schooling, cognitive skills, and wage in South Africa. *Economica* **65**: 263–284.

Morrisson, C. and F. Murtin (2007) *Education Inequalities and the Kuznets Curves 1870–2000*, Working Paper No. 12. Paris School of Economics.

(2008) *The Century of Education*, Working Paper No. 22. Paris School of Economics.

Murphy, K. M., A. Schleifer, and R. W. Vishny (1991) The allocation of talent: implications for growth. *Quarterly Journal of Economics* **116**: 503–530.

(1993) Why is rent-seeking so costly to growth? *American Economic Review* **83**: 409–414.

OECD (2010). *The High Cost of Low Educational Performance*. Paris: OECD.

O'Neill, D. (1995) Education and income growth: implications for cross-country inequality. *Journal of Political Economy* **103**: 1289–1301.

Peaslee, A. (1969) Education's role in development. *Economic Development and Cultural Change*, **17**: 293–318.

Pritchett, L. (2006) Does learning to add up add up? The returns to schooling in aggregate data. In: E. Hanushek and F. Welch (eds.), *Handbook of Economics of Education*. Amsterdam: North Holland.

Psacharopoulos, G. (1977) Measuring the welfare effects of educational policies. In: A. J. Culyer and V. Halberstadt (eds.), *Public Economics and Human Resources*. Paris: Cujas.

(1984) The contribution of education to economic growth: international comparisons. In: J. Kendrick (ed.), *International Comparisons of Productivity and the Causes of the Slowdown*. Pensacola, FL: Ballinger Publishing for The American Enterprise Institute.

(1994) Returns to education: a global update. *World Development* **22**: 1325–1343.

Psacharopoulos, G. and H. A. Patrinos (2004) Returns to investment in education: a further update. *Education Economics* **12**: 111–134.

Romer, P. (1986) Increasing returns and long-run growth. *Journal of Political Economy* **94**: 1002–1037.

(1990) Endogenous technological change. *Journal of Political Economy* **89**: S71–102.

Sala-I-Martin, X., G. Doppelhofer, and R. Miller (2004) Determinants of long-term growth: a bayesian averaging of classical Estimates (BACE) approach. *American Economic Review* **94**: 813–835.

Schultz, T. W. (1975) The value of ability to deal with disequilibria. *Journal of Economic Literature* **13**: 827–846.

(1961a) Investment in human capital. *American Economic Review* **51**: 1–17.

(1961b) Education and economic growth. In: N. B. Hentry (eds.), *Social Forces Influencing American Education*. Chicago, IL: National Society for the Study of Education.

Sianesi, B. and J. van Reenen (2003) The returns to education: macroeconomics. *Journal of Economic Surveys* **17**: 157–200.

Solow, R. (1956) A contribution to the theory of economic growth. *Quarterly Journal of Economics* **70**: 65–94.

(1957) Technical change and the aggregate production function. *Review of Economics and Statistics* **39**: 312–320.

Stokey, N. (1994) Comments on Barro and Lee. *Carnegie–Rochester Conference Series on Public Policy* **40**: 47–57.

Topel, R. (1999) Labor markets and economic growth. In: O. Ashenfelter and D. Card (eds.), *Handbook of Labor Economics*. Amsterdam: North Holland.

UNESCO (1953) *Progress of Literacy in Various Countries*. Paris: UNESCO.

(2010) *Global Monitoring Report*. Paris: UNESCO.

Wils, A. (2003) *National Transitions to Full Literacy: Patterns of Timing, Gender Inequality and Regional Diffusion*. Washington, DC: Academy of Educational Development.

Wils, A. and A. Goujon (1998) Diffusion of education in six world regions, 1960–90. *Population and Development Review* **24**: 357–368.

Wils, A. and R. O'Connor (2003a) *The Transition to Education for All: General Patterns and Timing*. Washington, DC: Academy of Educational Development.

(2003b) *The Causes and Dynamics of the Global Education Transition*. Washington, DC: Academy of Educational Development.

World Bank (1993) *The East Asian Miracle: Economic Growth and Public Policy*. New York: Oxford University Press.

(2005) *Equity and Development: World Development Report 2006*. New York: Oxford University Press.

Gender Inequality: A Key Global Challenge – Reducing Losses due to Gender Inequality

CHAPTER 6

JOYCE P. JACOBSEN

Introduction to the Challenge

Gender inequality pervades the world. In considering the dimensions of economic gender inequality, women still make less than men in the formal work sector, are more likely to live in poverty, are less likely to participate in the formal work sector, and do a larger share of work in the household sector. The dimensions of political gender inequality include women's lower representation in elected office and lower representation in political and corporate appointments. Social gender inequality has numerous dimensions, some of which are less favorable to men while others are less favorable to women: men are more prone to violence, imprisonment, and disability, while women are more likely to be the victims of domestic violence and sexual assault; in some countries men have lower educational attainment than women, while the pattern is reversed in other countries. Demographic gender inequality includes the fact that men live shorter lives on average than do women (65 years for men, 69 years for women) (CIA 2010), but there is also concern that many women are never given the chance to be born, and in the younger generations men now outnumber women, by large numbers in China and India in particular (with gender ratios respectively of 113 men and 117 men per 100 women in the under-15 age range) (CIA 2010).

While many of the costs of gender inequality are ultimately borne by particular individuals, they can also be calculated at a society or even worldwide level. If individuals of different genders are not given equal opportunity to develop their potential, then societies forgo the increased level of output and ultimately well-being that would derive from their higher productivity. If societies do not invest equally in educating and training men and women,

do not give them equal opportunities to engage in more productive forms of work, and do not give them equal opportunities to advance to more productive positions over time, then the societies do not harness the full potential of their members.

The goal of this chapter is to perform such a calculation, in which the costs to human society of gender inequality, measured as a percent of actual GDP worldwide and for sub-regions, are calculated for the years 1900 through 2050. These numbers can also be used to measure the total cumulative costs over the past 110 years of gender inequality and to project forward the expected additional costs over the next 40 years.

Background to the Challenge

While many readers are likely familiar with the main dimensions of gender inequality, this section provides a quick overview of the empirical patterns researchers have documented, particularly over the course of the twentieth century.

The nineteenth century saw the rise of the women's suffrage movement across Western countries and a general push for equal treatment of women and men under the law. In 1893 New Zealand became the first country to extend the right to vote to women; most countries followed suit in the first part of the twentieth century (e.g. Denmark in 1915, the USA in 1920), while other countries were much later (Liechtenstein in 1984; Kuwait in 2005).

Many other forms of legal discrimination against women persisted beyond suffrage, however. It was only in 1963 that the USA passed the Equal Pay Act, making it illegal to pay women and men different wages for equal work; it took a while for other countries to follow suit (e.g. Ireland in 1976; Japan in 1987).

Not surprisingly, women's participation in paid work was fairly limited before the latter half of the twentieth century. As an example, Figure 6.1 shows the growth for the USA in women's labor force participation (as compared to men's more static

Table 6.1 Labor force participation rates by sex and proportion of labor force that is female, countries grouped by income level

	%Labor force/population		
	Women	Men	Women/labor force
Low income	68	85	0.45
Lower middle income	54	84	0.38
Middle income	54	83	0.38
Upper middle income	53	79	0.41
High income	64	80	0.44

Source: Data are from most recent available year, 2007–2008, for persons aged 16–64.
http://genderstats.worldbank.org/

and eventually declining participation) from 1800 up until the present. Participation rises steadily throughout, but at an accelerated rate after 1940, with a recent downturn in participation since 2000. Women as a percentage of the labor force has leveled out at around 46%.

Table 6.1 shows comparable contemporary data to Figure 6.1 for sets of countries sorted by per capita income level. It is notable that there is still a wide range of participation rates found in the present day so that countries have not converged on a specific higher level of female participation in paid work. Interestingly, there is a convex shape with regards to women's participation, with lower participation rates for the middle-income countries compared to both the low- and high-income countries. Men's participation shows much less variation across income levels, but drops for higher-income groups.

One possible precondition for higher rates of participation in the labor force, as well as higher female earnings, is higher levels of female education. Table 6.2 shows the US ratios of women to men among high-school graduates and among tertiary-degree recipients over the period from 1870 to 1950 where they are also increasing, albeit at a low rate, their labor force participation. Interestingly,

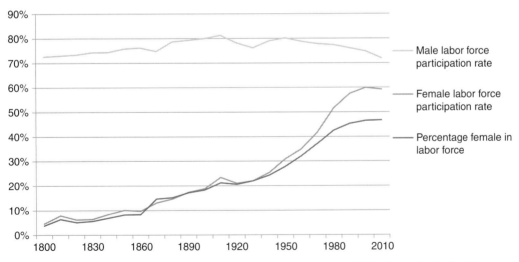

Figure 6.1 *US labor force participation rates by sex and percentage of labor force that is female, 1800–2010. Data for 1800–60 are for free persons only. Data for 1800–1930 are for persons ages 10 and over, for 1940 are for persons ages 14 and over, for 1950–60 are for persons ages 14 and over, for 1970–2010 are for persons ages 16 and over. Sources: 1800–60, Weiss (1986); 1870–1970, US Bureau of the Census (1976); 1980–2050, Economic Report of the President (2011)*

Table 6.2 US ratio of females to males among high-school graduates, and bachelor and first-professional degree recipients, end of each school year, 1870 to 1950

Year	High school	Bachelor's and first-professional degree
1870	1.28	0.17
1880	1.18	0.24
1890	1.31	0.21
1900	1.5	0.24
1910	1.48	0.29
1920	1.53	0.52
1930	1.22	0.66
1940	1.11	0.7
1950	1.1	0.31

Source is National Center for Education Statistics (1991), p. 105 (Table 95).

Table 6.3 Education enrollment rates by sex, percent of relevant age group, countries grouped by income level

	Secondary			Tertiary		
	Females	Males	Ratio	Females	Males	Ratio
Low income	34	41	0.83	4	6	0.67
Lower middle income	61	65	0.94	18	19	0.95
Middle income	67	69	0.97	25	24	1.04
Upper middle income	89	86	1.03	47	38	1.24
High income	100	101	0.99	74	60	1.23

Note: Data are from most recent available year, 2006–2008.
Source: http://genderstats.worldbank.org/

Table 6.4 Non-agricultural hourly earnings ratios, women to men, selected countries

Country	Women/men
Sweden	0.89
New Zealand	0.87
Denmark	0.86
Australia	0.86
France	0.83
Bulgaria	0.83
Netherlands	0.81
Finland	0.8
Egypt	0.78
Germany	0.76
Iceland	0.75
Singapore	0.73
Canada	0.72
South Korea	0.64
Japan	0.52

Source: http://laborsta.ilo.org; data are from 2000–2008.

over this period, women actually predominate over men in the pool of high-school graduates, but have lower rates of tertiary-degree recipiency and actually lose ground on this measure after World War II.

This pattern of relatively high rates for women relative to men of secondary education is still seen today across most countries. Relative rates by gender of tertiary education vary more substantially across countries. Table 6.3 indicates secondary and tertiary enrollment rates (more readily available than degree completion rates) for sets of countries sorted by per capita income level (as in Table 6.1). All country groups exceed the tertiary ratio seen in the USA as of 1950, but have lower secondary ratios than in the USA over the period reflected in Table 6.2. Thus education alone is clearly not the fundamental precondition for women's participation in the paid labor force, but education enrollment rates do rise with income level for both genders.

Finally, we can again contrast the growth in relative earnings in the USA since the nineteenth century, as shown in Figure 6.2, to comparable contemporary data for a range of countries as shown in Table 6.4. Notably, the US path is not a steady upward trend, pointing out that progress is not always linear, or irreversible.

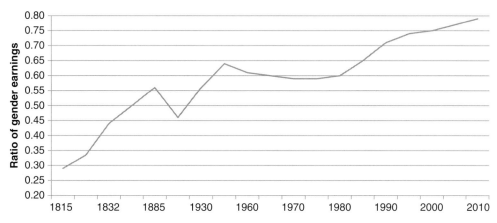

Figure 6.2 *US gender earnings ratios, 1815–2009.* Sources: *1815–1930, Goldin (1990); 1955–2009, Current Population Reports, Series P-60*

In Table 6.4, it is clear (as in Table 6.1) that the world has not yet converged on a standard gender earnings ratio, with a wide range of outcomes still occurring across different countries. These ratios are higher than the USA in many cases, though it is also the case that yearly earnings ratios are lower than these hourly ratios due to working women's lower hours in paid work.

The world clearly still does not yield equal outcomes for women and men. The question is how much these unequal outcomes by gender stem from unequal opportunities by gender. In addition, if opportunities were equalized, how might the world have looked different in the past, and how might it look different in the future?

Delimitation of the Challenge

The attempt to calculate an estimate of the world's losses due to gender inequality provides the opportunity to conduct a fascinating what-if exercise into how a gender-neutral world might look. It is always mind-stretching to construct a reasonable alternative to the current state of the world, let alone consider what a gender-neutral world might have looked like 110 years ago, or what it might look like 40 years into the future.

This brings up the standard question of whether to focus on gender equality in outcomes or in opportunities. For instance, a world in which economic outcomes were equal would be a world in which women and men participate equally across all sectors of activity, whether paid or unpaid, and make the same rate of pay. However, in a world where opportunities were gender-neutral, men and women would receive the same amount of education and training and have the same chances in life for economic, personal, and social advancement. But they could make choices that would lead to outcomes being significantly different on average by gender, such as women choosing to enter certain occupations at higher rates than men (and vice versa), choosing to spend more time in household production rather than in paid work, and thus ending up with different average earnings than men.

It is thus a challenge to interpret the differential economic outcomes by gender that we see in the world, as some component of them can be due to free choice rather than to gender discrimination in access to education in training, to gender discrimination in hiring, or to gender discrimination in pay (by which I mean that equally productive women and men are nonetheless paid different wages). In deciding what proportion of observable differences are due to free choice on the part of individuals as opposed to constraints imposed on individuals through the discriminatory actions of others, I rely on the results of some 40 years of research by economists and other social scientists that attempts to calculate the proportion of the gender earnings gap that is due to each cause. I also make assumptions regarding what proportion of women might have worked in the labor force at each point in time. But I also consider the case of equality of outcomes, in which women would work at the same rate in the formal sector as do men and would be paid the same wage rate as are men. This result gives me a potential maximum value for the gains that society could reap through achieving gender equality, not simply neutrality.

Throughout my calculations the focus is on measuring changes in the labor market and thus changes in the amount of labor income generated by movement to gender equality. Thus there are a number of other topics that I do not include in my calculations that could be considered in a much broader framework of how gender inequality affects societal efficiency. I exclude them from my analysis due to a lack of available research on how these factors might affect GDP overall. These include the potential effects on efficiency of increasing women's political participation in many if not all societies. It may be that women would run societies (or subunits thereof, like local governments) more efficiently than men, including potentially engaging in less corruption – for instance Swamy *et al.* (2001) find that women are less involved and accepting of bribery – and thus there might be gains from putting them in charge of more governmental bodies and agencies. In addition, if women leaders were less likely to lead their countries to war or other armed conflicts, there might be quite significant efficiency gains related to the lower level of societal violence.

There are also some very difficult questions relating to how the entire path of development might have been altered if gender equality had been already achieved in 1900. For instance, if women had been working more in paid labor in 1900, the world might well have begun demographic transition down to replacement-level birth rates much sooner (since we know that higher rates of female labor force participation in the formal sector are strongly related to smaller family sizes). Another factor not dealt with is the phenomenon that as women's participation rises in the workforce, men tend to work less, often starting work later in their lifespan and retiring earlier. I also do not consider the question of how societies might operate differently at this point if the many girls who were not born due to son-favoring had been born, instead

taking the society at each point as constituted by the people actually alive in it.

Definition of the Challenge

Thus this is a much less ambitious exercise in this chapter than could potentially be hypothesized, meant as a first pass at calculating the costs of gender inequality. I define costs of gender inequality as the forgone gain that would have occurred had women participated more fully in the formal work sector and been trained and then utilized up to their full productive capacity in the formal work sector. While I am assuming that workers in general are more productive in the formal sector than in the informal (including household) sector, I take the gain as the difference between the value of the output that workers produced in the informal sector and the value of the output that they would produce if moved to the formal sector. In addition, I take a portion of the gender wage gap as a calculation of the degree to which women are not able to be employed as productively as they could be if they were allocated efficiently to jobs, as well as educated and trained as much as men to participate in paid work.

I assume that the maximum additional gain achievable through gender equality – and thus the highest of my loss calculations attributable to gender inequality – would be if: (1) women worked at the same rate in the formal (paid) work sector as do men, both in terms of participation and hours worked, and (2) were paid at the same wage rate as are men. Subtracted from this is (3) an estimate of the value of forgone household (unpaid) sector production and (4) an estimate of the additional costs of expanding education and training so that women are educated at the same rates as men (noting that for a number of countries this has already been achieved). Thus the loss attributable to gender inequality drops over time and for areas in which the participation rate of women rises and the gender earnings gap narrows.

I contrast this maximum figure to a medium figure for each point in time from 1900 to 2050. My medium figures modify the above assumptions by considering the case where (1) women would still participate in the formal sector at a reduced rate relative to men; and (2) women would still receive a somewhat lower earnings rate than men. However, both of these phenomena would be due to women's free choice rather than due to gender discrimination in either the paid work sector or the household sector. Thus it is important to consider what proportion of women would choose not to participate in paid work and how much of the observed earnings difference between women and men may be due to choice rather than constraint. Note I do not also have a "low" or "minimum" estimate because that would be the same as the status quo; if we assume that observed gender differences in participation and pay are due to free choice on the part of women in terms of where they want to work and what skills they want to attain, then there would be no costs attributable to gender differences, and no cost of gender inequality (since inequality in outcomes here does not imply inequality of opportunity).

Relevant Research and Available Data for the Challenge

The literature on the economics of gender spends much time on four topics that are relevant to this analytical exercise: (1) measuring and explaining the gender gap in formal work participation; (2) measuring and explaining the gender wage gap; (3) calculating the value of work in the informal (mainly household) sector; (4) considering gender differences in educational attainment. These literatures thus provide both theoretical underpinnings for the current exercise, and calculations that are necessary inputs into the estimation of the social cost of gender inequality.

Gender Differences in Participation in Paid Work

Worldwide, women participate less in the formal or paid work, sector of the economy than do men. The International Labor Organization (2009) estimates total worldwide female participation in the paid workforce at 40%, with generally a lower rate in the less developed countries (closer to 35%) and a higher rate in the more developed countries (closer to 45% in the OECD). For our purposes, it will not make that large a difference if we assume a constant

rate of 40% participation versus assuming some variation.

This lower participation of women than men in the formal sector appears in large part due to their having much greater work responsibilities in the informal, or household, sector. Whether these responsibilities are assumed by free choice, by following of social norms, by coercion, or by lack of opportunities in the formal sector (whether due to gender discrimination or general lack of opportunities) can vary by person and by society. For the developed nations, it appears that women now exhibit free choice to participate to a greater degree in the household sector (as compared to men); for less industrialized nations, particularly where women may receive less schooling or training that is useful for paid work, the matter of choice is much less clear. However, studies across a wide variety of societies and times show that when opportunities for women's work expand in the paid sector, with the concomitant rise in women's wages, that women increase their participation in paid work significantly. This is well documented for the rise of manufacturing employment, particularly in textiles, in the USA and the UK (Goldin 1990; Simonton 1998; Costa 2000). Thus rising wages and rising female participation in the labor force rise hand in hand, implying that there are gains to the society from women's movement into the paid work sector at these times.

It is also the case that at many times there have been formal restrictions against women's full participation in paid employment, including work hours regulations (quite common from the turn of the twentieth century up through the 1920s and 1930s), marriage bars (requiring women to resign when they married), and banning of women from certain industries and occupations (often because they were banned from receiving the necessary training, such as bans on women's entering law school). Thus the current level of labor force participation for women represents for the most part a significant increase over the course of the twentieth century, a trend that will be reflected in our calculations below. This increase in participation will be modeled as partly due to decreased restrictions on women's participation – i.e. the factors leading to costs – and partly due to expanded opportunities for labor force participation, which will be viewed as a neutral force. These restrictions could be both formal and/or society-wide, as outlined above, and house-hold- or family-specific, if an individual woman is restricted by members of her family (husband, parent, brother) from participating in paid work. So both formal and informal restrictions comprise social inequality for women. Thus, as we calculate the costs related to lower participation of women in paid work going back to 1900, not all of the lower participation will be viewed as due to restriction, but rather related to the general lack of opportunities for full expansion of the paid labor force to accom-modate the full female population at each point in time. For my maximum cost calculations below, I assume that social inequality causes the entire par-ticipation gender gap and thus if it were eradicated, so would be the participation gender gap; while in my medium calculations, I assume that social inequality causes half of the participation gender gap, with the other half being caused by free choice on the part of women.

Gender Differences in Wages

There is an enormous literature that documents the existence of and explores the causes of the gender wage gap, mainly for recent years (1970–2010), but also for historical periods. The gender wage gap exists at all times and places. In the calculations below I benchmark the current gender pay ratio at 60% in developing countries and 75% in developed countries (women's to men's earnings) based on my own earlier surveys of gender wage gap studies (Jacobsen 2007, Chs. 10–13) and rely on calcula-tions from Goldin (1990) and other sources to esti-mate the pay ratio worldwide. Going back to 1900, fewer systematic studies exist of the pay ratio, particularly for countries other than the USA and the UK. I rely on the US calculations from Goldin (1990) and other sources that I had previously iden-tified (Jacobsen 2007, Chapter 14) for estimates of the pay ratio going back to 1900.

Interestingly, studies for both developed and less developed countries are quite consistent in attribut-ing about 40% to 50% of the gender wage gap in general to observable differences in characteristics, leaving as much as 50% to 60% unexplained and thus potentially attributable to discriminatory factors

in the labor market (though of course they could also be due to non-discriminatory unobserved factors; for one thing women may choose jobs with relatively more desirable characteristics such as lower proba-bilities of injury, or women may have the same level of formal education but less-valued specific training, such as a less mathematical – technical college major–comparative literature instead of engineering) (Jacobsen 2007, Chs. 10 and 12). However, even some of the differences in measured characteristics can either be attributable to underinvestment in women, such as lower rates of education and train-ing, including lower levels of on-the-job training. Also, factors such as whether a person is married or has children often affect earnings, but need not necessarily do so depending on support structures in the household sector, and thus are still potentially endogenous and capable of being re-engineered so that women could reach higher earnings levels. For example, if spouses share household work more evenly, or if other family members who are not in the workforce assist with childcare and other house-hold chores, these factors need not affect either spouse's earnings. Thus even part of the difference ascribed to measured characteristics could still be considered related to societal factors that increase gender inequality. As such, I provide both a "com-plete equality" calculation as a maximum figure for possible gains (i.e. assume pay is equalized between women and men) and medium calculations where 50% of the wage gap is assumed to exist due to differences in personal preferences by gender regard-ing type and intensity of paid work.

Valuing Household Production

While it has been intimated in the above sections that shifting women increasingly out of the house-hold sector and into the paid work sector leads to efficiency gains, such shifts are not costless as there is a significant opportunity cost in many cases of household work thus not being done. This could include less in-home production of food prepara-tion, childcare, and home-based agriculture such as growing kitchen gardens. In developed countries much food preparation and childcare has moved to the formal sector and a smaller proportion of people produce a significant share of their own food. Thus the gain in shifting women between sectors needs to be measured net of the loss of household production that is given up in exchange. Some of this may be mitigated as well over time as higher levels of capital in the household sector, such as has happened in countries like the USA, can increase efficiency in this sector as well, but then that can also reduce the net improvement in shifting women between sectors. Wagman and Folbre (1996) point out for example that the gain in well-being in the USA over the latter half of the twentieth century may be significantly overestimated if it is measured solely as gain in GDP per capita without any offset for lost household production, given that a large percentage of the gain in this period came precisely from women moving into the workforce in much higher numbers.

Landefeld *et al.* (2009) use an innovative approach of recent time-use data combined with a variety of estimates regarding the value of time spent in household production to come up with a range of values for the value of household production as a percent of measured GDP. They come up with a range of 12% to 62% of GDP.

A broader view that considers not only household production but unpaid work writ larger would increase these numbers. Richard Anker (1987), in his preface to Goldschmidt-Clermont's definitive book on valuation of unpaid work (1987) maintains that national income estimates would be increased by 25%–50% on average if unpaid work were taken into account. Thus it is quite clear that ignoring the shift in resources out of this sector would lead to a significant overestimate of the efficiency gains from employing more women in the formal sector.

I take these numbers as a cue to benchmark the opportunity cost of shifting people from the unpaid sector into the paid sector as 50% of the additional value of their paid work. As such, it represents not a cost of attaining gender equality, but simply an adjustment so that only net gains from the shift are counted as the benefit from attaining gender equality.

Gender Differences in Educational Attainment and Training

While there are still significant differences in educational attainment by gender, a number of countries have recently attained not only complete parity in primary education, but have even moved to the point where women in the younger cohorts appear to be receiving both more secondary education and now even more tertiary education than are men (World Bank 2010).

For instance, the 2009 ratio of female to male primary enrollment ranges from a low of 67 females per 100 males in Afghanistan to 108 females per 100 males in Mauritania, with parity achieved in all high-income countries. Nonetheless, in a number of countries women lag significantly behind men in literacy rates, enrollment rates, and degree attainment rates. In addition, women lag behind men in all countries where studies have been performed in terms of receiving on-the-job training and apprenticeships (Jacobsen 2007, Ch. 10).

King *et al.* (2009) spend a large part of their report discussing the importance of closing the education gap in order to reach gender equality. This closing represents both a necessary condition for women's achieving full parity in paid work participation and earnings, but also a significant cost as national governments would need to expand their spending on education in order to ensure that the genders receive equal education at each level, assuming that equality would be achieved through bringing up the group with lower attainment rather than reallocating the same level of resources so that the group with higher attainment were brought down. In addition, employers would need to spend more on training to accommodate the larger formal sector workforce. These costs may be viewed either as a necessary opportunity cost for society to achieve the higher level of social output, and thus should be an offset against the gains from these increases in training, or viewed as a separate issue from the total gains from bringing women into full equality with men. Government expenditure on education currently runs at about 5% of GDP across countries (CIA 2010); this does not include private household and firm costs for education and training, which I assume are of matching size. In the estimates below, I assume that additional education and training costs are included as an offset against gains and assume they are set at 10% of the added value of GDP to achieve a higher level of female education and training.

Calculating the Costs of Gender Inequality from 1900 to 2010

The numbers mentioned above delineate the differences in male and female paid work participation rates, earnings rates, household production, and educational attainment. A couple of additional numbers are necessary in order to finish the calculations necessary to calculate the costs of gender inequality. First, an estimate of how much of GDP and equivalently gross domestic income is attributable to labor rather than capital. Pakko (2004) indicates that labor has accounted for a relatively steady 70% share of US national income over the past 50 years where good data are available. Recent data for a set of OECD countries puts labor's share in this set at about 65% of GDP on average (with the USA on the high end at 70%) (Azmat *et al.* 2007). One might expect labor's share to be higher in lower-income countries which are characterized by lower capital stocks. However, it may well be lower in some other countries depending on other factors affecting labor's share such as regulations on earnings; for instance Cajing.Com.Cn (2010) argues that labor's share in China is less than 56% and dropping. At any rate, I assume that the percent change in GDP is the percent share of labor income, which I take as 70%, times the change in labor income generated by an increase in women's earnings and participation.

Second, in common with the other chapters in this volume I take the common set of numbers on estimated GDP and population year by year from 1900 to 2050.[1] These numbers include both a higher growth and lower growth scenario for GDP going forward from 2009 to 2050.

I construct two alternative scenarios. First I construct a maximum scenario in which the entire gender earnings gap and the entire gender participation gap is attributed to discrimination, and thus under full equality women would participate at the same rate as men and would be paid the same as men.

Alternatively, in my medium scenario, I assume that half of the gender earnings gap and half of the participation is due to free choice rather than inequality.

To start off these scenarios, I assume a worldwide participation rate whereby women comprise 15% of the labor force in 1900, rising to 25% in 1950 and 40% in 2010. In between these years I extrapolate growth at a steady rise. These numbers are averaged from a somewhat higher rate in the more developed countries and a somewhat lower rate in the less developed countries, with increasing convergence over the period. In 1900 in the USA, women comprised 18% of the labor force, rising to 30% by 1950 (Economic Report of the President 1976, Table B-34; US Bureau of the Census 1976, Series D13). Assuming these numbers mark the high end of the participation range, I adjust accordingly based on level of development over time and country to come up with the worldwide numbers.

For gender earnings ratios, I assume a worldwide gender earnings ratio of 0.50 in 1900, 0.45 in 1950 (as wages actually dropped for women relative to men compared to the earlier manufacturing era – see Goldin 1990, 60–62), and a rise back up to 0.60 in 2010.

For each woman that enters the market labor force, I assume an offset of 50% for reduced non-market production, and an offset of 10% for additional education and training.

As an example of the estimation technique, I will show here the calculations for 2010:

1. The assumed proportion of women in the workforce is 40% and the counterfactual is that there would be as many women as men in the workforce if it were not for gender inequality. Thus the new labor force can be calculated as an additional 20 women for every 100 people currently in the workforce (of which 40 are women and 60 are men, so an additional 20 women would yield equal numbers of women and men). Thus the workforce would increase by 20%.

2. The assumed gender earnings ratio is 60% and the counterfactual is that women would be paid the same as men if it were not for gender inequality. Thus the new wage bill can be calculated as an additional 40 cents for every $1.60 currently paid to workers (of which $0.60 is paid to women and

[1]   Data provided by Copenhagen Consensus Center based on United Nation, Department of Economic and Social Affairs, Population Division (2009) *World Population Prospects: The 2008 Revision*, CD-ROM edn and Maddison, A. (2008) *Historical Statistics of the World Economy: 1–2008 AD*, available at www.ggdc.net/maddison/Historical_Statistics/

$1.00 to men), where the workforce now consists of equal numbers of women and men. Thus the new wage bill is now 25% larger.

3. Thus the total earnings paid to workers would be 50% larger (1.20 times 1.25 = 1.50) if it were not for gender inequality.

4. Assuming that the wage bill is 70% of earnings, GDP now increases by 0.7×.05, or 0.35, so is 35% bigger.

5. Subtracting out half of this change to compensate for forgone household sector production, the net increase in production is 17.5% of GDP.

6. Subtracting out 10% of this change to cover education and training costs for the labor force increase, since the labor force increased by 20%, the additional educational and training cost is 0.2×0.1 or 2% of GDP, so the net change in total value due to gender inequality is 15.5% of GDP.

The medium scenario halves the labor force increase and halves the earnings increase before performing the calculation in (3) above and the subsequent calculations. For 2010 these adjustments yield a net change in total value due to gender inequality of 7% of GDP. Similar calculations are performed for the other years from 1900 up to 2010.

The only other study of which I am aware that tries to calculate the effects of eliminating gender differences in pay and employment is Tzannatos (2010), which provides a one-shot contemporary estimate of instantaneous adjustment to full equality. Using a two-sector model of the formal labor market (male occupations and female occupations), Tzannatos calculates a country-level average GDP gain of 4%, with regional differences ranging from a loss in the Nordic countries of −3 percent of GDP to a gain in high-income Asian countries of 6% of GDP. In his model, male wages decrease while female wages rise (always by more than the male wage decrease), and up to 32% of the labor force has to be reallocated, mostly from female-sector into male-sector occupations. His estimates, benchmarked to the late 1990s/early 2000s, do not include a reallocation of women out of the informal or unpaid sectors into the formal sector, and thus not surprisingly provide a lower bound to my calculations, which allow for female shifts into formal sector positions as well. In my maximum estimates,

I assume no drop in male productivity (and thus no drop in wages); my medium calculations by contrast can allow for part of the reduction to occur through a narrowing of the wage gain either because women's wage gain is smaller or because men's wages drop as well. Thus my medium estimates are much closer to his estimates but still higher due to the reallocation of women between sectors.

An alternative approach to measuring the effects of gender inequality on economic growth is taken by Klasen and Lamanna (2009), who estimate regressions of country-level GDP growth rates in the 1960–2000 period on measures of gender inequality, focusing in particular on education and labor force participation gender gaps. They find that these gaps explain part of the difference in growth rates between countries, and thus reduction of these gaps would lead to higher growth rates. Here there is no offset for reduced household production as women increase their formal labor market participation.

The Klasen and Lamanna regression-based approach could also be extended by including other societal gender differences of the types illustrated in the World Economic Forum's series of gender gap reports (e.g. Hausmann et al. 2010), which includes measures of political participation gaps such as the gender ratio of parliament seats, and life-expectancy differences. Thus one could measure the effects of a range of gender differences on GDP growth rates across countries. Again, this approach is somewhat more limited in serving as a basis for extrapolation out of recent experience (as the reports currently incorporate only about 5 years of data), particularly back to 1900.

Calculating the Costs of Gender Inequality from 2010 to 2050

Results going forward in time are calculated using the same technique as in the above historical calculations. I again use the two alternative scenarios of maximum, where all gender differences in participation and earnings are attributable to discrimination, and medium, where half of gender differences are attributed to free choice.

For women as a percent of the labor force, I use the estimate of 42% in 2030 and 45% in 2050. For the gender earnings ratio I use the estimate of 65% in 2030 and 70% in 2050. I use straight-line extrapolation to estimate the values in each case between 2010 to 2030, and 2030 to 2050.

Results going forward in time are calculated using both the low-GDP-growth and high-GDP-growth scenarios and comparing the different paths in terms of relative to 1900 figures.

Results for the Costs of Gender Inequality from 1900 to 2050

The results of my estimations are summarized below in Tables 6.5 and 6.6 and Figures 6.3 and 6.4.[2] Tables 6.5 and 6.6 give the numbers at the benchmark years for the challenge, while Figures 6.3 and 6.4 show the full time-series graphically. Table 6.5 and Figure 6.3 present the total/global loss for each year due to gender inequality as a percentage of GDP in the given year. Recall again that there is no "minimum loss" scenario depicted graphically, because the minimum loss would be zero at all points in time. Table 6.6 and Figure 6.4 present the total/global loss for each year due to gender inequality as a percentage of GDP in 1900 and as a total dollar figure as well in Table 6.6. They also show results for both a high-GDP-growth and a low-GDP-growth scenario going forward from 2010 to 2050, where the low-growth scenario assumes world GDP growth of 2.5% per annum over this period, and the high-growth assumes world GDP growth of 3.5% per annum.

As women have been increasing both their labor force participation and their earnings relative to men, the costs of gender inequality as a percent of current GDP have been dropping. However, these costs have been rising as a percent of 1900 GDP because the total amount of world GDP is so much higher now than in 1900. Thus the total dollar value of the loss is quite substantial by 2010, ranging from a low estimate of US$5 trillion to a high estimate of over US$13 trillion in 1900 dollars.

There are several obvious critiques of this exercise as we move back in time from the better-known present, where labor force participation rates are

[2] The Excel spreadsheet with my calculations is available from me upon request.

Table 6.5 Global loss from gender inequality as percent of GDP in the given year

	1900	1950	2010	2030	2050
Maximum estimate	37%	32%	16%	13%	9%
Medium estimate	17%	15%	7%	6%	4%

more similar between men and women. One is whether it is possible that the labor market of 1900 could really have employed this much higher number of women relative to the size of the labor force at that time. Of course in this scenario, it is not necessary to assume that gender equality only suddenly started in 1900. If gender equality had in fact started much earlier than 1900, the labor market would have had more time to adjust to this level of employment. Similarly, while it may be implausible to assume that the capital–labor ratio would have stayed the same in 1900 (thus providing the same relative returns to the higher level of labor), again if the formal labor market had had a higher inflow of women earlier than 1900, the capital–labor ratio would have had longer to adjust (i.e. investment in capital for the formal sector might have also been quite different in the nineteenth century). However, if either of these adjustments had not occurred, the returns to expanding female labor in the early stages of this calculations would have been lower.

Similarly, demographic and educational attainment effects of equality in the beginning of the twentieth century could have started much earlier, thereby likely causing an earlier demographic transition to lower fertility rates and changing the productivity of labor in the non-market sector as well as potentially changing the overall population growth rate. There could also have been many accompanying demographic changes in such variables as marital rates and age at first marriage, marital dissolution rates, child and adult mortality rates, life expectancies, and household size. Again, such additional effects are out of the scope of the current limited modeling exercise, and arguments could be made in both directions regarding whether incorporation of demographic dynamics would increase or decease the calculated amounts in this chapter. However, to the extent that many of such changes related to a lower fertility rate would have tended to

Table 6.6 Global loss from gender inequality as percentage/total in billions of 1900 GDP

Scenario	1900	1950	2010	2030	2050
Maximum estimate – high growth	37%	88%	429%	695%	1019%
Maximum estimate low growth	37%	88%	421%	561%	678%
Medium estimate high growth	17%	39%	202%	331%	493%
Medium estimate low growth	17%	39%	199%	267%	328%
Maximum estimate high growth	$736	$1730	$8301	$13,703	$20,093
Maximum estimate low growth	$736	$1730	$8301	$11,068	$13,365
Medium estimate high growth	$328	$776	$3916	$6529	$9713
Medium estimate low growth	$328	$776	$3916	$5273	$6460

Note: High growth assumes 3.5% GDP growth per annum from 2009 to 2050; low growth assumes 2.5% GDP growth per annum from 2009 to 2050.

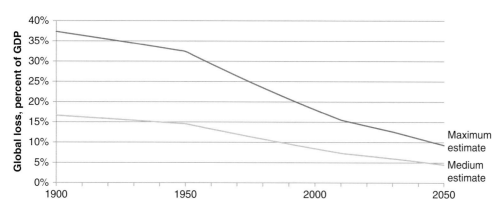

Figure 6.3 *Global loss from gender inequality as percent of GDP in the given year, 1900–2050*

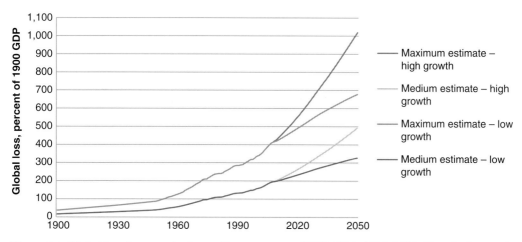

Figure 6.4 *Global loss from gender inequality as percent of 1900 GDP, 1900–2050. Note: high growth assumes 3.5% GDP growth per annum from 2009 to 2050; low growth assumes 2.5% GDP growth per annum from 2009 to 2050*

reduce both women's containment to the non-market sector and women's productivity in the non-market sector (fewer marriages, smaller families) while increasing human productivity in general (with smaller families, higher educational attainment and better health per child), one would tend to think that the results in the chapter are a lower bound rather than an overestimate of the gains from earlier gender equality. It is harder to see how these changes would have reduced total output per person.

Fundamentally, an analysis such as the one undertaken in this chapter, whether calculated as a partial equilibrium analysis or a general equilibrium analysis, will not satisfy all readers, and readers may well decide that the numbers presented herein are either too low or too high relative to what they believe to be the case, or that the time path is not as they would have construed it. However, it is also the case that this chapter attempts to put range values on which other more detailed studies may then compare with in the future. This chapter also makes clear that it is unlikely that the costs of gender inequality are zero – and also that they are not unlimited in scope and size.

Related Topics and Additional Considerations

There are a number of additional costs related to gender inequality that are not included in the above calculation, which focuses essentially on the costs related to women's reduced participation in paid work relative to what it would be if they were given equal access to education, training, and all occupations as are men. Unlike the systemic considerations mentioned in the earlier part of the chapter, they are smaller costs that can be calculated and added onto the above numbers if so chosen. One reason I do not include them in the main calculations above, other than their smaller size, is because less work has been done on the topics on a worldwide level, and there may be significant variations in their costs across societies that are hard to gauge without more studies. However, I mention them here because they underscore the way in which gender inequality permeates societies and leads to social costs in a variety of ways.

One topic that could be expanded is the calculation of the different returns to men and women to participation in the informal sector. In particular, while I have conceptualized the informal sector as essentially identical to the household sector, it can instead be conceptualized more broadly as including work in areas involving barter transactions, such as small-scale agriculture. There can also be paid transactions, so this adds in self-employment, including somewhat larger-scale agriculture and other forms of self-employment in the informal sector. While women would likely make less than men in informal transactions on average, it is the case that this factor combined with their greater representation in the informal sector could also lead to either an increase or a reduction of the measure of total cost of gender inequality. It is possible that there may be substantial efficiency gains by equalizing women's and men's access to inputs such as land in the agricultural sector (Udry 1996; FAO 2010; see in particular Peterman *et al*. 2010 for documentation of differences in inputs). On the other hand, O'Laughlin (2007) argues against the view as epitomized by Udry (1996) that there are large efficiency gains to be had by equalizing gender control of productive resources in the agricultural sector, in large part on the grounds that there is little to be gained in this impoverished sector by simply redressing the gender imbalances but not actually increasing total inputs.

Another topic is the costs of domestic violence. Most domestic violence takes the form of men abusing women. Both physical and mental abuse can lead to missed work in both the paid work and household production sector, and in the most extreme case domestic partner homicide leads to a loss of lifetime earnings. In addition there is the direct cost of hospitalization and other medical treatment for the victims, as well as the cost to society of having to set up systems to deal with battered domestic partners (such as halfway houses, help lines, and costs of the justice system in having to deal with such cases). A US study by the National Center for Injury Prevention and Control (2003) estimates the total annual costs in the USA as about US$5.8 billion, of which about 80% is the direct medical and mental healthcare costs. This means that for the USA, the cost of domestic violence as a percent of GDP is about 0.06%, or six-one-hundredths of 1 percent (in 2002, which reflects the last year of data available for the report: 5.8 billion divided by 10.4 trillion).

This is unfortunately large, but still small relative to the much larger costs estimated above for gender discrimination related to workforce participation and earnings.

Another topic is the costs related to discrimination on basis of sexual orientation, which fundamentally interacts with the social roles assigned by gender. In a survey of findings from labor economics studies of gender differentials between gay and straight, Jacobsen and Zeller (2007) summarize the evidence as finding a small differential favoring straight men over gay men, but also a differential favoring lesbians over straight women, the implication being that these differentials may be due both to on-the-job discrimination, but also to different decisions related to occupational choice and differential attachment to the household sector versus the paid workforce. Thus gender and sexual orientation interact to yield different results. The net effect of gender interacted with sexual orientation is non-zero, but not as significant in size as that found for the basic female–male divide in terms of both participation and earnings. Thus, while this can be viewed as another social cost related to gender inequality, it is much smaller in magnitude.

Another topic is how to deal with diseases and illnesses that have very different rates of prevalence by gender. Should we view an important element of gender equality as that somehow there should be equal spending on such diseases, or in some other way (rates of prevalence) should the disease burden be equalized across genders? In a large sense, namely lower life expectancy and high disability rates, men would appear to be net beneficiaries of attempts to equalize gender outcomes regarding diseases and other causes of death and disability. Currently they enjoy significantly fewer years of total life, with higher rates of dying at all ages, and have significantly higher rates of occupational injury as well as higher rates of dying from societal violence. However, this is a difficult topic to tackle on the gender dimension and it may be cleaner at this stage to consider the general challenge of reducing the costs of disease and illness rather than considering its gender dimensions.

Similarly, violence, which appears to be worldwide a predominantly male phenomenon in terms of its perpetrators, may be more effectively dealt with through an approach on reducing its level rather than considering its gendered nature. Nonetheless, the very predominance of men throughout the ages among both the victims and the perpetrators in most armed conflicts, whether civil war, war between nations, or terrorist activities, calls attention to the very real linkage of gender differences with many of the most pressing problems of our time.

Conclusions Regarding the Challenge

I conclude this interesting challenge with a newfound respect for the limitations of attempting a calculation of the sort found in this chapter, but also for the power of undergoing such an attempt to concretize the costs involved in gender inequality worldwide. The estimates presented in this chapter may strike some as large and some as small; they may strike others as too radical and others as too conservative. Nonetheless they provide a starting point for a debate on how much costs for gender inequality are we willing to bear, how much are we willing to spend to reap the potential gains from decreased gender inequality, and how these estimates might be modified by additional research and alternative conceptions of the challenge.

References

Anker, R. (1987) Preface. In: L. Goldschmidt-Clermont, *Economic Evaluations of Unpaid Household Work: Africa, Asia, Latin America and Oceania.* Geneva: ILO.

Azmat, G., A. Manning, and J. Van Reenen (2007) *Privatization, Entry Regulation and the Decline of Labor's Share of GDP.* London: London School of Economics and Political Science.

Caijing.Com.Cn (2010) China's labor share of GDP declined for 22 consecutive years. Available at: http://english.caijing.com.cn/2010-05-12/110437827.html.

Central Intelligence Agency (2010) *World Factbook.* Washington, DC: CIA.

Costa, D. (2000) From mill town to board room: the rise of women's paid labor. *Journal of Economic Perspectives* **14**: 101–122.

Economic Report of the President (2011) Washington, DC: US Government Printing Office.

Food and Agricultural Organization (2010) *Gender Dimensions of Agricultural and Rural*

Employment: Differentiated Pathways out of Poverty. Rome: FAO.

Goldin, C. (1990) Understanding the Gender Gap: An Economic History of American Women. Oxford: Oxford University Press.

Goldschmidt-Clermont, L. (1987) Economic Evaluations of Unpaid Household Work: Africa, Asia, Latin America and Oceania. Geneva: ILO.

Hausmann, R., L. Tyson, and S. Zahidi (2010) The Global Gender Gap Report. Geneva: World Economic Forum.

International Labor Organization (2009) Global Employment Trends for Women. Geneva: ILO.

Jacobsen, J. (2007) The Economics of Gender, 3rd edn. Malden, MA: Wiley-Blackwell.

Jacobsen, J. and A. Zeller (2007) Queer Economics: A Reader. London: Routledge.

King, E, S. Klasen, and M. Porter (2009) Women and development. In: B. Lomborg (ed.), Global Crises, Global Solutions: Costs and Benefits. Cambridge: Cambridge University Press.

Klasen, S. and F. Lamanna (2009) The impact of gender inequality in education and employment on economic growth: new evidence for a panel of countries. Feminist Economics 15: 91–132.

Landefeld, J., B. Fraumeni, and C. Vojtech (2009) Accounting for household production: a prototype satellite account using the American Time Use Survey. Review of Income and Wealth 55: 205–225.

O'Laughlin, B. (2007) A bigger piece of a very small pie: intrahousehold resource allocation and poverty reduction in Africa. Development and Change 38: 21–44.

National Center for Education Statistics (1991) Digest of Education Statistics. Alexandria, VA: NCES.

National Center for Injury Prevention and Control (2003) Costs of Intimate Partner Violence against Women in the United States. Atlanta, GA: US Department of Health and Human Services Centers for Disease Control and Prevention.

Pakko, M. (2004) Labor's Share. St. Louis, MO: Federal Reserve Bank of St. Louis.

Peterman, A., J. Behrman, and A. Quisumbing (2010) A Review of Empirical Evidence on Gender Differences in Nonland Agricultural Inputs, Technology, and Services in Developing Countries. International Food Policy Research Institute Discussion Paper No. 00975. Washington, DC: IFPRI.

Simonton, D. (1998) A History of European Women's Work: 1700 to the Present. London: Routledge.

Swamy, A., S. Knack, Y. Lee, and O. Azfar (2001) Gender and corruption. Journal of Development Economics 64: 25–55.

Tzannatos, Z. (2010) Decreasing the gender gap in employment and pay in the Arab world: measuring the gains for women, youth, and society. Paper presented at the International Conference on Women and Youth in Arab Development, Cairo, March 22–24, 2010.

Udry, C. (1996) Gender, agricultural production, and the theory of the household. Journal of Political Economy 104: 1010–1046.

US Bureau of the Census (1976) Historical Statistics of the United States. Washington, DC: US Government Printing Office.

Wagman, B. and N. Folbre (1996) Household services and economic growth in the United States, 1870–1930. Feminist Economics 2: 43–66.

Weiss, T. (1986) Revised estimates of the United States Workforce, 1800–1860, In: S. L. Engerman and R. E. Gallman (eds.), Long-Term Factors in American Economic Growth. Chicago, IL: University of Chicago Press.

World Bank (2010) World Development Indicators. New York: World Bank.

Human Health: The Twentieth-Century Transformation of Human Health – Its Magnitude and Value

DEAN T. JAMISON, PRABHAT JHA, VARUN MALHOTRA, AND STÉPHANE VERGUET

I have tried always to remember a simple truth about the past that the historically inexperienced are prone to forget. Most people in the past either died young or expected to die young, and those who did not were repeatedly bereft of those they loved ... the power of death cut people off in their prime and made life seem precarious and filled with grief. It also meant that most of the people who built civilizations of the past were young when they made their contributions.

– Niall Ferguson, *Civilization: The West and the Rest* (2011, pp. xxii–xxiii)

Ferguson refers to a past with mortality far higher than today, a past in which people not only died young but lived with frequent illness, undernutrition and (for women) the often debilitating consequences of high fertility. This past was not so very long ago. Section 1 will present long trends in life expectancy in the country where it is highest. From a period of virtually no change in mortality prior to 1790, improvements became rapid in the nineteenth century and extremely rapid in the period 1880–1960. During this latter period life expectancy in the leading country increased by 3.2 years per decade. And, as this chapter will document, not only did the leading country rapidly improve but much of the rest of the world converged toward the leader.

Our agenda in this chapter is, first, to review briefly the magnitude and likely origins of mortality decline in the twentieth century. While some of that decline results from improvements in income – and all the health-related goods that income buys – we conclude that improvements in health technology dominate the explanation for health gains. In Section 2, the core of the chapter, we develop measurements of twentieth century mortality reductions in terms of reduction in the expected number of years of life lost (YLLs) by a typical individual relative to an idealized norm. This norm is the United Nations' projected mortality profile for Japan in 2050. (An alternative to Japan 2050 as a norm is to use the lowest mortality country at any given time as the norm for that time. Annex 7.2 presents results obtained under this assumption.) Part 2 also presents money metric valuation of the YLL declines using methods standardized by the Copenhagen Consensus. The chapter conveys results for a number of individual countries and regions as well as for the world as a whole. Section 3 of the chapter presents examples to provide a more granular feel for the origins of mortality decline and the nature of remaining problems. Section 4 concludes.

It is worth noting at the outset that other chapters in this collection – on education, nutrition, water and sanitation and air pollution, for examples – explore in detail some of the underlying reasons for mortality change.

The Magnitude and Origins of Mortality Decline in the Twentieth Century

Figure 7.1 shows female life expectancy levels – in the country with the then highest female life expectancy – from the mid eighteenth century to the present time. Figure 7.2 shows the rate of increase in female life expectancy (in

This Chapter was prepared with support from the Copenhagen Consensus Center and from the Bill & Melinda Gates Foundation through the Disease Control Priorities Network Grant to the University of Washington.

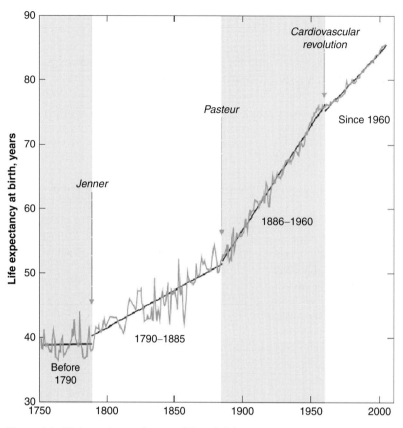

Figure 7.1 *Highest observed national female life expectancies at a given moment in the world (1750–2005). Source: Vallin and Meslé (2010).*

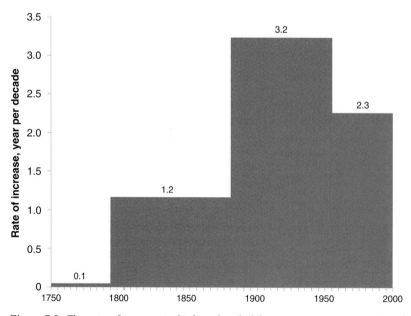

Figure 7.2 *The rate of increase in highest female life expectancy, years per decade*

years of life expectancy per decade) based on Figure 7.1. It is hard to overstate the magnitude of the improvements in longevity from 1800 on (or how little improvement there had been previously). And rapid as the leader's improvement was for many decades, at 3.2 years per decade, global convergence is more impressive. In India, for example, life expectancy grew at a rate of over 4.5 years per decade between 1960 and 2002.

Mortality declines in the twentieth century varied by age group – with the sharpest declines in childhood deaths below age 5 and less marked declines in middle age (defined here as age 30–69 years).[1] Mortality from infectious diseases fell far faster than did mortality from non-communicable diseases. Moreover, the main contributors to the declines varied over time, in part because the higher levels of income achieved by low-and middle-income countries in more recent decades have enabled them to purchase more technological progress (at any given level of income). Thus low-and middle-income countries have benefitted in the second half of the twentieth century from the diffusion of technological advances in higher-income countries in the first half of the twentieth century. In some cases, advances in education have enabled more effective use of these technologies, most notably from improvements in maternal education enabling better use of oral rehydration therapies or case management of sick children (Kidane and Morrow 2000).

Technological advances and their effective diffusion account for most of the large declines in premature mortality in the twentieth century worldwide, particularly for the declines in mortality observed in low-and middle-income countries from about 1950 onwards. Income and, to a lesser extent, education were less important predictors of these massive declines in premature deaths (Easterlin 1999; Jha *et al.* 2004;. Jamison *et al.* 2013). Two caveats on causality relations among income, technology, and mortality change are worth considering. First, most of the twentieth century had large gaps in evidence on diseases, expenditures, and their outcomes. The gaps persist. For example, less than a third of all deaths worldwide have reasonably reliable causes of death given to them, as they occur without any medical attention (Jha 2012). Second, income and education influence

many aspects of the use of technology. For example, higher income enables better access to improved water supply and to sanitation, which does (albeit quite expensively) reduce childhood deaths from diarrhea. Higher income also supports improved communication, changes in transportation, and other dimensions of infrastructure that might have more distal impacts on mortality reduction. There are also concomitant changes in changing occupation, such as safer, less manually demanding jobs, as well as changes in gender-participation in labour markets. All of these have an impact on reduced mortality. However, as reviewed elegantly by Easterlin (1999), the main contribution to the large declines in mortality arose from more proximate measures of public health including public health institutions.

Additionally, the specific choices made by households (or more commonly by governments) such as the use of smallpox vaccines in the late nineteenth and early twentieth centuries in turn depended on having some wealth (but smallpox eradication was independent of household decisions). In contrast, public health institutions and regulations that are quite important in interrupting the spread of infectious agents (say the ability of enforcing quarantine laws against suspected smallpox cases), or control of risk factors for chronic diseases (say enforced bans on smoking in public places) are often *poorly* correlated with income

---

[1] Avoidance of disability is also important. Mortality does not capture all illnesses, specifically neuropsychiatric and musculoskeletal diseases. However, the correlation of mortality with morbidity for most major diseases is quite strong, and in low-income countries, a greater proportion of the combined total of deaths and disability arise from mortality than is the case in high-income countries. Moreover, it is important to note that measurement error in disability estimates is much greater than for mortality, and often can exceed the desired change in health outcomes. For example, a health policy planner may desire a 10% improvement in an under-5 health outcome, but if measurement error exceeds 10% in the health outcome measure, she or he will not know if the intervention worked. Since it is usually possible to tell the difference between a dead person and a living one, restricting analyses to mortality should reduce measurement error in health policy-making. This chapter focuses on mortality reduction only and for that reason understates both the magnitude of health problems in, say, 1900 and the magnitude of subsequent progress.

levels. Thus, the impact on specific (and usually poorly measured) diseases (such as age-specific smallpox mortality) is difficult to quantify. There are also changes in the natural virulence of infectious agents over time (and much less likely increases in the resistance of humans to these agents). For example, there might well have been changes in unmeasured etiologic factors for tuberculosis that led to its declines in the early twentieth century, independent of treatment, which was not introduced widely until the 1950s (Nagelkerke 2012). These problems in measurement and attribution have contributed, along with ideological perspectives, to a wide range of interpretations on the reasons for mortality decline, ranging from factors like nutrition, changes in societal structures, or other more distal effects (see Easterlin 1999 for a relevant review). Even interpretations that suggest income to be an important driver of mortality declines (e.g. Pritchett and Summers 1996) allow ample scope for the importance of technical change. Moreover, some types of knowledge, such as the germ theory and the understanding of transmission of infectious disease, need little income to implement (Preston and Haines 1991). Analyses might well suggest that income played *no* role. The British-led army in India was instructed to march at right angles to the wind during cholera outbreaks, for example. Applied research that understood cholera transmission and clustering of outbreaks led to use of far more effective measures than wind avoidance (Davis 1951).

Some studies have attempted to assess what fraction of the decline in under-5 mortality arises from different sources. Jamison *et al.* (2013) for example estimate improved levels of education and technical progress are the largest contributors. Panel A of Figure 7.3 shows their results for all low- and middle-income countries for 1970–2000, and panel B shows their results for India.

Many of these interventions, particularly against infection and micronutrient deficiency, cost little and are highly efficacious. This is not to discount other more distal factors as having a role, for example by generating the wealth needed to purchase these interventions, the education to use them properly, or societal structures to ensure their widespread application. But in the absence of such specific technologies, it is hard to imagine that there would have been decline in mortality for these specific causes.

Estimation of the Number of Years of Life Lost (YLLs) and Its Money Metric Value

This section begins by describing the methods used in order to estimate the number of years of life lost (YLLs) for a given country or region and year. The countries and regions analyzed were China, India, Japan, the United States of America, sub-Saharan Africa, the world, the "Less developed regions" and the "More developed regions" as defined by the United Nations (2009). The time-span considered for the analysis was 1900–2050. Estimates of YLLs were calculated, for purposes of the Copenhagen Consensus Center analysis, using the United Nations' projected survival curve for Japan in 2050 as a reference.[2] Results are reported as a snapshot every 10 years for the years 1900, 1910, up to 2050. We then convert to money metric losses using a value of 2 for the ratio of the value of a statistical life year (VSLY) to per capita GDP.

2.1. Background and Methods

Notation

Consider a country or region i in year t. We note $e_{i,t}(a)$ the life expectancy at age a for the country/region i in year t. For country or region i in year t, we denote $s_{i,t}(a)$ to be the survival curve, which shows the probability that an individual of the population considered would survive from birth to age a given the age-specific survival rates at time t implied by the survival curve. Figure 7.4a displays survival curves for the Japanese population for the years 2005–2010 and for the Mozambican population for the year 1990. The age specific mortality rate at age a – or *hazard rate* – in population i in year t, $\mu_{i,t}(a)$, is given by:

$$\mu_{i,t}(a) = -\frac{s'_{i,t}(a)}{s_{i,t}(a)} \tag{7.1}$$

[2] An alternative reference population would be that of the best performing country in the year of the analysis. Annex 7.2 contains alternative calculations based on this assumption.

Panel A: All low- and middle-income countries

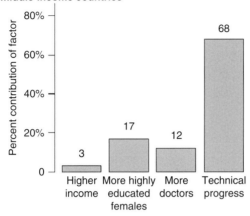

Note: Child mortality (5q0) across all low- and middle-income countries declined by 52% between 1970 and 2000 – from 130 per 1,000 to 62 per 1,000, i.e. at an average rate of 3.5% per year. This graph shows the fraction of the decline that can be attributed to several specific factors.

Panel B: India

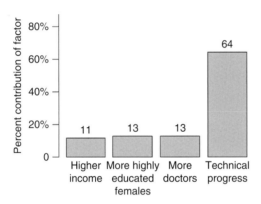

Note: Child mortality (5q0) in India declined by 58% between 1970 and 2000 – from 188 per 1,000 to 80 per 1,000, i.e. at an average rate of 2.9% per year. This graph shows the fraction of the decline that can be attributed to several specific factors.

Figure 7.3 *Factors accounting for decline in child mortality, 1970–2000*

Figure 7.4b displays hazard rates by age group for the Japanese population for the years 2005–2010 and for the Mozambican population for the year 1990.

We defined our *reference population*, as that of the country which had the highest (projected) life expectancy at birth, according to the United Nations, for the period we review (1900–2050). The Japanese population in 2050 thus serves as the reference population, which we named JPN2050. In 2050, a Japanese newborn would be expected to live about 87.2 years according to the United Nations (2009), and that is the highest life expectancy in their projections. We noted $e_J(a)$ the life expectancy at age a for a Japanese individual from JPN2050. Figure 7.5 displays life expectancy as a function of age for JPN2050, as well as for the Mozambican population in 1990.

For country/region i, and year t, we define the number of *years of life lost* $\text{YLL}_{i,t}$, relative to the Japanese population, to be:

$$YLL_{i,t} = \sum_a -s'_{i,t}(a)e_J(a) \tag{7.2}$$

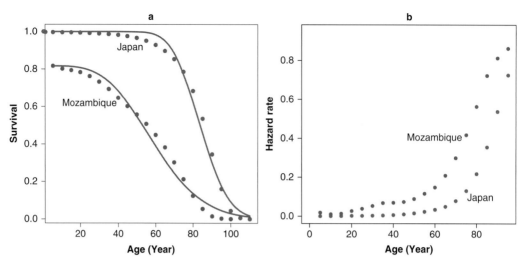

Figure 7.4 *Empirical and fitted survival curves (a), and hazard rates (b) as a function of age, for the Japanese population for the period 2005–2010 and for the Mozambican population for the year 1900*

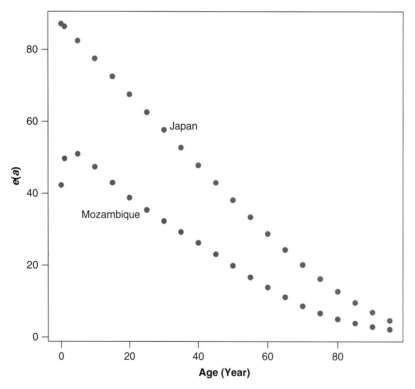

Figure 7.5 *Life expectancy as a function of age for JPN2050, and the Mozambican population in 1990*

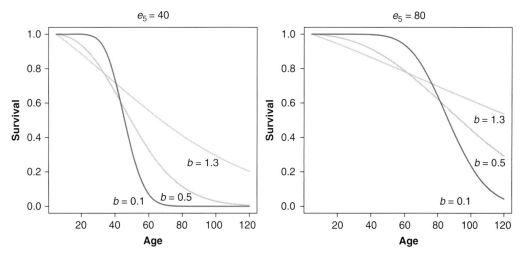

Figure 7.6 *Hypothetical survival curves for different values of the couplet* (e_5, b). *On the left-hand side,* $e_5 = 40$; *on the right-hand side* $e_5 = 80$. *On both figures,* b *takes the following values:* $b = 0.1$ *(purple),* 0.5 *(green),* 1.3 *(gray)*

s' is being used to denote a vector here and a scalar earlier. $e_J = (e_J(0), e_J(5), \ldots, e_J(100))$, and $s'_{i,t} = (s'_{i,t}(0), s'_{i,t}(5), \ldots, s'_{i,t}(100))$.[3] Recall $e_J(5k)$ is the life expectancy at age $5k$ for JPN2050, $-s'_{i,t}(5k)$ is the probability of dying between ages $5k$ and $5(k+1)$. This chapter uses YLL as its fundamental measure of health losses relative to the reference population.

We characterized a population from country or region i in year t by two indicators: (1) the number of $YLL_{i,t,u5}$ for deaths occurring at ages under 5, and (2) the number of $YLL_{i,t,a5}$ resulting from deaths above 5. The first kind of YLL is given by:

$$YLL_{i,t,u5} = -s'_{i,t}(0)e_J(0)$$

$$= (s_{i,t}(0) - s_{i,t}(5))e_J(0) = q5_{i,t}e_J(0) \quad (7.3)$$

where $q5_{i,t}$ is the probability of dying between ages 0 and 5 in country/region i, and year t. The over age 5 YLL is given by:

$$YLL_{i,t,a5} = -\sum_{k=1}^{20} s'_{i,t}(5k)e_J(5k) \quad (7.4)$$

where $s'_{i,t}(5k) = s_{i,t}(5k+5) - s_{i,t}(5k)$.

In this study we consistently estimate the YLLs arising from deaths before age 5 and those arising from age 5 and older. Hence in addition to q_5 we

need the survival curves for ages ≥ 5. For a given population, we estimated a survival curve $s_{i,t,5}(a)$ for $a \geq 5$. We approximated $s_{i,t,5}(a)$ by the following mathematical formulation:

$$s_{i,t,5}(a) = \frac{\Gamma(\frac{2-b}{b}, \frac{2-b}{b}\frac{a-5}{e_5})}{\Gamma(\frac{2-b}{b})} \quad 0 < b < 2 \quad (7.5)$$

where $\Gamma(x,s) = \int_x^{+\infty} t^{s-1}e^{-st}dt$ is the incomplete gamma function and $\Gamma(s) = \int_0^{+\infty} t^{s-1}e^{-st}dt$ is the complete gamma function; e_5 is the life expectancy at age 5 and corresponds to $e_5 = \int_5^{+\infty} s_{i,t,5}(a)da$. The parameter b captures the *rectangularity* of the survival curve and draws on the formal identity of survival curves and discount functions. Equation 7.5 is a survival curve based on the gamma discounting function of Jamison and Jamison (2011), and their speed parameter ρ (we have $b = 2 - \rho$). Figure 7.6 presents several shapes of hypothetical survival curves s for different values of the couplet *(e_5, b)*. Notice how for given e_5, varying b varies the rectangularity of the survival curve. Our purpose in using a parametric survival curve (equation 7.5) is to allow us to generate survival curves when only life expectancy is known by using an empirical relation between e_5 and b that we now describe in the next subsection.

[3] United Nations (2009) gives life expectancies at ages $a = 5k$ where $k = 0, 1, 2, \ldots, 20$.

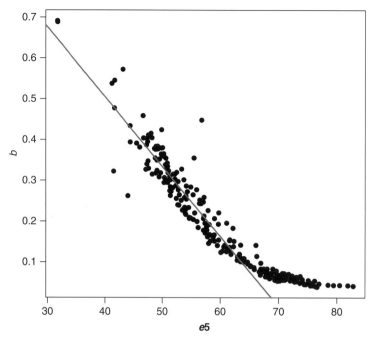

Figure 7.7 *Empirical relationship between rectangularity,* b, *of the survival curve age 5 onward as a function of life expectancy at age 5,* e$_5$. *The regression line for lower life expectancies (*e$_5$ < 65) is b = 1.19 – 0.017 e$_5$, R^2 = 0.86

This completes our development of notation and basic concepts.

Data and Empirical Relationship between *b* and *e$_5$*

We determined an empirical relationship $b(e_5)$ in order to estimate survival curves once given life expectancy at age 5, i.e. e_5. For that purpose, we fitted survival curves given by equation (7.5) to demographic life tables presenting a wide range of values for e_5. The life tables collected for our analysis were obtained from several sources. The Human Mortality Database (2011) provided life tables for England and Wales (1841–2009), France (1816–2007), Iceland (1838–2008), Japan (1947–2009), Sweden (1751–2009), and the United States (1933–2007). Davis (1951) provided life tables for India for the decades 1911–1921 and 1931–1941. We used life tables for 1990 and 2008 for males and females, provided by the World Health Organization (2010b) for 19

sub-Saharan African countries and Bangladesh, Brazil, China, Egypt, India, Indonesia, the Islamic Republic of Iran, Mexico, Pakistan, and the Philippines. The life expectancies at age 5 ranged from 31.8 to 78.1 years of age (corresponding to India in 1910: Davis (1951) and Japan in 2005–2007: Human Mortality Database 2011). The couplets *(e$_5$, b)* obtained after fitting of equation (7.5) are displayed on Figure 7.7.

Estimation of Survival Curves above Age 5

For China (CHN), India (IND), Japan (JPN), the United States of America (USA), sub-Saharan Africa (SSA), the "Less developed regions" (LDR), the "More developed regions" (MDR), and the world (WLD), over the period 1900–2050, we estimated a survival curve $s_{i,t,5}(a)$ for age 5 onward for each year starting a decade, i.e. 1900, 1910, 1920, …, 2040, 2050. For 2000–2050, all survival curves were estimated using direct fits to the life tables provided by the

United Nations (2009). For the USA and the period 1930–2000, and JPN in the period 1950–2000, the survival curves were estimated using direct fits to the life tables provided by Human Mortality Database (2011). For CHN, IND, SSA, LDR, MDR, and WLD, in the period 1900–2000, the survival curves were estimated using the relationship $b = f(e_5)$, once e_5 was known (Figure 7.7). The same approach was used to estimate the survival curves for USA in the period 1900–1930, and for JPN in the period 1900–1950. For CHN, IND, SSA, over the period 1980–2000, both e_0 and $q5$ (probability of dying before age 5) were given by United Nations (2009) and e_5 was derived in the following manner:[4]

$$e_5 = \frac{1}{1 - q_5}\left[e_0 - 5 + \frac{5}{2}q_5\right] \qquad (7.6)$$

All remaining e_5 values were either derived by linear extrapolation or through relationship (7.6) while using a relationship between e_0 and $q5$ extracted from the available data from the United Nations (2009). Input data were extracted from several sources including United Nations (2009), CDC (2004), Human Mortality Database (2011), Davis (1951), and Feachem and Jamison (1991). All data inputs used are collected in Table 7.1.

Money Metric Value of YLLs

For region or country i in year t, we estimated a money metric value of $YLL_{i,t}$, noted $MMVYLL_{i,t}$ in the following way:

$$MMVYLL_{i,t} = \gamma YLL^*_{i,t}I_{c,t} \qquad (7.7)$$

where we derived a weighted measure of YLL i.e $YLL^* = YLL_{a5} + 0.54\,YLL_{u5}$ as given by Jamison et al. (2006), I_c is the income per capita in 1990 International Geary–Khamis dollars (CCC 2011; Maddison 2011),[5] and γ is the value of YLL in units of per capita income, i.e. it is the VSLY. We take here $\gamma = 2$, the lower value given in Jamison et al. (2008).[6] We then estimated lifetime income per capita $LI_{c,i,t}$ in the following manner:

$$LI_{c,i,t} = e_{0,i,t}I_{c,i,t} \qquad (7.8)$$

where $e_{0,i,t}$ is the life expectancy at birth in country or region i in year t. Finally, we define the ratio a as:

$$a_{i,t} = MMVYLL_{i,t}/LI_{c,t} \qquad (7.9)$$

Reductions in YLLs

We estimated YLL_J i.e. the number of years of life lost for JPN2050, our reference population. We found $YLL_{J,u5} = 0.3$, $YLL_{J,a5} = 10.1$, leading to $YLL_J = 10.4$. (Note that the existence of non-zero YLLs in the reference population results from the non-rectangularity of the survival curve. Figure 7.7 suggests that after a life expectancy of about 75 years, life expectancy improvements cease to be accompanied by increased rectangularity.)

For each country and region i and year t, we subtracted the quantities associated with the reference population, i.e. we estimated:

$$YLL_{i,t,u5} = q5_{i,t}e_j(0) - YLL_{J,u5} \qquad (7.10)$$

and:

$$YLL_{i,t,a5} = -\sum_{k=1}^{20} s'_{i,t}(5k)e_J(5k) - YLL_{J,a5} \qquad (7.11)$$

which leads to the total unweighted YLLs:

$$YLL_{i,t} = q5_{i,t}e_J(0) - \sum_{k=1}^{20} s'_{i,t}(5k)e_J(5k) - YLL_J \qquad (7.12)$$

Table 7.2 lists the YLL_{u5} (7.10), the YLL_{a5} (7.11), and the total unweighted YLL (7.12) for each year

---

[4] This relation is derived from the identity expressing e_0 as the sum of integrals of the survival curve from 0 to 5 and from 5 to infinity and the approximation that the survival curve is linear between 0 and 5.

[5] For the period 2010–2050, projections of income per capita were estimated based on levels from Maddison (2011) in 2010 and assuming a constant growth rate of 2% for Japan and the United States, and of 5% for China and India for the period 2010–2050.

[6] Note that we could have values of γ varying with income as suggested by Hammitt and Robinson (2011). We chose here a constant value across income levels in the interest of simplicity of exposition.

Table 7.1 Input parameters – e_0 and e_5 (years), q_5 (per 1,000 live births), and b (millions of births), selected countries and country groupings, 1900–2050

Geographical area	Life expectancy at birth, e_0 (years)				Life expectancy at age 5, e_5 (years)				Under-5 mortality rate, q_5, per 1,000 live births				Births per year (millions)		
	1900	1950	2000	2050	1900	1950	2000	2050	1900	1950	2000	2050	1950	2000	2050
World[a]	32	47	66	76	40	53	67	73	335	167	77	31	98.3	133.9	121.7
China[b]	28	41	72	79	36	49	69	75	344	194	32	12	25.0	18.1	14.2
India[c]	23	38	62	73	32	43	63	71	464	227	90	39	16.9	27.6	19.8
Japan[d]	45	62	82	87	52	62	78	83	220	77	4	3	2.0	1.1	0.7
United States[e]	49	69	78	83	55	66	70	80	182	35	8	5	4.0	4.2	4.6
Sub-Saharan Africa[f]	20	38	50	66	31	43	54	65	500	270	161	58	9.3	28.9	35.1
More developed regions[g]	47	66	76	83	54	65	72	78	190	59	9	5	18.7	13.4	13.0
Less developed regions[g]	26	41	64	74	34	46	65	72	415	219	85	34	79.6	120.5	108.7

Note: Input parameters e_0 (years), e_5 (years), and q_5 (per 1,000) in 1900, 1950, 2000, and 2050; e_0 for 1950, 2000, 2050; e_5 for 2000, 2050, and q_5 for 2000, 2050 were taken from United Nations (2009).

[a] Acemoglu and Johnson (2007) and weighted average from other country/regions using CCC (2011) for the weights.

[b] Riley (2005) and weighted average from other country/regions using CCC (2011) for the weights.

[c] Riley (2005) and authors' assumption.

[d] Davis (1951) and authors' assumption.

[e] Kinsella (1992), Human Mortality database (2011), and authors' assumption.

[f] CDC (2004).

[g] Feachem and Jamison (1991) and authors' assumption.

Table 7.2 Years of life lost (YLLs) per birth, selected countries and country groupings, over and under age 5, and total, 1900–2050

	(a) Under-5 YLLs (YLL_{u5})				(b) Over-5 YLLs (YLL_{a5})				(c = a + b) Total YLLs (unweighted)			
	1900	1950	2000	2050	1900	1950	2000	2050	1900	1950	2000	2050
World	28.9	14.3	6.5	2.4	16.7	15.6	9.1	5.7	45.6	29.9	15.5	8.2
China	29.7	16.6	2.5	0.8	18.4	17.1	8.1	4.4	48.1	33.7	10.6	5.2
India	40.2	19.5	7.6	3.1	15.1	19.3	11.3	6.7	55.2	38.8	18.9	9.8
Japan	18.9	6.4	0.1	0	14.5	12.3	2.7	0	33.4	18.6	2.8	0
United States	15.6	2.8	0.4	0.2	14.0	10.4	6.5	1.8	29.6	13.2	6.9	2.0
Sub-Saharan Africa	43.3	23.3	13.7	4.7	13.7	17.7	14.6	10.8	57.0	41.0	28.3	15.5
More developed regions	16.3	4.9	0.5	0.2	14.3	11.3	7.1	2.5	30.6	16.1	7.6	2.6
Less developed regions	35.9	18.8	7.1	2.7	16.3	15.6	9.9	6.4	52.2	34.4	17	9.1

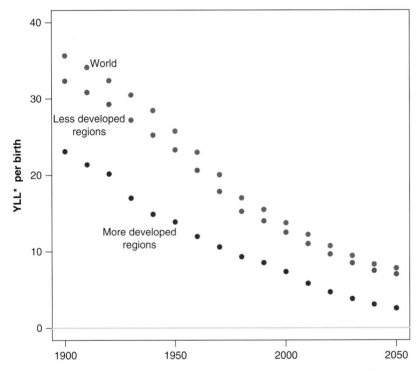

Figure 7.8 *Years of life lost (YLL*) over the period 1900–2050 for the world, the less developed regions, and the more developed regions*

and country/region, for the period 1900–2050. Figure 7.8 graphs the total number of YLLs per birth for the period 1900–2050 for the world, the "Less developed regions," and the "More developed regions."

YLLs due to "Mortality Shocks"

For each major "mortality shock" of the twentieth century including World War I, the "Spanish" pandemic flu of 1918, World War II, the Bengal famine

Table 7.3 Years of life lost (YLLs) per person, major mortality shocks of the twentieth century

Event	Excess deaths (millions)	Population affected (millions)	YLL per capita [a]
World War I (1914–18)	17	1,803	0.62
Influenza pandemic (1918)	50	1,843	1.22
World War II (1939–45)	71	2,275	3.14
Bengal famine (1943)	3	401	0.50
Chinese famine (1958–61)	29	637	3.03

[a] The YLLs per capita are calculated based on the total number of excess deaths over the indicated time period, not per year (as are most YLLs reported in this Chapter).

Source: Ashton *et al.* (1984), Devereux (2000), Wikipedia (2011a, 2011b), Johnson *et al.* (2002), Copenhagen Consensus Center (2011), United Nations (2009).

of 1943 in India, the Great Chinese famine of 1958–1961, we estimated YLLs per capita at the world level, except for the Great Chinese famine (at the China level) and for the Bengal famine (at the India level). For World War I and II, we used deaths data provided by Wikipedia (Wikipedia 2011a, 2011b). We estimated the YLLs corresponding to military casualties with $e_x(20)$. The YLLs corresponding to civil casualties were estimated using the age distribution of the world population in 1910 and 1940, while using a linear regression between the age distribution of the population as a function of life expectancy at birth for the period 1950–2000 extrapolated from United Nations (2009). For the "Spanish" pandemic flu, we used death numbers from Johnson and Mueller (2002) and attack rates from Luk *et al.* (2001) with the extrapolated age distribution of the world population in 1910 as above. Total world population numbers were obtained from the Copenhagen Consensus Center (2011). For the Bengal famine, we used death numbers from Devereux (2000), the extrapolated age distribution of the Indian population in 1940 as

above, and the total population of India in 1943. For the Great Chinese famine, we used death numbers from Ashton *et al.* (1984), the age distribution of the Chinese population in 1950, and the total population of China in 1957 (United Nations 2009). World population data at different times were obtained by the Copenhagen Consensus Center (2011). Table 7.3 lists the YLLs associated with each of the major mortality shocks.

Money Metric Value of YLL Reduction

Table 7.4 lists the values $YLL_{VSL,i,t} = \gamma YLL^*_{i,t}$, the $MMVYLL_{m,i,t}$ (equation 7.7), and the ratio $a_{i,t}$ (equation 7.9) for each year and country/region, for the period 1900–2050. Figure 7.9 graphs the ratios $a_{i,t}$ for the period 1900–2050 for: (a) China, India, Japan, and the United States; (b) the world, the "Less developed regions," and the "More developed regions."

Specific Health Problems: Accomplishments and Challenges

In this section, the statistical picture of gains provided in the previous section is illustrated by two specific examples of health accomplishments of the twentieth century: marked increases in child survival and the eradication of smallpox. The discussion then turns to one example of a major challenge that remains on the agenda of the twenty-first century: tobacco-attributable deaths. This is chosen to illustrate the importance of technological diffusion in affecting change (and also, in the case of tobacco and adult chronic diseases, the enormous returns possible if technologies were applied more widely). The other highly quantitatively significant challenge of the twenty-first century is the AIDS epidemic. That has been extensively covered in a recent Copenhagen Consensus Center publication so we discuss it no further here.

Accomplishments: Child Survival

Major declines in childhood mortality started in the late nineteenth century in the currently high-income countries, and in the mid twentieth century

Table 7.4 Value of statistical life years of life lost per birth (YLL$_{VSL}$), money metric value of years of life lost per birth (MMVYLL), and ratio a of MMVYLL over lifetime income per capita, selected countries and country groupings, 1900–2050

	YLL$_{VSL}$				MMVYLL($)				Ratio a			
	1900	1950	2000	2050	1900	1950	2000	2050	1900	1950	2000	2050
World	64.7	46.6	25.0	14.1	40,737	49,347	74,140	132,008	2.1	1.5	0.8	0.5
China	68.9	52.1	19.0	9.6	37,545	23,349	64,883	200,644	2.4	1.9	0.7	0.3
India	73.5	59.7	30.8	16.8	44,038	36,977	58,343	154,800	3.5	2.9	1.5	0.8
Japan	49.5	31.4	5.5	0	58,384	63,054	113,222	0	1.1	0.7	0.1	0
United States	44.8	23.8	13.5	3.8	179,985	221,036	370,334	212,861	0.9	0.5	0.3	0.1
Sub-Saharan Africa	74.2	60.5	44.0	26.7	22,305	27,688	31,398	40,643	3.9	3.1	2.3	1.4
More developed regions	46.2	27.8	14.7	5.1	56,588	65,027	128,389	112,704	1.0	0.6	0.3	0.1
Less developed regions	71.3	51.5	27.5	15.6	22,417	22,071	42,646	127,586	3.0	2.2	1.2	0.7

Note: YLL$_{VSL}$ are calculated from the per person YLLs reported in Table 7.2 in the following: YLL$_{VSL}$ = 2 (YLL$_{a5}$ + 0.54 YLL$_{u5}$); MMVYLL are calculated from the YLL$_{VSL}$ in the following: MMVYLL = YLL$_{VSL}$ × GDP per capita, where GDP per capita is expressed in 1990 International Geary–Khamis dollars; a is calculated as MMVYLL divided by the lifetime income per capita as defined by equation (7.8) in the main text.

in the currently low-income countries. The declines are much more complete in high-income countries, meaning that today 99% of children born in these countries can expect to reach their fifth birthday. However, the pace of decline has been rapid in low-and middle-income countries, especially since 1950.

Staggering Declines in Child Mortality

Declines in childhood mortality explain much of the remarkable improvements in life expectancy in the twentieth century as can be seen on Figure 7.10, which plots estimates and projections of the under-5 years of life lost as a percent of total years of life lost for the "More developed regions" and "Less developed regions" for the period 1900–2050.

Between 1900 and 2000, we estimate that crude death rates fell by nearly four-fifths and life expectancy at birth doubled from 32 to about 66 (Table 7.1); while death rates fell from about 40–50 to 10 per 1,000, the global population rose from 1.5 billion to over 6 billion. Thus, annual deaths totaled around 50–60 million throughout the last century. All told, there were about 5–6

billion deaths in the twentieth century. About 2 billion of these deaths were among children below age 5 years, despite the marked declines seen in recent decades. Child deaths far exceeded the several millions of deaths from more specific epidemics, such as the 20–60 million killed by the influenza epidemic of 1918–19, the 30 million (and growing) deaths from HIV, the 100 million deaths from tobacco, or the 200 million deaths from war and famine (see other chapters).

The staggering decline in child mortality is illustrated by a comparison of the levels and causes of child deaths in sub-Saharan Africa in 2008 to that from Liverpool, England in 1861–70 (Table 7.5).

Sub-Saharan Africa's real per capita income in 2008 was just over half of that of England around 1870. However, child mortality rates were two-thirds lower in Africa now than in England then (460 versus 140 per 1,000 live births). By 2008, the contribution of vaccine-preventable diseases, most notably diphtheria, measles, and scarlet fever, had fallen sharply. In contrast, the remaining causes of death arose largely from pneumonias, diarrhea and, in the African case, childhood malaria deaths (most of England had little malaria in the 1870s).

(a)

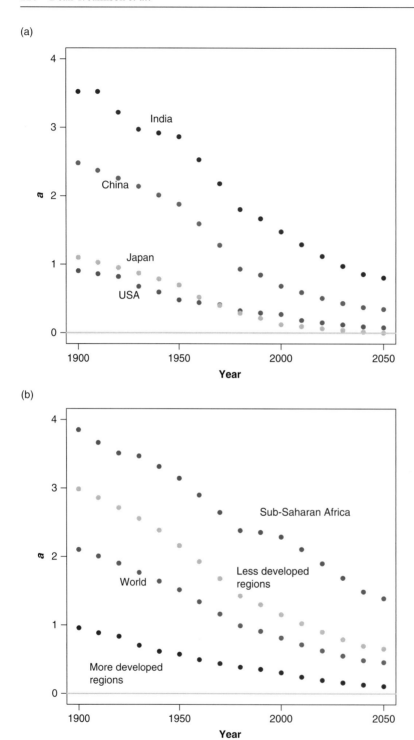

(b)

Figure 7.9 *Ratio of the money metric value of life years lost to expected lifetime income (a) over the period 1900–2050 for: (a) countries, i.e. India, China, Japan, the United States; (b) country groupings, i.e. the world, the less developed regions, the more developed regions, Sub-Saharan Africa*

Table 7.5 Child mortality in Liverpool (1860s) and sub-Saharan Africa (2008)

	Liverpool	Sub-Saharan Africa
Under-5 mortality rate (per 1,000 live births)	460	140
Per capita income (US$)[a]	3000	1700
Diseases		
Acute respiratory infections	17%	18%
Birth trauma/asphyxia	11%	8%
Diarrhea	12%	19%
Pulmonary vasculary disease	19%	6%
Tuberculosis	4%	–
Smallpox	1%	–
Malaria	0%	16%
Other infections	1%	18%
Injuries	4%	2%
Subtotal	**69%**	**87%**

[a] Adjusted to 1990 level.
Source: Farr (1889) and Lopez *et al.* (2006).

Put differently, if worldwide child mortality rates today were like those seen in England, or most Western countries near the beginning of the twentieth century, there would be about 30 million child deaths, rather than the 10 million deaths that occurred in children around 2001 (or 13.9 million if stillbirths are included (Jamison *et al.* 2006)). By 2000 child deaths in England had become quite rare. If the world had the same child mortality rates as seen in England today, only 1 million children would die worldwide (Peto 2006).

The Role of Technologies in Child Mortality Declines

Specific technologies have had different impacts on the decline in childhood mortality at different time periods. In the first half of the twentieth century, the available tools included knowledge of transmission of various infectious diseases (Preston and Haines 1991) including crude efforts around containment and isolation, contact tracing, improved sanitation, as well as specific vaccines. These tools, once

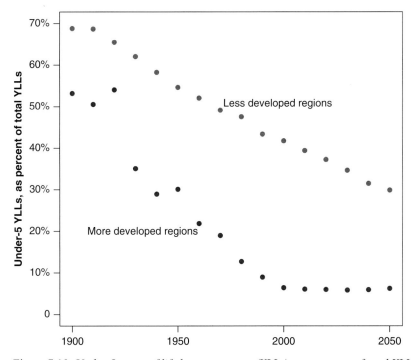

Figure 7.10 *Under-5 years of life lost per person (YLLs) as a percent of total YLLs, 1900–2050*

Table 7.6 Key discoveries in disease transmission and vaccines

Knowledge of transmission (and discoverers)	Vaccines and antibiotics (and discoverers)
1847 Measles (Panum)	1798 Smallpox (Jenner, plus tenth century China)
1847 Puerperal fever (Semmeweiss, Holmes)	1885 Rabies (Pasteur)
1854 Cholera (Snow)	1892 Diphtheria (von Behring)
1859 Typhoid (Budd)	1896 Cholera (Kolle)
1867 Surgical sepsis (Lister)	1906 Pertussis (Bordet-Gengou)
1898 Malaria (Ross)	1921 Tuberculosis (Calmette, Guérin)
1900 Yellow fever (Reed)	1927 Tetanus (Ramon, Zoeller)
1850–1920s Quarantine methods, sanitation improvements, case detection, contact tracing, and other public health efforts	1930 Yellow fever (Theiler) 1935 Sulfonamides (Ehrlich) 1941 Penicillin (Fleming) 1944 Streptomycin (Waksman) 1948 Broad-spectrum antibiotics (various) 1948 Diphtheria – tetanus – pertussis (various) 1950 Polio (Salk) 1954 Measles (Enders, Pebbles)

Source: Modified from Easterlin (1999).

implemented widely in Europe, led to substantial declines in child mortality in the early twentieth century. In the second half of the century, far greater reductions arose from childhood vaccinations (including the introduction of global campaigns to immunize children), oral rehydration therapies, antibiotic use and malaria control.

Easterlin (1999) describes some of the available tools in the first half of the twentieth century and their discovery years, and we have modified this table somewhat and added a table on more contemporary tools (Table 7.6).

The major tools of control in the early twentieth century comprised efforts to interrupt transmission of infectious diseases, often crudely. Plague epidemics and outbreaks were a major cause of childhood mortality worldwide. In India, plague deaths at all ages fell from about 500,000 in the period 1889–1918 to below 32,000 by 1935 with many of these deaths concentrated in children. The chief reasons for the decline were increases in rat immunity (rats transmit the *Yersinia pestis* bacteria into human populations). However, declines occurred also due to crude efforts to control the rat population, and to a much more limited extent the use of vaccines and, at a later point, sulfa drugs (Davis 1951). Similarly, cholera epidemics were substantial in many parts of the world, and the understanding of transmission from water sources and via fecal contact led to crude measures involving containment that reduce the spread and severity of periodic outbreaks. Notably, the periodic religious pilgrimages of several million Hindus often led to cholera outbreaks. Simple efforts to bring basic sanitation and (to a more limited extent) temporary vaccination to the large number of annual pilgrims reduced cholera outbreaks. Reductions in famines arising from better agricultural practices and irrigation supply (see chapter on nutrition) were also partly responsible for the reductions in cholera, as famines can lower human immunity and also contribute to spreading the virus more rapidly.

By 1950–4, the probability of newborns dying before age 5 was still about 23%, but fell to 14% by 1970–4, to 9% in 1990–4, and to about 6% in the present decade (Ahmad *et al.* 2000). The declines from about 1950 onward in child mortality mostly arose from the use of modern technologies. Table 7.7 describes the declines in infectious diseases, which is the leading cause of death among children that arose from specific technologies in the second half of the twentieth century. Improved environmental living conditions paired with the ability to identify new microbes and develop vaccines as well as antimicrobials account for the 90% or greater reduction in infectious disease mortality in the USA. In the last half century, more than 30 common infectious diseases are controllable with live or killed viral or bacterial vaccines, or those based on bacterial sugars and proteins (Jha *et al.*, 2004).

Table 7.7 Examples of science contribution to declines in infectious disease mortality in the second half of the twentieth century

Condition and intervention	Annual deaths prior to intervention (and reference year) in thousands	Annual deaths after intervention (and reference year) in thousands
Immunization services – against polio, diphtheria, pertussis, tetanus, and measles	~5,200 (1960)	1,400 (2001)
Eradication campaign – smallpox	~3,000 (1950)	0 (1979)
Diarrhea – oral rehydration therapy	~ 4,600 (1980)	1,600 (2001)

Source: Jamison *et al*. (2008).

In 1970, perhaps only 5% of the world's children under 5 were immunized against measles, tetanus, pertussis, diphtheria, and polio. The Expanded Programme on Immunization (EPI) has raised this to about 85% of children by 2000, saving perhaps 3 million lives a year (England *et al*. 2000). Diarrheal deaths among children have fallen by several million partly as a result of the development of oral rehydration therapy – much of which was the result of population research laboratories in Bangladesh. Delivery of a combination of anti-tuberculosis drugs with direct observation (or DOTS) has lowered case-fatality rates from well over 60% to 5%, and also decreased transmission. The percentage of the world's tuberculosis cases treated with DOTS has risen from about one in ten in 1990 to about one in three today (Dye 2000). The most spectacular success in immunization is the WHO-led eradication of smallpox, which culminated in the eradication of smallpox in human populations by 1979. We discuss smallpox in greater detail below.

Prior to 1950, the only major antibiotics were sulfonamides and penicillin. Subsequently, there has been remarkable growth in discovery and use of antimicrobial agents with different mechanisms of action effective against bacteria, fungi, viruses, protozoa, and helminths. These new agents have contributed importantly to the steady decline in child mortality.

The Uncertain but Perhaps Large Contribution of Malaria Control

Preston (1980) provides a useful set of estimates of the contribution of specific infectious diseases to reductions in mortality from 1900 to 1970. We provide an updated version in Table 7.8.

Preston's estimates of the contribution of technologies to mortality declines are consistent with others. However, he adds the important, and yet variable estimates of reduced mortality from malaria control. Perhaps 13%–33% of the overall decline in mortality during these seven decades might have arisen from malaria control, chiefly from indoor residual spraying, but also from early antimalarial drugs like quinine. Mandle (1970) finds that a very large part of the declines in mortality in British Guiana, especially in the period just after World War II, arose from malaria control (Figure 7.11).

In more recent years, artemisinin combination therapies have shown to be powerful tools to reduce malaria mortality (Gomes *et al*. 2009), and indeed childhood malaria deaths in Africa might be falling in response to expanded use of insecticide-treated nets and treatment. In this context, important findings from a large Indian mortality survey suggest that India might well have over 200,000 malaria deaths below age 70, as against the WHO estimate of 15,000 at all ages. Malaria appears not only to be a killer of children, but also of adults (Figure 7.12). Indeed, similar patterns are reported in Mozambique and other countries in Africa. If it is true that malaria remains a common killer of adults, then the same strategies that have been applied to reduce childhood deaths from malaria in Africa might well substantially reduce adult deaths from malaria worldwide.

Nutrition and Infection

How has nutrition reduced childhood mortality? Nutritional gains have been substantial (see

Table 7.8 Infectious diseases responsible for mortality declines in less developed countries and related control measures

Dominant mode of transmission	Disease	Approximate percent of mortality decline accounted for by disease, 1900–1970,	Principal method of prevention deployed	Principal methods of treatment deployed
Airborne	Influenza/pneumonia/ bronchitis	30		Antibiotics
	Respiratory tuberculosis	10	Immunization; identification and isolation	Chemotherapy
	Smallpox	2		Chemotherapy
	Measles	1		
	Diphtheria and pertussis	2	Immunization	Antibiotics
	Subtotal airborne	**45**		
Water-, food-, and feces-borne	Gastroenteritis	7	Purification and increased supply of water; sewage disposal; personal sanitation	Rehydration
	Cholera	1		Rehydration,
	Typhoid	1		antibiotics
	Subtotal water-, food-, feces-borne	**9**		
Vector-borne	Malaria	13–33	Insecticides, drainage, larvicides	Quinine drugs
	Typhus	1	Insecticides, partially effective vaccines	Antibiotics
	Plague	1	Insecticides, rat control, quarantine	
	Subtotal vector-borne	**15–35**		
	TOTAL	**69–89**		

Source: Modified from Preston (1980).

Chapter 8). For example, physical growth (height-for-age) rose among 10-year-old Norwegian females from 1920 to 1970 from 130.2 cm to 139.6 cm (and was only about 107.4 cm in 1800: Brundtland, *et al.* 1975). This massive increase of about 1.9 cm per decade or 0.84 standard deviation per generation has also been accompanied by increases in cognitive growth. Dutch males had, in 1982 1.2-fold higher IQ relative to their own fathers in 1952, and about 10-fold higher than men in 1800. This increase of about 7 IQ points per decade or 1.4 standard deviation per generation is also related to better nutrition (Ruger *et al.* 2006). Famines and mass droughts have become less and less common in the twentieth century (despite short-term fluctuations), in part due to better

food availability, and the effects of the Green Revolution on crop yields and durability. In turn, better diets, particularly but not only during early life, have substantially improved anthropometrics, schooling, adult cognitive skills, earnings, and wages of the next generation.

Nutrition is not only a function of available energy or protein, and diet alone fails to explain the widely variable prevalence of malnutrition in low- and middle-income countries. Nutrition is strongly correlated with childhood infections (Caulfield *et al.* 2006). Infectious diseases raise metabolic demands and decrease the absorption of food, and infection control from immunizations, and antimicrobials have helped reduce the worldwide prevalence of severe

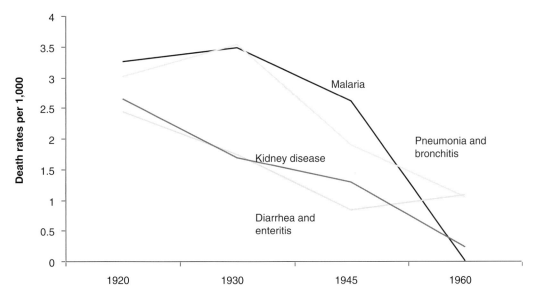

Figure 7.11 *Mortality trends and specific diseases in British Guiana*

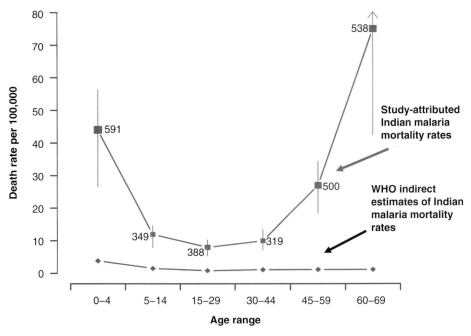

Figure 7.12 *Age-specific all-India malaria-attributed death rates estimated from a large mortality study and those estimated indirectly for WHO*

malnutrition, such as kwashiorkor or marasmus (Caulfield *et al.* 2006). Maternal breastfeeding is a key nutritional intervention to protect against infection. Indeed, Chile saw increases in child mortality among more affluent women than among poorer women, as a result of decreases in breastfeeding by the affluent women (Plank and Milanesi 1973). More recent efforts with specific micronutrients such as iron, folate, and zinc have been shown to be effective in reducing childhood anemia (Zlotkin *et al.* 2005) and subsequent mortality. Randomized trials of insecticide-treated mosquito nets and of specific respiratory antigens have often shown a bigger decline in child mortality than expected from malaria and pneumonia, respectively, and this might be attributed to lowering secondary causes of death from reduced malnutrition.

Current and Future Child Mortality

Despite these substantial achievements in child survival, major challenges still exist. As of 2008, about 9 million children still died before age 5. India alone had 2.3 million child deaths in 2005, of which nearly half occurred in the first month of life and 30% in the first week of life (Million Death Study Collaborators 2010). Indian child mortality has fallen by about 2% per year since 1971 as a whole in India and all states have shown declines. Differences in income levels and growth rates across Indian states do not appear to account for the variation in decline in child mortality (Measham *et al.* 1999). Rather, coverage with the EPI package, treatment of acute respiratory infection in a medical facility and use of oral rehydration therapy for diarrhea show a clear gradient from worst to best performing states on under-5 mortality (Jha 2001). Today, about three-fifths of all childhood deaths occur in just nine states. At ages 1–59 months, girls in some regions have four to five times higher mortality from pneumonia or diarrhea as boys in other regions (Million Death Study Collaborators 2010). Discrepancies in child mortality across states are so large that if the worst third and middle third states had under-5 mortality rates equal to that of the best third, over 1 million under-5 deaths would be avoided annually (Jha 2001).

Notwithstanding these challenges, child mortality declines are likely to continue. In Africa, for example, overall child mortality fell from 1990 to 2000 despite increases in childhood deaths from malaria and from mother to child transmission of HIV (Ahmad *et al.* 2000), and despite economic stagnation. Concerted efforts around reducing childhood mortality now focus on reducing neonatal mortality by improving prenatal and intrapartum care (skilled attendance, emergency obstetric care, and simple immediate care for newborn babies), postnatal family–community care (preventive postnatal care, oral antibiotics, and management of pneumonia), and tetanus toxoid immunization as well as expanding the use of highly effective newer antigens in immunization programs.

On current projection (Table 7.1), child mortality is projected to fall from about 77 per 1,000 live births in 2000 to 31 per 1,000 live births in 2050. These reductions are likely to continue as forthcoming analyses find the costs of reducing child mortality continue to fall yearly. This improving cost function is largely because of 40 years of public attention, donor assistance, and research funding have, together, created cost-effective and widely practicable interventions for child and maternal health, and more recently to control of HIV/AIDS, malaria and tuberculosis. Increasing coverage of inexpensive health interventions such as immunization, insecticide-treated nets, prevention of mother-to-child transmission of HIV, and micronutrients are contributing to the decline in child mortality and are getting cheaper by the year (Hum *et al.* 2013).

Accomplishments: Smallpox Eradication

In 1979 the WHO eradicated smallpox, a disease that perhaps had caused 300 million deaths in the course of the twentieth century. Successful eradication arose from a combination of two major factors. First, declines in smallpox in the first half of the twentieth century were substantial mostly due to widespread use of vaccination, as well as general understanding of isolation and control of outbreaks (paired with increases in general nutrition and hence resistance of humans to withstand the periodic outbreaks of smallpox). Second, in 1967 the WHO initiated a global eradication campaign which succeeded in the course of 12 years (Figure 7.13).

Smallpox before Eradication

Prior to any widespread control, smallpox may have been the leading cause of death worldwide. Smallpox may have killed perhaps 2–15 million of the total Aztec population of 30 million, and was responsible for periodic epidemics killing hundreds of thousands in cities as far apart as London and Tokyo. Nor did smallpox spare the rich and only strike the poor. Smallpox infected Egyptian pharaoh Ramses V in 1157 BC and Queen Elizabeth I in 1562 and it killed a Roman emperor in 180 BC (Fenner *et al*. 1988). In India in 1937–1941, smallpox accounted for between 12% and 20% of the deaths in the first year of life and about 19%–30% of the deaths between ages 1 and 9 years (Davis 1951). India had about half of the world's cases in the two decades prior to eradication. Between one in five and one in three of all cases died.

Introduction of smallpox vaccination began in crude forms as early as the eighth century in China. The technique, called variation, involved using the scabs of smallpox victims injected into healthy people so as to provide some protection. The Chinese even used inhalation approaches for vaccination. These technologies spread westward, and were brought from Constantinople to England in the early eighteenth century. Vaccination using Jenner's discoveries became widespread by the later nineteenth century, and was far more practicable and less painful than the variolation.

Where vaccination became commonly used, such as in Finland, death rates fell substantially (Figure 7.14). In many currently high-income countries, public health infrastructure expanded, including the ability to forcibly quarantine suspected cases, have mandatory examination of incoming ships, and require compulsory vaccination or revaccination of children and others.

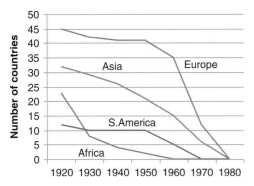

Figure 7.13 *Number of countries reporting smallpox by region, 1920–1980*

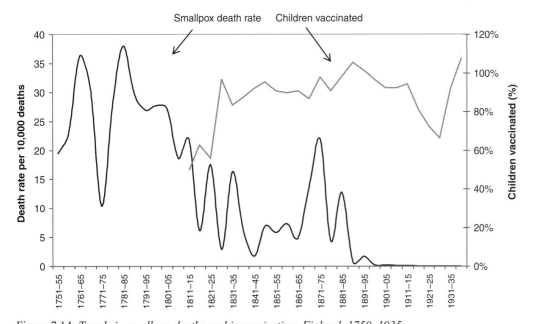

Figure 7.14 *Trends in smallpox deaths and immunization, Finland, 1750–1935*

London's public health act of 1875 gave broad powers to the police and public health officials to enforce these laws.

Smallpox vaccination spread widely, including to low-income countries. Banthia and Dyson (2000) describe how increases in vaccination were recorded in the Bombay census of 1881–91, and their comparison of coverage rates with self-reported smallpox shows remarkable declines. Nearly 80% of the roughly 30 million people in Bengal were inoculated and once replaced by vaccination around 1870, smallpox cases and mortality fell dramatically. A spectacular increase in vaccination occurred in Indonesia (then Netherlands East Indies). The numbers of vaccination rose from under 60,000 in 1890–9 to nearly 1.7 million by 1900–19 and to 7.3 million by 1920, from a total population of about 45 million Indonesians. This led to a marked decline in smallpox mortality (Davis 1951).

Global Eradication

The next major phase involved global eradication. A WHO effort organized all countries to launch a global eradication campaign. Eradication was technically possible as the causative virus for smallpox (with two variants *Variola major* and *Variola minor)* resides only in humans. The initial effort focused on increasing coverage of the routine vaccines. However, two key areas of operational research refocused the program so that it could achieve eradication. These were active case detection and ring vaccination. Under active case detection, mobile teams investigated outbreaks using local information. In the case of India, Bangladesh, Nepal, Pakistan, Ethiopia, and Somalia, country-wide house-to-house searches were conducted by a large number of health staff over the course of 3–4 weeks to discover possible cases. Ring vaccination involved finding people who were exposed to an infected person. Then the exposed person and those people he or she had been in contact with are given the vaccine. That is, the smallpox vaccine is given to those people who had been, or could have been, exposed to an infected person. This approach creates a "ring" of vaccinated people around the people who were infected with smallpox and stops the spread of the disease.

The smallpox eradication program cost an estimated $300 million over its 12-year life and displaced routine immunization costs that totaled $300 million in 1968 alone (World Bank 1993). These financial benefits, and the millions of lives saved annually, are more fully discussed in Fenner *et al.* (1988).

Challenges: Tobacco Control

On current smoking patterns, there will be an estimated 1 billion smoking-attributable deaths in this century, mostly in low- and middle-income countries. In contrast, there were "only" 100 million tobacco deaths in the twentieth century, mostly in high-income and Eastern European countries who took up smoking en masse generally before or around World War II (Peto *et al.* 1994; Jha 2009). Most of these future tobacco-related deaths will occur in low-income countries, and half or more will occur during productive middle age (defined here as about 30–69 years). A substantial proportion of these deaths will occur among the poorest or least educated members in each of these countries. Currently, about 70% of the 40 million deaths among adults over age 30 years worldwide are due to cancer, vascular and respiratory diseases, and tuberculosis (Lopez *et al.* 2006), each of which are made more common by smoking. Smoking currently causes about 5–6 million deaths annually worldwide from all causes (Jha 2009). About 50% of all current smoking related deaths occur in low-income countries.

Here, we review the twentieth-century development in tobacco hazards, and examine in particular, the benefits of cessation, which has now become widespread among males in high-income countries. We examine the importance of taxation to increase cessation. The key relevance here is not to the 100 million deaths in the twentieth century which have already occurred, but to the avoidability of the 1 billion deaths in this century.

Trends in Smoking in Developed and Developing Countries

Widespread automation of cigarette production in the early twentieth century turned cigarettes into a global commodity. Lung cancer was a rare disease prior to World War II, and the large increase in lung cancer rates lagged behind the onset of consumption by three or more decades. Among British doctors who were born in the first few decades of the twentieth century (1900–1930) and followed those born in the second half of it (1951–2001), death rates were three times higher among doctors who smoked than those who did not (Doll *et al.* 2004). Prolonged smokers lost about 10 years of life compared to non-smokers. Similarly, the main increase in cigarette smoking in the USA occurred from 1920 to 1940, and peaked at about 10 cigarettes per adult only around 1960 (Jha 2009). Yet the rates of lung cancer in middle age and at older ages, almost all of which are due to smoking, peaked almost 30 years later.

The full effects of smoking have not yet been observed in low- and middle-income countries. China has over 300 million smokers and India has over 120 million smokers, most of whom are male (Jha *et al.* 2013). Moreover, China reports a marked increase in cigarette production since 2000, which might be from increased smoking among younger adults. India's per capita adult male consumption is over six bidis (small locally manufactured smoked tobacco products) or cigarettes per day, although there is some uncertainty in this, particularly for bidi use (Jha *et al.* 2011). This is comparable to the per capita adult consumption in France prior to 1990, and higher than that seen for adults today in Canada, which has declined from about 11 cigarettes per capita in the 1960s to below five in 2010.

Effects of Cessation on Lung Cancer and Total Deaths

Widespread smoking cessation in high-income countries has afforded researchers the opportunity to study the impact of quitting at various ages on the risk of death from tobacco-attributable diseases. Doctors in the UK who quit smoking before the onset of major disease avoided most of the excess hazards of smoking. In comparison to those who continued smoking, the average gain in life expectancy for those who quit smoking at 60, 50, 40, and 30 years of age, was about 3, 6, 9,

and nearly 10 years, respectively (Peto *et al.* 2000). Cessation before middle age prevents more than 90% of the lung cancer mortality attributable to smoking, with quitters possessing a pattern of survival similar to that of persons who have never smoked.

Overall Current Risks from Smoking

Provided due allowance is made for the long delay between smoking onset and disease, reasonably consistent quantitative estimates of risk emerge: about one in two of all long-term smokers worldwide are killed by their addiction (Jha 2009). It is already apparent that a substantial proportion of tobacco-related deaths worldwide occur in middle age : 50% in the USA and UK, 50% in China (Liu *et al.* 1998), and a surprisingly high 70% in India.

At present, about 80% of worldwide smoking-related deaths occur in men (Jha 2009), but this is chiefly because men who died recently smoked more commonly and more intensively when they were young than did the female smokers. The smoker : non-smoker mortality risks in US women after 2000 are actually greater than in men (Jha *et al.* 2013). Additionally, the consequences of smoking vary by socio-economic group. For example, in several high-income countries and Poland, smoking-related deaths were shown to account for at least half of the differences in middle age risk of death between rich, educated men and poorer, less educated men (Jha *et al.* 2006).

Future Risks from Smoking and Estimates

The future risks of smoking among men in low- and middle-income countries and women worldwide will depend on the duration of smoking (and cessation rates) in the population, variation in the diseases which are made common by smoking, and in the products and patterns of smoking. First, the full effects of smoking will only be apparent when the death rates from smoking in middle age among those who have started smoking as young adults rise 30–40 years later. Death rates from smoking in older age will rise only about 20 years after this (Jha

2009). For example, of all US male deaths at ages 35–69, the proportion attributable to tobacco in 1950 was only 12%, rising to 33% in 1990, when the increase in US male tobacco-related deaths had been completed (about three decades after peak male tobacco consumption).

Plausible projections of future smoking-related deaths rely on smoking prevalence and uptake (cessation is minimal in low- and middle-income countries), growth in population and growth in the age-specific tobacco-attributable death rates. Sir Richard Peto (2006) estimates that global tobacco-related deaths will reach about 450 million between 2000 and 2050. Worldwide annual tobacco-related mortality will rise to about 10 million per year or 100 million per decade around 2030, with some further increases in later decades. Further estimations are more uncertain, but based upon current initiation and cessation rates and projected population growth, from 2050–2100 there would be, conservatively, an additional 500 million tobacco-related deaths (i.e. an average of 10 million deaths per year).

How Can Cessation Rates be Raised Rapidly Worldwide?

Cessation by today's smokers is the only practicable way to avoid a substantial proportion of tobacco-related deaths worldwide before 2050. Halving the worldwide per capita adult consumption of tobacco by 2020 (akin to the declines in adult smoking in the UK over the last three decades) would prevent about 160–180 million tobacco-related deaths over the next few decades (Peto *et al.* 1994; Jha 2009). In contrast, halving the percentage of children who become prolonged smokers (from about 30% to 15% over two decades) would prevent some 20 million deaths over the next few decades, but its main effect would be to lower mortality rates in 2050 and beyond.

Higher taxation is the single most important intervention to raising global smoking cessation rates. Other interventions, specifically on information for consumers, banning advertising and promotion, and restricting public smoking as well as cessation for smokers also raise quit rates. For brevity, only taxes are discussed here. Detailed reviews of tobacco control strategies are published elsewhere (Jha and Chaloupka 2000; Jha *et al.* 2006; Jha 2009).

Aggressive taxation is the key strategy for low- and middle-income countries to reduce smoking at a rate faster than that achieved by high-income countries. Powerful policy interventions to tax and regulate consumption and to inform consumers have reduced consumption in most high-income countries (WHO, 2010a). The US and UK each took about 35 years and Canada about 25 years to halve per adult cigarette consumption (from about ten per adult per day to about five: Forey *et al.* 2009).

However, France took only 15 years to halve consumption (Hill 2010). France's uptake of smoking was chiefly after World War II and its prevalence rose until the mid-1980s. From 1990 to 2005, cigarette consumption fell from about six cigarettes per adult per day. This sharp decline was mostly due to a sharp increase in tobacco taxation starting in 1990 under the then president Jacques Chirac (Figure 7.15). These price increases raised the inflation-adjusted price threefold. Among men, the corresponding lung cancer rates at ages 35–44, which is a good measure of recent smoking in the population, fell sharply from 1997 onward. During this period, revenues in real terms rose from about €6 billion to €12 billion. Tax levels stagnated from 2004 onward when Nicolas Sarkozy became finance minister as has the decline in per capita cigarette consumption.

An increase in cigarette taxes of 10% globally would raise cigarette tax revenues by nearly 7%, as the fall in demand is less than proportional to the price increase in most countries (Jha and Chaloupka 1999). However, taxes are underused in most developing countries (WHO 2010a). Taxes tend to be absolutely higher and account for a greater share of the retail price (71% as of 2006) in high-income countries. In low- and middle-income countries, taxes account for 54% of the final price of cigarettes. In South Africa, tax as a percentage of retail price fell to about 20% around 1990, but has subsequently risen to nearly 40% (Van Walbeek 2005). As a result, consumption fell from about four cigarettes per adult per day to two over a decade. Poland's recent tax increases have doubled the

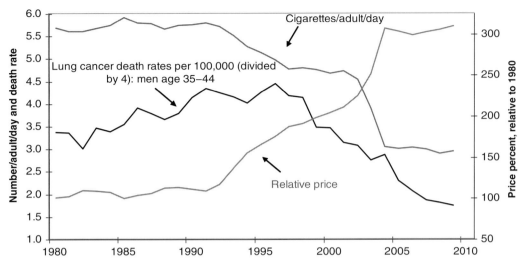

Figure 7.15 *France: smoking, tobacco prices, and male lung cancer rates at young ages, 1980–2010*

real price of cigarettes and lowered consumption. Mauritius and Mexico recently raised taxes by about 30%, which has already produced a drop in consumption.

A tax increase needed to raise the street prices of cigarettes by 70% would involve a 2- to 2.8-fold increase across countries (Jha 2009). The increase would raise the street price for a pack of 20 cigarettes from about US$0.7 to US$1.3 in low-income countries, from about US$1.3 to US$2.3 in middle-income countries, and from US$3.7 to US$6.3 in high-income countries. Such increases, while large, have been achieved in numerous countries, including Canada, France, Poland, and South Africa and within the various states of the USA. Indeed, the 2.5-fold increase in the US federal cigarette tax as of 2009 (rising by 62 cents to US$1.01 per pack) might get about 1 million Americans to quit smoking and deter another 2 million youth from starting, thus saving over 1 million lives.

Our purposes in this discussion of smoking are twofold. First, the growing consequences of the smoking epidemic provide a quantitatively important exception to the general rule of rapid progress in health. Second, we have attempted to show that knowledge-based approaches to control have every potential for ultimately yielding success of the sort experienced elsewhere in the health sector.

Conclusion

The twentieth century saw life expectancy rise by about 3 months for every calendar year. This extraordinary transformation of mortality is chiefly, but not exclusively, a result of the creation and widespread use of specific technologies. What was the value of this transformation? And what then are the implications for this century?

First, by any reasonable measure of value, the value of the health gains in the past century has been enormous.

Second, ongoing investments in widely applicable treatments and policies remain the best engine of future reductions. Specifically, the ongoing investments in child health and infectious disease control should continue to make possible the creation of new powerful interventions, and ongoing operations research and public support for child health should enable the use of these interventions much more widely. In contrast, the future looks less rosy for adult health. The costs of achieving adult survival are rising each year, in part due to the effects of the tobacco and HIV epidemic, (Hum *et al.* 2012). Moreover, the major enterprise of public support, research attention, and widespread operations research remain scanty at best. Nowhere is this demonstrated more powerfully than for tobacco taxation. A worldwide coordinated major increase in tobacco taxation is not hard to make practicable – the only obstacles are widespread indifference or misunderstanding of tobacco hazards among the public and politicians, and well-organized and funded opposition from the tobacco industry. Similar widely cost-effective strategies (Jamison *et al.* 2008) focused on long-term management with combination drugs for heart attacks and strokes are also widely practicable.

The third major implication has to do with institutions. Previous careful reviews (WHO 1996) have supported worldwide efforts to accelerate research on neglected and unfinished agendas (such as selected tropical diseases) and on chronic diseases. To some extent, the major philanthropy of the Bill & Melinda Gates Foundation will continue research on promising interventions for child health and infectious diseases, although there are limitations to how the foundation chooses and funds innovations (Black *et al.* 2009; McCoy *et al.* 2009). Major institutions, are, as seen above, central to gains in health. Similar efforts and philanthropy are needed for chronic diseases.

Finally, while mostly beyond the scope of this chapter, a rethink in developmental assistance around health is required. Given income growth, and increased affordability (at least of child health interventions), it can be fairly argued that most funding for delivery of effective interventions should be the responsibility of governments as well as major global funds (such as the Global Fund for AIDS, Tuberculosis and Malaria or the Global Alliance for Vaccines and Immunization). This suggests that a substantial part of traditional bilateral aid, such as by USAID or the UK DFID, should be redirected to operations research as well as to chronic disease intervention research. Facilitating the application and diffusion of new health technologies and policies will yield the highest return on the aid dollar.

Finally, as illustrated by Annex Figure A7.1 (below) presenting the total money metric value of years of life lost as percent of GDP for selected regions for the period 1900–2050, the biggest decline has taken place in less developed regions where the ratio has fallen from 35% to 12% in the last century and expected to fall to 6.5% in 2050. The world as a whole has experienced a development bringing it from 32% to 5% in the same period. This is both a result of improved human health and economic growth.

References

Acemoglu, D. and S. Johnson, (2007) Disease and development: the effect of life expectancy on economic growth, *Journal of Political Economy* **115**: 925–985.

Ahmad, O. B., A. D. Lopez, and M. Inoue (2000) *The decline in child mortality: a reappraisal. Bulletin of the World Health Organization* **78**: 1175–1191.

Aral, S. O. and K. K. Holmes (2008) The epidemiology of STIs and their social and behavioral determinants: industrialized and developing countries. In: K. K. Holmes, P. Sparling, W. Stamm, *et al.* (eds.) *Sexually Transmitted Diseases*, 4th edn. New York: McGraw-Hill.

Ashton, B., K. Hill, A. Piazza, and R. Zeitz (1984) Famine in China, 1958–1961. *Population and Development Review* **10**: 613–645.

Banthia, T. and T. Dyson (2000). Smallpox and the impact of vaccination among the Parsees of Bombay. *Indian Economic and Social History Review* **37**: 22–51.

Basu, A. M. and R. Stephenson (2005) Low levels of maternal education and the proximate determinants of childhood mortality: a little learning is not a dangerous thing. *Social Science and Medicine* **60**: 2011–2023.

Black, R. E., M. K. Bhan, M. Chopra, I. Rudan, and C. G. Victora (2009) Accelerating the health impact of the Gates Foundation. *The Lancet* **373**: 1584–1585.

Bloom, D. E., D. Canning, and J. T. Jamison (2004) Health, wealth, and welfare. *Finance and Development* **40**: 10–15.

Bloom, D. E., A. Mahal, L. Rosenberg, *et al.* (2004) *Asia's Economies and the Challenge of AIDS.* Mandaluyong City, Philippines: Asian Development Bank.

Breman, J. G., M. S. Alilio, and A. Mills (2004) Conquering the intolerable burden of malaria: what's new, what's needed: a summary. *American Journal of Tropical Medicine and Hygiene* **71** (2 Suppl.): 1–15.

Brundtland, G. H., K. Liestol, and L. Walloe (1975) Height and weight of school children and adolescent girls and boys in Oslo 1970. *Acta Paediatricia* **64**: 565–573.

Caldwell, J. and P. McDonald (1982) Influence of maternal education on infant and child mortality: levels and causes. *Health Policy and Education* **2**: 251–267.

Carter, R. and K. N. Mendis (2002) Evolutionary and historical aspects of the burden of malaria. *Clinical Microbiology* **15**: 564–594.

Caulfield, L. E., S. A. Richard, J. A. Rivera, P. Musgrove, and R. E. Black (2006) Stunting, wasting, and micronutrient deficiency disorders. In: D. T. Jamison, J. G. Breman, A. R. Measham, *et al.* (eds.), *Disease Control Priorities in Developing Countries*. New York: Oxford University Press.

Center for Disease Control and Prevention (2004). *United States Life Tables, 2002: National Vital Statistics Report*. Atlanta, GA: CDC.

Coale, A. J. and P. Demeny (1966) *Regional Model Life Tables and Stable Populations* Princeton, NJ: Princeton University Press.

Copenhagen Consensus Center (2011): Population Data.

Crawford, C. B., B. E. Salter, and K. L. Lang (1989) Human grief: is its intensity related to the reproductive value of the deceased? *Ethology and Sociobiology* **10**: 287–307.

Cutler, D. M. and S. Kadiyala (2002) The return to biomedical research: treatment and behavioral effects In: K. M. Murphy and R. H. Topel (eds.), *Measuring the Gains of Medical Research: An Economic Approach*. Chicago. IL: University of Chicago Press.

Davis, K. (1951) *The Population of India and Pakistan* Princeton, NJ: Princeton University Press.

(1996) The amazing decline of mortality in underdeveloped areas. *American Economic Review* **46**: 305–318.

de Vlas, S. J., N. J. Nagelkerke, P. Jha, and F. A. Plummer (2002) Mother-to-child HIV transmission and ARVs. *Science* **298**: 2129.

Devereux, S. (2000) *Famine in the Twentieth Century*, Institute of Development Studies Working Paper No. 105. Brighton, UK: IDS.

Dhingra, N., P. Jha, V. P. Sharma, *et al.* (2010) Adult and child malaria mortality in India: a nationally representative mortality study. *The Lancet* **376**: 1768–1774.

Doll, R., R. Peto, J. Boreham, I. Sutherland (2004) Mortality in relation to smoking: 50 years' observations on male British doctors. *British Medical Journal* **328**: 1519–1533.

Dye, C. (2000) Tuberculosis 2000–2010: control, but not elimination. *International Journal of Tuberculosis and Lung Diseases* **4**(Suppl): S146–152.

Easterlin, R. A. (1999) How beneficent is the market? A look at the modern history of mortality. *European Review of Economic History* **3**: 257–294.

England, S., B. Loevinsohn, B. Melgaard, U. Kou, and P. Jha (2000) *The Evidence Base for Interventions to Reduce Mortality from Vaccine-Preventable Diseases in Low- and Middle-Income Countries*, CMH Working Paper Series WG5 Paper No. 10. Available at: www.cmhealth.org/docs/wg5_paper10.pdf.

Farr, W. (1889) Life and death in England. Reprinted in N. A. Humphreys (ed.) *Vital Statistics: A Memorial Volume of Selections from the Reports and Writings of William Farr, Bulletin of the World Health Organization* (2000) **78**: 88–96.

Feachem, R. G. and D. T. Jamison, (1991) *Disease and Mortality in Sub-Saharan Africa* Washington, DC: World Bank.

Fenner, D., D. A. Henderson, I. Arita, *et al.* (1988) *Smallpox and its Eradication*. Geneva: WHO.

Ferguson, N. (2011) *Civilization: The West and the Rest*. New York: Penguin Books.

Forey, B. J. Hamling, and P. Lee (eds.) (2009) *International Smoking Statistics: A Collection of Historical Data from 30 Economically Developed Countries*. New York: Oxford University Press.

Giovino, G. A., S. A. Mirza, J. M. Samet, *et al.* (2012) Tobacco use in 3 billion individuals from 16 countries: an analysis of nationally representative cross-sectional household surveys. *The Lancet* **380**: 668–679.

Global Forum on Health Research (2003) *The 10/90 Report on Health Research 2001–2002*. Geneva: WHO.

Gomes, M. F., M. A. Faiz, J. O. Gyapong, *et al.* (2009) Pre-referral rectal artesunate to prevent death and disability in severe malaria: a placebo-controlled trial. *The Lancet* **373**: 557–566.

Hammitt, J. K. and L. A. Robinson (2011) The income elasticity of the value per statistical life: transferring estimates between high and low income populations, *Journal of Benefit–Cost Analysis* **2**, Article 1. Available at www.bepress.com/jbca/vol2/iss1/1/

Hill, C. (2010) *Prévention et Facteurs de Risque*, Institut de cancérologie. Available at: www.igr.fr/fr/page/prevention-et-facteurs-de-risque_80

Hira, S. K., K. Panchal, P. A. Parmar, *et al.* (2004) High resistance to antiretroviral drugs: the

Indian experience. *International Journal of STD and AIDS* **15**: 173–177.

Hum, R., P. Jha, A. M. McGahan, and Y. L. Cheng (2013) Global divergence in critical income for adult and childhood survival: analyses of mortality using Michaelis-Menten. eLife Sciences 1: e06051, 2007. *eLife* (in press).

Human Mortality Database (2011) Available at www. mortality.org.

Institute of Medicine (1985) *Diseases of Importance in the United States, vol. 1, New Vaccine Development: Establishing Priorities.* Washington, DC: National Academies Press.

Jamison, D. T. and J. C. Jamison (2011) Characterizing the amount and speed of discounting procedures. *Journal of Benefit–Cost Analysis* **2** Article 2.

Jamison, D. T. (2006) Economic benefits of investing in disease control. In: D. T. Jamison, J. G. Breman, A. R. Measham, *et al.* (eds.), *Disease Control Priorities in Developing Countries.* New York: Oxford University Press.

Jamison, D. T., J. D. Sachs, and J. Wang (2001) The effect of the AIDS epidemic on economic welfare in Sub-Saharan Africa. *CMH Working Paper Series* **13**: 1–27. Available at: www.cmhealth. org/docs/wg1_paper13.pdf

Jamison, D. T., S. A. Sahid-Salles, J. Jamison, J. E. Lawn, and J. Zupan (2006) Incorporating deaths near the time of birth into estimates of the global burden of disease. In: A. D. Lopez, C. D. Mathers, M. Ezzati, D. T. Jamison, and C. J. L. Murray (eds.), *Global Burden of Disease and Risk Factors.* New York: Oxford University Press.

Jamison, D. T., P. Jha, and D. E. Bloom (2008) Disease control. In: B. Lomborg, (ed.), *Global Crises, Global Solutions: Costs and Benefits.* Cambridge: Cambridge University Press.

Jamison, D. T., S. M. Murphy, M. E. Sandhu, and J. Wang (2013) Why has under-5 mortality decreased at such different rates in different countries? *Journal of Health Economics* (accepted pending minor revisions).

Jha, P. (2001) Avoidable mortality in India: past progress and future prospects. *National Medical Journal of India* **15**: 6.

(2009) Avoidance of worldwide cancer mortality and total mortality from smoking. *Nature Reviews: Cancer* **9**: 655–664.

(2009) Avoidable global cancer deaths and total deaths from smoking. *Nature Reviews: Cancer* **9**: 655–664.

(2012) Counting the dead is among the world's best investments to reduce premature mortality. *Hypothesis* **10**, Article 1.

Jha, P. and F. J. Chaloupka (1999) *Curbing the Epidemic: Governments and the Economics of Tobacco Control.* Washington, DC: World Bank.

(2000) *Tobacco Control in Developing Countries.* Oxford: Oxford University Press.

Jha, P. and A. Mills (2002) *Improving Health Outcomes of the Poor*, Report of Working Group 5 of the Commission on Macroeconomics and Health. Geneva: WHO.

Jha, P., J. D. Nagelkerke, E. N. Ngugi, *et al.* (2001) Reducing HIV transmission in developing countries. *Science* **292**: 224–225.

Jha, P., A. Mills, K. Hanson, *et al.* (2002) Improving the health of the global poor. *Science* **295**: 2036–2039.

Jha, P., F. J. Chaloupka, J. Moore, *et al.* (2006) Tobacco addiction. In: D. T. Jamison, J. G. Breman, A. R. Measham, *et al.* (eds.), *Disease Control Priorities in Developing Countries.* New York: Oxford University Press.

Jha, P. D. Brown, A. S. Slutsky, *et al.* (2004) Health and economic benefits of an accelerated program of research to combat global infectious diseases. *Canadian Medical Association Journal* **172**: 1538–1539.

Jha, P., E. Guindon, R. A. Joseph, *et al.* (2011) A rational taxation system of bidis and cigarettes to reduce smoking deaths in India. *Economic and Political Weekly* **46**: 44–51.

Jha, P., C. Ramasundarahettige, V. Landsman, *et al.* (2013) 21st-century hazards of smoking and benefits of cessation in the United States. *New England Journal Medicine* **368**: 341–350.

Johnson, N. and J. Mueller (2002) Updating the accounts: global mortality of the 1918–1920 "Spanish" influenza pandemic. *Bulletin of the History of Medicine* **76**: 105–115.

Johnston, R. (2002) Microbicides: an update. *AIDS Patient Care and STDs* **16**: 419–430.

Kidane, G. and R. H. Morrow (2000) Teaching mothers to provide home treatment of malaria in Tigray, Ethiopia: a randomised trial. *The Lancet* **356**: 550–555.

Kinsella, K. G. (1992) Changes in life expectancy 1900–1990. *American Journal of Clinical Nutrition,* **55**: 1096S–1202S.

Kumar, R. (2004) Plague outbreak in 2001 in Northern India. Paper presented at *Controlling the Risk: Science to Combat Global Infectious*

Diseases, Toronto, Ontario, November 9–10, 2004. Available at: www.healtheconomics.org/conferences/

Laxminarayan, R., *et al.* (2005) Drug resistance. In: D. T. Jamison, J. G. Breman, A. R. Measham, *et al.* (eds.) *Disease Control Priorities in Developing Countries*. New York: Oxford University Press.

LeGrand, J. (1987) Inequalities in health. *European Economic Review* **31**: 182–191.

Liu, B. Q., R. Peto, Z. M. Chen, *et al.* (1998) Emerging tobacco hazards in China: 1. Retrospective proportional mortality study of one million deaths. *British Medical Journal* **317**: 1411–1422.

Lopez, A. D., C. D. Mathers, M. Ezzati, D. T. Jamison, and C. J. L. Murray (eds.) (2006) *Global Burden of Disease and Risk Factors*. New York: Oxford University Press.

Luk, J., P. Gross, and W. Thompson (2001) Observations on mortality during the 1918 influenza pandemic. *Journal of Infectious Diseases* **33**: 1375–1378.

Maddison, A. (2011) *Statistics on World Population, GDP and Per Capita GDP, 1–2008 AD*. Available at: www.ggdc.net/MADDISON/oriindex.htm.

Mandle, J. R. (1970) The decline of mortality in British Guiana, 1911–1960. *Demography* **7**: 301–315.

Mathers, C. D., J. A. Salomon, C. J. L. Murray, and A. D. Lopez (2003) *Deaths and Disease Burden by Cause: Global Burden of Disease Estimates for 2001 by World Bank Country Groups*. Washington, DC: World Bank.

McCoy, D., G. Kembhavi, J. Patel, and A. Luintel, (2009) The Bill and Melinda Gates Foundation's grant-making programme for global health. *The Lancet* **373**: 1645–1653.

Measham, M. R., K. D. Rao, D. T. Jamison, J. Wang, and A. Singh (1999) Reducing infant mortality and futility, 1975–1990: Performance at all-India and state levels. *Economic and Political Weekly* **34**: 1359–1367.

Million Death Study Collaborators (2010) Causes of neonatal and child mortality in India: a nationally representative mortality study. *The Lancet* **376**: 1853–1860.

Munos, M. K., C. L. Walker, and R. E. Black, (2010) The effect of oral rehydration solution and recommended home fluids on diarrhea mortality. *International Journal of Epidemiology* **39**: 175–187.

Murphy, K. M. and R. H. Topel (2002) The economic value of medical research. In: K. M. Murphy, and R. H. Topel (eds.), *Measuring the Gains of Medical Research: An Economic Approach*. Chicago, IL: University of Chicago Press.

Nagelkerke, N. (2012) *Courtesans and Consumption: How Sexually Transmitted Infections Drive Tuberculosis Epidemics*. Amsterdam: Eburon Academic Publishers.

Nagelkerke, N. J. D., P. Jha, S. J. de Vlas, *et al.* (2002) Modelling HIV/AIDS epidemics in Botswana and India: impact of interventions to prevent transmission. *Bulletin of the World Health Organization* **80**: 89–96.

Nelson, K. E., D. D. Celentano, S. Eiumtrakol, *et al.* (1996) Changes in sexual behavior and a decline in HIV infection among young men in Thailand. *New England Journal of Medicine* **335**: 297–303.

Nordhaus, W. (2003) The health of nations: the contributions of improved health to living standards. In: K. M. Murphy and R. H. Topel (eds.), *Measuring the Gains from Medical Research: An Economic Approach*. Chicago. IL: University of Chicago Press.

Oeppen, J. and J. W. Vaupel (2002) Broken limits to life expectancy. *Science* **296**: 1029–1031.

Organisation for Economic Co-operation and Development (2003) *Trends in Developmental Assistance*. Paris: OECD. Available at: www.oecd.org/dataoecd/42/21/1860310.gif.

Perrin, L. and A. Telenti (1998) HIV treatment failure: testing for HIV resistance in clinical practice. *Science* **280**: 1871–1873.

Peto, R. (2006) Avoidable mortality. Paper presented at *Disease Control Priorities Launch Meeting*, Beijing, 2006. Available at: www.dcp2.org

Peto, R., S. Darby, H. Deo, *et al.* (2000) Smoking, smoking cessation, and lung cancer in the UK since 1950: combination of national statistics with two case-control studies. *British Medical Journal* **321**: 323–329.

Peto, R., A. D. Lopez, J. Boreham, M. Thun, and C. Heath Jr. (1994) *Mortality from Smoking in Developed Countries, 1950–2000*. Oxford: Oxford University Press.

Pitkanen, K. J., J. H. Mielke, L. B. Jorde (1989) Smallpox and its eradication in Finland: implications for disease control. *Population Studies* **43**: 95–111.

Plank, S. J., and M. L. Milanesi (1973) Infant feeding and infant mortality in rural Chile. *Bulletin of the World Health Organization* **48**: 203–210.

Preston, S. H. (1980) Causes and consequences of mortality declines in less developed countries during the twentieth century. In: R. A. Easterlin (ed.), *Population and Economic Change in Developing Countries*. Cambridge, MA: National Bureau of Economic Research.

Preston, S. H. and M. Haines (1991) *Fatal Years: Child Mortality in Late Nineteenth Century America*. Princeton, NJ: Princeton University Press.

Pritchett, L. and L. Summers (1996) Wealthier is healthier. *Journal of Human Resources* **31**: 841–868.

Riley, J. (2005a) Estimates of regional and global life expectancy, 1800–2001 *Population and Development Review* **31**: 537–543.

(2005b) The timing and place of health transitions around the world. *Population and Development Review* **31**: 741–764.

Ruger, J. P., D. T. Jamison, D. Bloom, and D. Canning, (2006) Health and the economy. In: M. H. Merson, R. E. Black, and A. J. Mills, (eds.), *International Public Health: Diseases, Programs, Systems, and Policies*. Sudbury, MA: Jones and Bartlett.

United Nations, (1998) *Revision of the World Population Estimates and Projections*. New York: Population Division, UN.

(2004) *Demographic Bulletin, Latin America: Life Tables, 1950–2025*. New York: Latin American and Caribbean Demographic Center, Population Division, UN.

(2009) *World Population Prospects: The 2008 Revision*. New York: Department of Economic and Social Affairs, Population Division, UN.

US Center for Disease Control (1999) *Achievements in Public Health, 1900–1999: Changes in the Public Health System*. Available at: www.cdc.gov/mmwr/PDF/wk/mm4850.pdf.

Usher, D. (1973) An imputation to the measure of economic growth for changes in life expectancy. In: M. Moss (ed.), *The Measurement of Economic and Social Performance*, New York: National Bureau of Economic Research.

Vallin, J. and F. Meslé (2009) The segmented trend line of highest life expectancies. *Population and Development Review* **35**: 159–187.

(2010) Will life expectancy increase indefinitely by three months every year? *Population and Societies* **473**: 1–4.

Van Walbeek, C. (2005) Tobacco control in South Africa. *Promotion & Education*, Suppl. **4**: 25–8, 57. (In French.)

Victora, C. G., J. Bryce, O. Fontaine, and R. Monasch, (2000) Reducing deaths from diarrhea through oral rehydration therapy. *Bulletin of the World Health Organization* **78**: 1246–1255.

Viscusi, W. K. and J. E. Aldy (2003) The value of a statistical life: a critical review of market estimates throughout the world. *Journal of Risk and Uncertainty* **27**: 5–76.

Vos, T. (2002) Shifting the goalpost: normative survivorship goals in health gap measures. In: C. J. L. Murray, J. A. Salomon, C. D. Mathers, and A. D. Lopez, (eds.), *Summary Measures of Population Health: Concepts, Ethics, Measurement and Applications*. Geneva: World Health Organization.

Weatherall, D., B. Greenwood, L. H. Chee, and P. Wasi, (2005) Science and technology for disease control: past, present, and future. In: J. G. Breman, A. R. Measham, D. T. Jamison *et al.*, (eds.), *Disease Control Priorities in Developing Countries*. New York: Oxford University Press.

Wikipedia (2011a) World War I casualties. *Wikipedia: The Free Encyclopedia*. Available at: en.wikipedia.org/

(2011b) World War II casualties. *Wikipedia: The Free Encyclopedia*. Available at: en.wikipedia.org/

Williamson, J. G. (1982) Was the Industrial Revolution worth it? Disamenities and death in nineteenth century British towns. *Explorations in Economic History* **19**: 221–245.

World Bank (1993) *World Development Report 1993: Investing in Health*. New York: Oxford University Press.

World Health Organization (1996) *Investing in Health Research and Development*, Report of the Ad Hoc Committee on Health Research Relating to Future Intervention Options. Geneva: WHO.

(2002) *Macroeconomics and Health: Investing in Health for Economic Development*, Report of the Commission on Macroeconomics and Health. Geneva: WHO.

(2003) *Global Forum for Health Research: The 10/90 Report on Health Research 2001–2002*. Geneva: WHO.

(2010a) *WHO Technical Manual on Tobacco Tax Administration*. Geneva: WHO.

(2010b) *Life Tables for WHO Member States, 1990, 2000, 2008, by Country and Region*. Geneva: WHO.

Zlotkin, S. H., C. Schauer, A. Christofides, *et al.* (2005) Micronutrient sprinkles to control childhood anaemia. *PLoS Med* **2**(1). DOI: 10.1371/journal.pmed.0020001

Annex 7.1

In this chapter, we developed measurements of twentieth-century mortality reductions in terms of reduction in the expected number of years of life lost (YLLs) by a typical individual relative to an idealized norm. The norm chosen in the main text of the paper is the United Nations' projected mortality profile for Japan in 2050, named "Japan 2050." This Annex 7.1 presents all the results obtained under this assumption (Annex Tables A7.1 – A7.5).

Annex Figure A7.1 illustrates the total money metric value of years of life lost as percent of GDP for selected regions for the period 1900–2050. The biggest decline has taken place in less developed regions where the ratio has fallen from 35% to 12% in the last century and is expected to fall to 6.5% in 2050. The world as a whole has experienced a development bringing it from 32% to 5% in the same period. This is both a result of improved human health and economic growth.

Table A7.1 Years of life lost per person under 5 (YLL$_{u5}$) (in years), selected countries and regions, 1900–2050

Year	China	India	Japan	USA	Sub-Saharan Africa	More Developed Regions	Less Developed Regions	World
1900	29.7	40.2	18.9	15.6	43.3	16.3	35.9	28.9
1910	27.1	40.2	16.4	13.8	39.3	14.1	34.3	27.1
1920	24.5	35.0	13.9	14.2	35.3	14.5	30.4	24.8
1930	21.9	29.7	11.4	6.7	31.3	7.1	26.5	19.8
1940	19.2	24.6	8.3	4.7	27.3	5.0	22.6	16.6
1950	16.6	19.5	6.4	2.8	23.3	4.9	18.8	14.3
1960	12.8	16.9	2.6	2.3	21.2	2.9	15.8	11.8
1970	9.0	14.3	1.1	1.7	19.1	2.2	12.7	9.8
1980	5.1	11.7	0.5	0.8	17.1	1.3	10.4	9.2
1990	3.2	9.4	0.2	0.6	15.8	0.8	8.4	7.6
2000	2.5	7.6	0.1	0.4	13.7	0.5	7.1	6.5
2010	2.0	6.1	0.1	0.3	11.3	0.4	5.9	5.3
2020	1.5	4.9	0.0	0.3	9.1	0.3	4.8	4.4
2030	1.2	4.1	0.0	0.2	7.1	0.2	3.9	3.5
2040	0.9	3.4	0.0	0.2	5.4	0.2	3.1	2.8
2050	0.8	3.1	0.0	0.2	4.7	0.2	2.7	2.4

Table A7.2 Years of life lost per person above 5 (YLL$_{a5}$) (in years), selected countries and regions, 1900–2050

Year	China	India	Japan	USA	Sub-Saharan Africa	More Developed Regions	Less Developed Regions	World
1900	18.4	15.1	14.5	14.0	13.7	14.3	16.3	16.7
1910	18.3	15.1	14.3	13.9	14.1	13.8	15.6	16.2
1920	18.1	14.7	13.9	12.7	14.7	12.3	16.0	15.9
1930	17.9	14.9	13.5	13.2	16.5	13.2	16.2	16.5
1940	17.5	17.1	12.9	12.2	17.2	12.2	16.2	16.3
1950	17.1	19.3	12.3	10.4	17.7	11.3	15.6	15.6
1960	15.2	17.2	10.3	9.7	16.4	10.4	14.5	14.3
1970	12.9	15.0	8.5	9.3	15.1	9.4	13.2	12.6
1980	10.2	12.5	6.2	7.6	13.7	8.6	11.4	10.3
1990	10.0	12.3	4.7	6.9	14.1	8.1	11.0	9.9
2000	8.1	11.3	2.7	6.5	14.6	7.1	9.9	9.0
2010	7.1	10.2	2.1	4.4	14.2	5.6	9.0	8.1
2020	6.2	9.0	1.4	3.6	13.4	4.5	8.1	7.3
2030	5.4	8.0	0.8	2.8	12.4	3.7	7.3	6.6
2040	4.7	7.1	0.3	2.2	11.4	3.0	6.7	6.0
2050	4.4	6.7	0.0	1.8	10.8	2.5	6.4	5.7

Table A7.3 Total years of life lost per person, selected countries and regions, 1900–2050

Year	China	India	Japan	USA	Sub-Saharan Africa	More Developed Regions	Less Developed Regions	World
1900	48.1	55.2	33.4	29.6	57.0	30.6	52.2	45.6
1910	45.4	55.2	30.6	27.6	53.4	27.9	49.9	43.3
1920	42.6	49.7	27.8	26.9	50.0	26.8	46.4	40.7
1930	39.7	44.7	24.8	19.9	47.8	20.3	42.7	36.3
1940	36.8	41.8	21.8	16.9	44.4	17.2	38.9	32.9
1950	33.7	38.8	18.6	13.2	41.0	16.1	34.4	29.9
1960	28.0	34.2	12.9	12.0	37.7	13.3	30.3	26.0
1970	21.9	29.3	9.6	11.0	34.3	11.6	25.9	22.4
1980	15.3	24.2	6.7	8.4	30.8	9.9	21.8	19.5
1990	13.2	21.7	5.0	7.5	29.9	8.9	19.4	17.5
2000	10.6	18.9	2.8	6.9	28.3	7.6	17.0	15.5
2010	9.1	16.3	2.2	4.7	25.5	6.0	14.9	13.5
2020	7.7	13.9	1.4	3.8	22.5	4.8	13.0	11.7
2030	6.6	12.0	0.8	3.0	19.5	3.9	11.2	10.1
2040	5.6	10.5	0.3	2.3	16.8	3.2	9.7	8.8
2050	5.2	9.8	0	2.0	15.5	2.6	9.1	8.2

Note: Values in this table are the sum of the values in the corresponding columns of Tables A7.1 and A7.2.

Table A7.4 Money metric value of years of life lost (MMVYLL), selected countries and regions, 1900–2050 ($)

Year	China	India	Japan	USA	Sub-Saharan Africa	More Developed Regions	Less Developed Regions	World
1900	37,545	44,038	58,384	179,985	22,305	56,588	22,417	40,737
1910	36,360	51,242	60,279	209,524	22,200	61,397	23,338	45,089
1920	35,106	42,665	72,592	219,538	24,049	68,458	24,410	48,913
1930	33,707	45,009	72,512	202,389	25,411	63,308	24,543	49,180
1940	31,373	41,759	101,726	201,551	25,947	60,974	24,499	49,545
1950	23,349	36,977	63,054	221,036	27,688	65,027	22,071	49,347
1960	29,267	39,726	93,383	240,188	30,018	78,018	25,765	57,497
1970	27,656	39,436	175,897	297,719	34,401	102,065	28,604	66,633
1980	27,424	35,273	174,749	291,074	34,556	114,580	31,135	68,588
1990	43,910	45,546	182,260	323,635	31,964	127,442	35,213	71,084
2000	64,883	58,343	113,222	370,334	31,398	128,389	42,646	74,140
2010	125,591	88,164	100,540	285,432	36,019	120,677	58,017	84,808
2020	151,431	110,980	80,206	276,589	35,347	115,508	66,593	89,386
2030	169,830	126,952	56,363	255,791	35,529	111,768	78,947	98,168
2040	181,503	138,210	24,224	222,368	36,229	109,962	96,236	109,584
2050	200,644	154,800	0.0	212,861	40,643	112,704	127,586	132,008

Note: Entries in this table are calculated from the per person YLLs reported in Tables A7.1 and A7.2 by multiplying those $YLL^* = YLL_{a5} + 0.54YLL_{u5}$ by twice per capita GDP expressed in 1990 International Geary–Khamis dollars.

Annex 7.2

In this chapter, we developed measurements of twentieth-century mortality reductions in terms of reduction in the expected number of years of life lost (YLLs) by a typical individual relative to an idealized norm. The norm chosen in the main text of the chapter is the United Nations' projected mortality profile for Japan in 2050, named "Japan 2050." An alternative to Japan 2050 as a norm is to use the lowest mortality country at any given time as the norm for that time, named frontier country. Annex 7.2 presents all the results obtained under this second assumption. Specifically, Annex Table A7.6 describes the characteristics of countries on this life expectancy frontier. Annex Tables A7.7 through A7.11 are the variants of Annex Tables A7.1 through A7.5. Annex Figure A7.2 compares the YLLs per birth for the less developed regions for the period 1900–2050 for the two different norms, Japan 2050 and frontier country.

Finally, Annex Figure A7.3 illustrates the total money metric value of years of life lost as percent of GDP for selected regions for the period 1900–2050. The biggest decline has taken place in less developed regions where the ratio has fallen from 23% to 12% in the last century and is expected to fall to 7.5% in 2050. The world as a whole has experienced a similar but less drastic development from 23% to 8% in the same period. For more developed regions the ratio has been declining and is expected to reach just 2.2% in 2050.

Table A7.5 Ratio *a* of money metric value of years of life lost (MMVYLL) per lifetime income per capita (LI) (no units), selected countries and regions, 1900–2050

Year	China	India	Japan	USA	Sub-Saharan Africa	More Developed Regions	Less Developed Regions	World
1900	2.4	3.5	1.1	0.9	3.9	1.0	3.0	2.1
1910	2.4	3.5	1.0	0.9	3.7	0.9	2.9	2.0
1920	2.3	3.2	1.0	0.8	3.5	0.8	2.7	1.9
1930	2.1	3.0	0.9	0.7	3.5	0.7	2.6	1.8
1940	2.0	2.9	0.8	0.6	3.3	0.6	2.4	1.6
1950	1.9	2.9	0.7	0.5	3.1	0.6	2.2	1.5
1960	1.6	2.5	0.5	0.4	2.9	0.6	1.9	1.3
1970	1.3	2.2	0.4	0.4	2.6	0.5	1.7	1.2
1980	0.9	1.8	0.3	0.3	2.4	0.4	1.4	1.0
1990	0.8	1.7	0.2	0.3	2.4	0.4	1.3	0.9
2000	0.7	1.5	0.1	0.3	2.3	0.3	1.2	0.8
2010	0.6	1.3	0.1	0.2	2.1	0.2	1.0	0.7
2020	0.5	1.1	0.1	0.1	1.9	0.2	0.9	0.6
2030	0.4	1.0	0.0	0.1	1.7	0.2	0.8	0.6
2040	0.4	0.9	0.0	0.1	1.5	0.1	0.7	0.5
2050	0.3	0.8	0.0	0.1	1.4	0.1	0.7	0.5

Note: Entries in this table are calculated from the money metric value of years of life lost MMVYLL reported in Table A7.4 divided by the lifetime income per capita as defined by equation (7.8) in the main text.

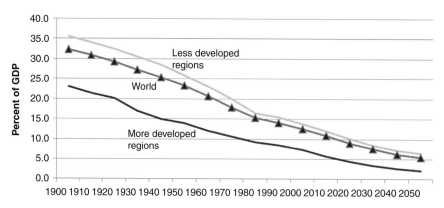

Figure A7.1 *Money metric value of years of life lost (MMVYLL), selected regions, 1900–2050, percent of GDP*

Table A7.6 Characteristics of countries on the life expectancy frontier

Year	Frontier reference (female life expectancy)	e_0 (females)	e_0 (males)	e_0 (both)	e_5 (both)	q_5 (per 1,000 live births)	YLLs under age 5 per birth	YLLs from age 5 per birth	YLLs per birth[a]
Estimates									
1900	New Zealand[b]	60.3	57.8	59.0	60.4	99	5.9	13.3	19.2
1910	New Zealand	63.6	60.6	61.9	61.8	73	4.6	13.0	17.5
1920	New Zealand	65.0	62.4	63.6	62.7	62	5.0	12.7	17.8
1930	New Zealand	68.2	65.5	66.8	64.7	43	2.8	12.4	15.2
1940	New Zealand	69.4	65.8	67.6	65.3	39	2.6	11.9	14.6
1950	Norway	74.4	70.8	72.6	69.8	30	2.2	11.0	13.2
1960	Norway	75.9	71.1	73.5	70.1	22	1.6	10.8	12.3
1970	Norway	77.6	71.3	74.4	70.5	15	1.1	10.9	12.0
1980	Iceland	79.9	73.8	76.8	72.4	8	0.6	11.3	12.0
1990	Japan	82.3	76.2	79.4	74.9	6	0.5	10.6	11.0
2000	Japan	85.1	78.2	81.9	77.2	4	0.3	10.6	10.9
Projections									
2010	Japan	87.2	80.1	83.7	79.0	4	0.3	10.6	10.9
2020	Japan	88.4	81.2	84.9	80.2	4	0.3	10.4	10.8
2030	Japan	89.5	82.2	85.8	81.1	4	0.3	10.3	10.6
2040	Japan	90.5	83.1	86.8	82.0	3	0.3	10.2	10.5
2050	Japan	91.0	83.5	87.2	82.5	3	0.3	10.1	10.4

Sources: Oeppen and Vaupel (2002), Human Mortality Database (www.mortality.org), United Nations (2009).
Note: The e_0 (females, males, both), and e_5 (both) columns are extracted from full life tables for the frontier country.
[a]This column shows YLLs for the frontier country relative to its own survival curve.
[b]The New Zealand estimates are for New Zealand's non-Maori population.

Table A7.7 Years of life lost per person under 5 (YLL_{u5}) (in years), selected countries and regions, 1900–2050 (variant of Table A7.1)

Year	China	India	Japan	USA	Sub-Saharan Africa	More developed regions	Less developed regions	World
1900	14.4	21.5	7.1	4.9	23.6	5.3	18.6	13.9
1910	14.9	24.2	7.3	5.4	23.6	5.7	20.0	14.9
1920	13.0	20.7	5.3	5.5	20.9	5.8	17.3	13.3
1930	14.1	20.1	6.1	2.5	21.3	2.8	17.7	12.5
1940	12.5	16.7	4.5	1.3	18.7	1.5	15.2	10.5
1950	11.9	14.3	3.4	0.4	17.5	2.1	13.7	10.0
1960	9.4	12.9	0.8	0.6	16.5	1.1	11.9	8.6
1970	6.8	11.4	0.1	0.7	15.5	1.0	10.0	7.5
1980	4.2	10.0	0.1	0.4	14.7	0.8	8.8	7.8
1990	2.7	8.4	0	0.3	14.2	0.5	7.4	6.7
2000	2.3	7.1	0	0.3	12.8	0.4	6.6	6.0
2010	1.8	5.8	0	0.2	10.8	0.3	5.6	5.1
2020	1.4	4.8	0	0.2	8.8	0.2	4.7	4.2
2030	1.1	4.0	0	0.2	7.0	0.2	3.8	3.4
2040	0.9	3.4	0	0.2	5.4	0.2	3.0	2.7
2050	0.8	3.1	0	0.2	4.7	0.2	2.7	2.4

Table A7.8 Years of life lost per person above 5 (YLL_{a5}) (in years), selected countries and regions, 1900–2050 (variant of Table A7.2)

Year	China	India	Japan	USA	Sub-Saharan Africa	More developed regions	Less developed regions	World
1900	5.2	3.3	1.7	1.2	2.4	1.4	3.9	3.9
1910	5.6	3.9	1.9	1.4	3.0	1.3	4.0	4.0
1920	6.0	3.9	2.0	1.0	3.9	0.8	4.6	4.2
1930	6.5	4.6	2.2	1.6	6.0	1.6	5.4	5.2
1940	6.4	6.5	1.9	1.0	6.7	1.2	5.6	5.2
1950	8.8	11.0	3.8	2.4	9.8	3.0	7.6	7.4
1960	7.0	9.1	2.0	1.6	8.7	2.4	6.6	6.1
1970	4.8	7.0	0.5	1.3	7.4	1.6	5.2	4.5
1980	3.5	5.6	0	1.1	7.0	2.1	4.6	3.7
1990	4.8	7.1	0	2.0	9.1	3.1	5.8	4.9
2000	4.9	7.9	0	3.4	11.3	3.9	6.6	5.8
2010	4.6	7.6	0	2.1	11.6	3.2	6.5	5.7
2020	4.5	7.2	0	2.0	11.6	3.0	6.4	5.6
2030	4.4	6.9	0	1.9	11.3	2.7	6.3	5.6
2040	4.3	6.7	0	1.8	11.0	2.6	6.3	5.6
2050	4.4	6.7	0	1.8	10.8	2.5	6.4	5.7

Table A7.9 Total years of life lost per person, selected countries and regions, 1900–2050 (variant of Table A7.3)

Year	China	India	Japan	USA	Sub-Saharan Africa	More developed regions	Less developed regions	World
1900	19.7	24.8	8.9	6.0	26.0	6.8	22.6	17.8
1910	20.5	28.1	9.2	6.8	26.6	7.0	24.0	18.9
1920	19.0	24.6	7.3	6.6	24.8	6.5	21.9	17.5
1930	20.7	24.7	8.3	4.1	27.3	4.5	23.1	17.8
1940	19.0	23.2	6.4	2.3	25.4	2.6	20.8	15.7
1950	20.7	25.3	7.2	2.8	27.2	5.2	21.4	17.3
1960	16.5	22.0	2.8	2.2	25.2	3.5	18.5	14.7
1970	11.6	18.4	0.6	2.0	22.9	2.7	15.3	12.0
1980	7.6	15.6	0	1.5	21.7	2.8	13.4	11.5
1990	7.5	15.5	0	2.3	23.3	3.6	13.3	11.6
2000	7.1	15.0	0	3.7	24.1	4.3	13.3	11.8
2010	6.5	13.4	0	2.3	22.4	3.5	12.1	10.7
2020	6.0	12.0	0	2.2	20.4	3.2	11.1	9.8
2030	5.5	10.9	0	2.1	18.3	2.9	10.1	9.0
2040	5.2	10.1	0	2.0	16.4	2.8	9.3	8.3
2050	5.2	9.8	0	2.0	15.5	2.6	9.1	8.2

Note: Values in this table are the sum of the values in the corresponding columns of Tables A7.7 and A7.8.

Table A7.10 Money metric value of years of life lost (MMVYLL), selected countries and regions, 1900–2050 ($) (variant of Table A7.4)

Year	China	India	Japan	USA	Sub-Saharan Africa	More developed regions	Less developed regions	World
1900	14,195	17,838	13,177	30,485	15,631	16,656	14,231	22,449
1910	15,091	23,637	15,127	42,644	16,729	20,083	16,426	27,579
1920	14,555	19,105	16,436	43,200	17.076	21,012	15,972	28,213
1930	16,008	22,422	20,218	35,544	20,770	16,758	18,589	32,184
1940	14,838	21,258	24,765	23,141	20,660	10,649	17,880	30,745
1950	13,658	23,167	21,507	48,725	24,855	24,327	18,308	36,640
1960	16,039	24,238	19,092	41,479	27,113	22,755	20,724	41,029
1970	13,153	22,784	10,816	49,263	30,893	25,998	21,882	44,670
1980	12,062	20,173	0	47,273	32,745	34,497	25,330	51,554
1990	23,394	30,425	0	96,596	32,809	53,976	30,215	58,898
2000	41,594	44,379	0	192,245	34,396	74,604	41,101	69,988
2010	83,412	70,117	0	139,174	39,745	72,822	57,542	82,495
2020	114,007	93,291	0	159,886	39,404	78,644	69,083	91,248
2030	140,065	112,921	0	174,357	39,889	85,297	84,826	103,942
2040	167,924	131,815	0	187,828	41,549	99,320	107,831	121,273
2050	200,644	154,800	0	212,861	47,012	112,704	148,850	154,638

Note: Entries in this table are calculated from the per person YLLs reported in Tables A7.7 and A7.8 by multiplying those YLL* = YLL$_{a5}$ + 0.54YLL$_{u5}$ by twice per capita GDP expressed in 1990 International Geary–Khamis dollars.

Table A7.11 Ratio *a* of money metric value of years of life lost (MMVYLL) per lifetime income per capita (LI) (no units), selected countries and regions, 1900–2050 (variant of Table A7.5)

Year	China	India	Japan	USA	Sub-Saharan Africa	More developed regions	Less developed regions	World
1900	0.9	1.4	0.2	0.2	1.6	0.2	1.2	0.7
1910	1.0	1.6	0.3	0.2	1.6	0.2	1.2	0.8
1920	0.9	1.4	0.2	0.2	1.6	0.2	1.2	0.7
1930	1.0	1.5	0.2	0.1	1.8	0.1	1.3	0.8
1940	1.0	1.5	0.2	0.1	1.7	0.1	1.2	0.7
1950	1.1	1.8	0.2	0.1	2.0	0.2	1.3	0.8
1960	0.9	1.5	0.2	0.1	1.8	0.1	1.1	0.7
1970	0.6	1.3	0.1	0.1	1.6	0.1	0.9	0.6
1980	0.4	1.0	0	0.0	1.6	0.1	0.8	0.5
1990	0.5	1.1	0	0.1	1.7	0.1	0.8	0.6
2000	0.4	1.1	0	0.1	1.9	0.2	0.9	0.6
2010	0.4	1.0	0	0.1	1.8	0.1	0.8	0.5
2020	0.4	0.9	0	0.1	1.7	0.1	0.7	0.5
2030	0.4	0.9	0	0.1	1.6	0.1	0.7	0.5
2040	0.3	0.8	0	0.1	1.4	0.1	0.7	0.5
2050	0.3	0.8	0	0.1	1.4	0.1	0.7	0.5

Note: Entries in this table are calculated from the money metric value of years of life lost MMVYLL reported in Table A7.10 divided by the lifetime income per capita as defined by equation (7.8) in the main text.

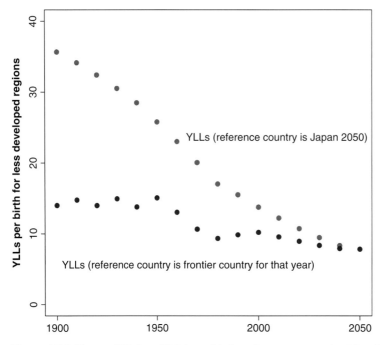

Figure A7.2 *Years of life lost (YLLs) per birth; reference country is either frontier country or Japan 2050, less developed regions, 1900–2050*

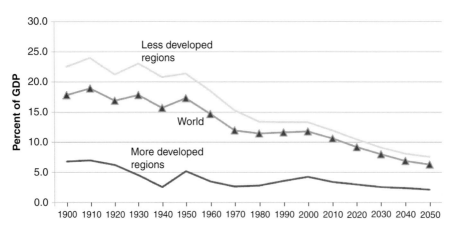

Figure A7.3 *Money metric value of years of life lost (MMVYLL), selected regions, 1900–2050, as percent of GDP*

Malnutrition: Global Economic Losses Attributable to Malnutrition 1900–2000 and Projections to 2050

CHAPTER 8

SUE HORTON AND RICHARD H. STECKEL

Introduction

The two-way link between improved nutrition and higher income is well known. Higher income allows people to obtain a more varied and nutritious diet. Higher income is associated with improved sanitation and health, such that there is less loss of nutrients associated with infection. More maternal education (associated with higher income) is associated with better infant feeding practices, and mothers who are better able to obtain care for themselves during pregnancy. Of course, higher income also can bring with it an overly sedentary lifestyle, excess consumption of fat and added sugar, and associated risks of non-communicable disease. However in this chapter we focus on the beneficial aspects of income for nutrition because a large share of the world's population was stunted during much or most of the twentieth century.

Similarly, better nutrition is associated with higher productivity. Better-nourished individuals are more productive in physical labor, because of higher stamina, higher maximal work output, etc. Better-nourished infants and young children have improved cognitive skills, which translate to higher productivity as adults. We use the results from micro-level data to disentangle the effect of nutrition on productivity from that of income on nutrition, making broad estimates over the past century for various world regions.

During the twentieth century, nutrition improved considerably in most regions of the world, as evidenced by increases in stature. This increase in stature was not uniform (some countries did not experience an improvement), and the timing and rate of this increase varied greatly. Data suggest that as living standards improve (associated with modern economic growth), mean height of young adults/all adults/

conscripts (a sample for whom data are readily available) in national populations can increase from 163 cm or even lower, up towards 178 cm. Mean heights lower than 160 cm have been observed in subpopulations of particular ethnic groups (pygmies and Bushmen, for example, in Africa; Maya, Quechua, and Yanomano in Latin America), as well as in regions of particularly low per capita income (for example, Japanese conscripts recruited in 1900). However, the assumption is that all populations have similar genetic potential for height, even though this may take more than one generation to achieve. Data on heights of wealthy households in different countries support this assumption (Eveleth and Tanner 1990; Bogin 1999).

Height is a good indicator of long-run nutritional status. In this regard it is useful to think of the human body as a biological machine that receives fuel as a mixture of protein, calories, micronutrients, and so forth, which it expends on basal metabolism (maintaining vital functions while at rest), physical activity, and fighting infections. Physical growth ceases if net nutrition is poor but children experience catch-up growth if conditions improve. Anthropometric studies around the globe show that individuals who are malnourished as young children are stunted as adults, and the extent of stunting depends upon the duration, timing, and severity of malnutrition. Stunting is commonly measured by height-for-age (by sex) relative to international standards. Evidence on children adopted from poor into rich countries shows that the

The authors would like to thank Harold Alderman and an anonymous referee for helpful comments received on a previous draft. Responsibility for remaining errors remains with the authors.

human capacity for catch-up or compensatory growth may be substantial (but still incomplete) depending upon the quality of nutrition and the age at which conditions improve.

Height does not capture all the beneficial effects of nutrition. For undernourished adults, improved diet (both in calories and micronutrients) can improve productivity. For children, improved micronutrient status can have effects on cognitive development independent of height. However we do not have worldwide data on calorie availability and distribution over the past century, nor on micronutrient status of children. Hence our estimates underestimate the benefits of improved nutrition.

In the next section we summarize the literature on the effects of height on wages or earnings, to obtain a range of coefficient estimates. This is not easy to do, since household decisions on investments in nutrition, health, and education of their children are correlated. Child nutrition impacts cognitive skills and education, and child nutrition and health act synergistically. Adult height, education, cognitive skills, and health are all known to affect earnings. We extract coefficients from a number of empirical studies to produce estimates of the effect of height (our proxy for nutrition) and earnings. We also summarize key references on the effect of nutritional status (as represented by height) on child mortality.

The third section of the chapter describes the height database and discusses the caveats associated with using height as a measure of nutrition, for our purpose. An international height database was assembled to provide broad trends in men's height over the time period 1900–2000. This is compiled for the five major geographic regions identified for this project (Africa, Asia, Europe, Latin America, and North America), as well as for developed and developing countries separately. Data on height for Australasia is lacking, and we assume there is a similar pattern to the USA; this region is included with Asia. There are very few data for Africa: the broadest coverage is only for women from DHS surveys (South Africa DHS 2002), and goes back only to about 1950. Given the data limitations for many countries and even whole regions (Australasia, Africa) these are broad estimates only.

We then turn in the fourth section to explain the model used to make the calculations, which combines the coefficients from the literature review with the height database, to estimate both the economic and human losses. This is the most technical section of the chapter, and less technically minded readers may prefer to gloss over the details in this section. The fifth section presents the detailed results for our estimates of income losses and mortality losses associated with nutritional deficiencies over the twentieth century, as measured by men's height. These are presented both for the five geographic regions, as well as the developed/developing country grouping. We present income losses for 1900–2010, as well as projections for 2010–2050, for the same two sets of groupings of countries. We follow this with estimates for the contribution of nutrition on child mortality for 1900–2010 (data are not available to project this number forward to 2050). We briefly consider the sensitivity of the results to the assumptions made. The sixth and final section discusses the findings and presents conclusions.

Empirical Evidence of the Effect of Height on Earnings, and Height on Mortality

Many studies have noted that taller individuals earn more, and that height is associated with higher occupational status. There are also plausible biological reasons why better nutrition (of which height is a marker) is associated with higher productivity: both in physical labor, due to effects of improved nutrition on stamina and maximal work capacity, and in other occupations via well-known effects of improved nutrition on cognitive development. Even more powerful evidence comes from long-term longitudinal studies following up on controlled nutritional interventions. One trial in Guatemala involved a nutritious food supplement which demonstrated strong effects on wages and earnings of men in adulthood, particularly in children supplemented below the age of 3 (Hoddinott *et al.* 2008). Another trial in Costa Rica demonstrated the long-term impacts of an intervention involving iron supplements in infants (Lozoff *et al.* 2006).

We do not have data on birth weights or micronutrient status for populations in different regions extending over decades in the past. We can however find data on height over extended historical periods. Height-for-age is used as an indicator of chronic nutritional status, and achieved height of adults is sensitive to nutritional status during the vulnerable early years. Deficiencies in utero and prior to age 3 cannot completely be reversed by subsequent improvements in nutrition. The height data will be reviewed in the next section.

Fogel (1994) made early estimates of the contribution of better nutrition to economic growth, and calculated that it accounted for 30% of the increase of per capita income in the UK between 1790 and 1980, based on greater availability of food as well as reduced infection which increased the efficiency of use of food. He used data on height as well as estimates of calorie availability, and what he terms a technophysio modeling exercise.

A large number of studies have correlated earnings with height for adults, using a variety of specifications (see Tables 8.1 and 8.2 below). When height is entered as an independent variable in earnings functions, there is general evidence of economic returns. Typically, higher returns are found when instrumental variables techniques are employed. These can improve the estimates if height is measured poorly, or if there is simultaneity.

We would expect the effects to differ significantly between developed and developing countries. In industrialized countries it is estimated that 80% of the variation in height observed is genetic, and 20% reflects differences in the environment (Silvontoinen 2003). However, it is likely that in developing countries with lower average heights a larger proportion of the variation observed reflects environment. We would also expect the estimates to differ between rural and urban areas. We would anticipate height to have greater effects on productivity in rural areas (if there are gains attributable to greater physical size and strength), whereas benefits

Table 8.1 Effect of increased height on wages, developed countries

Reference	Country	Results	Percent change in wages per cm height ↑, men
Case and Paxson (2008)	UK NCDS, born 1958	1 inch height leads to 2.3% ↑wages men, 1.9% women	0.9%
Case and Paxson (2008)	USA PSID	1 inch height leads to 1.9% ↑wages men, 1.2% women	0.7%
Heineck (2008)	UK BHPS	No effect: others criticize and say height affects work through education and occupational choice	0%
Heineck (2005)	Germany GSOEP	1 cm height males leads to 0.4% ↑ wage	0.4%
Kortt and Leigh (2009)	Australia	1 cm height males leads to 0.3% ↑ wage	0.3%
Persico *et al.* (2004)	UK NCDS Born 1958	1 inch height leads to 2.2% ↑ wage	0.9%
Persico *et al.* (2004)	USA NLSY	1 inch height leads to 1.8% ↑ wage	0.7%
Sargent and Blanchflower (1994)	UK NCDS, born 1958	1 cm height leads to 0.27% ↑ wage	0.3%
Twins study			
Behrman and Rosenzweig (2001)	USA	1 inch height women leads to 3.5–5.5% ↑ wage	1.4% to 2.2%

Note: Table constructed from literature survey in Gao and Smyth (2010); all references in Gao and Smyth (2010).

Table 8.2 Effect of increased height on wages, developing countries

Reference	Country	Methods used	Results	Percent change in wages per cm height ↑, men
Gao and Smyth (2010)	12 Chinese cities, 2005, individuals 16+	IV: urban data	↑ height 1 cm for men increases earnings 4.5%; same for women increases earnings 7.3%	4.5%
Haddad and Bouis (1991)	Philippines, agricultural work	IV: rural data	Elasticity wages with height is 1.38%	0.86%
Schultz (2002)	Brazil, 1989, national survey	IV: national data		8–10%
Schultz (2002)	Ghana, 1987–9, age 20–54	IV: national data		8–10%
Schultz (2003)	Côte d'Ivoire, 1985–7	IV: national data		11%
Thomas and Strauss (1997)	Brazil, 1989, national survey	IV: national data	1% increase in male height associated with 2.4% increase in wages	1.4%
Studies involving height and schooling				
Alderman et al. (2008)	Tanzania, children born 1984–94	Longitudinal data, IV using short-run drought shocks: rural data	↑ height from 80% to 95% of median, leads to↑ schooling 0.93 years and annual salary 8%; ↑height from 85% to 100% of median leads to↑ schooling 0.85 years, and annual salary 7%: heights measured in children	NA (only child heights used)
Alderman et al. (2006)	Zimbabwe, children born 1977–87	Longitudinal data, IV using major drought, civil war shocks: rural data	Drought led to height/age 1.25 SD lower (3.4 cm shorter) at adolescence: associated with 0.85 fewer years school achievement, and 14% lower lifetime earnings	4.12%
Longitudinal intervention studies				
Hoddinott et al. (2008)	Guatemala, children born 1969–77	Longitudinal study following up controlled intervention in rural area	Intervention below age 3 resulted in 2.9 cm ↑ in height, 46% ↑ in hourly wage for adult men; effect not significant for women	15.8%

occurring in urban areas are more likely to occur via cognitive skills and education.

Instrumental variables approaches can also help deal with simultaneous relationships between nutrition/health, schooling, and cognitive skills, all of which can affect wages. Taller children are more likely to enter school earlier and stay in school longer, and hence part of the observed schooling effect may

be attributable to height (i.e. preschool nutrition). Nutrition particularly prior to the age of 3 can affect cognitive skills, and cognitive skills may then affect schooling as well as wages. Schooling and nutrition both depend on possible unmeasured household characteristics which may also affect wages. Parents may make the education and health investment decisions simultaneously for their children, either investing more in schooling for those with higher cognitive skills (related to early childhood nutrition) if efficiency motives prevail, or investing less if equity motives prevail. See Alderman *et al.* (2006) for a simple model of this form.

A more sophisticated model is provided by Behrman *et al.* (2010). Here there are two periods (childhood and adolescence) in which parents can invest in physical capital (e.g. height) and human capital (education and/or cognitive skills), and there is more endogeneity. Such a model requires longitudinal data to estimate. Their results for Guatemala suggest that even in a low-income and rural environment, the dominant effects of nutrition on productivity occur via cognitive improvements, or, as they characterize it, the effects of nutrition occur primarily through brains and not brawn.

Twins data have also been used to explore the relationship. Case and Paxson (2008) summarize results from three other studies in developed countries. These suggest that the environment accounts for 65% of the height–intelligence relationship and genes 35% (using comparisons of monozygotic and dizygotic twins). Note that this is a higher effect for environment than that suggested by Silvontoinen (2003). Studies on monozygotic twins with different birth weights (reflecting differential nutrition in utero) find clear links between height and cognitive skills, and height and schooling.

Table 8.1 summarizes results from a literature survey by Gao and Smyth (2010), for eight studies for industrialized countries (the USA, UK, Germany, and Australia, where average height for adult men is currently about 178 cm). The estimates presented are all using instrumental variables (IV), to account for errors in measurement of height and simultaneous relationships between height and income, and height and education. All the IV estimates are higher than the ordinary least squares (OLS) estimates. The median effect is a 0.55% increase in earnings per additional 1 cm of adult male height. The effect from one study of twins is about three times higher.

Table 8.2 presents similar results for a sample of developing countries. The median effect (from eight studies from Brazil, China, Côte d'Ivoire, Ghana, Philippines, Tanzania, and Zimbabwe) is a 4.5% increase in earnings per additional 1 cm of adult

male height. Mean height of adult males in these countries is approximately 170 cm. The effect from the single longitudinal intervention study is about three times higher, for a population where adult male height is closer to 163 cm. The studies in Table 8.2 include three of rural areas only, one of urban areas only, and the others include both. The studies also vary in the quality of the instruments used, which may help explain the variation in findings.

Previous studies have also determined that there is a relationship between nutritional status of children, and mortality risk. Pelletier *et al.* (1994a) compare the predictive power of weight-for-age as compared to height-for-age and two other anthropometric indicators, using one prospective study. They conclude that the predictive power of the indicators varies. Height-for-age has greater predictive power 2 or 3 years after the child is measured, but other indicators have greater predictive power in the short term. Pelletier *et al.* (1994b) develop very useful odds ratios for different categories of weight-for-age, using eight prospective studies from developing countries. Severe malnutrition (weight-for-age less than 60% of the reference median) is associated with an odds ratio of 8.4; moderate malnutrition (as measured by weight-for-age 60–69% of the reference median) with a ratio of 4.6, and mild malnutrition (weight-for-age 70–79%) with a ratio of 2.5. In the model section we convert these to estimated odds ratio for height-for-age.

A similar relationship holds for the developed countries, using historical data. Data for men and women (Bozzoli *et al.* 2009), and men (Schmidt *et al.* 1995), show that postneonatal mortality for children is correlated with achieved adult height for the same cohort 20 years later, for European countries in the second half of the twentieth century.

Height Database: Trends in Height 1900–2010, and Projections 2010–2050

A database of adult heights was assembled for this project, containing approximately 400 mean heights from cohorts of adult males (defined here as age 18 or over), since 1900. Time-series from 1900 to 2010 could be constructed (although not for every decade) for approximately 30 countries

(19 in Europe, two in North America, five in Latin America, and four in Asia). There are also scattered data available for another 50 countries. The biggest gaps are for Africa, Australasia, and the Middle East, where historical data are least available.

We focus on male height since female height data are less readily available (for example, some series rely on conscripts, where the data are exclusively for men). Female height is a strong predictor of male height (an R^2 of 0.95 was obtained by one of the authors when the natural log of male height was regressed on the natural log of female height, for a data set containing male and female mean heights for 132 different samples, using data from Eveleth and Tanner 1976 and 1990). Empirical studies of the effects of height on income are also more readily available for men, since the proportion of women working in the wage-labor market is smaller. Many of the benefits associated with improved women's nutrition (for example intergenerational effects via their children) are harder to measure, although Behrman *et al.* (2009) provide useful estimates for Guatemala from the same longitudinal study of supplementation mentioned previously.

Figures 8.1 through 8.3 present trends for 11 indicator countries in four regions. These are countries with reasonably good time-series data. Figure 8.4 presents our informed guesses for trends

in those regions without historical data, namely Africa and West Asia. Figure 8.5 then presents trends for the five geographic regions included. Figure 8.6 presents the same data aggregated into developed and developing regions. Table 8.3 provides details and references for the data sources for the 11 indicator countries, and Table 8.4 (see below) the underlying population weights applied to the indicator countries to construct the regional and developed/developing aggregates. We will first describe the trends observed, and then discuss the data limitations and qualifications.

In 1900, adult male heights in Northern and Western Europe (represented by the UK) and the USA and Canada (represented by the USA) had already attained a mean of 170 cm or more, and heights have grown at a rate approximately 1 cm per decade to the end of the century, consistent with fairly slow but steady economic growth around 2% per capita per annum (Figure 8.1). Heights in Southern Europe (represented by Spain) began somewhat lower (165 cm) and took off around World War II but grew faster and were still a couple of centimeters lower by the end of the century (Figure 8.1). Height data for Eastern Europe are more fragmentary. Data for Hungary (prior to 1960) and Poland (starting in 1965) are similar to the pattern for Spain, but catch up with the UK by

Figure 8.1 *Trends in adult male height (in cm), representative countries from North America and Northern, Southern, and Eastern Europe, 1900–2000*

Table 8.3 Source of data to obtain trends for representative countries

Country	Population surveyed	Source	Years data collected	Age of subjects
Bolivia	National	Baten (2010)	1940, 1950, 1960, 1970, 1980	Adult
Brazil	?	Monasterio and Signorini (2008)	1910, 1920	?
	?	Strauss and Thomas (1988)	1930, 1940	?
	National	Baten (2010)	1950, 1960, 1970	Adult
	National	Monteiro et al. (1994)	1989	22
China	Shandong province	Zhen-Wang and Cheng-Ye (2005)	1956, 1972, 1985, 2000	18
	National	Yang et al. (2005)	1992–2002	17
Colombia	Conscripts	Meisel and Vega (2007)	1910–20, 1920–30	Adult
	National	Meisel and Vega (2007)	1930–5, 1936–40, 1940–45, 1946–50, 1950–55, 1956–60, 1960–65, 1966–70, 1970–75, 1976–80, 1980–85	18–48
		Meisel and Vega (2004)	2002	18–22
Hungary	Conscripts	Bodzsár and Zsákai (2002)	1900, 1905, 1910, 1915, 1920, 1925, 1935, 1940, 1945, 1950, 1960	Adult
India	National	Guntupalli and Baten (2006)	1915, 1916, 1917, 1918, 1919, 1920, 1921, 1922, 1923, 1924, 1925, 1926, 1927, 1928, 1929, 1930, 1931, 1932, 1933, 1934, 1935, 1936, 1937, 1938, 1939, 1940, 1941, 1942, 1943	Adult
	National	Indian Council of Medical Research (1972)	1972	18
	National	Deaton (2008)	2005–6	20
Japan	Conscripts	Mosk (1996)	1901–10, 1911–20, 1921–30, 1931–40, 1941–50, 1951–60, 1961–70, 1971–80, 1981–90	18
Poland	Conscripts	Bielicki and Szklarska (1999)	1965, 1976, 1986, 1995	19
		Bielicki et al. (2005)	2001	19
Spain	Conscripts	Maria-Dolores and Martinez-Carrion (2011)	1901–05, 1906–10, 1911–15, 1916–20, 1921–25, 1926–30, 1931–35, 1936–40, 1941–45, 1946–50	21
	National	Garcia and Quintana-Domeque (2007)	1951–5, 1956–60, 1961–65, 1966–70, 1971–5, 1976–80	Adult
South Korea	Prisoners	Choi and Schwekendiek (2009)	1900–10, 1905–15, 1910–20, 1915–25, 1920–30	20–40
	Students	Pak (2004)	1965, 1970, 1975, 1980, 1985, 1990, 1995, 2000	17–18
UK	Conscripts	Rosenbaum et al. (1985)	1931–5, 1936–40, 1941–5, 1946–50	Adult
	National	Hatton and Bray (2010)	1951–55, 1956–60 1961–65, 1966–70, 1971–75, 1976–80	Adult
	National	National Health Service (2008)	1996	25–44
USA	National	Steckel (2006)	1900, 1910, 1920, 1925, 1930, 1935, 1940, 1945, 1950, 1955, 1960, 1965, 1970	Adult

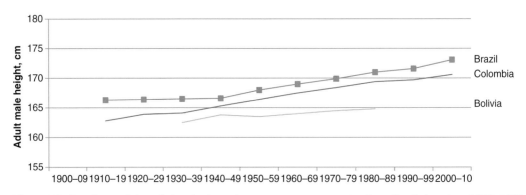

Figure 8.2 *Trends in adult male height (in cm), representative countries from South America, 1900–2000*

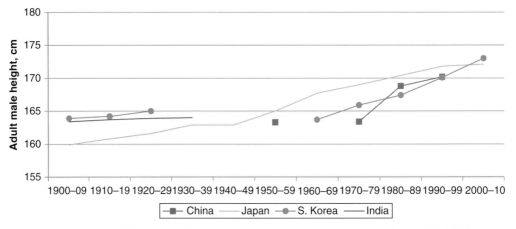

Figure 8.3 *Trends in adult male height (in cm), representative countries from Asia, 1900–2000*

the end of the century. The one national data point for Hungary after 1960 (in the 1980s) is in line with data for Poland at a similar date, suggesting that switching from Hungary to Poland mid-century does not do great violence to the trend.

In Latin America (Figure 8.2) heights in the richer countries (e.g. Brazil) started out somewhat similar to Spain (Argentine men – not presented – were if anything taller than those from Spain). Men in the poorer countries (represented by Bolivia) have heights about 5 cm below those of the richer countries (e.g. Brazil), and Colombia represents the trend for the intermediate countries. The trends for Mexico (not presented, due to a big gap in the data from 1970 to 2000 inclusive) are similar to those for Colombia. We do not have separate data for the Caribbean; however, the population of this region is quite small. Over the whole century, the increase in height

for Latin America averaged about 1 cm per decade, but there is greater variability consistent with a greater variation in economic growth both across countries and between decades, and the poorer countries lag increasingly further behind.

In Asia (Figure 8.3), we see the remarkable increase in height in the Asian "tiger" economies as they entered the phase of rapid modern economic growth, starting around 1950 for Japan, around 1960 for Korea, and around 1970 for China. Prior to this, average heights had been around 163 cm (and even lower for Japan in 1900). For India, even by 2000 recent economic growth has not yet manifested in increased height at the national level. The "tiger" economies experienced increases in height of up to 3 cm per decade during the fast growth periods, when per capita income was growing at 7% per capita per annum or even more.

Table 8.4 Representative countries, associated population weights for modeling, and regional nutrition groupings

Country	Developed/ Developing	Geographic region	Weight	Region represented (nutritional grouping)
Brazil	Developing	Latin America	0.021	Brazil
Colombia	Developing	Latin America	0.045	**Latin America and Caribbean (LAC)** excluding Brazil
Subtotal: LAC			**0.066**	
China	Developing	Asia	0.220	**China**
India	Developing	Asia	0.269	**South/Southeast/South Central Asia**
Japan	Developed	Asia	0.026	**Japan**
South Korea	Developing	Asia	0.020	**East Asia** (excluding China and Japan)
West Asia	Developing	Asia	0.020	Use Eastern Europe with 50-year lag
Australasia	Developing	Asia	0.005	Represent with North American data
Subtotal: Asia			**0.560**	
Hungary/Poland	Developing	Europe	0.087	**Eastern Europe**
Spain	Developed	Europe	0.043	**Southern Europe**
UK	Developed	Europe	0.087	**Northern Europe**
Subtotal: Europe			**0.217**	
US	Developed	North America	0.068	**North America:** also Australasia
Subtotal: North America			**0.068**	
Africa	Developing	Africa	0.088	No data: assume little change over the century, heights remain below 170 cm
Subtotal: Africa			**0.088**	
TOTAL: World			**1.000**	

Note: Population weights used are for 1950 (mid-century) throughout. *Source*: UNESA (2009); see also UNESA (2009) for countries included in regional groupings.

To put the developing country data from the twentieth century into perspective, note that in the UK mean height for adult men was 160 cm as late as 1750 (Steckel 2008), 168.9 cm by 1800, and was only 0.4 cm more by 1900. In France as late as 1800 mean height was 164 cm and life expectancy was only 34 years. The USA was an exception, in that mean height was already 170 cm by 1710 and (after various fluctuations) the same in 1900 (Steckel and Floud 1997).

We next use the data on individual indicator countries to represent regional trends. This requires strong assumptions, given the data gaps: however the fact that heights track economic growth and life expectancy (Steckel 1995) provides some support for these assumptions. The population weights are provided in Table 8.4.

North America is represented by the USA (the data for Canada are similar: and Mexico is included with Latin America and the Caribbean for our purposes). The trend for Europe is a weighted average of Northern and Western Europe (using UK data), Southern Europe (using Spain), and Eastern Europe (using data for Hungary/Poland).

Brazil has its own time-series, and the rest of Latin America and the Caribbean is represented by Colombia (Colombia has the best time-series, and also tracks Mexico well for those years when data are available). We assume that the richer countries (where men are taller) such as Chile and Argentina are balanced out by the poorer countries in the region such as Bolivia, Haiti, the Dominican Republic, Guatemala, and El Salvador, such that Colombia is a reasonable average.

For South-central and South-east Asia, we assume that the data for India represent the situation across that entire region prior to the initiation of modern economic growth, i.e. that height was around 163 cm and changed little. There was almost no time trend in India prior to 1940, and for two isolated years (1972 and 2005–6) for which later data are available (not visible on the chart) heights remained the same as during the period 1900–1940.

In the East Asian countries, prior to the initiation of modern economic growth, heights were similar to those in India (even lower than India in the case of Japan prior to 1930). For those economies which experienced the take-off into modern economic growth, such as Japan, Korea, and China, heights grew rapidly.

In Western Asia (Iran being the most populous country) we use the trend for Eastern Europe lagged 50 years reflecting a later start to modern economic growth, which is consistent with men's heights in Iran around 2000 of about 170 cm (Figure 8.4). The Asian regional average therefore reflects a weighted average of the economic take-off which began in Japan, and spread to Korea (and Taiwan, Singapore, Hong Kong), followed by China (and Thailand and Malaysia). Economic take-off has still not

affected heights in South Asia and the remaining countries in South-east Asia. Take-off in Western Asia followed (with a lag) the take-off in Eastern Europe, i.e. at a similar time to that in Japan.

For Africa, even for the modern period there are very limited data. The South African Demographic and Health Survey 1998 is one exception (South Africa DHS 2002), which provides national data for adult men (with a mean of 168 cm). Similar surveys for other African countries provide data for adult women but not men, and most other studies provide data for samples that are not nationally representative. We assume that mean heights in Africa did not change significantly, and remain below 170 cm by 2010 (Figure 8.4). Some support for this assumption comes from Deaton (2007), who examines the height of women born between 1950 and 1980 for Africa (using Demographic and Health Survey data), where no improvement is detectable.

Finally, there are no time-series data for Australasia. We assume heights in New Zealand and Australia tracked those of the USA over the century which would be consistent with data on migration patterns, economic growth, and modern height. We do not have separate sources for Micronesia, Polynesia, and Micronesia, but these populations are a very small fraction of the world.

Figure 8.5 presents the trends for the five geographic regions used in this project. Figure 8.6 displays the same data aggregated into developed and developing regions. These two figures also include projections to 2050, for which the estimation method is explained further below in this section.

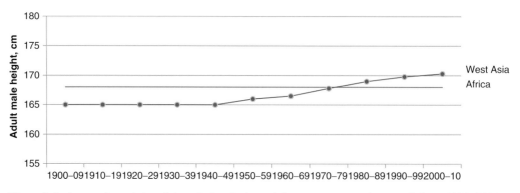

Figure 8.4 *Assumed trends in adult male height (in cm) for areas missing historical data, 1900–2000*

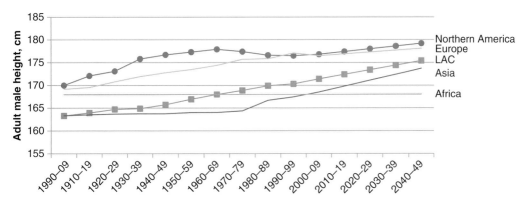

Figure 8.5 *Estimated trends in adult male height (in cm) by region, 1900–2010, and projections 2010–2050*

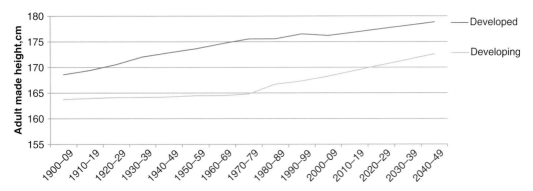

Figure 8.6 *Estimated trends in adult male height (in cm), developed and developing countries, 1900–2010, and projections 2010–2050*

Two major data limitations should be borne in mind. First, the population surveyed is as far as possible national data for adult men or conscripts (for whom series are often quite good): see Table 8.3. There are frequently data available for subpopulations which are not representative. Data for particular ethnic groups are often available (e.g. in Mexico, Bolivia, USA), or selected occupations (government workers, railway workers, employees of a particular firm, students), or selected cities or regions. We have avoided using these data, other than to confirm broad patterns, since they are not representative of the population. Members of ethnic groups or disadvantaged groups such as prisoners may be systematically shorter than the average, and other groups such as students or government employees may be systematically taller. Only for Korea were we forced to use a less than preferable

series (prisoners up to 1930, and students aged 17–18 from 1965 to 2000).

Second, the age of the men surveyed matters. Ideally we would want a consistent series for men in their twenties who have completed their adolescent growth spurt. Although in well-nourished populations this would be completed prior to age 18, in less well-nourished populations this might occur in the early twenties. Series for men aged 18 (and possibly conscripts, depending on the age of conscription) might therefore slightly overstate nutrition improvements over the century. Series for all adult males will reflect changes in young men or conscripts, but with a lag. The current adult male working-age population consists of men who recently completed their growth within the last decade, those who completed their growth one to two decades ago, two to three decades ago, and three to four decades ago, with appropriate weights dependent on population growth rates and normal retirement age. We have not made this further data refinement.

For the projections 2010–2050, we need forecasts of height. Three options to forecast are available: (1) extrapolate existing time-series of height; (2) use projections of per capita GDP; and (3) develop a model of height and life expectancy. The first two options are unsatisfactory because the time-series of height are lacking for a large share of countries, and second, GDP is notoriously difficult to forecast. Forecasts of life expectancy are widely available and arguably are more reliable than GDP. Moreover life expectancy and height are direct measures of health, whereas GDP per capita is only one determinant of human growth.

We estimate the relationship using data from 35 countries (from four of the five regions here) that conducted national height studies in recent years. There are many height studies for sub-Saharan Africa but unfortunately they cover only local populations or ethnic groups, and regrettably there are no data from these countries in our model. Estimates of life expectancy are readily available for every country since 1960 (World Bank 2010). Ideally we would compare life expectancy in the year that young adult men were measured but some

height studies included a wider range of ages such as 19–39. In these situations we approximated the desired life expectancy using an estimate for several years prior to the year the study was conducted, ranging from 5 to 15 years depending upon the age range of adults.

Previous studies have found that the relationship between life expectancy and average height is approximately linear (Steckel 1995, 2000). Here we use a quadratic function because ultimately there is an upper limit to height that does not apply (or applies less so) to life expectancy. Put another way, future gains in life expectancy for rich countries will come from falling mortality rates at older ages, but height reflects conditions in childhood, at ages where mortality rates are now exceptionally low. We then anticipate diminishing returns of life expectancy on height. Figure 8.7 provides a scatter diagram and the estimating equation.

In making projections we caution that extrapolations beyond the range of evidence can be hazardous, particular in polynomial models. We think this problem is notable at the lower end of forecast life expectancies, some of which are below 55 years. Unfortunately, this applies to almost all of sub-Saharan Africa for both 1950 and 2000. The heights for sub-Saharan Africa projected by the model for 2050 are too low to be credible – ranging

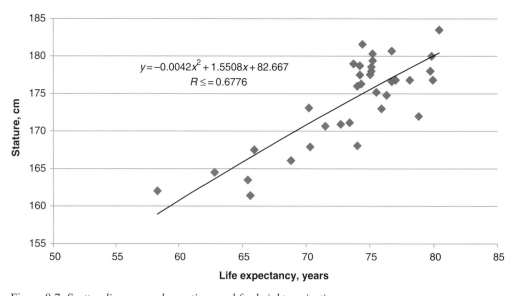

Figure 8.7 *Scatter diagram and equation used for height projections*

from below 150 cm for the countries with the lowest life expectancy, to barely over 170 cm. We simply project forward the same height for Africa as for the twentieth century.

Our projections are that the 5-cm differential between heights in developed and developing countries which existed in 1900, and which widened to 10 cm in 1960, diminishes again by 2050 (Figure 8.6). Heights in Latin America catch up to within 3 cm of those in the West by 2050, and in Asia to within 5 cm, while (by assumption) there is no change in Africa (Figure 8.5).

Model

In this section we first model the effect of nutrition (as measured by height) on economic productivity. We then model the effect on mortality (a human cost of undernutrition). This requires strong assumptions. Less technically minded readers may wish to gloss over this section and proceed to the results.

We assume that the effects of height on productivity and hence economic growth can be captured by the effects of height on wages (earnings), and further that these effects act on the share of wages in national income (approximately 50%). This is a conservative assumption, since it is possible that better-nourished individuals with higher cognitive skills could increase the rate of technical change, or

could enhance the productivity of other complementary factors of production.

We use the empirical estimates surveyed previously and summarized in Tables 8.1 and 8.2. At a height of 178 cm the median effect of height on wages is 0.55% per cm, and at a height of 170 cm the effect is 4.5% per cm. We do not have evidence on how this effect tapers off, other than some estimates of curvature in the relation of height with schooling for children in Alderman *et al.* (2008). We therefore assume a linear relation between the wage coefficient and height, between 170 cm and 178 cm (namely 4.5% at 170 cm, 4% at 171 cm, 3.5% at 172 cm, etc., up to 0.5% at 178 cm and zero thereafter). We also assume conservatively that there are no additional losses in productivity per centimeter of height lost below 170 cm.

If we then aggregate these losses, at a height of 170 cm (compared to 179 cm) the cumulative loss in wages is 22.5%; at 171 cm 18%; at 172 cm 14%; at 173 cm 10.5%; at 174 cm 7.5%; at 175 cm 5%; at 176 cm 3%; at 177 cm 1.5%; and at 178 cm 0.5%. The assumed loss function as a percent of GDP (plotted against current height) is depicted in Figure 8.8. The loss function as a percent of GDP allows for the assumption that lost earnings (attributable to poor nutrition) affect only labor income, approximately half of total GDP (Lübker 2007). It also assumes that at a given point in time,

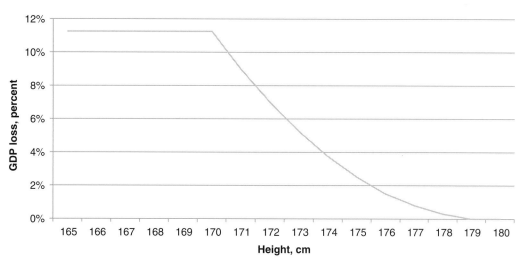

Figure 8.8 *Assumed GDP loss (percent) with height (cm)*

the percentage loss of earnings for those women who work in the market labor force is the same as for men.

We lack two sets of data to do a separate analysis for women. First, there are fewer data on women's heights (the data on conscripts do not include women). Second, the studies reported in Table 8.2 do not always include the effect of women's height on earnings. Women's market earnings are however typically less than half (in some regions much less than half) of total market earnings, and hence the overall losses (being based on the market labor share in national income) are less sensitive to women's than men's earnings.

These assumed productivity losses described above are then combined with the height trends and projections for each geographical region (Figure 8.5) and the developed/developing grouping (Figure 8.6) to give estimated productivity losses as percent of national income.

Undernutrition (as represented by height) affects not only economic productivity, but there are human costs in terms of increased mortality. We do not have data on child height-for-age worldwide throughout the entire twentieth century, unfortunately. Stein et al. (2010) examine longitudinal data on over 4,000 children from five cohorts in three developing regions. They conclude that birth length and conditional length at 12 months (i.e. growth since birth) were the most strongly correlated with adult height, and that "Growth failure (prior to age 12 months) was most strongly associated with adult stature."

Hence we use achieved adult height as an indicator for height in early childhood, and as such as an indicator for child mortality risk.

We then have to make three sets of assumptions, in order to associate mean adult height with odds ratios of postneonatal mortality. The assumptions are described in the next three paragraphs.

We first assume that the standard deviation of adult height does not change as mean population height changes. Although some researchers have suggested that the standard deviation of height may depend on the degree of inequality within a society (e.g. Deaton 2008), there is no evidence to suggest that it varies with height per se. We then calculate (using normal tables) the proportion of the population who would fall below two standard deviations from the reference population mean,

at each mean height in increments of 1 cm from 163 cm to 176.86 cm. Hence we have constructed estimates of the proportion of the child population severely or moderately malnourished on a height-for-age basis (SMM : HA), inferred from mean adult male height (column 2, Table 8.5).

We then link statistically the proportion moderately or severely malnourished using height-for-age, with the same group using the weight-for-age measure, in both cases using the z-score measure. Height for age reflects chronic nutrition status, whereas weight-for-age combines the effects both of chronic and acute nutritional status. Using data for 2006 (UNICEF 2006), we regress the proportion severely or moderately malnourished using weight-for-age (SMM : WA) on the proportion severely or moderately malnourished using height-for-age (SMM : HA). The 2006 data were used rather than the most recent data, since these use the same NCHS-WHO growth standards as for the Pelletier et al. (1994b) calculation. The equation estimated is:

$$\text{SMM} : \text{WA} = -2.14 + 0.808\,\text{SMM} : \text{HA} \quad (8.1)$$

F statistic $(1,114) = 373.29$; adjusted R^2 is 0.7640.

We then apply this equation to the data in column (2), Table 8.5, to estimate the proportion severely or moderately malnourished using weight-for-age (SMM : WA). The result is given in Table 8.5, column (3).

We then apply Pelletier et al.'s (1994b) conversion equations to convert the proportion moderately and severely malnourished using the z-score, to the different categories of malnutrition using the percent of median methodology (using the WHO-A methodology, Table 8.6 of Pelletier et al. 1994b). The equations are:

$$\text{WA} < 60 = \left(\text{WHO A1} < 2\acute{\text{Z}} \times 0.184\right) \\ -3.86 \text{ (severe malnutrition)} \quad (8.2)$$

$$\text{WA}60-69 = \left(\text{WHO A1} < 2\acute{\text{Z}} \times 0.421\right) \\ -4.41 \text{ (moderate malnutrition)} \\ (8.3)$$

$$\text{WA}70-79 = \left(\text{WHO A1} < 2\acute{\text{Z}} \times 0.399\right) \\ +13.59 \text{ (mild malnutrition)} \\ (8.4)$$

Table 8.5 Construction of estimated proportion of child mortality attributable to malnutrition, at different levels of achieved mean adult male height

Mean height (cm)	Percent of population SMM : HA	Percent of population SMM : WA	Percent WA < 60	Percent WA 60–69	Percent WA 70–79	PAR
176.86	2.30	0.00	0.000	0.000	13.590	0.169
176	2.94	0.24	0.000	0.000	13.684	0.170
175	4.01	1.10	0.000	0.000	14.029	0.174
174	5.37	2.20	0.000	0.000	14.467	0.178
173	7.08	3.58	0.000	0.000	15.019	0.184
172	9.18	5.28	0.000	0.000	15.696	0.191
171	11.7	7.31	0.000	0.000	16.508	0.198
170	14.69	9.73	0.000	0.000	17.472	0.208
169	18.14	12.52	0.000	0.860	18.584	0.236
168	22.06	15.68	0.000	2.193	19.848	0.274
167	26.43	19.22	0.000	3.680	21.257	0.311
166	31.21	23.08	0.386	5.306	22.798	0.360
165	36.32	27.21	1.146	7.044	24.445	0.414
164	41.68	31.54	1.943	8.867	26.173	0.461
163	47.21	36.01	2.765	10.748	27.956	0.503

See text for calculation method and explanation of column titles.

The calculated proportions are provided in columns (4), (5), and (6), respectively, in Table 8.5. If the predicted proportion in a category is negative, we set this to zero.

Finally, the PAR (population-attributable risk) for malnutrition deaths is:

$$PAR = \frac{(7.4 \times WA\!<\!60) + (3.6 \times WA60\!-\!69) + (1.5 \times WA70\!-\!79)}{1 + (7.4 \times WA\!<\!60) + (3.6 \times WA60\!-\!69) + (1.5 \times WA70\!-\!79)} \qquad (8.5)$$

This uses the odds ratios from Pelletier et al. (1994b), which we assume remained constant across the century. The calculated PAR is given in column (7) of Table 8.5 and displayed in Figure 8.9. We would expect the PAR based on height-for-age to provide a lower estimate of the mortality risk due to malnutrition, than if using actual weight-for-age data. Weight-for-age incorporates additional risks of death due to temporary food shortages which affect primarily weight-for-height, in addition to the risks which are correlated with chronic undernutrition and measured by height-for-age.

Table 8.6 shows the data used for the calculations, namely the under-5 mortality rates, birth rates, and population by region and by decade. The sources, and assumptions required to interpolate data prior to 1950, are described beneath the table. We are not able to project the human costs forward after 2010: although we have projected heights, we do not have the necessary projections of mortality rates.

Child deaths in the twentieth century predominantly occur in the developing countries. However, it is important to note that consistent improvements in height only began in Western Europe and North America after 1900. In the USA in 1850 infant mortality rates were as high as 200 per 1,000 births, higher than regional averages for Asia in 1960 and in Africa in 1980. In Austria, between 1820 and 1870 rates fluctuated between 250 and 310 per 1,000

Table 8.6 Selected demographic variables, by region, selected years 1900–2000

	1900	1910	1920	1930	1940	1950	1960	1970	1980	1990	2000
1. Under 5 mortality rate per 1,000 births											
Africa	259	259	259	259	259	259	250	215	180	158	151
Asia	217	217	217	217	217	217	188	147	114	86	82
N. America	132	120	109	111	99	82	36	26	15	10	9
L. America	151	151	151	151	151	151	131	105	71	48	42
Europe	181	153	112	86	67	58	48	35	27	20	18
2. Population (millions)											
Africa	110.00	121.14	133.41	160.79	193.80	227.27	285.05	366.79	496.22	640.72	822.37
Asia	877.87	959.35	1036.1	1136.92	1247.60	1415.69	1709.88	2145.03	2696.89	3225.87	3759.36
N. America	81.84	99.47	115.68	129.21	144.33	171.62	204.32	231.28	256.46	290.29	329.06
L. America	64.61	76.76	89.98	108.13	129.95	167.32	219.65	286.47	370.55	445.92	526.75
Europe	429.14	480.22	488.35	533.82	583.52	547.46	604.46	656.20	696.04	741.24	748.07
3. Birth rate per 1,000 population											
Africa	48	48	48	48	48	48	47.6	46.2	44.8	40.6	37.2
Asia	42	42	42	42	42	42	39	33.7	28.9	25.1	20.3
N. America	32.3	31.5	27.6	21.1	19.4	24.6	22	15.7	15.5	15.5	13.8
L. America	42.5	42.5	42.5	42.5	42.5	42.5	41	35.2	30.7	25.3	21.2
Europe	30.8	28.9	27	25.1	23.2	21.5	19.1	15.7	14.4	11.5	10.2
4. Child deaths (millions)											
Africa	1.368	1.506	1.659	1.999	2.409	2.825	3.398	3.638	3.997	4.120	4.620
Asia	8.009	8.745	9.444	10.363	11.372	12.918	12.512	10.618	8.893	6.932	6.248
N. America	0.349	0.376	0.348	0.303	0.277	0.346	0.162	0.094	0.060	0.045	0.041
L. America	0.415	0.493	0.577	0.694	0.834	1.076	1.181	1.057	0.807	0.537	0.464
Europe	2.389	2.128	1.481	1.155	0.901	0.684	0.549	0.358	0.270	0.169	0.135
Total	12.528	13.248	13.509	14.514	15.794	17.849	17.802	15.765	14.027	11.803	11.508

5. Malnutrition child deaths (millions)

Africa	0.222	0.244	0.269	0.324	0.390	0.458	0.550	0.589	0.647	0.667	0.748
Asia	2.403	2.256	2.437	2.674	2.934	3.333	3.228	2.740	1.654	1.289	0.900
N. America	0.044	0.043	0.038	0.031	0.028	0.035	0.017	0.010	0.006	0.005	0.004
L. America	0.124	0.136	0.142	0.171	0.180	0.200	0.191	0.152	0.102	0.068	0.056
Europe	0.344	0.268	0.178	0.132	0.097	0.074	0.059	0.037	0.028	0.017	0.014
Total	3.136	2.947	3.063	3.331	3.630	4.100	4.046	3.527	2.437	2.046	1.722
Share of all attributable to malnutrition	0.250	0.222	0.227	0.229	0.230	0.230	0.227	0.224	0.174	0.173	0.150

Sources and assumptions:

Block 1: Under 5 mortality rate

Source: Ahmad *et al.* (2000), for the 5-year periods beginning 1955–59 to 1995–9, using population weights to aggregate WHO regions to the five regions used here. Europe B (WHO category) uses data for Austria to extend the data back to 1900 (Corsini and Viazzo 1993); Europe A and C (WHO category) uses data for the UK to do a similar calculation (Hicks and Allen 1999). These data are for infant mortality, and we add an additional 15% to estimate under-5 mortality, using the ratio for the UK from Hatton (2009). North America uses data for the USA; we use data on mortality under 14 from Cutler and Meara (2001), which slightly overestimates the rate for under 5s. For the remaining regions, we assume that the rate remained constant between 1900 and 1950.

Block 2: Population

Source: Maddison (2007)

Block 3: Birth rates

Source: UNESA (2009) for data from 1950 onwards. The WHO regions have to be aggregated into the broader regions used in this analysis, using population weights. Prior to 1950, birth rates for the USA from Haines (2008). For Europe, the rate for 1900 for Western Europe was used from Maddison (2006) and a linear trend from 1900 to 1950 to interpolate values for 1910, 1920, 1930, and 1940. For the other regions, the rate was assumed not to have changed from 1900 to 1950, which is consistent with data provided in Maddison (2006) for India, China, Brazil, and Mexico.

Block 4: Child deaths

Calculated from U5MR × birth rate × population size.

Block 5: Child deaths attributable to malnutrition

Calculated as follows: we use achieved adult height 20 years in the future to obtain PAR. For 1990 and 2000 we use PAR estimated from child height-for-age from UNICEF 2000, to be consistent. However, this yielded PARs higher than 1980, hence we used the 1980 PARs for 1990 and 2000 instead. We assume that 40% of child deaths occur in the first month, based on WHO (2010), and that the relative risks from Pelletier *et al.* (1994b) can be applied to the other 60%. In practice, Pelletier *et al.* (1994b) derived those rates from ages 6 months to 5 years; but it is the first month which is most critical to exclude.

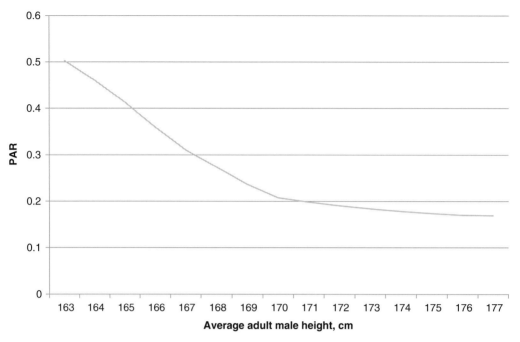

Figure 8.9 *Estimated population-attributable risk (PAR) due to child malnutrition*

(falling to 252 by 1880) (Corsini and Viazzo 1993), well above rates for any region in the twentieth century except Africa. Thus the twentieth-century patterns in developing countries likely existed in developed countries in the nineteenth century.

Results: Economic and Human Costs of Undernutrition

Figure 8.10 shows the trends in economic losses by region, and Figure 8.11 for the developed/developing countries and world aggregate, for 1900–2010, as well as projections for 2010–2050. Economic losses attributable to poor nutrition were already negligible in North America by the 1930s, and in Europe overall by the end of the twentieth century. Losses in Northern Europe virtually disappeared as the post-war babies reached adulthood, and similarly by 2000 in Eastern and Southern Europe.

In the developing world, although productivity losses began to diminish in individual countries, progress was not widespread enough to see any decrease at the level of the region until the turn of the twenty-first century, when improvements in

Latin America became evident. The improvements in Asia become evident as of 2020, and significant improvements are visible in both Latin America and Asia by 2050. According to our assumptions, no improvement is seen in Africa even by 2050.

Global productivity losses start to decline at the beginning of the twentieth century (Figure 8.11), since productivity losses are weighted by GDP and not by population, and hence reflect heavily the situation of the developed regions. As the share in global GDP of the developing countries increases, particularly since 1970, global productivity losses increase again for almost four decades (since heights in these countries have not yet attained the level of North America). Once heights in Latin America attain 170 cm in 2000, and in Asia in 2020, global productivity losses recommence their downward trend. Global losses average 8% over the twentieth century, and diminish to a projected 6% over the first half of the twenty-first century.

Table 8.7 provides some indications as to how sensitive these results are to the assumptions made. The assumptions made of the relationship between height and productivity (Figure 8.8) have a major effect, as do assumptions as to how the effect of

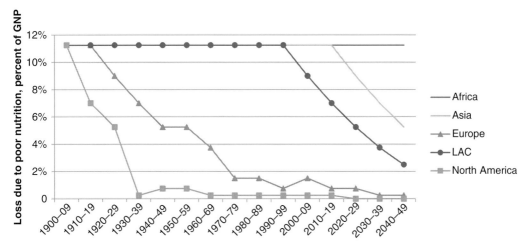

Figure 8.10 *Estimated percent of GNP lost due to poor nutrition, geographic regions, 1900–2010, and projections 2010–2050*

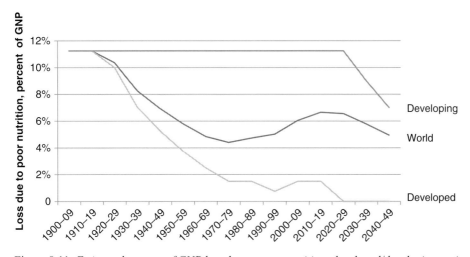

Figure 8.11 *Estimated percent of GNP lost due to poor nutrition, developed/developing regions and world, 1900–2010, and projections 2010–2050*

male height on individual productivity, translates into an effect of overall height on GDP. Assumptions which have a medium effect include our use of height as a measure of nutrition (which omits effects of higher calorie intake by adults, and higher micronutrient intake by children and adults), and the assumption that the benefits for women are similar to those for men. Assumptions which have the least impact include those concerning heights in Africa (since Africa contributes only about 3% of world GDP over this period), and errors in measurement of height trends.

In addition to the economic losses, there are human costs of poor nutrition. Given the assumptions required, our results should be treated as broad orders of magnitude. Figure 8.12 presents trends in the annual number of under-5 deaths from all causes by region over the twentieth century. Figure 8.13 compares the total actual annual number, and our estimates of what this number would have been in the absence of nutrition improvements. Figure 8.14 breaks down the estimates of deaths avoided due to nutrition improvements, by region. The underlying numbers are available in Table 8.6.

Table 8.7 Sensitivity analysis of effect of varying assumptions on estimates of economic losses

Assumption	Impact
There are additional productivity losses associated with heights below 170 cm (e.g. Hoddinott *et al.* (2008) find that early childhood food supplements are associated with an additional 2.9 cm of adult height, 45% higher wages, at mean height around 163 cm for men	Gains/losses 2× larger
Benefits of improved productivity affect all of GDP, not just the wage share (one-half)	Gains/losses 2× larger
Benefits of improved height for women have no effect on productivity (who are on average one-third of labor force)	Gains/losses 50% smaller
Using data on young men overstates the improvement in height (hence productivity) of the whole labor force	Gains/losses 25% smaller (depending on structure of labor force by age, and rate of nutritional improvement)
Additional nutritional productivity losses attributable to improvements in calorie intake and micronutrient intake which do not manifest in improved height	Gains/losses 25% larger or possibly more
Heights in Africa do not stay constant over the 150-year period	World GDP gains/losses at most 10% larger/smaller (1 percentage point change in world GDP): Africa accounts for 3% of world GDP
GDP growth between 2010 and 2050 is higher or lower than expected	Will affect estimates, but by an undetermined amount: the effect on height is estimated via changes in life expectancy (which depend partly on income): however UN has not produced life expectancy variants to correspond

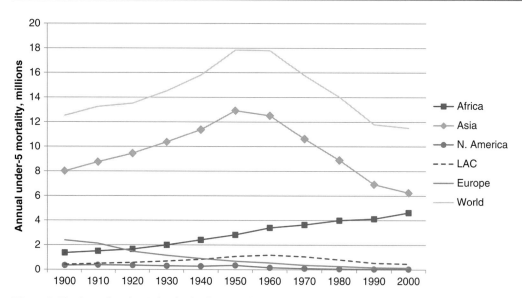

Figure 8.12 *Annual under-5 deaths (millions), all causes, by region, 1900–2000*

The results show that the mortality due to under-nutrition (as measured by height) is disturbingly large – accounting for a quarter of postneonatal child deaths from 1900 to 1970, on average 3–4 million child deaths annually. This only drops to 15% (and below 2 million deaths annually) by 2000. Note that since we conservatively assume no height growth in Africa over the century, there

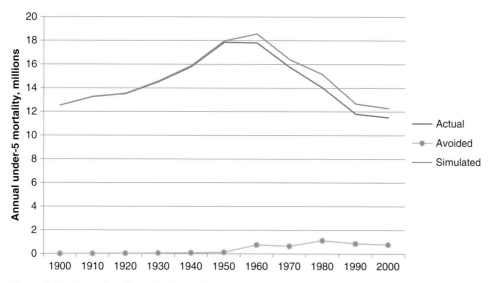

Figure 8.13 *Annual under-5 deaths (millions), all causes and deaths avoided due to nutrition improvements*

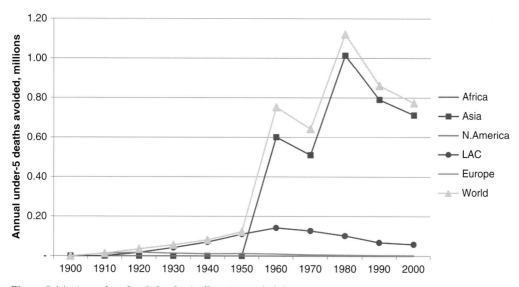

Figure 8.14 *Annual under-5 deaths (millions) avoided due to nutrition improvements, by region*

is no improvement in child mortality attributable to nutrition for that region. There is also no improvement in North America, but for the opposite reason: heights were already sufficiently large by 1900 that further increases had no noticeable impact on further mortality reduction. (Note that some of the apparently surprising patterns – e.g. absolute decreases in annual lives saved due to nutrition improvements between 1960 and 1970, and between 1980 and 1990 – are due to drops in birth rates.)

Although there are substantial nutritional improvements in some regions in the twentieth century (primarily Europe and Latin America), these are regions with lower population, lower birth rates, and lower child mortality. The end result is that these nutritional improvements save only about half a million lives a year worldwide prior to 1970, and just over 1 million worldwide thereafter, once nutritional improvements in Asia begin to take effect. We would expect major improvements between 2010 and 2050 as nutrition improves, particularly in Asia which is home to the majority of the world's children.

This estimate of mortality attributable to malnutrition focuses only on chronic malnutrition. In addition, there is a risk attributable to short-term variations in nutritional status (associated with hungry seasons, periodic crop failures, or famines). These affect weight-for-height and have separate effects on mortality. Our best estimate is that chronic malnutrition accounts for about three-quarters of the attributable risk due to malnutrition, based on the fact that our estimates around 2000 predict 1.7 million under-5 deaths annually. Black et al. (2008) by comparison use weight-for-age (which combines both chronic and acute malnutrition) and a more robust methodology for the same year, and obtain a higher estimate of 2.2 million under-5 deaths due to undernutrition.

It is interesting to contrast the differences in patterns between the gains in economic productivity, with those in lives saved. The function linking GDP gains to height (Figure 8.8) models all the improvements occurring above a height of 170 cm. By contrast, the function linking mortality risk to height (Figure 8.9) shows virtually all the improvement occurring at heights below 170 cm. The improvements in height in the developed world have a large impact on world GDP growth (since these countries account for a large proportion of world GDP). By contrast, the improvements in height in the developed world have only a modest impact on world mortality improvements (since these countries account for a small proportion of world mortality).

Discussion and Conclusions

The estimates suggest that undernutrition has been a cause of a significant, slowly declining, loss of global productivity. We estimate that this loss was 8% of world GDP over the twentieth century, and will decline to 6% of world GDP in the first half of the twentieth century. The losses are largely associated with impaired cognition which directly reduces productivity, with reduced educational attainment, as well as lower productivity of undernourished adults in manual work.

There is clearly some overlap between GDP gains in the twentieth century attributed to nutrition, and those attributed to increased education. Part of the improvement in nutrition allows children to stay longer in school, and part improves cognition and hence productivity even holding education level constant. Alderman et al.'s (2006) estimates for Zimbabwe suggest that an increase in height from the 85th to the 95th percentile is associated with an extra 0.75 years of schooling (i.e. an extra 10 cm in adult male height is associated with approximately 1 extra year in school). In the twentieth century, if heights increased on average by 10 cm and education by 10 years for some regions, that implies that about a tenth of the schooling effect is nutrition-related, and equally somewhere between a quarter and a third of the nutrition effect is schooling-related. This gives a rough idea of the double-counting implicit in improved education and improved nutrition.

Similarly, there is overlap between health and nutrition as explanations of human costs (excess deaths). In the 35% of child deaths attributable to undernutrition, the immediate cause of death is often infection; however, a well-nourished individual could have survived.

The results are highly sensitive to the assumptions made regarding the effect of height (as a measure of nutritional status) and productivity. These assumptions likely could affect the results by an order of magnitude four to eight times greater than variations in the assumptions made regarding height and mortality, errors in our estimates of height of adult males, and possible errors in the height projections to 2050.

Our results for productivity are lower than those of Fogel (1994) for the UK over the period 1790 to 1980. Fogel did not have access to the more recent econometric studies in Tables 8.1 and 8.2, and used a modeling exercise instead. Using height as a nutrition measure excludes the effect of higher calorie intake for adults on work output, as well as the benefits of improved micronutrient status on work output both directly and (via cognition and schooling) indirectly. Hence, our estimates are conservative. However, our estimates are somewhat larger than cross-sectional estimates of the costs of malnutrition for individual countries and regions at one point in time, since some of the effects take more than one generation to achieve.

We have carefully controlled econometric studies of the effect of an additional centimeter of height, both for industrialized countries and for countries with mean heights of 170 cm for male adults. We do not, however, have good measures of how the relationship tapers off as height increases (our assumption of a linear reduction in effect is not based on empirical evidence). We also do not have good measures of the effect at mean heights for male adults lower than 170 cm. Unfortunately, mean heights for male adults in most of the developing world are below 170 cm (often substantially below) for much of the twentieth century. The one longitudinal study available for Guatemala, where mean heights are around 163 cm, suggests the effects on nutrition on productivity might be even larger at that height. We have not assumed additional losses of productivity as height falls further below 170 cm, to be conservative.

The projections from 2010 to 2050 show much stronger impacts of improved nutrition on productivity, since our model is that heights of 170 cm have to be attained before productivity improves significantly. This happens in Latin America by 2000, and in Asia by 2020. Even by 2050, world economic losses attributable to undernutrition are still 5%. These are dominated by losses in Asia. Africa also likely has losses due to undernutrition, but the data on height for Africa are too limited to model the trends in this region; in any case Africa contributes only around 3% of world GDP over this period.

Our results for mortality using height are an underestimate of the effect of nutrition overall, since we measure chronic nutrition status (via height) and do not include the effects via weight-for-height, reflecting temporary food shortages and famines. Our own estimate is that these would add at least another third to the absolute losses. Our estimate of 41 million child deaths over the twentieth century is a huge number (especially if we are correct about the additional deaths due to acute undernutrition, which would contribute an additional 20 million child deaths).

Although using height to measure nutrition underestimates both the productivity losses and the mortality losses, unfortunately there is no other measure that can be used for the whole century, nor for a global study. Despite the limitations of the measure, the differences between regions and by decades are very informative.

We have not touched at all on what could have been done to improve nutrition – and hence reduce child mortality, and increase world GDP – during the twentieth century. The cost-effectiveness of nutrition interventions is another big topic in itself (Horton *et al.* 2009).

References

Ahmad, O. B., A. D. Lopez, and M. Inoue (2000) The decline in child mortality: a reappraisal. *Bulletin of the World Health Organization* **78**: 1175–1191.

Alderman H., J. Hoddinott, and B. Kinsey (2006) Long-term consequences of early childhood malnutrition. *Oxford Economic Papers* **58**: 450–474.

Alderman H., J. Hoogeveen, and M. Rossi (2008) Preschool nutrition and subsequent schooling attainment: longitudinal evidence from Tanzania. *Economic Development and Cultural Change* **57**: 239–260.

Baten, J. (2010) Latin American anthropometrics, past and present: an overview. *Economics and Human Biology* **8**: 141–144.

Behrman, J. and M. Rosenzweig (2001) *The Returns to Increasing Body Weight*, PIER Working Paper no. 01–052. Philadelphia, PA: Penn Institute for Economic Research.

Behrman, J. R., M. C. Calderon, S. H. Preston, *et al.* (2009) Nutritional supplementation in girls influences the growth of their children: prospective study in Guatemala. *American Journal of Clinical Nutrition* **90**: 1372–1379.

Behrman, J. R., J. Hoddinott, J. A. Maluccio, and R. Martorell (2010) *Brains versus Brawn: Labor Market Returns to Intellectual and Physical Human Capital in a Developing Country.* Philadelphia, PA: University of Pennsylvania (mimeo).

Bielicki, T. and A. Szklarska (1999) Secular trends in stature in Poland: national and social class-specific. *Annals of Human Biology* **26**: 251–258.

Bielicki, T., A. Szklarska, S. Kozieł, and S. J. Ulijaszek (2005) Changing patterns of social variation in stature in Poland: effects of transition from a command economy to the free-market system? *Journal of Biosocial Science* **37**: 427–434.

Black, R. E., L. H. Allen, Z. A. Bhutta, *et al.* (2008) Maternal and child undernutrition: global and regional exposures and health consequences. *The Lancet* **371**: 243–260.

Bodzsár, É. B. and A. Zsákai (2002) Some aspects of secular changes in Hungary over the twentieth century. *Collegium Antropologicum* **2**: 477–484.

Bogin, B. (1999) *Patterns of Human Growth.* Cambridge: Cambridge University Press

Bozzoli, C., A. Deaton, and C. Quintana-Domeque (2009) Adult height and childhood disease. *Demography* **46**: 647–669.

Case, A. and C. Paxson (2008) Stature and status: height, ability, and labor market outcomes. *Journal of Political Economy* **116**: 499–531.

Choi, S.-J. and D. Schwekendiek (2009) The biological standard of living in colonial Korea, 1910–1945. *Economics and Human Biology* **7**: 259–264.

Corsini, C. A. and P. P. Viazzo (eds.) (1993) *The Decline of Infant Mortality in Europe 1800–1950: Four National Case Studies.* Florence: UNICEF International Child Development Centre. Available at: www.unicefirc.org/publications/pdf/hisper_decline_infantmortality.pdf

Cutler, D. M. and E. Meara (2001) *Changes in the Age Distribution of Mortality over the Twentieth Century,* National Bureau of Economic Research Working Paper No. 8556. Cambridge, MA: NBER.

Deaton, A. (2007) Height, health, and development. *Proceedings of the National Academy of Sciences of the USA* **104**: 13 232–13 237.

(2008) Height, health, and inequality: the distribution of adult heights in India. *American Economic Review* **98**: 468–474.

Eveleth, P. B. and J. M. Tanner (1976) *Worldwide Variation in Human Growth.* Cambridge: Cambridge University Press.

(1990) *Worldwide Variation in Human Growth*, 2nd edn. Cambridge: Cambridge University Press.

Fogel, R. W. (1994) *Economic Growth, Population Growth, and Physiology: The Bearing of Long-Term Processes on the Making of Economic Policy*, National Bureau of Economic Research Working Paper No. 4368. Cambridge, MA: NBER.

Gao, W. and R. Smyth (2010) Health human capital, height and wages in China. *Journal of Development Studies* **46**: 466–484.

Garcia, J. and C. Quintana-Domeque (2007) The evolution of adult height in Europe: a brief note. *Economics and Human Biology* **5**: 340–349.

Guntupalli, A. M. and J. Baten (2006) The development and inequality of heights in North, West and East India 1915–44. *Explorations in Economic History* **43**: 578–608.

Haddad, L. J. and H. E. Bouis (1991) The impact of nutritional status on agricultural productivity: wage evidence from the Philippines. *Oxford Bulletin of Economics and Statistics* **53**: 45–68.

Haines, M. (2008) Fertility and mortality in the United States. In: R. Whaples (ed.), *EH.Net Encyclopedia.* Available at: http://eh.net/encyclopedia/article/haines.demography

Hatton, T. J. (2009) *Infant Mortality and the Health of Survivors: Britain 1910–1950.* Canberra: Australian National University. Available at http://espe.conference-services.net/resources/321/1533/pdf/ESPE2009_0099_paper.pdf

Hatton, T. J. and B. E. Bray (2010) Long run trends in the heights of European men, 19th–20th centuries. *Economics and Human Biology* **8**: 405–413.

Heineck, G. (2005) Up in the skies? The relationship between height and earnings in Germany. *Labour* **19**: 469–489.

(2008) A note on the height–wage differential in the UK: cross-sectional evidence from the BHPS. *Economics Letters* **98**: 288–293.

Hicks, J. and G. Allen (1999) *A Century of Change: Trends in UK Statistics since 1900*, House of Commons Research Paper No. 99/111. London.

Hoddinott, J., J. A. Maluccio, J. R. Behrman, R. Flores, and R. Martorell (2008) Effect of a nutrition intervention during early childhood on economic productivity in Guatemalan adults. *The Lancet* **271**: 411–416.

Horton, S., H. Alderman, and J. Rivera (2009) Hunger and malnutrition. In: B. Lomborg (ed.), *Global Crises: Global Solutions*, 2nd edn. Cambridge: Cambridge University Press.

Indian Council of Medical Research (1972) *Growth and Physical Development of Indian Infants and Children.* New Delhi: ICMR.

Kortt, M. and A. Leigh (2010) Does size matter in Australia? *Economic Record* **86**: 71–83.

Lozoff, B., E. Jimenez, and J. B. Smith (2006) Double burden of iron deficiency in infancy and low socio-economic status: a longitudinal analysis of cognitive test scores to 19 years. *Archives of Pediatric and Adolescent Medicine* **160**: 1108–1113.

Lübker, M. (2007) *Labour Shares*, International Labour Office Technical Brief No. 01. Geneva: ILO.

Maddison, A. (2006) *The World Economy: A Millennial Perspective*. Paris: OECD.

(2007) *Historical Statistics of the World Economy*, vol. 1. Available at: www.ggdc.net/maddison/Historical_Statistics/horizontal-file_03-2007.xls

Maria-Dolores, R. and J. M. Martinez-Carrion (2009) The relationship between height and economic development in Spain, 1850–1958. *Economics and Human Biology* **9**: 30–44.

Meisel, A. and M. Vega (2004) *A Tropical Success Story: A Century of Improvements in the Biological Standard of Living, Colombia 1910–2002*. Cartagena, Columbia: Banco de la República.

(2007) The biological standard of living (and its convergence) in Colombia, 1870–2003: a tropical success story. *Economics and Human Biology* **5**: 100–122.

Monasterio, L. M. and M. Signorini (2008) *As condicoes de vida dos Gauchos entre 1889–1920: uma analise anthropometrica*. Pelotas, Brazil: Federal University of Pelotas.

Monteiro, C. A., M. H. D. A. Benicio, and N. d. C. Goveia (1994) Secular growth trends in Brazil over three decades. *Annals of Human Biology* **21**: 381–390.

Mosk, C. (1996) *Making Health Work: Human Growth in Modern Japan*. Berkeley, CA: University of California Press.

National Health Service (2008) *Health Survey for England 2006: Latest Trends*. London: NHS Information Centre.

Pak, S. (2004) The biological standard of living in the two Koreas. *Economics and Human Biology* **2**: 511–521.

Pelletier, D. L., J. W. Low, F. C. Johnson, and L. A. H. Msukwa (1994a) Child anthropometry and mortality in Malawi: testing for effect modification by age and length of follow-up and confounding by socioeconomic factors. *Journal of Nutrition* **124**: 2082S–2105S.

Pelletier, D. L., E. A. Frongillo, D. G. Schroeder, and J.-P. Habicht (1994b) The effects of malnutrition on child mortality in developing countries. *Bulletin of the World Health Organization* **73**: 443–448.

Persico, N., A. Postlethwaite, and D. Silverman (2004) The effect of adolescent experience on labor market outcomes, the case of height. *Journal of Political Economy* **112**: 1019–1053.

Rosenbaum, S., R. K. Skinner, I. B. Knight, and J. S. Garrow (1985) A survey of heights and weights of adults in Great Britain, 1980. *Annals of Human Biology* **2**: 115–127.

Sargent, J. D. and D. Blanchflower (1994) Obesity and stature in adolescence and in young adulthood: analysis of a British birth cohort. *Archives of Pediatric Medicine* **148**: 681–687.

Schmidt, I. M., M. H. Jørgensen, and K. F. Michaelsen (1995) Height of conscripts in Europe: is post-neonatal mortality a predictor? *Annals of Human Biology* **22**: 57–67.

Schultz, T. P. (2002) Wage gains associated with height as a form of health human capital. *American Economic Review Papers and Proceedings* **92**: 349–353.

(2003) Wage rentals for reproducible human capital: evidence from Ghana and the Ivory Coast. *Economics and Human Biology* **1**: 331–336.

Silvontoinen, K. (2003) Determinants of variation in adult body height. *Journal of Biosocial Science* **35**: 263–285.

South Africa DHS (2002) *Demographic and Health Survey 1998: Final Report*. Pretoria: Department of Health.

Steckel, R. H. (1995) Stature and the standard of living. *Journal of Economic Literature* **33**: 1903–1940.

(2000) 'Alternative indicators of health and the quality of life.' In: J. Madrick, (ed.), *Unconventional Wisdom: Alternative Perspectives on the New Economy*. New York: Twentieth Century Fund.

(2006) Health. In: S. B. Carter, S. Gartner, M. R. Haines, *et al.* (eds.), *The Historical Statistics of the United States: Millennial Edition*. New York: Cambridge University Press.

(2008) Living standards: historical trends. In: L. Blume and S. Durlauf (eds.), *The New Palgrave Dictionary of Economics*, 2nd edn. Basingstoke, UK: Palgrave Macmillan.

Steckel, R. H. and R. Floud (1997) Conclusions. In: R. H. Steckel and R. Floud (eds.), *Health and Welfare during Industrialization*. Chicago, IL: University of Chicago Press.

Stein, A. D., M. Wang, R. Martorell, *et al.* on behalf of the Cohort Group (2010) Growth patterns in early childhood and final attained stature: data from five birth cohorts from low- and middle-income countries. *American Journal of Human Biology* **22**: 353–359.

Strauss, J. and D. Thomas (1988) Health, nutrition, and economic development. *Journal of Economic Literature* **36**: 766–817.

Thomas, D. and J. Strauss (1997) Health and wages: evidence on men and women in urban Brazil. *Journal of Econometrics* **77**: 159–185.

UNESA (2009) *World Population Prospects: The 2008 Revision*, CD-ROM edn. New York: United Nations, Department of Economic and Social Affairs, Population Division.

UNICEF (2006) *State of the World's Children*. Geneva: UNICEF.

WHO (2010) *World Health Statistics 2010*. Geneva: WHO.

World Bank (2010) *World Development Indicators*. New York: World Bank. Available at: http://data.worldbank.org/indicators.

Yang, X., Y. Li, G. Ma, *et al.* (2005) Study on weight and height of the Chinese people and the differences between 1992 and 2002. *Zhonghua Liu Xing Bing Xue Za Zhi* **26**: 489–493.

Zhen-Wang, B. and J. Cheng-Ye (2005) Secular growth changes in body height and weight in children and adolescents in Shandong, China between 1939 and 2000. *Annals of Human Biology* **32**: 650–665.

Trade Barriers: Costing Global Trade Barriers, 1900 to 2050

CHAPTER 9

KYM ANDERSON

Introduction

The potential net economic and social benefits available to almost every country if they were to open their economies to international trade have been well known and clearly articulated since at least the eighteenth century (Irwin 1996). Yet national governments continue to intervene in markets for goods, services, capital, and labor in ways that alter the location of production, consumer expenditure, and thus also international commerce. Certainly transport and communication costs of doing business across borders have fallen enormously over the centuries, lowering natural barriers to trade. Governmental barriers to trade, however, have fluctuated widely around both upward and downward long-run trends.

The objectives of this chapter are threefold: to review evidence on the changing extent of global trade restrictions resulting from government policies over the past 100+ years; to assess prospects for trade policy changes over coming decades, drawing on current political economy theory and evidence; and to estimate the annual cost in terms of economic welfare forgone in high-income and developing countries of those trade-restricting policies at various points in time retrospectively from 1900 and prospectively to 2050.

To keep the task manageable, attention is initially confined to restrictions on goods trade, leaving aside until the end the less-certain effects of barriers to trade in services including financial flows.[1] This is necessary because methods for estimating the extent of (let alone the market and welfare effects of) barriers to services and capital flows between countries are far less developed than methodologies applicable to trade in goods. Preliminary studies to date to fill these lacunae suggest, however, that potential gains from just goods trade reform today are very much lower than the gains that could come from removing barriers for all products and financial flows. A sample of these studies is reviewed in what follows, and the penultimate section of the chapter provides an indication of how much greater the global cost of trade barriers could have been at different points in time with this more-comprehensive coverage of trade barriers.

There is a paucity of detailed historical data even on goods trade restrictions. There are also virtually no global economy-wide models capable of estimating costs of distortions through most of the previous century. Precision about the past is therefore impossible. Also, there is a broad range of projections of the world economy available for coming decades, and each of them depends on explicit or (most commonly) implicit assumptions about future trade and other economic policies. Hence even baseline shares of different countries in global GDP and trade in 2050, let alone projected trade barriers, have an unmeasurable but wide confidence band around them. The use of global economy-wide models in estimating the costs of trade-distorting policies has grown considerably in recent years though (Anderson 2003; Francois and Martin 2010), so estimates of the cost of at least

Paper for the Copenhagen Consensus on Human Challenges 2011 Project. This draws to some extent on the author's earlier CC04 chapter and Anderson and Winters' CC08 chapter which appear in *Global Crises, Global Solutions*, edited by B. Lomborg, Cambridge University Press, 2004 and 2009. Research assistance by Signe Nelgen is gratefully acknowledged.

[1] How large the international movement of labor would be without restrictive immigration laws is impossible to guess, so it is ignored even though preliminary studies suggest the developing country and global economic welfare gains from even a modest expansion in access to jobs in high-income countries could be far greater than the gains from goods trade liberalization (Anderson and Winters 2009).

recent policies are available. They will be drawn on for their own sake, and also for providing guidance in estimating past and future costs.

The chapter begins, by way of background, with a brief history of trade policy and institutions. It then examines the changing extent of barriers to international trade in various parts of the world from the late nineteenth century to the present. That survey reveals the ups and downs of trade taxation over the past 100+ years. In the following section, a series of estimates of the global cost of trade barriers is presented: for 2004, for 2050 under two alternative scenarios (high and low protection) for 1980–84, and for earlier decades of the twentieth century. The penultimate section of the chapter then explores how much those estimates might need to be adjusted to account for missing elements of the calculus, which are identified in the review of recent literature summarized in the Appendix. Those two sections provide the basis for the estimates reported in the final section of the costs of those changing trade barriers, expressed as a percentage of GDP in high-income countries, developing countries, and globally.

The results suggest that while the cost of trade barriers may have come down over the past six decades, they are still high compared with those in 1900 (when transport costs were a more important barrier to trade: Jacks and Pendakur 2010; Jacks *et al.* 2010). The results also reveal that their cost may not fall significantly over the next four decades unless a comprehensive liberalization is agreed to under the current Doha Round of multilateral trade negotiations by member countries of the World Trade Organization (WTO). The chapter therefore concludes by exploring possible strategies to reduce remaining distortions over the next four decades. The most obvious of them is unilateral reform, but governments find it difficult politically to ignore protectionist lobbies unless there are counter-lobbies from other groups, such as exporters. Hence the ongoing effort to reform in concert with other countries, including multilaterally via the WTO's Doha Development Agenda but also via new or expanding preferential trading agreements.

[2] This section draws on the Introduction in Anderson and Hoekman (2006).

Trade Policies and Institutions since the Nineteenth Century[2]

During the seventeenth, eighteenth, and early nineteenth centuries, trade negotiations were "ever pending, never ending." Frustration with that state of affairs set the stage for unilateral tariff cuts by the major economic power in the nineteenth century, namely Britain, with the repeal of its Corn Laws in 1846. British policy-makers hoped that their European trading partners would see the benefits of unilateral liberalization and follow their example. That was not immediately forthcoming but, by 1860, with war clouds gathering over Austria's involvement in Italy, the governments of Britain and France felt a commercial treaty was needed to diffuse tensions and improve diplomatic relations. The resulting Cobden–Chevalier Treaty of 1860 contained a Most-Favoured-Nation (MFN) clause. This required that the agreed cut in the tariff on each item in their bilateral trade was to be applied also to their imports from other countries. It also meant that every European country that subsequently signed a trade treaty with either Britain or France (and most had done so by 1867) signed onto MFN. Especially important was the Treaty of Frankfurt concluded by Bismarck with France in 1871: its Article XI provided for permanent, unconditional MFN and was thereby a key stabilizer of European commercial policy. The systemic effect of the 1860 Anglo-French accord was thus of much greater significance than its importance to either country alone, as it led to a network of treaties that lowered hugely both the average level of tariff protection and the extent of trade discrimination in Europe.

During the years from 1860 to 1913 the world enjoyed relative serenity in terms of international trade and monetary relations. Even though economic growth then was proceeding at less than half the post-World War II pace, it was very rapid by previous standards. In contrast to Europe, the United States during this period sought mainly exclusive reciprocity agreements or, at best, conditional MFN treaties. While those agreements freed up some trade, they explicitly retained a degree of discrimination and meant America entered the twentieth century with among the highest tariffs of today's high-income countries.

When many of those European trade treaties were reaching their expiry date (nearly 50 of them were to expire in the first half of the 1890s), economic difficulties were making their renegotiation more contentious than earlier. Tariff wars ensued, so that the threat of retaliation – which had served as a deterrent to raising tariffs – was no longer a constraint on reform reversal. Even so, MFN was retained, and there was no recourse to anti-dumping[3] or countervailing duties or to export subsidies, despite the appearance of a "fair trade" movement in Europe in the 1890s.

Great though that trade policy achievement of the period from 1860 to 1913 was, including the establishment of non-discrimination in Europe via the widespread use of the unconditional MFN clause, problems remained. One was the absence of bindings on tariffs (to prevent backsliding), and of constraints on non-tariff trade-distorting measures. Another was that there was no legal means of resolving trade disputes. Furthermore, the unwillingness of America or others to adopt the unconditional MFN principle (see Viner 1924) meant the sustainability of the European commercial policy achievements of that period was far from certain. Indeed, the bilateral treaty regime ended abruptly with the outbreak of World War I in 1914.

Following that war, efforts to restore liberal trade centered on international conferences. However, despite the rhetoric in support of open markets, those meetings did not lead to renewed trade treaties with binding commitments to openness based on MFN. With no country willing or able to replace Britain as the hegemon, there was trade policy anarchy (Kindleberger 1989). When economic recession and low agricultural prices hit in the late 1920s, and the USA introduced the Smoot–Hawley tariff hikes of June 1930, governments elsewhere responded with beggar-thy-neighbor protectionist trade policies that together helped drive the world economy into depression. The volume of world trade shrunk by one-quarter between 1929 and 1932, and its value fell by 40%.

The first attempts to reverse that growth in protection were discriminatory, benefitting colonies at the expense of other trading partners. Thus between 1929 and 1938 the share of imports from colonies rose from 30% to 42% for Britain, from 12% to 27% for France, and from 20 to 41% for Japan (League of Nations 1939; Anderson and Norheim 1993). By the end of the 1930s protectionism was far more entrenched than in the late nineteenth century when only non-discriminatory tariffs had to be grappled with. Indeed non-tariff trade barriers were so rife as to make tariffs redundant and hence a return to MFN irrelevant unless and until "tariffication" of those barriers occurred.

Out of the inter-war experience came the conviction that a return to the beneficent non-cooperative equilibrium of the nineteenth century was highly unlikely. Instead, Britain and the United States were convinced that liberal world trade required a set of multilaterally agreed rules and binding commitments based on non-discriminatory principles. A proposal for such an agreement was put to the British War Cabinet in 1942 by Meade (1942), and was developed further at the Bretton Woods conference in 1944 out of which grew also the International Monetary Fund (IMF) and World Bank. In the Anglo-American view, the post-war international economic system was to be constructed in such a way as to remove the economic causes of friction that were believed to have been at the origin of World War II. An important element in this vision was the establishment of a stable world economy that would provide all trading nations with non-discriminatory access to markets, supplies, and investment opportunities. There was a strong perception that there was a positive correlation between trade and peace, and, as important, between non-discrimination and good foreign relations.

As it happened, the efforts in the latter 1940s to create an International Trade Organization (ITO) to complement the IMF and World Bank were unsuccessful (Diebold 1952). Nonetheless, many of the key elements of the ITO proposal were encapsulated in a General Agreement on Tariffs and Trade (GATT) that was signed in 1947 by 23 trading countries – 12 developed and 11 developing – who at the time accounted for nearly two-thirds of the world's international trade. The GATT provided

---

[3] The first anti-dumping legislation was not introduced until Canada did so in 1904. It was soon followed by similar legislation in most of the major trading nations prior to and just after World War I (Deardorff 2005).

not only a set of multilateral rules and disciplines but also a forum to negotiate tariff reductions and changes in rules, plus a mechanism to help settle trade disputes. Eight so-called rounds of negotiations took place in the subsequent 46 years, as a result of which many tariffs on at least manufactured goods were progressively lowered in most high-income countries. The last of those rounds culminating in numerous Uruguay Round agreements to further reduce trade barriers over the subsequent decade including – for the first time – in agriculture and services. Another of those agreements involved the GATT Secretariat being converted into the World Trade Organization (WTO) in January 1995, the membership of which now accounts for more than 95% of world trade.

Methodology for Estimating the Cost of Trade-Distorting Policies

The key trade-distorting policies include import or export taxes or subsidies, quantitative restrictions such as import or export quotas, licences, or bans (so-called non-tariff trade barriers or NTBs), or domestic policies that affect the price facing producers or consumers of tradable products. Multiple exchange rates also have been used in ways that effectively alter both exports and imports. The net effect of those measures on the domestic price of a tradable good is usually expressed in ad valorem terms as the percentage by which that domestic price exceeds the border price (ignoring domestic policies that may drive a wedge between the producer and consumer prices of a good, which are relatively minor apart from such generic and therefore less distortionary measures as taxes on consumption or value added). That percentage is often referred to as the nominal rate of assistance to producers and the consumer tax equivalent affecting buyers (NRA and CTE, which are equal if the

only distortions are trade measures). It will be negative if an export tax or import subsidy or equivalent is the sole trade distortion. In the absence of externalities and market failures, maximizing national economic welfare for a small economy typically requires those NRAs/CTEs to be zero.[4]

Import restrictions are the most common trade distortion, predominantly tariffs but also NTBs from time to time. Export restrictions have been less common, but certainly were used widely to tax exports of primary products in many (especially newly independent) developing countries in the 1960s and 1970s. At the same time those countries also protected some of their import-competing farm industries, just as in high-income countries. Production restrictions are even less common, the most notable exception being their use by members of the Organization of the Petroleum Exporting Countries (OPEC) since 1973. Trade subsidies are least commonly used, apart from some farm export subsidies by high-income countries in the 1980s and 1990s.

Raising the price of importables relative to non-tradables and exportables would appreciate the currency and draw mobile resources from the export sector. An export subsidy of the same size as the tariff could neutralize the trade- and welfare-reducing effects of the latter, whereas an export tax would exacerbate them. Thus it is important to have estimates not only of the tariff rate on imports but also of any trade taxes (or subsidies) applying to exportables.

It is not only the mean trade tax rates that matter though. Also relevant is their dispersion across industries/products within each sector. The greater the dispersion in price distortions within any sector in which productive factors are mobile, or within any group of products that are substitutes in consumption, the more production and consumption patterns will have been affected and so the greater will be the welfare cost (Lloyd 1974; Laborde et al. 2011). In the longer term, when non-natural resources (labor and capital) are more mobile between sectors, it also matters if there is a divergence of NRAs inter-sectorally.

If one had access to a global economy-wide model for each year of interest, with a great deal of individual country coverage and industry and product detail, and

---

[4] See Bhagwati (1971) or Corden (1997). The national welfare calculus is more complex than in simple international economic textbooks but is fundamentally based on the sum of changes in consumer surplus, in producer surplus, in government tax revenues and in the country's terms of trade as a result of introducing or changing a trade-related policy (Martin 1997).

for which NRA and CTE estimates were available, the task of estimating the cost of trade-related policies that distort product prices would be straightforward. Such models have become increasingly common in recent years, although most rely on a single database, including for price distortion estimates, that has been compiled by the GTAP (Global Trade Analysis Project) consortium. Those models are being used not only for contemporary trade policy analysis but also to project forward to obtain cost estimates of prospective policies under specified assumptions about growth rates. However, they are not available for the earlier part of the twentieth century, for which cruder "guesstimates" based on sectoral average trade tax equivalent rates are relied upon.

Estimates of Trade Tax Equivalents in the Twentieth Century

The potential importance of various economies to global trade distortions is reflected not only in their trade tax equivalent rates but also in their shares of global GDP and trade (which are candidates for calculating weighted average trade tax rates across countries). Table 9.1 shows that Europe and North America accounted for around two-thirds of global GDP and international trade through most of the 1900s, with Asia's importance growing only in the last quarter of the century[5] and other developing countries accounting for barely one-sixth of world GDP and trade throughout that period.

Manufacturing and agriculture are the two main sectors producing tradables, with trade in minerals, energy, raw materials, and services being relatively minor until their trade costs began falling and fossil fuel prices rose in the last quarter of the twentieth century.[6] Thus agricultural and industrial price distortions matter most and will be the focus here.

Most distortions in manufacturing since 1900 can be captured by tariffs plus (especially from the early 1930s to the 1950s) the tariff equivalent of non-tariff import barriers. Unfortunately there are no comprehensive time-series of those NTBs, so reliance will be on tariffs while keeping in mind that these provide a lower-bound estimate of overall import protection to manufacturing, particularly in the middle one-third of the twentieth century. Even

the available tariff estimates are imprecise, for several reasons associated with the differing methodologies adopted by those compiling and averaging them (see Lloyd 2008): unweighted vs. trade-weighted vs. production- or consumption-weighted averaging across tariff lines, the inclusion of all or only dutiable lines, whether tariffs serving as excise taxes on imported product are included (as with alcohol and tobacco, for example), the way specific tariffs are converted to ad valorem rates (that is, from a volumetric to a percentage-of-border-price basis), and whether account is taken of differing rates for different supplying countries (due to preferential trading agreements, for example).

When seeking a sectoral average rate of tariff protection, ideally the dispersion of rates across the import-competing industries in the sector should be taken into account, since the welfare cost of a barrier is proportional to the square of the tariff rate. The best way to capture that for obtaining a stand-alone measure is to estimate a trade restrictiveness index (TRI), as has been done recently for the United States by Irwin (2010) using the Anderson and Neary (2005) methodology as adapted by Feenstra (1995). Typically such an index will exceed the trade-weighted average tariff on dutiable items, which in turn will exceed the average over all tariff lines. However, TRIs are not available for other countries over the time period being considered here, and they are not needed when an economy-wide model is available since the latter takes into account the dispersion in rates across the products in that model.[7]

Bearing those caveats in mind, Table 9.2 suggests that Europe's manufacturing import tariffs were

---

[5] China was almost completely closed for all but the last two decades of the twentieth century (Keller *et al.* 2010). In 1900 it accounted for 11% of global GDP (and a low of 5% in 1953), but up until the mid-1980s it accounted for only 1% of global trade (Table 9.1).

[6] Services and non-agricultural primary products each accounted for less than one-sixth of global trade prior to the 1960s, while manufactured products accounted for less than one-half, the rest being agricultural products (Haberler 1958; GATT 1978).

[7] Such a model requires tariffs to be aggregated to the product categories identified in the model though, and for that it is important to use the TRI concept in aggregating up from, say, the 6- or 10-digit tariff lines (Laborde, *et al.* 2011).

Table 9.1 Shares of world GDP and merchandise trade, by region, 1913 – 2050

a) GDP shares (percent, based on 1990 International Geary–Khamis dollars except last 2 columns)

	1900	1913	1953	1983	2008	2050[a]	2010[b]	2050[b]
Europe (incl. CIS)	47	47	39	35	23	14	33	24
United States + Canada	17	20	29	23	20	15	31	21
Australia + New Zealand	1	1	1	1	1	1	1	1
Japan	3	3	3	9	6	6	10	5
All high-income (+CIS)	**68**	**71**	**72**	**68**	**50**	**36**	**75**	**51**
Developing Asia	22	20	14	15	35	50	12	32
of which China	*11*	*9*	*5*	*6*	*17*	*50*	*6*	*19*
Latin America	5	4	8	9	8	7	6	7
Africa	3	3	4	4	3	3	2	5
Middle East	2	2	2	4	4	4	5	5
All developing	**32**	**29**	**28**	**32**	**50**	**64**	**25**	**49**
WORLD	100	100	100	100	100	100	100	100
Value (1990 $ billion)	*1.972*	*2.733*	*5,911*	*19,633*	*50,974*			

b) Trade shares (average of export and import shares, percent)

	1913	1953	1983	2008	2008 (excl. intra-EU27)
Europe (incl. CIS)	57	45	49	45	17
United States + Canada	14	22	18	13	18
Australia + New Zealand	1	1	1	1	2
Japan	2	2	8	5	6
All high-income (+CIS)	**74**	**70**	**76**	**64**	**43**
Developing Asia	10	9	9	22	35
of which China	*1*	*1*	*1*	*8*	*11*
Latin America	8	10	5	6	9
Africa	4	7	4	3	5
Middle East	4	4	6	5	8
All developing	**26**	**30**	**24**	**36**	**57**
WORLD	100	100	100	100	100
EU[c]			31	38	
GATT/WTO members[d]		68	90	95	

[a] Projections provided by the Copenhagen Consensus Center.
[b] Projections provided by van der Mensbrugghe and Rosen (2010), in 2004 US$.
[c] Six members in 1963, 10 in 1983, 27 in 2008.
[d] 23 countries in 1948, 103 by 1986, 153 by 2010.

Sources: GDP data from Maddison (2008); trade data from Woytinsky and Woytinsky (1955) for 1913, and otherwise from WTO (2010, Tables 1.6 and 1.7).

Table 9.2 Import tariffs (percent) on manufactures, key trading countries, 1902 – 1970

	1902	1913	1925	1937	1950	1955	1962	1970
Europe								
Austria		16	27		18			
Belgium	13	9	15	11	11	7	11	6
Czechoslovakia		18	27					
Denmark	19	14	10		3			
France	34	20	21	17	18	19[a]	11	6
Germany	25	13	20	14	26	16[a]	11	6
Greece					39			
Hungary		18	27					
Italy	27	18	22		25	24[a]	11	6
Netherlands	3	4	6				11	6
Norway	12			14	11	10		11
Poland			32					
Portugal					18			
Russia	131							
Spain	76	41	41					
Sweden	23	20	16	13	9	6	7	7
Switzerland	7	9	14	13		8		3
United Kingdom			17[b]		23	17[a]		
Yugoslavia			23					
Other high-income countries								
Australia	32[c]	31	31	45	25	22	22	24
New Zealand						21	22	23
Japan	1	20	13	11		14[b]	16	12
United States	54	30	24	28	12	11	12	9
Canada	17	26	23	16		12[b]	12	14
Developing countries								
Argentina		28	29					
Brazil[d]		40[e]			70	29		
Chile					34	39		
India	3	4	16	29		30		

[a] 1952.
[b] 1931.
[c] 1903–04.
[d] Import duties as a percent of the value of imports were (often well) above 30% in 1913 also for Paraguay, Peru, Uruguay and Venezuela, according to Bulmer-Thomas (1994, pp. 141–142).

Sources: League of Nations (1927), Little *et al.* (1970), Woytinsky and Woytinsky (1955), Maizels (1963), Irwin (2010, Table A1) for the United States, Lloyd (2008, Table 5) for Australia and, for other 1970 estimates, GATT (1972).

mostly in the range 12–34% as of 1902 (and 9–20% as of 1913), key exceptions being Spain and Russia. The United States had very high industrial tariffs around that time (54% in 1902, 30% in 1913), but they were cut far more than Europe's by 1955 when they were slightly below those in the countries that formed Europe's Common Market (later to become the European Union). By contrast, industrial tariffs in Australia, New Zealand, and many developing countries had been rising over that period and by the mid-

1950s/early 1960s were two or three times those of Europe and North America.

In the middle of that period, however, was a rapid escalation of trade barriers that contributed nontrivially to the Great Depression of the early 1930s. That sudden beggar-thy-neighbor protectionism is not evident on the tariff estimates for 1925 and 1937 in Table 9.2, but can be seen in Table 9.3: between 1927 and 1931 the unweighted average across European countries of their tariffs on

Table 9.3 Import tariffs (percent) on food and manufactures, Western and Central European countries, 1913, 1927, 1931, and 1950

	Food				Manufactures	
	1913	1927	1931	1950	1927	1931
Austria	29	17	60	36	21	28
Belgium	26	12	24	7	12	13
Bulgaria	25	79	133		75	90
Czechoslovakia	29	36	84		36	37
Denmark				1		
Finland	49	58	102		18	23
France	29	19	53	27	26	29
Germany	22	27	83	27	19	18
Greece				45		
Hungary	29	32	60		32	43
Italy	22	25	66	22	28	42
Norway				8		
Poland	67	72	110		56	52
Portugal				42		
Romania	35	46	88		49	55
Spain	42	45	81		63	76
Sweden	24	22	39	5	21	24
Switzerland	15	22	42		18	22
United Kingdom				9		
Yugoslavia	32	44	75		28	33
Unweighted average of above	32	37	65	21	33	39
United States					26	35[a]
Australia					33	63

[a] 1932

Source: Liepmann (1938), plus Woytinsky and Woytinsky (1955, p. 285) for 1950 food, Irwin (2010, Table A1) for the United States and Lloyd (2008, Table 5) for Australia.

manufactures rose from 33% to 39%, while it rose in the United States from 26% to a peak of 35% and in Australia from 33% to 63%. Tariffs on foods rose even more, almost doubling in Europe to 65%. They gradually came down through the latter 1930s though, before war interrupted trade; and by 1950 those rates were only about one-third of their peaks in the early 1930s.

Import tariffs in developing countries are less well documented, but Clemens and Williamson (2010) generate an index of them for 17 of the largest developing countries (accounting for 76% of developing country GDP in 1900), for the period from 1870 to 1938. Their index is simply import tariff revenue as a percentage of the value of total imports, and so may understate considerably the true tariff average. For those developing countries in that period, most tariffs and imports were manufactured goods. The estimates, reported in Table 9.4, suggest Asia has been much less

Table 9.4 Import tariffs on manufactures, major developing countries, 1870–1938: import duties as a percent of total imports

	1870–99	1900–13	1913–38	Weight, based on GDP in 1900
Asia				
China	3	3	11	41.1
India	3	5	17	32.1
Indonesia	5	5	10	6.0
Myanmar	4	11	23	1.5
Philippines	10	21	8	0.9
Sri Lanka	6	7	13	0.9
Thailand	4	7	15	1.1
Average, Asia[a]	4	5	13	83.6
Latin America				
Argentina	26	23	18	2.5
Brazil	35	40	23	2.3
Chile	19	18	22	1.1
Colombia	34	47	29	0.8
Cuba	23	26	26	0.4
Mexico	17	22	21	3.5
Peru	32	23	16	0.6
Uruguay	30	33	20	0.4
Average, Latin America[a]	25	28	21	11.5
Egypt	11	14	26	1.9
Turkey	7	10	31	2.8
Average, all 17[a]	7	8	15	100

[a] Averages are weighted by this chapter's author, using 1900 GDP as weights (see final column), from Maddison (2008). This set of countries accounts for 76% of all of today's developing country GDP in 1900, which in turn is 35% of global GDP in 1900.

Source: Clemens and Williamson (2010, Table 8).

protectionist of its manufacturing sector than Latin America before 1940, just as it was in the post-war period. Those rates for Latin America are well above those for the higher-income countries reported in Table 9.2.

As for primary agriculture, there has been a general tendency for poor agrarian economies to tax the farm sector relative to other sectors but, as nations industrialize, to gradually change from negatively to positively assisting farmers relative to other producers (and from subsidizing to taxing food consumers). Following the famous repeal of Britain's Corn Laws in the mid-1840s and the passage of the 1860 Anglo-French Treaty of Commerce, Britain moved close to freer trade in farm (and other) products followed by France and gradually other European countries. However, agricultural protection returned before the end of the nineteenth century to some European countries, and became widespread in the early 1930s (Kindleberger 1975, 1989; Swinnen 2010). In contrast to tariffs on manufactures, however, agricultural protectionism increased further over the next five decades.

Japan provides a striking example of the tendency to switch from taxing to increasingly assisting agriculture relative to other industries. Its industrialization began later than Europe's, after the opening up of the economy following the Meiji Restoration in 1868. By 1900 Japan had switched from being a small net exporter of food to becoming increasingly dependent on imports of rice (its main staple food and responsible for more than half the value of domestic food production). This led to calls from farmers and their supporters for rice import controls. Those calls were matched by equally vigorous calls from manufacturing and commercial groups for unrestricted food trade, since the price of rice at that time was a major determinant of real wages and hence profitability

in the non-farm sector. The heated debates were not unlike those that led to the repeal of the Corn Laws in Britain six decades earlier. In Japan, however, the forces of protection triumphed, and a tariff was imposed on rice imports from 1904. That tariff then gradually rose over time, raising the domestic price of rice to more than 30% above the import price during World War I. The Japanese government then extended its protection to its colonies of Korea and Taiwan, shifting from a national to an imperial rice self-sufficiency policy. By the latter 1930s imperial rice prices were more than 60% above those in international markets (Anderson and Tyers 1992).

After the Pacific War ended and Japan lost its colonies, its agricultural protection growth resumed and spread from rice to an ever-wider range of farm products. In South Korea and Taiwan in the 1950s, as in many newly independent developing countries, an import-substituting industrialization strategy was initially adopted, which harmed agriculture. But in those two economies – unlike in most other developing countries – that policy was replaced in the early 1960s with a more neutral trade policy and then from the 1970s with ever-higher levels of protection of farmers from import protection (Anderson and Hayami 1986, Ch. 2).

The other high-income countries that were settled by Europeans are far less densely populated. They therefore have had a strong comparative advantage in farm products for most of their history following Caucasian settlement, and so have felt less need to protect their farmers than Europe or North-east Asia.

Many less advanced and less rapidly growing developing countries not only adopted import-substituting industrialization strategies from the 1930s and especially in the 1950s and 1960s (Little et al. 1970; Balassa and Associates 1971) but also imposed direct taxes on their exports of farm products.[8] It was common in the 1950s and 1960s and in some cases through to the 1980s for developing countries to use dual or multiple exchange rates as well, thereby indirectly taxing both exporters and importers (Bhagwati 1978; Krueger 1978). This added to the anti-trade bias of developing countries' trade policies. By the early 1980s, however, both high-income and developing countries began to

---

[8] The precise extent of taxation of agriculture in developing countries as a group prior to the 1950s is not yet well documented, but is at least hinted at in Lindert (1991). Certainly it was occurring in Latin America (Bulmer-Thomas 1994; Bértola and Williamson 2006), Africa (Bates 1981), as well as in the Soviet Union and China where farmers were squeezed more than urban dwellers to fund State activities and the industrialization drive (Sah and Stiglitz 1992; Lin et al. 1996).

lower their barriers to agricultural trade, including not just import tariffs but also export restrictions that were imposed in the 1960s and 1970s on numerous farm products in developing countries.

A recent World Bank project has captured the extent of those changes since 1955 for a sample of 75 countries accounting for more than 90% of the global economy, and for both agricultural and non-agricultural tradable goods (K. Anderson 2009). That study suggests industrial tariffs by the first half of the 1980s were already low in high-income countries, while they had risen to quite high levels in developing countries (NRAs of 3% vs 35%). Table 9.5 shows that two decades later, however, they not only were reduced further in high-income countries but also were substantially lowered in developing countries (to just 6%). As for agricultural trade distortions, high-income countries lowered their export subsidies (a two-thirds drop, from 22% to 7%) but retained high barriers to imports so their overall agricultural NRA fell, from 56% to 34%.[9] Meanwhile developing countries since the mid-1980s have lowered their export taxes (from 41% to 3%) but raised their tariffs on farm imports (from 17% to 23%), and Europe's transition economies' rates are converging on those in the European Union for both agriculture and manufacturing.

Even though these average NRAs for recent years may not seem very high, it needs to be kept in mind that within each sector of each country there is a great deal of dispersion in rates of assistance across various farm and non-farm industries. There is also a wide range of sectoral NRAs across the sample of 75 countries – and an even wider range when the relatively high distortions of many small least-developed countries not in that sample are taken into account (Anderson 2010, Ch. 2). The only feasible way to estimate the global welfare effects of that cross-product and cross-country dispersion of NRAs (and CTEs) is to employ global computable general equilibrium modeling. Such modeling can correctly capture the welfare effects of not only the intra- and inter-sectoral dispersion of price distortions within a country, but also of the effects of those and other countries' policies on each country's international terms of trade.

Before turning to such modeling, one final point needs to be made about price-distorting policies. It relates not to their longer-run trends but rather to their NRA changes from year to year as international product prices fluctuate. This is not a major issue for manufactured goods, apart from occasional use of anti-dumping duties on select products by a small (albeit growing) number of countries (Finger 2002). For agricultural products, by contrast, their annual changes in NRAs tend to be negatively correlated with movements in their international price, especially for food staples of developing countries. This is particularly evident when prices suddenly spike up or down, but it applies more broadly as well. It results from countries varying their trade barrier in the hope of not transmitting an international price shock to their domestic market: when the international price rises, importers lower their tariff and exporters raise their export tax (as happened in 2008), and when the international price falls the opposite tends to occur (Anderson and Nelgen 2012). The irony is that if both exporting and importing countries sought thereby to fully insulate their domestic market from the exogenous shock such as a crop shortfall, neither would succeed as the world trade volume would be the same as if neither country altered their trade barrier; yet both would cause the international price to spike more, so there would be an even larger transfer of welfare between importing and exporting countries than that due just to the initial external shock (Martin and Anderson 2012).[10] This is especially so for products in which most key countries are close to self-sufficient and so

[9] Domestic producer subsidies also were rife in high-income countries, but made a relatively small contribution to trade distortions compared with border measures (Anderson et al. 2006a; Anderson and Croser 2011).

[10] Large welfare transfers also occur between countries that are net exporters and net importers of fossil fuels. The transfer has been predominantly from importers to exporters since OPEC introduced production quotas in 1973, which caused petroleum prices to quadruple (and to double again in 1979–80). But net importing countries that are unilaterally taxing carbon emissions explicitly or implicitly for local and global pollution reasons are causing the opposite terms of trade effect. Since OPEC's quotas are not subject to international disciplines in the same way tariffs are under the GATT, and since without OPEC quotas other countries might have raised their consumption taxes on petroleum products earlier for pollution reasons, this distortion will not be considered below.

Table 9.5 Nominal rates of assistance (percent) to agricultural and non-agricultural tradables, by region, 1955–2004

	1955–59	1960–64	1965–69	1970–74	1975–79	1980–84	1985–89	1990–94	1995–99	2000–04
Developing countries[a]										
NRA agriculture	na	−24	−27	−32	−26	−21	−16	−4	4	7
exportables	na	−47	−45	−45	−44	−41	−36	−19	−6	−3
import-competing	na	13	14	8	13	17	38	23	22	23
NRA non-agriculture tradables	na	58	60	46	37	35	27	17	10	6
European transition economies										
NRA agriculture	na	na	na	na	na	na	na	10	18	16
exportables	na	na	na	na	na	na	na	−3	−1	−1
import-competing	na	na	na	na	na	na	na	33	35	36
NRA non-agriculture tradables	na	na	na	na	na	na	na	10	6	5
High-income countries										
NRA agriculture	23	31	37	27	35	43	56	48	37	34
exportables	4	7	14	10	11	12	22	16	8	7
import-competing	31	46	50	37	47	58	71	62	54	51
NRA non-agriculture tradables	7.5	8.5	7.7	5.4	3.6	3.4	3.2	2.5	1.7	1.3
World[a]										
NRA agriculture	na	6	8	1	3	6	19	20	18	19
exportables	na	-23	-20	-23	-25	-24	-17	-7	-1	0
import-competing	na	35	37	27	34	38	57	43	38	36
NRA non-agriculture tradables	na	19	21	16	14	10	10	8	6	4

[a] Estimates for China pre-1981 and India pre-1965 are based on the assumption that the agricultural NRAs in those years were the same as the average NRA estimates for those countries for 1981–84 and 1965–69, respectively, and that the value of production in those missing years is that which gives the same average share of value of production in total world production in 1981–84 and 1965–69, respectively.

Source: Author's derivation, using data in Anderson and Valenzuela (2008), based on a sample of more than 40 developing countries and more than 12 of Europe's transition economies in addition to all OECD member countries.

the share of global production traded internationally is small, as with rice. Large though the welfare transfer effects can be in any price spike year, they tend to be short-lived and to be offset by transfers in the opposite direction when the international price of the product spikes the other way. For that reason such fluctuations in NRAs around their longer-term trends will be ignored in the analysis below.

Modeling the Welfare Effects of Trade Barriers

The easiest years to estimate the welfare effects of trade-distorting policies are recent ones to which the databases of global economy-wide models have been calibrated. We therefore begin with that period. Such models have also been used to project prospective effects in future decades under various assumptions, so they will be considered next, before turning to the earlier decades of the twentieth century.

The so-called Global Trade, Assistance, and Production (GTAP) database is by far the most widely used by global economic modelers, providing data for more than 100 countries and country groups spanning the world. Its current version is for 2004 (Narayanan and Walmsley 2008). The price distortions in that database have been carefully compiled from 6-digit applied bilateral tariff data, thereby taking account of preferential tariffs due to regional and other sub-global trade agreements that have grown so much over recent years. They also incorporate the production and export subsidy estimates for high-income countries, as compiled by OECD (2006). They do not, however, capture the other measures that distort developing country production and consumption of farm products, most notably export taxes and various NTBs that can only be estimated by careful comparison of domestic and border prices. Thus in the case of agriculture in developing countries, the distortion levels in the GTAP database have been replaced with an alternative set based on the NRAs estimated for 2004 that have come from the recent World Bank project (Anderson and Valenzuela 2008), as calibrated by Valenzuela and Anderson (2008). For comparison purposes Valenzuela and Anderson also show the distortions as they were in 1980–84 on average, to

get a sense of the reform that has taken place since then and allow modelers to use backcasting to estimate the effects of those reforms.

According to this amended data set, the weighted average applied tariff in 2004 for agriculture and lightly processed food was 21.8% for developing countries and 22.3% for high-income countries, while for non-farm goods it was 7.5% for developing countries and just 1.2% for high-income countries.

Though export subsidies for farm products for a few high-income regions and export taxes in a few developing countries were still in place in 2004, these measures are generally small in their impact compared with tariffs, as are production subsidies and taxes (Valenzuela *et al.* 2009, Table 13). While those average rates obscure large variations across countries and commodities, the effects of the dispersion are captured in the economy-wide models used because of the detailed country and commodity disaggregation in such models.

The model whose results are to be drawn on for the contemporary period (and also prospectively, for 2050, and retrospectively, for 1980–84) is the World Bank's global model known as Linkage (van der Mensbrugghe 2005). For more than a decade, this publicly available model has formed the basis for the World Bank's standard long-term projections of the world economy and for much of its trade (and more recently migration) policy analysis. In the application summarized below, the full database has been aggregated to 24 sectors and 52 regions to make computations and reporting more manageable.

Linkage is a relatively straightforward computable general equilibrium (CGE) model but with some characteristics that distinguish it from other comparative static models such as the GTAP model (described in Hertel 1997). Factor stocks are fixed, which means in the case of labor that the extent of unemployment (if any) in the baseline remains unchanged. Producers minimize costs subject to constant returns to scale in production technology, consumers maximize utility, and all markets – including for labor – are cleared with flexible prices. There are three types of production structures. Crop sectors reflect the substitution possibilities between extensive and intensive farming; livestock sectors reflect the substitution possibilities between pasture and intensive feeding; and all other sectors reflect standard capital and labor substitution. There are two types of labor, skilled and unskilled, and the total employment of each is assumed to be fixed (meaning no change in their unemployment levels). There is a single representative household per modeled region, allocating income to consumption using the extended linear expenditure system. Trade is modeled using a nested structure in which aggregate import demand is the outcome of allocating domestic absorption between domestic goods and aggregate imports, and then aggregate import demand is allocated across source countries to determine the bilateral trade flows (Armington 1969).

Government fiscal balances are fixed in US$ terms in Linkage, with the fiscal objective being met by changing the level of lump-sum taxes on households. This implies that losses of tariff revenues are replaced by higher direct taxes on households. The current account balance also is fixed. Given that other external financial flows are fixed, this implies that ex ante changes to the trade balance are reflected in ex post changes to the real exchange rate. For example, if import tariffs are reduced, the propensity to import increases and additional imports are financed by increasing export revenues. The latter typically is achieved by a depreciation of the real exchange rate. Finally, investment is driven by savings. With fixed public and foreign saving, investment comes from changes in the savings behavior of households and from changes in the unit cost of investment. The model solves only for relative prices, with the numeraire, or price anchor, being the export price index of manufactured exports from high-income countries. This price is fixed at unity in the base year.

Only comparative static results are reported in this section, so it needs to be kept in mind that they do not include the (often much larger) dynamic gains that result from an acceleration in investment that would accompany a reduction in trade barriers. And because the version of the Linkage model reported here assumes perfect competition and constant returns to scale, it captures none of the benefits of freeing markets that came from accelerated productivity growth, scale economies, product variety, and the creation of new markets. There is also a dampening effect on estimates of welfare gains

from trade because of product and regional aggregation, which hides many of the differences in NRAs and CTEs across products and countries. The results therefore should be treated as providing lower-bound estimates of the net economic welfare benefits from policy reform, as is true of most currently available models (see Anderson and Winters 2009; Francois and Martin 2010). An attempt is made in the chapter's penultimate section to provide an order of magnitude of the extent to which the reported estimates should be raised to account for these missing elements in the calculus.

Cost of Trade Barriers as of 2004

What do the results show? Valenzuela et al. (2009) estimate that the gains from the removal of trade barriers as of 2004 could have added US$168 billion per year to the global economy. That is equivalent to 0.6% of the world's real income that year. They find that developing economies were being harmed by those policies nearly twice as much as were high-income economies on a percent of real income basis in 2004 (0.9% vs. 0.5%). They also find that 70% of those costs globally, and 72% of those to developing countries, are due to agricultural policies, thanks to the huge price distortions that remain in markets for farm products as compared with those in manufacturing. For developing countries, 57% of the costs stem from policies of developing countries themselves, and the other 43% from policies of high-income countries.

Cost of Trade Barriers in 2050 if Policies as of 2004 Are Unchanged

If policies as of 2004 were to remain in place until 2050, and given the projected faster growth of developing than high-income countries, liberalization of those trade barriers in 2050 would generate an even larger proportional gain to developing countries. According to results using the same global Linkage model as Valenzuela et al. (2009), a new study by van der Mensbrugghe and Rosen (2010) estimates that the gain to developing countries would amount to a real income improvement of 1.4% per year, compared with again 0.5% for high-income countries and thus 0.9% globally.[11] This global number is slightly larger than in 2004, even though rates of price distortions are assumed to be unchanged, because the developing countries are projected to grow in relative importance in the global economy and they were suffering relatively more in 2004 from trade barriers at that time, particularly as it affected South–South trade.

However, it is unlikely that trade-related policies will not change over the next four decades. We therefore consider two alternative scenarios in the next subsection. They provide an opportunity to amend the above numbers for 2050 down or up, according to whether one assumes policies will distort prices of tradables less or more in four decades than now. A key uncertainty is the WTO's Doha Round of multilateral trade negotiations.

Cost of Trade Barriers in 2050 if Policies Become More Liberal (Low Protection Case)

If the WTO's Doha Development Agenda were to be revived and eventually come to a successful conclusion such that the most comprehensive set of policy reform proposals as of 2008 were to be implemented, it would lock in recent reforms through lowered bindings on tariffs and subsidies and possibly lead to further opening of markets for services. The lower legal bindings would prevent temporary or long-term backsliding into protectionism (Francois and Martin 2004), and in addition there would be net gains from the phased liberalization itself. A study by Anderson *et al.* (2006a), again using the global Linkage model and hence again ignoring pro-competitive and dynamic gains from trade reform, suggests economic welfare in both developing and high-income countries would be around 0.2% higher after full implementation of the agreement (which would take until the early 2020s at least). A similar number has emerged from a forthcoming update of that study projected to 2025 (Martin and Mattoo 2011).

If the Doha Round did conclude so successfully, it would be reason to expect yet another WTO round of reform commitments to be concluded

and implemented by 2050. There would not be much liberalization of trade in manufactures to be done by high-income countries, but there would be ample scope for gains from reducing regulations in their services sectors as well as from providing greater market access in farm products. Hence another 0.2% of GDP gain could be expected for those countries. The scope for further gains from a successor to Doha is much greater for developing countries. Large middle-income countries in particular might be expected to forgo the "Special and Differential Treatment" still afforded developing country members of WTO, especially those also seeking membership of the OECD. That could lead to the gains (reduced costs) to developing countries of perhaps twice that estimated for the Doha Round, that is, an extra 0.4% of GDP from 2025 or a total of 0.6% of developing country GDP between 2004 and 2050.

In this liberal (low protection) scenario, the van der Mensbrugghe and Rosen (2010) estimates of the cost of barriers in 2050 could be adjusted downwards by the extent of those gains from trade reform, that is, to 0.8% for developing countries, 0.1% for high-income countries, and 0.5% globally (penultimate column of Table 9.6b).

Cost of Trade Barriers in 2050 if Policies Become Less Liberal (High Protection Case)

Alternatively, what if the Doha Round of multilateral trade negotiations were to collapse and there were no other external trade barrier disciplines placed on national governments? The trade policy counterfactual in that case may not be the status quo. Manufacturing tariffs may not change a lot, especially in middle- and high-income countries where applied tariffs are close to the relatively low rates at which countries bound them as part of the

[11] That projections study is based on 2004 US $. The developing country shares of global GDP on that basis are shown in Table 9.2 to differ from those based on Geary–Khamis dollars, but the proportional changes in developing country shares between the present decade and four decades hence are very similar and so no adjustment is made to the van der Mensbrugghe and Rosen (2010) estimates.

Table 9.6 Assumed NRAs and their estimated welfare cost to developing and high-income countries,[a] 1900–2050

(a) NRAs (percent)

	1900	1925	1931	1937	1962	1982	2004	2050 Low	2050 High
Developing countries									
NRA agriculture	−15	−15	5	−14	−24	−21	9	6	19
exportables	−20	−20	0	−20	−47	−41	0	0	0
import-competing	5	5	20	10	13	17	22	16	46
NRA non-agriculture tradables	10	15	30	30	58	35	8	4	8
High-income countries[b]									
NRA agriculture	10	10	30	30	31	43	16	9	15
exportables	0	0	0	0	7	12	7	0	5
import-competing	15	15	50	45	46	58	22	14	22
NRA non-agriculture tradables	30	23	37	21	11	3	1	1	1

(b) Lower-bound estimates of welfare cost (percent of GDP), extrapolated from simplest global economy-wide model for 2004

	1900	1925	1931	1937	1962	1982	2004	2050 Low	2050 High
Developing countries	0.8	0.9	2.8	1.7	2.2	1.9	0.9	0.8	1.8
High-income countries[b]	1.1	1.0	2.7	1.9	1.4	1.2	0.5	0.1	0.5
World	1.0	1.0	2.7	1.8	1.6	1.4	0.6	0.5	1.2

(c) Amended estimates of welfare cost (percent of GDP), after adjusting for some elements missing from the simplest global economy-wide modeling[c]

	1900	1925	1931	1937	1962	1982	2004	2050 Low	2050 High
Developing countries	3.1	3.4	10.7	6.5	9.2	8.6	4.3	3.8	8.6
High-income countries[b]	4.2	3.8	10.3	7.3	5.9	5.4	2.4	0.5	2.4
World	3.8	3.8	10.3	6.9	6.7	6.3	2.9	2.4	5.7

[a] The weights used to obtain regional and global averages for 1900 to 1937 are as follows: exportables are four-fifths of agriculture in developing countries and one-third in high-income countries; and developing countries are one-quarter of both global agriculture and global non-agricultural tradables. The NRAs for 1962 and 1982 are the averages for the 5-year periods 1960–64 and 1980–84, respectively. The "Low" and "High" in the final two columns refer to whether it is assumed that price distortions from trade barriers fall or rise between 2004 and 2050, as shown in the final two columns of part (a) above.
[b] High-income countries include Eastern Europe and the former Soviet Union (whose NRAs are assumed to equal the averages for high-income countries).
[c] Based on guesstimates of the impact of missing elements discussed in the text, from which the cost of trade barriers are made so as to be able to multiply the estimates in part (b) to obtain those in part (c) above (which do not include any adjustment for the growth dividend expected to result from openness).

Source: Author's compilation from Tables 9.2 and 9.3 and from global Linkage model results and as described in text.

Uruguay Round. Even in lower-income countries there is now a broad consensus that industrial openness is sensible in today's globalized world of fragmented production processes. As for agricultural distortions, export restrictions are likely to remain low apart from their sporadic use in times of upward spikes in international prices, and export subsidies may well be used less as high-income countries continue their move towards more targeted forms of farm income support (particularly in the EU as it gradually absorbs the new East European members). That same political force may restrain high-income countries from raising their agricultural import tariffs, even if it is insufficient, without external pressure from a new WTO agreement to lower them. In rapidly growing developing countries, by contrast, their continuing industrial and service sector growth and urbanization is in many cases being accompanied by social tensions as rural areas feel left behind. Such countries may therefore follow the earlier example of today's high-income countries in allowing agricultural protection rates to rise (Anderson and Nelgen 2011). Since the per capita income of developing countries is projected by 2050 to be similar to that of high-income countries in the early 1980s, the latter's NRA for import-competing agriculture at that time (58%) might provide a guide as to what to expect. However, developing countries already have binding commitments in the WTO that prevent their average tariff from legally rising much above 45% (Bouët and Laborde 2010). We therefore have chosen the high-income countries' NRA for import-competing agriculture in 1960–64 (46%) as the counterfactual for developing countries in 2050 in the event of no further disciplines being agreed to in the WTO before then.

With those assumed distortions rates for 2050 (see final column of Table 9.6a), the van der Mensbrugghe and Rosen (2010) estimates of the cost of developing countries' barriers in 2050 need to be adjusted upwards to some extent. Bearing in mind that in 2004 agricultural policies were responsible for no less than 70% of the cost of all goods market distortions for developing countries and for the world, the doubling of the agricultural distortions in developing countries by 2050 would add substantially to the cost of distortions to those countries. For present purposes we assume it would rise from 1.4% to 1.8%. It would also add a little to the cost to high-income countries that are net exporters of farm products, but we assume that would be exactly offset by the improved terms of trade for high-income food-importing countries. That is, the cost of barriers in this case would be 0.5% for high-income countries (as in 2004) and thus 1.2% globally (final column of Table 9.6b).

Cost in 2004 if Price-Distorting Policies Had not Changed since 1980–84

According to the global distortions data set as amended by Valenzuela and Anderson (2008), in 1980–84 developing countries had an average agricultural export tax of 11% compared with almost zero on average in 2004, while high-income countries had an average farm export subsidy of 21% in 1980–84 compared with just 7% in 2004. The average agricultural import tariff was lower for developing countries (16%) in 1980–84 than for high-income countries (26%), as opposed to the situation in 2004 when the two groups of countries had equivalent average tariffs on farm products of 22%. In addition, tariffs on non-agricultural imports were more than three times higher in 1980–84 than in 2004 for developing countries (26% vs. 8%), and twice as high for high-income countries but still small at an average of 2.4% as compared with 1.2% in 2004 (Valenzuela, et al. 2009, Table 13.1).

How much higher would have been the cost of trade barriers if the national policies in 2004 had instead been those that were in place in 1980–84? The Linkage model results reported in Valenzuela et al. (2009, Table 13.2) suggest that global welfare would have been lower by US$233 billion per year, or by 0.8%. Again, developing countries would have been hurt disproportionately, by 1.0% compared with 0.7% for high-income countries. These numbers, in conjunction with the earlier ones for 2004 policies, suggest that between 1980–84 and 2004 the world had come about three-fifths of the way towards free markets for goods. They imply that in 1980–84 the cost of global distortions would have been around 1.4% of global income, made up of 1.9% for developing countries and 1.2% for high-income countries. These higher numbers reflect not only the much higher rates of price distortion in the early 1980s than recently but also the facts that (a) welfare costs are proportional to the square of the price distortion rates and (b) developing countries accounted for just 32% of global GDP in 1982 (the proxy for 1980–84) compared with 46% in 2004.

Cost of Price-Distorting Policies prior to 1980

According to Table 9.6a, the extent of import protection in 1962 was slightly less than in 1982 for agriculture but much higher for manufacturing in both rich and poor countries. That would have been even more hampering for both North–North and South–North trade in manufactures. We therefore assume it would have raised the proportional cost of trade barriers by one-seventh for both groups of countries compared with 1982, hence to 1.6% of GDP globally for 1962.

The high-income countries' agricultural distortions in 1937 were similar to those in 1962, while their manufacturing tariffs averaged about twice those of 1962 (the latter having been lowered following the first few rounds of multilateral trade negotiations under the GATT). In developing countries, protection rates in 1937 were around half those of 1962, but the heavy taxation of agricultural exports that followed in the wake of those countries' independence around 1960 was also much less prior to World War II. That lesser export taxation helped high-income countries via better international terms of trade, offsetting somewhat the welfare-reducing effect for high-income countries of their higher manufacturing protection. The cost of global trade barriers in 1937 is thus assumed to be one-quarter lower for developing countries, and one-third higher for high-income countries, than in 1962.

The assumed agricultural distortion rates in 1925 were only one-third those in 1937 for high-income countries, while developing country manufacturing protection was only half that of 1937. That meant productive resources were far more efficiently employed globally in that earlier year, and so the welfare costs are assumed to be barely half as large in 1925 as in 1937 as a share of GDP. In 1900 manufacturing protection was higher in rich countries and lower in developing countries than in 1925 while agricultural distortions on average appear to

have been similar. That would suggest a slightly greater welfare cost for high-income countries and a slightly smaller one for developing countries.

The worst year of the Great Depression, 1931, was an outlier. Agricultural protection rates were more than three times, and manufacturing protection as much as double, their 1925 rates. Export taxation evaporated temporarily though, as is commonly the case when international food prices slump (Anderson and Nelgen 2012). Since the welfare cost is proportional to the square of the distortion rate, the welfare cost for both developing and high-income countries would have briefly spiked at nearly three times the 1925 cost as a percent of GDP.

Adjusting for Elements Missing from the Calculus

The above estimates of the costs of global trade barriers are based on the estimates for 2004 using a standard global economy-wide model (GTAP). That standard calculus is known to underestimate trade barrier costs for several reasons that relate to the following:[12]

- The measurement of the tariff equivalent of non-tariff barriers to goods trade
- The averaging of tariffs at the detailed tariff line level for use at a more aggregated level by CGE modelers
- The measurement of distortions in markets for services and their incorporation in CGE models
- The effect of allowing financial market integration
- The inclusion of economies of scale and imperfect competition in some sectors
- Allowing for product quality and variety differences, and for the emergence of new products
- Administration, compliance and lobbying costs and, perhaps most importantly
- The growth-enhancing impacts of trade openness.

When lower-bound guesstimates for all but the last of these are used to multiply the costs of global trade barriers in Table 9.6b – as discussed in the remainder of this section – they become those shown in Table 9.6c. Adding the dynamic gains is problematic, though, because they involve an increase in the annual *rate of growth* of capital

---

[12] If trade reforms were to be accompanied by reforms to domestic markets, the gains from trade opening would be further magnified, but this is ignored here. So too is greater freedom of movement for workers through less restrictive immigration policies (but see Anderson and Winters 2009).

and outputs, not just a permanent one-off increase in the *level* of GDP. Its continued omission almost certainly ensures that even the adjusted numbers in Table 9.6c are still very much lower-bound estimates of the retrospective and prospective costs of the world's trade barriers.

Measuring the costs of trade barriers/benefits of trade liberalization is still an inexact science, despite the improvements since the 1950s in quantifying the extent of price distortions due to trade-related policies and the huge amount of progress made over the past two decades in global economy-wide (CGE) modeling. The remainder of this section illustrates how the progress made is drawn upon to adjust the estimates in Table 9.6.

Non-Tariff Barriers (NTBs) to Goods Trade

It has long been recognized that the only practical way for NTBs to be incorporated comprehensively in global economic models is for their ad valorem tariff equivalent to be estimated through comparing domestic and border prices of like products (Baldwin 1991). This is inherently difficult and enormously time-consuming, which is why it tends to have been done only for a small sample of countries or products (Laird 1997). Fortunately there is now a set of NRA estimates from 1955 to 2007 for global agriculture that is based on price comparisons and so includes NTBs (Anderson and Valenzuela 2008), and those estimates have been incorporated in the Linkage model that is drawn on for the present study. Hence NRA adjustments need to be made only for manufacturing and for pre-1955 agriculture.

A study for four high-income countries by Roningen and Yeats (1976) suggests that the average tariff equivalents of NTBs on manufactures in 1973 were at least twice the average tariffs at that time, making the latter largely redundant other than for revenue collecting. The difference would have been at least as high in 1962 because NTBs were still being used for balance-of-payment reasons under fixed exchange rates, and could have been even higher in the beggar-thy-neighbor period of the 1930s, if not earlier. A more comprehensive study of 16 high-income countries, accounting for 60% of

world imports, reveals that NTBs became more extensively used in the early 1980s. This followed the conclusion of the GATT's Tokyo Round in 1979 when those countries' tariffs had been lowered to an average of less than 8%, compared with five times that in the mid-1930s (Nogues *et al.* 1986). The most prevalent were probably the import quotas and "voluntary" export restraints on textiles and clothing trade, but trade in cars and steel also were commonly restricted with quantitative measures. Since the mid-1980s many of these measures have gradually disappeared in high-income countries and to a lesser extent in developing countries.

Adjustments to the NRAs in Table 9.6a to include the tariff equivalent of NTBs might involve doubling those for manufactured goods from 1930 with more modest rises before that, and doubling those for import-competing farm products prior to 1940. The anti-agricultural bias of policies in the pre-World War II era might thereby not be altered greatly. As for the post-war era (for which NTBs on farm products are already incorporated in the NRAs in Table 9.6), the boost to manufacturing protection from NTBs would exacerbate the anti-agricultural bias in developing countries but reduce the pro-agricultural bias in high-income countries. These two effects might be offsetting. However, the anti-trade bias of policies in 1962 and 1982 would increase within sectors in both sets of countries.

Averaging of Tariffs for Including in Models

In the Linkage model application cited in this study, the world economy has been aggregated to just 24 sectors or product groups and 52 countries or country groups. This has a number of consequences. One is that it restricts the extent to which the model can capture the reality that firms in a policy-reforming environment could exploit the increasing opportunities to lower costs through the recent fragmentation of the production process into ever more pieces whose location is footloose internationally (Hanson *et al.* 2005). A more fundamental consequence is that it requires the averaging of price distortions from trade policy measures. This matters because trade barriers vary enormously across 10-digit tariff lines and across countries, and the cost of protection increases with the square of the tariff. Hiding that variation thereby leads to underestimation of the true cost of any given "average" level of protection.

Necessarily, some degree of aggregation is unavoidable in modeling the real world because the available information on the structure of production and consumption is at a much higher level of aggregation than information on tariffs and trade. Further aggregation is necessarily employed for computational reasons too.

Commonly tariffs are averaged using import values as weights. This adds an additional problem because, as protection rates rise, the weights associated with these measures decline, so that a tariff that completely blocks trade has the same measured impact as a zero tariff.

A relatively new approach to tariff aggregation provides a possible means of dealing with the aggregation problem (Anderson and Neary 2005). Since then J. E. Anderson (2009) has developed a superior tariff aggregator that captures the welfare impacts of a non-uniform tariff regime. Building on this approach, Laborde et al. (2011) generate a set of national tariff aggregates at the level used by CGE modelers in which the aggregate tariff for a product group is that which, if applied uniformly to all the tariff lines in that group, would allow the same level of expenditure on imported commodities in the group as the actual tariff structure. They then use the global Linkage model to see how much difference that method of aggregating makes to the results from liberalizing global goods trade as of 2004. They find that the global economic welfare cost of trade barriers is 46% greater than that generated using the standard tariff database (one-quarter larger for high-income countries, twice as large for developing countries). It may have been of more significance in the past – especially when NTBs are included – because there was probably more dispersion of tariff equivalents of border measures in the twentieth century, especially prior to the 1950s (including for agriculture).

A conservative adjustment to compensate for this missing effect and the NTB phenomenon is to raise the estimated welfare cost for both sets of countries

by 50% in 2004 and 2050, 40% in 1982, 30% in 1962, and 20% pre-World War II.

Barriers to Trade in Services

The potential gains from trade liberalization in services are rarely considered in CGE models, or at best are included only in rather rudimentary ways. This is because of a lack of good data on bilateral services trade, and methodological difficulties in modeling distortions in services markets. This is a serious omission, since there are indications that the costs of barriers to trade in services may be several times larger than the barriers presented by conventional trade measures such as merchandise tariffs and subsidies (Dee et al. 2003; Brown et al. 2005; Jensen et al. 2007; Francois and Hoekman 2010).

Konan and Maskus (2006) point out that the costs of services distortions are likely to be larger than those affecting merchandise trade because they typically involve restrictions not only on cross-border trade (Mode 1 of GATS), but also on supply by establishing enterprises in the country or by the movement of service suppliers (Modes 3 and 4 of GATS). That is, they raise the domestic cost of production of services, including those that are non-tradable internationally.

In the absence of reliable estimates of the welfare cost of services trade barriers, a conservative adjustment to compensate for this missing effect – after amending to include the influences of NTBs and tariff aggregation issues – is to raise by 50% the estimated welfare cost for 2004 and beyond. For earlier eras, when costs of trading services were higher and so provided more of a natural barrier, the cost of government regulation of the service sector was probably lower. We therefore raise the estimated welfare cost of goods trade barriers by 20% pre-World War II, 30% in 1962, and 40% in 1982 to account for policies inhibiting services trade of both developing and high-income countries.

Allowing Financial Market Integration

International trade requires international financial services to transfer the required payments and often to provide temporary credit to traders. Trade reform thus expands also the markets for financial services, which contributes to the long-term stability of financial markets. Openness also tends to reduce inflation. It can do so not only by increasing competition in domestic markets but also by providing more options for people to hold savings in foreign currencies, which reduces the ability of governments to inflate savings away (Rogoff 2003). Yet CGE models typically ignore financial markets. This is unfortunate also because their inclusion would allow an additional set of influences on real exchange rates (see, e.g., McKibbin and Stegman 2005).

A recent study by Hoxha *et al.* (2009) examines potential gains from financial integration and find that a move from autarky to full integration of financial markets globally could boost real consumption by 7.5% permanently, even assuming no productivity dividend. We therefore raise the amended welfare cost of goods and services trade barriers by 7.5% for both sets of countries and all years.

Allowing Economies of Scale and Imperfect Competition

We have assumed constant returns to scale and perfect competition rather than allowing firms to enjoy increasing returns and some degree of monopoly power for their differentiated product. The so-called "new" trade theory has shown how this can lead to underestimating the welfare gains from trade reform (Krugman 2009). Empirical case studies suggest that if opening an economy exposes monopolistic firms to greater competition and allows greater exploitation of scale economies, it generates additional gains from trade reform that could be several times the standard estimates based on constant returns to scale and perfect competition (see, e.g., Harris (1984) on Canada, Krishna and Mitra (1998) on India, Pavcnik (2002) on Chile).

A study by Francois *et al.* (2005) used the comparative static global GTAP model without and then with scale economies and imperfect competition and found that the estimated gains from freeing global trade as of 1997 were about half as large again in the latter case. Since small economies are more likely to benefit in this way than larger economies, other things equal, this difference may well

have been larger in earlier decades. A conservative adjustment to the amended welfare cost of goods and services trade barriers and restrictions on financial integration is to add for both groups of countries a further 50% for each of the years considered in the present study.

Allowing for Product Quality and Variety Differences, and New Product Emergence

Another product aggregation issue has to do with the fact that, within any product classification, there is a wide range of qualities and varieties available. The only way product quality or variety differences enter most CGE models is by distinguishing between a product's country of origin. This is done using so-called Armington elasticities which can ensure domestically produced goods are imperfect substitutes for imported goods in aggregate, and imports from one country are an imperfect substitute for goods imported from any other country (Armington 1969).

In the real world, however, there is an ever-increasing array of qualities and varieties available for any product from each supplying country. It appears consumers (including producers using those products as intermediate inputs) are willing to pay for a greater variety of different quality products, even though that product differentiation may be costly in terms of shorter production runs and more advertising. Hummels and Klenow (2005) suggest that these improvements in quality are sufficiently rapid that the prices received by countries for the products that they continue to export – as distinct from their new exports – actually rise by 0.09% for each increase of 1% in national income. This result is at variance with traditional Armington models, which generate a reduction in export prices when economies grow and exports expand.

In a study of US import data from 1972 to 2001, Broda and Weinstein (2006) find that the upward bias in the conventional import price index, because of not accounting for the growth in varieties of products, is approximately 1.2% per year. Feenstra *et al.* (1992) suggest the welfare cost of tariff protection can be underestimated by as much as a factor of 10 when this consideration is not included in the analysis.

Also, standard models used to assess the implications of trade reforms are based on the assumption that expansion of exports following liberalization involves increasing the volume of the products initially being exported, but not of any other products. The Armington assumption also rules out expanding the markets to which goods are being supplied: if exports to a particular country are initially zero, then in most CGE models they remain zero following reform.

Recent research, however, highlights the key role of the "extensive" margin, where export expansion involves increases in the range of products exported (Hummels and Klenow 2005) and expansion in the range of markets supplied (Evenett and Venables 2002). Hummels and Klenow conclude that only about one-third of the export expansion associated with economic growth comes from the "intensive margin" where greater quantities of the same products are exported. And Evenett and Venables find that about one-third of the expansion of exports from developing countries was obtained by exporting products to countries to which they had not previously exported.

In a world where importers exhibit a preference for variety in the goods they purchase, these observations on the importance of extensive margin growth have major implications. Increasing the volumes of the same products, as under the Armington assumption, has the inevitable consequence of driving down the price of exports and causing income losses to the exporter from deterioration in the terms of trade. Where exports are characterized by an expansion in the range of products supplied, the preference for variety exerts a counteracting force – helping to increase the demand for exports. In simulations introducing the Hummels–Klenow preference for variety in exports from China and India, Dimaranan et al. (2007) found that the terms of trade for these exporters need not deteriorate significantly, despite very high projected rates of export growth.

Common treatments of new varieties, such as those based on monopolistic competition and a love of variety inspired by Krugman (1980), typically assume they apply mainly to manufacturing. However, as Rodrik (2004) notes, the process of discovering efficient new exports is just as important and difficult in

primary and service sectors as in manufacturing. It may be even more important in emerging economies than in high-income countries. So too might issues of product quality. Jensen et al. (2007), for example, find that the benefits of reform in services trade, when allowing for productivity growth in trading a wider range of qualities of goods as the quality of business services rise (following Markusen et al. 2005), completely dominate as a source of potential benefits from reforms likely to follow Russia's eventual accession to the WTO.

To take account of these additional three missing elements, we raise the amended welfare cost of barriers to economic and financial integration for both groups of countries by a further 50% for 2004 and beyond and by 20% pre-World War II, 30% in 1962, and 40% in 1982.

Administration, Compliance, and Lobbying Costs

Savings in bureaucratic costs of administering trade barriers, in traders' costs of circumventing barriers (Bhagwati and Hansen 1973), and in lobbyists' costs of rent-seeking to secure or maintain trade-distorting policies are all non-trivial elements of gains that can come from removing trade barriers, none of which are captured in most global economic modeling. Lobbying costs potentially could absorb all of the rents received by private agents from trade barriers, for example (Krueger 1974). For want of reliable estimates, these costs will be assumed to add just another 10% each year to the amended welfare cost of barriers to economic and financial integration.

Growth-Enhancing Impacts of Reform

The comparative static GTAP model used here does not measure any of the dynamic gains that come from trade reform. Yet economists have long been convinced that participation in international trade provides a growth dividend additional to standard improvements in allocative efficiency. Dynamic gains arise in numerous ways. One of the more important is through encouragement of the more efficient firms to take over from the less efficient in each country (Melitz 2003; Trefler 2004; Bernard *et al.* 2007; Melitz and Ottaviano 2008). Another way is through multinational firms sharing technologies and knowledge across countries within the firm (Markusen 2002). Offshoring is yet another mechanism through which heterogeneous firms are affected by trade liberalization, including via relocating from small to larger nations (Baldwin and Okuba 2011). The greater competition that accompanies trade reform also can stimulate more innovation (Aghion and Griffith 2005), leading to higher rates of capital accumulation and productivity growth (Lumenga-Neso *et al.* 2005).

Based loosely on Arrow's (1962) concept of learning-by-doing, major empirical contributions to this literature include Feder (1983), Dollar (1992), and Sachs and Warner (1995), all of which find strong links between export performance and economic growth. Rodriguez and Rodrik (2001) raised concerns about the robustness of the estimated relationship between aggregate exports and productivity growth. During the same period, Clerides *et al.* (1998) questioned the learning-by-doing framework based on firm-level findings that exporting firms were more efficient before entering export markets, rather than because of learning-by-doing after entering these markets. However, more recent research on the aggregate links between exports and productivity growth has carefully re-examined the potential endogeneity of the relationship, and continues to find an aggregate positive relationship (Frankel and Romer 1999). A number of subsequent firm-level studies find evidence of productivity growth associated with learning-by-doing after firms enter exporting. Blalock and Gertler (2004) find an increase in firm productivity of between 2% and 5% after Indonesian firms enter export markets. Fernandes and Isgut (2007) find evidence of an increase in productivity from learning-by-exporting when Colombian firms entered export markets. Van Biesebrock (2005) finds that African exporting firms had higher productivity before entering export markets, and that their productivity levels, and their subsequent rates of productivity growth, increased after entering export markets. Girma *et al.* (2004) also find both higher initial levels of productivity and higher productivity growth rates after entry into exporting.

In a more macro study, Wacziarg and Welch (2008) estimate that countries that have liberalized their trade (defined as raising their trade-to-GDP ratio by 5+ percentage points) enjoyed 1.5 percentage points higher GDP growth compared with their pre-reform rate. Liberalizing international financial flows also has been shown to have boosted economic growth, especially in the first wave of globalization up to 1913 (Schularick and Steger 2010).

Synopsis

A single paper that brings several of the above omissions together using a numerical open economy growth model is that by Rutherford and Tarr (2002). Its simulation model allows for product variety, imperfect competition, economies of scale, and international capital flows. It is also dynamic, so it can trace out an adjustment path to trade reform. Furthermore, it is stochastic in that it draws randomly from uniform probability distributions for eight key parameters of the model. The authors simulate a halving of the only policy intervention (a 20% tariff on imports) and, in doing so, fully replace the government's lost tariff revenue with a lump-sum tax. That modest trade reform produces a welfare increase (in terms of Hicksian equivalent variation) of 10.6% of the present value of consumption in their central model. Systematic sensitivity analysis with 34,000 simulations showed that there is virtually no chance of a welfare gain of less than 3%, and a 7% chance of a welfare gain larger than 18% of consumption. Several modeling variants and sensitivity analysis on all the key parameters found that the welfare estimates for the same ten percentage point tariff cut ranged up to 37% when international capital flows are allowed, and down to 4.7% when using the most inefficient replacement tax (a tax of capital). The latter result shows that even a very inefficient tax on capital is superior to the tariff as a revenue raiser. Increasing the size of the tariff cuts beyond 50% results in roughly proportional increases in the estimated welfare gains.

Those results suggest the amendments proposed for each of the omissions discussed in this section are modest. In summary, the multipliers, not including any amendment for dynamic gains from trade are as in Table 9.7.

When these "Total" multipliers are used to reduce the underestimates in Table 9.6b they become those shown in Table 9.6c. Combining these effects in this way may overstate the required adjustments, because of interactions between them (that is, econometricians focusing on one or only a subset at a time may have spuriously captured the effects of some of the others). However, by not including an adjustment for the dynamic gains from trade we are still omitting what is probably the most important of the missing effects discussed above. Adding the dynamic gains is problematic, though, because they involve an increase in the annual *rate of growth* of capital and outputs, not just a permanent one-off increase in the *level* of GDP. Its continued omission almost certainly ensures that even the adjusted numbers in Table 9.6c are still lower-bound estimates of the retrospective and prospective costs of the world's trade barriers.

Table 9.7 Summary of multipliers

Source of multiplier to trade reform gain	1900–37	1962	1982	2004–2050
NTBs and tariff averaging	1.5	1.4	1.3	1.2
Services	1.2	1.3	1.4	1.5
Financial market integration	1.075	1.075	1.075	1.075
Scale economies and imperfect competition	1.5	1.5	1.5	1.5
Product quality, variety, and newness	1.2	1.3	1.4	1.5
Administration, compliance, and lobbying costs	1.1	1.1	1.1	1.1
Total	3.83	4.19	4.52	4.79

Summary and Conclusion

The above estimates of the cost of trade barriers to developing and high-income countries are summarized in Figures 9.1 and 9.2. If one leaves aside the spike in the Great Depression of the early 1930s,

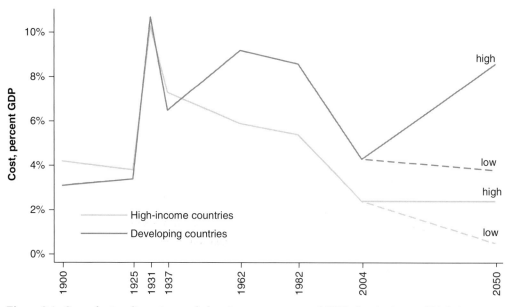

Figure 9.1 *Cost of price-distorting trade barriers as a percent of GDP, developing and high-income countries, 1900 to 2050. "Low" and "High" scenarios refer to whether it is assumed that price distortions from trade barriers fall or rise between 2004 and 2050 (see Table 9.6)*

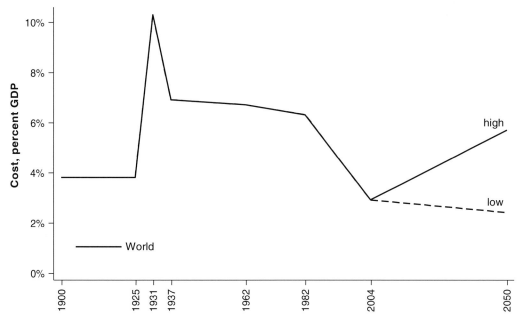

Figure 9.2 *Cost of price-distorting trade barriers as a percent of GDP, the world, 1900 to 2050. "Low" and "High" scenarios refer to whether it is assumed that price distortions from trade barriers fall or rise between 2004 and 2050 (see Table 9.6)*

the pattern begins with relatively low costs at the start of the twentieth century, which was the tail end of the world's first great policy reform-driven globalization wave. Those costs did not change greatly up to the late 1920s, were nearly three times as high in the early 1930s before falling back to two times as high by the latter 1930s, fell for high-income countries but rose further for developing countries after World War II (associated with the transition to independence for many former colonies), before falling rapidly during the second great globalization wave that began around the mid-1980s. Whether that fall continues over the next four decades is by no means certain. The difficulties WTO members are having in bringing the Doha Round of multilateral trade negotiations to a successful conclusion is worrying. A collapse of those talks means more than just not reaping the gains they are estimated to be able to provide, for two reasons: it would diminish the chances of completing and implementing yet another round before 2050; and it would leave open the possibility for countries whose WTO-bound tariffs and subsidies are above currently applied rates to raise their trade barriers. Clearly a great

deal hangs on the WTO membership finding the political will to fulfill the expectations of its Doha Development Agenda. Certainly countries have the additional option of creating or joining preferential trading blocs or even broader economic integration agreements – and they will proliferate even more if Doha fails. However, they are typically choked with exceptions such that they are poor substitutes for a comprehensive multilateral agreement from a global welfare viewpoint.

Three points need reiterating by way of conclusion. The first is to keep in mind the paucity of historical data available to estimate the extent of price-distorting trade barriers prior to the 1960s. It means that any estimates of the costs of trade barriers that are dependent on them necessarily are subject to a considerable degree of uncertainty. The second is that, despite huge progress being made in building global economy-wide models capable of analyzing trade policy issues, the type of model used in the present study still grossly underestimates the global cost of trade barriers/benefits from trade policy reform, since dynamic gains from trade are still omitted. And third, such models are best suited to analyze situations for which their database is pertinent. Using them to forecast or backcast many decades is necessarily an imprecise exercise, so the results for the outlying decades especially should be viewed with that in mind as well.

References

Aghion, P. and R. Griffith (2005) *Competition and Growth: Reconciling Theory and Evidence* Cambridge MA: MIT Press.

Anderson, J. E. (2009) Consistent trade policy aggregation. *International Economic Review* **50**: 903–927.

Anderson, J. E. and J. P. Neary (2005) *Measuring the Restrictiveness of International Trade Policy.* Cambridge MA: MIT Press.

Anderson, K. (2003) Measuring effects of trade policy distortions: how far have we come? *The World Economy* **26**: 413–440.

(2004) Subsidies and trade barriers. In B. Lomborg (ed.), *Global Crises, Global Solutions.* Cambridge: Cambridge University Press.

(2009) *Distortions to Agricultural Incentives: A Global Perspective, 1955–2007.* Washington, DC: World Bank.

(2010) *The Political Economy of Agricultural Price Distortions.* Cambridge: Cambridge University Press.

Anderson, K. and J. L. Croser (2011) Changing contributions of different agricultural policy instruments to global reductions in trade and welfare. *World Trade Review* **10**: 297–323.

Anderson, K. and Y. Hayami (1986) *The Political Economy of Agricultural Protection: East Asia in International Perspective.* Boston, MA: Allen and Unwin.

Anderson, K. and B. Hoekman (eds.) (2006) *The WTO's Core Rules and Disciplines.* London: Edward Elgar.

Anderson, K. and S. Nelgen (2011) What's the appropriate agricultural protection counterfactual for trade analysis? In W. Martin and A. Mattoo (eds.), *Unfinished Business? The WTO's Doha Agenda.* London: Centre for Economic Policy Research and the World Bank.

(2012) Trade barrier volatility and agricultural price stabilization. *World Development* **40**: 36–48.

Anderson, K. and H. Norheim (1993) History, geography and regional economic integration. In K. Anderson and R. Blackhurst (eds.), *Regional Integration and the Global Trading System.* London: Harvester Wheatsheaf.

Anderson, K. and R. Tyers (1992) Japanese rice policy in the interwar period: some consequences of imperial self sufficiency. *Japan and the World Economy* **4**: 103–127.

Anderson, K. and E. Valenzuela (2008) *Global Estimates of Distortions to Agricultural Incentives, 1955 to 2007.* Data spreadsheets available at www.worldbank.org/agdistortions

Anderson, K. and L. A. Winters (2009) The challenge of reducing international trade and migration barriers. In: B. Lomborg, (ed.) *Global Crises, Global Solutions,* 2nd ed. Cambridge: Cambridge University Press.

Anderson, K., W. Martin, and E. Valenzuela (2006a) The relative importance of global agricultural subsidies and market access. *World Trade Review* **5**: 357–376.

Anderson, K., W. Martin and D. van der Mensbrugghe (2006) Market and welfare implications of the Doha reform scenarios. In: K. Anderson and W. Martin (ed.), *Agricultural Trade Reform and the Doha Development Agenda.* London: Palgrave Macmillan.

Armington, P. (1969) A theory of demand for products distinguished by place of production. *IMF Staff Papers* **16**: 159–178.

Arrow, K. (1962) The economic implications of learning by doing. *Review of Economic Studies* **29**: 155–173.

Balassa, B. and Associates (1971) *The Structure of Protection in Developing Countries.* Baltimore, MD: Johns Hopkins University Press.

Baldwin, R. E. (1991) Measuring the effects of nontariff trade-distorting policies. In: J. De Melo, and A. Sapir (eds.), *Trade Theory and Economic Reform: North, South and East: Essays in Honour of Bela Balassa.* Cambridge, MA: Basil Blackwell.

Baldwin, R. and T. Okuba (2011) *International Trade, Offshoring and Heterogeneous Firms.* National Bureau for Economic Research Working Paper No. 16660. Cambridge MA, NBER.

Bates, R. (1981) *Markets and States in Tropical Africa: The Political Basis of Agricultural Policies.* Berkeley, CA: University of California Press.

Bernard, A. B., J. B. Jensen, S. J. Redding, and P. K. Schott (2007) Firms in international trade. *Journal of Economic Perspectives* **21**: 105–130.

Bértola, L. and J. G. Williamson (2006) Globalization in Latin America before 1940. In: V. Bulmer-Thomas, J. H. Coatsworth and R. Cortés Conde (eds.), *The Cambridge Economic History of Latin America*, vol. 2. Cambridge: Cambridge University Press.

Bhagwati, J. N. (1971) The generalized theory of distortions and welfare. In: J. N. Bhagwati, R. W. Jones, R. A. Mundell, and J. Vanek (eds.), *Trade, Balance of Payments and Growth*. Amsterdam: North-Holland.

(1978) *Foreign Trade Regimes and Economic Development: Anatomy and Consequences of Exchange Control Regimes*, Cambridge, MA: Ballinger.

Bhagwati, J. N. and B. Hansen (1973) A theoretical analysis of smuggling. *Quarterly Journal of Economics* **87**: 172–187.

Blalock, G. and P. Gertler (2004) Learning from exporting revisited in a less developed setting. *Journal of Development Economics* **75**: 397–416.

Bouët, A. and D. Laborde (2010) Assessing the potential cost of a failed Doha Round. *World Trade Review* **9**: 319–351.

Broda, C. M. and D. E. Weinstein (2006) Globalization and the gains from variety. *Quarterly Journal of Economics* **121**: 541–585.

Brown, D. K., K. Kiyota, and R. M. Stern (2005) Computational analysis of the Free Trade Area of the Americas (FTAA). *North American Journal of Economics and Finance* **16**: 153–185.

Bulmer-Thomas, V. (1994) *The Economic History of Latin America since Independence*. Cambridge: Cambridge University Press.

Clemens, M. A. and J. G. Williamson (2010) *Endogenous Tariffs and Growth: Asia versus Latin America, 1870–1940*, Cambridge, MA: Harvard University (mimeo).

Clerides, S., Lach, S., and Tybout, J. (1998) Is learning by exporting important? Micro-dynamic evidence from Colombia, Mexico and Morocco. *Quarterly Journal of Economics* **113**: 903–947.

Corden, W. M. (1997) *Trade Policy and Economic Welfare*, (revd edn.), Oxford: Clarendon Press.

Deardorff, A. V. (2005) A centennial of anti-dumping legislation and implementation: introduction and overview. *The World Economy* **28**: 633–640.

Dee, P., Hanslow, K., and D. T. Pham (2003) Measuring the cost of barriers to trade in services. In: T. Ito, and A. O. Krueger (eds.), *Services Trade in the Asia-Pacific Region*. Chicago, IL: University of Chicago Press for the NBER.

Diebold, W., Jr. (1952) *The End of the ITO*, Essays in International Finance No. 16. Princeton, NJ: Princeton University Press.

Dimaranan, B., E. Ianchovichina, and W. Martin (2007) Competing with giants: who wins, who loses? In: L. A. Winters, and S. Yusuf (eds.), *Dancing with Giants: China, India and the Global Economy*. Washington, DC: World Bank.

Dollar, D. (1992) Outward-oriented developing economies really do grow more rapidly: evidence from 95 LDCs, 1976–1985. *Economic Development and Cultural Change* **40**: 523–544.

Evenett, S. and A. Venables (2002) *Export Growth in Developing Countries: Market Entry and Bilateral Trade Flows*. Available at: www.alexandria.unisg.ch/Publikationen/22177

Feder, G. (1983) On exports and economic growth. *Journal of Development Economics* **12**: 59–73.

Feenstra, R. C. (1995) Estimating the effects of trade policy. In: G. N. Grossman and K. Rogoff (eds.), *Handbook of International Economics*, vol. 3. Amsterdam: Elsevier.

Feenstra, R. C., J. R. Markusen and W. Zeile (1992) Accounting for growth with new inputs *American Economic Review* **82**: 415–421.

Fernandes, A. and A. Isgut (2007) *Learning-by-Exporting Effects: Are They for Real?*, MPRA Working Paper No. 3121. Munich, Germany: University of Munich. Available at: http://mpra.ub.uni-muenchen.de/3121/.

Finger, J. M. (2002) Safeguards: making sense of GATT/WTO provisions allowing import restrictions. In: B. Hoekman, A. Mattoo, and P. English (eds.), *Development, Trade and the WTO: A Handbook*. Washington, DC: World Bank.

Francois, J. F. and B. Hoekman (2010) Services trade and policy. *Journal of Economic Literature* **48**: 642–692.

Francois, J. F. and W. Martin (2004) Commercial policy, bindings and market access. *European Economic Review* **48**: 665–679.

(2010) Ex ante assessments of the welfare impacts of trade reforms with numerical models. In: H. Beladi, and E. K. Choi (eds.), *New Developments in Computable General Equilibrium Analysis for Trade Policy* London: Emerald Group Publishing.

Francois, J. F., van Meijl, H., and van Tongeren, F. (2005) Trade liberalization in the Doha Development Round. *Economic Policy* **20**: 349–391.

Frankel, J. A. and D. Romer (1999) Does trade cause growth? *American Economic Review* **89**: 379–399.

General Agreementary Tariffs Trade (1972) *Basic Documentation of the Tariff Study*. Geneva: GATT Secretariat.

(1978) *Network of World Trade by Areas and Commodity Classes, 1955 to 1976*, GATT Studies in International Trade No. 7. Geneva: GATT Secretariat.

Girma, S., D. Greenaway, and R. Kneller (2004) Does exporting increase productivity? A microeconometric analysis of matched firms. *Review of International Economics* **12**: 855–866.

Gootiiz, B. and A. Mattoo (2009) *Restrictions on Services Trade and FDI in Developing Countries*. Washington, DC: World Bank (mimeo).

Haberler, G. (1958) *Trends in International Trade: A Report by a Panel of Experts*, Geneva: GATT Secretariat.

Hanson, G. H., R. J. Mataloni, and M. J. Slaughter, (2005) Vertical production networks in multinational firms. *Review of Economics and Statistics* **87**: 664–678.

Harris, R. G. (1984) Applied general equilibrium analysis of small open economies with scale economies and imperfect competition. *American Economic Review* **74**: 1016–1032.

Hertel, T. W. (ed.) (1997) *Global Trade Analysis: Modeling and Applications*. Cambridge: Cambridge University Press.

Hoxha, I., S. Kalemli-Ozcan, and D. Vollrath (2009) *How Big are the Gains from International Financial Integration?*, National Bureau of Economic Research Working Paper No. 14 636. Cambridge, MA: NBER.

Hummels, D. and P. Klenow (2005) The variety and quality of a nation's exports. *American Economic Review* **95**: 704–723.

Irwin, D. (1996) *Against the Tide: An Intellectual History of Free Trade*. Princeton, NJ: Princeton University Press.

(2010) Trade restrictiveness and deadweight losses from U. S. tariffs, 1859–1961. *American Economic Journal: Economic Policy* **2**: 111–133.

Jacks, D. S. and K. Pendakur (2010) Global trade and the maritime transport revolution. *Review of Economics and Statistics* **92**: 745–755.

Jacks, D. S., C. Meissner and D. Novy (2010) Trade booms, trade busts, and trade costs. *Journal of International Economics* **83**: 185–201.

Jensen, J., T. Rutherford, and D. Tarr (2007) The impact of liberalizing barriers to foreign direct investment in services: the case of Russian accession to the World Trade Organization. *Review of Development Economics* **11**: 482–506.

Keller, W., B. Li, and C. Hua Shiue (2010) *China's Foreign Trade: Perspectives from the Past 150*

Years. Centre for Economic Policy Research Discussion Paper No.8118. London: CEPR.

Kindleberger, C. P. (1975) The rise of free trade in Western Europe, 1820–1875. *Journal of Economic History* **35**: 20–55.

(1989) Commercial policy between the wars. In: P. Mathias, and S. Pollard (eds.), *The Cambridge Economic History of Europe*, vol. 8. Cambridge: Cambridge University Press.

Konan, D. and K. Maskus (2006) Quantifying the impact of services liberalization in a developing country. *Journal of Development Economics* **81**: 142–162.

Krishna, P. and D. Mitra (1998) Trade liberalization, market discipline and productivity growth: new evidence from India. *Journal of Development Economics* **56**: 447–462.

Krueger, A. O. (1974) The political economy of the rent-seeking society. *American Economic Review* **64**: 291–303.

(1978) *Foreign Trade Regimes and Economic Development: Liberalization Attempts and Consequences*, Cambridge, MA: Ballinger.

Krueger, P. (1980) Scale economies, product differentiation, and the pattern of trade. *American Economic Review* **70**: 950–959.

(2009) The increasing returns revolution in trade and geography. *American Economic Review* **99**: 561–571.

Laborde, D., W. Martin, and D. van der Mensbrugghe (2011) Measuring the benefits of global trade reform with optimal aggregators of distortions. In: W. Martin, and A. Mattoo (eds.), *The Doha Development Agenda*, Washington DC: World Bank.

Laird, S. (1997) Quantifying commercial policies. In: J. F. Francois, and K. A. Reinert (eds.), *Applied Methods in Trade Policy Analysis: A Handbook*. Cambridge: Cambridge University Press.

League of Nations (1927) *Tariff Level Indices*. Geneva: League of Nations.

(1939) *Review of World Trade 1938*. Geneva: League of Nations.

Liepmann, H. (1938) *Tariff Levels and the Economic Unity of Europe*. London: Allen and Unwin.

Lin, J. Y., F. Cai, and Z. Li (1996) *The China Miracle: Development Strategy and Economic Reform*. Hong Kong: The Chinese University Press for the International Center for Economic Growth.

Lindert, P. H. (1991) Historical patterns of agricultural policy. In: C. Timmer, (ed.), *Agriculture and the*

State: Growth, Employment, and Poverty. Ithaca NY: Cornell University Press.

Little, I. M., T. Scitovsky, and M. Scott (1970) *Industry and Trade in Some Developing Countries: A Comparative Study*. London: Oxford University Press for the OECD.

Lloyd, P. J. (1974) A more general theory of price distortions in an open economy. *Journal of International Economics* **4**: 365–386.

(2008) 100 years of tariff protection in Australia. *Australian Economic History Review* **48**: 99–145.

Lumenga-Neso, O., M. Olarreaga, and M. Schiff (2005) On "indirect" trade-related R&D spillovers. *European Economic Review* **49**: 1785–1798.

Maddison, A. (2008) *Historical Statistics of the World Economy: 1–2008 AD*. Available at www.ggdc.net/maddison/

Maizels, A. (1963) *Industrial Growth and World Trade*. Cambridge: Cambridge University Press.

Markusen, J. (2002) *Multinational Firms and the Theory of International Trade*. Cambridge, MA: MIT Press.

Markusen, J., T. Rutherford, and D. Tarr (2005) Foreign direct investment in services and the domestic market for expertise. *Canadian Journal of Economics* **38**: 758–777.

Martin, W. (1997) Measuring welfare changes with distortions. In: J. F. Francois and K. A. Reinert (eds.), *Applied Methods in Trade Policy Analysis: A Handbook*. Cambridge: Cambridge University Press.

Martin, W. and K. Anderson (2012) Export restrictions and price insulation during commodity price booms. *American Journal of Agricultural Economics* **94**: 422–427.

Martin, W. and A. Mattoo (eds.) (2011) *Unfinished Business? The WTO's Doha Agenda*. London: Centre for Economic Policy Research and the World Bank.

McKibbin W. and A. Stegman (2005) Asset markets and financial flows in general equilibrium models. Paper presented at conference. *Quantitative Tools for Microeconomic Policy Analysis*. Canberra: Productivity Commission.

Meade, J. (1942) A proposal for an international commercial union, unpublished Cabinet paper reproduced in *The World Economy* **10**: 399–407 (1987), and in S. Meade (ed.), *The Collected Papers of James Meade*, vol 3, *International Economics*. London: Unwin Hyman (1988).

Melitz, M. J. (2003) The impact of trade on intra-industry reallocations and aggregate industry productivity. *Econometrica* **71**: 1692–1725.

Melitz, M. J. and G. I. P. Ottaviano (2008) Market size, trade and productivity. *Review of Economic Studies* **75**: 295–316.

Narayanan, G. and T. L. Walmsley (eds.) (2008) *Global Trade, Assistance, and Production: The GTAP 7 Data Base*. West Lafayette, IN: Center for Global Trade Analysis, Purdue University. Available at: www.gtap.org.

Nogues, J. J., A. Olechowski, and L. A. Winters (1986) The extent of nontariff barriers to industrial countries' imports. *World Bank Economic Review* **1**: 181–199.

OECD (2006) *Producer and Consumer Support Estimates: OECD Database 1986–2005*. Available at: www.oecd.org.

Pavcnik, N. (2002) Trade liberalization, exit, and productivity improvements: evidence from Chilean plants. *Review of Economic Studies* **69**: 245–276.

Rodriguez, F. and D. Rodrik (2001) Trade policy and economic growth: a skeptic's guide to cross-national evidence. In: B. S. Bernanke, and K. S. Rogoff (eds.), *NBER Macroeconomics Annual 2000*. Cambridge, MA: MIT Press.

Rodrik, D. (2004) *Industrial Policy for the Twenty-First Century*. Cambridge, MA: Hanvard University (mimeo). Available at: http://ksgome.harvard.edu/~drodrik/UNIDOSep.pdf

Rogoff, K. S. (2003) Disinflation: an unsung benefit of globalization. *Finance and Development* **40**: 54–55.

Roningen, V. and A. Yeats (1976) Nontariff distortions of international trade: some preliminary empirical evidence. *Weltwirtschaftliches Archiv* **122**: 613–625.

Rutherford, T. F. and D. G. Tarr (2002) Trade liberalization, product variety and growth in a small open economy: a quantitative assessment. *Journal of International Economics* **56**: 247–272.

Sachs, J. D. and A. Warner (1995) Economic reform and the process of global integration. *Brookings Papers on Economic Activity* **1**: 1–95.

Sah, R. and J. E. Stiglitz (1992) *Peasants versus City-Dwellers: Taxation and the Burden of Economic Development*. Oxford: Oxford University Press.

Schularick, M. and T. M. Steger (2010) Financial integration, investment, and economic growth: evidence from two eras of financial globalization. *Review of Economics and Statistics* **92**: 756–768.

Swinnen, J. F. M. (2010) Agricultural protection growth in Europe, 1870 to 1969. In: K. Anderson (eds.), *The Political Economy of Agricultural Price Distortions*. Cambridge: Cambridge University Press.

Trefler, D. (2004) The long and short of the Canada–US Free Trade Agreement. *American Economic Review* **94**: 870–895.

Tyers, R. and K. Anderson (1992) *Disarray in World Food Markets: A Quantitative Assessment*. Cambridge: Cambridge University Press.

Valenzuela, E. and K. Anderson (2008) *Alternative Agricultural Price Distortions for CGE Analysis of Developing Countries, 2004 and 1980–84*, GTAP Research Memorandum No. 13. Lafayette, IN: Center for Global Trade Analysis, Purdue University. Available at: gtap.agecon.purdue.edu/resources

Valenzuela, E., D. van der Mensbrugghe, and K. Anderson (2009) General equilibrium effects of price distortions on global markets, farm incomes and welfare. In: K. Anderson, (ed.), *Distortions to Agricultural Incentives: A Global Perspective, 1955–2007*. London: Palgrave Macmillan.

van Biesebrock, J. (2005) Exporting raises productivity in sub-Saharan African manufacturing firms. *Journal of International Economics* **67**: 373–391.

van der Mensbrugghe, D. (2005) *Linkage Technical Reference Document: Version 6.0*. Washington DC: World Bank (mimeo). Available at: worldbank.org/prospects/linkagemodel

van der Mensbrugghe, D. and R. Rosen (2010) Climate, trade and development. Paper presented at the *13th Global Economic Analysis Conference*, Penang, June 9–11.

Viner, J. (1924) The Most-Favored-Nation clause in American economic treaties. *Journal of Political Economy* **32**(1), February. (Reprinted as Ch. 1 in his *International Economics: Studies by Jacob Viner*. Glencoe, IL: The Free Press.)

Wacziarg, R. and K. H. Welch (2008) Trade liberalization and growth: new evidence. *World Bank Economic Review* **15**: 393–429.

World Trade Organization (2010) *World Trade Statistics 2009*. Geneva: WTO.

Woytinsky, W. S. and E. S. Woytinsky (1955) *World Commerce and Governments: Trends and Outlook*. New York: Twentieth Century Fund.

Water and Sanitation: Economic Losses from Poor Water and Sanitation – Past, Present, and Future

MARC JEULAND, DAVID FUENTE, SEMRA ÖZDEMIR,
MAURA ALLAIRE, AND DALE WHITTINGTON

Introduction

Diseases associated with poor water, sanitation, and hygiene comprise on average 6–7% of the annual mortality in less developed countries (World Health Organization 2004; Prüss-Üstün *et al.* 2008). A growing body of research suggests that a variety of different types of water, sanitation, and hygiene (WASH) interventions are effective and capable of delivering large health benefits to target populations (Hutton and Haller 2004; Fewtrell *et al.* 2005; Luby *et al.* 2005; Clasen *et al.* 2007; Hutton *et al.* 2007). Many of these interventions – the provision of improved community water supplies, point-of-use water treatment, hygiene education, on-site sanitation – can be delivered at very low cost, but their adoption remains surprisingly low (Whittington *et al.* 2012). Piped water and sewerage services, the gold standard for water and sanitation in the developed world, do not seem to be necessary to achieve many of the health benefits from improving existing water and sanitation conditions. Household demand for these network services, however, is much higher than for low-cost interventions, perhaps because they bring other types of improvements that households value, such as time savings and greater convenience (Whittington *et al.* 2009).

In this chapter we present a global analysis of the "economic losses" associated with inadequate water and sanitation from 1950 to 2050. These estimates provide an entry point for thinking about the challenges of ameliorating water and sanitation services in poor countries. Using a simple simulation model, we calculate the economic losses from the morbidity and mortality associated with inadequate water and sanitation services, and from the

time spent collecting water from outside the home, in less developed countries during the period 1950 to 2008. We then use projections of GDP and population growth to forecast economic losses from 2008 to 2050. We compare total economic losses with non-monetary measures of disease burden, such as deaths due to WASH-related diseases.

We are forced to make many assumptions in our attempt to describe the associations that exist between socio-economic conditions, coverage with improved water and sanitation services, and reduced burden of disease. We confront problems related to both data availability and the difficulty of drawing causal inferences between improved health, the provision of improved water and sanitation services, and economic growth. We are forced to rely primarily on country-level data for which only short time-series and/or cross-sectional measurements exist. These data obscure important sub-national differences in

We are grateful to one anonymous reviewer of a previous version of this chapter. Kasper Anderskov and Bjørn Lomborg provided useful feedback throughout the development of this research effort. We also benefitted from discussions and comments from many colleagues – Alex Pfaff, Subhrendu Pattanayak, Peter McCornick, Duncan Thomas – as well as doctoral students in the University Program on Environmental Policy seminar at Duke University and students at the University of Manchester and the University of North Carolina at Chapel Hill. A preliminary version of this chapter was presented at the biannual meetings of the Latin America and Caribbean Environmental Economics Program (LACEEP) in April 2011. We benefitted from the discussion with LACEEP researchers, and thank Juan Robalino, from early LACEEP's Executive Director, for this opportunity. Courtney Harrison of the Nicholas Institute for Environmental Policy Solutions helped us to obtain data on bilateral aid flows for WASH. All errors are our own.

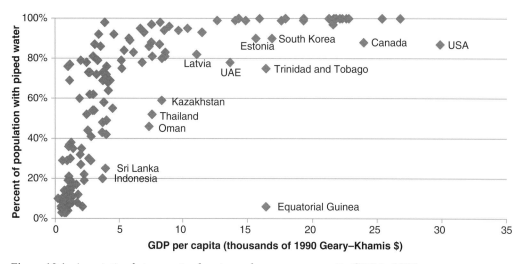

Figure 10.1 *Association between piped water and average per capita GDP in 2008*

income, coverage, and mortality. We use data on mortality due to WASH-related diseases, coverage with water and sanitation services such as piped water and sewerage, and "improved" access as defined by the World Health Organization (WHO), and various other socio-economic indicators such as per capita GDP and urbanization rates. Unfortunately, estimates of coverage with improved water and sanitation do not exist prior to 1990, and the data for many of our key socio-economic indicators are spotty for much of the estimation period.

Importantly, our analyses should not be interpreted as implying a causal link between coverage with improved water and sanitation services and decreases in morbidity and mortality. However, empirical evidence from many countries shows that there is a strong association between these factors. For example, Komives *et al.* (2003) show that coverage with conventional piped water and sewerage infrastructures initially increases very rapidly up to household income of about US\$4,000–5,000 per year, after which coverage grows more slowly. These associations also apply at the national level (Figure 10.1).[1] In a recent paper, Günther and Fink (2011) use household survey data to relate coverage with various levels of improved water and sanitation to child mortality and find a strong negative association.

These associations do not necessarily imply that expanding piped water and sewerage itself causes the changes in mortality, though some evidence from the literature suggests that it is likely to play a significant role (Van Poppel and Van Der Heijden 1997; Galiani *et al.* 2005). Many coincident changes – in infrastructure, the quality of health systems, diet and nutrition, etc. – occur simultaneously in countries undergoing rapid development, and it is difficult to isolate the causal impact of any single factor (such as coverage with piped water and sewerage) on mortality rates. Our backward projections and future forecasts of economic losses over much of the historical period for which data are unavailable are sensitive to assumptions about the strength of association between GDP, coverage with improved services, and mortality rates.

In the next section, we discuss findings from the literature that are critical for a nuanced understanding of the problems inherent in the estimation of country-level economic losses associated with unimproved water and sanitation. Many of these findings are puzzling, and their implications are not fully recognized by the global community. We then discuss a key issue regarding the interpretation of our simulated results in Section 3: whether inadequate water and sanitation should actually be conceptualized as creating "economic losses" in poor countries. In Section 4 we present the structural model that underpins our economic simulations. Section 5 describes

[1] In this chapter, all economic estimates are presented in 1990 International Geary–Khamis dollars.

the data and parameters for our simulation model and describes our simulation procedure and sensitivity analyses. Section 6 presents the simulation results, and Section 7 summarizes our findings.

Recent Findings from the Literature on Improvements in Water and Sanitation

This second section of the chapter summarizes recently published findings from the literature on water and sanitation interventions in less developed countries that we believe are relevant for understanding the challenge and potential benefits of expanding access to such services.

Finding 1 – Household demand for non-piped water and sanitation interventions is low, while many households in less developed countries appear to want piped services but cannot afford to pay for their full cost.

It is surprisingly difficult to obtain high-quality information on the demand for improved, non-piped water and sanitation services, such as community taps or handpumps, point-of-use household treatment, on-site sanitation, and hygiene education for stimulating hand-washing. During the pilot phase of program development, most WASH interventions are provided to beneficiary households in target communities for free or at highly subsidized rates (Whittington *et al.* 2012). Then, scaled-up programs (such as the large, recent campaigns to stop open defecation in South Asia) rarely charge users the full cost of new services, or collect the type of information needed to understand the relationship between user fees and uptake rates (Water and Sanitation Program 2005).[2] A few recent studies provide limited information on this issue. In one recent intervention in ten panchayats in Kerala, India, for example, capital subsidies were very high (75%), but the increase in latrine ownership varied considerably (by 26–62% depending on the site) (Cairncross *et al.* 2005). Trémolet *et al.* (2010) summarize results from six countries that provided capital subsidies for sanitation facilities ranging from 12% to 82%; uptake rates varied from 15% to 70% in these programs. Pattanayak *et al.* (2009) provide the most specific information on the effect of prices on adoption of improved sanitation, for latrines in Orissa. Uptake

among households living below the poverty line and who were eligible for subsidized prices of US$ 7.5 increased by 31% during a recent promotion campaign, whereas uptake among households living above the poverty line and paying the full cost (about US$ 50) was 19%.

Field evidence on the demand for point-of-use water treatment and community water systems (spring protection, community standposts, or pumps) is even harder to obtain. Point-of-use technologies such as household filters or bottles of chlorine are almost always provided free of charge during intervention studies, and usage estimates are difficult to maintain once these interventions and associated subsidies come to an end (Olembo *et al.* 2004; Arnold and Colford 2007). A recent study found that very few households in rural Kenya were willing to pay anything for chlorine for point-of-use water treatment, which is cheap, effective, and readily available in numerous less developed countries (Ahuja *et al.* 2010).

Finally, household demand for piped water supply appears to be much greater, but there are significant economic and financial hurdles to providing these services to the majority of a population (Whittington *et al.* 2009). Devoto *et al.* (2009) conducted a randomized experiment to investigate the effect of home water connections on self-reported health and other outcomes among households in urban Morocco. Households randomly selected into the treatment group were informed of an offer of credit toward a new connection, and received administrative assistance for applications to connect. Uptake for the treatment group was 69% (compared with 10% in the control group). Despite the widespread perception that stated preference methods lead to inflated willingness-to-pay estimates, the evidence on demand for community water improvements from contingent valuation studies is consistent with this picture of low and heterogeneous household demand (Whittington *et al.* 2009; Pattanayak *et al.* 2010).

---

[2] Capital subsidies in large-scale sanitation campaigns supported by the Water and Sanitation Program of the World Bank, in India and Bangladesh, vary from 40% to 100%, depending on the program location, technology, and income of recipients.

Finding 2 – Many interventions to improve water and sanitation reduce baseline diarrhea incidence by 10–50%, but multiple interventions do not seem to further increase health benefits.

A large number of evaluations, some of which are randomized controlled trials, suggest that a variety of interventions to improve water, sanitation, and hygiene lead to reduced incidence of self-reported diarrheal disease. Point-of-use treatment interventions (chlorination, filtration, etc.) seem to reduce morbidity by 20–60% (Fewtrell *et al.* 2005; Arnold and Colford 2007; Clasen *et al.* 2007), though the effects are lower in urban and peri-urban environments (Fewtrell *et al.* 2005). Hand-washing interventions also appear to generate large reductions of 25–65% in self-reported incidence of diarrhea (Curtis and Cairncross 2003; Luby *et al.* 2005; Ejemot *et al.* 2009). Fewtrell *et al.* (2005) find effects of similar magnitude for sanitation campaigns.

The effects of water supply and source improvements on diarrheal disease incidence are less clear. Fewtrell *et al.*'s (2005) meta-analysis suggests a relative risk of 0.90 for households obtaining new in-house connections, and 0.94 for those using new standpipe connections; the relative risk associated with source water quality improvements is similar (0.89).[3] The absence of sizeable health gains from water-supply interventions may be due to the fact that water can easily become contaminated during transport to the home (in containers or via poorly designed and maintained pipe systems) or because of unhygienic water handling within the household. The random experiment conducted by Devoto *et al.* (2009) revealed that the incidence of self-reported diarrheal disease among households with new water connections in urban areas in Morocco was no different than that in a control group with much lower access to piped water. This may be due to the fact that the water quality from alternative

sources – communal taps with chlorinated water – was generally good. Households with private connections did increase their water use substantially, however, suggesting that they experienced other benefits.

However, evidence from five studies that assessed the joint introduction of water, sanitation, and hygiene/health education measures also showed that risk reductions were also about 25–60% (Fewtrell *et al.* 2005). Given that point-of-use, hygiene, and sanitation interventions address different routes of contamination, the lack of additional gains from interventions that combine more than one of these components is puzzling. Several other studies have obtained similar results (Esrey *et al.* 1991). Fewtrell *et al.* (2005) offer several possible explanations for these findings: (a) "piecemeal implementation" of programs; (b) an overall lack of focus or lack of sufficient attention to sanitation and hygiene education components; and c) the lack of assurance of water quality at the point of consumption.

Finding 3 – Access to reliable piped water supply is highly correlated with decreases in mortality in countries experiencing rapid economic development, but not in low-income countries or among the poor.

Jalan and Ravallion (2003) used propensity-score matching methods to estimate the causal effects of piped water (a tap inside the house or a public tap) on diarrhea prevalence and duration in children under 5 in India.[4] Children living in households with piped water had significantly lower prevalence and duration of diarrhea than the comparison group. However, the health gains were not significant for the poorest 40% in terms of income, and were lower for children in households with less educated women. Two hypotheses have been advanced for why health gains from increased piped water access among the poor are elusive: (a) there may be a mortality penalty associated with living in cramped urban environments in poor countries due to poor sanitation, which could be made worse by increasing households' supply of water (Miller and Cutler 2005; Bennett 2012); or (b) poor areas may experience low reliability of piped water supply due to cost recovery problems and/or mismanagement, which undermines the quality of water delivered (Hunter *et al.* 2009).

---

[3] Relative risk is the risk of a developing a disease relative to exposure (in this case to improved water supply), and is the ratio of the probability of illness in the exposed group versus the non-exposed, control group.

[4] Propensity score matching is a statistical technique that aims to limit bias in the measurement of an intervention's effects by matching treated units with control units that are similar on observed pre-treatment attributes that influence selection into the treatment group (Rosenbaum and Rubin 1983).

Gamper-Rabindran *et al.* (2010) investigated the impact of piped water on the infant mortality rate in Brazil. They used quantile regression models with panel data to examine whether the provision of piped water reduces infant mortality, controlling for potential time invariant confounders. They found a highly non-linear relationship between coverage, income, and mortality rates. The provision of piped water services had a small effect on mortality in the poorest counties, but rose rapidly as counties experienced economic development. However, once a certain level of economic development was achieved, decreases in mortality slowed, and the most developed counties experienced limited health gains from extension of piped water services. Surprisingly, they also found that piped sewerage did not have any significant effect on infant mortality. Their results lend support to the threshold-saturation hypothesis, i.e., that the relationship between water supply and mortality rates varies with changing socio-economic levels (Shuval *et al.* 1981). They conclude that studies that fail to find associations between mortality reductions and the expansion of coverage with piped water services must therefore be interpreted with caution.

Finding 4 – Increasing knowledge about the health benefits of preventative health interventions, such as water and sanitation infrastructure, does not always increase household demand.

There are many examples from the literature that lend support to the idea that social marketing or information related to the benefits of WASH services can be effective in increasing uptake of improved technologies (Waterkeyn and Cairncross 2005; Pattanayak *et al.* 2009). In one recent study, Jalan and Somanathan (2008) found that providing information about an individual household's water quality did modestly affect the behavior of households in a relatively affluent suburb of Delhi, India. A random sample of households was given a water quality test, and half of these households were informed of their result. A follow-up visit 8 weeks later revealed that households who were told that their drinking water might be contaminated (following a positive test for fecal contamination), were 11% more likely to change water purification, storage, and handling practices (incurring average out-of-pocket expenses

of US$7.24 more for these changes) than those who were not informed of their test result. The effect was strongest among the wealthiest households. Hamoudi *et al.* (2012) recently found that providing households in rural Andhra Pradesh, India with information about the quality of their drinking water increased the purchase of water from advanced community treatment facilities by about 50% in communities with low levels (10%) of baseline uptake – a much larger information effect than reported by Jalan and Somanathan (2008).

However, two other recent studies suggest that some caution is warranted regarding the effect of social marketing and information. In a randomized evaluation of a deworming program in rural Kenya, Miguel and Kremer (2004) found that school health education did not increase household demand for the deworming treatment, in spite of the fact that deworming is highly effective at reducing infection. A social mobilization campaign also failed to increase demand, and a modest cost recovery program reduced uptake by 80%. The researchers even found that uptake was lower among households with more knowledge about the health benefits of deworming. Also, Kremer *et al.* (2011) found that almost no households were willing to purchase a water-treatment product called WaterGuard after 6 months experience using it, even though diarrhea rates among users had decreased by 35–40%. Moreover, they found only modest positive effects of social networks on uptake (i.e. households were only slightly more likely to use WaterGuard when they saw their neighbors using it). The researchers concluded, "We find no evidence that valuation of the product is higher among households who stand to benefit most from it." The limitations of social marketing have been highlighted in studies of other health prevention technologies as well (Snow *et al.* 1999).

What are the Implications of These Findings for Our Analysis?

These facts suggest a set of dynamic, complicated causal relationships between investments in water and sanitation infrastructure, public health, the demographic transition, and economic development. We suspect that these relationships are unstable and non-stationary, and are mediated by household income, education, and awareness of disease pathways. Today's industrialized countries escaped from the constraints of the Malthusian economy so long ago that most people have forgotten its cruel logic. In a Malthusian economy, high morbidity and mortality reduce the labor supply and drive up real average wages (Clark 2007). Conversely, interventions that reduce mortality and morbidity, with a simultaneous increase in economic opportunities, drive down average wages. Water, sanitation, and hygiene interventions that focus solely on improved health may thus have the direct effect of improving the well-being of households who do not become ill, but also the indirect effect of driving down average household income in the community, which then leads to lower health. In a Malthusian economy, increasing investment in preventative health is not a way out of a poverty trap.

As a result, one should be cautious about claims that improvements in water, sanitation, and hygiene will automatically translate into better health and economic outcomes. Given the complexity and uncertainty in these relationships, we do not claim that our simulation model unravels the conflicting causal claims in the literature. Rather we rely on relatively robust associations between key variables that enable us to simulate future developments with modest confidence. We prefer to think of the results of these simulations as "plausible scenarios." We do not claim that improved water and sanitation services are the fundamental cause of the reduced mortality rates we project. But before we describe the simulation model and present these forecasts, we turn to the question of how best to frame the problem of "economic losses" from unimproved water and sanitation infrastructure.

Problem Framing: What Precisely are We Trying to Measure?

Before the twentieth century people living in countries that are now industrialized suffered greatly from poor water and sanitation conditions in both urban and rural areas. Today, in industrialized countries,

almost all of this acute suffering from poor water and sanitation conditions has been alleviated due to the installation of piped water and sewer infrastructure, good housing, food safety, and modern healthcare systems. Diseases such as cholera and typhoid are no longer a concern for citizens of countries like the United States, Britain, or Japan. This is not true for the nearly 6 billion people in less developed countries, where the position today is similar in important respects to conditions in the nineteenth and early twentieth centuries in industrialized countries that have now largely solved their water- and sanitation-related health problems.

By definition economic losses and gains are measured as a change from some reference point. "Economic value" is defined as the change in human well-being that results from a move from one state of the world to another. For people in industrialized countries today the reference point – or status quo state of the world – is improved water supply and sanitation infrastructure. If they had to live in conditions that exist in many parts of the developing world (where they would be at risk of contracting diseases such as cholera and typhoid), this change would reduce their well-being, and they would experience this change as an "economic loss."

On the other hand, the reference point for many people living in less developed countries is poor water and sanitation conditions, and any improvement in water supply or sanitation infrastructure is experienced as an improvement in well-being, i.e. an "economic gain." This difference in perspective (or reference point) between people in industrialized and less developed countries is important because psychologists and behavioral economists have demonstrated convincingly that people value losses much more than commensurate gains (Kahneman and Tversky 1979).[5] If economic growth in less-developed countries (LDCs) proceeds and these countries invest in improved water supply and sanitation infrastructure, people living in these countries will experience this change as an economic gain. Trying to empathize with people in LDCs, people living in industrialized countries will likely perceive the same improvement as a reduction in economic loss – and are likely to place higher value on what is actually an improvement over the status quo. It is thus natural for donors to believe that the welfare

---

[5] In fact, the feelings associated with gains and losses are different – and are experienced in different parts of the brain.

gains from improved water and sanitation infrastructure are much more important to people in LDCs than people who live in LDCs are likely to feel themselves.[6] As Jack Knetsch and others have argued (Knetsch 2010; Knetsch *et al.* 2012), preferences are reference-dependent.

From our perspective, the most appealing, logical way to report the consequences of improved water supply and sanitation infrastructure are as economic gains to the populations affected because we believe this is how people themselves perceive these changes. In other words, the correct measure of the welfare gain to poor people in less developed countries is their willingness to pay (WTP) for the economic gains that result from infrastructure improvements. This WTP measure could be compared with the cost of installing those infrastructures to determine whether the net benefits of an intervention are likely to be positive.

However, for the purposes of this chapter, we call these economic gains "reductions in economic losses" (i.e. the industrialized world's or donors' perspective) so that our estimates are reported in a manner that is consistent with that of the other chapters in the Copenhagen Consensus Center project. Moreover, to ensure a standard terminology, we refer to status quo conditions in LDCs as "economic losses." We caution that this approach of referring to economic gains as reductions in economic losses, and to status quo conditions as "economic losses" can be confusing for several reasons.

The first problem is simply that it re-enforces a donor bias on global challenges (Whittington 2010). For people in industrialized countries, who empathize with the suffering of people in less developed countries, and perceive status quo conditions as "losses," the appropriate measure of economic value will appear to be their willingness to accept (WTA) compensation to move to a state of the world with such poor water and sanitation conditions. This perceived WTA measure will be very high both because citizens of industrialized countries are relatively rich and because they have a different reference point. If people in industrialized countries and donors shift the reference point (to their own state of the world), and measure or conceptualize the potential gains from investments as economic losses to be reduced by investments, then the economic value of the resulting welfare change may be greatly exaggerated. It may also be very difficult for donors to understand poor peoples' behavior.

A second problem occurs when we look back in time and try to characterize the state of the world in a country such as Brazil in, say, 1900. In this chapter we attempt to estimate the number of fatalities due to poor water and sanitation infrastructure in Brazil in 1900, and this estimate will show the suffering that occurred in 1900 in this status quo "state of the world." This suffering is expressed in monetary terms as an economic loss compared to a state of the world in which all the citizens in Brazil in 1900 had modern water and sanitation infrastructure and modern healthcare facilities similar to those that citizens of industrialized countries experience today. Obviously this is a hypothetical reference point that did not happen, nor could it ever have happened.

A third problem arises when one tries to express these "economic losses" as a percentage of a country's GDP at a point in time in the past. For example, the GDP estimates for Brazil in 1900 have embedded in them the actual state of the country's water and sanitation infrastructure existing at that time. If in 1900 Brazil had invested more in modern water supply and sanitation infrastructure, these investments would have reduced investments elsewhere in the Brazilian economy in 1900 (perhaps investments in roads, hospitals, or schools). It is practically impossible to know what the net effect of shifting investments to water and sanitation infrastructure in 1900 would have been on mortality or growth rates in Brazil. When we compare our estimates of "economic losses" due to poor water and sanitation conditions to GDP estimates in 1900, we are thus implicitly forced to assume that someone outside of Brazil "donated" the funds for these investments in water and sanitation infrastructure. In other words, we measure "economic losses" in Brazil in 1900 relative to a state of the world in which someone outside of Brazil gave all the citizens of Brazil modern water

---

[6] Similarly, donors appear to believe that the value of mortality risk reductions, perhaps as conceptualized in the value of a statistical life (VSL), is higher than many people who actually live in LDCs, who face a wide array of mortality risks every day.

and sanitation infrastructure. Such a conception of losses is unrealistic and quite confusing.

Modeling Framework

This section describes the modeling strategy we use to determine historic and future economic welfare "losses" associated with the challenge of water and sanitation. Conceptually, the economic benefits of improvements in water and sanitation to households consist of three main components: (a) health, (b) time savings, and (c) aesthetic and convenience improvements (at the household and business level, including reductions in individuals' psychological stress result from utilization of unimproved infrastructures for water and sanitation) stemming from increased consumption due to the drop in the marginal "price" of acquiring additional water (Whittington *et al.* 2009). These benefits (gains) are the converse of our desired measure of welfare losses due to inadequate water and sanitation. We thus define the economic cost (measured in monetary terms) of not having improved services ($Loss_i^{WSH}$) as:

$$Loss_i^{WSH} = \sum_j \left[H_{ij} + T_{ij} + A_{ij} \right] \qquad (10.1)$$

where H_{ij}, T_{ij}, and A_{ij} are the health, time, and aesthetic gains forgone, respectively, from not having access to improved water and sanitation, summed over all individuals j in location i to yield the overall costs for location i. Note that the reduction in losses related to improved water quality is already included both in health benefits, which increases when water quality is improved, and aesthetic benefits, which may or may not increase

depending on individuals' tastes for improved water quality.

The risk of illness from WASH-related diseases decreases with access to improved water and sanitation services. Health damages consist of morbidity and mortality losses. Each of these two components of health damages is heterogeneous across individuals in a population, and depends on income Y and other socio-economic characteristics X of the affected individuals (including factors related to an individual's water and sanitation situation):

$$H_{ij} = I_{ij}^{WSH}\left(Y_{ij}, X_{ij}\right)$$
$$\times \left[morb\left(Y_{ij}, X_{ij}\right) + CFR_{ij}^{WSH}\left(Y_{ij}, X_{ij}\right) \right.$$
$$\left. \times mort\left(Y_{ij}, X_{ij}\right) \right], \qquad (10.2)$$

where the first term in the bracketed expression represents the cost of morbidity and the second term corresponds to the cost of mortality; I_{ij}^{WSH} is the incidence (or risk of illness) of WASH-related disease for individual j in location i, CFR_{ij}^{WSH} is the case fatality rate (risk of death given illness), and *morb* and *mort* are the economic cost of illness and mortality, respectively, measured in monetary terms.[7] All of these terms depend on income Y_{ij} and the other individual and household characteristics X_{ij}.

The incidence and the case fatality rate are a function of income because richer households are better able to invest ex ante in preventive health technologies such as water and sanitation, as well as ex post treatment of illness. As discussed, empirical data support the assertion that coverage with water and sewerage infrastructures increases rapidly as countries move from low GDP per capita to middle-income status (Komives *et al.* 2003). After this transition, coverage reaches high levels and thereafter grows much more slowly. Interestingly, the kink in the relationship between coverage and average household income (Figure 10.1 above) occurs around US$4,000–5,000, which coincides almost exactly with the kink in the "Preston curve" which relates per capita GDP (a proxy for income) and longevity (Preston 1975).[8] The kink in water and sanitation coverage may not be the only factor so closely associated with the Preston curve; others for example have found similar transition points between

---

[7] To express mortality risks in monetary terms, we rely on the economic concept of the value of a statistical life (VSL), which is obtained by scaling up the willingness to pay for small mortality risk reductions to a single death measured at the population level (see Appendix 10.1 for details and discussion).

[8] The Preston curve grew out of an empirical study of the relationship between life expectancy and real per capita income. It shows that individuals born in richer countries, on average, can expect to live longer than those born in poor countries, but that the link between income and life expectancy flattens out beyond a certain level of income.

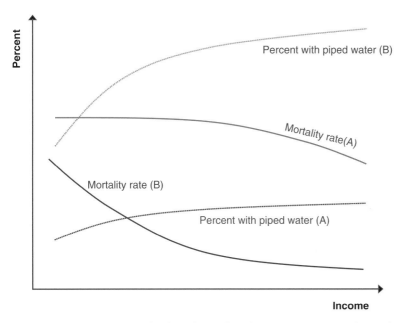

Figure 10.2 *Two scenarios for the relationships between coverage with piped water, WASH-related mortality rate, and income*

income and environmental quality, or income and happiness indices (Grossman and Krueger 1995; Dasgupta *et al*. 2002; Inglehart and Klingemann 2003). Indeed, many coincident improvements occur with rising incomes, including factors such as improved healthcare systems and better nutrition.

Of course, this stylized description is complicated by the fact that income is endogenous in the production of better health. In fact, the argument that increasing income leads to declines in disease incidence and mortality hinges on the extent to which households acquiring health-improving technologies experience health improvements. Figure 10.2 presents two possible cases (A and B) that depict how mortality rate might be associated with income. In Case A, coverage with improved water services is low and increases slowly with income; the mortality rate also decreases slowly with income. In Case B, income growth is associated with rapid increases in

coverage and decreases in the mortality rate, perhaps due to a virtuous cycle in which income and health are self-reinforcing.

The economic health cost of WASH-related disease for a representative individual with average income $\overline{Y}_i$ and characteristics $\overline{X}_i$ in location i is:

$$H_i = I_i^{WSH}\left(\overline{Y}_i, \overline{X}_i\right)$$
$$\cdot \left[morb\left(\overline{Y}_i, \overline{X}_i\right) + CFR_i^{WSH}\left(\overline{Y}_i, \overline{X}_i\right) \cdot mort\left(\overline{Y}_i, \overline{X}_i\right)\right]$$
(10.3)

Differentiating equation (10.3) with respect to income and dropping the subscripts, yields equation (10.4) (the signs of each term are shown in parentheses below the equation):

We expect that incidence (I) of WASH-related dis-

$$\frac{dH}{dY} = \frac{dI}{dY} - [morb + CFR - mort] + I\left[\frac{dmorb}{dY} + \frac{dCFR}{dY} - mort + CFR - \frac{dmort}{dY}\right]$$
(10.4)

$$(?) \quad (-) \quad (+) \quad (+) \quad (+) \quad (+) \quad (+) \quad (-) \quad (+) \quad (+) \quad (+)$$

eases and the risk of death among those who fall ill (*CFR*) both decrease as income increases (Figure 10.3). As shown in Figure 10.2, we expect

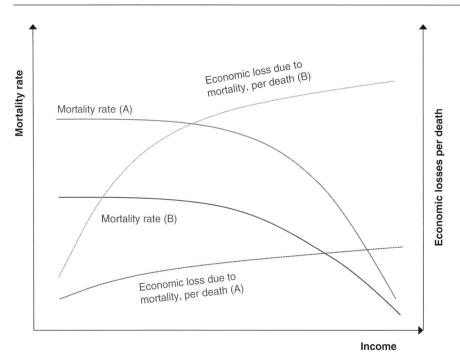

Figure 10.3 *Illustrations of possible relationships between the mortality rate, "economic losses" per death, and income*

that these changes are strictly monotonic; however they could either be slow (Case A) or rapid (Case B), depending on the cost of health improvements and the income available to individuals who would make such investments. The terms and – the "economic losses" in monetary terms due to illness and death per case, respectively – are increasing in income, because richer households are willing to pay more to reduce the negative consequences of poor health (Figure 10.3). This positive relation between income and the economic value of reduced mortality risks is well documented (Viscusi and Aldy 2003). As development proceeds and income grows, the sign on the change in WASH-related health damages per capita is ambiguous, and depends on the respective rates of change of the terms in equation (10.4). In Case A in Figure 10.3, "economic losses" decrease overall: mortality rates decrease sharply while "economic losses" per death increase slowly. In Case B, however, "economic losses" increase, as decreases in mortality do not keep pace with the increasing "economic losses" of additional deaths. As shown, it is possible that H (measured in absolute terms) will

increase with income, even as incidence of WASH-related diseases falls, if increases in $mort(Y)$ outweigh decreases in $I(Y) \times CFR(Y)$. Whether the economic value of health losses and income are positively or negatively related is thus an empirical question.

It is useful to contrast equations (10.2)–(10.4) with a non-economic measure of the burden of disease for an individual j, such as the total burden of disease, perhaps as represented by the number of disability-adjusted life years (DALYs):

$$DALY_{ij} = I_{ij}^{WSH}$$
$$\times \left[w^{WSH} \times Dur^{WSH} + CFR_{ij}^{WSH} \times LE_{ij} \right]$$
$$(10.5)$$

where the first term is a measure of morbidity, and the second reflects the mortality burden. w^{WSH} is the DALY weight for WASH-related disease (a measure of the relative pain and suffering associated with illness; see Mathers *et al.* (2004) for details); Dur^{WSH} is the duration of illness; and LE_{ij} is the discounted life expectancy of those who fall ill. All terms in expression (10.5) are decreasing in income, except perhaps

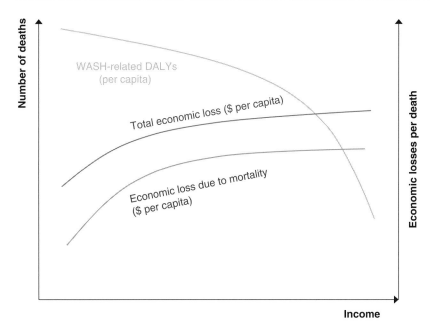

Figure 10.4 *Illustrations of possible relationships between DALYs, "economic losses" per capita, and income*

w^{WSH}(which will depend on how the relative proportion of relevant diseases, such as diarrhea, typhoid, and cholera, change with income) and LE_{ij}, since longevity increases in income (as shown by the Preston curve). DALYs per person are thus certain to decrease in income for WASH-related diseases given the strong negative relationship between income and the incidence of infectious diseases (i.e. the "environmental risk transition") (Smith and Ezzati 2005).[9] Thus, while measures such as DALYs would likely decrease with rising GDP, "economic losses" per case or death would increase (Figure 10.4).

Similar to health losses, the time costs and aesthetic benefits forgone due to lack of access to improved water and sanitation services depend on income and other socio-economic characteristics:

$$T_{ij} = t_{ij}^{collection}\left(Y_{ij}, X_{ij}\right) \times v_{ij}^{t}\left(Y_{ij}, X_{ij}\right) \qquad (10.6)$$

and

$$A_{ij} = q_{ij}^{water}\left(Y_{ij}, X_{ij}\right) \times v_{ij}^{water}\left(Y_{ij}, X_{ij}\right) \qquad (10.7)$$

where $t_{ij}^{collection}$ corresponds to the time required for members of household to collect water or reach sanitation facilities outside the home; v_{ij}^{t} is the

shadow value of the time spent by individuals in household j; q_{ij}^{water} is the quantity of additional water that would be used if supplies were more conveniently located (i.e. if the shadow price of water were reduced via enhanced access to water and sanitation services) for household j; and v_{ij}^{water} is the net economic value of the additional units of consumed water, in location i.

As with equation (10.4) for dH/dY, the signs of dT/dY and dA/dY – the rates of change in time savings and aesthetic burden with respect to income – are ambiguous. The term $dt^{collection}/dY$ is negative, since richer households and communities are better able to invest in improved technology to obtain time savings (for example private handpumps or more convenient connections to piped water networks), but the change in the shadow value of time with respect to income dv_{ij}^{t}/dY is also positive. Similarly, dq^{water}/dY is negative, since richer households are able to purchase technologies or services (for water delivery) that

[9] There is actually one odd situation where DALYs per capita could increase even when income is rising and mortality is falling, if increases in life expectancy and thus years of life lost are increasing faster than mortality is dropping.

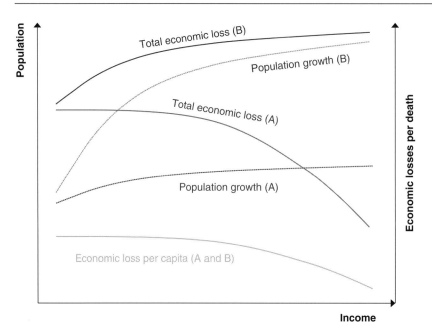

Figure 10.5 *Illustrations of possible relationships between per capita "economic losses," total "economic losses," population growth, and income*

improve convenience and allow them to more easily obtain additional water. However, the change in the net economic value of additional units of consumed water with respect to income dv_{ij}^t/dY may (or may not) be positive, depending on the relative magnitude of the income elasticities of the terms in equations (10.6) and (10.7).

Finally, many LDCs are in the midst of the demographic transition. It is theoretically possible that per capita losses could decrease while overall "economic losses" at the country level would increase, due to increased population (Figure 10.5). In both cases shown, per capita *Loss* decreases, but Case A is characterized by low population growth while Case B has high population growth. The consequences for total "economic losses" measured at the country level would be very different in these two situations, increasing in Case B but decreasing in Case A.

Our simulations for different countries therefore need to reflect differences in population growth, baseline mortality rates, the costs associated with WASH-related deaths and illnesses, the costs associated with collecting and hauling water over long distances, and the trends of each of these with respect to historical income and future income projections.

Data, Model Parameterization, and Analytical Approach

This section describes our approach for estimating and parameterizing the relationships described in the previous section. Our unit of analysis for this global analysis is the country rather than the individual household. We consider only the health losses and time costs from equation (10.1), and do not include aesthetic costs, due to the limitations on country-level data availability with respect to the latter. Our analytical approach is summarized in the flow chart shown in Figure 10.6. We first describe the specification of the key relationships between coverage with improved water and sanitation services, income, and WASH-related health burden and time costs, which allow us to value outcomes. Then we present the regression results that provide the parameter estimates for our modeling of outcomes and losses. Finally, we explain the analytical approach used for our simulations and sensitivity analyses. We utilize country-level data collected from secondary sources for the regressions and simulations whenever possible, and regional data otherwise.

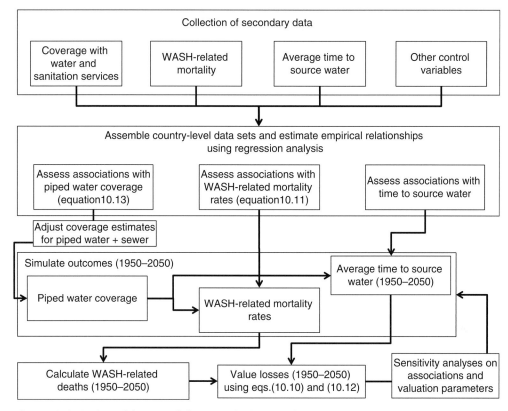

Figure 10.6 *Analytical framework for our calculations of economic losses associated with poor water and sanitation*

Data considerations and Model Specification

The literature and existing empirical analyses do not provide much insight on the relationships between WASH-related disease incidence and case fatality rates, income, and access to various levels of improved water and sanitation. Reliable measures of incidence of WASH-related diseases in different countries are nearly impossible to obtain. The mortality attributable to WASH (expressed as the percentage of mortality attributable to all factors), though also uncertain and subject to measurement problems, has at least received some attention.[10] We rely on 2004 country-level data from the World Health Organization's Environmental Burden of Disease project; the methodology used to calculate overall mortality burden is outlined in Fewtrell *et al.* (2007).[11] The mortality attributable to poor WASH conditions includes: (a) infectious diarrhea;

(b) malnutrition, about 50% of which is estimated to be attributable to inadequate WASH and its consequences,[12] the WASH-related fraction of which is estimated by the authors; and (c) intestinal nematode

[10] In the description that follows, we use the term mortality attributable to WASH as the ratio of the total number of deaths due to WASH to the total number deaths. The terms WASH-related death rate and WASH-related mortality refer to the ratio of the total number of deaths due to WASH to the number of population in a country.

[11] Available at: www.who.int/quantifying_ehimpacts/national/countryprofile/intro/en/index.html. The data are only available for 2004.

[12] More precisely, the diarrhea rate attributable to WASH was calculated based on access levels to safe water and adequate sanitation service levels, as explained in Fewtrell *et al.* (2007). For malnutrition, Prüss-Üstün and Corvalán (2006) estimate that 39–61% is attributable to WASH-related factors, based on analysis of expert surveys. Malnutrition rates are highest in South Asia and sub-Saharan Africa.

infections, schistosomiasis, trachoma, and lymphatic filariasis, 66% of which is attributed to poor WASH (Prüss-Üstün and Corvalán 2006).

We convert country estimates of the mortality attributable to WASH as a percentage of all deaths into a WASH-related death rate by multiplying this percentage by the total number of deaths and dividing by the total population of each country in our data set for 2004 (132 countries in all):

$$d_{it}^{WSH} = pd_{it}^{WSH} \times \frac{Deaths_{it}}{Pop_{it}} \qquad (10.8)$$

where d_{it}^{WSH} is the death rate that is attributable to poor water, sanitation and hygiene; pd_{it}^{WSH} is the mortality attributable to WASH; and $Deaths_{it}$ and Pop_{it} are the total number of deaths and population, all for country i in year t. The WASH-related death rate (or WASH-related mortality) is thus equivalent to the combined term $I_i^{WSH} \times CFR_i^{WSH}$ from equation (10.3). In our sample of less developed countries for 2004, these death rates range from a low value of 0 in several countries to roughly 5.5 deaths per 1,000 people per year in Angola, with a mean value of 0.58 deaths per 1,000.

To obtain annual country-level health losses due to inadequate water and sanitation, we use the economic concept of the value of a statistical life (VSL) to represent the cost of mortality (*mort*) per death, and cost-of-illness (COI) to represent the cost of morbidity (*morb*) per case, and multiply by the population size in each year. We also explicitly separate coverage with improved water and sanitation services $\overline{W}_{it}$ (we use various measures for this variable, which are defined further below) from the other control variables $\overline{X}_{it}$ that determine the health outcomes of interest, and thus rewrite equation (10.3):

$$H_{it} = Pop_{it} \times \left[I_{it}^{WSH} \left(\overline{Y}_{it}, \overline{W}_{it}, \overline{X}_{it} \right) \times COI \left(\overline{Y}_{it}, \overline{X}_{it} \right) \right.$$
$$\left. + d_{ij}^{WSH} \left(\overline{Y}_{it}, \overline{W}_{it}, \overline{X}_{it} \right) \times VSL \left(\overline{Y}_{it}, \overline{X}_{it} \right) \right] \qquad (10.9)$$

Given the paucity of country-level data on incidence rates, it is not possible to specify the first term in equation (10.9). Instead, our analysis applies estimates of the cost of WASH-related morbidity relative to mortality based on the calculations

presented in Whittington *et al.* (2009), which suggest that morbidity makes up roughly 25% of the economic cost of WASH-related disease (we vary this from 10% to 40% in sensitivity analysis). We therefore obtain equation (10.10), where f_{COI} is this fraction of morbidity burden:

$$H_{it} \simeq (1 + f_{COI}) \times Pop_{it} \times d_{it}^{WSH} \left(\overline{Y}_{it}, \overline{W}_{it}, \overline{X}_{it} \right)$$
$$\times VSL \left(\overline{Y}_{it}, \overline{X}_{it} \right)$$
$$= (1 + f_{COI}) \times Pop_{it} \times d_{it}^{WSH} \left(\overline{Y}_{it}, \overline{W}_{it}, \overline{X}_{it} \right)$$
$$\times VSL \left(\overline{Y}_{it}, \overline{X}_{it} \right)$$
$$(10.10)$$

As shown above, we ultimately specify VSL in our model to be solely dependent on income. The available evidence on VSLs from meta-analyses in the literature suggests the need to develop a function that accommodates both low income elasticities for the VSL in rich countries, and higher income elasticities for the VSL in less developed countries (Viscusi and Aldy 2003; Hall and Jones 2007; Hammitt and Robinson 2011). We describe our procedure for developing such a function in more detail in Annex 10.1. The VSL and all economic values in our model are specified in 1990 International Geary–Khamis dollars. Also, given the fact that the diarrheal disease burden (and especially mortality from diarrheal disease) is concentrated on the poor in less developed countries, we value these deaths using $VSL \left(\overline{Y}_{it,80} \right)$, which is the VSL calculated from the average income among the bottom 80% of the population, which in part accounts for the amount of inequality in the income distribution in different less developed countries. This adjustment is made to address concerns over the relevance of using average per capita GDP when calculating health losses. We evaluate the importance of this adjustment in sensitivity analysis.

We next use regression models to better understand how the WASH-related death rate d_i^{WSH} is associated with income and coverage with improved water and sanitation services:

$$d_i^{WSH} = \alpha_0 + \alpha_1 \times ln\left(\overline{Y}_i \right) + \beta \times \overline{W}_{il} + \gamma \times X_{ik} + \epsilon_i$$
$$(10.11)$$

where $\overline{Y}_i$ is per capita GDP (in 1990 IGKD), obtained from Angus Maddison's GGDC

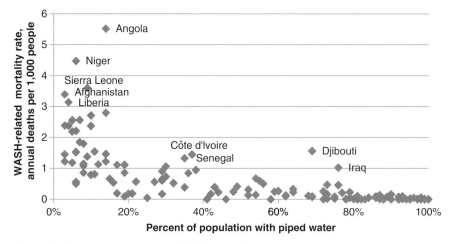

Figure 10.7 *Association between WASH-related death rate and percent coverage with piped water in 2004*

database.[13] $\overline{W}_{il}$ is the set of l variables that relate to improved water and sanitation, which we take to be the percentage of population with (a) access to in-house piped water; (b) access to other improved water supply; and (c) access to improved sanitation, in country i, obtained from the Joint Monitoring Program (JMP) for Water Supply and Sanitation.[14] We use separate variables for coverage with piped water, coverage with other improved sources, and coverage with improved sanitation, because the empirical data suggest that WASH-related mortality only really drops to zero in countries with high coverage with adequately treated piped water and sewerage (see for example Figure 10.7 and Figure 10.8 which show the associations with piped versus unimproved water sources, respectively, for 2004). Unfortunately, unlike for piped water, country-level estimates of sewerage are not widely available, so we cannot separately test for associations with improved sanitation versus piped sewage system.

When estimating equation (10.11), we use coverage data for piped water from 2005, since these are the data closest to the year for which mortality burden was determined (2004). X_{it} is a vector of other control variables (regional dummy variables, percent urban population, income inequality, fertility, literacy, and several governance variables: democracy–autocracy score (polity), regime durability, and an indicator for coups d'état) and ε_i is an error term.[15] The coefficients α_0, α_1, β, and γ are estimated by

ordinary least squares (OLS) regression. We expect α_1 and β to be negative since the WASH-related mortality should be negatively related to access with improved services, although we acknowledge that the broad definitions of improved access may lead to less than expected effects.

In similar fashion, we estimate a relationship for the average time to water in minutes, using the limited data available for different countries and years in the Demographic and Health Surveys (DHS), the Multiple Indicator Cluster Surveys (MICS), and the World Health Surveys (WHS) of the WHO.[16] We do not include the time spent due to lack of improved

---

[13] Available at www.ggdc.net/databases/ted.htm.

[14] Available at www.wssinfo.org/datamining/tables.html. Improved sources that are not piped water include: plot or yard tap; public tap/standpipe; tubewell/borehole; protected dug well; protected spring; and rainwater collection. Improved sanitation includes: flush or pour-flush to piped sewer system, septic tank, or pit latrine; ventilated improved pit latrine; pit latrine with slab; and composting toilet.

[15] Annex 10.2 presents additional details on the data sources for the control variables in our regression models; Table A10.3 in Annex 10.3 presents the regional country groupings.

[16] The MICS data can be found at: www.unicef.org/statistics/index_24302.html; DHS data are available at: www.measuredhs.com/accesssurveys/; and WHS at www.who.int/healthinfo/survey/en/. There are quality and consistency problems associated with the time-to-source data from these sources. In terms of consistency, the DHS summaries by country only report the *median* time to water, which is not precisely the same as the *mean* time to water obtained from MICS.

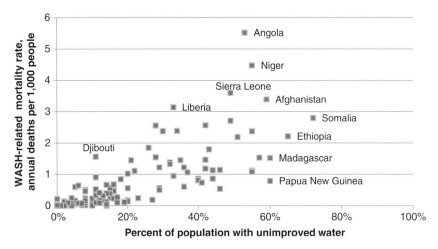

Figure 10.8 *Association between WASH-related death rate and percent coverage with unimproved water in 2004*

sanitation because of insufficient data. That model is similar to the one shown in equation (10.11), except that the dependent variable is replaced by the average time spent to reach water in country i and year t $\left(\bar{t}_{it}^{collection}\right)$ among all households, whether connected to piped networks or not, and the control variables other than coverage do not include literacy and fertility. We then value the time lost due to collection of water at the country level using equation (10.12) (adapted from equation (10.6) in the previous section):

$$T_{it} = \left(2^{trips \times Pop_{it}} / hhsize_{it}\right)$$
$$\times \bar{t}_{it}^{collection}\left(\bar{Y}_{it}, \bar{W}_{ilt}, \bar{X}_{it}\right) \times v'\left(\bar{Y}_{it,80}\right)$$
$$(10.12)$$

where the opportunity cost of time spent gathering water is assumed to be a fraction of the average per capita GDP among the bottom 80% of the income distribution (converted to a per-hour value assuming that the GDP is generated from a work week of length L^w); $hhsize_{it}$ is the average household size;

Similarly, the WHS data are not ideal because they only collect time-to-water data in categories that range from <5, 5–30, 30–60, 60–90, and >90 minutes per trip. Converting these to mean times by country requires assumptions; we assume that average time to water is zero in countries with 100% of responses in the group for <5 minutes per trip, and otherwise we multiply the percentages in each category by the midpoint of that category.

and *trips* is the average number of trips to collect water per household per day. The factor of 2 is to account for the round-trip collection time. We expect that time to water sources drops significantly as income and the opportunity cost of time increase, as suggested in Figure 10.9.

To extrapolate historic and future levels of coverage with piped water and sewerage, which are required to project changes in mortality and time spent collecting water that accompany those changes, we also estimate the relationship between piped water coverage and GDP using regression methods:

$$P_{it} = k_0 + k_1 \times \ln\left(\bar{Y}_{i,t-1}\right) + k \times Z_{ij,t} + \delta_{it} + v_{it}$$
$$(10.13)$$

where $\bar{Y}_{i,t-1}$ is the income from the previous wave of data (period $t-1$), $Z_{im.t}$ is a vector of m control variables (WHO region dummy variables, linear time trend, year dummy variables, percent urban population, income inequality, several governance variables, bilateral aid received for WASH, and a set of time–region interaction variables), measured at time t for country i, δ_{it} is a time-varying error term, v_{it} is a time-invariant error term, and k_0, k_1, and k are coefficients estimated using regression models. The year and region dummy variables are important to control for differences in technology, access to capital, and other factors that influence uptake of water and sanitation technologies over time and space. In

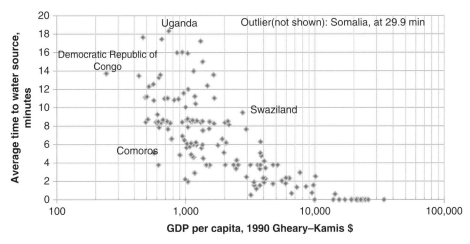

Figure 10.9 *Association between time to water and GDP per capita (GDP per capita on a log scale)*

estimating equation (10.13), we use the Joint Monitoring Programme (JMP) data for all five available years – 1990, 1995, 2000, 2005, and 2008. We estimate both fixed effects and random effects models. We expect k_1 to be positive since higher income should be associated with higher piped water coverage.

Estimates of Associations between WASH-Related Death Rates, Income, and Coverage with Improved WASH Services

The results of our OLS regressions for WASH-related death rates (equation 10.11) are presented in Table 10.1. Results for piped and improved water access are similar whether or not developed countries are included. Column (1) presents results from a reduced form specification that does not include variables relating to coverage with improved water and sanitation services, and instead relates the mortality rates directly to income. In this specification, a 1-log increase in per capita GDP is associated with a decline of WASH-related death rates of roughly 0.4 per 1,000 per year (in other words increasing income by a factor of about 2.7 decreases the death rate by 0.4 thousand per year).

Columns (2)–(4) provide evidence that both piped water and improved water coverage have significant and negative associations with the WASH-realted death rate, and that the magnitude of these associations is similar. The fit for this model is improved

over that of the reduced form specification. A 1% increase in piped water coverage or improved water coverage is associated with a decrease of 0.03 deaths per 1,000 people per year due to WASH-related diseases. Similarly, a 1-log increase in income is associated with a decline in WASH-related deaths by 0.3 per 1,000 per year; this is the effect of income that excludes its indirect association with coverage with improved services. Given the mortality rates across countries in our sample (ranging from 0 to 5.5 per 1,000), these are large declines. Somewhat surprisingly, coverage with improved sanitation is not significantly associated with the WASH-related death rate, though this may be due to high correlations (over 0.8) with the water coverage variables. Percent urban population, percent coverage with improved sanitation, inequality, the democracy–autocracy index, and the number of years since a regime change do not have significant associations with the WASH-related death rate. The association with literacy, however, is negative and significant, as expected, since higher education levels would be correlated with lower death rates. A 1% increase in literacy is associated with a decline of 0.02 deaths per 1,000 people per year.

These results are sensitive to the assumed functional form of the regression relationships. We find some evidence that the associations between coverage variables and death rates may be non-linear. Additional robustness tests (provided in Annex 10.3, Table A10.4) reveal that the coefficient

Table 10.1 OLS regression for WASH-related mortality (annual deaths per 1,000 people)[a]

	All countries, reduced form model		All countries, base model		Developing countries only, base model		Developing countries only, full model	
	Coefficient	Standard error[b]	Coefficient	Standard error[b]	Coefficient	Standard error[b]	Coefficient	Standard error[b]
Piped water coverage (%)			−0.031[***]	0.0086	−0.031[***]	0.0088	−0.029[*]	0.015
Improved non-piped water coverage (%)			−0.030[***]	0.010	−0.030[***]	0.010	−0.029[*]	0.016
Improved sanitation coverage (%)			0.0048	0.0052	0.0049	0.0053	0.010	0.0067
Ln GDP per capita	−0.43[***]	0.10	−0.30[***]	0.089	−0.31[**]	0.095	−0.27[**]	0.14
Urban population (%)	−0.00093	0.0041	0.0049	0.0053	0.0053	0.0059	0.0061	0.0065
Fertility rate							0.00067	0.0030
Literacy							−0.019[***]	0.0061
Percent of GDP to lowest 80% of population							0.0071	0.016
Developed countries	−0.34	0.24	−0.24	0.20				
Countries in LAC region	−0.87[***]	0.19	−0.69[***]	0.20	−0.69[***]	0.20	−0.60[**]	0.27
Countries in MIDEAST region	−0.69[***]	0.26	−0.39	0.26	−0.40	0.27	−0.55	0.37
Countries in SOUTH ASIA region	−0.96[***]	0.17	−0.40[*]	0.23	−0.40[*]	0.23	−0.44	0.34
Countries in EAST ASIA/PACIFIC region	−0.88[***]	0.20	−0.69[***]	0.19	−0.69[***]	0.19	−0.34	0.28
Countries in EASTERN EUROPE region	−0.79[***]	0.19	−0.46[**]	0.20	−0.46[**]	0.21	−0.13	0.31
Democracy–autocracy score	0.0043	0.0092	0.016	0.0096	0.016	0.0099	0.015	0.0099
Years since last regime change	0.00017	0.00083	0.0004	0.00087	0.0007	0.0024	0.0011	0.0025
Constant	4.7[***]	0.69	5.4[***]	0.98	5.4[***]	1.0	5.6[***]	1.25
Number of observations	148		132		115		104	
Adjusted R^2	0.617		0.693		0.672		0.697	

Significance: *, 90%, **, 95%, ***, 99%

[a] The omitted region in these regressions is sub-Saharan Africa (SSA).

[b] Robust standard errors.

estimates and significance of coverage variables are sensitive to functional form (changing for example with inclusion of higher-order squared terms, or with log coverage terms). When higher-order terms are included alongside the linear coverage terms in the model, the coefficient for the linear piped water coverage increases by about 65% (to –0.50), and the squared piped water coverage is positive and significant. This suggests that there is a concave relationship between death rates and piped water coverage, whereby declines in WASH-related deaths decrease as coverage increases. Neither non-piped improved water nor improved sanitation remain significantly associated with the WASH-related death rate in this model. With log coverage terms, the strength of association between the decrease in

mortality and piped water coverage is roughly two and a half times as strong as that with improved water coverage, and the association with improved sanitation remains insignificant. Taken together, these results suggest that the death rate is more closely associated with piped water coverage than with the other coverage variables. Similar tests on inclusion of different income terms reveal that the log income specification outperforms models with linear or higher-order income terms.

Estimates of Associations between Average Water Collection Time, Income, and Coverage with Improved WASH Services

Regression results for the average water collection time (equation 10.12) are presented in Table 10.2.

Table 10.2 OLS regression for average water collection time (in minutes per one-way trip)[a]

	All countries, base model		All countries, full model	
	Coefficient	Standard error[b]	Coefficient	Standard error[b]
Piped water coverage (%)	−0.039	0.037	−0.0040	0.026
Improved non-piped water coverage (%)	0.0073	0.061	0.068[*]	0.038
Ln GDP per capita (lagged)	−1.21[*]	0.65	−1.16[**]	0.58
Urban population (%)	−0.060[***]	0.023	−0.063[***]	0.023
Percent of GDP to lowest 80% of population			−0.051	0.038
Developed countries	2.1	7.0	8.3[*]	4.8
Countries in LAC region	−1.5	1.0	−0.42	0.82
Countries in MIDEAST region	0.8	1.6	2.1	1.3
Countries in SOUTH ASIA region	−4.7[***]	1.4	−5.7[***]	1.1
Countries in EAST ASIA/PACIFIC region	−2.6[**]	1.0	−2.9[***]	1.1
Countries in EASTERN EUROPE region	−2.4[**]	0.99	−2.6[**]	1.0
Democracy–Autocracy Score			−0.052	0.045
Years since last regime change			−0.0041	0.011
Multiple Indicators Survey	4.9[***]	1.1	3.7[***]	0.83
World Health Survey	2.9[***]	0.59	2.6[***]	0.55
Constant	16.3[***]	5.2	15.3[***]	4.2
Number of observations	184		175	
R^2	0.614		0.682	

Significance: *, 90%, **, 95%, ***, 99%.
[a] The omitted region in these regressions is sub-Saharan Africa (SSA).
[b] Robust standard errors.

For this model, as with the mortality model, we use simple OLS but cluster standard errors by country, since a few countries have more than one observation. Once again, the log of per capita income (lagged) is significant in both the base and more complete model, and negatively related to the average water collection time. An increase in per capita GDP of 1 log is associated with a decrease of roughly 1.2 minutes per trip. Higher urbanization is also associated with lower water collection times; a 10% increase in the percentage of urban population is associated with a decrease in collection time of 0.6 minutes per trip. The constant of 13 or 16 minutes (depending on the model) represents the baseline collection time in a country in sub-Saharan Africa (the reference group for this regression) with zero values for all other right-hand-side variables. Both the MICS and WHS survey dummy variables are significant and positive; these represent the higher "mean collection time" obtained for similar countries in those surveys relative to the DHS surveys, which only reported median collection times. We find no significant associations between coverage with piped or improved water sources and average water collection times when controlling for GDP, perhaps because of lack of variation and collinearity among these variables. Omitting lagged GDP, the piped water coverage variable becomes significant; specifically a 1% increase in coverage with piped water is associated with a reduction in average time to water of 0.07–0.09 minutes (results not shown). Coverage with improved water however remains insignificant. The governance variables and inequality are also not significant in the model.

We also consider several other model specifications for understanding the associations between average time spent collecting water and these variables. We find that the model with log per capita income performs better than one with linear and squared per capita GDP terms (results available upon request). Also, use of random effects and random effects tobit models (with lower-bound censoring at 0 minutes per trip) do not yield results that are qualitatively different, though the coefficients on the income term in such models decreases to 0.9 and 0.7, respectively.

Estimates of Associations between Water and Sanitation Coverage, Income, and Other Variables

Regression results for equation (10.13) (fixed effects and random effects models) are reported in Table 10.3. In both models GDP in the previous period and the percentage of urban population have significant and positive effects on piped water coverage. In the random effects model, a 1-log increase in per capita GDP in the previous period is associated with a 12% increase in piped water coverage in the current period. Percent urban population is also significant and positive – a 0.4% increase in piped coverage for a 1% percentage increase in urban population. The regional dummy variables for all regions except South Asia are significant and positive relative to sub-Saharan Africa. The governance variable for regime durability is marginally significant and negative, but none of the other governance or inequality variables have significant associations with piped water coverage. Year dummy variables for early years are significant and negative, suggesting higher coverage expansion in later years.

In the fixed effects model, a 1-log increase in per capita GDP in the previous year is associated with roughly a 7% increase in piped water coverage. Percent urban population is significant and positive, and similar to the estimate from the random effects model. Of the governance variables and inequality, only regime durability is marginally significant and unexpectedly negative, but the linear trend is significant and positive, and the early year dummy variables are significant and negative in the basic model, suggesting that access to piped water may have accelerated in these countries in the recent past, relative to the early 1990s.

A Hausman test rejects the hypothesis that the fixed and random effects model estimates are the same, suggesting that the coefficients estimated in the random effects model are biased, probably due to autocorrelation in the error term. We thus use the fixed effects estimates in the simulation, i.e. the more conservative estimates of the association between GDP and piped water coverage. Also, the full model with complete interactions yields estimates of this association that are about 2.5 percentage points lower, i.e. a 1-log increase in GDP per

Table 10.3 Estimation of population coverage with piped water (robust standard errors presented in parentheses, clustered at the country level)

	Random Effects[a]		Fixed effects	
	Simple model	Full model[b]	Simple model	Full model[b]
Lagged ln (GDP per capita)	11.5*** (2.03)	9.25*** (1.87)	7.17*** (2.33)	4.49** (2.20)
Percent of GDP to lowest 80% of population	0.070 (0.09)	0.075 (0.09)	0.071 (0.10)	0.072 (0.09)
Urban population (%)	0.42*** (0.10)	0.45*** (0.08)	0.48*** (0.17)	0.45** (0.21)
Countries in LAC region	29.2*** (6.06)	33.4*** (5.6)		
Countries in MIDEAST region	31.1*** (6.33)	33.9*** (6.8)		
Countries in SOUTH ASIA region	4.4 (3.53)	5.0 (3.9)		
Countries in EAST ASIA/PACIFIC region	11.5* (7.04)	14.5** (7.3)		
Countries in EASTERN EUROPE region	44.1*** (5.61)	35.3*** (4.6)		
Developed countries		40.7*** (7.0)		
Linear time trend	0.14 (0.11)	−0.12 (0.07)	0.21** (0.10)	−0.022 (0.08)
1995	−1.64** (0.73)	−0.53 (0.64)	−1.4** (0.61)	−0.96* (0.58)
2000	−0.66* (0.38)	0.42 (0.31)	−0.66* (0.36)	−0.03 (0.31)
Democracy–Autocracy score	−0.065 (0.13)	−0.0027 (0.11)	−0.15 (0.14)	−0.17 (0.13)
Years since last regime change	−0.048 (0.06)	−0.073* (0.04)	−0.084 (0.05)	−0.12** (0.05)
Coup	−1.20 (0.89)	−1.06 (0.84)	−0.74 (0.97)	−0.64 (0.82)
Constant	−82.4*** (11.9)	−63.3*** (12.6)	−36.0** (17.9)	−1.8 (21.6)
Number of observations	361	493	361	493
Adjusted R^2 (overall)	0.888	0.889	0.730	0.693
(within)	0.508	0.489	0.523	0.511
(between)	0.897	0.895	0.739	0.709
Hausman test for simple model χ^2 (p-value)	70.0 (0.000)			

Significance: *, 90%, **, 95%, ***, 99%.
[a] A random-effects tobit model that allows censoring at 0% and 100% coverage does not yield qualitatively different results.
[b] Includes all countries (including developed and former Soviet republics dropped from the simple model) and full set of year–region interactions (as in the other regressions the omitted region is sub-Saharan Africa).

capita is associated with a 4.5–9% increase in piped water coverage, relative to the 7–11.5% increase suggested by the simple model. Returning to a comparison of the base and reduced form models for WASH-related mortality presented in Table 10.1, we would thus calculate the net effect of log income to be −0.3 + (−0.03 × 4.5) = −0.43 to −0.3 + (−0.03 × 7) = −0.51 if we use the associations obtained from the fixed effects models for coverage. These seem reasonable given the –0.43 coefficient on log income obtained from the reduced form model.

Finally, we also explored whether controlling for aid flows for WASH would affect our estimates. This variable was not significant, and its inclusion did not qualitatively change the results in Table 10.3, though the limited data for aid flows reduced the sample size to less than 150 observations (results not shown).

We estimated several additional models in order to assess the sensitivity of these results to assumptions about functional form and coverage variables. In terms of functional form, we estimated random and fixed effects models with linear and squared per capita GDP terms, as well as log and squared log per capita GDP terms. The model fit for the models with per capita GDP terms (rather than the log GDP terms) was not as good as the simple log GDP model, and adding squared log GDP terms only provided small improvements in model fit. Furthermore, this squared log GDP term was only statistically significant, and negative, in the fixed effects model that included all countries (rather than less developed countries only). We interpret this as evidence that a diminishing rate of expansion of piped services may only apply late in the development path of countries, once they approach full coverage. With regards to the specific coverage variables, we estimated models for coverage with improved water and improved sanitation (see Annex 10.3, Table A10.5). The results for these are generally similar to those for piped water coverage, though urban population is less significant in the models for improved water.

The Simulation Model for Health Losses

The final step of our analytical approach involves use of a spreadsheet simulation model that incorporates the most important associations obtained from the country-level regression models for coverage with improved water and sanitation services, WASH-related mortality, and average time to water. Our simulation model, like the regression analyses of the previous section, is a country-level model. We use single-year time steps from 1950 to 2050. The model is calibrated with the historical time

series data on (a) coverage with piped water from the JMP (1990–2008), (b) purchasing power parity (PPP)-adjusted actual per capita GDP from Angus Maddison's GDCC data series (1950–2008), and (c) actual population recorded by the United Nations population division (1950–2008). When data for particular years are missing, we conduct simple linear interpolation between the available data points. For simulation of future projections, we use the regional population and two sets of economic growth projections based on historical country averages over the recent past (1990–2008) and over the long term (1950–2008).[17]

Given the results of our empirical analysis, we focus in our calculations of losses from WASH-related mortality and time spent collecting water on how these change with piped water coverage, income, and urbanization. We use the simulation model to make both backward and forward projections of the three left-hand side variables from our regression analysis – coverage with piped services, WASH-related death rates, and average time to water. We assume that:

1. Piped water coverage increases as a function of the log of per capita GDP and the proportion of urban population;
2. WASH-related mortality decreases with piped water coverage and the log of per capita GDP; and
3. Average time to water decreases as a function of the log of per capita GDP and the proportion of urban population.

We backcast and forecast coverage with piped water, WASH-related mortality, and mean time-to-source over the periods of missing data by applying the income and coverage elasticities shown in Table 10.4, which are obtained from our regression model estimations. For mean time to water, we must also impute values for countries that are missing data, which we do using the full model presented in Table 10.2. We test the sensitivity of our model results using the lower-bound, base case, and upper-bound estimates of the parameters.

The lower and upper bounds for our sensitivity analyses of piped water coverage to income come from the 90% confidence intervals from the base

---

[17] The Copenhagen Consensus Center did provide regional estimates for economic growth for low growth (GDP rising from 1.5% per annum in Europe to 3.5% per annum in Asia, with other regions in between) and high growth (GDP rising from 2.5% in Europe to 4.5% in Asia, respectively) scenarios. We show results using these projections in the Annex 10.3, but prefer in this chapter to comment on the more nuanced picture that arises when heterogeneous country trends are used. Historical growth trends in many developing countries have outpaced these regional averages, particularly over the recent 1990–2008 period, the recent economic downturn notwithstanding.

Table 10.4 Elasticities and ranges used in projections of water and sanitation coverage, WASH-related mortality, and average time spent collecting water

	Low	Base case	High
A. Elasticities of percent coverage with improved water and sanitation services			
For piped water and sewerage			
Ln(per capita GDP) elasticity	2	7	12
Percent urban population elasticity	0.3	0.45	0.6
For non-piped improved water only			
Ln(per capita GDP) elasticity	5	7.5	10
Percent urban population elasticity	0.1	0.2	0.3
For improved sanitation only			
Ln(per capita GDP) elasticity	8	11	14
Percent urban population elasticity	0.2	0.35	0.5
B. Elasticities of the WASH-related death rate (in deaths per 1,000)			
Ln(per capita GDP) elasticity	−0.1	−0.3	−0.5
Percent piped water coverage elasticity	−0.02	−0.03	−0.04
Sensitivity analysis only: percent improved water coverage elasticity	−0.02	−0.03	−0.04
C. Elasticities of average time to collect water (in minutes to source)	−0.5	−2.5	−4.5
Ln(per capita GDP) elasticity	−0.3	−1.2	−2.1
Percent urban population elasticity of average time to collect water	−0.025	−0.06	−0.095

case fixed effects regression model estimates shown in Table 10.3. We also make one other adjustment to our simulated results because the JMP data do not report sewerage rates, to account for the fact that coverage with sewerage is generally about 10–15% lower than coverage with piped water (Komives *et al.* 2003). To forecast piped water + sewerage, we therefore reduce the piped water estimates by 12% for all countries in which piped water coverage is greater than 20%; and by a linear factor down to no difference at a coverage level of zero for those in which piped water coverage is less than 20%. Finally, for calculation of the economic benefits of reduced illness and time savings from improved coverage with water and sanitation services, i.e. VSL, COI and the opportunity cost of time savings, we explore the effect of varying simulation model assumptions between the bounds presented in Table 10.5, which are based on work in Whittington *et al.* (2009).

Since the Copenhagen Center scenarios assume positive economic growth in all regions, and since we use UN projections for urbanization rates (which also strictly increase over time), the model predicts that piped network coverage will increase

and WASH-related mortality rates and average time spent collecting water will decrease on a per capita basis. This trajectory does not necessarily hold in absolute terms, however, due to population growth. Similarly, economic losses may increase even as per capita trends improve, since the economic opportunity cost of time and the economic cost of mortality will increase with rising income. We track the following regional and global indicators over time, focusing on the period 1950–2050:

1. Percent coverage with piped water and sewerage (and improved water and improved sanitation only), and population not covered by these services;
2. Regional WASH-related mortality rates (as a percentage of population) and total numbers of deaths; and
3. The value of a statistical life and health-related "economic losses," and the opportunity cost of time lost collecting water (in dollars and as percent of GDP).

We do not extrapolate before 1950 because of insufficient data on the variables required to make those calculations.

Results

This section of the chapter presents our estimates of historical and future coverage, WASH-related mortality, and "economic losses" due to poor water and sanitation services. We first present base case estimates for four large countries (China, India, Brazil, and Nigeria) because these results illustrate several interesting features of the global water and sanitation problem, yet also highlight some of the limitations of these projections. Second, we turn to aggregate regional and global estimates of historical, present, and future coverage with various levels of improved water and sanitation. Third, we show historical and future projections of the WASH-related mortality risk. Fourth, we present our calculations of regional and global health burden (in deaths) and "economic losses" related to poor water and sanitation from WASH-related illnesses, and time spent collecting water. We also conduct analyses to test the sensitivity of our projections to the model parameters shown in Tables 10.4 and 10.5.

The Evolution of Water and Sanitation Coverage and WASH-Related Economic Losses in China, India, Brazil, and Nigeria

China, India, Brazil, and Nigeria are among the most populous countries in the world, and represented 51% of the total population in the developing world in 2010 (2.9 out of 5.6 billion). They are thus critical to understanding the global picture of water and sanitation in poor countries. Also, the data available suggest that they have very different levels of coverage with water and sanitation services, WASH-related mortality rates, and accessibility to water. As a result, our projections for these four countries illustrate the complexity of the water and sanitation challenge.

Over the period 1990–2008 China and Brazil increased coverage with piped water and sewer services relatively quickly from moderate levels (40–65%) to 70–80% (Figure 10.10; the period for which data are available is shown in gray). The extension of these services occurred at a particularly rapid rate in China. In contrast, baseline coverage started from low levels in India and Nigeria (<10%), and increased very slowly in India and actually decreased in Nigeria. These changes took place despite the fact that all four countries were experiencing economic growth during this period (growth in Nigeria and Brazil was slowest, followed by India, and finally China). In Nigeria, the slow expansion of piped water and sanitation services could not keep pace with rapid population growth. Our model projects that coverage will continue to increase most quickly in China, followed by India (as a result of the higher growth projections

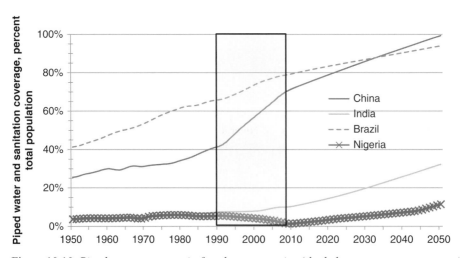

Figure 10.10 *Piped water coverage in four large countries (shaded area represents years with actual data; coverage in other years is estimated; future projections based on economic growth trajectory for 1950–2008)*

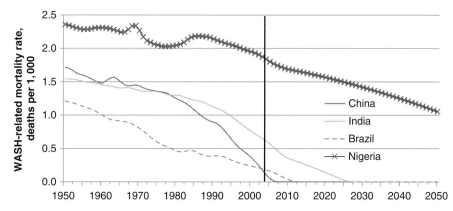

Figure 10.11 *WASH-related mortality in four large countries (dark line shows the year with mortality data from which predictions are made; future projections based on economic growth trajectory for 1950–2008)*

for these two countries), but that coverage in India will remain relatively low due to its low starting point.

Our predicted WASH-related mortality rates mirror these trends (Figure 10.11). Brazil's and China's mortality rates were lowest in 2004, the year for which we have data (China = 0.04 and Brazil = 0.16 deaths per 1,000 people). If these data are accurate, China has largely solved the problem of mortality from such diseases, and Brazil is getting close. India, on the other hand, had a WASH-related mortality rate nearly four times that of Brazil (0.57 deaths per 1,000), and Nigeria's was even higher (1.8 deaths per 1,000). In the base case, the simulation model suggests that the WASH-related mortality rate in India could decline to nearly zero over the next 20 years, but Nigeria, with slowly expanding coverage and a lower growth trajectory, could continue to have high WASH-related mortality through 2050. A key puzzle in the 2004 data is that the WASH-related mortality rate in India appears to be so much lower than that in Nigeria, despite the low piped water coverage in both countries. This could be due to better economic conditions in India, higher general health services, and/or the higher levels of access to more general "improved" water sources (58% in Nigeria vs. 88% in India in 2008).

These projections of the mortality rate are used to estimate the number of deaths associated with

poor water and sanitation (Figure 10.12, top panel). Despite mortality rates that are mostly flat or decreasing over the simulation period, the model suggests that the number of deaths in all countries was increasing throughout much of the twentieth century, largely because population growth was outpacing projected declines in mortality rates. In China, a dramatic transition occurred in the late 1970s and early 1980s, when population growth slowed dramatically even as the mortality rate probably declined at an increasing rate, as shown in Figure 10.11. These two trends led to rapid declines in the number of WASH-related deaths in China. In Brazil, WASH-related deaths fell slowly, in part because population growth was slower and slightly outpaced by predicted mortality declines. The model suggests that the number of WASH-related deaths in India may have peaked in the early 1990s, but that deaths in Nigeria, where the demographic transition is only beginning and mortality rates remain very high, could continue to increase until the middle of the twenty-first century.

Next we turn to the economic losses associated with WASH-related illnesses. Because the economic cost per case or death increases with GDP, the relative position of the peak in health losses depends on the relative rates of decline in mortality rates and of increase in GDP and the VSL (Figure 10.12, bottom panel). For China, our base case suggests

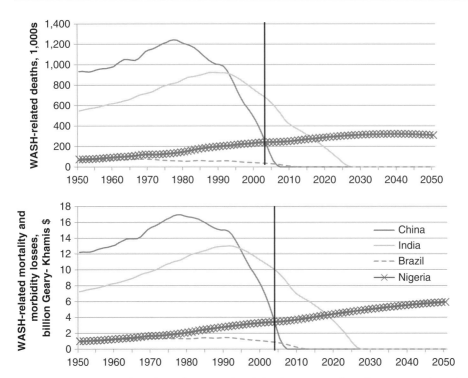

Figure 10.12 *Predicted number of WASH-related deaths (top panel) and "economic losses" due to WASH-related health problems (bottom panel) in four large countries (dark line shows the year with data from which predictions are made; future projections based on economic growth from 1950–2008)*

that this peak occurred around 1980, close to when deaths began to decline. Brazil, on the other hand, saw increasing "economic losses" up to a peak around 1990 in spite of decreasing deaths over time. In India, the peak in economic losses from WASH-related illnesses occurred just after the peak in deaths in the early 1990s. The trajectory in India lags that in China by about 15 years. In Nigeria, the

economic losses from WASH-related illnesses have been increasing, and continue to do so throughout the simulation period, even though deaths peak around 2040. Nigeria's trajectory represents a case where both incomes and population are increasing quickly and where WASH-related mortality starts from a high level, such that economic losses increase even as death rates are reduced.[18]

The data on average time to water suggests that the convenience of access to water supplies is also varied across these four countries. China and Brazil have the lowest one-way time to water, with 2.0 (in 2002) and 2.3 (in 2003) minutes, respectively. India is next, at 6.2 minutes (2003), followed by Nigeria (8.5 minutes in 2003). As with the WASH-related mortality rate calculations, model projections for time to water over the simulation period are made from a single year of measurements (Figure 10.13, top panel), and forecasts (and backcasts) are driven by the associations with GDP and urbanization rates.[19] These

[18] We note that these results, and the issue of whether the peak in health losses in aggregate will lag the peak in deaths, are sensitive to the values of the parameters in the model (and the same also applies to time costs associated with poor access to water supplies). This is also illustrated by the variation across these countries with different baseline GDP and WASH-related mortality rates.

[19] Unlike the WASH-attributable mortality data, which is all for 2004, however, the time to water is available for different countries in different years, and several countries, for example Nigeria, India, and Benin, have measures in several years, since several of the surveys producing those data were conducted in those countries.

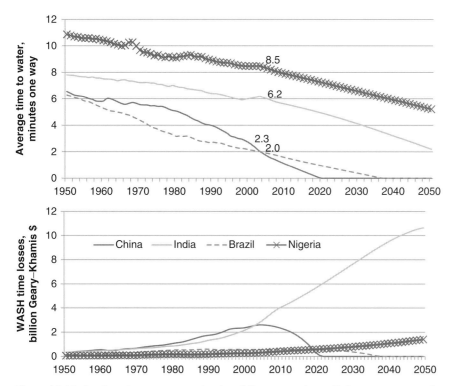

Figure 10.13 *Predicted time to water (top) and "economic losses" due to time costs (bottom) in four large countries (actual data points from which predictions are made are identified by diamonds; future projections based on economic growth from 1950–2008)*

suggest that average travel times will drop to zero in China just before 2020, and in Brazil about 10 years later. In India, average time to water is predicted to fall to 2 minutes on average by 2050, while in Nigeria it will decrease to about 5 minutes.

For these countries, the modeled trajectory of time costs for collection of water is somewhat different than that for health losses (Figure 10.13). Collection times are less strongly associated with income than are mortality rates (see Table 10.4), and thus remain well above zero for most of the simulated time period. Thus, falling average time to water does not so easily offset the higher aggregate costs associated with rising population and income. Only in China and Brazil time costs peak and then fall to zero in the base case (around 2002 and 2013, respectively). In India, time costs peak only around 2050. India's total time costs rise to very high levels (about G–K$10 billion per year) relative to the

other countries, due to a combination of factors: (1) its low coverage with in-house water and sanitation, (2) its large population, and (3) its relatively high income trajectory. In Nigeria, time costs rise steadily throughout the simulation period, owing to a similar combination of factors, and reaches about G–K$1.5 billion per year in 2050.

Finally, we turn to aggregate "economic losses," represented by the sum of the health losses and time costs (Figure 10.14). For China, Brazil, and India, there is an early peak that corresponds exactly with the peak in health losses, followed by a decrease over some period of time. Time costs, which start from much lower levels, lag behind the peak in health losses, and eventually lead to newly rising total costs in India. China and Brazil's trends slow but continue their downward trend, dropping to zero only when time costs also fall to zero. In contrast, aggregate costs in Nigeria are forecast to rise throughout the period because both health and

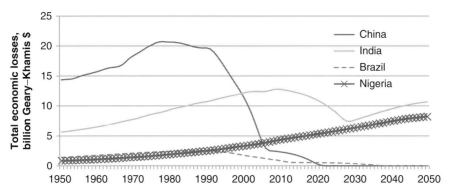

Figure 10.14 *Predicted aggregate "economic losses" due to poor access to water services in four large countries (future projections based on economic growth trajectory for 1950–2008)*

time costs are increasing over the whole simulation period.

Before moving to our global projections, a few brief observations on limitations are necessary. First, coverage with piped water in these four countries over the data period (1990–2008) does not exactly follow the projected trends from our model. There are two primary reasons for these deviations. One is that the country forecasts are based on average associations across all developing countries in our data set, and thus individual countries may see faster or slower expansions depending on their own particular situations, which are not captured by the covariates in our regression model. Some of these particularities may have to do with individuals' demand for improved services, and some may be related to government intervention such as investment in infrastructure. As shown in Figure 10.10, coverage expansion in India, and especially Nigeria, has been slower than expected, while China's has been faster.

Another reason for these differences is that we use historical GDP growth from a longer period of about 60 years, rather than the 18-year period that coincides with the water and sanitation coverage data. During the latter period, China's economy grew very quickly. In fact, one might expect that rising economic costs (in time or health) would create pressure and demand for improved services. Our model does not account for such endogenous feedbacks, so it is unclear precisely how realistic it is to think that economic losses in Nigeria, or

time costs in India, for example, would continue to rise until 2050. There is certainly nothing inevitable about such forecasts of economic losses. In the interest of space, we have not presented sensitivity analysis of the forward and backward projections for these four countries, though we do present such sensitivity analyses for the global analysis.

Progression of Water and Sanitation Coverage in Less Developed Regions

Figure 10.15 shows our base case estimates of the percentage of population with access to piped water and sewerage in different regions. These estimates are from the base case parameterization for the association between coverage and urbanization and historical GDP growth (see Table 10.5). There are four noteworthy aspects of these results. First, the backcasts for the transition from coverage levels between 1950 and 1990, like the forecasts starting from 2008, are highly uncertain; no data exist for this period so our estimates are based solely on changes in GDP and urbanization since 1950.

Second, the increase in global coverage (the double black line) from 1990 to 2008, appears slightly faster than our past and future projections. This increase was partly driven by robust economic growth of 6–7% in several regions: East Asia/ Pacific (EAP), the Middle East (MIDEAST), and Latin America (LAC). The most dramatic expansion of piped water and sewerage occurred

Table 10.5 Assumptions for valuation of changes in WASH-related mortality and time spent collecting water

Model parameter (*symbol*)	Low	Base case	High
Value of a statistical life $[VSL(\overline{Y}_{it,80})]$	See Annex 10.1		
Cost of illness adjustment, as a fraction of mortality benefits (f_{COI})	10%	25%	40%
Average household size (*hhsize*)	4	5	6
Average trips to collect water per day (*trips*)	1	1.5	2
Assumed work hours per week; for deriving opportunity cost of time from per capita GDP (L^w)	30	40	50
Opportunity cost of time spent collecting water, as a fraction of hourly wage (v^t)	0	0.25	0.5

Other variable assumptions:
  Inclusion of (1) piped water and sewerage only, or (2) all improved water
  GDP growth trajectory: (1) 1950–2008 or (2) 1990–2008
  VSL and opportunity cost of time using average (1) per capita GDP or (2) per capita GDP for bottom 80%
  VSL based on (1) curve fit to empirical data or (2) income elasticity of 1.5, as outlined by Hammitt and Robinson (2011). See Annex 10.1 for details.

in East Asia and the Pacific, due largely to the changes in China discussed in the previous section, which may be related to factors besides economic growth. Since China is such a large part of the global population in the developing world, but only represents one data point in the multi-country regression used to obtain model elasticities, the rapid expansion of services there explains much of the difference between the observed data and the trends. In contrast, recent increases in coverage in South Asia (SA), sub-Saharan Africa (SSA), and Eastern Europe (EURCA) appear somewhat lower than our projected trends. SSA and SA stand out with their low baseline levels of coverage and slow rates of increase in coverage, despite recent accelerated economic growth in SA. If these trends continue, coverage with piped water and sanitation services will not exceed 30% in these regions, even in 2050.

Third, despite increases in global coverage rates, the total population without piped water and sanitation was actually increasing in most regions (except perhaps EURCA) up until the early 1990s, and has only recently begun to decline in the MIDEAST, EAP, and LAC regions, where the demographic transition has taken hold (Figure 10.16). The population without access continues to increase rapidly in SA

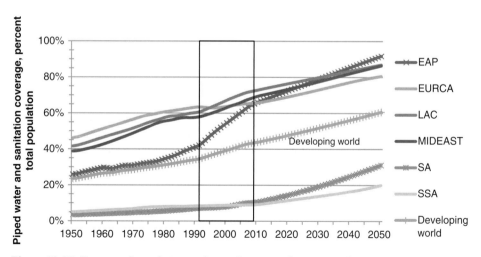

Figure 10.15 *Percent of population with piped water and sewerage, by region, with base case coverage elasticities (actual data period shown in shaded box; future projections use growth rates for 1950–2008)*

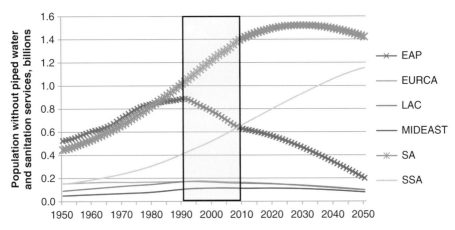

Figure 10.16 *Population not covered with piped water and sewerage, with base case coverage elasticities (actual data period shown in shaded box; future projections use growth rates for 1950–2008)*

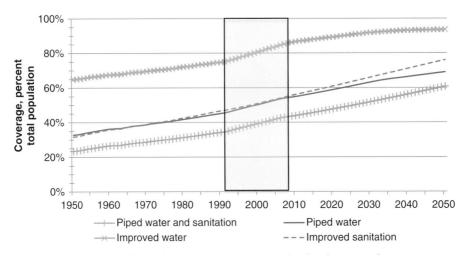

Figure 10.17 *Percent of global population with various levels of water and sanitation services, assuming base case elasticities of coverage (actual data period shown in shaded box; future projections use growth rates for 1950–2008)*

and SSA. Our base case projections suggest 1.2 billion and 1.4 billion people still could be without piped services in 2050, in SSA and SA respectively. The population without coverage peaks in SA around 2030, and increases in SSA throughout the simulation. The base case projection shows global population without piped water and sanitation peaking just before SA does, around 2027.

Fourth, if we consider global coverage with "improved water," "improved sanitation," or piped water only, rather than piped water plus sewerage,

the percentages served look much better (Figure 10.17). Globally, coverage increases with improved water – up to 85% in 2008, and projected to rise to 94% in 2050 – in particular have been slightly faster during 1990–2008 than our base case projections predict. Again, this is partly the effect of expansion in water services in EAP, LAC, and MIDEAST, but increased access to improved water has also been more broadly based than that for piped water. In SA, for example, access to improved water has risen dramatically over the

Table 10.6 Ranges of projected coverage with different levels of water and sanitation services in 1950, 2008, and 2050[a]

	Improved water	Improved sanitation	Piped water	Piped water + sewerage
Worldwide coverage (%)				
Backcast 1950	65 (61–69)	32 (26–37)	33 (26–40)	23 (17–30)
Year 2008 data	86	56	55	44
Projection 2050	94 (92–95)	76 (70–85)	69 (62–76)	61 (50–69)
Population unserved (billions)				
Backcast 1950	0.7 (0.6–0.7)	1.3 (1.2–1.4)	1.2 (1.2–1.4)	1.4 (1.4–1.5)
Year 2008 data	0.8	2.4	2.5	3.1
Projection 2050	0.5 (0.4–0.5)	1.9 (1.4–2.4)	2.4 (1.9–2.6)	3.0 (2.4–3.4)

[a] Low and high estimates shown in parentheses following base case; estimates derived using the elasticity parameters in Table 10.3, and with both economic growth scenarios.

data period.[20] Global coverage with improved sanitation and piped water (around 55% in 2008) is much lower than it is for improved water alone. Access to piped water plus sewerage is lowest, at about 42%. The association we use for our base case projections between improved sanitation and economic growth is stronger than it is for piped water, such that our predictions of improved sanitation coverage rise to about 76% by 2050 (in comparison with 70% for piped water and 60% for piped water and sewerage).

There are important regional differences in coverage with non-piped water and sanitation services. SSA lags far behind all regions in coverage with improved water (60% in 2008), despite large improvements from 1990 to 2008. SA is only slightly behind EAP, and all regions except SSA have improved water coverage exceeding 85%. Our base case simulations project coverage levels with improved water above 90% in 2050 in all regions except SSA, which could rise to nearly 70%. For improved sanitation, SA and SSA are similar, and both had coverage rates below 40% in 2008 (other regions are at 60% or better). The trend in coverage in SSA, however, is nearly flat, whereas coverage increases in SA were high from 1990 to 2008. Our base case simulations suggest that coverage with improved sanitation in 2050 could increase to 40% in SSA, nearly 60% in SA, and more than 90% in other regions.

These projections are sensitive to the strength of association between economic growth and urbanization, and coverage with the different services (Table 10.6). Between 1950 and 2008, even while the percentage of people covered was increasing, high rates of population growth led to larger numbers unserved by any level of improved services. This was especially true for improved sanitation and for piped water and sewerage services; the unserved global population for both of these levels of service increased by over 1 billion. We expect coverage rates with piped water and sewerage to increase from about 44% today to 50–69% in 2050. With the upper bound for the respective elasticities of coverage, and using the higher 1990–2008 growth rates, the percentage of people with piped water would rise to 76%; improved water and sanitation coverage levels could reach 95% and 85%, respectively. Conversely, with the lower-bound elasticity and using long-term growth rates, coverage rates would increase slowly, to 62%, 70%, and 92% for piped water, improved sanitation, and improved water. Accounting for population growth, whether the numbers unserved will increase or decrease depends on the type of service as well as the strength of associations between income,

[20] See Appendix 10.3 for additional regional graphs for improved water and sanitation only.

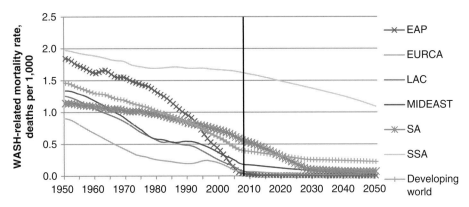

Figure 10.18 *The WASH-related mortality rate, by region, assuming base case elasticities of WASH-related mortality rate (data for 2004 shown by dark line; future projections use growth rates for 1950–2008)*

urbanization, and coverage. For improved water, the numbers unserved will probably continue to decline; for improved sanitation and piped water alone, these numbers will either stabilize or decline. For piped water and sewerage, either decreases or increases are possible, and the total number unserved could move from 3.1 billion in 2008 to 2.4–3.4 billion people in 2050.

Historical and Future WASH-Related Mortality

Our model simulations suggest that WASH-related mortality rates have been and will continue declining in most regions over much of the period 1950–2050, reflecting trends in economic growth and coverage with piped water and sanitation services (Figure 10.18). The mortality rate was 0.39 deaths per 1,000 across all less developed regions in 2008, down from 1.5 deaths per 1,000 in 1950 (at which time rates ranging from just under 1.0 deaths per 1,000 in EURCA to 2.0 deaths per 1,000 in SSA). Simulated declines are slowest in SSA due to its relatively low economic growth and low coverage with piped water and sanitation services. The drop is steepest in EAP, followed by the MIDEAST and LAC regions; these large declines are driven by the modeled associations with rapid economic growth and the coverage expansions in these regions (particularly China). At the end of the simulation period, the average mortality rate across less developed regions

is predicted to be 0.22 in the base case. The non-zero WASH-related mortality at the global level in 2050 is mostly driven by the high mortality rates in SSA, which becomes relatively more important as SSA's population continues to expand.

However, the data on which these projections are based, from the year 2004, contain several puzzles. In those data, the entire SSA region, like Nigeria by itself, stands out with its very high WASH-related mortality rate. This high baseline mortality is the primary factor driving the model result that WASH-related mortality remains much higher in SSA than in the other regions over most of the simulation period. In contrast, SA appears to have very similar levels of piped water and sanitation coverage to SSA, but much lower WASH-related mortality rates in 2004. By 2050 the model projections for WASH-related mortality in SA drop to nearly zero. It is not clear why the WASH-related mortality rates in the WHO data are so different in these two regions. The discrepancy could arise from real differences in access to other services, for example better health systems, treatments, and technologies, greater access to "improved" (not piped) water and sanitation, or greater connectivity due to higher density. It could also be the result of measurement error or other limitations of the WHO analysis.

It is also difficult to know whether WASH-related mortality rates dropped as much as we predict in other regions. WASH-related mortality rates in less

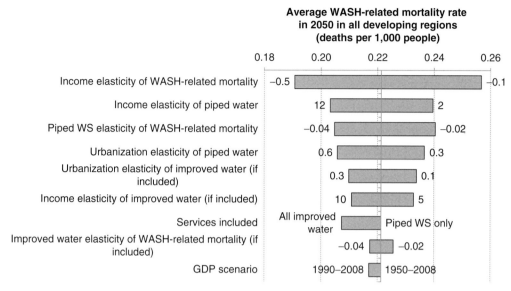

Figure 10.19 *Ranking of factors influencing model projections of the average WASH-related mortality rate across developing regions in 2050*

developed regions other than SA and SSA are currently low (relative to those regions), and overall, non-WASH-specific mortality rates have been in decline across many parts of the globe over the past two decades. Thus, though we have doubts about the specific levels of mortality in SA and SSA, we believe that the general trajectory in the projections is probably realistic, and is consistent with other calculations of declining mortality from infectious and diarrheal diseases (Kosek *et al.* 2003; Mathers and Loncar 2006). In most regions, WASH-related mortality rates will likely be very low by 2030, due to the many health improvements that come with economic growth, as well as higher coverage with water and sanitation services.

Our sensitivity analyses suggest that the projected global mortality rates due to WASH-related disease are most sensitive to their assumed association with income (Figure 10.19). The 90% confidence interval range from our empirical analysis, for the value of this parameter alone, implies a range in average mortality rates of about 0.19–0.26 deaths per 1,000 in 2050 (the base case estimate was 0.22). The other most important parameters driving uncertainty in our projections of mortality rates are the income and urbanization elasticities of piped water services,

and the piped coverage elasticity of mortality. The inclusion of improved water, and its own income and urbanization elasticities, as well as the GDP projections, are relatively less important in driving variation in the predicted mortality rate. If we set all parameters to the values that lead to the highest projected mortality rate in 2050, we obtain a "worst case" value of 0.34 deaths per 1,000, which would represent a very small decline in these rates (and the best case outcome is 0.13).

Combining population growth and these mortality rates, we next predict the WASH-related deaths over the simulation period. The base case calculations suggest that the number of deaths in SSA alone could increase from about 1.2 to about 1.6 million per year between now and 2050, peaking around 2045 (Figure 10.20). This is not much less than the global total of WASH-related deaths today (2.1 million). In 2050, the only other region with significant numbers of WASH-related deaths in the base case is SA, but this is due to a single country, Afghanistan, for which mortality rates (3.3 deaths per 1,000) start from levels that are higher than all but the three very highest mortality countries in SSA: Angola, Niger, and Sierra Leone. The number of future deaths and the trajectory of

Table 10.7 Ranges of projected WASH-related mortality and deaths in 1950, 2004, and 2050[a]

	Year		
	1950	2004	2050
WASH-related mortality rate (deaths per 1,000)			
All developing regions	1.5 (0.82–2.1)	0.43	0.22 (0.13–0.34)
South Asia (SA)	1.1 (0.81–2.0)	0.64	0.1 (0.01–0.24)
Sub-Saharan Africa (SSA)	2.0 (1.8–2.7)	1.7	1.1 (0.60–1.5)
WASH-related deaths (millions)			
All developing regions	2.7 (1.5–3.9)	2.3	1.7 (1.0–2.7)
South Asia (SA)	0.53 (0.37–0.93)	0.9	0.14 (0.03–0.50)
Sub-Saharan Africa (SSA)	0.32 (0.29–0.43)	1.1	1.6 (0.87–2.1)

[a] Best and worst estimates shown in parentheses following base case; estimates derived using the elasticity parameters in Table 10.3, and with both economic growth scenarios.

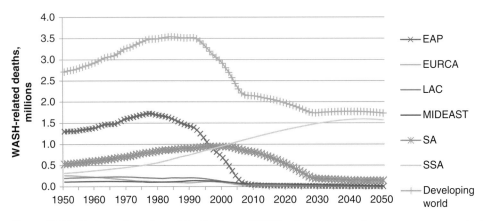

Figure 10.20 *Estimated number of deaths due to WASH-related disease for base case parameterization of the mortality rate, by region (future projections use growth rates for 1950–2008)*

mortality declines in SSA and SA vary substantially based on our parameter assumptions, and our sensitivity analyses suggest that the global number of deaths from WASH-related disease could range from 1.0 million per year (high growth and high elasticities) to 2.7 million per year (low growth and low elasticities) in 2050 (Table 10.7).

Predictions of Average Time to Water

As a result of gradually rising income and urbanization, our model shows declining average time to water in most regions and countries over the

simulation period (Figure 10.21) – similar to the projections of WASH-related mortality rates. Because of the model structure, increases in time to water coincide only with either (1) periods of economic slowdown, or (2) a small set of individual countries for which several years of data are available and show rising collection times. Predicted one-way collection times in 1950 ranged from 4 to 5 minutes in EURCA, and LAC in 1950, to about 11 minutes in SSA. By 2000, when these data first became available, the first two of these regions had average times of about 2 minutes, and SSA was at 9 minutes. We project continued declines to nearly

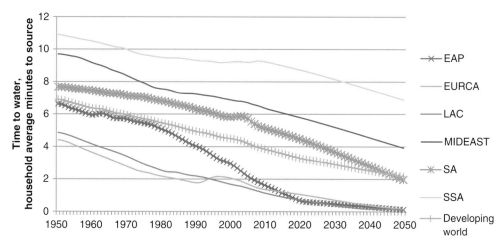

Figure 10.21 *Estimated base case simulation of one-way time to water, by region (future projections use growth rates for 1950–2008)*

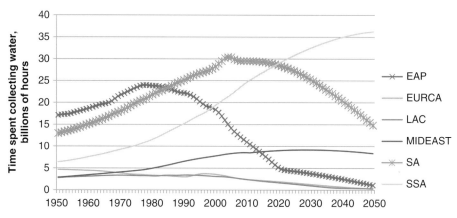

Figure 10.22 *Estimated base case simulation of total time spent collecting water, by region (future projections use growth rates for 1950–2008)*

zero in EAP, EURCA and LAC around 2030 (where economic growth projections are highest) and to 2–4 minutes in SA and MIDEAST by 2050.[21] Time to water remains somewhat higher in SSA in 2050, at about 7 minutes. The average one-way time to water across all less developed regions decreases from about 7 minutes in 1950 to just over 2 minutes in 2050, and is most sensitive to the income elasticity parameter of average time to source.

We convert these average collection times into total time spent collecting water by multiplying time to water by the number of households, and

the number of round trips per household per day, to yield the aggregate regional totals shown in Figure 10.22 (assuming base case parameter values from Table 10.5). The resulting trajectory shows that the total time spent collecting water in EAP, LAC, EURCA, and SA is now declining, but that it may still be climbing in the MIDEAST (to about 2030, though the data may overestimate

[21] Only three MIDEAST countries have data, however, and these are likely higher than in other countries. They are Yemen, Tunisia, and Morocco.

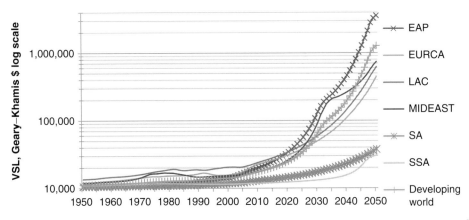

Figure 10.23 *Average value of a statistical life, by region (projections from 1950–2008 growth rates)*

average time to water in this region; footnote 21) and SSA regions (no peak over the simulation period), due to population growth. Total time spent collecting water is declining in the other regions (EAP and LAC) which are further along in the demographic transition or have lower average time to water. Globally, aggregate time spent collecting water for the base case simulation rose from about 47 billion hours in 1950 to a peak of 82 billion hours around 2003, and is projected to decline to 60 billion hours in 2050.

"Economic Losses" from Lack of Piped Water and Sanitation

Finally, we turn to our calculations of the "economic losses" associated with WASH-related disease, to investigate how rising incomes, and thus the VSL and opportunity cost of time, interact with these various factors of declining mortality rates and time to water, as well as demographics. As shown in Figure 10.23 , the VSL, or "economic losses" per statistical life lost, have been increasing over time across all regions, especially in EAP, because

incomes have been increasing (these reach about G–K\$ 4 million in 2050 in EAP, which is very close to levels in the developed world today). The countries in EURCA present an interesting exception to the general upward trend in VSLs since 1990. After the fall of the Soviet Union, real incomes declined in many of these countries; the VSL therefore decreased somewhat in the early 1990s.

If declines in mortality compensate for the rise in the VSL, it would still be possible for "economic losses" to increase on *aggregate* (not on a per capita basis) due to population growth alone. Population in all less developed regions increases rapidly throughout much of the period simulated in this study. Wherever the number of deaths was increasing over time (in EAP until the late 1970s, the MIDEAST until 1990, SA until 2000, and still in SSA), "health losses" would have been increasing over time as well, given the positive trend in real incomes. The same would also hold true with regard to time costs from collecting water wherever aggregate time to water and incomes were increasing.

Figure 10.24 shows our base case estimations of "economic losses" by region, based on future GDP growth projections for 1950–2008. Panels A and B present health losses and time costs, by region, and Panel C presents the global totals (totals by region can be found in Annex 10.3). Total aggregate "economic losses" in trillions of G–K\$ over the entire period are then summarized in Table 10.8, which also presents best- and worst-case sensitivity analyses.[22]

---

[22] Note that these aggregate losses are undiscounted and occur over a 100-year period, and are therefore perhaps hard to interpret. Considering the annual amounts at different points in time may be more intuitive: in the base case, we find that these losses are GKD40, 56, 54, 45, and 57 billion in 1950, 1975, 2000, 2025, and 2050, respectively, as shown in Figure 10.24.

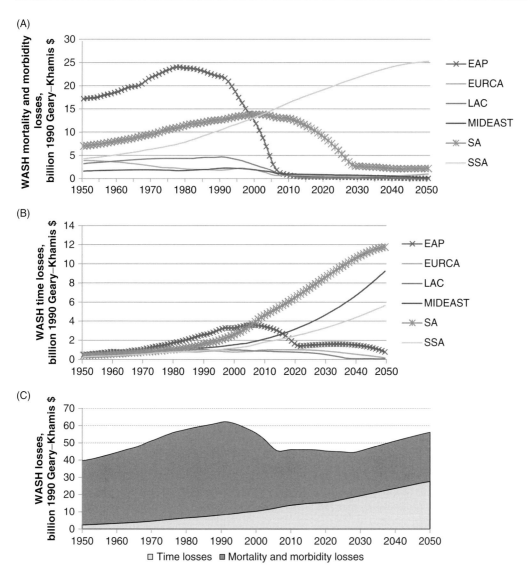

Figure 10.24 *Base case "economic losses" associated with WASH: (A) health losses, by region; (B) time costs, by region; and (C) aggregate global losses (projections from 1950–2008 growth rates)*

In EAP, LAC, and the MIDEAST, economic losses due to WASH-related illnesses peaked in the early 1980s or 1990s. Health losses declined in EURCA until the late 1980s and then increased briefly after the fall of the Soviet Union before declining more quickly. Our base case simulations suggest that SA reached a peak in economic losses due to WASH-related illnesses of about G–K$14 billion around the turn of the century. In contrast, economic losses due

to WASH-related illnesses for SSA only approach a peak of G–K$25 billion around 2050.

The trajectory of time costs is quite different because the average time to source declines much more slowly in our base case model than mortality, and does not always outpace the combination of increasing value of time and the mostly upward trend in population. In SA, MIDEAST, and SSA, time costs rise throughout the period, and the model

Table 10.8 Ranges of aggregate "economic losses" associated with WASH, summed over the time horizon 1900–2050 (in trillions of 1990 G–K$ and as percent of GDP)

	Low		Base case		High	
	Total	Percent of GDP	Total	Percent of GDP	Total	Percent of GDP
All developing regions	0.7	0.01	5.1	0.1	114	2.4
East Asia and Pacific	0.2	0.01	1.3	0.1	33.1	1.3
Europe and Central Asia	0.07	0.01	0.24	0.05	10.7	2.2
Latin America and Caribbean	0.1	0.02	0.29	0.05	10.1	1.8
Middle East and N. Africa	0.03	0.01	0.40	0.1	12.0	3.4
South Asia	0.09	0.01	1.3	0.2	36.5	5.9
Sub-Saharan Africa	0.2	0.1	1.6	1.2	11.4	8.6

Notes: Derived using the elasticity parameters and other uncertain parameters in Table 10.4, for two scenarios of GDP growth, VSL assumptions (as outlined in the Annex 10.1; high estimate uses Hammitt and Robinson (2011) extrapolation with an income elasticity of VSL = 1.5), inclusion of coverage type (improved water or piped water and sewer only), and use of alternative GDP measures (average GDP to lowest 80% or average GDP overall).

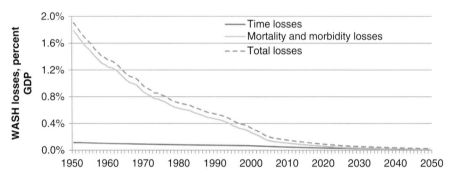

Figure 10.25 *Base case "economic losses" associated with WASH-related diseases as percent of GDP for all developing regions (projections from 1950–2008 growth rates)*

predicts that total losses could begin to increase again in the period leading up to 2050. And whereas economic losses due to WASH-related illnesses seem to have been larger than time costs for much of the historical period when mortality rates were high, time costs will become relatively more important over time.

It is also useful to put the base case results in perspective by comparing them to the total GDP for the regions involved (Figure 10.25). We use GDP to contextualize predicted "economic losses" simply to provide a sense of the relative magnitude of these losses. These losses as a percent of GDP should not be interpreted as the net economic effect of improved service. In our base

case, the calculation shows that health and time costs have and are likely to *decline* as a fraction of GDP, even as absolute "losses" go up. This is because population and economic growth also raise aggregate income, and do so faster than these "losses," at least in relative terms. In the base case "economic losses" start out at about 2% of developing world GDP in 1950, and decline to about 0.02% of GDP by 2050. A few of the countries with the highest losses at different points in time in the base case, for example Angola, Niger, Sierra Leone, or Afghanistan, are in the range of 10–14% of GDP.

As shown in Table 10.8, the base case results are highly sensitive to the value of model parameters.

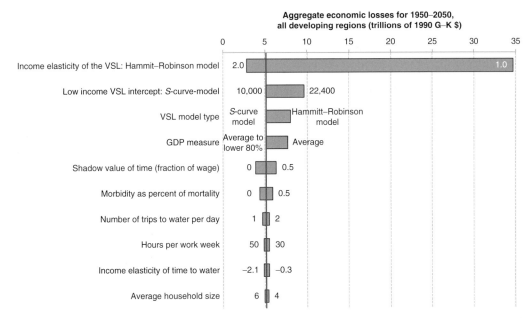

Figure 10.26 *Ranking of factors influencing model projections of the aggregate economic losses over the simulation period 1950–2050*

Worst-case model results project "economic losses" that are over one order of magnitude larger than those in the base case (and the best-case outcomes are about 15% as large). For aggregate losses, by far the most critical factors for varying outcomes are those that determine the assumed relationship between the value of a statistical life (which scales health losses) and income (Figure 10.26). These are followed by several parameters related to the cost of time spent collecting water (i.e. the shadow value of time, GDP measure, and number of work hours used to derive the opportunity cost of time, and the number of daily trips to collect water) and the relative size of morbidity costs from WASH-related diseases. Inclusion of improved water access as well as piped water and sewer makes a relatively minor difference in these estimates. Finally, although aggregate losses are more sensitive to the valuation parameters in the model, the precise timing of the different regional maxima in health and time losses shifts considerably depending on the values of the elasticity parameters shown in Table 10.4. For this reason, one should not make too much of the points where the base case predicts those peaks to occur.

Assumptions about the VSL play a dramatic role in determining the "economic losses" predicted in our simulation model. Typically an analyst would assume a constant income elasticity and extrapolate from rich world VSLs to obtain less developed country VSLs (an approach described by Hammitt and Robinson (2011) that is discussed more thoroughly in Annex 10.1). This is problematic from an analytical perspective because the choice of the appropriate income elasticity of the VSL for less developed countries is not empirically based, but rather relies on the judgment of the analyst. As shown in Figure 10.26, varying this parameter between 1 and 2 has an enormous impact on the economic analysis of the problem at hand, shifting estimates of "economic losses" from poor water and sanitation from about G–K\$ 3 to 35 trillion, and explains a great deal of the variation identified in Table 10.8. Some familiar with the literature on the relationship between the VSL and income might even advocate using an income elasticity of 0.5, which would raise aggregate losses over the period to G–K\$ 203 trillion. This would imply that losses in 1950, for example, were nearly 75% of developing world GDP, which is clearly unreasonable.[23] In contrast, variation in the intercept parameter of the more empirically based S-curve relationship that we develop in Annex 10.1 generates a smaller, though still substantial range of uncertainty in loss estimates of G–K\$ 5.1–9.6 trillion.[24]

We also note that there is considerable uncertainty in where the peaks in "economic losses" actually occur, though the trajectory of rising and falling economic costs appears consistent across most regions. Many poor countries initially experience high population growth and modest GDP growth, both of which raise per capita and aggregate losses, and often at a faster rate than declines in mortality rate and time to water sources. With growth, however, these declines begin to outpace the drivers of increasing health and time losses. With economic losses due to WASH-related illnesses, this seems to occur much earlier than with time losses, because the income and urbanization elasticities of mortality are larger than those of time to water sources. Due to the positive relationship between economic losses and GDP, we find that the peak in WASH-related health losses lags slightly behind, and is more pronounced than, the peak in deaths in many countries. (This is not the case in China which represents a special case where high growth and demographic changes occurred concurrently.) Similarly, because of the positive relationship between income and time losses, the peak in time losses lags (or will lag) the one in total time spent collecting water in these countries.

In addition, we find that assuming smaller elasticities or associations between income and urbanization and our model outcomes (coverage, mortality rates, and time to water) tends to increase aggregate losses overall, and tends to push the peaks in losses further into the future. Indeed, in SSA, our base case model results do not show a peak in "economic losses" because (a) population expansion continues to be high, (b) the mortality rate and time to water is high and remains high over the simulation period, and (c) economic growth raises the "economic loss" per death and hour spent collecting water at a rate that exceeds these declines. This rising trend of "economic losses" in SSA is relatively robust to changes in the assumptions in the simulation model. Given our derived associations between coverage, mortality, and GDP growth, and assuming the data on WASH-related mortality rates are correct, additional sensitivity analyses suggest that "economic losses" in SSA are only likely to peak before 2050 if at least two things happen: (1) GDP growth increases considerably, to at least 5–10%, and (2) the negative associations between time to water and income growth in SSA are much stronger than our empirical estimations would suggest.

Discussion

To the best of our knowledge, this chapter describes the first attempt to estimate the global economic burden of health losses and time expenditures associated with poor water-, sanitation-, and hygiene-related illnesses over a long historical and future time horizon. The analysis provides what we believe to be a useful and broad perspective on the scope of this problem and on the transition that takes place as countries proceed along different economic and demographic growth trajectories. It also highlights important data gaps and methodological challenges. In this discussion we summarize the most important of these issues.

First, economic losses per case of WASH-related illness or death, and time losses per unit of time spent collecting water, both increase with income because of the positive relationships between income and the value of mortality risk reductions and the opportunity cost of time. At the same time, disease incidence, mortality rates, and time to water decrease in income. It is therefore not clear a priori whether total economic losses will increase or decrease with economic growth. Indeed, the

---

[23] Some might wonder why this is so unreasonable. After all, poor water and sanitation do seem like big problems. However, if losses were this large, it would so obviously be beneficial to invest in improved services that one would have to confront the odd reality that few individuals in these countries invest heavily in such services.

[24] We also note that the constant elasticity approach outlined in Hammitt and Robinson (2011), with an elasticity of 1.5, ultimately does not yield estimates that are so different from our empirical model.

modeling conducted in this research shows that "economic losses" sometimes increase even as economic development is occurring and mortality rates are falling.

Second, the rise in "economic losses" can accelerate with development, and this creates endogenous pressure to invest in WASH technologies. So long as the income growth is broad-based, this pressure may be especially important for the expansion of technologies that are subject to economies of scale such as piped water and sewerage. The massive expansion in coverage with piped and improved water and sanitation in China and Latin America between 1990 and 2008 did not occur by chance: it accompanied quickly rising incomes, which contributed to increased household demand for those services, and the public sector's financial resources to provide them. People in less developed nations want piped water and sewer networks, and their ability to pay for these improvements increases sharply as their incomes rise. WASH-related health losses typically rise sharply when populations grow and countries transition to middle-income status, (between G–K$1,000 and G–K$5,000 income per capita) because the value of mortality risk reductions increases rapidly. Once demand pressures and subsequent investment kick in, there is a slowing of this rise in economic losses which is then followed by an eventual decline. This is shown by the regional peaks in our model simulations of health losses (see for example Figure 10.24). Wherever economic development is successful, as has happened in EAP, the problem of WASH-related mortality will likely be solved quickly from a historical perspective and without new technological breakthroughs. This is not to say, however, that such places will easily solve all of their water problems: this chapter has not considered issues of industrial pollution, climate change, or water scarcity, for example.

Also, conventional piped water and sewerage are expensive, and impose real resource costs on poor countries, so these "old world" technologies may not be the best solution in all places and at all times. Simply financing these services with upfront investment is not sufficient to ensure their long-term success; operation and maintenance must be supported, debt repaid, and new capital infusions are continually required. It is useful to consider what

it might cost to achieve the high levels of coverage with piped water and sewerage (found for example in EAP and LAC) in the regions that lag behind (i.e. SSA and SA). For this illustrative calculation, we use data from 2008, the last year for which we have coverage data. In that year, about 1.4 billion and 0.65 billion people did not have piped water and sanitation in SA and SSA, respectively, out of 1.5 and 0.7 billion total population. To raise coverage levels to 35–40%, as were found in EAP when mortality rates began to fall, a total of 0.6 billion and 0.3 billion people would need to have access to these services. This would entail providing these services to 0.45 and 0.25 billion new people. Assuming that the average household size is five people and that the full economic cost of piped water and sanitation per household is US$40 per month (Whittington et al. 2009), the annual costs of covering these additional people would be US$43 and US$24 billion, respectively. This amount represents 1.0% of GDP in South Asia and 2.3% of GDP in sub-Saharan Africa in 2010.

Given our focus on piped water and sewerage, our projections of future "economic losses" associated with inadequate water and sanitation could be viewed as an upper bound because international donors such as the World Health Organization, UNICEF, and others are actively working to reduce the problems related to water and sanitation using lower-cost innovations and interim solutions where piped services are unaffordable. One would hope that the uptake of such innovative technologies would be successful in providing economic benefits and therefore be subject to the same demand-side forces which push people with rising incomes to invest more heavily in piped water and sanitation. Then, mortality declines could accelerate independently of large-scale and costly initiatives to expand piped water and sewerage. However, the empirical evidence reviewed above (pp. 305–308) suggests that the demand for cheap and decentralized interventions in the WASH sector is much lower than the demand for convenient piped services; thus, sustaining widespread use of these technologies may remain a major challenge.

At the national level, we find that there are important differences in the burden of WASH-related illnesses and time costs across the developing world.

At the beginning of the simulation period, around 1950, when WASH-related mortality was much higher than it is today in most less developed countries, we find that health losses associated with mortality make up a relatively larger share of the total costs of poor services. However, mortality has dropped quickly over the second half of the twentieth century in many regions, in parallel with economic development and increases in coverage with better water and sanitation services. Our calculations suggest that this has reduced the relative fraction of losses due to poor health particularly in East Asia and the Pacific, Latin America and the Caribbean, the Middle East, and Eastern Europe. In contrast, in South Asia and especially sub-Saharan Africa, WASH-related mortality remains high today and still causes many deaths and economic losses.

These regional disparities are important because many parts of the globe have made tremendous strides in reducing the number of deaths related to inadequate water and sanitation, even without achieving universal coverage with piped water and sewerage. However, our simulation results suggest that it is unlikely that economic losses from WASH-related diseases will decrease soon in SSA. WASH-related mortality remains much higher in SSA than in other regions. Average incomes in SSA are also much lower than in other regions, such that the demand for preventative health improvements is limited. Also, the average statistics for South Asia, which has lower mortality rates than SSA, mask the fact that hundreds of millions of very poor people live there. For example in the Ganges Plain which spans from the Terai in Nepal across Bihar and Uttar Pradesh and into Bangladesh, there are more people living on less than US$2 per day than in all of SSA. As a result, health losses in sub-regions in SA and throughout much of SSA could accelerate over the next half century, especially given the projected rise in the populations of these areas. These trends seem likely to maintain strong pressure for government and donor action.

In addition, access to water remains inconvenient in many more countries than those in SA and SSA, and time expenses appear likely to grow over time relative to health losses. Because the average time to sources is less strongly associated with economic growth than is the WASH-related mortality rate, our analysis projects that the aggregate time spent collecting water will increase rapidly over the first half of the twenty-first century in many regions. This will be true particularly where coverage with convenient piped services is low or where water supplies in rural areas are inadequate, and where population growth remains high, e.g. in SA, poor countries in MIDEAST, and in SSA. In general, the mortality problems associated with poor water and sanitation are more quickly reduced than the time burden of water collection. Indeed, the only real way to decrease collection times for water is through in-house connections, whereas health gains follow from economic growth as well as uptake of such technologies.

We conclude by emphasizing that data constraints and measurement problems severely limit our ability to make accurate projections of "economic losses." As described in this chapter, there are very large uncertainties associated with extrapolations of mortality data beyond the single year available from the WHO. The data on time to source in different countries are spotty and only cover a fraction of the countries in our model. Our coverage data, while better, only span 18 of the 100 years in our simulations. If the associations we found in the data are unstable over time, our extrapolations back to 1950 and forward into the future will be erroneous. More work on collection and analysis of these data is needed, as is work on factors such as convenience and/or aesthetic costs unrelated to the time burden of collecting water. As summarized in Table 10.8, the ranges of the losses we calculate by varying parameter assumptions are very large, and the precise timing of the regional maxima in losses is unstable.

Climate change is another source of uncertainty that is ignored in our simulations. Climate change may affect both the costs of improved water supplies (and thus governments' financial resources to deliver such services) and the epidemiology of WASH-related illnesses. Finally, we especially caution against drawing any conclusions with regards to the causal nature of relationships between income, coverage with improved water and sanitation services, and reduced mortality from WASH-related diseases and average water collection times.

References

Ahuja, A., M. Kremer, and A. P. Zwane (2010) Providing clean water: evidence from randomized evaluations. *Annual Review of Resource Economics* **2**: 237–256.

Alberini, A., M. Cropper, A. Krupnick, and N. B. Simon (2004) Does the value of a statistical life vary with age and health status? Evidence from the US and Canada. *Journal of Environmental Economics and Management* **48**: 769–792.

Arnold, B. F. and J. M. Colford (2007) Treating water with chlorine at point-of-use to improve water quality and reduce child diarrhea in developing countries: a systematic review and meta-analysis. *American Journal of Tropical Medicine and Hygiene* **76**: 354–364.

Baranzini, A. and G. Ferro Luzzi (2001) The economic value of risks to life: evidence from the Swiss labour market. *Swiss Journal of Economics and Statistics* **137**: 149–170.

Bellavance, F., G. Dionne, and M. Lebeau (2009) The value of a statistical life: a meta-analysis with a mixed effects regression model. *Journal of Health Economics* **28**: 444–464.

Bennett, D. (2012) Does clean water make you dirty? Water supply and sanitation in the Philippines. *Journal of Human Resources* **47**: 146–173.

Bhattacharya, S., A. Alberini, and M. L. Cropper (2007) The value of mortality risk reductions in Delhi, India. *Journal of Risk and Uncertainty* **34**: 21–47.

Black, D. A., J. Galdo, and L. Liu (2003) *How Robust are Hedonic Wage Estimates of the Price of Risk?* Washington, DC: US Environmental Protection Agency.

Blomquist, G. C., T. R. Miller, and D. T. Levy (1996) Values of risk reduction implied by motorist use of protection equipment: new evidence from different populations. *Journal of Transport Economics and Policy* **30**: 55–66.

Bowland, B. J. and J. C. Beghin (2001) Robust estimates of value of a statistical life for developing economies. *Journal of Policy Modeling* **23**: 385–396.

Cairncross, S., K. Shordt, S. Zacharia, and B. K. Govindan (2005) What causes sustainable changes in hygiene behaviour? A cross-sectional study from Kerala, India. *Social Science and Medicine* **61**: 2212–2220.

Clark, G. (2007) *A Farewell to Alms: A Brief Economic History of the World*. Princeton, NJ: Princeton University Press

Clasen, T., W. Schmidt, T. Rabie, I. Roberts, and S. Cairncross (2007) Interventions to improve water quality for preventing diarrhoea: systematic review and meta-analysis. *British Medical Journal* **334**: 782.

Costa, D. L. and M. E. Kahn (2003) The rising price of nonmarket goods. *American Economic Review* **93**: 227–232.

Cousineau, J.-M., R. Lacroix, and A.-M. Girard (1992) Occupational hazard and wage compensating differentials. *Review of Economics and Statistics* **74**: 166–169.

Cropper, M., J. K. Hammitt, and L. A. Robinson (2011) Valuing mortality risk reductions: progress and challenges. *Annual Review of Resource Economics* **3**: 313–336.

Curtis, V. and S. Cairncross (2003) Effect of washing hands with soap on diarrhoea risk in the community: a systematic review. *The Lancet Infectious Diseases* **3**: 275–281.

Dasgupta, S., B. Laplante, H. Wang, and D. Wheeler (2002) Confronting the environmental Kuznets curve. *Journal of Economic Perspectives* **16**: 147–168.

Devoto, F., E. Duflo, P. Dupas, W. Parienté, and V. Pons (2009) *Happiness on Tap: The Demand for and Impact of Piped Water in Urban Morocco*, Working Paper. Available at: siteresources.world bank.org/DEC/Resources/

Dreyfus, M. K. and W. K. Viscusi (1995) Rates of time preference and consumer valuations of automobile safety and fuel efficiency. *Journal of Law and Economics* **38**, 79–105.

Drèze, J. (1962) L'Utilité sociale d'une vie humaine. *Revue Française de Recherche Opèrationelle* **6**: 93–118.

Eeckhoudt, L. R. and J. K. Hammitt (2001) Background risks and the value of a statistical life. *Journal of Risk and Uncertainty* **23**: 261–279.

Ejemot, R., J. Ehiri, M. M. Meremikwu, and S. A. Critchley (2008) Hand washing for preventing diarrhoea. *Cochrane Database Systematic Review* (**1**): CD004265.

Esrey, S., J. Potash, L. Roberts, and C. Shiff (1991) Effects of improved water supply and sanitation on ascariasis, diarrhoea, dracunculiasis, hookworm infection, schistosomiasis, and trachoma. *Bulletin of the World Health Organization* **69**: 609–621.

Evans, M. F. and G. Schaur (2010) A quantile estimation approach to identify income and age variation in the value of a statistical life. *Journal of Environmental Economics and Management* **59**: 260–270.

Fewtrell, L., R. Kaufmann, D. Kay, *et al.* (2005) Water, sanitation, and hygiene interventions to reduce diarrhoea in less developed countries: a systematic review and meta-analysis. *The Lancet Infectious Diseases* **5**: 42–52.

Fewtrell, L., A. Prüss-Üstün, R. Bos, F. Gore, and J. Bartram (2007) *Water, Sanitation and Hygiene: Quantifying the Health Impact at National and Local Levels in Countries with Incomplete Water Supply and Sanitation Coverage.* Geneva: WHO.

Gaba, A. and W. K. Viscusi (1998) Differences in subjective risk thresholds: worker groups as an example. *Management Science* **44**: 801–811.

Galiani, S., P. Gertler, and E. Schargrodsky (2005) Water for life: the impact of the privatization of water services on child mortality. *Journal of Political Economy* **113**: 83–120.

Gamper-Rabindran, S., S. Khan, and C. Timmins (2010) The impact of piped water provision on infant mortality in Brazil: a quantile panel data approach. *Journal of Development Economics* **92**: 188–200.

Gayer, T., J. T. Hamilton, and W. K. Viscusi (2000) Private values of risk tradeoffs at superfund sites: housing market evidence on learning about risk. *Review of Economics and Statistics* **82**: 439–451.

Gibson, J., S. Barns, M. Cameron, *et al.* (2007) The value of statistical life and the economics of landmine clearance in developing countries. *World Development* **35**: 512–531.

Giergiczny, M. (2008) Value of a statistical life: the case of Poland. *Environmental and Resource Economics* **41**: 209–221.

Grossman, G. M. and A. B. Krueger (1995) Economic growth and the environment. *Quarterly Journal of Economics* **110**: 353–377.

Günther, I. and G. Fink (2011) *Water and Sanitation to Reduce Child Mortality: The Impact and Cost of Water and Sanitation Infrastructure*, World Bank Policy Research Working Paper No. 5618. Washington, DC: World Bank.

Guo, X. and J. K. Hammitt (2009) Compensating wage differentials with unemployment: evidence from China. *Environmental and Resource Economics* **42**: 187–209.

Hall, R. and C. Jones (2007) The value of life and the rise in health spending. *Quarterly Journal of Economics* **122**: 39–72.

Hammitt, J. K. (2000) Valuing mortality risk: theory and practice. *Environmental Science and Technology* **34**: 1396–1400.

Hammitt, J. K. and M. E. Ibarrarán (2006) The economic value of fatal and non-fatal occupational risks in Mexico City using actuarial and perceived-risk estimates. *Health Economics* **15**: 1329–1335.

Hammitt, J. K. and L. A. Robinson (2011) The income elasticity of the value per statistical life: transferring estimates between high and low income populations. *Journal of Benefit–Cost Analysis* **2**(1). Available at: www.bepress.com/jbca/vol2/iss1/1.

Hammitt, J. K. and Y. Zhou (2006) The economic value of air-pollution-related health risks in China: a contingent valuation study. *Environmental and Resource Economics* **33**: 399–423.

Hamoudi, A., M. Jeuland, S. Lombardo, *et al.* (2011) *Know Thy E. Coli: Household Responses to Water Quality Testing in Rural India.* Durham, NC: Duke University.

Hintermann, B., A. Alberini, and A. Markandya (2010) Estimating the value of safety with labour market data: are the results trustworthy? *Applied Economics* **42**: 1085–1100.

Hunter, P., D. Zmirou-Navier, and P. Hartemann (2009) Estimating the impact on health of poor reliability of drinking water interventions in developing countries. *Science of the Total Environment* **407**: 2621–2624.

Hutton, G. and L. Haller (2004) *Evaluation of the Costs and Benefits of Water and Sanitation Improvements at the Global Level.* Geneva: WHO.

Hutton, G., L. Haller, and J. Bartram (2007) Global cost–benefit analysis of water supply and sanitation interventions. *Journal of Water and Health* **5**: 481–502.

Inglehart, R. and H. D. Klingemann (2000) Genes, culture, democracy, and happiness. In: E. Diener and E. M. Suh (eds.), *Culture and Subjective Well-Being.* Cambridge, MA: MIT Press.

Jalan, J. and M. Ravallion (2003) Does piped water reduce diarrhea for children in rural India? *Journal of Econometrics* **112**: 153–173.

Jalan, J. and E. Somanathan (2008) The importance of being informed: experimental evidence on demand for environmental quality. *Journal of Development Economics* **87**: 14–28.

Jenkins, R., N. Owens, and L. Bembenek Wiggins (2001) Valuing reduced risks to children: the case of bicycle safety helmets. *Contemporary Economic Policy* **19**: 397–408.

Jeuland, M., M. Lucas, J. Clemens, and D. Whittington (2009) A cost–benefit analysis of vaccination programs in Beira, Mozambique. *World Bank Economic Review* **23**: 235–267.

Johannesson, M., P.-O. Johansson, and K.-G. Lofgren (1997) On the value of changes in life expectancy: blips versus parametric changes. *Journal of Risk and Uncertainty* **15**: 221–239.

Kahneman, D. and A. Tversky (1979) Prospect theory: an analysis of decision under risk. *Econometrica: Journal of the Econometric Society* **47**: 263–291.

Kim, S. W. and P. V. Fishback (1999) The impact of institutional change on compensating wage differentials for accident risk: South Korea, 1984–1990. *Journal of Risk and Uncertainty* **18**: 231–248.

Knetsch, J. (2010) Values of gains and losses: reference states and choice of measure. *Environmental and Resource Economics* **46**: 179–188.

Kniesner, T. J., W. K. Viscusi, and J. P. Ziliak (2010) Policy relevant heterogeneity in the value of statistical life: new evidence from panel data quantile regressions. *Journal of Risk and Uncertainty* **40**: 15–31.

Komives, K., D. Whittington, and X. Wu (2003) Infrastructure coverage and the poor: a global perspective. In: P. Brook and T. Irwin (eds.), *Infrastructure for Poor People: Public Policy for Private Provision*. Washington, DC: World Bank.

Kosek, M., C. Bern, and R. L. Guerrant (2003) The global burden of diarrhoeal disease, as estimated from studies published between 1992 and 2000. *Bulletin of the World Health Organization* **81**: 197–204.

Kremer, M., J. Leino, E. Miguel, and A. Zwane (2009) *Spring Cleaning: Rural Water Impacts, Valuation and Property Rights Institutions*, National Bureau of Economic Research Working Paper No. 15280. Cambridge, MA: NBER.

Lindhjem, H., S. Navrud, and N. A. Braathen (2010) *Valuing Lives Saved from Environmental, Transport, and Health Policies: A Meta-Analysis of Stated Preference Studies*. Paris: OECD.

Liu, J.-T, and J. K. Hammitt (1999) Perceived risk and the value of workplace safety in a developing country. *Journal of Risk Research* **2**: 263–275.

Liu, J. T., J. K. Hammitt, and J. L. Liu (1997) Estimated hedonic wage function and value of life in a developing country. *Economics Letters* **57**: 353–358.

Lott, J. R. and R. L. Manning (2000) Have changing liability rules compensated workers twice for occupational hazards? Earnings premiums and cancer risks. *Journal of Legal Studies* **29**: 99–130.

Luby, S. P., M. Agboatwalla, D. R. Feikin, *et al.* (2005) Effect of handwashing on child health: a randomised controlled trial. *The Lancet* **366**: 225–233.

Mathers, C. D., and D. Loncar (2006) Projections of global mortality and burden of disease from 2002 to 2030. *PLoS Medicine* **3**: e442.

Mathers, C., A. Lopez, C. Stein, *et al.* (2004) *Deaths and Disease Burden by Cause: Global Burden of Disease Estimates for 2001 by World Bank Country Groups*, Disease Control Priorities Project Working Paper No. 18. Geneva: WHO.

Maskery, B., Z. Islam, J. Deen, and D. Whittington (2008) *An Estimate of the Economic Value that Parents in Rural Bangladesh Place on Ex-ante Mortality Risk Reductions for Their Children*, Working Paper. Chapel Hill, NC: Department of Environmental Sciences and Engineering, University of North Carolina.

Melhuish, C., A. Ross, M. Goodge, *et al.* (2005) *Accident Costing Report AC5: Malaysia*. Manila, Philippines: Asian Development Bank, Association of Southeast Asian Nations, Regional Road Safety Program.

Meng, R. and D. A. Smith (1999) The impact of workers' compensation on wage premiums for job hazards. *Applied Economics* **31**: 1101–1108.

Miguel, E. and M. Kremer (2004) Worms: identifying impacts on education and health in the presence of treatment externalities. *Econometrica* **72**: 159–217.

Miller, G. and D. Cutler (2005) The role of public health improvements in health advances: the twentieth-century United States. *Demography* **42**: 1–22.

Miller, T. R. (2000) Variations between countries in values of statistical life. *Journal of Transport Economics and Policy* **34**: 169–188.

Mrozek, J. R. and L. Taylor (2001) What determines the value of life? A meta-analysis. *Environmental and Resource Economics* **30**: 313–325.

Olembo, L., F. A. D. Kaona, M. Tuba, and G. Burnham (2004) *Safe Water Systems: An Evaluation of the Zambia CLORIN Program*, Final Report. US Agency for International Development Environmental Health Project. Available at: www.ehproject.org/pdf/others/zambia%20report%20format.pdf.

Ortuzar, J. D., L. A. Cifuentes, and H. C. W. L. Williams (2000) Application of willingness-to-pay methods to value transport externalities in less developed countries. *Environment and Planning A* **32**: 2007–2018.

Pattanayak, S. K., J.-C. Yang, K. L. Dickinson, *et al.* (2009) Shame or subsidy revisited: social mobilization for sanitation in Orissa, India. *Bulletin of the World Health Organization* **87**: 580–587.

Pattanayak, S. K., C. Poulos, J.-C. Yang, and S. R. Patil (2010) How valuable are environmental health interventions? Evaluation of water and sanitation programmes in India. *Bulletin of the World Health Organization* **88**: 535–542.

Preston, S. (1975) The changing relation between mortality and level of economic development. *Population Studies* **29**: 231–248.

Prüss-Üstün, A. and C. Corvalán (2006) *Preventing Disease through Healthy Environments: Towards an Estimate of the Environmental Burden of Disease*. Geneva: WHO.

Prüss-Üstün, A., R. Bos, F. Gore, and J. Bartram (2008) *Safer Water, Better Health: Costs, Benefits and Sustainability of Interventions to Protect and Promote Health*. Geneva: WHO.

Robinson, L. A. and J. K. Hammitt (2009) *The Value of Reducing Air Pollution Risks in Sub-Saharan Africa*, Final Report. Available at: www.regulatory-analysis.com/robinson-hammitt-air-pollution-africa.pdf.

Rosenbaum, P. R. and D. B. Rubin (1983) The central role of the propensity score in observational studies for causal effects. *Biometrika* **70**: 41–55.

Scotton, C. R. and L. O. Taylor (2011) Valuing risk reductions: incorporating risk heterogeneity into a revealed preference framework. *Resource and Energy Economics* **33**: 381–397.

Shanmugam, K. R. (1997) Compensating wage differentials for work related fatal and injury accidents. *Indian Journal of Labour Economics* **40**(2).

(2000) Valuations of life and injury risks. *Environmental and Resource Economics* **16**: 379–389.

(2001) Self selection bias in the estimates of compensating differentials for job risks in India. *Journal of Risk and Uncertainty* **22**: 263–275.

Shogren, J. F. and T. Stamland (2002) Skill and the value of life. *Journal of Political Economy* **110**: 1168–1173.

Shuval, H., R. Tilden, B. H. Perry, and R. N. Grosse (1981) Effect of investments in water supply and sanitation on health status: a threshold-saturation theory. *Bulletin of the World Health Organization* **59**: 243–248.

Siebert, W. S. and X. Wei (1994) Compensating wage differentials for workplace accidents: evidence for union and nonunion workers in the UK, *Journal of Risk and Uncertainty* **9**: 61–76.

Simon, N. B., M. L. Cropper, A. Alberini, and S. Arora (1999) *Valuing Mortality Reductions in India: A Study of Compensating Wage Differentials*. Washington, DC: World Bank.

Smith, K. and M. Ezzati (2005) How environmental health risks change with development: the epidemiologic and environmental risk transitions revisited. *Annual Review of Environment and Resources* **30**: 291–333.

Snow, R. W., E. C. McCabe, C. N. Mbogo *et al.* (1999) The effect of delivery mechanisms on the uptake of bed net reimpregnation in Kilifi District, Kenya. *Health Policy and Planning* **14**: 18–25.

Trémolet, S., P. Kolsky, and E. Perez (2010) *Financing On-Site Sanitation for the Poor: A Six Country Comparative Review and Analysis*. Washington, DC: World Bank.

US Environmental Protection Agency (2010) *Valuing Mortality Risk Reductions for Environmental Policy: A White Paper*. Prepared for consultation with the Science Advisory Board – Environmental Economics Advisory Committee. Washington, DC: US EPA.

Van Poppel, F. and C. Van Der Heijden (1997) The effects of water supply on infant and childhood mortality: a review of historical evidence. *Health Transition Review* **7**: 113–150.

Vassanadumrongdee, S. and S. Matsuoka (2005) Risk perceptions and value of a statistical life for air pollution and traffic accidents: evidence from Bangkok, Thailand. *Journal of Risk and Uncertainty* **30**: 261–287.

Viscusi, W. K. (2004) The value of life: estimates with risks by occupation and industry. *Economic Inquiry* **42**: 29–48.

Viscusi, W. and J. Aldy (2003) The value of a statistical life: a critical review of market estimates throughout the world. *Journal of Risk and Uncertainty* **27**: 5–76.

Wang, H. and J. Mullahy (2006) Willingness to pay for reducing fatal risk by improving air quality: a contingent valuation study in Chongqing, China. *Science of the Total Environment* **367**: 50–57.

Water and Sanitation Program (2005) *Scaling-Up Rural Sanitation in South Asia: Lessons Learned from Bangladesh, India, and Pakistan*. Washington, DC: World Bank.

Waterkeyn, J. and S. Cairncross (2005) Creating demand for sanitation and hygiene through Community Health Clubs: a cost-effective intervention in two districts in Zimbabwe. *Social Science and Medicine* **61**: 1958–1970.

Whittington, D. (2010) What have we learned from 20 years of stated preference research in less-developed countries? *Annual Review of Resource Economics* **2**: 209–236.

Whittington, D., W. M. Hanemann, C. Sadoff, and M. Jeuland (2009) The challenge of improving water and sanitation services in less developed countries. *Foundations and Trends in Microeconomics* **4**: 469–609.

Whittington, D., M. Jeuland, K. Barker, and Y. Yuen (2012). Setting priorities, targeting subsidies among water, sanitation, and health interventions in developing countries. *World Development* **40**: 1546–1568.

World Health Organization (2004) *Environmental Burden of Disease Data*. Geneva: WHO. Available at: www.who.int/quantifying_ehimpacts/national/countryprofile/intro/en/index.html.

Annex 10.1: Estimating the Value of the Statistical Life (VSL) for Calculating Global Losses from Inadequate Water and Sanitation

Introduction

This annex provides a more detailed explanation of the value of a statistical life (VSL), the concept we use for valuing mortality losses associated with poor water and sanitation. We review the literature on VSL estimation, focusing on developing countries, and explain the strategy we employ to develop VSL estimates for use in our simulation model. There are now numerous high-quality VSL estimates for industrialized countries (Viscusi and Aldy 2003). These are methodologically sophisticated and typically use large data sets that include multiple variables associated with individuals' preferences for mortality risk reductions.

Preferences for mortality risk reductions are heterogeneous and vary across a number of important dimensions including income and wealth, level of background risk, and cultural preferences towards risk (Viscusi and Aldy 2003; Cropper *et al.* 2011). One would not expect that individuals in countries at different stages of development would place the same value on mortality risk reductions. Economic theory and empirical evidence suggest that mortality risk reduction (and the corresponding VSL) is a normal good; individuals' willingness to pay (WTP) for mortality risk reduction increases as income increases. Thus, it would be inappropriate to use the same VSL estimates in developing countries as in industrialized countries. Our challenge in this chapter is to develop VSL estimates for the more than 100 developing countries over a period of 100 years during which real incomes change dramatically so that we can estimate the economic value of mortality losses.

The next section of this annex provides a brief overview of the concept of the VSL, describes the methods most commonly used to estimate VSLs, and then summarizes the principal limitations of these methods. Section 3 reviews the global literature on estimating the VSL, with special emphasis on studies from low- and middle-income countries. Section 4 provides a critique of the benefit transfer strategy that is typically used to predict the VSLs in low- and middle-income countries when primary data are not available. Section 5 then presents a different strategy that we employ to estimate VSLs in our analysis.

The Concept of VSL

Dreze (1962) first formulated the standard model for estimating the economic value of mortality risk reduction, often termed the value of a statistical life. This model relates individuals' marginal rate of substitution between mortality risk and wealth over a defined period of time. More formally, the VSL is the local slope of the indifference curve between wealth and mortality risk (Cropper *et al.* 2011). The VSL does not represent the value of a specific life. Rather, the VSL is an economic measure derived from risk–income tradeoffs that individuals routinely make (e.g. investing in preventative health, purchasing smoke detectors, buying point-of-use water filters, etc.). The VSL represents the value of small changes in mortality risk spread across a specific population.[25]

The VSL is calculated by scaling individuals' willingness to pay (or accept compensation) for a

---

[25] Readers interested in a more thorough summary of the conceptual foundation of the VSL concept should refer to Hammitt (2000), Viscusi and Aldy (2003), Evans and Schaur (2010), and Bellavance *et al.* (2009).

small reduction (or increase) in mortality risk up to the unit of a statistical life. A typical formulation of VSL is presented in equation (A10.1), where ΔP represents a change in mortality risk.[26]

$$VSL \approx WTP/\Delta P \approx WTA/\Delta P \qquad (A10.1)$$

For example, an individual willing to pay $600 per year for reducing their mortality risk by 0.0001 in that year would have an implied VSL of $6 million. This does not mean that a specific individual would be willing to pay $6 million to avoid certain death over that year, nor that she would be willing to accept $6 million in compensation for certain death during that period. The VSL of $6 million implies that 10,000 similar people would collectively pay $6 million to eliminate a risk that would kill one of them, selected at random, during that year or defined period of time (Hammitt 2000).

Because individuals have heterogeneous preferences, the VSL will vary both within and across populations. Various dimensions of heterogeneity that have been found to be associated with the VSL include income, age, the type and magnitude of risk considered, the level of background risk, and cultural attitudes or preferences towards risk. The most robust research findings on these VSL covariates

are age and income: specifically, the VSL has been found to increase in income and decrease in age (see Viscusi and Aldy (2003) for further details). In our study we are primarily concerned with the effect of income on the VSL and we ignore effects related to changes in the age structure of the population.

The two most commonly used approaches to estimate the value of mortality risk reductions have been (1) compensating wage differential (wage–risk) and (2) stated-preference (SP) techniques.[27] The following sections briefly describe these approaches, and some of their most important limitations. We note, however, that there are very few applications of either method in developing countries.

Compensating Wage Differential (Wage–Risk) Approaches to Estimating VSL: Theory and Challenges

The value of mortality risk reduction is most commonly estimated via hedonic wage studies that examine the tradeoff workers make between job-related mortality risk and wages. This approach is based on the assumption that a competitive labor market should compensate workers in jobs with higher occupational mortality risks, holding other worker, firm, and job characteristics constant (Hammitt 2000; Viscusi and Aldy 2003; Cropper *et al.* 2011; Hammitt and Robinson 2011). Workers' willingness to pay (accept) for marginal changes in job-related mortality risk (increase) is captured by the wage differential between jobs with different levels of risk.

Hedonic wage–risk studies generally adopt the form of equation (A10.2) (Viscusi and Aldy 2003):

$$w_i = \alpha + H_i\beta_1 + X_i\beta_2 + \gamma_1 p_i + \gamma_2 q_i + \epsilon_i \qquad (A10.2)$$

where w_i is a worker's wage, α is a constant intercept term, H_i is a vector of individual characteristic variables for worker i (e.g. age, education, race, etc.), X_i is a vector of job characteristic variables for worker i (e.g. industry, whether the job is white-collar or blue-collar, the degree of physical exertion required, etc.), p_i is the fatality risk, q_i is the non-fatal risk of injury for worker i's job, and ε_i is a random error term.[28] β_1, β_2, γ_1, and γ_2 are

---

[26] Critically, and more formally, the VSL is equal to the limit of WTP/ΔP or WTA/ΔP as ΔP approaches zero (Cropper *et al.* 2011). In other words, this expression is only valid for small (marginal) changes in risk. Also, this expression assumes that the value (or demand) function for changes in risk is symmetric, which may not be the case since individuals appear to treat economic gains and losses very differently (as discussed in the main chapter).

[27] A third class of studies which generate VSL estimates are revealed preference studies which examine individuals' private spending for goods that reduce mortality risks, for example purchase of drinking-water treatment technologies or vaccinations, see for example Kremer *et al.* (2009) and Jeuland *et al.* (2009).

[28] Studies employ a range of model specifications including log-linear and log-log to estimate the parameters in equation (10.A2). While individual studies and convention may favor a particular specification (Viscusi and Aldy 2003) there is no a priori theoretical basis for favoring a particular functional form.

[29] Studies often include additional covariates and interactions between covariates motivated by theory. For example, studies often include an interaction between non-fatal risk (q_i) and workers' compensation payable for an injury on the job.

parameters estimated via regression,[29] and γ_1 represents the change in wage (or WTP) for a 1-unit change in job-related mortality risk.

Wage–risk studies face both theoretical and econometric challenges. The VSL literature is rich with detailed discussions of estimation challenges, including model specification, omitted variable bias, the endogeneity of job-related mortality risk, the collinearity of fatal and non-fatal job-related mortality risks, and small sample sizes (Cousineau *et al.* 1992; Miller 2000; Mrozek and Taylor 2002; Shogren and Stamland 2002; Black *et al.* 2003; Viscusi and Aldy 2003; Viscusi 2004; Hintermann *et al.* 2010; Cropper *et al.* 2011; Knieser *et al.* 2011).[30]

There are several other threats associated with using compensating wage differentials estimated from wage–risk studies to estimate VSLs in developing countries. First, workers may not be well informed about job-related mortality risk. Second, labor markets may not be competitive. With respect to the former, there is little convincing evidence that subjective perceptions of risk are biased (Mrozek and Taylor 2002). However, Gaba and Viscusi (1998) do find that education affects whether individuals consider a job "dangerous." The assumption of competitive labor markets is problematic for some developing countries, given that they may have dual wage economies. It may be that labor markets for semi-skilled and skilled workers are competitive in some places. Several researchers have successfully used the wage–risk approach to estimate VSLs for subpopulations in poor countries; see for example Liu *et al.* (1997), Simon *et al.* (1999), Shanmugam (2000, 2001), and Guo and Hammitt (2009). However, one should be cautious extrapolating these VSL to an entire country's population (or in our case the population of people most exposed to diarrheal disease risks).

Another problem with using estimates from wage–risk studies is that they only apply to a specific class of mortality risks from occupational hazards. Selection effects aside (e.g. the fact that not everyone chooses to work), people may not treat these risks as equivalent to infectious disease and environmental risks. Recent work by Scotton and Taylor (2011) suggests that even in the context of on-the-job mortality risk, workers place a higher

risk premium on workplace homicide than on other types of job-related mortality risk. Industry and occupation dummies are consistently significant in wage hedonic regressions, which may reflect differences in the type of mortality in different employment contexts.

Stated-Preference Approaches to Estimating VSL: Theory and Challenges

Stated-preference techniques (e.g., the contingent valuation method) also have been used to estimate the value of mortality risk reductions, especially from risks such as air pollution and road hazards. Stated-preference techniques have two primary advantages over hedonic wage methods. First, the scenarios presented to respondents in stated-preference surveys can be tailored to specific mortality risks. As a result, stated-preference techniques have been most widely used to estimate the VSL for a number of environmental risk applications, most notably air pollution and road safety. Second, stated-preference techniques allow the researcher to specify and vary the magnitude of the risk reduction presented to respondents. Best practice in stated-preference studies of the VSL is to consider the effect of varying these mortality risks, and determine whether results are consistent with standard economic theory (i.e. whether WTP depends on income, levels of baseline risk, etc.), as shown in equation (A10.3) below:

$$\text{WTP}_i = \alpha + p_i\beta_1 + \gamma_1 r_i + X_i\beta_2 + \gamma_2 q_i + \epsilon_i$$
$$(A10.3)$$

where WTP_i is a dichotomous variable that takes a value of 1 if a respondent agrees to pay some price p_i for a good or policy intervention that reduces his/her mortality risk by an amount r_i, α is a constant intercept term, X_i is a vector of socio-economic

---

[30] Because of these types of issues, Cropper *et al.* (2011) caution against using the results from studies conducted prior to 2000 because they often omitted important explanatory variables and did not address threats of endogeneity or unobserved worker characteristics. Hintermann *et al.* (2010) go so far as to say that "if compensating differentials for risk exists, econometric problems and the changing nature of labour [sic] markets prevent us from observing them" (p. 1085).

characteristic variables for individual i (e.g. income, education, age, etc.), q_i is the baseline mortality risk (if it varies across individuals in the sample), and ε_i is a random error term.[31] The parameters in equation (A10.3) are typically estimated using a probit or logistic regression model.

In spite of their flexibility, stated-preference techniques, like wage–risk hedonic approaches, present econometric challenges (Alberini *et al.* 2004).[32] More generally, stated-preference techniques are often criticized as being susceptible to a variety of biases (Carson *et al.* 2001; Whittington 2010). Perhaps most relevant in work on mortality risks are claims that respondents' answers in surveys may not reflect their true preferences because individuals misunderstand the hypothetical scenario (i.e. the nature of the risk reduction) with which they are presented. Risk reductions presented to respondents in stated-preference studies are generally small, on the order of 1 in 10,000 or 1 in 100,000. Individuals often have difficulty understanding and valuing such very low probability risks, and stated-preferences researchers commonly use visual aids such as colored grids representing risk and risk ladders to try to communicate the magnitude of the risk reduction to respondents (see Lindhjem *et al.* (2010) for a more complete review of these types of tools).

Cropper *et al.* (2011) recommend various scope tests to check the validity of survey responses. Economic theory suggests that the willingness to pay for risk reductions should be sensitive to the magnitude of the risk reduction and should increase proportionally for small changes in risk, such that the VSL derived over a range of modest risk reductions should remain approximately constant. In a review of VSL studies using stated preference techniques, the US Environmental Protection Agency (2010) found that only half of the studies incorporated such scope tests. Ninety percent of the studies that used scope tests reported that WTP varied with the magnitude of risk reduction. However, only 15% reported changes in WTP that were roughly proportional to the change in risk reduction.

Perhaps surprisingly, stated-preference techniques have yielded lower estimates of VSL than hedonic wage studies (Cropper *et al.* 2011). However, it is unclear whether these results are artifacts of estimation technique, the type of risk examined in each study, or differences in the populations studied, including perceptions and comprehension of mortality risks.

Overview of VSL Estimates in Less Developed Countries

The majority of studies that seek to value mortality risk reduction have been conducted in industrialized countries and in particular in the USA and Canada. In a review of VSL studies conducted globally, Miller (2000) lists 30 studies conducted in 12 countries, none of which were from developing countries. Viscusi and Aldy (2003) examine 50 studies (27 in the USA), only three of which were in non-industrialized countries (and all in India). More recently, Hammitt and Robinson (2011) provide a review of international VSL studies to date, including 17 studies from nine countries, none of which is a low-income country.

Table A10.1 provides a summary of the 30 international VSL studies from 19 countries we identified in our literature review.[33] We found 11 wage–risk studies in developing countries, none of which are classified as low-income countries by the World Bank, and all with very limited sample sizes.[34] Moreover, all of the studies focused on very specific subpopulations of individuals, and yield VSL estimates that are vary considerably. The high estimates are more than one order of magnitude greater than

---

[31] As with the wage-hedonic models, stated-preference models often consider a range of model specifications including log-linear and log-log to estimate the parameters in equation (10.A3).

[32] For example, using data reported in Johannesson *et al.* (1997), Cropper *et al.* (2011) report a difference of more than six orders of magnitude in WTP estimates derived using different distributional assumptions about the demand for risk reductions.

[33] We identified a total of 48 VSL studies published in the international literature. Eighteen studies were excluded from our sample due to the fact that they: (1) were conducted prior to 1995, before significant advances in both econometric and stated-preferences methods of estimating VSL, or (2) presented a range of VSL estimates that differed by more two orders of magnitude.

[34] These sample sizes are much smaller than the more than 100,000+ observations common in studies conducted in industrialized countries. Note: Shanmugam (1997) and Simon *et al.* (1999) do not report a sample size.

Table A10.1 Summary of international studies reviewed for this annex

Study	Type[a]	Country	Per capita GDP	Reported VSL
Developing Countries				
Jeuland *et al.* (2009)	CV/SP	Beira, Mozambique	504	11,700
Kremer *et al.* (2009)	RP	Kenya (rural)	892	500
Maskery *et al.* (2008)	CV/SP	Bangladesh (rural)	896	12,075
Simon *et al.* (1999)	WR	India	2,084	263,575
Shanmugam (2000)	WR	India (Chennai)	2,084	910,000
Shanmugam (2001)	WR	India (Chennai)	2,084	1,885,000
Bhattacharya *et al.* (2007)	CV/SP	India (Delhi)	2,084	9,068
Shanmugam (1997)	WR	India (Chennai)	2,084	877,500
Guo and Hammitt (2009)	WR	China (urban)	4,547	52,650
Hammitt and Zhou (2006)	CV/SP	China (urban and rural)	4,547	78,163
Wang and Mullahy (2006)	CV/SP	China (Chonging)	4,547	28,470
Vassanandumrongdee and Matsuoka (2005)	CV/SP	Thailand (Bangkok)	5,558	1,072,500
Vassanandumrongdee and Matsuoka (2005)	CV/SP	Thailand (Bangkok)	5,558	1,105,000
Gibson *et al.* (2007)	CV/SP	Thailand (rural)	5,558	182,000
Melhuish *et al.* (2005)	CV/SP	Malaysia	8,154	397,800
Hammitt and Ibarrarán (2006)	WR	Mexico City	8,857	209,950
Ortuazar *et al.* (2000)	CV/SP	Chile (Santiago)	9,329	2,067,000
Ortuazar *et al.* (2000)	CV/SP	Chile (Santiago)	9,329	421,850
Giergiczny (2008)	WR	Poland	10,644	1,202,500
Kim and Fishback (1999)	WR	South Korea	17,098	650,000
Liu *et al.* (1997)	WR	Taiwan	20,811	422,500
Liu and Hammitt (1999)	WR	Taiwan	20,811	455,000
Siebert and Wei (1998)	WR	Hong Kong	25,600	1,105,000
Industrialized countries				
Meng and Smith (1999)	WR	Canada	26,505	3,380,000
Baranzini and Ferro Luzzi (2001)	WR	Switzerland	27,571	4,842,500
Lott and Manning (2000)	WR	USA	30,225	2,346,570
Dreyfus and Viscusi (1995)	RP	USA	30,225	3,598,075
Blomquist *et al.* (1996)	RP	USA	30,225	4,536,703
Gayer *et al.* (2000)	RP	USA	30,225	3,637,184
Jenkins *et al.* (2001)	RP	USA	30,225	1,916,366

[a] CV, contingent valuation; RP, revealed preference; SP, stated preference; WR, wage–risk.

those obtained using other methods in similar countries, e.g. Shanmugam (1997, 2000, 2001), Simon *et al.* (1999), and Hammitt and Ibarrarán (2006). For example, Shanmugam (2000) developed VSL estimates from surveys of university employees in the city of Chennai; Hammitt and Ibarrarán (2006) worked with a sample of approximately 600 urban workers from the industrial, commercial and public sectors in Mexico City. One should not rely on such wage–risk data to describe developing country VSLs that apply to the general population.

Because there are few VSL studies in developing countries, researchers have often adjusted VSL estimates from industrialized countries, and then transferred these adjusted estimates to developing countries. Adjustments have been made for geographic and population characteristics (e.g. baseline risk, income, age, and health status) using the results of meta-analyses. Meta-analyses typically construct a pooled sample from existing primary studies, and estimate a regression that explains differences in estimated VSLs as a function of differences in research design, samples, and model specification (Miller 2000; Bowland and Beghin 2001; Mrozek and Taylor 2002; Viscusi and Aldy 2003). For example, in their meta-analysis, Mrozek and Taylor (2002) include covariates to capture variation in VSL, risk, and earnings, 12 dummy variables to control for variation in samples, eight variables to control for differences in specification across studies, and four industry/occupation variables. Published meta-analyses to date have included both old and relatively recent studies that vary considerably in quality and econometric sophistication.

Researchers who want to transfer VSL estimates from such meta-analyses to a range of developing countries could then use the parameter estimates from such a regression model to adjust for the characteristics of the population of interest, such as income. For this approach to work, it is essential to understand the relationship between income and the VSL. Several of the meta-analyses described above have attempted to estimate the income elasticity of the VSL, i.e. the percent change in VSL for a 1% change in income, as shown in equation (A10.4):

$$VSL_2 = VSL_1 \times (income_2/income_2)^\gamma \quad (A10.4)$$

where γ is the elasticity of the VSL with respect to income. In this formulation an income elasticity of one implies that a 1% increase in income yields results in a 1% increase in the VSL. Similarly, an income elasticity of zero implies that the VSL does not change with income. Suppose for example that an individual in the USA (per capita GDP of $45,600) were willing to pay $600 (or just over 1% of income) for a 0.0001 reduction in mortality risk, yielding a VSL of $6 million (VSL = $600/0.0001). An income elasticity of zero would imply that an individual in Bangladesh (with average PPP-adjusted income of $1,500), would also be willing to pay $600. This would constitute 40% of annual income for the average Bangladeshi, which is clearly unrealistic.

As shown in Table A10.2, estimates of the income elasticity from meta-analyses of VSL studies conducted in industrialized countries range from approximately 0.4 (relatively insensitive to income changes) to 1.0,[35] with a general consensus that the income elasticity associated with a range of incomes in industrialized countries is approximately 0.5 to 0.6. This implies that the VSL increases as income

Table A10.2 VSL income elasticities from meta-analyses

Study	Original reported elasticity	Re-estimate of elasticity
Liu *et al.* (1997)	0.53	0.51
Miller (2000)	0.85–1.00	0.53
Bowland and Beghin (2001)	1.52–2.27	0.61
Mrozek and Taylor (2002)	0.37–0.49	0.52
Viscusi and Aldy (2003)	n.a.	0.46–0.60

Source: Adapted from Hammitt and Robinson (2011)

---

[35] Bowland and Beghin (2001) report an income elasticity ranging from 1.5 to 2.3. However, using data from Viscusi and Aldy (2003) Hammitt and Robinson (2011) estimate an income elasticity of 0.6 using the model presented in Bowland and Beghin (2001). Similarly, Hammitt and Robinson (2011) provide a re-estimate of 0.5 for the income elasticity reported in Miller (2000).

increases but at a decreasing rate (i.e. the relationship between income and the VSL is concave).

There are two main problems with extrapolating income elasticities derived from VSL studies in rich countries to low-income populations. First, this assumes that individuals in developing countries have the same basic preferences regarding mortality risk reduction as individuals in industrialized countries (i.e. all other covariates and unobserved differences across individuals are the same). However, it seems more reasonable to believe that safety and mortality risk reductions are normal goods, and that demand for them may be similar to the demand for coverage with improved water and sanitation services, for environmental quality (the environmental Kuznets curve), or for longevity (as in the Preston curve). The notion that preferences for mortality risk reduction change as countries progress through different stages of economic growth is in fact supported by longitudinal studies of VSLs in industrialized countries, as well as estimates of VSL across a range of low-income countries. Hammitt and Ibarrarán (2006) and Wang and Mullahy (2006) report income elasticities for the VSL in Mexico and China of 1.4–2.0. Working with longitudinal data, Hammitt et al. (2009) and Costa and Khan (2003) estimate elasticities of 2.0–3.0 for Taiwan, and 1.5–1.7 for the USA, respectively. Kniesner et al. (2010) use quantile regression methods and report that income elasticity declines as income increases, from 2.2 in the lowest quantile and 1.2 in the highest quantile.

Second, using income elasticities of 0.5–0.6 from industrialized countries to estimate VSLs in developing countries assumes, somewhat counterintuitively, that the percentage of income invested in the specific mortality risk reductions of interest will decrease as income increases.[36] This seems unlikely because poor households in developing countries spend much more of their income on basic needs such as food (the Engel curve), clothing, and shelter. Note that increased expenditures by a very-low-income household on food, clothing, and shelter could reduce mortality risk, whereas marginal increases in such expenditures by a household in an industrialized country would be unlikely to affect mortality. Additionally an income elasticity in the range of 0.5 to 0.6 is inconsistent with much of the recent empirical evidence from VSL studies in developing countries, which is discussed further below.

Critique of the Standard Benefit Transfer Approach Based on Income Elasticity

If we accept the conventional wisdom and large body of evidence supporting the fact that the income elasticity of the VSL is between 0.5 and 0.6, we soon run into difficulties explaining empirical findings for the demand for mortality risk reductions in poor countries. Indeed, the recent literature recognizes that extrapolation from industrialized country VSLs using income elasticities greater than 1.0 may be appropriate when deriving VSL estimates for low-income countries (Robinson and Hammitt 2009; Hammitt and Robinson 2011).[37] Using a high-income elasticity to extrapolate VSLs to developing countries accommodates findings in the empirical literature for lower VSLs (see Table A10.1). However, this approach does not explain how the VSL changes with income or the stage of economic development – which is our focus.[38] Assuming a constant high-income elasticity in low-income countries does not explain how or when a country transitions from a state where it is appropriate to use a high-income elasticity to a state where it is appropriate to use the well-established low-income elasticities used in industrialized countries. Changes in VSLs could be attributable not only to changes in income, or to changing attitudes towards risk that accompany economic growth, but also to reduced background mortality risk, and

[36] Hall and Jones (2007) for example assert that health, and by extension mortality risk reduction, is a superior good with an income elasticity that should be greater than 1.0.

[37] These authors use a range of 1.0–2.0, but point out that VSL estimates derived with income elasticities above 1.5 may lie below expected discounted future earnings or consumption, which would be inconsistent with economic theory. In light of this, they recommend using expected future consumption as a lower bound for the VSL. However, implementation of this cut-off is difficult without detailed information on individuals' time preferences.

[38] Costa and Kahn (2003) find that the VSL in the USA increased fivefold from 1940 to 1980, a period that saw dramatic decreases in mortality and improvements to quality of life.

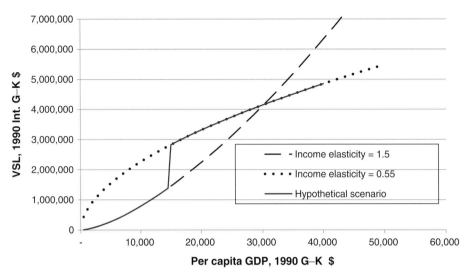

Figure A10.1 *VSL estimates derived from income elasticities. Low-income elasticity line is dashed; high-income elasticity line is solid; the hypothetical scenario is bolded in blue*

other changes that occur alongside the demographic transition.[39]

Figure A.10.1 illustrates this point. It shows VSL estimates for PPP-adjusted per capita incomes ranging from 0 to $50,000. These are projected from a base VSL of $6.3 million for a GDP of $46,500, following Hammitt and Robinson (2011). The top curve shows VSL estimates assuming an income elasticity of 0.55, which is representative of income elasticities reported in meta-analyses for industrialized countries. The bottom curve shows VSL estimates derived using an income elasticity of 1.5, the main income elasticity used by Hammitt and Robinson (2011).

An approach that relies on a constant income elasticity for the VSL cannot generate reasonable estimates over a wide continuum of income. If individuals in industrialized and low-income countries have different preferences regarding mortality risk

reduction, and if differences in these preferences can be captured by different income elasticities, it is unclear how a country (or population) will transition from the low- to high-income VSL curves. Wherever this transition is assumed to occur, there would appear to be a sharp change between VSL estimates on either side of the transition.

For example, suppose a policy analyst believes that the threshold at which one should transition from deriving the VSL with an income elasticity of 1.5 to an income elasticity of 0.55 occurs at a per capita GDP of $15,000. If a country has a per capita GDP of $14,990 at a particular point in time the analyst would apply an income elasticity of 1.5 to derive an estimate of the VSL, which would yield a VSL of approximately $1.4 million (Figure A10.1). However, if this country experienced economic growth and recorded a per capita GDP of $15,010 6 months later, the analyst would then use an income elasticity of 0.55 to derive an estimate of the VSL. This would yield a VSL of approximately 2.8 million, twice the VSL estimated using an income elasticity of 1.5. It does not seem plausible that individual preferences towards mortality risk reduction could change so sharply over such a small increase in income. In many benefit transfer applications, this would not be an issue because VSL estimation is not

[39] Eeckhoudt and Hammitt (2001) find that high levels of background mortality and financial risk can substantially reduce the VSL. They argue: "…when the competing risk is large, willingness to pay to reduce the first [mortality] risk can fall nearly to zero. Intuitively, in the presence of a large background risk, there is little benefit to reducing the first source of mortality risk" (p. 262). They term this the "why bother" effect.

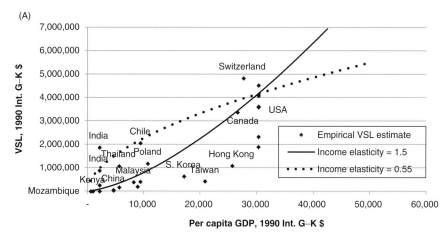

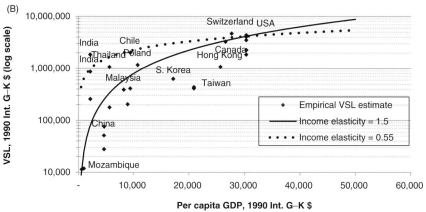

Figure A10.2 *Scatter plots of VSL estimates published since around 2000 for industrialized and middle-income countries, with low- and high-income elasticity curves superimposed. Note: panel B is on a log scale*

required in both low- and high-income countries in the same year. However, because our analysis projects changes in income over a long period of time, we inevitably find that some countries cross whichever ad hoc transition point we define in our model. As a result, the constant income elasticity benefit transfer approach described in the recent VSL literature is insufficient for our purposes.

Our Modeling Approach for the Economic Analysis of Global Losses from Inadequate Water and Sanitation

To address these challenges, we use an approach that incorporates the findings from both (1) the

meta-analysis literature on the relationship between income and VSL in industrialized countries; and (2) the limited empirical data on the VSL for developing countries in Table A10.1. Figure A10.2 provides scatter plots of these published VSL estimates expressed in 1990 international dollars, along with the high- and low-income elasticity curves presented above, which are estimated using the Hammitt and Robinson (2011) benchmark for VSL of US$4.1 million at per capita GDP of US$30,225.[40]

---

[40] GDPs are in international dollars as reported in the Penn World Tables for 2007 deflated to 1990. Hammitt and Robinson (2011) use a base VSL of US$6.3 million and a base GDP of US$46,500. These figures have been deflated to 1990 for consistency with the chapter.

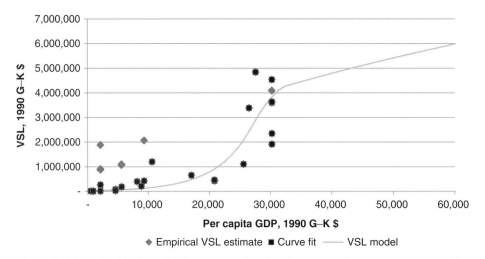

Figure A10.3 *Hybrid S-shaped VSL curve used in this chapter, combining an exponential function fit to empirical VSL estimates and an income elasticity of 0.55 at higher incomes*

As shown, the estimates derived using an elasticity of 1.5 are generally consistent with the lower end of estimates for developing countries found in the literature up to a per capita GDP of about US$10,000. We do not believe that the VSL estimates for India, Thailand, and Chile (which appear considerably larger than suggested by this curve) are representative of developing country VSLs because they were conducted in urban settings with semi-skilled or skilled workers, or among individuals owning motor vehicles. Also, even the high elasticity curve appears to overestimate VSLs over the range of per capita GDP of about $10,000 to $25,000. When deflated to 1990, the VSL estimates derived in recent studies for industrialized countries do indeed cluster around the US$4.1 million benchmark used by Hammitt and Robinson (2011).

In order to preserve the relatively well-established VSL–income relationship for rich countries while acknowledging the empirical evidence from developing countries, we use a functional relationship

[41] Five studies were excluded from the curve estimation. Four of the studies (Shanmugam 1997, 2000, 2001; Vassanadumrongee and Matsuoka 2005) were conducted in urban areas among a relatively well-off segment of the population. Ortuzar *et al.* (2000) present two estimates of the VSL, one of which is 500% larger than the base estimate, and which is also excluded.

that does not depend on constant income elasticities. Examining the published estimates, it appears that VSLs are initially very low, before rising steeply with incomes between US$20,000 and US$30,000, and then leveling off with the income elasticities of 0.5–0.6 documented by Viscusi and Aldy (2003). To accommodate this s-curve relationship, we fit an exponent thereafter, assuming that the income elasticity of the VSL is 0.55, as shown in Figure A10.3.[41] Although this S-shaped curve is admittedly ad hoc, we believe that it is the best characterization of the VSL estimates available in the published literature. The household budget shares available for investments in specific mortality risk reductions (e.g. bed nets, vaccines, point-of-use water treatment) are very low at low levels of income. Additionally, at low income levels households may face high levels of background risks, which can result in very low VSLs (Eeckhoudt and Hammitt 2001). We speculate that after the demographic transition occurs, baseline levels of mortality risk decline and households then increase their expenditures (i.e. they place an increasingly high economic value) on mortality risk reductions up to the point where diminishing returns to investments in reduced mortality set in. This story is consistent with the recent literature (e.g. Hammitt and Robinson 2011) that suggests that income elasticities of the VSL in developing countries may exceed 1.0 over some ranges of income.

In the sensitivity analysis for our chapter, we use a relationship with a constant elasticity over all income levels at the central estimate of 1.5 used by Hammitt and Robinson (2011), and we also show separately using a tornado diagram the implications of varying this elasticity over a range of 1 to 2, which would still be higher than the estimate obtained from rich world meta-analyses.

Annex 10.2: Data Sources for Control Variables in the Regression Models

This section describes the sources for the control variables included in the models (equations 10.11–10.13):

a. *Urban population* Percentage of total population in a country that is located in an urban area. This variable was created by dividing urban population by total population, both of which were reported by the WHO/UNICEF JMP. Urban population projections for the future were obtained from: http://esa.un.org/unpd/wup/index.htm. We expect that higher levels of urbanization will be associated with higher piped water coverage.

b. *World region dummy variables* We generated dummy variables for the major world regions in order to control for regional differences that might influence piped water coverage and WASH-related death rates. We use the following country groupings: (1) Sub-Saharan Africa (SSA); (2) Latin America and the Caribbean (LAC); (3) Middle East (MIDEAST); (4) Eastern Europe (EURCA); (5) South Asia (SA); and 6) East Asia and the Pacific (EAP). The full list of countries in each of these regions is given in Table A10.3 below.

c. *Inequality* We obtained the percentage of national GDP for the lowest 80% of the income distribution from the World Bank database, as a measure of inequality. Higher percentages imply greater equality.

d. *Fertility* Fertility rates were obtained from the United Nations. Only year 2008 rates are available.[42] Because fertility rates are highly endogenous, we use this variable mainly to test whether the associations of greatest interest to us (specifically the effect of improved water services on mortality rates) are robust to model specifications that include it.

e. *Literacy* Adult literacy rates for 2005 were also obtained from the United Nations. We expect that death rates will be negatively correlated with literacy rates.

f. *Governance variables* Obtained from the Center for Systemic Peace's Integrated Network for Societal Conflict Research (INSCR).[43] We expect that higher coverage levels with infrastructure and lower deaths will be associated with positive governance and stability measures.

   1. Democracy–Autocracy score: this is a governance measure that seeks to account for the extent of democracy and autocracy in a country. The variable is derived by subtracting a country's autocracy score (−10 to 0) from its democracy score (0 to 10). A democracy–autocracy score of +10 indicates the most strongly democratic country possible; −10 is the most autocratic.

   2. Regime durability: this variable indicates the number of years since the most recent regime change. A regime change is defined by a three-point change in the democracy–autocracy score over a period of 3 years or less.

   3. Coups d'état: we used the coup indicator to create a dummy variable indicating a successful coup in the last 5 years.

g. *Bilateral aid for WASH* Data on total aid received for WASH by country was obtained from the OECD for many countries after 1996, in three

---

[42] Available at: www.un.org/esa/population/
[43] Available at: www.systemicpeace.org/inscr/inscr.htm. The INSCR data cover all independent countries with population of at least 500,000. In 2009, 163 countries were included in INSCR.

categories: aid for large systems (water-treatment plants and networks), aid for basic systems, and water resources planning and management. As far as we know, these are the only comprehensive data available for WASH aid.

h. *Linear time trend and/or year dummy variables*
For the piped water coverage model, we defined a linear time trend variable as equal to the year of the observation minus 1990, which was the first year in our data set. We also created dummy variables for each year to control for non-linear effects over time, and created a set of time–region interactions as additional controls for regionally differentiated time effects.

Annex 10.3: Additional Tables and Figures

Table A10.3 Region groupings of countries in our analysis

Region	Countries included
Developed countries (DEV_ECON)	Australia, Austria, Belgium, Canada, Cyprus, Denmark, Finland, France, Germany, Greece, Iceland, Ireland, Italy, Japan, Luxembourg, Malta, Netherlands, New Zealand, Norway, Portugal, Singapore, Spain, Sweden, Switzerland, United Kingdom, United States
Sub-Saharan Africa (SSA)	Angola, Benin, Botswana, Burkina Faso, Burundi, Cameroon, Cape Verde, Central African Republic, Chad, Comoros, Côte d'Ivoire, Democratic Republic of Congo, Equatorial Guinea, Eritrea, Ethiopia, Gabon, Gambia, Ghana, Guinea, Guinea-Bissau, Kenya, Lesotho, Liberia, Madagascar, Malawi, Mali, Mauritania, Mauritius, Mozambique, Namibia, Niger, Nigeria, Republic of Congo, Rwanda, Senegal, Seychelles, Sierra Leone, Somalia, South Africa, Sudan, Swaziland, Tanzania, Togo, Uganda, Zambia, Zimbabwe
Latin America and Caribbean (LAC)	Argentina, Belize, Bolivia, Brazil, Chile, Columbia, Costa Rica, Cuba, Dominican Republic, Ecuador, El Salvador, Guatemala, Guyana, Haiti, Honduras, Jamaica, Mexico, Nicaragua, Panama, Paraguay, Peru, Suriname, Trinidad and Tobago, Uruguay, Venezuela
Middle East (MIDEAST)	Algeria, Bahrain, Djibouti, Egypt, Iran, Iraq, Israel, Jordan, Kuwait, Lebanon, Libya, Morocco, Oman, Palestinian Territories, Qatar, Saudi Arabia, Syria, Tunisia, United Arab Emirates, Yemen
Eastern Europe and former Soviet Union (EURCA)	Albania, Armenia, Azerbaijan, Belarus, Bosnia, Bulgaria, Croatia, Czech Republic, Estonia, Georgia, Hungary, Kazakhstan, Kyrgyzstan, Latvia, Lithuania, Macedonia, Moldova, Poland, Romania, Russia, Serbia, Slovakia, Slovenia, Tajikistan, Turkey, Turkmenistan, Ukraine, Uzbekistan
South Asia (SA)	Afghanistan, Bangladesh, Bhutan, India, Maldives, Nepal, Pakistan, Sri Lanka
East Asia and Pacific (EAP)	Cambodia, China, Indonesia, Lao PDR, Malaysia, Mongolia, Myanmar, North Korea, Papua New Guinea, Philippines, South Korea, Thailand, Vietnam

Table A10.4 OLS regression for mortality death rate (annual deaths per 1000, people) due to inadequate WASH; alternative model specifications

	All countries, log coverage terms		All countries, higher-order coverage terms	
	Coefficient	Standard error[a]	Coefficient	Standard error[a]
Log % Piped water coverage	-0.48^{***}	0.12		
Log % Improved non-piped water coverage	-0.19^{***}	0.073		
Log % Improved sanitation coverage	-0.11	0.22		
% Piped water coverage			-0.049^{***}	0.013
% Improved non-piped water coverage			-0.0065	0.020
% Improved sanitation coverage			-0.0022	0.017
Squared % Piped water coverage			0.00024^{*}	0.00012
Squared % Improved non-piped water coverage			-0.00022	0.00024
Squared % Improved sanitation coverage			0.000057	0.00012
Ln GDP per capita	-0.29^{***}	0.11	-0.32^{**}	0.094
% Urban population	0.0030	0.0053	0.0043	0.0053
Developed countries	-0.39^{**}	0.25	-0.34^{*}	0.19
Countries in LAC region	-0.54^{**}	0.24	-0.54^{**}	0.23
Countries in MIDEAST region	-0.28	0.32	-0.35	0.26
Countries in SOUTH ASIA region	-0.73^{***}	0.21	-0.33	0.25
Countries in EAST ASIA/PACIFIC region	-0.66^{***}	0.22	-0.63^{***}	0.20
Countries in EASTERN EUROPE region	-0.34	0.25	-0.44^{**}	0.19
Democracy–Autocracy Score	0.0041	0.0096	0.0086	0.0088
Years since last regime change	0.0018	0.0015	0.00046	0.00084
Constant	3.8^{***}	0.86	3.0^{***}	0.55
Number of observations	118		132	
Adjusted R^2	0.656		0.709	

Significance: *, 90%, **, 95%, ***, 99%.
[a] Robust standard errors.

Table A10.5 Estimation of population coverage with improved water and sanitation (clustered standard errors presented in parentheses), basic model specification

	Random effects[a]		Fixed effects	
	Improved water	Improved sanitation	Improved water	Improved sanitation
Lagged ln(GDP per capita)	8.0*** (1.7)	12.6*** (2.9)	6.5** (3.1)	9.4** (4.6)
% of GDP to lowest 80% of population	−0.21* (0.12)	−0.15 (0.12)	−0.30** (0.13)	−0.13 (0.14)
% Urban population	0.20*** (0.06)	0.22* (0.12)	0.27* (0.15)	0.43* (0.23)
Countries in LAC region	6.4* (3.8)	17.7** (7.1)		
Countries in MIDEAST region	7.1* (4.1)	26.9*** (6.9)		
Countries in SOUTH ASIA region	16.7*** (3.8)	9.7 (9.2)		
Countries in EAST ASIA/PACIFIC region	3.1 (4.5)	15.0** (6.4)		
Countries in EASTERN EUROPE region	12.4*** (4.5)	34.1*** (6.9)		
Linear time trend	0.30*** (0.08)	0.23** (0.10)	0.29*** (0.10)	0.20 (0.13)
1995	−0.80 (0.70)	0.37 (1.18)	−0.72 (0.66)	0.50 (1.08)
2000	−0.38 (0.31)	−0.14 (0.44)	−0.35 (0.29)	−0.17 (0.41)
Democracy–Autocracy Score	−0.086 (0.17)	0.19 (0.33)	0.076 (0.19)	−0.18 (0.38)
Years since last regime change	−0.0073 (0.03)	−0.0030 (0.05)	0.010 (0.04)	−0.019 (0.06)
Coup d'état	−1.44 (0.90)	−1.29 (1.16)	−1.29 (0.89)	−0.85 (1.23)
Constant	64.7*** (6.5)	28.3*** (8.2)	72.2*** (8.5)	33.0*** (12.9)
Number of observations	374	374	374	374
Adjusted R² (overall)	0.676	0.749	0.586	0.629
(within)	0.492	0.263	0.498	0.271
(between)	0.688	0.765	0.593	0.640

Significant:*, 90%, **, 95%, ***, 99%.
[a] A random-effects tobit model that allows censoring at 0 and 100% coverage does not yield qualitatively different results, though coefficients for the income term are somewhat larger.

Coverage with Improved Water and Sanitation, Regional and Global Estimates and Sensitivity Analyses

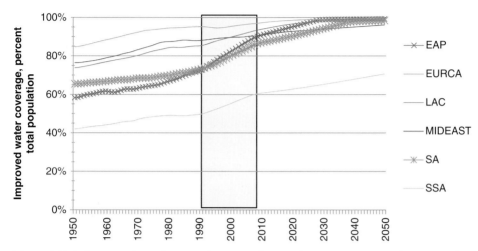

Figure A10.4 *Percent of population with improved water, by region, assuming base case elasticities of coverage and using 1950–2008 GDP growth for future projections (actual coverage data shown in shaded box)*

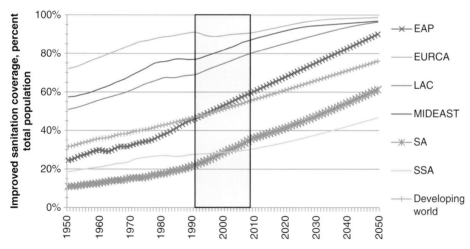

Figure A10.5 *Percent of population with improved sanitation, by region, assuming base case elasticities of coverage and using 1950–2008 GDP growth for future projections (actual coverage data shown in shaded box)*

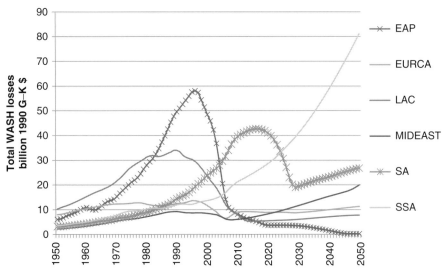

Figure A10.6 *Base case total "economic losses" associated with WASH, by region (projections from 1950–2008 growth rates)*

Index